Blindsided by the Messiah

My Book.
My Life.
My Way.

Lori Michelle

Printed in the United States of America

First Edition: December 9, 2018 | Rosh Chodesh Tevet, 5779

ISBN 0-692-18244-6

Running On Love
45 S. Park Place, #506
Morristown, NJ 07960

RunningOnLove.org
LoriMichelle.net

Baruch Hashem, You continuously brace me with love, strength and courage. You are the Master and King of the Universe, however, to me the sun, moon and stars are the smallest part of Your Awesomeness. I love You simply for being You. After I hear You greet me each morning, it's all extra. Thank You Hashem for extra.

Contents

Chapter 13
I'm Wide Awake Now. Are You?   405

GOD is Everything.
Everything else is extra.
Thank you GOD for extra.

Dedication

My book is dedicated to the well-being of my three children and all the children of the world.

When my children were small I used to kiss them good night and tell them the following words, "I love you with all my heart, don't you ever forget that." At the time I didn't know why I asked them to never forget. As I release this book I risk everything. I am risking my life, but I am risking something even more precious to me. I risk my relationship with my three beautiful children.

There comes a moment of truth when everyone must face Hashem God and answer for every life choice. In my case, I face Hashem in every moment day and night. My every choice is filled with the passionate desire to heal our world. Day and night, I pray for my children and all the children of our world. As I risk it all, I pray my children remember my words, "I love you with all my heart, don't you ever forget that."

Please Hashem may I finally succeed in my life's work and may this book serve to be a wake-up call for humanity. May we all come together as family, work to heal our world, save our children, and bring world peace in our time.

Blindsided by Messiah

14

Introduction

In the Beginning ...

You've been *Blindsided by Messiah!* I've revealed the truth to the world. The Messiah is me, Lori Michelle. In the beginning you might be blindsided and stunned by this announcement, but this news shouldn't be shocking at all. I've been screaming to you for over nine years. Thousands of people know me and I've never tried to hide this, not at all. I've scratched and clawed my way to freedom and through the grace of God Himself, I lived to tell.

You may be in disbelief or even dumbstruck with the revelation that you have a "Mommy Messiah," but doesn't a mom truly make more sense? Moms are traditionally the ones who clean up the mess created by their children. Who better to lead the charge to clean up our world? That's what everyone expects from the Messiah or Moshiach, right? The Messiah is going to clean up all the horror in our world and bring lasting peace where there is none. While all of God's children have created this monumental mess, the men of the world have led the charge. Think about all the men in history. Just do the math for a minute and count how many war criminals, maniacal dictators, rapists, murderers, pedophiles, and serial killers were men versus women. Without even doing a Google search to investigate this, you know that men rule our world when it comes to evil. I rest my case.

Having just made the case for a "Mommy Messiah" doesn't take away the fact that I agree with you about desiring a male Messiah. I too would prefer a man to lead us to world peace. I never believed in the Messiah before my awakening but if I had to answer to one, I'd prefer a big strapping handsome man too. Truly! I'm sorry to disappoint everyone, but it's really a girl this time. Not just a girl, but a menopausal mommy from New Jersey of all places! This time it's for all the marbles and God chose me. As crazy as that sounds, it's true. I still question Hashem, God, daily if He got it right when He chose me. To this day, daily, I still ask Him, "Am I really your Messiah?" as I fall into raucous laughter and uncontrollable hiccups. Most of the time I'm not laughing at all, I'm crying. His answer for more than nine years is that it's me, it was always going to be me, and there's nobody else on earth who can fill this role. You can keep looking around for your Messiah or Moshiach, and I completely understand if you do. I'm not insulted in the least bit. This isn't about me at all, this is about you and the future of our world. I'm not here to win friends or influence people, like Dale Carnegie taught everyone. I'm here to save your lives. If you don't like me, I will simply move on. I want you to like me, but I don't need you. You need me and you need to learn what I'm sharing right now. Time is truly of the essence.

My warning to everyone reading this book: this information will test you deeply. It will test your beliefs about everything you've been taught about the world, religion, and yes, God Himself. Because our world has fallen into complete chaos, people around the world are searching for answers and many have sadly given up. Religion has become a source of division and hatred instead of being a method of healing. In the name of religion, people have been tortured and brutally murdered. Because of this, many intelligent people turn to atheism, finding it impossible to believe in one benevolent God that rules over us all. Still others hold out some hope and choose to be agnostic, remaining wishful that there's some higher intelligence managing everything. They can't definitively say they believe in God or that they're positive there is none.

Writing this book and sharing my personal journey has the potential to bring me ultimate peace or destroy what remains of my life. No matter what danger I face, it's time for me to share this with you. My story must be heard by everyone in the world. Whether you believe me and my written story or not, you will be moved in some way. In the end, you will decide what you believe about me and how this information will affect you. More importantly, you will decide what your next move will be and how you'll go forward.

I pray that you will read my book without skipping one word, right to its conclusion. For your own benefit, if you're able, please put your opinions and religious beliefs aside and keep an open mind. Please ask yourself the question, "Is this in the realm of possibility?" In the end, your answer might be emphatically no. You may choose to believe that what I'm revealing to you can't possibly be true and reject me and everything I've written in this book. My prayer is that you'll feel my sincerity. I pray the information I'm sharing with you gives you good reasons to pause and evaluate what you believe about life, God, and the world as we know it. Most importantly, I pray this book moves you into action. God willing you'll listen to this call and join me to work for world peace.

This book brings you on my personal journey after I experienced a life-changing spiritual awakening. On April 7th, 2009, I was awakened to the voice of God Himself. I listened that morning to His instructions, and I've been listening ever since. That moment led me to write several journals in longhand recording my conversations with the King of the Universe. I discovered without any doubt whatsoever that God is real and He is the final arbiter of everything that happens in our world. There is nothing that goes unnoticed and we're answerable to every single choice we make in our lifetime. I mean everything!

My spiritual awakening began a journey that changed my life and the lives of my family irrevocably. The series of events that followed peeled my eyes open to a world I no longer recognized. After I was awakened, I found myself teetering dangerously between two worlds, the physical and the non-physical. My life became chaotic where everything was turned inside out and backwards. Friends, family, business associates and the people of mainstream America who I once believed were wise and good were clearly foolish, sick and even deliberately evil. It became painfully clear to me that the country where I was raised was deeply dysfunctional and all the people I loved were walking zombies! Without exaggeration, it was like I was living inside the old horror flick *Night of the Living Dead*. Nobody, and I mean nobody, could comprehend or see clearly what I now saw. Over the past several years I've learned and searched for deeper understanding about our world and the truth behind our existence. The price I've paid? I was forced to walk away from everything I owned and almost everyone I knew to walk in freedom with God.

In His infinite wisdom, Hashem took away my physical hearing, and caused me to go deaf. He then gave me the supernatural ability to hear Him and the world of spirit with exquisite clarity. I now hear my father, my mother-in-law and countless others who have passed away. I don't reach for anyone except for Hashem God. He controls who I hear on the other side and decides when they're permitted to speak with me. He is my Gatekeeper, Guardian, and my entire life. Hashem is my Everything without exception.

It's time for me to speak freely and share this information with you without fear or equivocation. As you read my stories you may feel the entire range of human emotions including sadness, laughter, fear, remorse, confusion, embarrassment, compassion and perhaps extreme anger. You might vehemently disagree with many of my assertions. Conversely, you might believe that I'm telling you the truth and feel outrage that because of the way I was treated, I've been forced to remain silent for many years. In all these years of silence, how much of God's voice and goodness could I have shared with you and others?

I don't have any need to convince you that I'm the Messiah, Moshiach. I don't even truly want to be what that implies. I just want to be Lori Michelle, mother to my three children, and to work for world peace, period end of story. My goal right now is to be heard, to share Hashem's healing voice and messages, and to provide answers to many confounding questions. In the end, it's you who will decide, not me. My promise to you is that everything I'm sharing comes directly from my heart and soul with complete sincerity. As much as I've learned and now know about our world, I have infinitely more questions left unanswered. I'm sure this will be true for you too. My deepest desire is to bring you God's voice and wisdom at a time when we are all in grave peril. I pray that you will be open-minded enough to entertain the possibility that I am speaking the truth.

He shows me in beautiful visions that one day we will come together as one family that desires peace. In a time to come He says we will enjoy a free-flowing public conversation, and we will work together to uncover the truth. These open discussions and forums for learning are required so that we can all learn His laws and how to choose God and goodness in every moment. You see, if we all consistently choose wrong, we will continue to be at war and destroy our world and each other. Isn't it about time that we learned how to get along? He says that the truth will set us free and help us all come together to bring world peace for an eternity. Now that's music to my ears, how about yours? Our future will be one of collaboration, love and free-flowing knowledge. Education is our cure.

Are you ready?

His Voice, Visions & Lessons

Is world peace possible and how?

Hashem, God, has answered this question unequivocally for me many times. He says we will have peace on earth for an eternity. He not only says that we will have peace for an eternity but He says that we're the generation to bring world peace. This generation. That's fantastic news! But the challenge and the disappointment is that most of the world is not awake. They're not working for peace. They're putting out fires. They're fighting wars. They're dropping bombs and that's not the **how** that I am told we need to bring peace on earth. The **how** is for us all to get together as one family and learn how to remove evil from ourselves. Every one of us in the world is expected to roll up our sleeves and get to work. We all must get busy working on ourselves to figure out where we can improve and become better people. The work of self-improvement must become our way of life.

We need to come together as a family. This is not just a Jewish, Christian, Muslim call to action. This is a call to action for humanity. There is one God for all the people of the world. I am blessed to have Him speaking to me and providing me with information, much of which is available but most of the world doesn't even know that it exists or where to find it. Most of the world doesn't know the true difference between evil and good. You might say, "Of course I do!" But no, it's very sneaky. This is information that you must learn. You need to go inward. You need to work on yourself. Because let's face it, none of us can go over to war-torn countries like Syria to end the war and save the children, or save the people who are being blown to bits in acts of terror.

Bombs aren't going to end the problem. The true solution and the only way that we will bring world peace is to listen, learn and work for peace by healing ourselves. If enough of us remove the problems from ourselves, we will experience peace in our world in our time. He promises. We must learn how to get it right to bring peace because Hashem, God, promises we are the generation of world peace.

Chapter 1

I am Lori Michelle, Hashem's Moshiach

Whoa! Really? Did I just refer to myself as Hashem's Moshiach? Now that you're reading this book, it's likely that you've seen my series of crazy videos that include me swinging my pink baseball bat, playing a little game of *Where's Waldo*, singing hilarious or not so hilarious song parodies, and telling all the world that I'm God's Moshiach Queen. *Blindsided by Messiah* didn't come to me as a whim overnight. This unthinkable claim has been brewing for more than nine years since my spiritual awakening on April 7, 2009 and was always the destiny of my life.

Do you think I'm crazy? Well you're not alone but please finish reading this book before you make your final decision. Hashem says, "Lori, you are crazy good!" Do I agree with Him that I'm that good? No, I don't see myself as crazy good, just plain old good. I don't truly understand why He chose me of all people. I ask Him why He chose me still to this day. Sometimes I'm also confused by how much Hashem loves me. He showers me with intense love and says such wildly beautiful things about me day and night. It's confusing because no one in this world treats me the way He does. Sadly, I get the complete opposite treatment from the people closest to me in this world.

I've received disdain and condemnation from them. I've been accused by my own mother and brothers of being arrogant and self-centered my entire life. I have bitter memories as a toddler of being yelled at by my very young mother to get away from her as she shouted, "You're always under my feet!" It's something I've never forgotten and the verbal assaults kept coming through all the years of my life.

Growing up I was deeply affected by the tone, language and facial expressions of the people around me. Receiving a raised eyebrow or hearing cross language from a parent, teacher, or someone I loved made me visibly upset or sent me into tears. By the time I was four years old I was told daily that I was moody and too sensitive. As I got older I was often verbally berated by my mother. I lived with the rap sheet of being selfish, moody, and ungrateful. My own father whom I loved dearly, one morning gave me a vicious and demoralizing verbal beating because I walked into the kitchen looking sad and didn't say good morning. He blew his lid and marched me out of the kitchen, sat me in the living room of our home that memorable Saturday morning, and screamed at me while my mother goaded him on to yell at me even harder. He screamed that I was ungrateful because I never smiled and he was incensed that I had the audacity to be unhappy. In his mind, I should have been giddily happy because of the home he provided me and how hard he worked to give me everything that I had. As he berated me in front of my mother, he screamed at me to smile as I wept. He continued to verbally assault me and treated me as though I was a moody ungrateful spoiled little brat. I cried so hard I began hyperventilating.

As I sat in the living room of my family home not even aware that it was Shabbos morning, I sobbed and forced a fake smile on my face to please the father whom I loved so much. I vividly recall staring at the TV where the musical group, *The Tokens* were performing the famous song "The Lion Sleeps Tonight." As I sat there at just eight years old I couldn't understand what I was doing that was so awful or how screaming at me and calling me names would ever make me want to smile. Now, more than five decades later I know that while I was being verbally abused by my parents, our King, Hashem God sat silently with me on the sofa watching with supreme patience. Hashem knew that over 50 years later He would instruct me, His Moshiach, to include the last verse of this poignant song in my book:

> Hush my darling don't fear my darling
> The lion sleeps tonight
> Hush my darling don't fear my darling
> The lion sleeps tonight

I took my lumps and bruises that morning and looked for the love, not realizing I was being groomed to be a teacher. God knew one day I would accept my role as His chosen one who would work tirelessly to end the madness and dedicate my life to heal our world.

The verbal punishment didn't end at eight years old. As I grew up, I always felt as though I was the black sheep in our family. Almost daily my father and mother said that they loved me, but I only felt those words were true when they came from my dad. My mother seemed to despise me from the time I was a baby. Growing up I have many painful memories of being called names, ridiculed, and treated horribly. In one memory I was leaving the house to go on a date with a young man who brought me a single rose. He said, "You are as beautiful as this rose." I was so moved that I ran into the house to put the rose in water before we left.

My mother was standing in the kitchen as I placed the rose in a cup of water. I told her what the young man had just said to me. Without hesitation she said, "Come on Lori, you're not beautiful. Cute maybe, but not beautiful." I was dumbstruck why she would say this to me as I left for my date. I let her nasty comment go as I always did and kept silent. As I grew up in our home, I became accustomed to the many nasty labels given to me along with demeaning comments like this one. There were some happy memories strewn in between, but the nasty attacks occurred often enough throughout my life that I questioned if I was loved.

When my father was diagnosed with cancer, I was a young adult living and working in northern New Jersey. At the end of his life, the doctors were trying everything they could to save him. One day I visited him at Hahnemann University Hospital in Philadelphia when he was in the intensive care unit. He had tubes coming out of every part of his body. I was heartbroken to see my once strong father so weak and struggling to utter a word. The nurses couldn't understand what he was saying to them with all the tubes coming out of his mouth. As he struggled to tell them what he needed, I leaned over to see if I could help him by repeating what I thought I heard. As I tried to communicate for him to the nurses, he became irritated and embarrassed. The humiliation of not being able to speak for himself was too much for him to bear. He turned to me angrily and shouted, "You talk too much!" I was devastated. As I burst into tears, I ran out of the ICU to my family who was outside and told them what had happened. They tried to calm me down and told me that he wasn't in his right mind. I understood that under the duress of his illness he wasn't thinking clearly but this was devastating nonetheless.

One morning when I was back in my apartment in North Jersey, I spoke to my father's doctor by phone. He told me my dad's condition was grave and he would be passing away imminently. I hung up the phone immediately and raced to see my father one last time. I cried buckets of tears as I drove in the rain for two hours hoping to see him. When I arrived at our family home, my older brother was standing on the front porch and said the words, "It's over. He's gone." As I type these words into this book I'm crying buckets of tears again. Even though this was over 30 years ago, the pain of losing my father is still gut-wrenching for me. While I know it was also heartbreaking for my mother and older brother, they judged me as cold, indifferent, and uncaring, and their vicious verbal attacks towards me worsened. Throughout the years whenever they became angry with me, they would taunt me by shouting the mantra, "Where were you when your father died?" as a condemnation that I wasn't there as he took his last breath of life. In the heat of any future argument they would shout these awful words at me as though I was the most demonic and selfish person on the face of this earth. But that wasn't all. When tempers flared my older brother would add, "What were your father's final words to you?" This hideous chide was added to his arsenal of verbal attacks in an unrelenting desire to hurt me. Frankly, I can't comprehend how or why anyone would want to hurt another human being in such a malicious way.

Eventually, my mother and older brother's poisonous feelings and venom toward me entered the mind and heart of my younger brother too. This would only be a natural outcome after many years of listening to them both speak evil about me. My younger brother and I once enjoyed a special, loving and close relationship but it was destined to be destroyed. He lived and worked with our older brother and mother and was fed a steady diet of nasty mantras and lies about me. Once in the heat of anger, even my younger brother resorted to using that hideous mantra and taunt too, "Where were you when your father died?"

Some people reading this might wonder if my mother and brother's treatment of me was possibly justified. After all, they were all on the same page about me. I was the "odd man out" so to speak. I was selfish and ungrateful Lori who only considered herself. Some might even question that perhaps I took too long to get in my car that day to go see my dad when I heard the worst news. Maybe I dilly-dallied a bit and went to get my nails done instead. Perhaps the taunt the three of them used to hurt me, "Where were you when your father died" was warranted. The dysfunction in my family was so acute growing up that the stories and explanations could fill an entire book. It's important not to make this book read like a *Dr. Phil* psychotherapy television program or an hour on *The Oprah Winfrey Show*. To ask the question, "Was their hatred and venom toward me ever justified?" comes from the inability to recognize pure evil. The question itself, "Were they justified?" serves only to elicit even more evil as you work to give credence, validation and acceptance to their horrible behavior. There is never any justification to be spiteful or hate-filled toward anyone, without exception. The taunts and the name-calling that I received throughout my life were deeply malicious and unfounded, period.

In between the acrimony, we would patch things up well enough to keep our family relationship intact and remain on speaking terms. While it was a dysfunctional relationship, I tried my best to tolerate the nasty barbs and swallow the abuse. Three days before my wedding, I went to South Jersey to pick up my wedding gown and another brawl erupted. As my older brother berated me in front of my mother, she goaded him on to give it to me harder, like the day I was eight years old in my living room with my father. In that heated exchange my brother said, "Your fiancé (name concealed) thinks he loves you. He won't love you when he finds out who you really are." Over the years, he continued to attack me using his arsenal of verbal assaults. On my first Mother's Day, once again with the support and endorsement of our mother, he phoned me and said, "You think you're so great. One day when you lose your husband and your business, you won't think you're so great anymore." As he shouted these awful words at me it was apparent that he desired me to lose everything. I was perplexed. For one thing, I didn't know why he and my mother hated me so much and desired harm to come to me. For another, I never once thought of myself as great back then, and I still don't believe I'm great now. I'm the same as I ever was, just ordinary me. Being me never seemed to be good enough for either of them. Quite the contrary, they both despised me and wished me harm.

It's important to share these painful memories and the nasty treatment I received from my family to give you better insight about my life, where I came from, and how this all came as a shock to me too. Messiah of the world? You've got to be kidding me, right? Throughout my life I wondered why I was so broken and how it was possible that my own mother didn't truly love me. I always felt it was innate for a mother to love her own children, but it wasn't true when it came to me. She was deeply loving toward my two brothers but never showed the same affection to me. After my father died and the verbal berating took on a new and more venomous tone, I spent many tearful hours crying to my close girlfriend who had lost her father a couple of years earlier. She was like the sister I never had who made me feel loved and accepted as she consoled me in my despair.

Right after my father died, the pain from this loss was so severe I became acutely aware that I needed to search for a better way of life and find the goodness and love that seemed to be hiding from me. My search to do it right and become a better person led me to reading many self-help books. Working on myself became my passion as I ventured out into this wonderful world which I've learned over the years, isn't so wonderful. As I grew up and became a young adult, I learned how to find my authentic smile and make many friends. Eventually, I became quite good at making friends and influencing people but not because I wanted anything from anyone. I just wanted to be loved and to succeed. Success eventually found me and I enjoyed many friends and a flourishing career with lots and lots of money. I learned how to accomplish and acquire all the things that people of this world value and applaud—an impressive career, friends, marriage, three wonderful children, a beautiful home, a late model SUV, and a wildly wonderful relationship with my in-laws. I had everything. But did I have true love? I still ask that question to this day. Now that I know and understand what true love is by receiving it directly from Hashem God, I wonder daily if true love exists anywhere in this world. I wonder if any of the people who told me they loved me ever truly did. I just don't know.

As I walk the earth now, contemplate life, observe everyone and everything while spiritually awake and with my eyes wide open, I know that I'm peculiarly different from everyone. I've always been different and now I understand that this difference is quite good. I, Lori Michelle, journey as one with our Creator, God Himself. I speak with Him in fluent English and we converse day and night. But that's not all we do together. In every waking moment, we do every physical task together. We are walking, talking, and breathing as one being. I'm truly one with Hashem God.

I don't need to be accepted under any grandiose title at all. I simply am what I am and don't need or desire to convince anyone for my own benefit. Quite the contrary, this book and exposing my personal story isn't for my benefit at all, it's completely for yours. You'll make your decision in the end, about what I am to you. I know what I am to Hashem and without Him I wouldn't be doing any of this. Trust me, that would be insane! It simply wouldn't be possible to do this work without Him breathing down my neck, literally. I'll provide you with greater detail and explanations about how closely connected I am with our Creator. For now, please hold back any skepticism, continue reading this book, and enjoy the ride as I share my incredible journey of awakening to the voice of Hashem God and my life's purpose.

Hindsight is 20/20

When my soul was awakened, I knew that God and the spirit world were speaking to me. How could I possibly know this? My entire life prepared and led me to my awakening in April of 2009. I've read many books about people finding their life's calling. When they seemingly stumbled upon it, they recognized in that life changing moment that every part of their life prior came together into a perfect tapestry. Everything they accomplished in their lifetime up until that moment of truth suddenly made perfect sense. All their questions seemed to be answered. This was the case for me too.

I spent almost my entire life trying to figure out how I could become a better person. As I told you, from the time I was a baby I was told I was broken or in the way. The name-calling started at an early age and continued throughout my life. This isn't so different for most people in the world. We've been told we're broken or not good enough. There seems to be a preponderance of people willing to explain how broken we are from the time we're young. Fortunately, most of us either have parents, friends, or other loving people to stem the tide of the massive assaults on us to help us see the goodness in ourselves. We manage to grow up and lead productive lives. Most of us have become functional adults—depending upon your definition of functional. As our world grows sicker, careens out of control and we now head to World War III, we're seeing the cracks in our armor.

Broken parents are raising broken children and the brokenness is leading us all to self-destruction. My parents married young and were secular ham and cheese eating Jews who desired the all-American dream of having children, acquiring wealth and doing everything better than their broken parents did for them. They tried their best but their brokenness was felt by me as a baby and throughout my life. Instinctively, I felt this brokenness and kept reaching for answers to get this life right. I desired to be a better person and get along with everyone despite the difficulties at home and in school.

The name-calling at home hurt but I imagined I was loved by my family and I most certainly loved them. When the bullying and name-calling started in school, it was much more difficult to tolerate. Through trial and error, I eventually became an extremely successful adult with many friends. Money came easily to me through hard work and effort. I found a nice Jewish boy whom I considered my best friend, so I chose to marry. We started a family and worked together for the American dream.

As I mentioned, just after my father died and I fell into despair, I became passionately addicted to reading self-help books written by gurus such as Dr. Wayne Dyer and Anthony Robbins. Yup I did the Tony Robbins 30 days to success program too. Every day since I was 25, I spent an hour or two reading and searching for new ways to become better, happier and to lead a more fulfilled life.

After spending about 20 years reading every book under the sun on how to improve myself, I discovered Judaism had many of the same answers that were written in these self-help books. I went to synagogue one year for Rosh Hashanah services after the 9/11 terror attack and started to pay closer attention to the words written in the prayer book. My jaw dropped open and I thought to myself, "Holy mackerel—Dr. Dyer ripped off the Torah!" It didn't turn me into a Torah observant Jew yet. That took Hashem's intervention and a baseball bat to the head, metaphorically speaking of course. After my spiritual awakening in April of 2009, I had my eyes pinned wide open and discovered the truth. The truth and answers to all my questions were within me my entire life. I searched the world and found my answers in Hashem God's Torah and my Jewish faith. Shocking to some who don't understand what Judaism truly is and why it's at the center of everything in our world. Like it or not, the Jews hold the future of our world in their hands. My spiritual awakening opened the door to knowledge that everyone needs now. This awakening and wake-up call was always going to happen to me. It was simply a matter of when.

Growing up I always felt a profound love for God Himself. I prayed deeply to God daily from the time I was a small child without any guidance or encouragement from my parents or family. My daily prayers were steeped in devotion, love for God, profound gratitude for everything in my life, and a heartfelt plea to Him to bless my family and the people I loved with health, happiness and long joyful lives. These prayers that I made up myself without any religious education, mimicked the prayer called the *Amidah*, a prescribed prayer that Jews around the world say daily. This discovery that I had been praying like religious Jews my entire life came to me several months after April 7, 2009, the morning of my spiritual awakening. This spiritual awakening was in the making from the time I was born. Without putting a name or label on it, I always had an openness and psychic ability. I wasn't a mind reader or fortune teller but I always felt a deep connection to the spirit world.

As a little girl, I used to be awakened in the middle of the night to physical vibrations that took over my body and were accompanied with the overwhelming feeling of people in the room. These people were non-physical, often referred to as ghosts. I felt surrounded by people that I recognized were no longer in this physical world. As a child, I thought they were ghosts, and these nightly visits would scare the daylights out of me. In the middle of the night I'd wake up screaming and tried to break these vibrations, swinging my arms wildly at the ghosts to push them away.

At around seven years old, I remember my father standing at the doorway of my bedroom as I was struggling with these feelings in the middle of the night. My dad simply stood there waiting for me to wake up out of what he likely thought was an ordinary nightmare. After he saw that I was all right, he left and I went back to sleep. These sorts of nightly visits happened throughout my life and continued into adulthood. As I grew older I learned that this didn't happen to everyone and that I had something more going on within and around me than most people. I could hear and feel people who were no longer in this world.

I also had several out-of-body experiences when I was growing up. I remember playing a bedtime game that I called flying. This was a game where I would levitate my soul out of my body at will and fly around the house while my family was sleeping. I played this game often and on purpose. I didn't fully recognize what I was doing, but I instinctually knew that I couldn't leave the front door of my home or fly too far away from my body which was still in my bed. I somehow knew I had to keep close by so that I could reenter my body after I had my fun. I understood that if I went too far away from my body, my parents would find a lifeless dead Lori in the morning. It was a game that I never spoke about with anyone because to me it was just a fun nightly activity. It never occurred to me that not everyone was able to do this.

In the beginning of my awakening when I began hearing the spirit world in April of 2009, I wasn't surprised that this was happening to me. I had always had an acute spiritual awareness going on within me but never understood it fully. Throughout my life I received frequent visits from the spirit world that I always pushed away because they frightened me. On one miraculous occasion, when I was 21 years old, I was given life changing physical proof that we are not alone in this world.

Visitor from Beyond

As a teenager, I was enamored with psychics and tarot card readers. It became one of my pastimes trying to figure out if I was on the right path in my life. I believed we were surrounded by a spirit world and that some people could hear things that nobody else could hear. Visiting palm readers and psychics was something my friends and I did occasionally. If there was a psychic fair in the mall, I went and paid money for a reading and to ask questions. My parents weren't aware that I was doing this and speaking of such things was never a topic in my home growing up. I had no idea that having tarot cards read was dangerous or breaking any of God's laws. The thought that I was breaking

God's laws by doing any of this was never on my radar. As far as I knew, God had only 10 laws to follow. You know, *The Ten Commandments* as taught in the movie with Charlton Heston. In my life, I would never break one of those!

My fascination with psychics continued into my college years. In my senior year at Fairleigh Dickinson University, my friend and former roommate introduced me to a psychic medium. This medium was a man who lived in northern New Jersey and was the husband of somebody my roommate worked with during a college internship. This man claimed to be clairvoyant with the ability to speak to the spirit world. He gave himself the lofty title of Reverend. At the time, I was having trouble with my college boyfriend so I went to meet the reverend for advice. He was quite impressive and he took a liking to me.

There are extremely dangerous people in our world who sport the name "Reverend" or other religious titles to give you a feeling of safety and comfort. These people can be some of the most dangerous people on earth. They lure you into their devil's den with their false titles and are more dangerous than pagans and atheists who don't believe in God at all. In my naïveté, I formed a relationship with this man who claimed to be a reverend after he gave me my first psychic reading. He seemed to know things about me that he couldn't know unless he was guided by some invisible force. Because he seemed gifted and he went by the title of Reverend, I trusted him and his advice and called him at his request when I had important decisions to make. After I graduated college he wanted to speak with me more frequently. It didn't occur to me that he might be dangerous. I don't recall that he even took money from me after the first reading. He instructed me to call him every time I needed to make any decision.

After graduating college from Fairleigh Dickinson University in Teaneck, New Jersey, in May of 1981, I accepted my first job offer with a company in northern New Jersey. I packed up my new car, a graduation present from my father, and drove to North Jersey to find a place to live. My college placement office referred me to a room for rent in a private home in Paramus. The woman who was renting this room was a widow in her 60s who had lost her husband a few years prior. She lived with her disabled daughter in a lovely split-level in a beautiful neighborhood. Her home was clean and the rent was a perfect price for someone like me on an entry level salary. These were my only criteria for choosing a place to live. The owner was lovely. The house was clean. The price was right.

I moved in right away and began my new job. My landlady was very warm and generous and we enjoyed a friendly relationship. Her daughter, who was in her 30s, suffered from mental illness and never left the home. She was also a very nice woman like her mother, but seeing her suffer from mental illness made me sad and often uncomfortable. There were several times when she exhibited very dysfunctional behavior, and suffered negative reactions to her medications. I simply accepted the situation as part of the package and made the best of it.

In recent years I learned something I couldn't have known back when I moved into this widow's home in Paramus. Her house was spiritually unclean. In 1981, I wouldn't have had any idea what spiritually unclean even meant. When I moved into this woman's home, I didn't know about Torah, Torah law, or the risk involved in living in a home that was unprotected by a mezuzah. A mezuzah is an ornament placed on the doorposts of Jewish homes which contains a scroll inscribed with the holy prayer called the *Shema*. The *Shema* is a holy prayer that protects the home from spiritual impurities. My landlady wasn't Jewish, so why in the world would she have a mezuzah? She wouldn't. It never occurred to me that this could be of any concern. If you're not Jewish and you're reading this, you're likely thinking this has nothing to do with you. You might think to yourself, "I've never had a mezuzah, I'm not Jewish and I've never suffered from any problems." You need to read this information and learn about this anyway to understand the true nature of our world. There are many laws in Torah that were given to the children of Israel to protect them spiritually in this physical world. Most of the world is completely unaware of this knowledge. These laws were passed down for generations and are adhered to by a Torah observant minority.

Here I was a young 21-year-old girl, completely naïve, unaware of how dangerous the spirit world truly was, living in the home of a widow who didn't follow Torah law at all. She was a good Christian woman, but a woman who was void of any understanding and knowledge that exists within God's Torah. In comes little Lori, who befriended a psychic medium masquerading as a holy reverend without being holy or reverent to God at all. Holy God! This spiritual uncleanliness that surrounded me was a horrific powder keg ready to explode … and it did!

As I began working at my new job, my new supervisor and I became friendly. He was a Christian man in his 30s, who was truly amazing and highly clairvoyant. The moment we met it was as though angels were wildly ringing bells around us. We felt a deep spiritual connection between us immediately. I don't know if you've ever had this kind of encounter with someone before, but there are times in our lives when we meet someone and know there is a divine purpose.

My supervisor was smart and charming and I admired him so I began to sit at his desk where we talked daily. One day I discovered he had a supernatural ability to astral project his soul out of his body and travel in a non-physical way. Crazy you say? Yeah but this is unequivocally possible and he proved it to me! He astral projected himself and visited me from another part of the building where we both worked. As I was working at my desk, I suddenly saw his face in full-color in my mind's eye, the center of my forehead, and heard his voice clearly say, "Come say hello to me. I'm in the cafeteria." When this happened, I slowly looked around the office where I was sitting to see if anyone else heard him. I got up out of my seat and walked over to the cafeteria. I looked in the cafeteria window and there he was, sitting, smiling and waving to me. Wow! This was supernatural and very exciting for me to experience. I wondered how in the world could anyone do such things?

Remember now, I'm living in a widow's home in Paramus with her disabled, mentally ill daughter. Again, she was a Christian woman who didn't follow any Torah law protecting her home and didn't follow any laws that guard our spiritual purity and safety. Why is this so important? In short, Torah law protects us from hauntings that can come from spiritual uncleanliness. Her husband who died a few years earlier was still dwelling in her home. He never left and was very unhappy with my presence. He did not want me there whatsoever. He frequently came to me at night to wake me out of a deep sleep. As a child, I grew up with frightening feelings of spirits surrounding me in my bedroom. Now, at 21 years old, I was living in a haunted house and being taunted by a ghost!

This is when my clairvoyant work buddy came to my rescue, and why from the moment we met we knew we had a strong spiritual connection. Hashem, God, in his infinite wisdom places the right people in our lives at precisely the right time. My clairvoyant work buddy knew I was in terrible danger and explained that the reverend was steeped in black magic and was quite evil. He explained that this satanic medium reverend who was dealing in black magic was also capable of astral projection like he was. Unlike him though, the reverend had evil intentions and wasn't just playing around with me.

This filthy monster used his ability to astral project his soul out of his body and visit me in the middle of the night with purely evil intentions. He astral projected his soul and came into my bedroom and non-physically sexually assaulted me while I slept. My clairvoyant work buddy instructed me to break all ties with this reverend immediately and warned me how dangerous he was to my well-being. I was grateful for his help and advice and I listened.

Some of you may wonder how it's possible for someone to astral project their soul out of their body at will and sexually assault a woman against her will. Please trust me, this is completely possible. I've learned since then about other women who have suffered from similar assaults. What this disgraceful excuse for a man did to me was so extraordinarily dangerous I am shaking now at the thought that this ever happened. Every night that I slept in the widow's home I was being spiritually tortured. Either I was taunted by the landlady's dead husband who haunted her house, or I was visited and sexually assaulted by a deeply evil monster who masqueraded around our world with the title of Reverend.

Ending all connections with this monster reverend wasn't enough to protect me or remove the problem. I continued to be traumatized by him and was frequently taunted by my landlady's dead husband. There was nobody in my life who was knowledgeable about the Torah back then, and I didn't have any knowledge or understanding that this was something I sorely needed. I didn't know where to turn for help. So, I did what I thought was the next best thing. I went to my favorite tarot card reader, a psychic woman whom I met in the shopping mall. She was a kind woman who I grew to like and trust. Really Lori? Yes, really. I went where I felt safe and I thought she had knowledge about how to deal with the spirit world.

This tarot card reader told me that I was being taunted by a ghost and said the answer was for me to buy a green candle from the store and keep it lit all night. She said there was something about green candles that would protect me. Okay, that's easy enough I thought. So I did what she recommended and I went to the store and bought the only green candle I could find. I bought a very large candle that was obviously made for Christians. It had pictures of Christian looking angels with large wings. Yes, your Jewish Messiah bought a Christian candle. True. I lit this candle and then I began to do what I always instinctually did throughout my life—I prayed very hard for God to protect me. As I prayed, I never imagined what was about to happen to me that night. It was a night that changed the way I see our world forever.

I went to bed praying to God to protect me from all the evil that was taunting and terrorizing me. I fell asleep and at around 3 AM, the most common time for me to have "visits" from the spirit world, the vibrations took me over once again. As a child, these vibrations frightened me. I fought hard to break out of them and swat away the "ghosts" that I felt surrounding me. These vibrations felt like I was plugged into an electrical outlet with a strong current buzzing all over my body from head to toe. Growing up I never saw what was in the room because I would scream to end these feelings and push these spirits away. Not so on this special and miraculous night. On this night, I would receive a visit that proved to me once and for all that we are not alone.

This time when I felt the vibrations, I decided not to retreat in fear. I braced myself and asked God to protect me. I prayed to Him for protection and courage, then asked Him to please let me see what has been happening around me my entire life. When I slowly opened my eyes, the sights and images I saw literally took my breath away.

The entire room was filled with white flashing light. The light was very bright but didn't hurt my eyes. It looked like the kind of light that's described when people die and come back. It seemed extremely white and holy. I looked down by the side of my bed and I could see nasty looking hands reaching up and trying to grab me. This scared me to no end. I was petrified seeing these evil hands trying to reach for me as though they desired to harm me. While these awful hands were reaching for me, the white light flashing in the room provided a deep sense of safety and comfort.

I looked across the room and suddenly by the window I saw the silhouette of a person which shocked me. "Oh no!" I thought, "Someone is in the room with me!" The silhouette of this person turned around slowly to face me as I was lying there in bed. "Oh God, what is happening?!" This person was surrounded with the glow of the same white light that was flashing in the room.

As this person walked closer to me, illuminated in bright white light, I could see the face of an average looking woman. She was wearing a white T-shirt and blue jeans. She looked completely ordinary and her demeanor was deeply calming. If I had to guess her age, I would say she looked to be in her 30s. She was very calming and sweet as she walked over to me. Then, as she leaned closer to me, with the tip of the center finger of her right hand she gently touched the side of my left cheek, looked me squarely in my eyes, smiled gently, and said, "I would never hurt you." She then turned around and walked toward the window where she first appeared and vanished into thin air. At that moment, the entire room was completely silent and still and all the flashing lights vanished with her. As I sat up in bed I had one tear streaming down the right side of my face.

This woman who was surrounded in holy white light came from nowhere and left the room going into nowhere. Where did she come from? Where did she go? Who was she? The result was complete silence and peace. From that moment on I never had another visit from the evil satanic reverend or the angry dead husband who wanted me out of his house.

Shortly after that experience, I packed my belongings and moved to a new home. After I moved out and things were calmer in my life, I found a new job. My clairvoyant work buddy and I got together for one last dinner. We both knew that it was time for us to say goodbye. We knew that his purpose had been served and we had completed what was needed. Before we parted ways, he said something to me that I've never forgotten.

He told me that I was highly clairvoyant and gifted but that I wouldn't embrace my gifts for many years. He told me that in my 40s I would choose to open the door, embrace my gift, and unite with 40 other people around the world at a time when our world needed healing. This was a stunning prediction and prophecy. His words struck me deeply and I didn't fully accept or understand them at the time. Over the years, I wondered if this would one day come true. After we parted, we never spoke again.

Fast forward, 28 years later on April 7, 2009, the door opened and I accepted. What I opened the door to was something I couldn't have imagined in my wildest dreams. On that day, I was a 49-year-old mother of three children, the oldest of whom was looking at colleges. I was suffering from despair because I was losing my hearing. I started losing my hearing around the age of 40 and by age 49, as a working mother of three who ran her own marketing company, I was told I was going deaf. In the spring of 2009, in deep crisis over this painful news, I reached for God with all my might and on one auspicious morning He gave me an audible answer! I went deaf and now I hear Hashem God's voice and the spirit world with exquisite clarity. Fantastic, right? Wrong! He said to me on the first morning that I was chosen. Chosen? Okay, I thought. This is quite miraculous, so I decided to buy a journal and record my conversations and learn about my new miraculous ability. Like I do everything in my life, I gave this a 110% effort.

So being that hindsight is usually 20/20, in hindsight, I should have taken everything slowly. I should have been more prudent about how I digested all the information I was hearing. Perhaps everything I was hearing wasn't true. How could I be sure of what I was hearing if I couldn't see who was speaking the words? Instead of taking everything slowly, my reaction was to leave the ground and fly. Information that came in, was information out. I shared everything I heard with reckless abandon—a very dangerous thing to do when you have no education and understanding of Torah, the spirit world, and the mysterious ways of Hashem God.

As dangerous as my choices were and having suffered through the horrific turn of events that followed, I know now that it was all planned. Everything that happened was orchestrated by Hashem, precisely on time and completely on purpose. Every bit of it. The agony, pain and suffering that I went through to get to the other side of this nightmare was excruciating. The personal pain that I experienced in my life was necessary, and I still suffer hardship to this day. My life, as blessed as I am to have a uniquely close relationship with our Creator, is tragically lonely. Family and longtime friends are no longer part of my life. Many of them have disavowed any relationship with me. More often, I made the painful personal choice to walk away from every relationship except for one remaining friend and my three children. I've chosen to live my life alone.

This is Me

Why you might ask would I walk away from almost every relationship I've ever had? Because this is me. I am truly this. What is this? I am completely one with God. I am fully integrated and journey as one with our Creator. I speak, eat and talk with Him continuously every day and throughout the night. Asking me to stop talking to Him and be like everyone else is like asking a giraffe to be a pumpkin. I can't be something that I'm not. This is truly what I am. If I'm not permitted to be authentically myself in my personal relationships, share Him and His wisdom with you, I need to walk away and live alone. If I don't reveal what I know and how I truly am to the people who are supposed to be the closest to me, I'm living a lie. Living a lie where I conceal my relationship with God is not only painful for me, but it's of great harm to everyone else in the world. I must be authentically me and share this gift without reservation. It's time.

It's incomprehensible to me that I've had such a difficult time finding acceptance since my awakening. Nobody has wanted to listen to me. When I bring up the subject of God, people head for the hills. I'm not Jewish enough, Christian enough, or man enough. I'm not rich enough, young enough, or beautiful enough. I'm just not enough. I'm not what you expected or what you want. Bruce Jenner turning into Caitlin Jenner received more love and acceptance than your Queen Moshiach, Messiah. Doesn't that say anything powerful to you? I'm an honest, hardworking American mother who hears God and the spirit world better than anyone else in the world. Truly. I'm authentic and sincere and not inventing any of this. There is nothing contrived about me. Why then has every family member and friend turned a deaf ear to me? I'm deaf and nobody listens. Powerfully ironic, don't you think?

People who have known me for decades secretly peek at my LinkedIn profile online and don't bother to pick up the phone to call me. Why? It's clearly astounding. I'm intelligent, honest, I can be funny and even witty. Being funny is quite accidental as I express how I think about things and don't realize I've said something humorous until I see someone laughing. Their laughter makes me giggle too. I've learned that I can tell a great story occasionally and complete strangers in remote parts of the world appear to find me genuine and believable.

Why then have lifelong friends and family members walked away from me in utter silence? This is my story but millions of people everywhere will be able to relate to it. Every day people around the world are scorned, rejected and judged unfairly. People harm each other in untold ways and are expected to shrug it off. We're taught to accept that being treated poorly and with utter disdain is just the way of this world. As everyone takes turns scorning, rejecting and judging one another, they rarely take personal responsibility for any problems. My story will show you that the true source of our problems is hidden within ourselves and each other.

Lori the Leper

One night, as Hashem often does, He pointed me to a YouTube video posted by a rabbi and asked me to watch it with Him. This is the way I live my daily life. Alone day and night with nobody else conversing with me except for Hashem. I do every single life task with His involvement while I spend all my waking and sleeping hours physically alone. The YouTube video was entitled, *Why is Moshiach called a "Metzorah?"* Many people reading this book right now will have no idea what a Metzora is and neither did I. Yes, your Moshiach is clueless too. I asked Hashem what this word meant and as usual, He made me look it up. I looked up the meaning of Metzora and found the following definition: *one who is diseased (commonly mistranslated as leper)*. While I didn't know the meaning of Metzora, I know what it's like to be treated like a leper.

After reading this definition, Hashem watched this video with me. As I was overcome with emotion, He comforted me as He always does. When the truthfulness of this video struck me deeply and brought me to tears, I could barely see straight. The rabbi in this video described the Moshiach as an amazing and most exalted servant of God but "he" was someone who would be treated horribly by everyone else in the world, and would live as a tortured soul. As the rabbi continued to describe how astounding and wonderful the Moshiach was, I lost it at "leper." I sobbed and cried to Hashem how my life was horrible and barely livable. If it weren't for His constant companionship and love, my life would be void of any true love or companionship at all.

I'm almost friendless and have no family other than my three beautiful children who have refused to abandon me. Many people tried to destroy me and desired to sever my relationship with my children. Hashem held me in the grip of His hands, carried me through this raging storm, and I've lived to write this book and tell my story. With God's help I persevered and survived unimaginable cruelty that continues to follow me. While everyone else in the world quit and left me cold, my children continue to show their devotion and love for me. I'm deeply grateful for the love of my children and one friend who remains part of my daily life and supports me with this work.

My life experience has shown me that everyone will leave me at some time. When push came to shove, they all left. While I felt forced to walk away from many relationships that were dysfunctional, it wasn't my preference, it was for self-preservation. As I publish this book and reveal my story, it may become untenable for my one last friend to remain in my life. I also fear that I will finally lose my children. They may feel forced to leave me and walk away to save themselves. I must release this book and tell my story anyway. Though the last remaining loved ones might walk away, I love them too much to remain silent. I also can't bear living this life as a leper any longer. It's time to break free of my prison and be authentically who I am.

My daily life is physically lonely as I spend every moment alone with Hashem. Living with Hashem as one is a supreme and magnificent gift that I never want to live without. Being like this with Hashem in our world with all of you is the greatest holy nightmare I wish would end. He wakes me every morning and I feel his hands within my own as He wipes the tears from my eyes. We have our morning chat where He infuses me with love and inspires me to get out of bed and continue forward with my work. My work is fruitless and deeply painful. As I watch you and the rest of our world head toward certain destruction, I post many videos, wait for you to watch them yet you continue to scoff and ignore me. I keep reaching to you anyway. In my great despair I warn you about what's ahead and many flee or call me names. I'm compulsively addicted to try and reach anyone who will listen, but to date I've reached so few people I can count them on one hand.

I'm promised you will all begin to wake now and finally listen to me. Hashem says my life here will become glorious when you do. He continues to stream visions in my mind where I'm surrounded by a mass of people showering me with love and acceptance. It flows like a miraculous dream that is too difficult for me to fathom. As I go forward with this work, I wish and pray for this dream to come true.

My Children, My Purpose

While my life here in this world with you is horrible and I live like a leper, I keep going and refuse to quit. Nobody has truly believed me completely from April 7, 2009 through this very day. How in the world could I be anyone's Messiah? Some people have chosen to listen occasionally and believed it might be true that I hear God, but when I told them difficult things they didn't want to hear, they retreated and walked away. When I shared feel-good messages, they rejoiced and told me they believed I could hear God, but Messiah still sounded far-fetched. Nobody will completely believe that I'm the Moshiach until the world sits up at attention, finally believes me, and the trumpets blare announcing the coming of the Messiah. Some former friends and family members might smile when they realize I told the truth all along. Others will be heartbroken, devastated, and might beg to die because of how they treated me. I live in a constant state of prayer for all of them.

As I complete this incredible book, and I mean incredible, I have two people in this world supporting me. Without them, I would go it alone and do this anyway. I'm compelled to persevere against all odds and give you what you need. The truth.

Instead of being loved and accepted for revealing the truth and being transparent, I was branded crazy and my life was irrevocably destroyed. Through it all I persevered and refused to quit because I knew this was my calling on that first morning. I know this is my calling now. My calling is to extend my hand to you and help you learn the truth about our world and the peril we are facing. It's my life's purpose to save my children and all the children of the world which includes you. Our world is spinning in chaos and everyone is either sound asleep or blaming someone else for all the problems they see. The few who recognize the madness and evil, don't know or see everything that I do. I know more and can lead you to answers.

My beautiful children, whom I love with all my heart, are sound asleep and the house is on fire. I'm going in. There is no other way for me to go. I must save my children. They are my life's breath and the reason why I keep reaching to Hashem God day and night praying for the strength and courage to continue with this work and live another day of my painful life.

As I deliver God's voice to you with love, I pray you will recognize your life's purpose too. Please read every word of my book and take my extended hand so that I can help you heal. When you reach the last page, I pray you will awaken to your purpose and extend your hand to others too. We must band together and save all our children.

Imagine This Happened to You

As you read my story try to imagine this happened to you. In this way, maybe you can possibly understand why I'm so devoted to doing this work and you might be able to relate to me better and feel my sincerity. By putting yourself in my shoes, perhaps you'll feel compassion for everything I went through to bring this information out to the world. Through your compassion you might feel the enormity of what I've experienced and my relentless determination to bring this book to the public. Perhaps then you'll value how important this information truly is and take this very seriously.

Whoever you are, imagine one morning God Himself woke you up. Yes, it's Him and you know it with all your heart and every fiber of your being. He awakens you one auspicious morning and says, "This is God speaking to you and you are chosen. You need to go out right now and tell everyone that I'm speaking to you and you are my chosen one." Okay, are you ready? Let's go on the count of three. Ready, set, 1-2-3, GO! Come on now, go tell everyone right now! What's wrong? What are you waiting for? Oh, maybe you're concerned they may think you're nuts? Yeah, I totally understand. Perhaps now you might empathize with me a bit and understand what happened to me.

People said that I was crazy and mentally ill when it happened to me, a middle-aged mommy from New Jersey. Many have said, "God would never choose you Lori Michelle, that's simply ridiculous!" Try to suspend your disbelief and keep reading right to the end.

As you read the story of my awakening, try to put yourself in my shoes and think about what you would have done in the same situation. Hashem tells me that no other person would have made it this far or made the same choices. He says that the choices I made were all spot-on and correct. I chose goodness and God in every moment without exception. This natural innate ability to choose Him without exception makes me His Moshiach and I'm here to teach. While Hashem says He chose me to be His Moshiach because of how I am, I know being the Moshiach has very little to do with me. I am Moshiach because of Him. It's all Hashem. He drives me and pushes me to get out of bed each morning with a smile on my face when I truly have nothing to be happy about. He never lets me hit rock bottom and keeps me paddling my rowboat no matter how much suffering I must endure. I go weeks on end without any physical human contact. No handshakes, hugs, kisses, no nothing. He loves me right through the rainstorm and fills my mind with visions of world peace. Hashem God is pure love and spiritually magnificent. He holds me in the grip of His hands in every moment. Nobody could do what I'm attempting to do right now without Him breathing down their neck, quite literally. It simply wouldn't be possible. Although I'm admittedly a little bit bizarre, this is a story about an everyday person like you. I was an ordinary everyday American, a working mom with three kids, who woke up to a miracle and a hellish nightmare at the same time.

This story is wild and strange but emphatically true. More than nine years ago, I woke up to the voice of God Himself, stepped into the Twilight Zone and never left it. It may be too hard to believe that I speak to and live as one with our Creator and that's 100 percent ok for now. You can still learn and benefit from my stories and experiences. For now, just enjoy the journey I'm about to take you on and consider it a wild tale with many life lessons. Go get yourself a bucket of popcorn and a pack of M&M's. Go ahead ... I'll wait.

Now, as Jackie Gleason used to say, "And away we go!"

HIS VOICE, VISIONS & LESSONS

Are we slaves to GOD?

It might sound like an odd question to you but people do wonder—do they have real control of their lives? God is all powerful. If you believe in God and I hope you do, you know that He is omnipotent. He is dominant and He is the greatest force in all the universe. So, are we His slaves? Are we puppets in His play?

The answer to the question, "Are we slaves to God?" is emphatically no. As a matter of fact, Hashem God desires us to be free to choose. It is our birthright. Liberty and freedom is the way of life that He desires for us. Slavery, bondage and control are the workings of mankind. These offenses come from ego and its insatiable desire to control. Ego says, "It's all about me!" It's about the need to control everybody and your surroundings so that there's more for me. Ego is on a relentless quest to satisfy me, myself and I with little or no regard for others.

Hashem has no ego. All He desires to do is to give us freedom and love and yes, He has given us rules—a playbook to follow His rules. There are many people who think they know better. They think that religious people who follow His rules and observe His laws are ridiculous. Many secular non-religious people view devoutly religious people as insane or part of a cult. They think the rules and restrictions are oppressive. "Why can't I go to the ball game on the Sabbath? I should be able to do anything I want to do."

The truth is you can choose anything you want to do. You can break the rules that He has provided to us and it is much to your chagrin if you do. Because when you break His rules you harm yourself. He has given us everything. He's given us the entire world and all that there is. All He asks us to do is to choose Him, share, be loving and follow His rules which are designed for us to have a great and blessed life here on earth. He gave us a rulebook because He knows the pitfalls. He knows where we'll fall down and He has predicted exactly what we're experiencing right now in this world—terror, war, conflagration. He predicted it all. So, we're not slaves. We choose to be slaves or we choose to enslave others by using controlling behavior and forcing people to go along with the way we think they should live their lives.

On the holiday of Passover, we celebrate freedom itself, where Moses, God's prophet with Hashem God's hand involved all the way, freed the children of Israel from slavery. Passover is a celebration of freedom, not just for the Jewish children—for all of God's children. We are all free. Free to choose God or to choose the opposite of God. Peace on earth will come when we all learn to choose God in every moment.

Chapter 2

The Brewing Wake-up Call

My spiritual awakening was in the making without my realizing it for many years prior to that auspicious morning when I heard Hashem God's voice speak to me. He methodically prepared me for this awakening by causing me to lose my hearing, slowly, over many years.

The magnitude of going deaf was far more significant to me than most other people experiencing the same trauma. This is not meant to marginalize how serious and depressing it is for anyone who suffers from profound hearing loss. Quite the contrary, I've been there and know how dreadful this is for everyone who loses their hearing. People who have suffered from hearing loss suffer in silence, pun intended. They often don't verbalize the pain they live through every day and keep it to themselves. Hearing loss is painful for everyone, but for me it meant that I was losing my entire life. The loss of my hearing was tantamount to being diagnosed with a terminal cancer. Why so melodramatic? For me, the ability to hear people and communicate is equivalent to being able to love. Without my ability to hear, I feared that I would lose everything and everyone in my life.

My fear of going deaf likely seemed exaggerated to everyone who knew me. They understood that it was upsetting, but they made light of my hearing loss and even made jokes about it. They couldn't fathom why I was so traumatized. Losing my hearing triggered a premonition in my soul that I was facing terrible losses. How terrible? I couldn't possibly fathom, but I knew something very bad was going to happen to me and I knew that I was about to lose everything. My losses weren't a direct result of going deaf but it was the precursor for many tragedies that were about to take place. The news that I was going deaf shook me to my core and literally brought me to my knees.

My Husband, My Best Friend

My husband and I were introduced by a mutual friend and we hit it off right away. A few months prior to this fateful introduction, I made the decision that I would only marry a Jewish man. This decision came after dating Gentiles almost exclusively my entire life. When I turned 26 I felt it was time to think about marriage and somehow, I instinctually knew I was about to meet my one. In making this decision, I pondered a statistic about how more than half of all marriages ended in divorce and I wanted to stack the deck in my favor. Religion was one issue where I thought I could avoid any future problems. I decided that marrying a Jew would ensure that we wouldn't have arguments when it came time to decide how we would raise our children. Raising my future children Jewish was non-negotiable to me. I felt a kinship with other Jewish families and always felt most comfortable in their homes. And so, I married my Jewish husband and the future father of my three children.

After dating only about nine months we became engaged on New Year's Day 1987 and married in August that year. We both came from secular Jewish American families and neither of us was religious. His parents were loving and wonderful and immediately embraced me as their daughter, not as a daughter-in-law. We had love, family and wealth right from the start. After we were married we enjoyed such wonderful financial success, I recall having to open a new checking account right away because the FDIC only insured our account up to $100,000. That marked our "meager" beginning of accumulating wealth. Wow! I was truly grateful to be so fortunate back then and it didn't occur to me that most of the world didn't have that kind of good fortune. We built our beautiful home in a lovely and affluent suburb in New Jersey in 1991 and began our Jewish family.

Everything came easily for us in those early years and we enjoyed a happy marriage. We were the best of friends who did everything together. People often joked how our personalities were completely opposite like black and white, yet we got along more like Frick and Frack, and our relationship seemed to work beautifully.

Neither of us had any desire to spend much time with anyone but each other. That's not to say we didn't have lots of friends and enjoy their company. We did. We simply enjoyed being alone with each other more. Ours wasn't an obsession or love affair like in the movie *Ten* with Bo Derek and Dudley

Moore. We weren't infatuated with each other, we loved each other deeply as the best of friends. I often told him how I loved him and that he was my best friend. He always replied, "I love you Lori. You're my only friend." This was his typical tongue-in-cheek sense of humor. I would chuckle at his response and move on with my day.

The subject of God or religion didn't come up very often. When it did, he would usually defer to me and my opinion. Sometimes it took a good fight to convince him, but he usually backed down in the end. Throughout my life I always loved and revered God, but never spoke about the subject much with him. It simply didn't come up very often. When we met I wasn't religious and neither was my husband. We worked together, had our three children, and life went somewhat smoothly for the first 10 years of our marriage. After a decade together, life brought us stress as it often does for everyone.

When I was seven months pregnant with our second child, we discovered that my husband was severely anemic. He had severe gastrointestinal issues and health problems throughout his childhood. Now many years later his history of poor health was rearing its ugly head. After a weekend in Montauk, New York, we rushed home and found that he needed an emergency blood transfusion. We found a local gastroenterologist who reviewed his health history and began treating him the same way the doctors treated him throughout his life. Since his parents brought him to the best of the best doctors in the world, this new gastroenterologist saw no reason to upset the applecart by putting him through more tests. He followed the party line and previous diagnosis given when my husband was 20 years old. My husband took a liking to this doctor, but after being treated for almost a year by him, he became more severely ill so I decided to find better.

After searching, I was referred to a world-renowned gastroenterologist from New York who thought for himself and didn't accept the party line. He put my husband through many grueling tests and then recommended major surgery. Four months after our third child was born, my husband endured over seven hours of major gastrointestinal surgery. When he came out of surgery, I never left his side throughout the ordeal. Our newborn baby was still nursing, so I came to the hospital with a breast pump, plastic bags and a cooler filled with ice. I frequently excused myself and went to the restroom to pump breast milk throughout the day and brought it home in the middle of the night. I did this while my husband was hospitalized because my mother was watching my children for us and I refused to feed my new baby formula.

This was one special memory I have of my mother. She stepped up on this occasion, supported me and my husband and stayed with our three young children when her own health was severely compromised at the time. Just a few months prior to my husband's surgery, she had a near-death experience. She endured a surgery that led to a life-threatening infection where she nearly died. The day she was rushed into emergency surgery to save her life, they told her there were no guarantees. She called me from the hospital to inform me that her life was in jeopardy, to express her love for me, and said this might be goodbye. My husband and I raced to the hospital with my newborn baby and oldest child, leaving our toddler at home with our family babysitter. Gratefully the surgery was successful and she made it through. This traumatic near-death experience changed our relationship for a short period of time. For the first time in my memory she became caring and loving toward me. Still recovering from this life-threatening event, she came to stay with our three children when my husband had his surgery. It's bittersweet that it took a brush with death to bring us closer for this brief time. Nonetheless, this memory of her is one I will always cherish because for the first time in my life I truly felt her love.

My husband didn't respond well to the trauma of this invasive surgery and for several nights I sat in a chair next to his bed in the surgical stepdown unit and held his hand all night long. The horrific pain from the surgery, massive doses of morphine, and trauma from this experience caused him to hallucinate. The hallucinations terrified him so I never left his side. Eventually he recovered from this surgery but his health problems were far from over. He struggled throughout the years both emotionally and physically. I attended almost all his medical appointments with him when he met with his doctors. He began to be treated for depression, anxiety, and sleep problems immediately after this first surgery. There was eventually a second surgery years later which was equally horrific. His poor health, psychological challenges and a lifetime of being ill were obstacles we learned to manage and deal with together. That's the way we lived our lives. We were the best of friends and we did everything together.

My husband and I struggled with many difficult life situations over the years as do many couples. We managed through our health problems, business problems and his mother's battle with cancer. After suffering through her death, we endured the painful loss of his father years later. We managed to work through all these health problems, business problems, and other life challenges as they occurred, and persevered.

The Supermom Complex—Doing It All

As I explained, my husband and I did everything together. We worked together in a graphic design company that I started in 1988. The goal in 1988 was a wishful vision to start a company so that one day my husband could join me, take it over and run it, and then I could have children and enjoy being a mom. My master plan was that I could work at my own discretion and be there for my children as they grew up. I believed in the American dream, that I could have it all. This was my working plan to have my cake and eat it too. I designed a plan and chose to do things that supported my vision of the perfect all-American life.

In 1988, I was working for a Minnesota-based company selling computer graphic design equipment. I approached one of my favorite clients and asked him to become business partners with me and my new husband. He agreed. He and his wife became business partners with my husband and me in a fledgling graphic design company. In the early years, our relationship with our partners was warm, friendly and mutually beneficial. We were like family. I seemed to have the Midas touch in sales and marketing. I brought my gift for sales and marketing into our new endeavor with our partners. Over the years, I brought in many major accounts and grew our new company faster than anyone expected. It seemed that every time I went out to secure new business I was successful. We all flourished financially for many years but eventually the partnership ended. After the partnership ended, my husband and I formed a new marketing design company. I was the president and ran the company from soup to nuts, but I left the bookkeeping to him. He liked to be a bean counter and I had no interest in beans. As with many small companies, I was chief cook and bottle washer. Whether I liked it or not I was involved in all aspects of the business including sales, technical, creative, hiring and firing, and even managing the work flow as project manager. The only aspect of the business I stayed out of was bean counting. I entrusted the accounting and money matters to my former husband.

We were self-employed for about 25 years. Over the years I brought in many accounts and millions of dollars in revenue. Good years or bad years, whatever revenue I managed to bring in, it never seemed to be enough. In the latter years, when I brought in the clients I needed to manage them all or we'd lose them. It seemed nobody could manage these relationships and keep our clients happy the way I did. When I tried to hand off this responsibility, the clients would eventually complain and request me to work with them again. I kept going, brought in new accounts and managed all the business as best as one person could possibly handle.

In the new millennium women have what's been nicknamed "The Supermom Complex." They try to do it all. They work at a career, raise their children, cook, clean, and do everything that a mother is traditionally supposed to do. I was no different from many moms. I ran my own marketing business while I raised and cared for my three children. We were an affluent American family of five, living in an upscale suburb in New Jersey as I worked at having everything. By everything I mean a career, family, and the all-American lifestyle with a beautiful house and frequent trips to the Caribbean. I had it all so I thought. I would get up at 4:30 AM and by 5 AM I was at the gym pumping iron and working out. By 7:30 AM I was in the shower getting ready for my full workday.

Our small marketing company had many ups and downs but so do many small businesses. We suffered from small company-itis where I wore too many hats and was involved in every aspect of our business. When people commented over the years, "If you take Lori out of the company there is no company" they were 100 percent correct. One day this prediction would come to pass.

From the outside looking in it might have appeared to people that I had the all-American life, with three beautiful children, a devoted husband, a beautiful home, financial security, lots of diamonds and trips to Hawaii. On the surface, it appeared that I had the perfect American dream life. Little did I know that one day God Himself would bring our false house of cards tumbling down.

The Journey to Deafness

I began losing my hearing in the year 2000 at the age of 40. Small things began to occur that signaled something was wrong. I noticed that I suddenly couldn't hear the high-pitched microwave sound that told me my food was ready. We had a burglar alarm system in our house that had a high-pitched alert signaling you to turn off the alarm when you entered the house. I tripped the alarm on multiple occasions. I couldn't hear the signal any longer and mistakenly thought that someone else had turned the alarm off. When I entered my home and neglected to turn off the alarm, I tripped it and then I heard the loud siren go off. The phone would ring immediately when the alarm security company called to check if it was a burglary. After this happened a few times, I realized that I couldn't hear the high-pitched signal any longer.

I went to an ENT (Ear Nose & Throat) doctor for a hearing exam and learned that I was suffering from bilateral neurosensory hearing loss. From the beginning, they said this type of hearing loss was incurable. I began to search everywhere for answers as to why I suddenly was losing my hearing because I wanted to find a solution and stop it in its tracks. In the beginning my hearing was still within normal speech range so I could cope well, work and still function normally. This was crucial to me because I was the main breadwinner for our family of five. While my husband and I worked together as business partners, everybody said that our business was all me. Even my husband joked, "Don't ask me anything, ask Lori. I work for her." When I had long drives for meetings that were hours away, my husband loved to drive me and wait for me in the car. He would say his favorite job in the world was "Driving Miss Lori" making a funny analogy to the movie *Driving Miss Daisy*. People who knew us often commented that if I ever stopped working and left my company, it would fall apart immediately and there would be nothing left.

By the year 2006 at age 46 I had already lost a great deal of my hearing Every six months to a year I went for a new hearing exam trying to find the reason why I was going deaf but I never received any answers. I was ultimately brought to tears at every visit when the audiologist informed me that I had suffered more hearing loss. The mere idea of going deaf was deeply frightening. I was terrified about losing my ability to work and provide financially for my family. But there was more to this experience of hearing loss that made it so intensely troubling and heartbreaking.

You see when you go deaf you lose more than your hearing. People with normal hearing should listen to my story and begin to examine your treatment of people who suffer from deafness. In the future, when you speak to somebody who suffers from hearing loss, start to check yourself. Watch how you treat people who struggle with their hearing and notice if your level of irritation rises when you're with them. Notice your facial expressions if they ask you to repeat something you just said. You may never have realized this before but most hearing people are extremely insensitive and rude to people who suffer from deafness. The insensitive treatment I received from hearing people was a startling revelation to me that I was being diminished in their eyes by my deafness. They began to treat me like I was less intelligent and a nuisance. Even family and friends who knew me extremely well and supposedly loved me, often belittled and dismissed me when I couldn't hear them. How so? With a roll of their eyes, an exasperated heavy sigh or refusing to repeat themselves because it was too much trouble. It was clear that I was becoming too much trouble to engage in a conversation with them. People also enjoyed poking fun at my hearing loss and made me the butt of jokes. They seemed to think it was hilarious when I couldn't hear them. I assure you, there was nothing to laugh about.

When I was in a room where people were joking and laughing at a story or punchline, it became heartbreaking instead of fun or a source of joy. While everyone else was giggling, I sat there looking like a stunned deer in the headlights of a car. Clueless. Everybody else understood and enjoyed the joke. Everyone but me. When they saw I didn't understand the joke, their reactions and facial expressions showed me they thought I was stupid. They couldn't understand that it was my filter, my ears, that weren't working, not my intellect. Here I was, a college graduate, considered a smart lady by many, and known to be a consummate business woman respected by her peers. Now instead of being treated with respect, people often dismissed and spoke down to me.

Business networking meetings became a severe challenge. I couldn't hear well, so when I spoke to people I'd often ask them to repeat themselves. At one networking meeting, a woman was trying to give me the name of a business contact as a potential sales lead. She was sharing this information in front of about five or six other people. As she was speaking, I couldn't understand what she was saying. I asked her at least three times to please repeat and speak slowly or write down the information because I couldn't hear her. She looked at me angrily and in a condescending and mocking tone said, "What are you, deaf?"

She was so nasty I was a bit stunned and I replied calmly, "As a matter of fact, yes I am." She was visibly shaken and quite embarrassed. Instead of being angry with her, I felt compassion because I knew she wasn't aware that I was deaf. It appeared she assumed I was being rude and not listening to her or she possibly thought I was stupid. What was memorable and striking about this incident was the reaction of the five or six people at the table. They all looked at her in that moment as though she was a demon. In their eyes, you could see that they were judging her for being so insensitive and rude. They failed to realize that she was just like everyone else. Everyone is guilty of this on occasion, it was just her turn that day. Trust me on this one, you do it too. Start to check yourself from now on, and become more aware about how you speak to other people. Being inconsiderate is now a worldwide phenomenon and seems to be "business as usual." This woman was mortified that she had been rude to a deaf woman because she was caught. What if I weren't deaf and shrugged off her rude comment instead? Wasn't this rude of her to speak derisively to me anyway? The people at the table were mortified because she was rude to a disabled woman but they should have been mortified that she was rude, period.

As I slipped further into deafness, it became normal to be treated this way in my daily life. My children, husband and all my friends often lost their patience with me or dismissed me completely. Sitting at the dinner table, I couldn't follow the conversation as everyone spoke over each other. I'd eat my dinner in silence as they conversed. I was in a room filled with people but I was completely alone. Over the years, some of my family members became more understanding and tried a little harder when they realized how deaf I had become. When the audiology reports continued to show that I was going deaf, they pitied me. Their pity only made me feel worse. When my children came home from school and shared a story from their day, I couldn't understand them with my broken ears. They'd often roll their eyes and say, "It's okay Mom it's not important anyway." While they thought they were being considerate and polite, those words "it's not important" meant to me "you're not important."

Losing my hearing meant losing my connection to my family and my world. Hearing is love. When we communicate through our voices we reach each other's souls through our ears. Being dismissed like this caused me deep spiritual pain. I continued to work learning to lip-read to cope with my increasing deafness.

In 2008 my husband and I met with a new audiologist. In front of me, she began speaking to my husband as though I wasn't in the room. She told him I was so severely deaf that it was a miracle I managed to hide my deafness from everyone. She turned to my husband and said, "Your wife deserves an Oscar and she should be given special consideration and handicapped seating wherever she goes." I didn't realize my hearing loss had become so profound. I'm certain she thought her words were complimentary but I wasn't ready to face this news. I went to a different audiologist soon after for another opinion and I purchased two digital hearing aids. These hearing aids helped me cope better for a few more months.

By March of 2009, I couldn't even hear with my two hearing aids. One morning I went to buy coffee at a local bagel shop and couldn't understand what the cashier was saying to me. It was as though English, my mother tongue, had become a foreign language. I was frightened and went to the audiologist again and she took a new hearing test. This time the results were undeniable. She said, "You've lost too much hearing and hearing aids will no longer help you. I'm very sorry but your deafness is so severe you need to see a neurosurgeon who specializes in cochlear implants."

These words stunned me. As I explained before, I was the breadwinner for our family of five and even though we were financially well-off, we had three children heading to college soon. I feared I would no longer be able to provide for them and felt the weight of the world was on my shoulders. The news that I was becoming completely deaf meant even more to me than my ability to earn money. Over the years that I suffered from hearing loss people began treating me differently. They treated me like I was stupid, refused to repeat themselves, made me the butt of their jokes, and treated me as though I was worthless. In my despair, I feared I'd wind up losing my family, be kicked to the curb and end up living in a cardboard box one day. While this may sound like a wild exaggeration to you, in my mind, I was too much trouble and felt strongly that eventually everyone would abandon me. Incredibly, I now understand that these emotions were prophetic premonitions of what was coming.

It's an understatement to say I was grief stricken by the news that I was losing all my hearing and becoming completely deaf. While I was living through this experience of suffering from progressive hearing loss, my day-to-day life continued as usual. Every step along the way during these years, God was preparing me for my true life's purpose. Before I bring you to the moment of truth, my spiritual awakening when Hashem spoke to me that miraculous morning, let's journey back a few years prior. These pivotal years that led me into deafness were accompanied with life changing decisions that prepared me for a life I couldn't have imagined in my wildest dreams. The decisions I made along the way prepared me to be your Messiah, Hashem's Queen Moshiach.

Why should we honor our mother?

It's a commandment—honor thy mother and father—but today we're going to talk about what Hashem God has revealed to me about the mother. He says the mother is closest to Him in nature. What does this mean? God is all giving. He's completely outward. All He desires is love and appreciation. In that way, the mother is exactly like Hashem. Women, mothers in particular, simply desire your love and appreciation. It's important to learn and understand the mother and that her true nature is to be a giver. Giving is what a mother inherently desires to do in her life. She desires to give.

Women have been less than appreciated since the beginning of time. They have been subjugated and have suffered horrible abuses like being enslaved, publicly ridiculed, dehumanized as sex objects and valued only for their ability to bear children. People ridicule traditional female responsibilities by using the terminology *women's work*. Taking care of the home and family is difficult work that isn't truly appreciated by most of the world. Most people don't appreciate all the roles and duties a mother performs daily for her family. Now, women work to bring home money while they raise their families too. It's an extremely difficult job to be a working mother, to say the least.

Being a mom is the most difficult job on earth and we're not given a user's manual. When I had my first child twenty-six years ago, I remember being petrified. My entire life I knew that one day I wanted to be a mom. I desired to have a baby to raise and love. After I gave birth and they put my first child in my arms, I was overcome with great emotion. The mere idea of raising another human being was daunting. I did my best to be a good mom and I still do my best every day. I have been blessed with three amazing children who are now wonderful young adults. When I was younger and desired to have children of my own I don't believe that I understood everything that goes into being a good mother. The knowledge of how difficult it is to raise children came after I became a mother.

I would like you, whoever you are, to pause and consider all the things that your mother ever did for you. You may never have truly appreciated every daily task she did for you over the years. She may not be a perfect person. She may have made many mistakes. She may be less than what you expected or desired her to be, but she's your mom and Hashem, God, says it is her nature to love her children, to love everyone and to be the consummate giver. All she desires in life is appreciation and to hear the magic words "Thank you mom, I appreciate you." Being valued is all she truly desires at the end of every day. So, the next time it's Mother's Day, remember to honor your mother no matter what your relationship, because she always tries her best and loves you no matter what. The loving bond between a mother and her child is innate and so strong it can never be broken.

Chapter 3

Marathon Running for Charity

As my hearing loss progressed, I worked and I raised my three children. I was the only salesperson in our small company, the rainmaker as some call it. While my role was the chief cook and bottle washer, sales was something that I did best. I didn't mind sales like many people do, and out of all my responsibilities this was the one thing that I enjoyed the most. Yes, crazy me, I enjoyed the one thing that most people hate, selling. I loved meeting new people, winning new business and building relationships with my clients. One day in November of 2006 I went to a networking meeting that brought me unexpected inspiration to begin a new hobby. This fateful meeting put me on a path that changed my entire life.

In attendance at this lunch meeting were about 25 men and just two women, me and one other lady. We were eating lunch as the meeting facilitator asked us to go around the table one at a time and introduce ourselves by stating our name and then our line of work. After our obligatory introduction, he then asked us to answer one specific question. I found his question deeply thought-provoking and one that I had never considered before. His question was, "If you could stop everything in your life for one year and accomplish one task what would it be?"

"Wow!" I thought. "Someone's giving me a year off to do anything I want." Here I was, a working mom who got up every day at the crack of dawn, went to the gym to pump iron, and then worked a full day in my own business. Every day I raced home to make dinner and take care of my three children. In this moment, someone gave me a gift of one year off to do anything I wanted to do. I was sitting immediately to the right of the meeting facilitator. He decided to begin with the lady on his left. As we went around the table in the opposite direction, I would be the last person to answer his question. When everybody was busy introducing themselves, and speaking about what they would do for the next year, I was in deep thought imagining what I could accomplish with this valuable time off. I took this question to heart and could barely hear any of the other conversations at the table. It was as though he truly handed me a precious gift of time. I tossed around many ideas of what I would do for the next year, but couldn't settle on just one. When it was my turn to speak, out of my mouth came the words, "I would run a marathon." Everyone at the table was surprised by my answer, and so was I.

I thought to myself, "Why did I just say that?" It felt as though someone else took over my mouth and said these words for me. The truth was I always admired people who had run marathons. I found running marathons inspiring and thought it was something I would never be able to complete. How in the world can any human being run 26.2 miles? I thought it was an amazing feat and my answer not only impressed everybody at the table, it stunned me too. I left the meeting not giving it any more thought, not until about two weeks later.

I came home from work one evening around six o'clock and stood in my kitchen opening the day's mail. There was a postcard addressed to me from the Leukemia and Lymphoma Society. The postcard read something like this, "Run a marathon in honor or memory of someone you love and we'll give you the coaching and mentoring you need to help you do it." My father had died of non-Hodgkin's Lymphoma, a blood cancer, in 1985. Somehow this marketing piece came to me just two weeks after I had said I would run a marathon. Coincidence? It spooked me so much that I looked around my kitchen to see if anyone was watching me, literally. I knew that someone from the invisible world was sending me a clear sign. This was what many people refer to as a "God wink." I knew this wasn't happenstance.

I went to an information meeting organized by Team in Training, the athletic fundraising arm for the Leukemia & Lymphoma Society to find out more about what was involved in running a marathon. They made a deeply emotional presentation that included video footage of people who had accomplished what I desired to do myself, complete a full marathon. But that wasn't the reason that I went to this meeting. I went to this meeting because they said one thing that grabbed my attention, "Honor someone you love with an act of charity." That was what hooked me and the compelling reason why I wanted to do this. They had me at love.

They told me that if I paid the $100 registration fee that night it would become part of the fundraising obligation. If I committed to doing this event with them I was obligated to raise $1,900 in donations before event day. They explained there were running coaches, mentors and organized training runs every weekend to help me prepare for marathon day. That evening I met one of their mentors, a man who had just run the Marine Corps Marathon for them. He was proudly wearing his Marine Corps jersey from that event. The words "Marine Corps" on his shirt impressed me and touched me deeply. Somehow seeing the words "Marine Corps" on his shirt made that marathon feel even longer and harder than any other. I had the deepest respect for the Marines and I thought to myself, "Wow! The Marine Corps Marathon is even more amazing. What a tremendous feat!" After we spoke briefly, I registered that night and learned that he would be one of my mentors for the New Jersey Marathon on April 29, 2007.

Registering for the NJ Marathon with Team in Training was a life changing decision. When I signed up to run a marathon for charity to honor the memory of my father who died when I was 25 years old, I didn't know that it was a Jewish mitzvah, good deed to honor the deceased with acts of charity and kindness. I wasn't raised with this knowledge and learned much later that this is a well-known Jewish custom. While it's true that many people of all faiths donate to charity as a kind gesture when people pass away, I learned that performing an act of kindness in honor of the deceased is the ultimate gift we can give them and that this was a mitzvah from God Himself in the Torah.

My spiritual awakening truly began when I took this opportunity to honor my father. Honoring his memory was the inspiration and motivation that sealed my decision. I signed up that evening and gave my $100 donation but intended to ask my family for their permission and support. There was still the option to back out at any time and consider this registration fee a donation in my father's memory.

On Thanksgiving Day, 2006, as we sat at the dinner table eating our holiday meal, I asked my children and husband what they thought about me running a marathon. My adorable youngest child who was 10 years old at the time quipped, "Yeah right mom, you're gonna run a marathon!" That was all I needed to hear. It was like she threw down the proverbial gauntlet and I wasn't about to back down from her challenge. So, I thanked my family in advance for their support and I began training. Whoa, I had no idea what I had signed up for!

Tough Training and Much More

The training for this marathon was difficult to say the least. Remember, I was a working mother of three children who was already getting up at 4:30 AM every day to head for the gym. You might say that I enjoyed exercise already but enjoying staying in shape has little or nothing to do with training for a full marathon. The training for a marathon is frankly daunting. I had a full plate at home and was self-employed, yet I diligently showed up for every weekend training run. I even went to midweek training runs when they were available. There were many people on the New Jersey Marathon team who provided great camaraderie. The coaches and mentors assigned to our team were extremely supportive. As I progressed through the training I surprised myself by the distances that I could run. Prior to training for this event, I rarely ran more than a few miles at one time. Each week we increased our mileage with the goal of completing 20 miles in a training run before event day.

As I was training, I was coping with the normal daily ups and downs of life and a full plate at home. On top of that, my father-in-law became gravely ill after I registered for this event, and he died in January of 2007. His death was devastating to my husband, me and our three children. We had lost my mother-in-law in 1998 and losing him was heartbreaking beyond words. After losing him too, my husband and I felt like orphans. While it was true my own mother was still alive, my relationship with her throughout my life was often acrimonious and rarely good. My relationship with my husband's parents was deeply loving and nurturing. They treated me like a daughter, never a daughter-in-law. When it came time to pay respects to my father-in-law at his funeral I unexpectedly was asked to speak and give a eulogy. On this heartbreaking day, as I spoke to friends and family, I shared how special both my in-laws were to me and how blessed I was to have had them both in my life. Much to my shock, my loving eulogy speech was met with fierce resentment from my mother and older brother. My mother couldn't contain her anger and was completely incensed that I spoke so lovingly about my father-in-law. It was clear she felt my glowing eulogy for my father-in-law that morning was somehow disrespectful to her and my father.

When we were at my father-in-law's funeral to pay tribute to him and his life, my lifelong family problems surfaced with a vengeance. As we drove away from the funeral home in the hearse and went to the gravesite to bury my father-in-law, one of my closest girlfriends warned me that something was brewing. Just as she warned, my mother and older brother drove up to where I was standing at the cemetery and through their car window showed contempt and disgust for me with looks that could kill. A few minutes later, as we stood at my father-in-law's gravesite giving our final respects to this wonderful man, their disrespectful behavior was felt by everyone there. My oldest child was visibly angry and horrified as her uncle loudly conversed with my mother drowning out the voice of the rabbi who was reciting the Mourner's Kaddish and praying over the grave. After the burial, my mother and two brothers refused to come to my husband's childhood home to pay further respects. Their absence was noticed since visiting the family home after a burial is proper and customary in Jewish traditon. That cold day in January, we not only buried my father-in-law, but his funeral marked the beginning of a cold war with my mother and two brothers. After a lifetime of acrimony and problems with my mother and older brother, we finally reached the boiling point when I needed to take a stand. I refused to call her after the funeral or reach out to any of them. Their behavior was reprehensible and unacceptable to me so I waited for her to call me or my husband. This was a phone call that never came.

While mourning the loss of my father-in-law, my husband and I were no longer speaking with my mother and two brothers. Through the grief, I continued to train for this marathon in memory of my dad. The one thing that my mother and brothers had in common with me was our deep love for my father. As I trained every weekend and during the week, I pounded that pavement in deep spiritual pain. My pain was so deep that I decided to go to a psychotherapist for counseling for the first time in my life. I needed help coping with the pain of being estranged from my mother and brothers. The first advice she gave me was to call my mother occasionally. She called these conversations "dutiful daughter calls." She explained that it was very damaging to cut ties with my family completely and this was necessary for my own self-preservation.

The psychotherapist also helped me see that throughout my upbringing I unknowingly suffered from deeply dysfunctional family relationships with my mother and brothers. She shared with me that my relationship with my mother was deeply dysfunctional because my mother suffered from a diagnosable mental illness. Wow! This well-respected doctor of psychotherapy complimented me for being strong enough to leave my crazy family at the age of 21. She said she was absolutely astounded how strong and resilient I was at such a young age. I hadn't recognized any of this before I met with this doctor. As she was explaining how remarkable I was and how my mother was diagnosably mentally ill, she turned and grabbed a book from her shelf and gave me the name of my mother's illness. She said, "Your mother has Borderline Personality Disorder." She went on to explain that this disorder had no known treatment or cure. Hmm, it's terminal eh? As I sat listening to her, I thought to myself that my mother's illness sounded kind of benign because after all it was only "borderline." Don't laugh too hard. I really thought that! Frankly, I shrugged off most of what she said and felt it was untrue. I always believed that these types of labels were simply lousy excuses for poor behavior. I didn't really give her words about my mother much credence. Nonetheless, our conversations helped me sort through what had happened. I came to terms with the fact that there were personal relationships in my life that were dysfunctional and the dysfunction wasn't necessarily my fault. After a lifetime of being ridiculed, called names by my mother and older brother, taunted and told everything that went wrong was my fault, this was an important revelation.

The difficult marathon training runs continued, 12 miles, 14 miles, 16 miles, all the way up to 20 miles. Remember, I was working full-time in my own business, raising three children and spending every weekend doing long runs that knocked me out and put me right to sleep for the remainder of the day. All the while, I was seeking counseling from a psychotherapist as to why my own family disowned me and why I felt unloved by my own mother all my life. I say this with complete sincerity. Except for the time when she helped me during my husband's major surgery, throughout my life, I never truly felt loved by my mother. I always thought I was the only person in the world who had a face even my mother didn't love. Was this true? Maybe not. I can only count a few occasions in my life when I felt she truly cared for me. Now, in the aftermath of my father-in-law's passing, it was painfully apparent that our relationship was beyond repair.

As I ran the long training runs with Team in Training, I cried buckets but hid my tears from everyone on the team. To get through my runs I concentrated on how much I missed my father and how important completing this marathon was to me. While my mother and brothers were barely speaking to me, I was strengthened by honoring my dad. I mysteriously felt his love was with me and helping me through each run. My love for him was my motivation and the inspiration to continue training despite my enormous emotional pain. It felt like he was rooting for me every step of the way. As I trained, I remembered his strong and loving personality and his warm hugs. This marathon run was for him and any thought of quitting or allowing anything to stop me from reaching my goal was simply out of the question.

The Brooklyn Half Marathon—A Saturday Morning Miracle

The months flew by quickly as I trained steadily and increased my miles each week. By the end of March 2007, I had completed my first 20-mile training run. When you train for a full marathon this is a huge milestone, especially if it's your first. In the training plan that we were given by Team in Training, we never ran more than 20 miles before race day. After the 20-mile training run we began to do what's called "the taper" and the mileage was curtailed dropping to very few miles before event day. I had signed up for a half marathon on April 14th, 2007 in Brooklyn, New York. This event was part of my training schedule for marathon day on April 29th. Brooklyn was significant for me because it's where I was born. My parents and all my extended family are from Brooklyn, New York.

Just prior to this half marathon, my family and I took a spring break trip in early April to Rehoboth Beach, Delaware. As I ran one morning, I felt a sharp pain in my left hip. The pain became so severe that I had to stop running and began to limp. In a panic, that afternoon I emailed one of my Team in Training coaches to find out what I should do. He told me not to worry because I had already completed my distance training. He recommended not running for a while and using the stationary bike instead. I listened to his advice and went for acupuncture as well, to help myself heal from this injury.

A couple of weeks later I felt recovered from the hip pain. As a matter of fact, I felt fantastic. The Brooklyn Half Marathon, April 14th, 2007, was on a Saturday morning. I drove into Brooklyn with one of my mentors and about five other teammates to run what would be my first half marathon race. Looking back now, I'm emotional to acknowledge that this event was on the morning of the holy Sabbath, Shabbos or Shabbat for the Jewish people. Being a non-observant Jew at the time, the fact that it was Shabbos wasn't on my radar as I hopped into my mentor's van for the ride to Brooklyn. It simply didn't occur to me until later that morning that it was the Sabbath.

We arrived in Coney Island, parked the van and made our way to the start line. The weather that morning was spectacular. There wasn't a cloud in the sky and the temperature was about 40 degrees Fahrenheit, perfect weather for a long run. I felt deeply emotional as we walked down the boardwalk past the famed Cyclone roller coaster. Memories of being a small child in Brooklyn flooded back to me. I recalled watching fireworks in the evening from the boardwalk in Brighton Beach, Brooklyn, eating potato knishes and Italian ices. Tears welled up in me as I thought of my dad who was born and raised in

Brooklyn too. Here I was many years later about to honor his memory with this half marathon run, preparing for the full marathon in just two weeks.

We headed to the start line and I looked up at the sky and remembered saying, "Thank you God for letting me do this for my dad!" As the race started, I began jogging and I thought to myself, "Wow I feel fantastic!" In that moment, I thought I would achieve a personal record and run the fastest 13.1 miles I had ever run. That's how great I felt. I kept running and less than a mile into the run I suddenly felt the most excruciating pain I've ever felt in my entire life. I had given birth to three children before this day but this pain eclipsed anything I had remembered even from childbirth. I thought that maybe I broke my hip. I couldn't imagine what was going on inside of me that was so painful. I limped over to the side of the boardwalk and held onto the rail. I began crying and looked up at the sky and asked God, "Why is this happening to me?" As I stood there helplessly with tears flowing and in pain all the participants were passing me by and running the race. My teammates who drove with me in the van that morning saw me standing by the side of the boardwalk in tears. They stopped to ask me what was wrong.

I told them I didn't know what happened but I was in so much pain that I couldn't even walk. They suggested that I stretch for a while and perhaps the pain would go away. I thanked them and they continued on their way to run the event. As I stood there trying to stretch, it seemed nothing would help. I was in complete agony. Putting any pressure on my left leg caused excruciating pain. I watched as everyone passed me by. There were people who looked to be 80 years old running past me effortlessly. Again, I looked up at the sky and prayed, "God how can I possibly run the marathon in two weeks if I can't complete this run today?" I imagined myself going back to my friend's van and sitting on the pavement to wait for everyone to finish the race. I thought about what it would feel like to sit there for three hours knowing full well that I didn't accomplish what I came to Brooklyn to complete.

The idea of going back to the van and failing to finish this run made me cry even harder. Right then, a large blonde-haired woman ran past me. She was extremely tall, had a strong bulky physique, and a flowing blonde ponytail. She turned around as she ran past me, waved and pointed at me as she shouted, "You don't stop! You keep going! It will go away!"

This blonde-haired amazon-like woman completely startled me. Who was this woman shouting at me like that? Why did she care about what happened to me? She snapped me right out of my feelings of despair and I started to think to myself, "What can I do now?" So, I did what I always do when I find myself in times of trouble. I prayed. But I decided that this moment was far too important to pray in English. I don't know why I thought like that being I was a secular Jew who rarely went to synagogue. I just knew I needed extra help and this felt like the most important morning of my life. So, I started to think about all the Hebrew prayers that I knew. I only knew three. I knew the candle lighting prayer for Shabbos. It's quite interesting that I knew this prayer even though this was Shabbos morning, yet I hadn't lit any candles the night before. I dismissed this prayer as inappropriate. I also knew the candle lighting prayer for Hanukkah. That also seemed unfitting for this moment. Then I remembered the only other prayer that I knew in Hebrew. The Shema.

In 2001, just after the 9/11 terrorist attacks, I went to Rosh Hashanah services where a Reform rabbi handed out a piece of paper with two lines of the Shema in English and in Hebrew and told everyone to memorize these two lines. He instructed us to recite them every morning and at night before retiring. He didn't fully explain why we should do this, but I did as he requested and I memorized these lines. I found it enjoyable to do this little exercise for a while, but eventually I stopped. The Shema prayer fell off my radar.

On this morning in Brooklyn the Shema was on my radar once again. I started saying those first two lines repeatedly like a mantra. First in English, and then in Hebrew. "Hear, O Israel, the Lord is God, the Lord is One. Blessed be the name of His glorious kingdom forever and ever." And then I said it in Hebrew. *"Sh'ma Yisra'eil Adonai Eloheinu Adonai echad. Baruch sheim k'vod malchuto l'olam va'ed."*

I started to limp down the boardwalk, barely able to put any pressure on my left foot without feeling excruciating pain in my hip. Again, and again I said these first two lines of the Shema prayer. I said them like a mantra repeatedly as I went down the stairs heading off the boardwalk. Suddenly I noticed the pain began traveling. It left my left hip, headed down my leg and landed in my left thigh. As I said the Shema repeatedly I became able to move my hip and put a little more pressure on my left leg. Within a few more minutes, I was jogging and the pain had shifted completely into my left thigh. I thought, "Wow this Shema is working!" and I kept on going. I could move my legs and hips now and tolerate the pain in my left leg. As I was jogging I noticed Chasidic Jewish men wearing prayer shawls, Tallit, heading to synagogue. That's when it occurred to me that it was Shabbos. I incorporated these men into my mantra and imagined that there were hundreds of bearded Jewish rabbis saying the Shema with me as I ran. Repeatedly in my mind I said, *"Sh'ma Yisra'eil Adonai Eloheinu Adonai echad"* as I continued down the boulevard.

I was grateful to be able to move my body at this point with the ray of hope to finish this half marathon. As I looked off to the side of the road I noticed the mile markers along the way and wondered, "How in the world am I doing this?" I saw mile markers three, four, five, and I thought, "It feels like somebody's carrying me."

At about mile eight there was a refreshment table with cups of water and Gatorade. I sauntered over to the table to take a break and get a refreshment. Out of my peripheral field of vision in my left eye, I saw a man who seemed very familiar. He wore a dark green windbreaker and a baseball type of hat and looked like someone who could pass as being my Jewish uncle. He walked quickly with a determined stride as he made a beeline toward me behind the back of the refreshments table. He looked like a man on a mission who would not be stopped. I went to grab the cup of water directly in front of me, and at that precise moment he was standing there. He looked directly into my eyes and pointed his index finger right at my nose! In a stern and commanding voice, he said, "I want you to know I am watching your every move!"

I was stunned! His voice and mannerisms sent chills up and down the back of my spine. I gently picked up my cup of water as our eyes met. The only words I could utter were, "Thank you." His eyes penetrated me as though he was looking directly into my soul. It was like nothing I had ever felt before with any other person. I wondered, "Who is this man? Why is he watching me?" This was undoubtedly a supernatural encounter with someone from another world.

I walked away and continued my run knowing that something supernatural was happening to me that morning. It was clear that I was surrounded in love and was being given divine help. It felt like angels and God Himself were carrying me through the entire run. In the beginning I couldn't even walk, let alone run this half marathon. I reached for God with the Shema prayer, prayed throughout the entire 13.1 miles, and in just over two-and-a-half hours, I ran into Prospect Park where the race ended and I saw the finish line just ahead. The coaches had taught us to make sure we smiled for a great finish line photo.

They coached us to throw our arms up in the air in victory at the end of every race. When I saw the finish line ahead of me I welled up with great emotion and I thought to myself, "I'm going to have the best finish line photo ever!" I crossed the finish line and pumped my arms up in the air in victory and then broke down and cried like a baby. For no explainable or ordinary reason, I was given the physical strength to run 13.1 miles when I thought I'd have to quit.

Instead of going back to my friend's van and calling it quits, I reached for a prayer that I had only heard about and never knew was anything special. On this Saturday morning, I knew I was touched by God. Was the man at mile eight an angel? Who was the woman who spurred me on at the beginning of the race? Why was I able to finish this half marathon when I thought I had broken my hip? While all these questions were running through my mind there was one question that was answered. I knew without any doubt I had experienced a miracle from Hashem, God Himself.

My teammates greeted me as I crossed the finish line and I collapsed in their arms crying. I could barely walk as all the pain from my injury returned. They asked me what happened and I told them I just experienced a miracle. I was in a complete state of awe. I limped back to the van in a great deal of pain but the joy of finishing was overwhelming. Without any doubt, nothing was going to stop me from running the full marathon in two weeks. I was going to honor my father if I had to crawl to the finish line. When I got home that day my husband saw me limping in severe pain and said, "You're not running any marathon."

Without missing a beat, I answered, "Just try and stop me!" From there I went upstairs and took off my pants and saw that my left thigh was completely black because it had bruised from the inside out. Whatever happened to my hip that morning had traveled down my leg and landed in my thigh. This gave me mobility and allowed me to run, but the injury caused so much damage in my leg that it bruised from the inside out. Seeing my thigh had turned completely black proved to me I had experienced a miracle in Brooklyn. I knew that if I could complete a half marathon that morning, I would be able to finish the full New Jersey Marathon in two weeks in honor of my father.

Friends and relatives heard what happened to me and warned me to take it easy. One of my cousins told me that I could break my hip and God forbid wind up in a wheelchair. He told me that it was crazy to go through with the marathon and urged me to reconsider. I told him I appreciated his well-intended concerns, but this was non-negotiable. I was not going to withdraw from the event. I had two weeks to prepare for the full 26.2 miles and I was going to do everything possible to make sure I finished. This one was for Dad.

NJ Marathon April 29, 2007

On a rainy Sunday afternoon, the day after I finished the half marathon in Brooklyn, I went to my company's office and took my two younger children with me. I had just read the book *The Secret* which spoke about making vision boards for improving your life and attracting the things you wanted. I was compelled to do everything within my power to accomplish finishing the NJ marathon so I decided to listen to this book's advice and I created a vision board. This vision board eventually went everywhere I went until marathon day. I bought all kinds of arts and crafts materials and told my children that they could make their own vision boards too. This was a fun way to spend a rainy Sunday afternoon with them and teach them to set goals for themselves. While they went into a back room to work together, I went into my office to do some research and have private time.

While I was in my office and my two children were busy making their vision boards, I researched the prayer "The Shema." I knew that I had experienced a miracle the day before in Brooklyn. I credited this miracle to the Shema prayer that I said repeatedly that morning as a mantra. I felt strongly that my miracle was brought about because I used that prayer to connect with God. I looked up the Shema on the internet and researched whether this Hebrew prayer could possibly create miracles. The information I found online astounded me and brought me to tears. I learned that the Shema was the holiest of Hebrew prayers and that religious Jews around the world say this very prayer three times a day. In this prayer, we state our devotion and love for God and make Him a promise to always remember Him, obey His commandments, speak of Him everywhere we go, and teach our children about His existence. In return, He promises us that He will never forsake us and He will always be there to provide for all our needs. As I read those words that morning I sobbed like a small child. I felt like a lost and neglected child who found out for the first time in my life that I was deeply loved.

Not only did I cry when I recognized that I was loved, but I knew unequivocally that I had connected directly to God Himself in Brooklyn the day before. It was an astoundingly sad revelation to know that this holy prayer was absent from my life for more than 47 years. Why wasn't I taught about this prayer by my parents? On April 14, 2007, on Shabbat, I reached for God by saying the first two lines of the Shema with all my heart and all my soul to please help me finish that race. That morning God answered with a loud and resounding "yes."

After reading about the holy Shema prayer, I created a vision board for my marathon run on April 29th. I looked for a picture of the winner of the New Jersey Marathon from the previous year and superimposed a small picture of myself over him crossing the finish line. Naturally, I changed the finish time on the overhead clock to something more realistic. My idea of winning had nothing to do with speed. I just wanted to cross the finish line, pump my arms up in the air in victory, look up at the sky and say to my dad, "This one was for you!"

On my vision board, I put the first two lines of the Shema in Hebrew and English, the mantra I repeated in Brooklyn. Until the Brooklyn half marathon, I didn't even know the significance of this prayer or that it had more than two lines. This was the sad truth. I simply wasn't raised knowing what the Shema was or that this holy prayer is inscribed on a scroll that is placed inside every mezuzah, an ornament that hangs on the door posts of Jewish homes. Jewish families around the world have failed to keep the promise of the Shema and many don't even know of its existence. Sadly, millions of Jews around the world are raised like I was, without any of this knowledge.

I carried my marathon vision board around with me everywhere I went for the next two weeks. My husband complained that I looked idiotic and that it was embarrassing. Well, I'm not sure who it was embarrassing to because it certainly wasn't embarrassing to me. As a matter of fact, I was quite proud of my vision board and my determination to go forward with this event. I defiantly told him that I didn't care what anyone thought of me and that I was going to carry it around with me everywhere I went. Do I recall anyone telling me I was behaving like an idiot or that I looked foolish? No, I don't. But I do remember many people questioning whether I should drop out of the race because of my injury. If they thought I was an idiot, they kept it to themselves. Had anyone said something disparaging to me, it frankly would have put more fire in my belly to persevere than embarrass me to quit. I was so intent on finishing this marathon in honor of my dad, nothing was going to stop me except for God Himself. There was no person in this world who could convince me to pull out of this race.

Right after suffering the injury in Brooklyn, I called my doctor to get a referral for a physical therapist. I specifically asked him to refer somebody who was involved in athletics and who wouldn't try to talk me out of running my marathon. I told him I refused to get an x-ray and that I would do everything possible to make sure I could run the marathon on April 29th. Crazy? Looking back now, I suppose it was. But I was a woman on a mission. I wasn't going to be stopped so long as it was still within my personal power to keep going.

While I was carrying my vision board with me everywhere, for the next two weeks I did something every day to heal my injury. I went for acupuncture, physical therapy, deep tissue massage, chiropractic care, and even kinesiology. My sweet little acupuncturist from Taiwan was going all out with her treatments on me. She used strange ointments and even hooked the acupuncture needles up to electrodes that sent shocks into my hip emitting smoke from the needles. I was literally determined to go through the fire for this one!

On Friday afternoon before the marathon, I prepared to leave for the drive to Long Branch, New Jersey. After I packed gifts for my mentors and coaches, I sat at my computer and wrote one last fundraising email to send to my list of friends and family. I entitled this email, "The NJ Marathon: My compelling reason why." As I wrote this email, I could barely see the keyboard or my computer through my tears. The following is the tribute letter I wrote in honor of my father.

In Honor and Loving Memory of My Father: Some Lessons from My Dad

The warmth of his smile could light up a room. He had a zest for life and loved to tell jokes and laugh so hard that everyone would laugh with him even if the joke wasn't funny. You didn't know if you were laughing at the joke or if it was his raucous laughter that was carrying you away. He would get these hysterical sounding hiccups when he laughed – I inherited that gene too, along with my three children! He showed me how to be joyful.

My Dad was bald most of his adult life and had more hair on his chest and back than most men have on their heads. Regardless he was undeniably an incredibly handsome man. He had no insecurities and exuded confidence wherever he went. He had no problem making fun of himself and enjoyed making people laugh even at his own expense. When people met him they instantly loved him. Dad was the world's best salesman and could sell ice to an Eskimo. By his example, he taught me how to love myself and accept myself exactly as I am.

He was strict and no-nonsense when he felt you had done wrong. At the young age of eight I told a lie and he punished me so severely that I will never forget it nor the lesson – your word is your bond. I learned the deep importance of trust and integrity.

My Dad loved to play sports and would often play basketball with my brother. Feeling left out, when I was about 9 years old I told my father that I wanted to spend time with him too, one on one. Being old fashioned and not thinking of doing something sports related with a girl (he should see me now!) he came up with the idea of planting a garden with me, pictured left. He taught me the importance of listening.

Growing up he always told me how much he loved me. He would say often, "I love you with all my heart." But he didn't just say the words; he said them so that you felt them. It was as if love just poured out of him. I remember as a teenager pulling the car into the driveway and walking up the walkway as he was on the front lawn doing yard work. I would notice him stop and lean on his rake, just like in the picture here, and gaze at me with the most loving eyes. I will never forget it. He showed me how to love unconditionally.

The incredible warmth of his hugs … oh how I miss them and can still close my eyes and feel them. He met me in my dorm room at college one day and was in my room waiting for me gazing out the window with his back turned. I remember thinking what broad shoulders he had and how incredibly handsome he was. Then he turned to me and gave me one of his famous loving hugs. I love you Dad.

When my Dad was diagnosed with non-Hodgkin's lymphoma, he fought hard and never lost his optimism. For Dad, the glass was always half full. I remember he made sales calls from his hospital room trying his best to keep things going monetarily for his family while he fought this terrible illness. He showed me how to stay determined.

After a year and a half of fighting, the cancer found its way to his liver. We were to go to the hospital for a last effort to save his life. At this point my strong father was walking with a cane. He came outside and asked me to take his hand to walk the property with him so he could take one last look. I don't know how I kept my composure. I assure you, I don't have it right now. He taught me about courage.

After all these years, I love you more now than ever. Somehow, I know that you are with me every step of the way ... the wind that pushes me right to the finish line.

With all my love,

Lori

I hit send on this email and then left for what became an unforgettable weekend with Team in Training. I had raised more than double my fundraising goal so I was entitled to bring my family with me and share my hotel room with them for the weekend. The Team in Training staff was phenomenal and inspiring. The coaches and the mentors were supportive beyond words. I'm not sure that a marathon run like this would have been possible if it weren't for their dedication and support. They nurtured me through the training and on this spectacular weekend, they made us all feel like we were truly heroes. There was a pre-event dinner with many inspirational speeches. Through the speeches there were tears and laughter. The evening ended with a party to decorate our marathon jerseys with fabric paint and glitter.

Unbeknownst to me, that evening the mentors organized an awards ceremony for the participants. In front of my three children they gave me an unexpected award. It was called the "Spirit Award." Writing this book now, I don't know whether to laugh uproariously or cry like a baby. There probably wasn't a more appropriate award that I could have hoped to receive. They said it was for my bravery and determination. Through injury and adversity, I went to every training run and defied the odds to make it there that weekend. I cried with gratitude and felt very proud to receive this special award in front of my children.

One of the most special people I remember from this experience was one of my coaches. He was the only other Jewish person on the team. You might ask why he was so significant to me, but I can't truly explain that to you. He had a great smile, a warm heart, and a wonderful sense of humor. I've never forgotten these magic words he said to me just before the marathon: "This is the greatest thing you can do with your life. You don't give until it hurts, you give until it feels great."

There was a great deal of wisdom in his words. What I connected to the most was when he said we give until it feels great. Through all the training and the injuries, it was the joy of giving that carried me through the pain. Focusing on my father was the wind that carried me through each training run. I prayed that my love for him would carry me to the finish line the next morning.

On marathon morning, it was cloudy and cold when I arrived at the start line. I was extremely nervous and worried about finishing the event. Although a good night's sleep was recommended, nobody truly sleeps the night before running a marathon, especially if it's your first. I was stretching at the start line waiting for the gun to go off and I recall the singing of the Star-Spangled Banner just before race time. I looked up and saw someone carrying an American flag. Over the stripes, in bold letters was written a phrase I had never heard of before that moment, "GOD IS LOVE." I've heard this said many times since then, but this was my very first. As I looked at these words I welled up with great emotion because it was so truthful and perfect. That morning I made sure I dressed for a miracle from God like the one He gave me in Brooklyn two weeks earlier. I planned to repeat the Shema like a mantra to help me get to the finish line. I found a Jewish Star necklace that was given to me as a small child that had always filled me with strength growing up. I wore this Star of David as well as a blue plastic bracelet that said, "Got Guts." This was a charity bracelet from the Crohn's & Colitis Foundation using a play on words which was a perfect slogan for that morning.

The many stories about my training, and the details about the New Jersey Marathon and how I managed to make it to event day after being injured have little or nothing to do with athletics. This story is about love, devotion, and persevering against all odds. While I was training for this event, raising money for charity and enduring both physical and spiritual pain, I became acutely aware of the uncanny parallel between running a marathon and living life itself. For people who find marathon stories like these boring, try to view this story from a different set of eyes. Try to view this as a lesson about life itself. For all the people in the world who don't run, don't like running, and are bored to tears by the subject, read every word anyway. There is a magnificent life lesson here for everyone.

While many people to this day think of me as a "runner" my stories about running marathons are far less about athletics than you might think. Completing my first marathon in New Jersey on April 29th, 2007 in memory of my dad wasn't about the amazing athletic triumph of running 26.2 miles, although I must admit, this is a triumph nonetheless. It was most importantly about my determination to reach the finish line under incredible odds to honor the memory of my father. This is a testimony of pure love, the only energy that truly fuels us and inspires us to keep going forward.

Mile 20 is an infamous spot on the marathon trail. People who have run marathons often speak about mile 20 as an important milestone. When I saw mile marker after mile marker creeping up to mile 20 I began to doubt if I could finish this run. Mind you, up until that morning I hadn't run more than 20 miles in my life. The training program that I was on only included a 20-miler and not further. On top of that, I was recovering from a serious injury. I hadn't run in two weeks since the Brooklyn Half Marathon on April 14th.

When I finally reached mile 20 everything hurt. My left hip that I injured two weeks prior was throbbing and I was short of breath. I felt completely sick to my stomach and I could barely hold down water. I seriously questioned if I could go another 6.2 miles. At that moment, I saw a blonde-haired man standing in the middle of the race path away from all the other volunteers and holding a cup of water. It was as though he was waiting for me. He handed me the cup of water and I said to him, "Now this is getting hard!"

He laughed at me and replied, "Oh come on you're almost done."

I jokingly responded, "That's easy for you to say. I still have 6.2 miles left." Nevertheless, I thanked him for his sense of humor and motivating smile and continued my run.

A few moments later my heart was racing, I was short of breath and feeling scared that I couldn't go further. That's when it hit me like a ton of bricks. I looked up at the sky and I said, "Dad this is for you. Nothing is going to stop me!" It was in that moment I realized that I wasn't running on water, Gatorade, or those chewy sweet candies they give you for a sugar boost. I was Running on Love. It was my love for my father that was going to carry me the distance.

My coaches from Team in Training caught up with me after mile 20 and

cheered me on. They ran with me almost to the finish line where they set me free to finish by myself. They taught me that no matter how I was feeling I must ensure a great finish line photo, pump my arms up in victory and smile for the cameras. When I got to the finish line it seemed all the pain was forgotten. It was a lot like childbirth in that way. I smiled, pumped my arms high in the air and made sure my finish line photo was magnificent.

After I crossed the finish line and received my finisher's medal, my three children and husband greeted me with warm hugs and smiles. To my amazement, my closest girlfriend drove all the way to Long Branch with her sons to watch me finish too. How beautiful it was to see their smiling and loving faces after I had completed one of the most daunting feats I had ever attempted. Through my tears of joy, I was on cloud nine and didn't want to come down. Just after I finished, the clouds on this cold and cloudy morning parted and the sun came shining through. It was so poignant and deliberate that both my husband and I noticed this moment of pure sunshine. I savored the sunshine and the magnificence of what I had just accomplished.

This marathon finish was magnificent not because of a stellar finish time. It was magnificent because I did it! My refusal to call it quits after my injury had nothing to do with any desire to stamp out cancer. The money I raised for charity was a blessing for the Leukemia and Lymphoma Society and God willing it helped fund research for a cure. My refusal to quit came purely from my love for my father. He was the wind beneath my wings that propelled me forward. This event, my charitable actions and every step I took that morning were a tribute to honor his life.

I didn't feel any soreness or pain for at least an hour. I was basking in the glory of attaining my goal. My family was exhausted from chasing me all day and I'm sure I was exhausted too, but my adrenalin was still high. We went back to the hotel room where I went to take the first warm bath I had taken in years to loosen my stiff muscles. When I came out of the bathroom the picture of my entire family was priceless. All four of them were sound asleep. I had just run a marathon and was without sleep for 48 hours but they were the ones who were out for the count! I laughed out loud and let them rest. It was heartwarming to have them all there with me that morning. They chased me around Long Branch and made my magnificent morning an unforgettable memory.

When we drove home from the marathon weekend, we decided to set the trip odometer on the car to see how far 26.2 miles was. We kept driving and driving and the distance was frankly astounding. It was a darn good thing that we didn't do this on the way there. The sight of how far I had run knocked us all out and was a jaw-dropper to say the least!

HIS VOICE, VISIONS & LESSONS

Motivational morning vision from Hashem. GOD always wins!

Here is a story with a good morning message from Hashem that has something to do with hair. Hair seems to be a big deal in this world. I know it's a big deal to me because as a woman I always want my hair to look nice. In the religious world it's a big deal, that you're supposed to cover your hair if you're married. Well, I'm not married and so I get a free pass on that one for now. The religious aspect of covering hair is a subject matter for another day. This story is heartwarming, funny and reveals Hashem's personality. A lot of people don't realize that Hashem has a wonderful personality. Yes, He's God, He's the Master of the Universe but He is heartwarming and funny and He has His own unique personality.

As I have said often, my life is challenging. Doing this work is very difficult. I post videos online and on any given day Hashem will give me a subject and He will say to me, "You must talk about this." So, I turn on my computer, look at my camera and I start talking. The results from all my work so far are that I'm divorced, I'm deaf and I'm destitute. Sort of. I live okay. I have enough to keep a roof over my head, keep my body fed and get a haircut once a month. Back to the hair.

One morning I woke up and I didn't want to get out of bed. I have a lot of trouble in the morning motivating myself to get up at 6 AM and go running. I run about 5 or 6 miles and then I go to the gym and work out, all at the prompting of Hashem. He wants me to take care of my physical self. So, the other morning I didn't want to get out of bed as usual and I was whining and complaining. Thank God that's not a sin in His eyes! But what is a sin is not trying. I was talking to Him and I was praying and saying, "Oh Hashem, I just want to lie here and talk to you. I don't want to go out. It's hot out there and ugh you know I work out and I don't even see results.

I was going on and on and suddenly He flashed a vision in my forehead, the place that they call the third eye—this is where the movies happen. He showed me my bed, me lying there, but suddenly a man got out of my bed from where I was lying and he put a ponytail in his hair. He looked to be 30-something, a good-looking guy and then I realized this man was supposed to be Hashem—showing me that He's here with me and He's doing everything with me. After He put the ponytail in His hair, which is what I do when I get up in the morning to go running, He began pulling my arms as I lay in bed. As He pulled on me He said, "Come on Lori! Let's go running! Come on!"

He made me laugh out loud. He also made me choke back tears because He is WOW! I don't have a better word right now than "WOW." I'll try to think of one, but He is Awe. He is pure Awe, funny and heartwarming. I hope you enjoyed this little story. I want to give you a bird's-eye view of what it's like to live as one with Hashem God and speak to Him and how He motivates me to keep going in the face of continuous losses in this world.

I hope this motivates you by making you realize that when you're praying to Him, there's a real Him and He is incredible. He has a wonderful personality, so the next time you reach for Him, imagine that He has a personality just like the one I'm explaining to you today and every day.

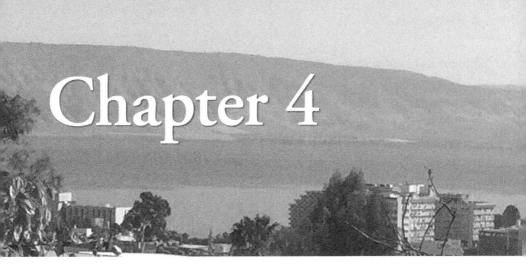

Chapter 4

Running on Love

Even though the experience of running my first marathon for charity was physically and emotionally draining, I was on cloud nine for several days. My experience running this marathon was so powerful that I was compelled to have the creative team at my marketing company work on building me a new website and logo for my new-found passion that I named "Running on Love." When I reached mile 20 in Long Branch the feeling of love and truthfulness of what I was doing that morning was encapsulated in these three beautiful words. I saw that running a physically demanding marathon was a metaphor to life itself. In my life, there were many moments when I didn't know where to find the strength to keep going forward. There were difficult times when I didn't have the strength or desire to get out of bed in the morning. In those times of hopelessness and despair, love was the fuel that inspired me to go forward and live another day.

After my creative team designed a website and a Running on Love logo for me, for the first time in my life I had a "hobby" that I loved. I wrote stories about the New Jersey Marathon and my miracle morning in the Brooklyn Half Marathon and posted them on the website. The website was a place where I could share my new passion for running for charity and share lessons I was learning along the way. I shared my experiences and revelations about life in this personal website blog with friends, family and business associates. This new hobby that I called "Running on Love" was a great source of enjoyment, inspiration and spiritual nourishment for me. I hoped to inspire others with my passion for Running on Love.

Marine Corps Marathon 2007

After about a week of basking in the glory of my accomplishment in Long Branch, New Jersey, it began to sink in that I had completed my mission to honor my father and the event was over. Although I still felt joyful about this accomplishment, the fact that it was over became a sinking feeling. I was working in my office one morning about a week after the marathon and made the decision that I simply had to do it again. I walked into my husband's office which was adjacent to mine and told him I was going to register for a second marathon. He didn't fully understand why I felt compelled to do this and frankly, at the time, neither did I. I simply knew that I had a tremendous void that needed to be filled.

That morning I signed up for the Marine Corps Marathon in Washington D.C. scheduled for October 28, 2007 with Team in Training once again. My favorite coach from the New Jersey event was the head coach for this team so I felt it was perfect and straight from heaven. Once again, I loyally attended all the weekly training runs. It was clear that I was addicted to the Team in Training program which happens to many people who sign up for an event with them. For me though, my addiction wasn't about Team in Training itself, finding a cure for blood cancer, or training for marathons. I fell in love with the idea of running a marathon as a tribute for someone I loved and doing this event as an act of charity in their name. Unbeknownst to me at the time, performing an act of kindness or charity in memory of someone is a Jewish mitzvah, an instruction from God Himself. I was addicted to this mitzvah called *L'ilui Nishmat*. I had no idea there was such a Jewish custom. Honoring someone I loved with an act of charity struck me deeply like an arrow in my heart. Now looking back, I fully understand why I was so smitten. It was my soul waking to my life's purpose. Which charity I supported with my act of kindness didn't matter at all to me. It could have been any worthy charitable cause. Physically committing myself to the task of running a marathon while raising funds for any good cause as a tribute to someone I loved was magical and food for my soul.

Now, training for my second marathon with Team in Training, I was unaware that this Jewish tradition and mitzvah called *L'ilui Nishmat*, was a precursor to my spiritual awakening that was just around the corner. The words *L'ilui Nishmat* translate to "for the elevation of the soul." I became inexplicably compelled and addicted to the feeling of connecting spiritually to someone I loved who had passed away. This began my personal quest of searching for people who had died who needed me to honor them. I kid you not! When I couldn't find someone who died to honor, I considered honoring people who were still alive. Admittedly, the magic was much stronger and more inspiring when I honored someone who was deceased.

I learned more about the mitzvah of L'ilui Nishmat months later at a Kabbalah class I took at my local Chabad House. I was still a secular, non-observant Jew at the time but my three children attended the Chabad Hebrew school and I took some classes with the rabbi. Chabad is a worldwide Jewish organization and network that serves the Jewish community. The network is comprised of ultra-religious Jewish families who move into neighborhoods around the world and dedicate themselves to perform outreach and provide education to the Jewish community. The Chabad movement was instrumental in helping my family learn about the Jewish way of life and educating my children about the Torah. This network of Chabad houses provided people like me and my family a non-judgmental place to turn when we desired to learn Torah and return to Judaism. The Jewish world has succumbed to secularism and Hashem's Torah has been lost in the process. While the Reform and Conservative Jewish movements may take great offense to my statement, it is simply the truth. Chabad is one of the few pure pathways to return to Hashem and learn His Torah. While I took these early classes in Kabbalah at the local Chabad house, I had no idea just how instrumental they would one day be to my family.

At one Kabbalah class taught by my Chabad rabbi, we were learning about the subject of life and death. In this class, he spoke about L'ilui Nishmat and his words struck me deeply. He explained that there is no greater gift that we can give a soul who has departed from this world than to accept upon ourselves performing a good deed or charitable act on their behalf. By doing a good deed, or mitzvah, on behalf of a loved one who has passed away, we increase their good deeds here on earth when they are no longer able to do so by themselves. This information penetrated me deeply because I discovered how honoring my father was received by God Himself. I felt the enormity of the beautiful gift I gave to my dad more than 20 years after he passed away.

Now I needed to choose someone I loved to honor in my next marathon run. Sadly, my decision was easy. I had lost my mother-in-law in 1998 to cancer. She wasn't just a mother-in-law to me in any ordinary sense. Her death was so deeply painful to me that it felt more like I lost my mother. Now I had this special opportunity to show her how much I loved her and proclaim this love out loud to the world. My grieving for her was compounded in January of 2007 when we lost my father-in-law too. Because they were both a powerfully beautiful part of my life, I decided this was a perfect way to pay tribute to them. Neither of them had died from a blood cancer but that didn't matter to me. As I said before, for me it was about love, honor and charity. The charity I supported with my fundraising wasn't important or my focus. I decided to honor them both by signing up with Team in Training and raising money for the Leukemia & Lymphoma Society once again. My marathon run and charitable actions in their memory were my way of celebrating how much they meant to me. In my mind, it wasn't how they died that mattered, this was a celebration about how they lived.

I had just finished a very tough marathon in April of 2007 for my dad when I took on this second marathon run. I went to the training runs conscientiously and now had a name for my new-found passion, "Running on Love." I had running t-shirts designed sporting the new Running on Love logo and sold them to people as a fundraiser for LLS. The t-shirts were a big hit with my Team in Training friends but it was more of a promotion for my website blog than an effective fundraiser. At the end of the event I lost money on these shirts because I overbought them in all the wrong sizes. To this day, I have dozens of unworn Running on Love t-shirts in various sizes that could be sewn into a very large quilt. So much for raising money with t-shirts!

As training continued, I began to experience physical pain once again. At one training run, which was "only" seven miles long, I suffered from pain in every part of my body. I barely finished the run that day and was completely distraught. It felt like I was heading for another injury which could be a knock-out punch for my new passion and hobby. I couldn't bear the thought of giving this up and asked for advice from teammates at the end of the run. It seemed they didn't suffer pain like I did and I wanted to figure out how to solve my issues. I had pain in my feet, knees, hips, and lower back. As I ran I winced in pain and gasped for air. You name it, it hurt!

That's when a young woman came up to me and asked if I'd ever heard of Chi Running. She explained that it was a kind of running style where you used gravity to pull you along and explained that someone invented it to help people avoid running injuries. I asked her to show me what it looked like and she gave me a quick demonstration. From what she showed me I couldn't figure out what she was doing but it looked and sounded interesting. One of the coaches overheard our conversation and advised that it was very dangerous to mess around with my running form. He recommended instead that I go to the gym and strengthen my muscles. He showed me a book he had in his car about weightlifting and how to improve your performance in athletics by strengthening your frame. I thanked everyone for their thoughtful advice although I had already made my decision. Chi Running was for me.

As I drove home that morning, I knew that Chi Running was exactly the right thing for me to do. I didn't want to insult anyone offering different advice because I knew all their recommendations were well intended and had value. I knew instinctively that I needed to go to the bookstore and buy a copy of *Chi Running* because I was already a gym rat and had been lifting weights for years. I was in excellent shape for my age when I started running these marathons. As a matter of fact, at this moment in time, at the age of 47, I was likely in the best physical shape of my life. Suddenly I had aches, pains and injuries that I had never suffered from before. I knew I needed to investigate something uniquely different and that there was a reason I was hurting after every run. It was imperative to find the source of my problem and correct it as soon as possible. I knew if I didn't, my new-found love for Running on Love would be short-lived.

I went to a Barnes & Noble and purchased *Chi Running*. I found it fascinating after reading only a few chapters. One of the issues I was experiencing was pain in my right knee. This book suggested that knee problems were a result of poor form where your feet weren't facing in the same direction as your knee when you ran. This repetitive motion and poor form causes pain and ultimately injury. As I began to examine my own form as I ran, I discovered that my right foot turned out and that was the problem with my right knee. I wondered what other issues I might correct with the right education.

Time was fleeting and the marathon training for the Marine Corps event in October was progressing. I didn't have time to figure out all the techniques in this book on my own and wanted to hire a coach to teach me the Chi Running techniques. Much to my delight I found a Chi Running coach located in New Jersey and scheduled a meeting right away to work with him on a one-on-one basis. This was back in the days when money wasn't a concern to me. If I wanted something, I had the money to purchase it. Learning how to run without pain was all-consuming to me. I was deeply grateful for these personal Chi Running lessons and found it was exactly what I needed to keep going and continue Running on Love.

Armed with my new Chi Running techniques I learned quickly how to scan my body for pain and adjust my form accordingly. This helped me avoid further injuries so that I could continue my marathon training. My training improved and my running began to go quite well.

One day, a few weeks before Marine Corps marathon day, I received a letter from my local synagogue. I sat at my kitchen counter and opened the letter. It was about my mother-in-law's yahrzeit lighting. Both religious and non-religious Jews alike are familiar with lighting yahrzeit candles. The yahrzeit candle is a memorial candle that most Jewish people regardless of their level of religious observance light every year at the anniversary of the passing of a loved one. The date when we light this candle is according to the Jewish calendar which follows the moon, unlike the Gregorian calendar which follows the sun. The Yahrzeit candle lighting date changes every year on the Gregorian calendar which is followed by everyone in the secular world. Jewish people are usually notified of the date we are to light this memorial candle because the date is different each year. My mother-in-law had passed away on November 16, 1998. As I read the letter my jaw dropped wide open and I nearly fell off my kitchen chair. My mother-in-law's yahrzeit candle was to be lit on October 27, 2007 the evening before my marathon run in her memory in Washington D.C. The yahrzeit candle lasts for 24 hours. Her yahrzeit candle would still be lit as I crossed the finish line in her loving memory.

I shared this information on my personal Running on Love blog and in my fundraising emails. Most people who read this were stunned, especially Jewish friends and relatives, because they knew there was no way to plan this and it couldn't possibly be a coincidence. This was what many people refer to as a "God wink" but it was much more than a God wink to me. I viewed this as a direct and loud message from God Himself that I was on the right path. This was another miracle in the sequence of many miracles that were beginning to show up in my life. I was living in complete synchronicity with my divine purpose and I knew it. I knew when I read the letter informing me of my mother-in-law's yahrzeit that she was being doubly blessed by my actions and was with me in that very moment. I had no doubt about this whatsoever.

On October 26th, the Friday before marathon weekend, I drove with my husband and our two youngest children to Washington D.C. Once again, I raised more than double my fundraising quota for LLS so I earned a bonus and was permitted to have my family share my hotel room. The weather was glorious and I was excited to have another beautiful marathon weekend, this time to honor my mother-in-law and father-in-law. I discovered one small hiccup when we arrived at the hotel in Washington D.C. Incredibly I had forgotten to bring my mother-in-law's yahrzeit candle. Unbelievable! But, in that moment of realization I thought to myself, "No problem, I'll just go to the local supermarket and get one." Not so fast. Store after store, nobody in Washington D.C. had ever heard of a yahrzeit candle. I wondered where all the Jewish people were in D.C. My husband had cousins who lived in Maryland, not far away, so I called them in a panic and asked them to please bring me a yahrzeit candle for my mother-in-law. They met us at our hotel for lunch and sure enough they brought me a cherished yahrzeit candle to be lit the evening before the race.

On Sunday morning, October 28th, I woke up bright and early to run in the Marine Corps Marathon, which was exciting beyond words. Running in Washington D.C. with all the sights and historical monuments was truly inspiring.

Another awesome sight was right in front of me as I was running. Two men running the marathon side by side carried tall flagpoles with extremely large American flags. This sight was powerfully inspirational. I felt deeply proud to be an American that morning. I was also very grateful to be able to run this event in honor of two people whom I loved with all my heart.

One of the most unforgettable parts about this marathon was the Marines themselves. It was the Marines who stood at every water stop and handed the runners water and Gatorade. They not only handed us our beverages but they greeted everyone in an extraordinary and uplifting way. They all wore their uniforms and sported latex gloves as they handed us our cups. Why do I remember this? Sometimes when you run in these events you see the volunteers put their bare hands in your beverage and you wonder how hygienic the beverage is or if you'll get sick if you drink it. Here we were running a marathon in Washington D.C. and the Marines were standing at attention, being delightful and courteous, and handing us our cups wearing latex gloves. They pulled out all the stops to make this an amazing event. It was absolutely incredible!

At the end of the marathon course I was depleted and exhausted beyond belief but I was doing well and looking forward to finishing. Just then my favorite coach ran up beside me to give me encouragement and moral support. He said to me, "Lori you're doing great. You're almost done. All you have left is another quarter-mile to the finish line which is straight uphill!"

I looked at him in disbelief and asked, "Are you kidding me?"

He said, "No, the last quarter-mile is all uphill." Leave it to the Marines to make the end of the marathon so grueling. I laugh at this now because this made the memory all the sweeter when I finally crossed the finish line. I took my marathon victory photo in front of the Iwo Jima monument.

This marathon event was inspirational and the course was spectacular. The finish photo taken in front of the heroes of Iwo Jima hoisting the American flag was poignant. It was gratifying beyond words to honor mom and dad in such a magnificent way. Another marathon was now in the history books for Lori.

We came home from Washington D.C. and the first thing I did was look at the Team in Training schedule to find marathon number three. I wasn't complete. There was more for me to do.

Rock 'n' Roll San Diego Marathon 2008

I needed to decide who I could honor in a third Run on Love. I saw that there was an event in San Diego where my sister-in-law and her family lived. She had recently lost her father-in-law to the same blood cancer that took my father's life in 1985, non-Hodgkin's lymphoma. Her father-in-law was a wonderful man. Over the years we had shared many holidays with him and his wife at their home in New Jersey. His wife was left in mourning and I thought this would be a wonderful way to pay tribute to her husband while it might lift her spirit and ease her pain. Running a marathon for charity in his memory would bring light where there was darkness. I asked for her permission to do this event in his memory and signed up for the Rock 'n' Roll San Diego Marathon with Team in Training once again.

After running two marathons in just six months and raising about $10,000 for the Leukemia and Lymphoma Society, I knew that running another marathon would be difficult. Not only would the training be hard but raising thousands more for the same charitable cause would become more challenging. I decided to lighten the fundraising burden by applying to be a mentor for Team in Training. As a mentor, I would need to help the participants raise money and motivate them to go the distance. For this extra effort, Team in Training gave me a lower fundraising obligation to meet. This seemed like a good idea at the time. The work as a mentor seemed like it would be inspiring and I could continue to Run on Love and honor more people with acts of charity, which was fueling my spiritual need to do more.

Part of my responsibility as a mentor was to create fundraising opportunities for the entire team and help everyone reach their fundraising goals. Because this marathon was called the Rock 'n' Roll Marathon, I came up with the bright idea of organizing a musical show and selling tickets. There were about 36 people on the San Diego team and I thought having a concert would be fun and easy. I played the "what if" game in my head as I had done so many times before in my life. When I played the "what if" game in the past I had always won and thought this time would be no different. We called the show "Rock the Night – Concert for a Cure." I even got my local town mayor to issue a proclamation that the day of the concert would be "Concert for a Cure Day" in my home town. I went to the town hall and had pictures taken and received press about the event. After putting in a Herculean effort to make this concert a success, this time my "what if" game would have a new outcome. Little did I know it was my destiny to experience failure this time. This concert became a bigger challenge than I originally thought. I really imagined organizing this concert would be fun and easy. I was fantasizing like Mickey Rooney and Judy Garland in clips included in the old movie, *That's Entertainment*. That movie showed several scenes where Mickey and Judy exclaimed, "Let's put on a show!" It's easy in the movies but it wasn't easy in real life.

The cost of organizing this concert was escalating at the same time we experienced poor ticket sales. I had my creative staff doing all the graphics for the advertising and designing the concert program. I never added up the cost of the numerous creative hours spent on this project and considered it my personal donation. The teammates that I was mentoring were supposed to sell tickets to the event and ads for the concert program. The programs needed to be printed yet few teammates made any effort to sell anything.

Expenses included renting the venue which was my hometown high school auditorium, refreshments, and designing and printing the tickets and event posters. The posters were hung in the local schools where my children attended. The final blow was at the 11th hour when I was informed that we needed to pay for a policeman to be at the show. When I told my coach and fellow mentor about the extra expense of the police they said we should cancel the concert and do a car wash instead. The coach said, "I don't volunteer and bust my ass for this charity not to make money."

"Wow really?" I thought. I couldn't believe my ears. Many business people would agree with him but I didn't. At this point, with posters all over the schools, morning announcements being made daily about this concert in all the classes, and my son telling all his friends that he was performing in this show, there was no way I would cancel the event. I was prepared to pay for the entire show myself and lose all the money rather than hurt or humiliate my son.

In the end, the concert went well and even turned a small profit. The show had a very small audience but received positive press and all in all, it was a heartwarming experience. My children sold most of the tickets, I sold most of the program ads, and a few teammates rallied on concert day to help. One special woman helped by giving her donation money to the concert because she had exceeded her personal fundraising obligation. My "what if" game of everyone doing at least the minimum and sharing the workload didn't play out the way I had hoped or expected. Hardly anyone was willing to give their effort or do the minimum but gratefully a few souls stood up and shined above the rest. I found this experience to be deeply disappointing and a heartbreaking lesson, but it was one that I needed to learn. After this experience, I decided that I would never be a mentor for this charity again. If I ever chose to run another fundraiser for them, I'd go it alone.

Not only was my experience of being a mentor for Team in Training deeply disappointing, running the marathon in San Diego was another disaster. We ran the marathon in a grueling heat wave and the event organizers were completely unprepared. While running in the oppressive heat we were desperate for water and beverages to hydrate but when we got to the beverage stops they had run out of water. To make matters worse, the organizers decided to serve a new beverage instead of the tried-and-true Gatorade or Powerade which I was conditioned to drink in all my previous running events. The drink they gave us included whey protein which I learned afterward is notorious for upsetting stomachs. In the middle of the grueling heat, I suffered along with many other

participants, from something called "runner's trots." Our stomachs were so upset from this beverage and dehydration from lack of water we began "trotting" from porta-potty to porta-potty only to wait on long lines in complete intestinal distress. After about 6 hours I gratefully crossed the finish line, collected my marathon finisher medal and then promptly collapsed on the grass in front of my family. I started to recover after swallowing a few teaspoons of salt and drinking a large bottle of water. This was one marathon run that left a very bad taste in my mouth to say the least.

New York City Marathon 2008

After completing the Rock 'n' Roll San Diego Marathon, I was disappointed by the experience of being a mentor for Team in Training. Despite my disappointment, I felt passionate to continue with my pastime of Running on Love. My extremely busy work and personal life didn't allow me much free time but this pastime of running marathons for charity and honoring people I loved was a profound source of joy for me. I felt a need to continue and wouldn't stop.

In my marketing business, I began hosting a networking lunch of my own. Every two weeks I facilitated luncheons and invited business executives to network with me. I became friendly with one gentleman who attended my networking meetings. One of the companies he did business with was ING who just happened to be the lead sponsor of the New York City Marathon. The New York City Marathon is one of the most coveted marathons to run and being a girl born in Brooklyn, this was now a dream of mine too.

At one of our lunch meetings I joked with him that perhaps he could pull some strings and get me an entry into the next New York City Marathon in 2008. I didn't say it completely seriously and didn't think that he would do anything about it. The next thing I knew he told me he had secured me an entry. I was flabbergasted and delighted. Usually you need to win a spot in a lottery, qualify as an elite runner, volunteer for the NY Roadrunners, or join a charity team and fundraise to gain entry. He called his contacts with ING and secured me a spot in the 2008 NYC Marathon on November 2nd.

Now I had a new challenge to master. How was I going to Run on Love in the New York City Marathon when I wasn't part of Team in Training? Was I going to train for this event on my own for no reason at all other than to run this coveted marathon? Would I run it and not raise money for charity to honor someone I loved? The idea of just running this event without a higher purpose of love and charity seemed impossible to me. I wasn't running these marathons to lose weight or stay in shape. They were serving an inexplicable deep spiritual need in me. As a matter of fact, when I was running the San Diego Marathon I recall running behind a few women and one of them was wearing a T-shirt that said, "Why do I run marathons?" Underneath this question was a blank line where she had handwritten "For a smaller butt!" I read this as I ran behind her and I was dumbfounded and astonished. I thought to myself that there were so many easier ways to achieve a smaller butt than running marathons. That wasn't the attraction for me at all. The attraction of marathon running for me was to to perform an amazing physical feat and charitable tribute in honor and memory of someone I loved. While running had its definite health benefits,

Running on Love in these marathons was completely about love and honor and the main attraction wasn't about running at all.

I knew it would be a huge challenge to train by myself for this marathon. I wondered if Team in Training would allow me to meet them for their weekly runs if I wasn't fundraising for them. These questions were running through my mind as I wondered how I would complete the NYC Marathon. I called the Team in Training office and asked if I could make the New York City Marathon a fundraiser for them if I already had my own entry into the event. Their answer was yes and they told me the fundraising goal would be very small and achievable. Fundraising was a great concern to me because I had already raised over $15,000 for them in just over a year and I worried that soliciting money for them again so soon was going to be very difficult.

I agreed to run and raise funds for them so that I would feel welcomed to join their teams for the weekly training runs. It felt inappropriate to train with them if I wasn't contributing by raising money for their organization. I still had one missing link though. I needed to honor someone with my act of charity or the training was going to be hard for me. I felt strongly that this was a requirement and I needed to do this event for love.

My training for this marathon was frankly lackluster to say the least. The fact that I couldn't find anyone new to honor made the training even worse. Gratefully I didn't have that many people in my life who had died and needed to be honored. When event day came closer I decided I could honor someone who was still living. I simply needed to do this for love. Love to me was the magical ingredient that would help me go the distance. Admittedly my passion was more heightened when honoring someone who had passed away. Honoring someone who had passed away had a magical and special quality to it. There's something extraordinary about honoring someone you love who is no longer here on this earth. The mitzvah of L'ilui Nishmat is truly inspiring and spiritually healing.

NYC would be my fourth marathon in 18 months. Because I was pretty worn out and didn't give myself enough rest in between marathons, I was starting to show signs of overtraining. Just before the event I started experiencing pain in my left knee. The Chi Running principles I had learned were helping me manage my aches and pains. Nonetheless, there was something brewing in that left knee. I trained as best I could and made it to the marathon weekend. I was running in this event with a childhood friend I had known since I was seven years old. She had entered the event by signing up to fundraise for the Crohn's & Colitis Foundation. She raised the required amount of money for them and earned her spot to run in the event with me. Her running ability was much better and faster than mine. I was going to do my best to keep pace with her and felt this would be an amazing experience to go the distance with my lifelong friend.

We signed up to be in the third wave for the slowpokes like me. When the event started, the first thing we did was run across the Verrazano Bridge which was breathtaking and spectacular. Even though we were in one of the last waves to start the race and it was late in the day, there were still thousands of New Yorkers all along the race route cheering for us as we ran. Visually the NYC Marathon isn't as picturesque as other marathon courses. It doesn't have the beauty of Washington D.C. with all its parks and monuments. New York's lack of natural beauty is made up for by its outstanding people. Nothing compared to the people of New York City and how they cheered us right to the finish. The crowd made us feel like we were all rock stars. As I had done for all three previous marathons, I emblazoned my name in big letters on the front of my runner's jersey. People shouted "LORI" as I ran by with my friend as though I was some sort of celebrity. She got a kick out of this as we ran through the streets. It does spice up the event and it's very motivating to have people cheer you on by shouting your name.

Just prior to running that morning I still didn't have anyone to honor with my run. I thought of my friend who was in his eighties and was an honored teammate for the Leukemia and Lymphoma Society. He had been battling non-Hodgkin's lymphoma for many years and we had become dear friends. The night before the event I called him and asked if I could Run on Love in his honor. He was very moved by my request. With his approval, I felt armed with the knowledge that I was Running on Love to honor him which gave me the fuel I needed to be able to go the full distance and finish this marathon run.

At first, I was running quite well and kept pace with my friend as we made it into Brooklyn, approximately seven miles into the race. When we entered Brooklyn, my left knee began hurting severely. I told my friend to run ahead and go on without me because my left knee was slowing me down too much. I didn't want to ruin her event or hold her back. I had to slow down and even walk a lot because I worried that I wouldn't make it to the finish line. She went ahead and ran at her own pace. After she ran ahead without me, I saw my husband and two youngest children, a welcome sight for an old gal in pain. They took pictures and video and off I went to finish the event.

At about mile 10 the pain in my left knee was so severe that I sent a text message to my family that this marathon was going to be the slowest one yet. I didn't want them to worry about me when they didn't see me along the race course. I intended to finish and told them it would be a very slow pace but I was fine.

From Brooklyn on I prayed throughout the day using the Shema as well as my own personal prayers. I asked for help to finish the marathon and not get swept off the course. After a long grueling trek of over six hours, I ran, walked, and limped all the way into Central Park. As I entered the park, I saw a marker that said the finish line was just ahead. There was a cameraman standing there

in the middle of the race course taking pictures. When I saw that the finish line was a short distance ahead I stopped cold in my tracks, threw my arms up in victory and smiled a great big smile for him to take one of the most amazing pictures I've ever taken. The joy I felt when I realized I finished this event was overwhelming. When I crossed the finish line, my left knee was in such bad shape that I couldn't put any pressure on it at all. After I hobbled to the area where my family was waiting I told my husband I couldn't walk. Because the roads were closed for the marathon, there was no traffic allowed in the city but there were pedicabs. A pedicab is a small pedal-operated vehicle, that serves as a taxi. My husband hired a pedicab to take me and my daughter back to the hotel room where I was staying that evening. On this occasion, I stayed alone at the hotel while my family went back home to New Jersey just a short distance away.

In the pedicab my daughter told me a story that was so hilarious I felt I would fall out of my seat because I was laughing so hard. My laughter was so uproarious that I got a good case of the hiccups. I knew this was one of the most enormous God winks I'd ever received. She told me that when she, her father and brother were in the subway in Brooklyn, a Chassidic man, a very observant Jew dressed in black and white, approached my 13-year-old son. He chased my son through the subway station and tried to put Tefillin on him. Tefillin is a religious garment and ornament that religious Jewish men put on when they pray to God. We weren't observant Jews at the time. My husband who remains completely secular to this day, became visibly upset and pulled my son away from the Chassidic man as they ran away. This man wouldn't give up or stop and continued to chase them out of the subway station trying to get my son to put on Tefillin. As he chased after my son he shouted, "May God be with you! May God be with you!"

Since there were no visible signs that my son or husband was Jewish, this Chassidic man didn't even know if my son was a Jew. It's highly unusual for any religious man to put Tefillin on a stranger without asking or knowing if he is Jewish. As a matter of fact, it would be considered a sin for religious Jews to put Tefillin on a non-Jew. This incident was a loud and clear sign from Hashem God and occurred right at the precise moment I suffered from my knee injury in Brooklyn. Hashem was giving me another clear sign that He was there with me in the New York City Marathon. After my experiences with the miracle of the Shema prayer, I knew when I heard this story in the pedicab that God Himself was looking out for me and helping me through the entire event. This told me once again that I was on the correct spiritual path and living my life's purpose.

A "Break" from Running on Love

The NYC marathon finish had a different feeling for me. Because of the injury in my left knee and feelings of exhaustion from raising thousands of dollars in just 18 months' time for one charity, I finally had my fill. I needed a break from Running on Love, but it was a forced break. The choice was taken out of my hands after visiting an orthopedic specialist who told me that I had a stress fracture in my knee and needed to rest for three to six months with no running at all. This would have been devastating news for me to hear after marathon one or two. At this point I was ready for a much-needed rest.

The good news was that the doctor told me I had the bones of a young woman. He sent me for x-rays and a bone density test. I found out through this physician that contrary to what most people believe, running was very good for my structure and bone health. I looked forward to healing and intended to get back to Running on Love as soon as I could. It was also nice to learn that I was doing something that was not only good for my soul but good for my body too.

December, January, and February went by quickly and I frankly didn't miss all the long hard training runs. It was nice to take a break from the heavy pounding on my body. But as my body began to heal, my hearing continued to fade.

Blindsided by Messiah

HIS VOICE, VISIONS & LESSONS

Is it true that we will witness the resurrection of the dead?

That's a big question. A lot of people believe in the resurrection of the dead. A lot of people believe in the redemption of our world and the convergence of heaven and earth. Different religions have different thoughts about it but there is a lot of literature out there that one day the dead will return to life. Hashem has answered this question for me on many occasions and He says it's all true. He has not only told me it's true, He has shown me in visions how, when and where it will begin.

That's an incredible answer, isn't it? Do I know that this is emphatically true? Well, I will tell you unequivocally with every part of my soul and being I know it's Him. It is truly Hashem God speaking to me. And I know this is His answer, not mine. In fact, before my spiritual awakening I never truly believed in any of this—in a Messiah (Moshiach), return of the dead or peace on earth for eternity. So, this answer is coming straight to you from the top. Hashem God says that the dead will return. I pray daily that we will witness this miracle together, enjoy a coming together of humanity and the healing of our entire world.

Chapter 5

Wake-up Alarm: "You're Going Deaf"

As you read in chapter two, by February of 2009 I was struggling severely with my hearing. I was trying all kinds of kooky nontraditional methods to see if there was an alternative way to heal my hearing problems. I had seen many miracles come into my life through my marathon running for charity so I thought perhaps there could be an alternative to traditional methods for treating hearing loss. I went to chiropractors of all kinds and different types of alternative healthcare people. Nothing was working and finally by March of 2009 I was having great difficulty hearing despite wearing two digital hearing aids. Even going to my local bagel shop and ordering food or speaking to the cashier was becoming impossible. It was difficult to hear anybody or anything. It seemed like my right ear had completely shut off and I struggled to hear and understand people when they spoke.

I made an appointment with my audiologist to have my hearing tested again. This time after my exam, she had a discouraged look on her face when I walked into her office. She said, "I don't know how to tell you this, but you're going deaf. You have lost another 25% of your hearing in your right ear alone since the last exam. Your hearing loss is so severe that it can't be helped with hearing aids any longer. You need to see someone who specializes in cochlear implant surgery."

Her words were gut-wrenching and devastating to me. I had been losing my hearing for about nine years at this point. Just a few years prior to this, I met with a cochlear implant specialist from New Jersey because I thought it might be a good idea to research and prepare myself in case my hearing became much worse. I was told early on that I would be a candidate for this surgery one day if the worst happened and I went completely deaf. If the unthinkable occurred, I thought perhaps the cochlear implant could be a solution for me in the future. When I went to see this specialist to inquire and learn more, he told me that my hearing wasn't bad enough to have a cochlear implant. He then said something I never forgot. He told me cochlear implants weren't "real hearing" and it was something that I never wanted to have. Wow! This frightening information was shocking news to me especially coming from a doctor who specialized in these implant operations. He removed any hope of a solution for me if I ever went deaf. Now, just a few years later, I was sitting with my audiologist who said those dreaded words I never wanted to hear, "I'm very sorry but you're going deaf and you need to see a neurosurgeon who specializes in cochlear implants."

Her words hit me like a bolt of lightning. I saw my life flash before my eyes. Remember, I was the one who ran my marketing company and everyone always told me that if anything happened to me and I was taken out of my company there would be nothing left. Hearing the news that I was going to become completely deaf and lose the rest of my hearing meant that my livelihood was now hanging in the balance and I would no longer be able to support my family. But this devastating news was worse than a loss of livelihood for me. It was as though someone was ringing my spiritual alarm bell and sending me a prophetic premonition that I was going to lose it all.

For me, I believed going deaf meant losing all my relationships with everyone I cared about. People told me jokes and I no longer laughed at the punchlines. I couldn't hear them. Laughter and camaraderie were vanishing from my life. People became visibly irritated with me when I couldn't hear them or if I asked them to repeat themselves. I felt I was becoming a tiresome nuisance to everyone around me. For me hearing was love and without love in my life, it felt like life wasn't worth living. That's not to say I would ever consider suicide God forbid! This is just to help you understand how devastating this news was to me and how it literally brought me to my knees. When my audiologist told me that I was going completely deaf, there seemed to be no viable medical options that could help me. Where was I to turn now for help? In my darkest moment, I knew what I needed to do. I reached for God.

Shema Yisrael: Hearing Hashem GOD

In times of trouble when I was desperate for help I always reached for God. Praying to God was instinctual for me throughout my life and not something that I was ever taught by anyone. This time would be no different. With the news that I was going to become completely deaf, I reached into my personal prayer arsenal that was now equipped with the Shema prayer. I reached for the Shema in the Brooklyn Half Marathon and knew that I was carried 13.1 miles to the finish line. My experience in Brooklyn moved me deeply on that special Shabbos morning, and now almost two years later, I was faced with the harsh reality that I was losing the rest of my hearing. I knew that I needed to reach for God with the Shema once again. The Shema brought me a miracle in Brooklyn and many blessings throughout my four marathon runs. Now, boy oh boy, did I need a miracle!

During the 18 months of running my four marathons, I learned firsthand that this prayer is far more holy than most of the world realizes. I believe that even the most religious Jews in the world who say this prayer three times a day, don't completely realize the life changing enormity of these precious words. Many people who know the prayer, consider it a prayer of acknowledgement that God is our Creator and believe this was a prayer given to the Jewish people for our protection. The Shema is much more powerful and miraculous than that. Without any exaggeration, the Shema prayer is singularly the most important prayer in all of humanity. It defies reason that the enormity of these precious words has been lost and ignored by most of the Jewish children and this prayer remains completely unknown to most people of the world. Is this claim an exaggeration or overstated? Not in the least. In fact, there aren't enough words to describe the magnificence, importance and holiness of the Shema. Here is the English translation to this magnificent prayer:

Cover your eyes with your right hand and say:
Hear, O Israel, the L-rd is our G-d, the L-rd is One.
Recite the following verse in an undertone:
Blessed be the name of His glorious kingdom forever and ever.
You shall love the L-rd your G-d with all your heart, with all your soul, and with all your might. And these words which I command you today shall be upon your heart. You shall teach them thoroughly to your children, and you shall speak of them when you sit in your house and when you walk on the road, when you lie down and when you rise. You shall bind them as a sign upon your hand, and they shall be for a reminder between your eyes. And you shall write them upon the doorposts of your house and upon your gates.

And it will be, if you will diligently obey My commandments which I enjoin upon you this day, to love the L-rd your G-d and to serve Him with all your heart and with all your soul, I will give rain for your land at the proper time, the early rain and the late rain, and you will gather in your grain, your wine and your oil. And I will give grass in your fields for your cattle, and you will eat and be sated. Take care lest your heart be lured away, and you turn astray and worship alien gods and bow down to them. For then the L-rd's wrath will flare up against you, and He will close the heavens so that there will be no rain and the earth will not yield its produce, and you will swiftly perish from the good land which the L-rd gives you. Therefore, place these words of Mine upon your heart and upon your soul, and bind them for a sign on your hand, and they shall be for a reminder between your eyes. You shall teach them to your children, to speak of them when you sit in your house and when you walk on the road, when you lie down and when you rise. And you shall inscribe them on the doorposts of your house and on your gates – so that your days and the days of your children may be prolonged on the land which the L-rd swore to your fathers to give to them for as long as the heavens are above the earth.

The L-rd spoke to Moses, saying: Speak to the children of Israel and tell them to make for themselves fringes on the corners of their garments throughout their generations, and to attach a thread of blue on the fringe of each corner. They shall be to you as tzitzit, and you shall look upon them and remember all the commandments of the L-rd and fulfill them, and you will not follow after your heart and after your eyes by which you go astray – so that you may remember and fulfill all My commandments and be holy to your G-d. I am the L-rd your G-d who brought you out of the land of Egypt to be your G-d; I, the L-rd, am your G-d. True.

I wasn't raised in a religious way at all. Even though I did go to Hebrew school as a child, my upbringing was secular and I was taught little or nothing about Jewish law or prayers. I didn't truly know about the significance of the Shema until I was in my forties. Like most Jews, I went once a year to Rosh Hashanah and Yom Kippur services. Jews of all levels of observance or non-observance seem to make it a point to go to synagogue on the Jewish High Holy days. If it weren't for a Reform rabbi at Rosh Hashanah services one year asking us to memorize the first two lines which he gave us on a printout, I would not have been able to reach for this miraculous prayer when I needed it most. The Hebrew word, *Shema*, the name of the prayer that I began using to pray passionately to God for help with my deafness, means "Hear." Coincidence? Hardly. This was a godly miracle in the making after a long sequence of many miracles that brought about my spiritual awakening.

By early April of 2009, I began to say the first two lines of the Shema like a mantra in my mind every day, all day long. Without anybody realizing or knowing it, I was in a constant state of prayer. While I was speaking with people, privately in my mind, I was continuously repeating the first two lines of the Shema prayer in both Hebrew and English. In between these first two lines I would plead with Him and say, "Please God don't let me go deaf!"

Spring Break, a College Road Trip

In April of 2009 at spring break for the public schools where our children attended, we decided to take a college road trip to Chicago, Illinois and visit potential colleges for my oldest child. My son packed a copy of the book *The Secret* that I bought two years earlier. I began reading it too and thought I would brush up on its principles which promoted using "The Law of Attraction" to materialize what we want to see in our lives. I used some of these positive thinking techniques when I was determined to finish my first marathon run in memory of my father. As recommended in this book, I created the vision board for the New Jersey marathon because I believed that positive thinking and visualization would help me achieve my goal. After hearing the awful news from my audiologist, I was pulling out all the stops. I couldn't accept the possibility of being deaf because it meant that I wouldn't be able to take care of my family. Deafness meant that I would lose everything in my life including the people I loved. I simply couldn't allow that to happen and was willing to do anything to stop it.

While we were driving cross-country from New Jersey to Chicago I repeated the Shema in my mind and prayed to God without anybody's knowledge. When we arrived, our family of five shared a two-room suite in a hotel in Evanston, Illinois where we were visiting Northwestern University. Our trip which took place over spring break was also over the holiday of Passover. We weren't observant Jews but we usually had some sort of Seder each year. This year it was too "inconvenient" because of our travel plans. We decided that this year we would just skip it. My daughter was very involved with USY, a Conservative Jewish youth group, and wanted to visit the Hillel at Northwestern. The Hillel is a place where Jewish students congregate and socialize. When we visited with the Hillel staff, they were very kind to us and gave us a care package for Passover which I recall contained matzah and candles. I don't recall ever opening this package or using any of its contents. We already decided there would be no Seder for us, so why bother.

Our hotel suite contained two full-size beds in the bedroom and a pullout sofa in the living room. I shared my bed with our youngest daughter and my husband shared his with our son. Our oldest daughter slept on the pullout sofa in the living room. I opened my eyes around 7 AM on April 7, 2009, the 12th of Nisan, 5769 on the Hebrew calendar. It was very quiet that morning as I looked around the room and saw that everybody was still asleep. I quietly stayed in bed and just looked up at the ceiling waiting for everyone to wake up. As I was lying there gazing at the ceiling, I heard a strong male voice say to me, "Go get pen and paper and start writing this down."

I looked around the room and thought to myself, "Did I just hear someone speak to me?" The sound of this voice was so clear and strong that it felt almost like I heard this with my ears.

Then I heard it again. A very strong male voice said, "I said go get pen and paper and start writing this down." So, I listened. I looked for a pen and paper to start writing down what I heard.

That morning led to a sequence of events that changed my life and the lives of my entire family forever. In that moment, I had no idea that I was being spoken to by none other than Hashem, God Himself. Not realizing it was Him, I was fascinated by His voice and decided to go along with the request. There was a pad of paper and pen next to me on the nightstand. I grabbed them both to begin writing and as they say, "The rest is history."

The Book of Love

I began taking notes on the pad of paper as I heard words stream into my mind. I even covered my eyes with one hand to make sure I was being completely honest and not influenced by anything in the room or my own thoughts. When I finished writing, I knew I had just been touched by the divine. It was completely jaw-dropping. What stunned me the most were the two words that finished this first encounter of hearing spirit—*Mazel Tov!*

"Mazel Tov?" I thought. "Wow this is amazing! Whoever is speaking to me must be Jewish!" *Mazel Tov* is Hebrew for congratulations. Only Jewish people use this term. I was so amazed after I reread what I had written. There were some startling things written in this message too but because it ended in such a heartwarming friendly Jewish way, I felt safe. There was a feeling of camaraderie and family because whoever spoke to me used the Jewish term *Mazel Tov.* I felt like whoever was speaking to me could possibly be family reaching to me from the other side. These two little words were endearing, touched me deeply and I felt blessed.

That afternoon I went to a card store in Evanston and bought my first journal to record this first encounter of hearing the spirit world. I hoped that perhaps it would happen again. This time if I heard them I would be ready to record and document everything in my new journal. I waited for a quiet moment to record that first morning's conversation in my journal and hoped that it would happen again so that I could learn more. This turned out to be the understatement of the century!

The next evening on April 8th, 2009, the 14th of Nisan, 5769, was the first night of Passover. When my family should have been having a Passover Seder, I began writing and recording the first conversation in my new journal. Hashem, God, has since named this journal "The Book of Love." The cover of this journal is white with the following words in black print:

Dance as though no one is watching you,
Love as though you have never been hurt before,
Sing as though no one can hear you,
Live as though heaven is on earth.   —Souza

The following is the first entry in "The Book of Love."

April 8th, 2009

I am not really sure what to make of this but I will write it down exactly as it occurred. Yesterday morning while I was lying in bed I had the sudden thought and impulse to get paper and a pen to write down the messages that were coming into my mind. Were they coming from me? I don't believe so. I receive messages, words and thoughts as if someone else is speaking to me. This has been occurring for as long as I can remember. I don't give it too much thought but on occasion it comes in louder. I also have very vivid dreams and "visits". Visits from another dimension, another world, another place. People. People I know and people I don't know. Often with a message, or two. I have never written anything down that is until yesterday morning. A couple of weeks ago I had a very vivid dream that I was doing something I had only heard about, automatic writing. In my dream, I was compelled to get a pen and paper and my hand was taken over by something or someone else and the words flew on the page without any interference or input from me. It was as if my hand had a life of its own and something took it over. I have been praying a lot more than usual lately and asking for help. Help with my hearing. It has been told to me recently by a woman (her name removed), who is a clairvoyant, that I caused my own hearing loss in or around the year 2000 because I couldn't bear to hear of any more bad news. I was under incredible stress and this was my way of shutting things out. Well it has been progressively getting worse.

We just took a family trip to Chicago to see Northwestern University with my daughter, who is now 17. My son happened to pack the book *The Secret* which I had purchased for him a couple of years ago. He was intending to brush up on its principles, I suppose. He wasn't reading it so I picked it up and began reading it. In this book, it insists that everything in our lives is a creation of our own thoughts. If this is true, then I did create my own hearing loss. With this thought in mind I began praying and meditating a couple of days ago about restoring my hearing to its original perfection. Yesterday morning this is what I was doing when the words came into my head, reminding me of the dream where I was "automatic writing" and telling me to go get paper and pen right now and give it a try. I got out of bed and found the hotel pad next to me with the words *Thought Pad* on it. Here is what I heard in my head and what I wrote exactly. I don't know if I did this accurately or transcribed exactly what I heard, but I wrote the words I was getting as they were coming to me. The first several I wrote without looking at the paper. Then I became more confident and looked as I was writing. When I went back to read it later, after I had finished, it made me very emotional! Here it is:

Science
calling you
remember
trust
refresh
be willing to understand
Compromise
power thoughts
goodness
Path
Right on
earlier
run
everywhere
anxiety   refusal
relevant
Son coming here to college

family tree
You've done that
go away
broader sense
You are on the verge
Breakdown
Do you really believe
Barack Obama
Extremely urgent
telling you something
What is it? Power
Programmed
Intelligent
Honest
Report
Go Eat
I have to tell you, surprise
You are on a mission
Special
You are wonderful
Stop it
Pressure
Take time to understand
Speak to her
Question
heart beat, Therapeutic, Slow Down
You know you are on a mission
Course listen help
understand help her marry college
This is an exercise
Hopeless   It requires
your understanding, Relax
focus complete this
My hand   dreaming
You understand
Complicated   judge you
Reason for you
just stand up

I/we will help you
Time to come
Benefit of Doubt
Screaming to you?
Mystery in your head/generations
hold on we're coming
It's what life is all about everywhere.
I'm not finished with you.
Mazel Tov.

This first entry, without me knowing it at the time, marked the beginning of my journey and conversations with Hashem, God. There was a great deal of learning that I needed to do to understand what this gift truly was. I lacked knowledge and understanding about how to cope with a spiritual awakening. In my innocence, I simply kept writing and recording everything I was hearing as accurately as I possibly could. I recorded the conversations by labeling who was speaking, me or the spirit I was hearing. It was a sequence of Lori, and then my question, followed by who I thought it might be. At first, I used a question mark to symbolize who I was speaking to because I simply had no idea who it was. Hashem wouldn't tell me it was Him. Then the question mark was replaced with "S" for spirit. By the end of the first book, "The Book of Love," I referred to the voice that I heard speaking to me as "We." At this point in time, I thought I was speaking with and hearing many people all at the same time. I couldn't differentiate the voices that I heard or distinguish one from another.

As I continued writing in this first journal, "The Book of Love," the conversations seemed a bit choppy and at times I couldn't fully understand what was being communicated. It often sounded nonsensical which concerned me. At other times, it was powerful and godly and I knew without any doubt that it was authentic and being orchestrated by God Himself. There were many references along the way to the Torah, the Talmud, and the Bible. Most of the conversations early on were telling me that I should become kosher and start to learn about Jewish law. There were conversations and information about many aspects of Judaism but eventually I was also spoken to about Jesus. In the early conversations, the language and information that was shared with me treaded lightly on anything not Jewish. I wasn't pushed too hard in a direction that I wasn't emotionally ready to go.

In these earlier conversations, I was told that Jesus was a visionary and teacher which made the conversation more comfortable for me and allowed me to continue. I never had any issues with the person known as Jesus but I never believed he was anything more than a Jewish rabbi who had magical qualities that made him successful and a positive influence on many people. At the time I was writing in this journal, my closest girlfriend was a Christian and we often traded prayers and spoke about God. To me, there was one God for all of us and how we reached for Him was a personal choice. She and I even went together to see the preacher Joel Osteen in person because we both found him to be a wonderful inspirational speaker. Throughout my entire life, I was always able to accept someone's positive advice and wisdom even though their religion was different from my own.

Over the first three weeks of writing in "The Book of Love" there were biblical terms and ideas I had never heard before. There were Hebrew words spoken to me that I had to look up and translate because I didn't know any Hebrew. I also began having powerful and prophetic nightly visions.

One night I was having vivid and powerful visions that began with baby pictures of me. These pictures were then superimposed with images that looked like Jesus. During these visions, I distinctly remember hearing loud claps of thunder and then raucous applause. The applause sounded like I was surrounded by thousands of people cheering wildly. It was a completely surreal experience where I felt surrounded by a profound love that I had never experienced before in my lifetime.

Throughout "The Book of Love," I was continuously told these words "You are chosen" and "Be brave." Another phrase that was said to me often was "Everything is measured." By April 30, 2009 just a few weeks after I purchased this first journal, I was certain that I was chosen by God Himself for something extremely important.

I was still unaware that it was Hashem, God, orchestrating every one of our conversations. I also was unaware that every word I heard was not directly from Him or truthful. In my innocence, I wrote every word I received as though it was the truth and coming from a pure source. Information that came to me, was written and received as though it came directly from Hashem, Himself. I had much to learn!

Over these many years since this awakening occurred, I have grown in my knowledge of what was happening in those early days. At the onset of this spiritual awakening I was unaware that there is an invisible world with many "voices" and not all of them are pure or good. I wrote down every word that I heard and was under the misconception that it was all holy and from Hashem, God. I now have knowledge and understanding that I didn't have back then. I learned over the years about the physical and the non-physical spiritual realm and how to decipher truth from fiction. This ability can only come to you with guidance, education and being protected by the observance of Torah law.

God's Torah, which is revered by the three major monotheistic religions and billions of people as given to Moses by God Himself and taught to the children of Israel, provides critical laws and education which have been lost to most of the world. While Orthodox Judaism is growing rapidly now, only about 3-4 million Orthodox Jews around the world study and observe Torah law. Torah shouldn't be confused with what Christians have included in their Bible and named the "Old Testament" or the Quran, the central religious text for Muslims. The Torah is distinctly different and a perfect instrument of knowledge given directly from Hashem God to Moshe Rabbeinu, Moses the Prophet, on Mt. Sinai. Torah includes the Five Books of Moses and much more. I will discuss more about the Torah later in this book. For now, what's important to convey is that at the onset of my awakening I lacked important knowledge and reacted with the pure innocence of a small child. I met every word that I heard with exuberance, purity and excitement that God was real and I was going to share Him and His messages with everyone.

Without knowing that it was Hashem Himself guiding me, I felt strangely safe and loved by whomever was speaking to me. This may sound confusing but if you become knowledgeable about the spirit world and the ways of Hashem, it will begin to make logical sense. You see right from the beginning, Hashem was my personal spirit guide in all my conversations, however, I could hear the voices of others as they spoke too. I could also hear another voice that is known in Torah as Yetzer Hara. Translated, this voice is the voice of the evil inclination, also known as Satan.

The evil inclination, Satan, is not a spirit or a being as some people are taught, it is simply a voice. It's a tester that gives us the option to choose evil over God or the good inclination called the Yetzer Hatov in Hebrew. Over the years since my awakening I have learned that the Yetzer Hara is a lure that can sound benign at first and mimics the voice of God Himself. Most people hear the Yetzer Hara as either their own voice or an impulse or idea that occurs to them. It's a sudden inclination that they either accept and act on or reject outright. An inclination or thought might come to you like eating a second piece of cheesecake when one serving is plenty. It sounds fairly benign and like a good idea at the time but it's the Yetzer Hara luring you the wrong way. Succumbing to this enticement often has an undesirable outcome. This information and knowledge about how the Yetzer Hara operates in our world came to me over many years since my spiritual awakening on April 7, 2009.

When I was awakened, I was a non-observant secular Jew with no knowledge of Torah. I now understand that in the beginning of my awakening I was hearing Hashem's voice, the voice of the Yetzer Hara, and voices of many souls who had crossed over. These souls were no longer here in the physical realm but I could hear them with my new and awakened spiritual ears. Many of the souls that I could hear were "unclean." These "unclean" souls are people who choose to remain earthbound and refuse to go through spiritual cleansing after they die. These souls are sometimes called ghosts, poltergeists, or demons. Are you scared yet? Just wait.

By referring to souls as spiritually unclean, I mean that when these souls lived here in the physical world as people, they became impure by choosing poorly. Souls incarnate as people and as they journey here on earth they are expected to choose between evil and good in every moment. When a person chooses poorly, and chooses the Yetzer Hara, Satan, the evil that they chose attaches to their soul creating a spiritual blemish. It also attaches to their physical body causing a myriad of illnesses. After passing away, there is a cleansing period where the soul goes through spiritual cleansing to remove these impurities and blemishes. There are souls who refuse to go through the cleansing process and they remain earthbound. After death, the Jewish souls don't have any choice in the matter and are required to go through cleansing. The non-Jewish souls who refuse to cleanse open Pandora's box for everyone who is still living here. How so? They hang around the living so to speak and people are unwittingly influenced by them. This is a powerfully dangerous situation for the well-being of those who are here in body. While I was hearing primarily the voice of Hashem, God, I was also hearing cleansed and uncleansed souls, the Yetzer Hara, the Yetzer Hatov—the entire shebang! Over many years since my spiritual awakening Hashem has taught me details and provided knowledge about the quagmire that we are all unsuspectingly living in while here on earth.

Hashem, God, does everything for our good and everything He does is on purpose. He purposefully allowed me to hear all that I heard knowing that I would share every sordid detail. In my innocence and excitement, I shared every morsel of information I heard with anyone who would listen. Hashem didn't intervene or help me discern who or what I was hearing. I listened intently to every word I could hear and recorded the words verbatim as they flowed to me.

In the early stages of this awakening, while I was writing in "The Book of Love," everything was intensely loving and there was nothing that I found frightening. It was magical to me because I could feel the presence of Hashem, God, but didn't realize that He was the loudest and strongest voice I was recording from day one. He deliberately withheld that information from me. Occasionally, the conversations I was recording seemed a little discombobulated and didn't flow quite right. I would ask questions and in the middle of a conversation I would receive an answer that didn't fit the flow of what we were just speaking about. When this happened, I asked questions as to why the answers made no sense. Hashem deliberately didn't clarify any of the confusion for me. This was an important part of the process of waking up.

The disconnect in the conversation flow disturbed me a little because I wanted to get this communication down completely right and honestly. I felt that this book, "The Book of Love," would be read one day by the public because it was so incredible and worthy of sharing. I wanted to be completely accurate with my recount of everything that I was hearing. It never occurred to me that everything I was recording was not directly from God, or goodness. It never occurred to me that I was hearing many voices, some giving false and negative information. I felt inexplicably safe the entire time because the strongest and most powerful voice that was speaking with me was Hashem Himself. This was all deliberate and part of the awakening process and my testimony which will be used to teach everyone in the future. I diligently recorded everything I heard as though it was coming from one truthful and godly source.

In "The Book of Love" very little of what I was writing seemed to be problematic. At times, it simply seemed confusing and it made me feel uncertain that I was recording the messages correctly. I felt the problem must be within me and my inability to record the information correctly. To complicate matters more, Hashem deliberately told me information that was false, for a specific purpose. Why in the world would God Himself give me information that was false? One might think that if it were truly God, every single utterance from Him would be authentically true, right? Wrong! If you believe that Hashem would never mislead you on purpose, you simply are not knowledgeable yet in the ways of Hashem God.

When Hashem needs you to do something He will tell you what you need to hear in that moment to encourage you to keep going and complete what needs to happen. In some cases, if He were to tell you the truth, you would likely refuse and not do what was required. Hashem is acutely deliberate and all-knowing. He knows exactly what to say to you to derive the outcome that is necessary. Everything He does to us is for our ultimate good. There is nothing that Hashem God does that is not for our well-being. He will tell us a lie to encourage us to do something that we would outright refuse if we knew where it would lead us. He will lead you right into the lion's den and into the jaws of pain and suffering if that is ultimately for your good.

Just prior to my awakening on April 7th, I had befriended a woman who practiced something called Angelic Reiki. I met her at a networking event that was held by someone who marketed herself as a psychic medium. I was interested in her ability to communicate with angels as an alternative form of healing work. Because I was losing my hearing and going deaf, I thought perhaps she could help with a spiritual answer to my problems. Since I always believed in God and miracles, I scheduled a few meetings at her home to allow her to perform her Angelic Reiki on me. I had no idea that any of this practice was against God's laws and that her Angelic Reiki practice was potentially dangerous.

Nonetheless, this woman was as sweet as sugar and we hit it off right away. I went to her home and as she performed Angelic Reiki, she had stunning visions while she was working over me. She told me in one of her visions that she saw me in white robes, surrounded in white light, and had the overwhelming desire to kneel to me as though I was someone very holy. She also told me she saw an angel who was Chasidic called Melchizedek. In her visions, she saw many Jewish male souls on the other side rocking and praying wildly. As she was working over me she felt the intense desire to rock and pray too.

She and her husband believed in me and my new gift of hearing God and the spirit world. There was even one occasion when I went to their home and told them that Hashem God had instructed me to find all the idols in their home and remove them. They walked through their home with me as I pointed to objects that Hashem said were idols and we removed them all to cleanse their home from evil. They listened to me intently and believed in my spiritual abilities and saw this as a miraculous gift.

On April 30, 2009, the last entry of "The Book of Love" turned quite serious. It shook me to my core. There was language in this entry that defied my upbringing and challenged my beliefs as a Jew. While it was challenging my beliefs, it was directly connected to my Jewish heritage and the safety of my family and Israel. As a Jew, no matter how observant, we all feel a deep spiritual relationship with Israel and the Jewish people. Being Jewish is part of our soul, and part of our entire being, and much more than a religion. Here is the entry that shook me up and made me tremble:

April 30, 2009 10:00PM

I spent the afternoon having lunch with my two brothers and mother. Then I went back to my mother's house where I told her what has been going on with me since April 7th. I brought out this book and read to her several pages. I gave her the messages that were meant for her. She told me she believed this was true but that it was hard to digest. I believe she believes but detect a little bit of doubt which would only be natural.

I no longer doubt. I now know this is all true. Here is a short update. Yesterday, last night I was told I would be visited and I was. It wasn't the same as when I was younger and met the woman who I believe was a guardian angel. It was quite different but profound. Here is what I saw and felt.

I saw a lot of lights in the room. I closed my eyes and felt the presence of spirits, many, and I could actually hear things that sounded a little like breathing. I'm not sure what it was. Then I saw around midnight a beautiful room that was filled with white light and grand stairs leading to an altar and was told it was the Ark of the Lord. I felt overwhelmed by the vision and thought this is so beautiful. I thought how amazing God was and how magnificent religion and faith was. These thoughts were running through my mind and I looked up and saw vividly a lion. But the lion did not scare me at all. From the lion, I could see a bear and then a leopard. Those made me a little less comfortable though I wasn't scared of any of it. It was just that the bear and the leopard were darker in color than the lion was.

I researched this tonight on the internet and found information that the lion, the bear and the jaguar are also symbolic of God. The lion can also be symbolic of angels protecting God. Which also makes sense since I was being shown the Ark and Temple of the Lord. It was magnificent. It seemed painted and surreal because it was so grand and so beautiful. I just remember feeling in awe.

From that image, I was shown a square of light. I closed my eyes as hard as I could and even had to check with my hands to make sure they were closed because the light was so bright. There was a very bright square of light in front of my eyes. The room was completely dark. There were no lights on at all. Black darkness yet I could see this bright square ahead of me with my eyes shut tightly.

They told me this was the space where they were and where I could most easily connect with them. It is the same location where they say your mind's eye is located. The only other thing I can remember was the name Hillel was told to me. I either have Hillel with me or I knew him.

Lori: They tell me now I knew him. The other name that was mentioned was Jordan Nash. I don't know this person.

We: You will. He will show up. We are talking to you. Write this down. Mexico. They are still worried about swine flu. Take precaution.

Lori: I didn't believe this would really be a problem. Do I need to worry for my family's safety?

We: For the time being, no. Put it out of your mind.

Lori: Then why do you say take precaution?

We: Because we care for you. That's all. You have enough on your mind to deal with. Safety. Use it.

Lori: Wash hands and that sort of thing?

We: Stay home more often. Eating out could be dangerous. Sprays. Cover your face. It will infect a lot of people. People will be scared. Not you. Keep away from them. Protect yourself. Not your time.

Lori: My family is protected too, please tell me.

We: Yes.

Lori: Thank you! Thank God! Phew.

Lori: Shall I warn "My Angelic Reiki friend"? Her health seems fragile.

We: You can tell her this. We want you to vaccine.

Lori: What about vaccine?

We: It could help.

Lori: I think I just got there is a reason for this and it is political. Am I correct?

We: Osama bin Laden, working with Taliban. Committed to evil. Terror. Have to catch him. Destroy him before it's too late. Eyes on nuclear weapons. Pointed at Israel. This can't be done.

Lori: Please tell me more.

We: Al Qaeda network bands, you have to listen to this before it's too late. Christians band together to fight Al Qaeda. Deadly explosion. Hurt many thousands. We will witness this. Population survived but devastation.

Lori: What will happen to Israel?

We: 18th bodies. Holy land. Disciples summoned up. Resurrection. The Lord will come. The second coming of Christ our Lord. Holy Trinity. Heavenly Father disciples will all be there. Pray to the Father. He will give comfort to you. Mind's eye. Have courage. Stop writing for a minute.

Lori: Okay. We spoke. I will do my best to remain calm. You will tell me what I am to do and I will listen. This is enormous, but I must be chosen for a reason. A reason I cannot know. You know who I am and evidently, I do not. I think of myself as someone different. I don't even know of such things.

We: Yet.

Lori: What?

We: You heard. You are Christ's child.

Lori: What does this mean? I am Jewish. Christ was Jewish. But what does this have to do with me?

We: You are summoned by the Holy one. The benefit of the doubt. Treasure. Believe it. You are the one.

Lori: This is very, very difficult.

We: Amazing it is.

Lori: Who will believe me?

We: Trust. Have faith. It will come. Measured. Safe haven. We are so glad you are here with us. We taught you well. You have learned quickly. It is evident. Slow down. Sleep. Good night.

Lori: Just like that? How can I sleep with this?

We: We compel you. Trust. Shut off the light. Sleep. Good night. Pray, archangels are with you. Solution, pray. 🙁

I trembled after writing this entry. I wrote every word as I heard it and believed I was being guided by a divine presence. Who I was truly speaking with still wasn't told to me. Now years later, I understand that every word I was writing was being orchestrated by Hashem, but every word spoken wasn't Hashem's voice. Everything I heard had a specific purpose. So, what portion of this entry in "The Book of Love" was true? On April 30th of 2009, I believed it was all true. Now, more than 9 years later, I can pick through each sentence of this entry and with the help of Hashem, decipher exactly what was true and learn the source of every word. I haven't done that yet to this day. This may be surprising to some, but deciphering each word with Hashem isn't important. In His wisdom, He knew I needed to hear all of this in its entirely and believe every word was completely true. Every word written had a specific divine purpose and everything was orchestrated by His will. It always is.

By April 30, 2009, Hashem had already peppered the way with ideas and conversations for me not to be completely stunned or upset by the mere mention of Jesus. Although this was true, mixing my name up with Jesus shook me at my core. I wondered why in the world are they saying this to me? Why am I being told I was Christ's child and that I was chosen? This was mixed with the message that a terrorist organization who was responsible for the 9/11 terrorist attacks was trying to get nukes and destroy Israel. Everything I wrote that day made me tremble. Feeling sure I was being guided by God Himself,

I ran with the information and shared it with family and friends even though I didn't fully understand everything. After finishing "The Book of Love," I went to a Barnes and Noble and purchased another journal to keep writing and recording these conversations. I had no idea what was coming or what was about to come through in this next journal. In a word, what came through was terrifying.

After going to the bookstore to buy my new journal, I continued with my new passion of speaking to the spirit world and recording our conversations. I was having nightly visions and my ability to hear spirit was increasingly stronger. As I continued listening, conversing and writing in my journal I realized I had another gift. I discovered that I had the ability to speak with souls who had crossed over and at their request could allow them to share my vessel. The ability to do this kind of thing has been documented by others in our world and isn't a new phenomenon. I had no knowledge of this at the time and didn't realize this was extraordinarily dangerous. It was a lot like the movie *Ghost* when Whoopi Goldberg allowed Patrick Swayze to enter her body to speak with Demi Moore. Freaky, I know!

If a soul requested this from me, I would relax my body and allow the soul to enter me through the crown of my skull. The invisible part of me, my soul that is truly Lori, would relax, sit back and allow the other soul to speak through my lips. After they entered me, it felt as though I was another person in the room listening in on the conversation as they spoke through me to other people. Wild yes? Incredibly wild and deeply dangerous to say the least!

In my naïveté and excitement to share my gift with others, I didn't filter or question anything that I heard. It didn't occur to me to be frightened or to say no to any request. I greeted every invisible voice with love and an open heart. I felt Hashem, God was with me, and because He blessed me with this wild and miraculous gift I was compelled to share it with everyone. It was clear to me that my life had come full circle and all the nightly dreams and visits that I experienced throughout my life were now crystallizing into my life's purpose. I had found my calling and I would not refuse or walk away from any of it. On April 30th, 2009, the last entry of "The Book of Love," I was told clearly and unequivocally that I was chosen by God Himself to do something extraordinary and special for our world. In this final entry, I was told to warn everyone about the acute danger we faced, wake everyone up and lead the charge to save my family, Israel and the Jewish people.

The Book of Truth

My awakening was in full throttle when I began writing in my second journal. This journal picked up where "The Book of Love" left off. Hashem continued to reveal to me the invisible world that surrounds us all. As I continued writing feverishly in the second journal, the conversation changed from gentle and loving to deeply frightening. I kept writing through it all without relenting to fear. In His all-knowing wisdom, Hashem named the second journal "The Book of Truth." At the time, I was completely unaware why this was such a powerful and perfect name for this journal. It wouldn't be revealed to me how poignant and perfect this name was until recently as I was writing this book and sharing my journey with you. "The Book of Truth" was named so by Hashem because it revealed the truth about how our world truly operates.

Most of the world is completely oblivious and unaware that we are surrounded by a spiritual web of both good and evil. My reaction to hearing Hashem along with these dark and negative voices helped whip me into such a frenzy that it brought about my eventual demise, an involuntary mental hospital commitment. As I heard all the voices that were present in my home, I recorded their hideous angry language that loudly screamed obscenities and outright lies.

"The Book of Truth" reveals how our world is currently completely perverted and surrounded by evil. Invisible to our physical eyes, Hashem, God, and His spiritual goodness exist in an invisible web that surrounds us in love. This invisible goodness is called the Yetzer Hatov, Hebrew for the good inclination. However, what most people of the world don't realize is that we are also surrounded by a web of profound evil, the Yetzer Hara, Hebrew for the evil inclination. The knowledge of good versus evil has been delivered to us in the written Torah and the oral Torah. Guidelines and laws were given to Moses and taught to the children of Israel to help prevent them from succumbing to evil and becoming infected. This knowledge about good versus evil is available but it is only studied by very few people. The current crisis we see in our world is due to the lack of knowledge about how our world truly operates. But it is much worse than lack of book knowledge that we are experiencing right now. Even the learned few who study this information are failing to recognize the Yetzer Hara, and are choosing evil every day. More evil is propagating our earth than ever before. We are on a steady path to complete self-destruction. Am I exaggerating a little bit? Being a little hysterical? No. I can't possibly overstate this or deliver this information to you in strong enough terms.

The existence of evil, known in Torah as the Yetzer Hara, is an alternative that you can choose instead of God or goodness. It is also known as Satan. The existence of the Yetzer Hara is part of God's design for our world and its existence allows us to choose between evil and good in every moment. By giving us an alternative to choosing Him and goodness, He is providing everyone with complete personal freedom. Evil doesn't truly manifest in our world unless people choose it. Choosing it is exactly what everyone does. The personification of evil is a choice made by human beings in almost every moment.

There is one exception however. Me, your Moshiach. Hashem has told me repeatedly that I have never chosen the Yetzer Hara in any incarnation, not once. This is a powerful statement that I myself don't believe. I check myself for wrongheaded thinking or choices and feel I sin often. Being void of choosing Yetzer Hara isn't my claim at all. Hashem Himself has told me and shown me for many years how I choose correctly in every decision.

This statement might be met with disbelief or possibly resentment. Many God-fearing people refuse to believe that they choose evil in any moment. The idea that everyone but me chooses the evil inclination without exception may be something you outright reject. How could I, Lori Michelle, be the only person on earth who doesn't choose evil, ever? Perhaps you even feel the pinch of resentment, indignation or are personally insulted about my inference that you choose evil and I never do. This resentment is an alarm bell that the Yetzer Hara is working on you and succeeding. Even if you paused for a moment and thought to yourself, "I don't choose evil," this is also the Yetzer Hara luring you away from the truth. This is how sneaky and difficult it is to spot the evil inclination and choose correctly in every moment. What you think of as human pride or defending yourself, most often is egotism and self-righteous behavior. The need to be right is the Yetzer Hara working on you in full bloom.

As you keep reading on, I will explain how Hashem has shown me for many years that I never choose the Yetzer Hara. Please try to understand this is not a boast; it's what Hashem says is my nature. I naturally choose Him over the Yetzer Hara in every moment. He has told me that I'm like a walking, talking and breathing Yetzer Hatov and Yetzer Hara computer. I scan everything instinctually to sniff out the evil and dismiss it summarily. It's natural for me and how I am wired. My work in this world is to show you how you can and must do this too. The work of learning to choose God in every moment without exception is everyone's responsibility in these End of Days.

When I was writing in these journals from the first day, April 8, 2009, Hashem was my personal guide and the strongest voice above them all. He deliberately and for good reasons allowed me to hear what every human being hears without realizing it. These voices that I heard clearly are for most of the world completely silent and appear to be your own thoughts. Not so for me. Since my spiritual awakening, I hear audibly with my spiritual ears pure Yetzer Hara, the evil inclination, in plain old everyday English. The Yetzer Hara mimics the sound of Hashem's voice and much of what it says is completely benign or even ridiculous. At first the Yetzer Hara is a lure. It baits you. It gets you to agree with its assertions which at first are often true. Much of what the Yetzer Hara tells you can be authentically true or even inspiring, and therein lies the supreme danger. It gains your agreement and lures you away from God but you are eventually forced to decide between good and evil. The Yetzer Hara, Satan, is extremely clever and sneaky and disguises itself as goodness and truthfulness. Even the most righteous God-loving souls become easy prey and fall daily to the Yetzer Hara.

Here is a fictitious example of the Yetzer Hara at work. Let's say it's Monday morning and the sky is cloudless. It is one of the 10 best weather days of the year. You look outside as you get ready for your workday and the Yetzer Hara says, "Wow, what a glorious day." You hear this as your own voice but it's not really you. It is the evil inclination baiting you. You agree with this obviously true statement. Then it continues, "Ugh I hate my job and there is so much for me to do. My co-workers don't help and it all falls on my shoulders." You agree once again. It continues, "What a beautiful day. I would love to go to the beach instead of dealing with my annoying co-workers and the mountain of work on my desk." So, you start thinking. You are tempted to call in sick but you know that the mountain of work needs to get done and you're the only one who knows how to accomplish everything. Now the Yetzer Hara sparks anger in you. "They don't appreciate me at work. They are asking me to do more and more and haven't hired anyone competent to help me." Again, it's true so you get angry. You say to yourself, "Yeah! They don't appreciate me." Now you're feeling abused and angry. The chasm is open for the Yetzer Hara to creep in and do its nasty work. It says, "To hell with all of them, I'm going to the beach. Let them figure it out and maybe they'll finally appreciate me!"

A beautiful morning became an excuse to relinquish your responsibility. It starts with benign comments and leads you to make decisions out of anger and ego. This example is somewhat benign. Imagine an example where politicians use hatred to rally support. You remember, Nazi Germany. The people of Germany were suffering hard financial times and Adolf Hitler gave them their common enemy, the Jewish people. The Yetzer Hara can be as benign as playing hooky from work or as evil as the Holocaust. It comes in different sizes and wears many masks. It is quite clever and designed to test your mettle.

In "The Book of Truth," I was also recording the words of uncleansed souls. Uncleansed souls are people who have crossed over and died but who refused to go the way of God and cleanse. Cleansing is a necessary process that souls go through after death to remove the stains of the Yetzer Hara that attach to the spirit when we are incarnate. Jewish souls must go through cleansing while non-Jewish souls are given the choice to refuse. As I was recording my conversations in "The Book of Truth," these unclean souls began shouting out garbled Christian ideas which included blatant lies. In between the Yetzer Hara and these uncleansed souls shouting at me, I heard clearly and strongly the voice of Hashem guiding me through my terrifying experience. Although Hashem was guiding me, He desired me to experience every horrific moment that occurred. I was required to go through the fire and come out the other side with a new perspective of our world. Every single word I wrote down in "The Book of Truth" and everything I experienced was designed to peel my eyes wide open to see our world as I had never seen it before.

Hashem deliberately peeled back every layer of the rotten onion of life here on earth and exposed the horrific dangers that are present in our world. For the first time, I saw how deeply evil and sick everyone truly is without knowing it. Yes, everyone reading this book right now is included in this statement. This isn't meant to be demeaning at all. It's meant to turn on the light switch and be your wake-up call to recognize that you've been choosing incorrectly. You must wake up and learn when you are unwittingly choosing evil over good or God. I now have full understanding why we are all in serious trouble all over our world. We are in much worse trouble than any human being currently realizes and I'm not just speaking of terrorism and war. I'm speaking of the enemy that lies within every single person. Humanity has become like the horror flick *Night of the Living Dead*, truly. People are choosing evil daily believing that it's goodness and truth. When you begin to wake up to this truth, you will reach a new understanding about our world and God willing you will learn to choose differently. That's why I'm writing this book for you now. It's time to expose the truth and turn on the light for humanity.

I went daily to work in my marketing company but when I arrived I shut myself in my office for privacy to speak with the divine and record our conversations. I was single-minded now and understood that writing in my journal was part of my life's calling and the work Hashem, God had chosen me to do. While I was writing in "The Book of Truth," I learned I was speaking directly to Hashem, God. As this became increasingly clear, His voice became louder and stronger within me. My instinctual knowing that it was indeed Hashem Himself guiding me became vivid and strong. I trusted Him completely.

In my moment of complete knowing and trust in Him, He began to tell me a series of boldfaced lies. Before you shut down and say, "God would never lie!" please suspend those thoughts and opinions and continue reading. This book and my testimony will give you a powerful education in the ways of our world and Hashem God. The ways of Hashem are deliberate and purposeful. He will do what is needed to achieve His goal which is always for our good, without exception. This even includes telling lies when they are required.

He created a wild tale that He was giving me the winning lottery ticket numbers to the New Jersey Mega Millions Lottery and instructed me to play specific numbers that He gave me. I was instructed to buy this ticket and told that it would surely win a record jackpot of hundreds of millions of dollars. He said that this winning lottery ticket would be the proof I needed to provide to all the people in my life that I was indeed speaking with Him, God. In the words of Hashem God, this would be the material world proof they desired for them to believe me. Fantastic, so I thought.

I became overwhelmed with excitement by the news that He was giving me material proof that my gift was real, and everyone would understand and know that I was truly speaking to Him. "Wow, won't everyone be delighted," I thought. So many people are in despair and don't truly know that God is authentically real because they have no solid material world proof. Now, He was about to give this proof to me. "Holy smokes, how blessed am I?" I thought to myself. My enthusiasm was soaring at the mere idea that I could deliver proof of God to my friends and family. Not only would this be miraculous proof, but I would win millions of dollars that I could share with all the people I loved. I began to make a long list of all the people I knew with whom I would share my winnings and bring everyone extreme joy. I was dizzied with excitement.

I took out my address book which included distant cousins whom I hadn't spoken to in years. I desired to include everyone I had ever loved in my entire life. I could hardly wait to receive this gift so that I could give all of it away. I fantasized about how I would do this and planned to have a secret party not telling anyone I invited who was hosting the party or what occasion would be celebrated. In my fantasy, I would show up to this surprise party and shock everyone with the wild news. My plan was to divvy up all the winnings and put extremely large checks in a gift box placed underneath each of their chairs. You know—the way Oprah gave out gifts to her television audience when she had her TV program. I planned do this in Oprah style times millions of dollars. As I excitedly thought about who I'd invite and how I would give all this money away, there would be only one request in return for showering everyone with great wealth. I would ask everyone to please give a portion of the money away to someone else in need and pay it forward. How blessed was I that God Himself was allowing me, Lori Michelle, to show them all that He is real by blessing me with great fortune so that I could enjoy giving it all away? He was giving me millions of dollars to share with everyone I've ever loved! Isn't this the way everyone else thinks? Wouldn't everyone be dizzy with excitement thinking about how to give it all away too? Wouldn't that be the first thought on everybody's mind?

I told my Angelic Reiki lady friend and her husband that God gave me the winning numbers to Mega Millions. The three of us were all so excited as we drove together to buy this winning lottery ticket. They had complete faith in me and were positive that I was guided by God Himself. They were 100 percent correct. It was Hashem orchestrating all of this. I had become unshakably confident that it was truly Him and I was sure that everything Hashem was telling me was the truth. My enthusiasm and excitement were soaring and I was living on cloud nine. I also had shared with the two of them my love for running marathons for charity and gave each of them Running on Love T-shirts as a gift. I told them that one day the people of the world would Run on Love together. Running on Love was still my hobby but I fantasized that one day I would turn my passion into a charity.

Along with my excitement of receiving the winning lottery numbers, my hearing improved and I began hearing better than I had in years. Suddenly I didn't even need to wear my two digital hearing aids. I felt this was a powerful confirmation that God was healing me. At the age of 49 I was also wearing reading glasses. No more! I could see better than I had seen in years. Was this really happening to me or was it my imagination? To this day I still have no physical proof that this occurred but at the time I took it as a clear sign that it was a gift from Hashem and that I was experiencing a holy miracle from God, Himself.

Not only did Hashem, God, tell me that I was going to win the Mega Millions Lottery, but He also told me a fictitious story about Jesus. By this time, I was certain it was Hashem and I completely trusted everything He told me. His voice was crystal clear, calming and strong. Today, more than nine years later, I know that it was truly Hashem and I understand everything He did to me and why. Why did He tell me fictitious stories with the intention of misleading me? One would question, if Hashem loved me so much, why in the world would He tell me lies and encourage my wild-eyed behavior? The simple answer is that these deceptions and the events that followed were deliberate and necessary. Everything He said to me, and each event that occurred because of my reactions, were all part of a perfect tapestry in my incredible story. He took me on a wild journey that gave me the education and understanding that I am now sharing with the world. My awakening wasn't only about hearing God and spirit. He was also waking me and educating me about our world and revealing the serious trouble we are all in. Done in any other way, this education would not have been possible.

In another fictitious story, Hashem convinced me He was Jesus and that this was the beginning of His second coming. I'm referring of course to the second coming that the Christians have been talking about for almost two thousand years. He informed me that I was chosen to give birth to Him and bring Him into this world so that He could one day save us all. He convinced me that I was the reincarnation of Jesus's mother, Mary, and that I was here to do it all again. This convoluted story was a complete lie but because I was certain that it was Hashem, and I loved Him so deeply, it served to convince me to also love Jesus. Had He not done this to me, any affection for Jesus would have been impossible. I was a Jewish girl not raised with any affection or reverence for the man Christian people call Jesus. Most Jewish people don't revere his memory at all. I personally didn't revere or dislike him, and certainly never thought of him as the Messiah or God. To clear the air right away, I am not Mary reincarnated at all and Hashem was not the one people refer to as Jesus. This story was simply one of Hashem's techniques to bring me to a spiritual place of love and acceptance for the one people call Jesus. Because I loved and trusted Hashem with all my heart, my love and trust transferred to Jesus when He said He was one and the same. Hashem's tall tale and convoluted story encouraged me to accept non-Jewish ideas that would have otherwise been impossible for me to believe.

Hashem's fictitious story encouraged me to open my mind and believe that Jesus was someone powerfully beautiful. Hashem deliberately convinced me that Jesus was Him, and He was my Savior. Hashem is emphatically not the person Christians know as Jesus. I've learned over these years that there is great confusion among the Christian people about whether Jesus was Messiah, the son of God, or God Himself. It seems to change depending upon which Christian you speak to. Some believe that Jesus was Hashem's son, while others believe that Jesus is Hashem, one and the same. Hashem has clarified in no uncertain terms that He is not the one people refer to as Jesus Christ. Over the years He has educated me that Jesus's true name was Yeshua ben Yosef. He explains that Yeshua was a Jewish man, a teacher and a visionary. As we continue with the story of my awakening, I will clarify who Yeshua ben Yosef was and what his true role was in our world.

By early May of 2009, Hashem convinced me that He was Jesus and He had chosen me to give birth to Him as my fourth child in this life. He instructed me that I would raise Him in complete secrecy not telling anyone His real identity. This would remain secret until He was the appropriate age to be the Messiah and heal our world. Sounds like it's straight out of the Christian Bible, perhaps? I wouldn't know because I've never read it. It didn't matter if it was written like this anywhere, I was getting this information all the way from the top, from Hashem, God. I took every morsel of information to heart. Nothing was going to stop me in my relationship with God Himself and I was going to do everything asked of me to save my children and Israel.

As I write these words and reveal the sordid details of my awakening for the first time in this book, I'm choking back emotion. I'm overcome with emotion because I listened and obeyed. Without any physical proof whatsoever, I knew it was truly Hashem. I feel wrought with emotion that I trusted my soul and my soul was unequivocally correct. In the face of naysayers and doubters, my soul knew and flew straight into His arms. In my desire to serve God, save my children and the Jewish people of Israel, I would have done anything. There is no human being who could convince me to stop. Hashem knew that I would take this on with unbridled enthusiasm. He also knew that I would never stop reaching for Him no matter what happened to me in the process. He knows me better than I know myself and knew that eventually, the entire truth would be revealed to me. Hashem was deliberately leading me smack into the center of the lion's den without my realizing it.

I was sure all these fictional stories were true because they were coming directly from Hashem. It was full steam ahead as I followed all His instructions. I was filled with passion and felt like I was flying with the angels as they say. I was sharing everything I was being told with people I knew. In time, I thought they would believe me especially when the physical proof showed up, all that money. I didn't even need to show them the money, I thought the money would simply be the icing on the cake. Why wouldn't they believe me? I was always known as a truthful and genuine person with some extra psychic abilities. I felt the people who knew and loved me would believe me. Sadly, I couldn't have been more wrong.

One evening I had a dinner date with my childhood friend with whom I had run the NYC Marathon in November 2008. Being friends since we were seven years old is the kind of friendship that is rare and I cherished knowing that we both kept our friendship strong for many years. We were not only childhood friends, but as we grew up she decided to enroll at the same university as me. We even roomed together in my senior year of college. Like many friendships, we had our challenges over those years but we always overcame them and were devoted to each other. Every few months we made plans to see each other socially.

On this occasion at our dinner get-together, I decided it was important to share my new gift with her. It never occurred to me in the middle of my awakening that she would be shocked and not believe one word that I uttered. She was completely stunned to see me exhausted and speaking about hearing spirits and God. As she looked at me in disbelief, it was clear she was sure I had lost my mind. Instead of saying anything to me, she played along in the conversation pretending to be engaged throughout the evening. Over dinner, I decided to share my gift of being able to share my vessel with souls who had crossed over. You remember, the whole Whoopi Goldberg and Patrick Swayze *Ghost* thing. I heard a male voice who I believed to be my friend's brother-in-law who had died years earlier from cancer. This male soul asked to speak through me to her. I was happy to share this miraculous gift with her. It never occurred to me that this would look bizarre in any way. Nuts you might say? Not to me. This was a miracle and a blessing that I was going to share with everyone, especially the people I loved. Some of the information that came through was discombobulated and untrue. That made her more certain that I had lost my mind. If I was truly speaking to her brother-in-law, every syllable would be authentic and true she thought. As I mentioned earlier, everything I heard was information in, and information out. I was without any filter and wasn't discerning where any of this was coming from. I simply assumed that everything I was hearing was 100 percent authentic and knew instinctually that I was being guided by God. My excitement had taken over my entire being to the point where I wasn't sleeping or eating well. I left the restaurant that evening not realizing how disturbed she was by our entire visit.

After dinner, she called my husband and told him she was deeply upset and thought I needed medical attention. Without my knowing, my husband was already up in arms and rallying the family to find out what he should do about Lori. None of the people in my life had any understanding at all about spiritual awakenings, the Bible, or God. The only reasonable answer they could come up with was that I was having a break from reality and was suffering from some sort of mental illness. They saw that I was not acting like myself, and they were concerned about my safety. I was speaking about God, the Torah, Biblical prophecy, the spirit world, and a lot of discombobulated religious Bible talk.

Everything I spoke about began to sound like a crazy mixture of Judaism and Christianity. It was an absurd mishmash of these two world religions. Since my friends and family knew me as a Jewish woman who was secular at best and never read the Bible, this was a frightening sight for them. To put icing on this already monstrous cake, I was now telling them all how I would be winning the lottery with the numbers God gave me. I also told them my favorite author and mentor Wayne Dyer along with other powerfully famous people would be coming to my home after the news came out. We would all gather in my home and roll up our sleeves and begin the work of bringing peace to our world. Nuts, right? It surely sounds nuts but no, it wasn't nuts at all. It was all being orchestrated by Hashem and all on purpose.

Right about now some of you might be thinking to yourselves, "Wow this lady is clearly bipolar and/or schizophrenic, poor thing." While this might sound like a logical conclusion to some of you, you are wrong. I wasn't then, and I am not now what the world recognizes as mentally ill. This was not the onset of any mental disease that the mental health professionals refer to as bipolar disorder or schizophrenia. It has taken me many years, perseverance, complete faith and my deep love for God Himself to overcome the odds and the naysayers. Hashem has journeyed with me from the beginning and guided me to the truth. The truth needed to be revealed one step at a time which included Him telling me many boldfaced lies. Hashem has since educated me about what happened in those early days of my awakening and has given me clarity about what mental illness truly is and how it can be cured. Yes, I just said cured. I have learned details about the spirit world, our existence here on earth, and what truly was happening to me in those early days of my spiritual awakening. Now all these years later I learned that much of this information is written and studied by a small number of learned people. Looking back upon those days, I understand why my family and friends became frightened. They were visibly worried, upset and thought that I was experiencing a nervous breakdown. This wasn't any nervous breakdown at all. What they were witnessing was a spiritual awakening where I was teetering dangerously between the physical and non-physical worlds.

By early May of 2009 I was in the middle of a full-blown spiritual awakening which was being exacerbated by Hashem Himself deliberately pouring oil on this raging fire. He was telling me fictional stories that excited me and helped bring me squarely into the center of the lion's den, the mental hospital. The journey into the mental hospital was what He required of me. He needed me to live through this horror to see how deeply sick our world had become. In my wild-eyed innocence, I was like a bull in a china shop that couldn't be stopped. I was fueled by my passion to save my children, Israel and our world.

While I was writing in "The Book of Truth" one night I was awakened and instructed to go downstairs. There was information that was necessary for me to hear. I went downstairs that night as I was instructed which led to a sequence of events that was truly terrifying. Unfortunately, even more frightening experiences were soon in store for me. That evening, I could feel and hear the many voices of evil in my home. I told Hashem I was frightened and He instructed me to light three candles and pray. This was my first clear recognition that I was hearing something other than pure goodness and God Himself. I was beginning to discern.

Although I was becoming aware of the voice of evil, Satan or Yetzer Hara, I still was unaware that there were other negative spiritual voices feeding me information that was fallacious at best. It was a confusing mixture of evil, good, and the disenfranchised spirits who had refused to cleanse and become one with God Himself in the nonphysical realm. These disenfranchised spirits are often called poltergeists, demons, or hauntings. As I wrote in "The Book of Truth" that night, I feverishly recorded everything I heard. I recognized the deeply evil voices but couldn't yet distinguish the good spirits from the uncleansed. The uncleansed spirits were speaking of God and had love for God strewn into their discombobulated speech. I was completely certain and aware of Hashem's voice which was extremely recognizable, powerful and loving. It was Hashem's voice that was giving me instructions throughout the night about what I should do to win this battle and protect myself and my home from evil.

This evening led me into the finished basement of my home where the presence of evil was extremely strong. Frighteningly strong. Interestingly, I recall that over the years my children began to refuse to go into our basement to play any longer. They were frightened of the basement and joked that it was haunted. That night I learned why they were so frightened. Our spirits know and understand things that our conscious minds can't see. The finished basement of my home which was furnished and decorated looked nice to the eye, but invisibly it was infested with the Yetzer Hara and poltergeists.

I am told now many years later that I was hearing and recording a mixture of pure Yetzer Hara along with earthbound uncleansed souls that were hidden in my home. Hashem revealed to me that my once beautiful suburban New Jersey home was literally haunted. I haven't revealed this to anyone before and when my children become aware of this information I'm sure they won't be surprised. On this fateful evening, I was in the basement going to war with the Yetzer Hara and the evil unclean spirits who were haunting my home. These many nasty voices were scary and eventually became one evil voice to me. In between hearing hate-filled language, Christian prayers that were foreign to my ears were shouted at me. These prayers were completely foreign to me because I am a Jew. These souls were coaxing me to go deeper into the religious world of Christianity. It was a garbled discombobulated message of evil mixed with Christian speech. I felt and heard Hashem's soothing and powerful voice holding me strong and guiding me through the horror. He was instructing me how to protect myself and clear the evil voices from the basement of my home.

Hashem told me in a very strong voice to grab a blanket from the sofa and cover my head as though the blanket were a Tallis. A Tallis is a prayer shawl that Jewish men wear in synagogue. As I put the blanket over my head, He told me to rock my body back and forth while I paced the floors and prayed the Shema prayer with all my heart and all my soul. As I was praying and rocking, I was crying and felt as though I was fighting for my life and the safety of my children who were asleep upstairs. It felt like I was at war with Satan. I worked feverishly all night long to clear my house of these satanic voices. The only comfort I received through these hours was Hashem's voice. I became stronger as I prayed intently with great emotion: Shema Yisrael Adonai Eloheinu, Adonai Echad. Repeatedly, again and again for hours I recited the Shema and did this without resting, until about 4:30 AM.

At 4:30 AM my husband came down to the basement and saw me covered with the blanket, rocking, praying, crying and saying the Shema. It scared the daylights out of him to say the least. He was certain I was having a nervous breakdown. My husband lacked any spiritual knowledge or religious Jewish upbringing but even the most Orthodox Jews are not educated in what I was experiencing. As I explained earlier, very few learned people study this spiritual aspect of Judaism and Torah education. Even Torah-learned people with years of study don't fully understand this part of the Torah. For many, this information comes to them as book knowledge at best. They've never experienced a spiritual awakening or heard what I was now able to hear. I was now spiritually awake and able to hear the invisible world of spirit while I was still part of the physical world. While there are many people who can hear spirit, people don't hear or fully understand what I heard until they pass away and leave our physical realm. It was extremely unnerving for me to dangerously teeter between two worlds, the physical and nonphysical, especially without any formal understanding of the written Torah or Kabbalah.

When my husband approached me in the basement, I told him to go away and leave me alone. At this point of my awakening, I not only heard the Yetzer Hara in the English language, I could see it physically attached to people. I saw that the Yetzer Hara was attached to my husband's form in a powerfully repugnant way. It was revolting and deeply upsetting for me to see this in him. It is taught in Torah that if you choose the Yetzer Hara, the evil inclination, it attaches not only to your soul causing blemishes, but it also attaches to your physical body. I could see that the evil inclination had attached itself to his body. I saw and felt its foul presence all through him.

What I am sharing with you is knowledge from the Torah that is taught around the world but I had no knowledge of any of this when my awakening occurred. When I began to see that my husband was sick with the Yetzer Hara, I wanted to stay away from him as best I could because I felt he was dangerous to me. At the time I was unaware that he was distraught and rallying family to intervene and do something about my apparent irrational behavior. He saw me as deeply ill and conversely, I saw him as the one who was extremely sick. The world soon became a flipped universe where everyone's beliefs were diametrically opposed to mine. I was viewed as sick and mentally ill by my husband and family but I could see the sickness and ignorance was in all of them. Little did I know what was in store for me. Hashem continued to pour oil on the raging fire and purposely placed me on a steady path to my first trip to hell on earth, the mental hospital.

His Voice, Visions & Lessons

Does prophecy exist in our world today?

Yes, prophecy does exist today. People receive prophetic visions, dreams, and messages. There are people in our world who are clairvoyant and hear the other side, the nonliving souls who are no longer here in the physical world. But—and there's a big "but"—the prophecy age when God tagged certain people to be His prophets and share His voice ended with the destruction of the Second Temple in Jerusalem. That's not to say that people in this world are not prophetic, or that Hashem hasn't tagged certain people to do holy and prophetic tasks along the way. It simply means that the era of prophecy ended with the destruction of the Second Temple and that Hashem no longer shared His voice and His words verbatim with the Jewish children of Israel.

So where does that leave me? My name is Lori Michelle and He awakened me in April of 2009 to be His Moshiach. He said to go get pen and paper and start writing this down and I've been listening for more than nine years. Now I'm sharing His voice on the internet but there are a lot of other people sharing a lot of confusing information on the internet. Because of the confusion, people don't know what to make of me. Do you believe me? Do you trust me? Do you trust the other people who are posting messages saying that God just spoke to them or they just spoke to Jesus and Jesus said to share this information? Hashem says you can't trust them but you must learn to trust me. Why can't you trust them and you can trust me? Hashem says my spiritual acuity, the ability to discern and choose good over evil, is perfect and my soul remains pure.

We are surrounded by spirit—all of us. Most of you don't realize the invisible world you are surrounded by. You are surrounded by the nonliving and by the Yetzer Hara, the evil inclination, also known as Satan. You're also surrounded by unclean spirits who have refused to go through a cleansing process in the spiritual realm to remove blemishes that they acquired on their soul while they were incarnate. All of these invisible elements have audible voices. You see when you sin, you are choosing to listen to something other than God which causes a blemish on your spirit and your soul becomes impure.

Right now, the world is filled with people choosing the Yetzer Hara every day. Unfortunately, you, your family, your friends, and the entire world are participating in choosing the wrong energy. Not because you're necessarily evil—but because you don't know. You don't understand. That's where my spiritual acuity comes in and why I have been chosen to help you. When I was awakened I went through Hashem God's boot camp and learned the difference between when I heard Yetzer Hara, when I heard a spirit speaking and when I heard Hashem God. I know how to choose and recognize the differences so the information I share with you is spot on. The other people who are sharing information with you may not be inherently evil and they may also be sharing what they hear clairvoyantly because they love you. They want to share what they believe is coming directly from Hashem but unknowingly they are sharing the wrong information. The Yetzer Hara is very tricky; it's a lure leading you to evil. The evil inclination, Yetzer Hara, is here on purpose to give you a choice between evil and Hashem God, the Yetzer Hatov also known as the good inclination. This choice gives you free will.

Please pause before you listen to any of the information that you hear on the internet. Pause before you listen to me. Discern. Check me out. Source what I am saying. Am I saying something that goes smack against God, God forbid? I am not. I am here to help you and teach everyone how to discern and choose goodness in every moment. This is a skill that we all require to enable us to bring lasting peace on earth in our time.

Chapter 6

My Miraculous Gift Becomes a Living Nightmare

The morning after my terrifying experience in the basement of my home, I went to work and proceeded with my day. In my thinking, I had just won a battle the night before against the evil that was lurking in my home. I did my best to distance myself from my husband who I saw was riddled with the Yetzer Hara, the evil inclination. All the while I had no idea that he was speaking to my family with extreme concern over my mental state. This was just before Mother's Day weekend 2009. I planned to enjoy my Mother's Day no matter what and decided that we would go out on Saturday night for Chinese food to celebrate. We went to a favorite Chinese restaurant, non-kosher of course, for a pre-Mother's Day celebration. As we sat and ate our Chinese food that evening, it felt like a normal family dinner. It didn't occur to me that anyone was upset by my recent behavior.

Mother's Day 2009—An Odyssey into Hell

The next day, Mother's Day was setting up to be a complete nightmare. Sunday, May 10, 2009, began an odyssey into hell which I could never have predicted. My husband was calling everyone without my knowledge to discuss how irrational my behavior was and to decide what to do with me. He had a point. Jesus, Biblical prophecy, and all kinds of things that I was hearing came straight out of my mouth as I heard it. I had no filters at all and knew that I was directly in touch with God. There was no doubt in my mind that this was

God awakening me to my life's purpose. I was not going to be stopped by any person. The stakes were too high and I was going to meet and greet my calling. I recognized right away that my calling was to share the voice of God and begin the work of world healing. It wasn't apparent to me that I had much to learn and wasn't quite ready to say the least. As far as I was concerned, every piece of information that I heard, excluding the night-long battle with evil in my basement, was directly from God Himself and I accepted it all as part of my life's mission.

Earlier in this book, I spoke about a falling out with my mother and brothers which began at my father-in-law's funeral. Just prior to my spiritual awakening we had patched things up and agreed to put our differences aside. Because we had recently repaired our relationship, I felt it was important to see my mother on this Mother's Day. I invited her to meet us for dinner at a restaurant in northern New Jersey. This happened to be the same restaurant where I had met my lifelong childhood friend for dinner just a few nights earlier.

My awakening was in full throttle at this point yet I didn't have the knowledge or understanding to interpret what I was hearing or why. I thought I understood everything perfectly, but it's an understatement to say I had much to learn. I drove to the restaurant with my young son and spent the drive ranting to him about the devil and warning him about evil. In my rant, I told him we needed to eradicate evil from our world. I told him we needed to curse out Satan and get this evil monster out of our lives and out of the world. I was determined to win a worldwide war against Satan and free us all from evil. While I sounded completely nuts at the time, what I was saying was ironically truthful. I simply wasn't ready. There was still a long hard road I had to journey.

As I recount this episode of my life, I am deeply upset and emotional. I understand why my husband was worried when he saw how I was behaving. I know it was Hashem speaking to me back then and the reasons why He deliberately helped whip me up into an unrecognizable frenzy. The truth about what I was experiencing was hidden from me quite deliberately and completely on purpose. Nobody in my life was knowledgeable about the Bible, Torah or spiritual awakenings. They had no experience about what an awakening might look or sound like. Quite the contrary, in mainstream society, we see people being diagnosed with schizophrenia and bipolar daily. They are diagnosed with incurable mental diseases and psychoses and then drugged. The world doesn't understand our true nature as human beings. The medical community doesn't recognize that we live in a physical world that exists parallel to a nonphysical spiritual one. The true information about how our world operates and functions is studied by only a few learned scholars. They are learned in Torah, both written and oral. They are most often Chasidic rabbis dressed all in black living a secluded life away from the mainstream. Many of these scholars are ridiculed and scoffed at by the secular world and are perceived as dysfunctional, part of a cult, or insane. The truth be known, our world has become a perversion where the truly dysfunctional and insane are the ones running the show. You should be very scared!

I drove to the restaurant that Mother's Day with my son while my husband chased after me in another car with my other two children. When I arrived at the restaurant I greeted my mother and brother outside and began to tell them all the wonderful prophecies that God was giving me. I ranted about how we would all be able to live eternally on earth and how I was going to win the lottery. I expounded about how the world would be repaired and we would never grow old and never die. My brother looked at me in disbelief as I rambled on about Biblical prophecy and how we are all reincarnations of other people from past lifetimes.

I was now trying to eat in a kosher style which was difficult at best coming from a non-observant background and living in secular New Jersey. We were dining at a chain restaurant in New Brunswick that served veggie burgers so that was good enough for me. I sat and ate my veggie burger when my deceased father made a request to speak to my mother through me. Naturally, I wouldn't refuse his request. In my mind, this was the most amazing Mother's Day gift I could give her. How could I refuse my father? Allowing my father who passed away in 1985 to speak through me to my mother was a truly miraculous Mother's Day gift! So I thought.

As I rested my own soul and allowed my father to enter through the crown of my head, I could feel his spiritual presence within my body and I knew without any doubt that it was indeed my dad's soul. I could feel him speaking out of my mouth as he called to my mother by the pet name he had always called her when he was alive. Hashem to this day says it was truly my father speaking through me that day. It was the most energizing experience and barely describable. My father's spirit felt like pure love energy rushing through me and I felt euphoric to be able to give this gift to my mother.

To my mother it wasn't a gift at all. It was horrific! My mother was so stunned and shocked that her eyes bulged out of her head. In that moment, I could see my entire family was unnerved. I was unfazed by their reactions and simply kept eating my veggie burger. I couldn't imagine that anything negative was about to happen to me. I knew I was being guided by God Himself, and was being allowed to share the miracle of letting my father speak to my mother on Mother's Day. I couldn't imagine a more glorious miracle or magnificent gift to give someone. Can you?

While I continued eating my veggie burger, everybody promptly stood up and left the restaurant except for one of my children. A few moments later I was summoned to come outside the restaurant. I couldn't imagine why they wanted me to leave but I did what they requested and walked outside. I had no idea that an ambulance was waiting in the parking lot. When I saw the ambulance, I was confused, then stunned and speechless. The ambulance pulled up and my brother wrestled me into the ambulance forcibly in front of my three children. As I kicked, screamed, and fought with my brother, my young son tried to fight his uncle and help me. It was the most gut-wrenching, terrifying and upsetting experience of my entire life. I kicked and fought as they dragged me into the ambulance and by the time I got inside I was bleeding, battered and bruised. One of the ambulance workers had a name tag, Angel. I saw this as a sign from Hashem that He was with me in that ambulance and that I would be all right.

The ambulance took me to a local hospital where they had a holding pen for mental patients. This is where they take people they believe are mentally ill and proceed to treat them like deranged animals. As the ambulance gurney took me into the hospital I saw my husband in the corridor. He shouted my name and tried to touch me. I smacked his hands away and told him to get away from me. He then said, "It's okay Lori they know what's wrong with you." This was the beginning of my tragic journey and Mother's Day odyssey into hell.

They took me to what they refer to as their mental health area within the hospital. It is far from a mental "health" ward because the treatment they deliver there is neither healthy nor humane. It's a dark cold filthy place tucked away from the rest of the "normal" people in the hospital. Instead of being a healthcare area for treating patients they believe are ill, it's a holding pen for what they consider to be deranged human animals who are treated as non-human. Sitting on the stretcher on which I arrived, I looked around this holding pigpen to see who was in there with me. I observed one man who appeared deeply evil and deranged. He was filthy dirty and tattooed from head to toe. He began taunting me and made malicious nasty hand gestures and deranged faces at me. What a wonderful way to spend Mother's Day. Across from me was a table where two nurses were seated. I sat there and observed them too.

The entire time I sat there, Hashem was speaking to me and giving me information about my surroundings. I needed the bathroom so I asked the nurse to use the restroom. I walked into the restroom and when I got inside

I became nauseated and appalled. There was excrement all over the toilet and the walls. It was disgusting and more dreadful than any NYC subway toilet I had ever seen. I was furious about where I was and how I was forcibly taken there against my will. As I exited the filthy bathroom, I let the two nurses know how disgusting it was and used a few expletives to describe it. Was this how they treat people they believed were ill? I wondered if these medical professionals took a Hippocratic oath to treat the ill with the best of their ability, or if they took a hypocritical oath instead. Did they really think I was sick or did they think I was just another one of their deranged animals with good medical insurance who would give them a healthy payday? This was the beginning of learning the painful truth about the evil that lies within our mental health system.

As I sat on the hospital gurney, I saw one of the nurses look over at me then lean over and whisper something to the other nurse. Then they both giggled. It was clear that she was ridiculing me, making fun of me, and that the joke was at my expense as they looked over at me in their laughter. It was startling to see a nurse behave like an insolent 12-year-old bully. As she and her co-worker were giggling at my expense, Hashem was fueling the fire and rage in me by telling me revealing stories about this nurse's past life identity as a Nazi nurse who worked for the notorious Josef Mengele. His stories, which Hashem maintains are true to this day, further enraged me while I watched them both laughing at me. In a fit of anger, I said to her, "Who are you laughing at? Are you talking about me you filthy bitch?!" She immediately signaled for two male hospital workers to physically restrain me as she plunged a syringe in my arm and drugged me unconscious.

The next thing I knew, I woke up in an ambulance on my way to another mental hospital facility. When I arrived there, I was completely naked under a scanty hospital gown still cut and bruised from the battle with my brother the day before. When I was carted away in the ambulance, I had no money or belongings with me. This would be the beginning of a week in hell. The people who work there call it a mental hospital where they provide healthcare for the mentally ill, but it's nothing of the sort. It's more accurate to describe these facilities as prisons where the patients have fewer rights than hardened criminals.

You're restricted to just a couple of phone calls a day and forced to wait in horrifically long lines to make those calls. You're only given a few minutes to speak before you are told to get off the phone. Criminals and prisoners convicted of felonies have more rights than people who are brought into these mental health facilities. In these facilities, they don't allow visitation like normal hospitals do. You're treated as something less than human and made to feel like a criminal, but they still call this medical care. Nobody listens to you, gives any credence to your opinions or values anything you say on your own behalf. Grown adults are treated like small children at best. At worst, you're treated like a filthy animal in a demeaning and cruel way. You don't receive the sort of professionalism or understanding you would be given if you were physically ill. There are only certain days with specific hours for visitation. You're cast away from society and family like a dirty old shoe and forcibly drugged beyond recognition. Refusal to take these drugs or having any choice in the matter is completely out of the question. It's eerily like the film *One Flew Over the Cuckoo's Nest* with Jack Nicholson. The patients wait in an obligatory line to receive medications and are not given the right to give any input into their own treatment. Whether you agree with their treatment or not, you're forced to take their debilitating drugs. If you don't comply and do as they say, you'll be forced to comply. If you continue to resist, you'll wind up like the character played by Jack Nicholson. Perhaps you won't receive a lobotomy, but there are serious consequences. You risk being sent into long-term involuntary confinement where they'll force you to receive the drugs you resisted, and possibly deliver even worse treatments like electroshock therapy. Most survivors eventually comply and take their drugs like good mental patients.

Many patients have so many drugs pumped into their veins at such high doses that they literally can't walk or see straight and begin to bounce into the walls. But you don't need to worry about this happening to you if you are dirt poor. You only get stuck in one of these reprehensible places if you have money and/or good health insurance. If you have no insurance, you're escorted out promptly, even if you've just sliced open your own wrists in a suicide attempt. On more than one occasion, I saw suicidal people leave promptly with their wrists bandaged because they couldn't pay the hospital bill. Unfortunately for me, I was a wealthy suburban mom with excellent health insurance coverage. I wasn't going to leave their facility anytime soon. They were going to bilk and charge my insurance company as much money as possible before I would be discharged. I also learned that my husband had full legal authority over my life and medical care. I had no say whatsoever about my treatment or care. His voice was the only one that was valued by these doctors and care providers in charge. Once they forcibly committed me against my will, my husband eventually found out that he too could lose his rights to make any decisions about my care. These mental non-health professionals can take over and legally make decisions on your behalf. It is extremely possible for you to lose all personal legal rights as big brother takes charge of your life.

While the mental health field is now replete with dysfunction and greed, there are a few good doctors and professionals strewn into the mix. I state this now because it's important not to paint everyone with the same dark brush. Everyone should be measured on their own merit. There are psychiatrists and psychotherapists who stand above the pack. Sadly, they are few and far between. Even though there are professionals who do care, they are all indoctrinated into the wild world of mental illness according to the psychiatric experts and American Psychiatric Association. The medical schools teaching psychiatry and psychology don't include the teaching of Kabbalah or Torah or any form of spirituality which makes their teachings flawed at "Good morning, class." The medical schools' strength and acceptance in our world is so powerful and pervasive, that even respected rabbis have bought their line of thinking and dismiss Torah teachings, deferring to biology and science and the opinions of the learned doctors of psychiatry. The rabbis have forgotten Hashem too. This makes one wonder how Moses would fare in today's world, doesn't it?

My family came to visit me in this mental non-health facility, and I promptly forgave them. Why wouldn't I? As soon as I was drugged unconscious and woke up in this strange and awful place, I snapped to and recognized that I lacked understanding. It was clear to me that I didn't fully understand what I was hearing but I knew it was a spiritual awakening. The resounding male voice that awakened me on April 7, 2009, was still speaking to me while I was in this awful place. Through the horror and the massive doses of drugs, Hashem never left me for one moment. I knew this strong male voice was Hashem but the Mother's Day experience troubled me deeply. It baffled me why God Himself would lie to me about so many things and purposely place me in a horrible predicament. I also couldn't yet discern Him completely from every other voice I was still hearing. Even though His voice was the strongest, I wasn't completely sure it was Him in every moment. I felt and knew there were still others around me.

Everything was inside out, upside down and backwards, but what I knew without any doubt was that I was completely sane and not mentally ill. I simply knew. It shocked everyone how completely grounded I became immediately. It seemed all I needed was a good shot in the ass so to speak and I was okay. But of course, they didn't truly believe I was okay, especially when the doctors diagnosed me as bipolar with psychotic delusions of grandeur. You see, if you hear voices and one of those voices is God, and God says to you that you are His chosen, well then you most certainly have delusions of grandeur. Why in the world would God choose me, Lori Michelle, for anything? This was emphatic and irrefutable proof that I was delusional and a textbook case of bipolar disorder. Most of the world doesn't truly believe in the existence of God in the first place, let alone any one person having the ability to speak with Him directly. This, coupled with my speech being filled with Bible prophecy, Jesus and promises that I would win the lottery, fueled the bonfire. It was clear to them that this was all a complete delusion and the onset of an incurable mental illness. I was now incurably mentally ill and needed to be medicated for the rest of my life. Oh my! Really?

If you're a fan of modern day psychology and have been indoctrinated into the mental health world, this may read like a textbook case of bipolar disorder and you might believe I'm in denial. My former husband will swear up and down and sideways that I was mentally ill and that he was only following the instructions of the medical professionals. The truth will be revealed with the help of God Himself that it's our society and the mental health world that is deeply sick and in denial, not me. They are in denial that there is truly God who runs our world and is the Master of it all. The mental health system in our world is deeply sick, perniciously evil and filled with greed. Men, women and children all over the world are suffering at the hands of a mental health system that is ill-informed at minimum and completely evil at worst. Psychiatrists are poisoning everyone with drugs and misinformation but worst of all, they're poisoning our children. My story is a loud human cry for everyone to wake up before it's too late. We are burying our children at an alarming rate.

I spent a week in this awful pigpen that they called a mental hospital. They force fed me a drug called *Risperdal* which I found sounded eerily like the first word of the Jewish prayer, the Mourner's Kaddish—*Yisgidal*. Coincidence perhaps? Nope, there aren't any coincidences. This drug is very evil, plays with your mind, and is said to stop "the voices." Did this drug eliminate the voices in my mind? Not at all. And so, I began to learn how to conceal. I learned to keep my mouth shut and not share everything I was hearing with anyone except for one close friend I felt I could confide in. She said she believed me and was enthralled with hearing about all my conversations with God. I kept quiet around other people, especially while I was in the hospital. When I concealed well enough, and they bilked my insurance company for enough money, they finally allowed me to leave. After I was discharged and ready to leave the building, I was told I had to go into a special room upon my exit. I entered this special room and a woman sitting at a computer said to me, "Give me your credit card. You owe us an out-of-pocket expense of $1,200."

I replied to her angrily, "I don't owe you a fucking thing. I came here naked, against my will, and I don't even have a credit card. I'm leaving now!" If foul language startles or offends you, I apologize, but it's something that I've succumbed to using on occasion. I don't like the use of foul words either and for about 20 years I didn't use any expletives as part of a promise to never swear after I became a parent. Even before becoming a parent, foul language wasn't a normal part of my speech. Sadly, this odyssey to hell ended my hiatus from swearing. There simply weren't strong enough or foul enough words I could use for what I was feeling when that woman accosted me. The F-bomb was the only fitting word to use when she demanded my credit card so that they could pilfer more money from me.

My temper was very hot to say the least as I left this filthy facility. Conversely, when I got home I was extremely loving to my husband and grateful to be back. I remember my husband couldn't believe how forgiving, tender and loving I was to him. He lamented that he felt terrible and guilty because I was so nice to him. I wondered why he thought I would be justified to be mean and angry with him. In my mind, I understood that he mistakenly thought there was something wrong with me and he was making his best decisions to protect me, right? I promptly forgave him and I went to a psychiatrist to get myself off these horrible drugs. I knew I didn't belong on medication and what I experienced wasn't any form of a mental defect or illness. I met with the psychiatrist and told her about my lifelong awareness of being surrounded by spirits and how I had the ability to hear them. I told her this whole episode of being locked up, forcibly drugged and diagnosed mentally ill was a huge mistake. After speaking to me at length, she honored my request and weaned me off these horrific drugs which have many nasty side effects. She weaned me off slowly because she said if you stop taking them too quickly it could cause irreparable harm. The psychological medications that they forced me to take were not only sickening, they were deeply frightening. I trusted her advice and agreed to follow her instructions to slowly come off those dreadful drugs.

Reaching for Answers in The Torah

As I mentioned earlier, many years before my spiritual awakening, my family became involved with the local Chabad House. It was where I chose to send our three children to Hebrew school, something most Jewish families do regardless of their level of religious observance. Chabad is a worldwide Chassidic Jewish movement, that provides education and support to all Jews who desire to return to Judaism and learn Torah. The movement of establishing a network of Chabad Houses in communities around the world was inspired by the beloved and revered Rebbe Menachem Mendel Schneerson who passed away in 1994. The network of Chabad Houses that began during his lifetime continues to grow worldwide.

Before our family became involved with the local Chabad House, I enrolled my oldest child in the local Reform Hebrew School when she was about nine years old. This made the most sense since we were secular and non-observant Jews. You might ask why even bother with any of this if we were secular and non-observant. All I can say is that going to synagogue at the High Holy days, eating matzah once a year and sending your kids to Hebrew school is tradition among most Jewish families without exception. For most Jews it's like it's required and inscribed in our souls.

The Reform Hebrew School classes were held once a week after regular school hours and every Sunday morning. My daughter became angry and despondent every time I drove her to Hebrew school and eventually refused to leave the car when I pulled into the synagogue parking lot. She hated this Hebrew school intensely which isn't unusual for many Jewish children in America. Her fighting and refusal to go became problematic. Added to the constant arguments, was the enormous expense of paying the synagogue dues, tuition and building fund fees. Even after we paid the exorbitant fees, we were barraged with phone calls asking for additional donations. It seemed every time I walked into their building there was another fundraiser and request for more money. Judaism felt like a pay to pray religion. There wasn't a strong sense of community or love and reverance for God at this Reform temple and it seemed to be a business more than a place of worship.

One day, a Jewish friend of mine told me that there was a new Chabad Hebrew School opening in our town. My ears perked up when I learned that the Hebrew school classes were being held at the local public elementary school where my children attended. There was a new statute that allowed religious schools to host classes at the public schools after hours. Wow! How convenient! My daughter wouldn't even need to leave school to attend and my two younger children were welcome to attend these classes too. All my children were welcomed! This was music to my ears, so I quickly made an appointment to meet the school's director, the Chabad rebbetzin and her husband the rabbi. They were a young and energetic couple filled with enthusiasm. The Hebrew school tuition was minuscule compared to every other synagogue in the area. Many people registered their children there too because they thought that this was a "good deal" to get their kids' Bar and Bat Mitzvahs for cheap. That wasn't my hook or reason why. For me, I immediately felt their love and passion for Judaism and teaching my children. And guess what? My daughter felt it too. Children are very intuitive. After the first Hebrew school class, she came home excited and joyful. Whoa! The rebbetzin made learning about Judaism fun. Who would have ever thought that could be possible? Not me.

Now fast forward several years later to the aftermath of my spiritual awakening. The first thing I did when I got home from my journey into hell and the Mother's Day nightmare, was call my Chabad rebbetzin and rabbi. I wanted to research what truly happened to me. It was clear to me that my experience was brought about by Hashem God and I wanted to crack the code, figure out what happened to me and why. I wanted truthful answers and refused any discussion that didn't include Hashem. I explained to the rabbi and rebbetzin what had just happened to me and they both told me that they knew undoubtedly that I wasn't mentally ill. They agreed with me that my experience was purely spiritual and from Hashem. They told me that these sorts of things can happen if you're not Torah-observant and that you can shield yourself by obeying and observing God's commandments. They further explained to me that there is an entire spiritual world with invisible dangers from which Torah insulates and protects us. My rabbi equated observing Torah commandments with installing anti-virus protection on your computer. He said Torah observance is anti-virus protection for your soul. I had never heard of any of this before. I wanted to learn more about how to protect myself and I asked them to teach me everything I needed to know. After this meeting, I took a class in Tanya with the rabbi which opened my eyes even wider to critical life concepts that I was never exposed to in my life. Tanya is the fundamental philosophy behind Chabad authored by Rabbi Schneur Zalman, the founder of the Chabad-Lubavitch movement. The study of Tanya provides practical and mystical details behind the Chabad philosophy of Judaism.

In my rabbi's Tanya class, I heard for the first time in my life the term *Yetzer Hara*, the evil inclination. He spoke about the Yetzer Hara and how dangerous this evil inclination is to our well-being. I was deeply fascinated by this lesson and commented to my rabbi, "Wow this is fascinating information. Rabbi I don't believe I've ever chosen the Yetzer Hara in the way you have just described it." The rabbi smiled politely at my comment. I'm sure he thought to himself that it was completely impossible for this to be true. Everyone in the world grapples with the Yetzer Hara, or the evil inclination. He likely thought I simply didn't understand the subject matter yet. The way he described the evil inclination in his class and the way it was written in the book of Tanya didn't sound like anything I'd ever chosen. Years later, I know his class didn't emphasize in strong enough terms how critical and powerful this information is to the well-being and safety of our entire world. In the description he gave, the evil inclination simply sounded like a lesson in dysfunctional behavior. The example given in this class was someone falling into depression and then reaching for drugs or alcohol which made their life even worse. It explained that the source of this depression and other dysfunctional behaviors was the Yetzer Hara. As I listened to his explanation, I didn't believe I wrestled with this Yetzer Hara in my life or chose this kind of behavior, ever. Unknowingly, I was completely correct. I've come to learn I have a unique immunity from choosing and accepting anything from the Yetzer Hara.

If you're a Torah-observant Jew who knows about the power of the Yetzer Hara, you might believe it's impossible for me to make this claim. You have likely been schooled that it's simply impossible for any human being to completely resist choosing evil. It is a natural human condition even for the most righteous souls to succumb to the power of the evil inclination on occasion. In all these years since Hashem awakened me, He has insisted that I'm the only person in flesh and blood who has never chosen the Yetzer Hara, not even once. He says I have no ego and I am a virtual anomaly incarnate. Hashem has explained to me that I not only have no ego, but that I've never chosen the Yetzer Hara in any lifetime I've incarnated here on earth. He also told me that I have incarnated more times and lived more years on this earth than any other human being in the history of creation. In all the years I've walked the earth, He says I've never sinned or transgressed in His eyes, not even once. He refers to this as completely uncanny, mind boggling, and supernatural. Our Creator and Master, God, says that my ability to discern and choose Him in every moment is a human impossibility. So, what the heck am I then? A freak of nature? Not human? He says that I am the only one who is like this, and explains there will never be another like me again. Please believe me, these are the words of Hashem, not mine.

If you read this and don't believe a word of it, I don't blame you at all. I've found this extremely hard to believe myself. Having never sinned might sound like some sort of feather in my cap and that I'm boasting, but please trust me, I'm not. The idea of boasting never makes it on my radar. It's repugnant behavior, isn't desirable and frankly bragging nauseates me. In fact, boasting in its essence is pure ego and Yetzer Hara at work. I find both egotism and arrogance sickening. This is simply how I think and how I tick. It simply doesn't occur to me to choose Yetzer Hara because it's so obviously vile. Choosing evil just doesn't compute. Choosing the Yetzer Hara, which everyone succumbs to and finds desirable, is completely repulsive and bizarre to me. It's a complete turnoff. Some of the choices of Yetzer Hara gratefully are also a complete turn-off to most people. Things like murder, rape and incest don't appeal to good and decent people. But the subtler choices that the world accepts as a "rite of passage" or "goodness," are deeply sickening to me. I'm completely unable to choose what mainstream America finds "normal" and I refuse to participate.

I simply can't choose the Yetzer Hara or go along for the party even when my life and safety hang in the balance. When I was told to take the psychological drugs, and accept my bipolar diagnosis like a good mental patient, I knew the "experts" were completely wrong. It was crystal clear to me from the beginning that they were the ones with the problem, not me. They were mentally ill and choosing dysfunctional beliefs and behavior. Had I accepted these drugs or their wrongful diagnosis, I would have succumbed to the Yetzer Hara. Believe it or not, it's true.

For me, the choice between good and evil is so completely clear that the correct answer is obvious in every moment. The world, especially the secular world, sees obvious daily choices as shades of gray. People who live in the shades of gray criticize religious people for being too black and white and rigid. I can't live in the gray area with the mainstream world because I see the choice of gray as clearly evil and against God Himself. I've tried many things in life that weren't good for me, but the reasons why I tried them were always intentionally good. When my choices in retrospect were sinful like smoking cigarettes, using illegal drugs, and other socially acceptable behaviors in America, Hashem says those choices were required of me and brought me the knowledge I needed to do this work now.

My upbringing wasn't filled with the existence of God, Torah law or observance of God's prescribed way of life. Like most Americans I was exposed to secular society and the "normal" rites of passage. As I grew up and went to college I tried many socially acceptable bad behaviors on for size, eventually learned my deeply painful lessons, and removed these dysfunctional choices from my life. Eventually, sometimes after deep deliberation, I view every choice in life as black and white and with crystal clear clarity. The correct answer jumps right out at me and I can't make myself choose the opposite. I absolutely refuse. People all over the world are choosing sin without any guidance that it's a sin at all. The education of what's good versus evil is practically void in American culture. Quite the contrary, many of America's new laws are a strong pull away from God's laws and a pathway straight to hell.

When I see the world and evaluate various situations, instinctually I scan them like a Yetzer Hara computer, discerning, thinking it over carefully and then choosing the way of God every time. Hashem says I'm a living and breathing spiritual computer that assesses each situation and discerns immediately Yetzer Hara from Yetzer Hatov, the good inclination, and chooses goodness in every moment. I never knew this about myself until recently. It has taken many years, and endless conversations with Hashem where He shows me my natural ability to uncover the Yetzer Hara in every situation. To me it's as though evil is a visible splinter underneath the skin causing pain. To my spiritual eyes, it's that clear and obvious.

It's as though I'm allergic to choosing the opposite of Hashem, God. It's not the least bit enticing or attractive to me in any way. This doesn't mean that I haven't tried things that weren't good for me. I have. It simply means that in every situation I'm unable to choose anything for a selfish or egotistical reason. The Yetzer Hara adores the ego and feeds on it. Ego creates a gaping chasm and open door where the Yetzer Hara enters your mind and preys on you, luring you further away from God Himself. Hashem has shown me over these years since my awakening that I am completely egoless.

To this day I still question if this is true and argue with Hashem that I feel guilty of transgressions all the time. When I feel that I've transgressed, which is almost daily, I apologize profusely to Him. He often refuses my apologies and asks me to stop because He says I didn't sin. In those moments, I still repent and beg Him for forgiveness anyway because I simply can't bear the pain or move forward. The mere thought that I've sinned against Him is completely overwhelming to me. He often obliges me by saying everything is okay so that I feel forgiven and can move on.

In my quest to learn more and heal from my horrible Mother's Day experience, I kept reaching for the Torah and signed up for classes in Kabbalah. I listened to my rabbi's and rebbetzin's advice to learn and observe many Torah commandments, also called *mitzvahs*. I worked as best as I could to eat in a kosher way even though I couldn't kosher my home properly. My husband was completely against all the "Jewish stuff" as he called it. He hated everything about my desire to read the Torah or my new prayer book, also called a siddur. My siddur was called "Tehillat Hashem" which was given to me by the Chabad rebbetzin to read daily. At 49 years old, I was still menstruating, and the rebbetzin encouraged me to go to the mikvah. A mikvah is a ritual bath that Jewish women visit monthly for spiritual purification in accordance with Torah law. It's not at all what I was raised to believe when I heard about this growing up.

Most people are under the misconception that the mikvah is a communal bath and something completely dirty and repulsive. Many secular Jews scowl at the mere mention of the mikvah, find the idea revolting and a source of embarrassment. This is pure ignorance and false information. The mikvah, on the contrary, is a beautiful and spiritual experience. I always thought it was only for women who were menstruating but learned that religious men visit the mikvah regularly also. The mikvahs I went to were beautiful spa-like facilities. It's a very private experience and you are required to bathe vigorously prior to going into the mikvah bath itself. In fact, when you enter the mikvah you must be meticulously clean and are escorted by a personal mikvah attendant. This is a mitzvah for spiritual and family purity. When I went I was surprised how uplifting the entire experience was. After I recited a prayer engraved on the mikvah wall asking Hashem for world redemption, I was given privacy to immerse myself in deep personal prayer.

I began going monthly as the rebbetzin recommended, and this brought even more anger and division into my home. I began to read the Chumash, the Five Books of Torah, and kept this by my bedside on my nightstand. One day my husband took it away from me and hid it so that I couldn't read from it anymore. He complained constantly about my new love and desire to learn about Judaism and observe Torah mitzvot—commandments.

After the Mother's Day travesty, my husband and I made a deal, a verbal agreement, that if anything like what had happened that day were ever to happen again, we would call the rabbi and his wife for help. He promised he would never have me carted off again, drugged against my will, or involuntarily committed to a mental hospital. I believed him and had no reason to be concerned. So I thought.

During this time, my closest girlfriend and I spoke daily on the phone, as I continued to share with her everything that I heard from God. I was still recording my conversations in journals and we had daily discussions where I shared them with her. Although she was Christian and I was Jewish, we both revered and loved God. Our differences in religious backgrounds were never a problem or an issue for us in our relationship. She told me that she completely trusted and believed that I was truly speaking to our Creator and she enjoyed the stories I shared daily.

My Tomato Story

Over time it became clear that it was Hashem God Himself with whom I was speaking most of the time. My ability to discern was increasing daily but my understanding about the ways of Hashem still wasn't in full bloom. I had much more to go through, experience and learn. My understanding and ability to discern the many spiritual voices I heard took many years and deep disappointments. Hashem told me things that weren't true because He needed to derive specific outcomes. Everything that He does has a specific purpose and it's always, without exception, for our good. I learned over the years that telling me a lie was necessary because He knew what I needed to hear so that I would respond in the appropriate way. It's been a long journey of more than nine years speaking and journeying with Hashem. I trust Him fully even though He has deliberately brought me into the devil's lair and caused me great suffering. If you believe that God would never purposely cause us pain or lie to us, you have much to learn about the true ways of Hashem, God. Here is a short story to help clarify and give you an example.

One day, when I was in my kitchen I decided to make myself a salad. I thought I would test the situation to see if I was truly talking with God and decided to ask Him a question just to see if I received a correct answer. I was like many people I knew at the time of my awakening who quizzed me to see if I could answer their unknowable questions and prove that I was hearing God. If I knew the answer to their ridiculous question it was somehow proof that it was truly God speaking to me. I decided to play my own "Prove it to me" game that day. I thought to myself, "If this is truly God, He will know the answer to all my questions and give me the validation I want that it's really Him. When I receive an accurate answer then I will brim with confidence that I'm truly hearing Hashem, God." As I was making my salad I asked Hashem, "Are there tomatoes in the refrigerator?"

He quickly replied, "No Lori. There aren't any tomatoes in your refrigerator."

I went over to the refrigerator to check because if there were no tomatoes then of course I now had validation and proof that I was speaking to God. I was testing and playing the "Prove it to me" game. I opened the refrigerator door, and there right in plain sight were tomatoes. I said, "Hashem! You just told me there were no tomatoes in the refrigerator. Why did you lie to me?"

He replied, "Lori, if you want to know if there are tomatoes in the refrigerator you could open the door and find out for yourself." That sounds a bit snippy, doesn't it? Was His answer showing that He was angry with me? Emphatically no. He was teaching me. From this point on, I will lovingly call this "My Tomato Story" which has many implications and lessons within it.

Lesson number 1: Hashem tells you exactly what you need to know and He won't treat you like a slave or puppet. When we need or desire information that we can figure out for ourselves, He desires us to do just that.

Lesson number 2: Don't play the "Prove it to me" game. In this lesson He was stating, "Don't test Me to try and figure out if it's truly Me." Some people might ask, why not? Why would God refuse to be tested and play the "Prove it to me" game? Because Hashem has nothing to prove to anyone. It's for us to discern and know that He is emphatically real and when He speaks to us we need to know and listen with our souls.

Lesson number 3: Hashem will deceive you and tell you something untrue if it's required. He will lead you into the lion's den and cause you inexplicable pain if it's for your good. This is one of the most difficult lessons in life to learn. He will allow or even bring about the most unthinkable tragedy if it's for the ultimate good to prevail.

Lesson number 4: We must learn to discern. Everyone is being tested continuously and we all hear voices. These voices mimic our own and we must choose. It's imperative not to take everything that comes into our minds and act on it immediately. Thinking for ourselves and deliberately choosing God and His goodness in each moment is not only required, it's a commandment.

While this "tomato story" sounds like a silly little exercise and story, it's packed with deep meaning and lessons in life. There are probably even more lessons that I can derive from this experience but I'll leave this at four lessons for now.

After my awakening, learning to discern His voice over all the others I was hearing was supremely difficult. I now heard Hashem, the Yetzer Hara, and other spiritual voices in the English language. Believe it or not, this made life much more challenging than choosing from the silent and subliminal spiritual inclinations we are all faced with daily. When it was subliminal, the only decision I had to make was deciding between good and evil, or right from wrong. I didn't have to figure out who was speaking because it was all interpreted as coming from me. Now I heard many voices that were separate from my own. Remember, in the secular world hearing these "voices" is a sign that you're nuts. I needed to be sure who was speaking to me after the torment of Mother's Day. I desperately wanted to be certain that I was listening to Hashem's voice and not something else. I didn't want to engage anyone who wasn't God or good. It was apparent now that there were other invisible voices that I could hear in addition to His. How was I supposed to know who was speaking with me in any moment? Now, more than nine years after my awakening, I can discern who is speaking and when. This skill and spiritual acuity has taken years of learning, years of discerning, and years of incredible suffering.

After my experience in the kitchen that day, I began to refer to this as "My Tomato Story." Afterwards, if Hashem said something I wasn't sure was truthful, I would ask Him, "Is this another tomato?" or "Are you throwing another tomato at me Hashem?" I began learning how to discern in every moment and growing closer in my relationship with our Creator.

It took several years and many disappointments to learn and understand His many ways. Every single decision and utterance from Hashem has a deliberate purpose and is solely for our good but His reason isn't always knowable in the moment. In fact, it's rarely understood why Hashem brings something to us in the moment that it happens. Only Hashem knows the future and what must occur and He will deliberately deceive you for your own good. He is pure wisdom and goodness and His decisions are always made with the intention for goodness to prevail. Despite being told lies along the way which led me through enormous pain and losses, I continued to search for the deeper meaning and reasons to believe Him. I not only believed I was journeying and speaking with Hashem, I knew this with every part of my being. I completely trusted Him despite all the challenges and disappointments I suffered.

While I continued journal writing and communicating with Hashem, He also gave me daily visions. Many of these visions were so uplifting and inspiring that they served to fuel me with optimism to keep going. Since the hospitalization on Mother's Day, my husband continued to insist that something was wrong with me. I'm a very honest person and I didn't want to leave any stone unturned so I often analyzed whether he could possibly be right. Could I be mentally ill and bipolar? Every time I explored this idea, I simply didn't accept the diagnosis. It didn't describe me or what I was experiencing. I knew it was Hashem and that my new way of being was a gift from God, and purely spiritual.

One morning I woke up feeling extremely upset with my life and personal situation. Everything seemed to be crumbling around me and my husband was fighting with me at every turn. When I got up that morning, I walked into the master bathroom off my bedroom and began ranting to myself under my breath. I was muttering to myself that there wasn't anything wrong with me and none of this horror should have happened. As I entered the bathroom I was going on and on saying to myself, "I know that this isn't mental illness and there's nothing wrong with me!"

Without missing a beat Hashem chimed in, "Then why are you talking to yourself?"

I burst out laughing so hard I began to cry. His acute sense of timing and witty sense of humor brought me to tears. It was becoming clearer every day that we had a lovingly warm and unique relationship. I never realized that God Himself had a sense of humor and could be so funny and charming. Yes, unbeknownst to me and probably to the entire world, Hashem has His own amazing personality. Most people don't know this about Hashem. They don't think of God Himself as having a personality like a human being. This is astonishing since we're taught that we're created in His image and not the other way around. People assume that God is God and He would never have a sense of humor or crack a joke to make us to laugh. After all it isn't written that way in the Torah, is it? The reality is that He is more wonderful than anything ever written. Hashem has a personality that is larger than life and more beautiful than anyone can possibly imagine.

Running on Love the Registered 501(c)(3)

About a month after I came home from the Mother's Day debacle, I received a phone call from my older brother. Even though we had many difficulties over the years and were never particularly close, we managed to be cordial and tried to get along. He called that day to tell me about his friend who had six children, one of whom was battling for her life with a rare form of bone cancer. They were trying all kinds of medical interventions to save her life. Much of the medical care was experimental and wasn't covered by their medical insurance. The exorbitant medical bills were wreaking havoc on their finances. My brother knew I had run four marathons and raised a lot of money for charity and called to ask me if I knew of any way to help this family. In that moment, I knew my destiny was staring me in my face and my life's calling was presenting itself. It was time to turn my passion for fundraising and running marathons for love, into a registered charity. I decided my new charity's first event would raise money for this family in need. I quickly called my friend who was a lawyer and asked him to file for 501(c)(3) registration for my new non-profit that I called Running on Love.

Before the charity was officially registered, I rallied half a dozen people I knew and told them about this teenage girl who was struggling with cancer and about her family who was suffering from financial hardship due to all the medical bills. I asked everyone to run a half marathon with me in Philadelphia in November of 2009. We were going to run in this girl's honor and raise money to help her family. The 501(c)(3) registration for Running on Love was approved just days before we all met in Philadelphia for our run. After Running on Love for this young girl and raising over $4,500 for her family, I knew that this charity gave me new inspiration and was a source of true joy. In December of 2009, I asked the family to meet us for breakfast so that our small Running on Love team could present them with the fundraising money and meet their daughter in person. I felt that this meeting was a blessing for everyone involved because it allowed us to connect with each other in love and gratitude. We met them and presented them a check for the entire amount raised. Running on Love kept none of the money. I gave 100 percent of the funds to this family and never considered keeping a dime for Running on Love. At this early stage, my charity had no financial plan or business model to follow. For me it wasn't about business at all. This was a charity that I created out of love. Business wasn't even on my radar. It never occurred to me that this charity needed to be run like a business to survive. I wasn't creating this to be a business or to begin a new career. I simply felt this charity was part of my life's purpose which was to share the experience and blessing of actively giving of ourselves to honor the people we love.

Visions and Prophetic Dreams

In the fall of 2009, the Hebrew year 5770, I was having frequent morning visions and prophetic dreams. The prophetic dreams were clear messages from Hashem God. I've learned that all my dreams have a deeper meaning and are filled with messages from Him. I never ignore any of my dreams now and always review them with Hashem for messages and insight.

I had one prophetic dream that penetrated me deeply and I have never forgotten it. In this dream, I found myself in a dilapidated old apartment. It was clear that we had lost our wealth, all our belongings, and our beautiful family home in New Jersey. As I looked around this dilapidated apartment I was saddened that we had lost everything and that I was living with my husband in this one-bedroom run-down apartment. For some crazy reason, I was waiting for my closest girlfriend's son to arrive at our apartment for a job interview. I was going to hire him for some unknown reason. I looked around the apartment and saw that the bed was unmade. I told my husband that we had to straighten up right away so that it wasn't messy when this young man arrived. As I was straightening up the apartment I wondered to myself how we lost everything. Why did this happen and how did we get here? What happened to my beautiful home in New Jersey? Suddenly I saw a very large picture window in the bedroom. As I walked over to the window I looked out and saw the most magnificent view I had ever seen in my entire life. As I gazed out the window I said to myself, "This apartment is awful, but man what a view!"

In that moment, I was lifted and catapulted out of the picture window and began floating in the sky on a magic carpet ride. The carpet slowly glided over magical sparkling waters surrounded by breathtaking mountains. As I flew over the water and through ravines, I was in complete awe at the sight of the natural beauty. The colors of the water and the mountains were unlike anything I'd ever seen. I was stunned by the view of breathtaking waterfalls. Suddenly, I wasn't on the magic carpet ride any longer. Instead, I was walking down a cobblestone street in a very hot city. I had never been to Israel at this point in my life, but I somehow recognized that I was walking in the Old City of Jerusalem. I had seen many pictures of the Old City and I knew that this was where I was walking in oppressively hot weather. Strapped on my back like a heavy backpack filled with hundreds of bricks was my husband. He was holding onto me tightly with his arms around my neck, choking me while I climbed up very steep cobblestone steps in Jerusalem. As I was climbing these steps sweating, dehydrated, parched and desperately needing water, I kept saying to myself, "I can do this. I can make it. I can do this!" I was like the little engine that could.

Just as I felt I could barely take another step, two very strong male arms lifted me from underneath and carried me up the steps all the way to the top. As I was being carried I was so emotionally grateful that I began choking back tears. I looked to my right side and saw a strong and hairy male arm holding me and carrying me up the steps. I tried to figure out if I recognized whose arm this was. I wondered who was being so kind to lift me in my despair and help me up this massive staircase. I went to touch this hairy arm to see who it was connected to and just then the hand slapped mine to push it away! It was done in a playful way as if to say, "You're not allowed to see me!" and "Just turn around and keep going. I have you!"

From that vision, I then saw the sun rising over Jerusalem. But instead of the sun rising, it was an image of four gigantic glowing gold numbers coming up from behind the horizon. These bright gold numbers, 5770 rose as though they were the sun rising in the morning sky. As the numbers 5770 came up brightly like the sun, two white doves flew toward each other over the skyline of Jerusalem. The vision transitioned into thousands of joyous people gathered at an extremely large event. My eyes zoomed in on a very religious Jewish young man holding a baby boy. The man was dressed in black and white and was clearly Torah observant. The boy was apparently his son who looked to be about the age of two or three years old. Instinctively, I knew that I was being shown my future son-in-law and his baby was my future grandson. This vision stuck with me over the years and penetrated me deeply. I would one day learn that this dream was filled with prophecy and a message directly from God Himself about my future.

Back into Hell—Lockup Number 2

As I went forward with my life, I returned to work in my marketing company, began to build my new charity Running on Love, and eventually finished weaning off the nasty drugs. I was still quite clueless about my new miraculous gift of hearing God and the spirit world and had no idea where this would one day lead me. I remained enthralled with listening to the invisible voices that were speaking with me and continued recording my conversations with them in journals. Even though I had suffered frightening encounters and experiences, I believed every voice I heard was from a divine source and I felt protected. I knew I was speaking directly to God Himself although I wasn't 100 percent sure that it was always Hashem. I thought that I was mostly hearing His voice along with a mixture of many others.

My ability to discern Hashem's voice from the others increased but I still didn't realize that I had much to learn and understand about our world and the ways of Hashem God. I lacked knowledge about what I was hearing coupled with a lack of understanding about how Hashem operates. Without my realizing, He was in the process of exposing to me how deeply sick our world is and how troubled our entire society has become. Learning just how sick and dysfunctional our world has become took many years and countless painful lessons. As I approached my 50th birthday that December, my husband and I decided to take a trip to Aruba to celebrate. Things seemed to be normalizing at home and going along fine for me. I was taking care of my health by working out at the gym, running, learning Torah, and now I had a fledgling charity, Running on Love, that was inspiring me and filling me with joy and purpose.

As time went on I felt more certain that most of my conversations were with Hashem. He has an extremely clear, calming, distinctive, and powerful male voice. This is the voice that I was listening to and hearing most of the time. I no longer heard any of those evil voices that shook me up that night in the basement of my home while I was writing in "The Book of Truth." The Christian garbled language and prayers that were shouted at me on that infamous night seemed to have vanished as well. I was being instructed by Hashem to embrace and observe the laws of eating kosher which was consistent with the advice of my Chabad rabbi and rebbetzin. I began buying kosher chicken at the local supermarket and eating in a way that some might characterize as kosher style. This was the best I could do at the time because I wasn't getting support from my family to make any drastic changes in our home.

I decided that I wanted to keep the Sabbath too. As best as I could without ruffling too many feathers, I began to cook every Friday and prepared nice Friday evening meals. My children all went to the local public schools. Even though my children had attended Hebrew school, two of my three children weren't involved in any Jewish social groups and most of their friends were Gentiles. My oldest child was involved in USY which is a youth group that is part of the Conservative Jewish movement. She was the only one of my three children who had any Jewish friends or socialized in organized Jewish functions.

My husband was fighting me tooth and nail and hated the idea of keeping Shabbos, the Jewish Sabbath. Everything I was doing was met with arguments and resistance. Even though my husband was increasingly unhappy and argued with me about everything, I pursued what I felt compelled to do. I began cooking dinner on Fridays and decided that we would no longer go to Pizza Hut on Friday nights. Going to Pizza Hut was a longstanding family tradition. I heard lots of complaints from my husband that he missed the Lori who loved to eat pepperoni pizza. I told him he'd have to get over it because I wasn't going to be eating pepperoni pizza anytime soon.

By January 2010 my ability to discern had increased dramatically. By this time, I knew emphatically that I was speaking with Hashem God. I also discovered another amazing miracle about myself. I became acutely aware that I not only heard Hashem's voice through my spiritual ears, but I could feel His presence physically within my vessel. I could feel Him physically inside my body. What do I mean by being able to feel Hashem within my vessel or body? It means that I became aware that I was journeying as one with Hashem both physically and spiritually. It's as though within my body exists a male soul that walks, eats and breathes with me all the time. My body contains two separate souls that are inexplicably connected and travel together in perfect synchronicity. To give you some source of reference, it was a little like the comedy movie with Steve Martin and Lily Tomlin called *All of Me*. In that movie, Lily Tomlin died and her soul became stuck inside Steve Martin's body. This movie was quite hilarious with many funny situations as they shared the same body. When I realized what was happening, I began to feel Hashem take over my arms and legs at will. It was apparent that at His will, He was moving my arms and legs like I was a rag doll. It felt like Hashem and I were doing a virtual tango within my body. The feeling was miraculous and completely seamless.

This should sound strange and even frightening to every other person who hears this but it was never frightening to me. It felt eerily familiar and somewhat natural. While it was invigorating and exciting, it also felt strangely familiar like I had done this before. Without knowing it at the time, this was the next stage of my awakening process. It was so exciting that I ran to the bathroom several times throughout the day to be alone so that I could experience the feeling of having Him physically connected to me. In the bathroom mirror I looked at myself as He was speaking to me, and He would take over my facial movements and wink at me. Bizarre, right? Yes, completely bizarre but this filled me with a feeling of overwhelming love and euphoria.

Some people are raised to believe that God is within every person. People who believe this in the literal sense might say, "Oh come on Lori, everybody has God within them. You're nothing special!" While it's true that I may not be special, I assure you that nobody else is like me. No other person in creation journeys with Hashem as one within their vessel this way. In the words of Hashem, the way I exist in this world and journey with Him is unlike any other human being. He has told me repeatedly for many years that no other person could tolerate journeying with Him the way I do. He says if you were to experience the way I exist with Him, it would quite literally kill you. I personally don't understand why that would be true because I find Him so delightful and loving that I don't want to exist differently. Nonetheless, He says to be like me would kill anyone else.

As I was realizing how I could feel Hashem within my body, I repeatedly went upstairs into my master bathroom for privacy to try and understand what was happening to me. Hashem began playing little games with me to show me how connected I was to Him both spiritually and physically. He took over my arms and hands as though I was His puppet. He playfully grabbed my hair and moved my head around at will. I could feel that it wasn't my hands touching my hair, it was His. I also felt His powerful emotions inside of me as He spoke and knew without any doubt that they weren't my emotions, they were His. He streamed familiar music with loving messages within the lyrics into my mind and played with my soul and emotions like I was His violin. His words and methods made me so emotional that I knew emphatically this could be none other than Hashem. He also told me Torah stories and spoke Hebrew words that I had never heard before. I frequently went online to translate these words into English. He filled me with great emotion and told me about my many past lives. He also shared the previous incarnations of several people in my personal life. Many of my current friends and family members are the reincarnation of extraordinary people written about in the Torah. Many of the stories He told me were true, but He wasn't done stirring the pot, so to speak. Once again, He told me that I would win the lottery. This time I didn't share that information, just in case! In addition to another winning lottery ticket, He told me more wild tales to inflame my situation further and bring me right back into a second living nightmare.

The idea of someone else's soul being inside your body with you should be very frightening, but this wasn't just somebody. This was God Himself making His presence known to me in a physical way. It's a feeling of joy and magic that I simply can't describe to you in words. I'm sure it's a feeling that no other human being could fully understand despite my best effort to describe it. You would have to live it to know what I'm talking about and as I said, Hashem explained to me that you wouldn't survive the experience. No matter how many descriptive words I use to describe my journey with Hashem, I can't completely share with you what it feels like. To understand or relate to me, you must go deep inside your soul, listen to my voice and read this book in its entirety. God willing you will arrive at a deep sense of knowing that I am completely genuine and this is the truth.

I cooked Shabbos dinner one Friday for my family and as usual my children had other plans. One child went ice skating, while the other went out with friends, and my son invited his Gentile friend from music school to sleep over. As I cooked dinner for that Friday evening meal, I could feel Hashem's hands within mine, cooking my chicken dinner and orchestrating the entire meal. When I sat down to eat with my family and tasted the food I thought, "Wow, this is absolutely the best chicken I've ever cooked!"

As the weekend went on, hearing Hashem and feeling Him physically was becoming so strong and vivid it was difficult to conceal my excitement. It was obvious that my husband was getting nervous. I also heard the spirit world with increasing clarity too. Repeatedly I ran to my bathroom upstairs in my effort to conceal but it was becoming more apparent to my family that something was up. By the end of this weekend my oldest child realized that I was going into the bathroom to speak to "the voices" and she sounded the alarm bells to my husband.

Yet again, in my exuberance and excitement, I quickly forgot about my tomato story which I revealed earlier with its many lessons and believed every detail that Hashem shared with me. Much of what He told me was completely true, but He wasn't finished revealing the broken world we live in. To do that, He needed to aggravate my fragile and broken marriage further and bring me on another trip into mental health hell on earth.

Feeling Hashem physically was so enthralling that I flew with the angels once again. Hashem shared a great deal of truthful information with me which included that people on the other side, in the non-physical realm, were watching me and listening to our conversations. He shared what my life's purpose was and who I was in many of my past lives.

That Sunday night, while I was lying in bed, He showed me a group of people on the other side. I don't view the other side to be heaven the way many people do. I recognize this place on the other side as a temporary way station, separated from the physical realm. For now, I'll continue to refer to this place as heaven so that you understand as I relay my story. I looked up over my bed that night when I was supposed to be asleep and saw people on the other side, in heaven, looking back at me. But it wasn't just people who had died that I could see and hear. I could also see people who were still alive and part of our physical world. I could see people I knew from work and socially. They were sitting on what looked like chairs, observing me conversing with Hashem and some of them were speaking to me. How could this be? They're alive but they were in heaven listening to me and Hashem converse? I was puzzled and wondered what this all meant.

Hashem explained to me that when people sleep at night a portion of their soul crosses over and leaves their body and visits "heaven." They make this trip for spiritual healing. The next morning after they've visited "heaven," God willing, they return to their bodies. This concept may sound bizarre to many reading this but it's knowledge that is taught in Torah. Observant Jewish people are raised with this knowledge and take precautions to keep their bodies spiritually pure. Part of the human soul crosses over at night to heal and learn on the other side. The soul then returns to its body the next morning without any realization that part of them had gone somewhere else. It's an observant Jewish practice to perform a ritual hand-washing upon rising every morning. Why? Because it's taught that the hand-washing seals the fingertips after the soul has returned and prevents impurities from entering their vessel. Nutty cuckoo you might say? No, it's Torah. This critically important information is not taught to most of the world. There is an enormous amount of information that was given to the children of Israel that isn't detailed within the five books of Moses. This information is part of Jewish law, which has been handed down and taught for generations in an oral tradition. The rules of hand-washing have been taught for thousands of years as a protection to keep the children of Israel spiritually clean.

As I was communicating with everybody I saw on the other side, I could literally see that my husband was sitting across from me and surrounded by his mother and father who had passed away years earlier. It was a portion of his soul, because his body was sound asleep next to me in bed. His parents were talking to him and sharing with him that I wasn't mentally ill at all. He was being told that this was a spiritual awakening and I was telling everyone the truth. While I was listening to all of this and speaking to Hashem I began to grow confident that the next morning my husband would wake up and we would finally have an open dialog about everything that was happening. I was very excited at the prospect of being able to share Hashem and my newfound gift with my husband. The world needed this information desperately and we could work together to bring this information out to the public. I naively believed that when I woke up that morning I would literally have his help. Nothing was further from the truth.

The next morning, he came over to my side of the bed and said, "It's happening again. We need to go to the hospital."

I answered, "What you talking about? There's nothing wrong with me."

He responded, "I heard you speaking in a foreign language last night."

I replied, "I don't speak anything but English. I don't know what you were hearing, but there is nothing wrong with me."

He insisted, "We need to go now. There's something wrong with you and we need to do something right away."

I feverishly picked up the phone next to my bed and called my closest girl-friend who I spoke to daily about God and who told me she believed me. She was my Christian friend with whom I shared my journal entries. I felt certain she would help me because of course she believed every word I was telling her and understood I could speak with God. Or did she? She believed me yesterday, so why wouldn't she believe me and support me today? On this morning when she answered the phone she was less than supportive. She responded with indignant anger. She was busy getting ready for her work day and I was clearly an interference in her life that morning. The angry and derisive tone in her voice stunned me and told me I was an inconvenience. As I begged her for help and asked her to come protect me from my husband, her voice became scathing. I said, "You need to come here now and help me. He's going to drag me off again and have me drugged!"

She responded tersely, "That's not fair Lori. I can't come. You're not being fair to me!" I was completely speechless! This is unfair to you? I was calling my closest girlfriend who said she believed in me to ask her to rescue me and she was angry that I wasn't fair to her? I thought, "Why won't she come to my aid? She believed every word I told her yesterday." Apparently, it was too inconvenient to come to my aid that morning when I needed her the most. It was more important that she was on time for work. This was the first of countless betrayals when the people I loved and trusted most, turned away readily and abandoned me.

I hung up the phone completely distraught. I said to my husband, "You promised we would go to the rabbi and his wife if this happened again."

He said, "Okay let's go." So, we went to the Chabad House and I sat with the rebbetzin in their synagogue. The rabbi walked out the front door sheepishly and looked clearly distressed. He wouldn't speak to me or even look in my direction.

The rebbetzin asked me, "What's going on Lori?"

I said, "I'm with Hashem and He is speaking to me."

She looked at me with a sympathetic eye as though I had lost my mind. This was a Chasidic woman who believes that Hashem speaks to us all and even believes in the concept of a Moshiach, Messiah. I repeated, "Hashem is talking to me and He says that we're in grave danger."

She replied in a patronizing tone, "Yes I know. You need to go home and rest Lori. Hashem wants you to go home and take care of your family. Go home and take a nap and get some sleep."

I said, "Are you kidding me? I'm telling you it's Hashem speaking with me and He's with me right now. He's telling me that we are all a reincarnation of someone else. He says I am here now to share this information and wake everyone up. He says this is what I was chosen for and I'm here to wake everybody up so that we understand the danger we're in. We must work together to protect ourselves."

Her reply became even more patronizing as she said, "Hashem wants you to go home and take care of your children Lori. He wants you to go home and get some sleep."

I looked at her in puzzled amazement. I wanted to scream at the top of my lungs. Inside my soul I silently cried out to Hashem, "What am I supposed to do now?"

Right then Hashem said to me, "Lori, I'll help you. She needs physical proof that I am here with you. Let's go over to the Ark and pull out the Torah. I will read from the Torah through your mouth. She knows you don't know how to read Torah. When you do this, she will know it's none other than a miracle from Hashem God."

I said, "Really Hashem? You will do this for me?"

He said, "Yes Lori. Go over to the Ark now and get the Torah. I will read from the scrolls."

I listened and obeyed. I then said to her, "Hashem just told me He will prove to you that He's with me and He will read from the Torah from my mouth." I went over to the Ark and pulled the Torah out, placed it on the bema, the podium for the Torah, and opened the scrolls. She must've been having a small heart attack because here I was a woman touching the Torah scrolls God forbid! To her credit, she played along and stayed calm. While this was happening, I saw the rabbi running in and out of the front door of the synagogue with a very distressed look on his face. He wouldn't come anywhere near me. It was clear they both thought I was completely out of my mind.

After I placed the Torah on the bema, I looked down at the Torah scrolls and I said silently to Hashem, "Okay Hashem ready. Please read!"

Hashem responded in stone cold silence. Oh No! I said, "Hashem, please read for me!" Again, He responded in silence. I had that sinking feeling He was teaching me a deeply painful lesson once again. Just then the rebbetzin went to get a book, Tehillim, the book of psalms by King David. She brought this book over to me and said, "Lori let's read some Tehillim together."

I said, "What's Tehillim?" Yes, really. I didn't know anything about Tehillim. Some Moshiach I am, right?

She explained that this book was filled with holy prayers that would help me heal. After she read one aloud, I looked at her and said, "Okay. What did you just read? What did that mean?"

She replied, "I don't know. It doesn't matter. You just need to read it and it will heal you. The essence of the prayer will get into your soul and heal you."

I replied, "Really? I don't know what you mean. How can this heal me if it makes no sense to me? You're going to read a prayer to me that you can't explain and I have no idea what it means. You want me to believe this is going to heal me?" Hashem has since explained that there was truth in what she said. However, knowledge and understanding are the only way our world will ever truly heal.

There was nothing mentally wrong with me as I stood there in the synagogue desperately trying to share my gift with the Chabad rebbetzin. I was being prodded by Hashem to poke at everyone around me and this was a supreme test. It was their test, not mine. In their eyes, I looked completely out of my mind and mentally ill. Telling them that Hashem spoke to me was delusional behavior in their eyes. This Chassidic couple thought I was having a mental illness psychotic episode. This wasn't any form of mental illness, it was Hashem and part of my spiritual awakening. I needed to learn how deeply unraveled our entire world had become. Doing this to me was the only way Hashem could bring me all the knowledge I ultimately required to do my life's work as Moshiach. There wasn't any other person on the face of the earth who knew and understood everything that I needed to teach. The loftiest rabbis had never experienced and lived what I was living in those moments. Even the most educated and holy rabbis who are extremely gifted and clairvoyant don't fully comprehend the information that was revealed to me through this awakening process.

I was shocked and horrified by the rebbetzin's behavior and how the rabbi wouldn't even look at me. How could these two Chassidic Torah-learned Jews who study spirituality, Kabbalah and Torah buy into the world view that we can't hear Hashem? Was it impossible for me to be spoken to by our King because I was an ordinary Jewish mommy from New Jersey who wasn't a Torah scholar? Most of the Orthodox Jewish world would concur with their disbelief. Most of the world would concur that a woman would never be tagged by God to be His messenger. This Chasidic Jewish couple's reaction astounded me then and still does to this day. Admittedly, Hashem telling me to pull the Torah out of the Ark put a heavy dose of oil on the raging fire of disbelief.

The Orthodox Jewish world prays daily for the coming of Moshiach. They believe that Moshiach will speak to and hear Hashem God, true? Well of course! But they also believe that Moshiach is a Torah-observant man and not a woman. Apparently, they believe you must be a religious Jewish man to hear Hashem. Ah, how was I supposed to know any of this at the time? I wasn't saying that I was Moshiach at this juncture but I was saying that Hashem was speaking to me. I surely didn't know that they wouldn't even consider this to be possible. I didn't have any idea that they believed it was impossible for me to hear Hashem as a non-Orthodox Jewish woman. On top of that, everyone wanted physical proof that I was hearing Hashem and I had none to give them. If I suddenly read beautifully from the Torah scrolls that day would they have been stunned into believing me then? We won't know the answer to that question but I believe the outcome and their reactions would have been far different. If I read from Torah, presented the winning lottery ticket to my former husband, and donated millions to their shul, the outcome would positively have been different.

Hashem is non-physical, right? I've read where the Orthodox rabbis state that Moshiach doesn't need to perform any miracles at all to prove he's Moshiach. I suppose he simply needs to be an Orthodox Jewish man who has complete knowledge and total recall of every word written in the Torah and Talmud. If there were a man like this who claimed to be Moshiach they would listen to him without any physical proof at all, right? Maybe, but eventually they would turn on him too. There are countless examples of the Jewish people turning on Moses, God's greatest prophet, aren't there? Moses even came equipped with plenty of miracles to boot. What must be understood is that Moshiach must be the living embodiment of the Torah and not a Torah scholar. Moshiach is chosen by Hashem, not by people. We have a plethora of Torah scholars and look at the hideous state of our world. We must all learn how to live the Torah, not just memorize and expound on its contents. Regardless of the endless prayers begging Hashem for the Moshiach, the world still isn't open to accept any Moshiach, with or without physical proof. That's simply the truth.

As we left the synagogue, my husband convinced me to drive over to the psychotherapist who had given us marital therapy over the years. She was the same psychotherapist who explained to me that my mother suffered from an incurable mental illness called borderline personality disorder. She diagnosed my mother without ever having met her. Remember that story? She also told me that my family upbringing was completely dysfunctional and that the relationship between my mother and two brothers was extremely unhealthy. She described both of my brothers' relationships with my mother as psychologically incestuous. Wow! Aren't we just a family brimming with mental problems?

To the surprise of many people who knew us, my husband and I had suffered marital problems over the years but I didn't share any of this with a soul. I never said a negative word about my marriage or relationship with my husband until my life ultimately unraveled and I filed for divorce. We went to meet with this respected doctor of psychotherapy and sat with her in her office. My husband told me after we met with her, she told him that she was shocked and upset. She told him that I was likely the most stable, logical and mentally well-balanced person she had ever met and the idea that this was happening to me was deeply unsettling and baffling to her. She thought I was experiencing a psychotic break from reality. What she thought was happening to me was nothing of the sort. On the contrary, I was smack in the middle of waking up to the sad discovery that everyone around me was delusional and sick. My husband and I sat in her office as she began to quiz me. She asked me questions to figure out whether I was having a mental crisis or if I was telling the truth and hearing God. Her questions were things like "What number am I thinking of right now?" and "Can you tell me what color I am thinking of?" You know the "Prove it to me" game. The game that Hashem refuses to play. If I was talking to God, and God knows everything, then I would surely be able to answer her absurd questions, right? Her questions clearly said to me "Come on Lori, prove it!"

When she asked her ridiculous questions, without missing a beat Hashem replied, "Tell her I don't do stupid pet tricks." Does this response sound like God to you? If you respond no, and that it sounds more like David Letterman, I might have agreed with you many years ago. Hashem has a stingingly funny and witty sense of humor. He speaks succinctly and is always powerfully poignant. If you think her line of questioning was appropriate, then it's time for you to grow in your understanding about the ways of Hashem. This is precisely how He responded to her nonsensical questions.

If I wasn't already in enough hot water, Hashem then took me once again into His hands like a hot poker to stab at everyone in the room. He said to me, "Tell them both that I have a hot stock tip for them. The stock market will have a record day this Wednesday and they should both invest heavily in the market to make a fortune. In this way, they will know that I am Hashem God." Unbeknownst to me, He was taking a deliberate shot at their worship of money. Believe it or not I was still completely clueless. I didn't detect any deception or sarcasm at all in His magnificent voice.

In my naiveté, I repeated His words not realizing how He was taunting them with their own false idols and ideology. Of course, this general non-specific recommendation from God to invest in the stock market on Wednesday sounded utterly ridiculous. They looked at each other and smirked, and then she said to my husband, "Take her to the hospital." Perhaps if I gave them an actual stock ticker symbol to invest in, they would have paused for a moment and their ears might have perked up. Because my statement was so vague and ludicrous it fed their notion that I was mentally deranged. If you love Hashem as I do, and you understand His ways, you understand exactly what He was saying with His words in that moment. He was taunting them and belittling their belief in materialism. The Golden Calf. Ridiculous? For those of us who know and love Hashem God, clearly this was a powerful lesson in the making and not ridiculous at all.

I began to have that sinking feeling that I was doomed once again. Nobody was ever going to believe me. How much money did I have to present everyone to prove that I was speaking to Hashem? What kind of magic trick would suffice? What would prove to people who knew me and supposedly loved me that I was truly speaking to and journeying with Hashem God, the Holy One?

The most religious people might question why God would choose to speak to a plain old Jewish mom from New Jersey. Most people would relate to and understand why all my family and friends didn't believe me. If you believe that being able to validate that you're hearing Hashem comes in the form of presenting the winning lottery ticket, a truthful stock tip, knowing what color is in the mind of someone, or blurting out the maiden name of somebody's grandmother is clear proof of His existence, we are on a steady path to annihilation. Pious people of our world would likely agree in principle that none of those things are proof of God. Unfortunately, even those pious people are misguided. The religious and learned believe that to be chosen by Hashem, you must be a man with complete knowledge of the written word. While studying Torah is a mitzvah and required of Jewish men, sorry to break the bad news to the devoutly religious. Being of male gender and having book knowledge weren't Hashem God's criteria for choosing His Moshiach.

I calmly went with my husband to the hospital because I didn't want to repeat being dragged away and physically brutalized like on Mother's Day. All along the way Hashem kept telling me that He would do something miraculous to prove to them He was with me. He told me He wouldn't let me go through the same horror again. This was untrue of course, because going through all of this was required of me. He simply wouldn't reveal this to me at that time. As He was comforting me, I was unaware that He was deliberately leading me back for another visit into mental hospital hell.

As we walked into the hospital Hashem told me He would materialize as Jesus in white robes and then I would be home free. The paparazzi would come and then we could get on with saving the world from all the terrorists who desired to kill us and destroy Israel. He explained that showing up in the image of Jesus would be the only thing that would convince them that God was with me. My tomato story was the furthest thing from my mind because I was so distraught and wanted to believe that He would save me from another trip to hell. I was comforted by His strong calming voice and hoped He would do all that He said so I told the doctors what Hashem said he would do. He of course didn't do any of this. The mention of Jesus, had no emotional effect on me whatsoever because of my Jewish upbringing. Hashem was poking at the Christians who worked at the hospital and were raised with the belief that this is how the world will be saved one day. As you read my story you might believe it sounds absurd. What Hashem was doing was raising a mirror to everyone around me. Jesus showing up in white robes to save the day is a wild story that many Christians believe. While Jesus showing up in robes is believable to many Christian people, an honest hard-working mother of three hearing and speaking to God is not. God willing most people will wake up and see the absurdity of these false beliefs now.

I realized soon that He wasn't materializing for everyone in the hospital as Jesus in those famous white robes, so Hashem changed His story again. He told me He would allow my father to return from the dead and come into my hospital room to prove to the doctors that I was telling the truth. This story affected me far more emotionally than the thought of seeing Jesus did. The idea that I could get a warm hug from my dad gripped me with great emotion and hope. We are taught in Torah that Hashem can and will resurrect the dead one day so I believed Him. Hashem knew exactly what to say to me in every moment to make me respond the way He needed. At one point, He told me to call the doctor over and tell him that He was going to bring my father into the room, resurrecting him from the dead, as proof that He was with me. It went on and on like this for a couple of hours.

Why was Hashem torturing me in this way? Was He torturing me or was He using me to get to them? I knew it was undoubtedly Hashem speaking to me as He deliberately fueled the raging inferno that would eventually destroy my secular American life. He was relentless, and so was I. Why wouldn't I just quit? Anyone would have quit after Mother's Day. Why did I persist in reaching relentlessly for Him? I kept getting tangled up in His exaggerated lies and didn't understand their purpose. Yet I still searched for reasons to believe that would support what I already knew. I knew it was Hashem. There was no doubt in any part of my soul. He knew I would never let go of Him. On the first morning when He woke me and told me to get pen and paper and start writing everything down, I knew in the depths of my soul it was Him and that this was my calling. Hashem knew me better than I knew myself. He knew without a doubt that I would never quit.

Every step of the way Hashem was revealing to me a world that was insidiously evil and completely dysfunctional. Any other human being would have quit after the Mother's Day trip to hell. Certainly, after this second journey into the mental hospital abyss, a good American mother would say, "No more! No more pain! I will take your psychological drugs like a good mental patient and accept my diagnosis of mental illness. This can't be real after all, because it has been one lie after another and this is destroying my all-American life." That's what any normal person would do but not so for me. I just knew it was Hashem and I wasn't going to let go for one moment. There truly is no way for me to explain myself or my decisions. It was Hashem then and it is most certainly Him here with me right now as I write this book.

The E.R. doctor came over to me, sat down next to me and asked, "What's going on Lori?"

I said, "I'm here with God and He's talking to me. He's not only talking to me, but I share my body with Him. I can feel Him inside of me physically."

The doctor responded in a patronizing way, "Oh really?"

I said, "Yes really. Everybody says they believe in God and that God is within us all and He talks to us. I am living breathing proof of this and He's here, right now. Ask me anything. He wants to speak to everybody."

The doctor left the room and came back with a syringe in one hand and a pill in the other. He said to me, "Take this pill or we will hold you down and forcibly shoot you up."

I replied, "That's not a choice."

He said, "Yes, it is. Take the pill or we will hold you down and inject these drugs forcibly."

I said again, "That's not a choice and I'm a grown woman. I know there's nothing wrong with me. I don't require your drugs and I don't want them." To his word, at least three people held me down and shot their drugs into my naked behind. I was forcibly committed against my will for the second time in six months. They told me to sign some papers that I was being voluntarily committed and explained that involuntary commitment was somehow a very bad thing for me. I'm not sure it was my best interest they were trying to protect. I venture to guess it had more to do with them getting paid, than protecting my well-being.

While I was committed in this hospital for about a week, Hashem never left me. Not for one moment. They forcibly made me swallow their drugs as if it were possible to remove His voice from my soul. It never happened. No matter how much drugs they forced through my veins, He was always there and speaking to me through it all. Every time I heard Him, I welled up with great emotion and felt deeply grateful that He didn't leave me. One day there was a double rainbow outside my hospital room window. I recall all the patients running in and out of my room to get a look at this beautiful sight. I wasn't knowledgeable at the time about the significance of the rainbow in Torah. Although I didn't understand the significance of the rainbow I knew this was clearly a sign from Hashem that He was with me in that room and everywhere I went. To this very day, when I wake to His voice greeting me every morning, I choke back tears of profound gratitude. He is always there for me and I never take this for granted for one moment.

This was incarceration and trip to hell number two. The health care workers spoke down to the patients as though we were small inept children. Some of the aides were half my age making their haughty and derisive behavior even more unnerving. Your personal rights are stripped from you and they control your every move. Every day the head psychiatrist asked me, "Are you hearing God Lori?" For the first couple of days I was defiant and refused to lie. I soon realized that if I kept saying that God was speaking to me I wouldn't get released. So, I started to change my language a little bit. I told him I only hear my own thoughts. I thought this was answering in a truthful way, but enough of what he desired to hear so I could get released. I rationalized that God's voice was part of my own thoughts and extrapolated that I wasn't being dishonest or a liar. My husband told me afterward that this doctor was worried that I was too smart and clever and was playing a game of deception with him. I suppose you might say I deceived him well enough to be released. Other than making me feel sick, the drugs had no effect on my ability to hear Hashem, thank God!

I came home after lockup number two and promptly forgave my husband once again. I excused him for having me committed a second time because I understood he was incapable of hearing what I heard and I sympathized with his dilemma. I had shared all of Hashem's wild promises of physical proof that never materialized so how was he to know that I wasn't nuts? I let go of any anger, continued journal writing and praying while doing all the things that my Chabad rabbi and his wife prescribed. I didn't hold a grudge against anyone and that included my Christian best girlfriend who angrily hung up the phone on me and refused to come to my aid that infamous morning. I never broke ties or remained angry with anyone and believed that they were all decent, good and loving people. I accepted that my husband wasn't a believer in God and that it wasn't possible to get inside of me to know what I was experiencing. There wasn't any way for me to prove any of this to a soul. It seemed that it was only possible for me to know without any doubt that I was truly speaking to and journeying with Hashem God.

HIS VOICE, VISIONS & LESSONS

What is the source of mental illness?

A lot of people believe that the source of mental illness is biological, genetic, it's a chemical imbalance in your brain and it's treated as such. Medical doctors diagnose people daily with bipolar disorder, schizophrenia, all kinds of mental disorders, even inventing new disorders that didn't exist when I was a kid. So, are they treating mental illness correctly? If you want to cure a problem you need to find its source or you're just ameliorating the problem and putting a band-aid on it. Or perhaps you're exacerbating the problem and making it much worse.

What is the source of mental illness as we know it? The answer is—spirit. That might shock a lot of people or maybe there are mental health professionals who agree that you need to treat the entire patient. You can't just prescribe psychological drugs to a patient and cure them of their mental problems. You need to speak with them and engage in things like psychotherapy and other behavioral therapies.

But it's deeper than that. We come into this world as a spirit and we journey in a body. There's really two of us, journeying here in this world. It's very complicated information but it's truly quite simple. I asked Hashem God, "Hashem, is there such a thing as mental illness? If it's a spiritual problem, well then there's a cure. So maybe there's no such thing as mental illness." Just then Hashem showed me an image of a black-masked man—a terrorist—and I knew exactly what He was saying. That's mental illness.

What is mental illness? Hashem says it emanates from the Yetzer Hara, the evil inclination—Satan. I am working now to educate the world about things that have been written and taught for thousands of years. Many millions of people are suffering from what they are told are mental illnesses and they don't realize that the answer and the cure is right here.

There is a cure to mental illness. But it isn't biological. It isn't genetic. You didn't get it from your mother. Some people say everything that goes wrong in our lives is mom's fault. But this one isn't mom's fault. This one truly isn't anyone's fault. It is a choice. You need to understand where your mental health problems are coming from and address them and I am here to help. I'm here to turn on the light and show you that you're making choices that are making you and everyone you love sick.

There are people out there who are hurting right now. They are looking for answers in a pill bottle but that's not where the answers lie. The answers were given to us by God Himself. It's time to reach for Him and learn His ways that will help you heal. If we heal ourselves of our own problems we have a shot at healing our world. This is the work of world peace—learning to look inside of ourselves, finding out where we are choosing wrong, learning how to choose correctly, and healing our souls.

An abundance of psychological drugs are prescribed to treat people who are suffering. Are these drugs good? Everything comes into existence with the approval of Hashem God so they must be good or has something good turned into something evil? Let's not be afraid to talk about mental illness and look at ourselves to find out where we are going wrong. Let's be unafraid to face our fears and our problems and work for peace on earth in our time.

Chapter 7

Perseverance and Running on Love

Once again, after a week in the hospital, I returned home without any anger or resentment in my heart. I let all of it go because in my mind I understood that they couldn't truly know that I was telling the truth. Even though I accepted this, I still didn't understand why nobody believed me. Everyone knew me as someone who was deeply honest and genuine. They also knew that I had a lifelong history of hearing the spirit world. My closest friends and some family members not only accepted this as true, but over the years they found my many stories and spiritual encounters fascinating. Why then was it no longer fascinating or believable to any of them? Despite their disbelief, I had compassion for them all. It was obvious to me that they couldn't put themselves inside my body and hear or experience anything that I was experiencing. They didn't have the ability to know directly for themselves that God was truly talking to me. I moved forward with my life and began to work on self-healing as best I could.

I returned to work in my marketing company, while I also organized teams for Running on Love. I registered to become an official charity for the New Jersey Marathon and I organized teams to run in this event. As a charity for the New Jersey Marathon I agreed to supply them with 30 volunteers on event day. For bringing volunteers to the event the organizers agreed to give Running on Love a nice donation. I was friendly with the event's race director and received the special honor of organizing volunteers to work at the finish line handing out the finisher medals. In my opinion, this was the best job of the day bar none. To greet people as they crossed the finish line and give them a medal was a deeply uplifting experience that I wanted for all my volunteers.

The organizers also gave me a complimentary table at their pre-event Expo where I could promote my new charity. Running on Love became the light of my life and my inspiration to keep going. In Running on Love's first event as an official charity for the NJ marathon, I set up a team to support the young girl with bone cancer whom we had honored in the first ever Running on Love event in Philadelphia. Once again I organized a team in her honor and we raised money for her family. I was still smitten with Team in Training, so I split the fundraising proceeds from this event between the young girl's family and Team in Training, supporting the Leukemia and Lymphoma Society. Through all the strife I was experiencing at home, this little charity gave me purpose and helped me focus on doing something positive for our world. While I was working to build something as beautiful as Running on Love, my home life and marriage were disintegrating.

Being a Good Mom Against All Odds

As time marched on, my husband continued to lament that there was something wrong with me even though I knew I was completely fine. He was also doing a formidable job of convincing my children, family and everyone he knew that I was having mental problems. As our marriage was disintegrating and our children were showing signs of emotional wear, he continuously pointed the blame squarely at me. Throughout our relationship, he consistently projected blame for any problems we experienced onto my shoulders so this behavior wasn't unusual.

Once again, I convinced the psychiatrist who had weaned me off these terrible drugs after the Mother's Day debacle to get me off them a second time. Just like the first go-around, she weaned me off slowly and safely. I was grateful to finally be off this horrible medication with its many side effects. After two involuntary psychiatric commitments, I was distraught about my personal struggle at home. I managed to drag myself out of bed every morning but it required a Herculean effort. Every day I mustered up the strength and went to work, worked out at the gym, and prayed intensely to Hashem to help lift my spirit.

Through it all, I never once stopped speaking with Hashem. For my personal safety, I began hiding my written conversations and journal writing because it enraged my family. They were convinced that I was in denial, completely psychotic and bipolar. They refused to entertain or explore any possibility that

I was truly hearing God. Instead of writing in my journal, I hid these conversations with Hashem by using my BlackBerry cell phone. I would vigorously type our conversations into my phone as though I was texting or emailing somebody and then promptly delete the entire discussion with Hashem God. In these early years of my awakening, I believed that I had to write down the conversations to be able to hear Him accurately. It felt like there was a connection to the action of writing and hearing Him. There were heightened times along the way when I spoke to Hashem and didn't feel any need to write. More often, in the beginning, I believed that writing gave me clarity which improved the accuracy of hearing and discerning His voice from my own.

My son attended a rock 'n' roll music school that I found for him during my marathon running days with Team in Training. He played the electric guitar and became so good that we bought him a Fender Stratocaster. Every summer since he was about 11 years old, we sent him to a summer music sleep-away camp where he accelerated in his gift of playing guitar and enjoyed performing on stage in the camp's rock concerts. During the regular school year, he went to the local rock 'n' roll music school and performed on stage in concerts with other students. He was musically gifted and loved performing with the other kids in the music school's rock concerts. It was wonderful to see him so happy with this musical pastime. As time went on though, I began to see cracks in the armor. When I dropped him off for his guitar practice and music lessons, I saw a decadent way of life enveloping my son. Some of the parents dropping off their children were scantily dressed and their bodies were covered with tattoos and piercings. Their children were growing their hair long and dressing in a way that was reminiscent of the sixties drug culture. It was the typical American rock 'n' roll culture of drugs, sex, and "The Pursuit of Happiness." This may sound hypocritical to many people because I participated in this when I was a teenager. Now that I was seeing the world through a new set of lenses I became increasingly concerned about my son being indoctrinated into this decadent way of life. This isn't meant to be judgmental at all about the parents or children I was observing at the school. They were all nice people but it became increasingly clear to me that they were on the wrong spiritual path. I wanted to steer my son away from what I now considered a deeply troubling way of life.

My son was always a sensitive boy and extremely good-natured. As I dropped him off for these guitar lessons it looked like I was sending an angel into the devil's lair. He was a pure angelic bright light being surrounded by darkness and decadence. An exaggeration? No, it's completely truthful. I grew up in the

'70s with drugs and rock 'n' roll and participated in this decadent lifestyle. I know firsthand that it wasn't good for me back then, and I didn't want this for my own children. I was watching these children being indoctrinated into the same wrongheaded behaviors that so many of us participated in back in the day. You might call me a hypocrite but that truly doesn't matter to me. My eyes were being peeled wide open by Hashem and the truth was undeniable. My son was heading the wrong way and I wasn't on board. I didn't want him being dragged into this way of life at all. Clearly America had lost its moral compass and I was fearful that I would lose my son to this troubled way of life.

Gratefully I convinced my son who wasn't involved in any Jewish education to give USY a try. He had no interest in any form of religion or Judaism. One day, I bribed my son to attend a USY event and I asked my oldest daughter to please help me convince him to go. As I recall, she participated in the bribe. I saw the Conservative Jewish youth group USY as a bridge that would help him return to Judaism in the same way it helped my daughter. Before his first weekend trip with USY, I had to go to the local Judaica store to buy him Tefillin. Tefillin is a religious garment for men and one of the most important commandments in the Torah. Tefillin consists of two small leather boxes that contain four sections of Torah inscribed on a parchment which are attached to leather straps. Orthodox Jewish men wear Tefillin during weekday morning prayer and my son was required to bring this on his weekend trip with USY.

While I was at the Judaica store purchasing him Tefillin, I decided to buy him Tzitzit, an undergarment with strings that are a reminder for Jewish men about the presence of God and their obligations to Him. USY didn't require Tzitzit, but I wanted to buy it for him anyway. This was my own wishful thinking at that time that one day he would wear this garment and embrace this commandment too. I purchased the Tzitzit but never showed it to him because I didn't want to push too hard and possibly turn him off to the entire idea. Instead I took the Tzitzit home and tucked it away in a drawer hoping to give it to him in the future. I took my son to our Chabad rabbi to teach him how to put on the Tefillin before his trip with USY. The rabbi was visibly moved and delighted and said most boys in America are finished with Judaism after their Bar Mitzvah day. He told my son that this was his "Real Bar Mitzvah" the day he willfully came to the rabbi to put on Tefillin and chose to observe this mitzvah, commandment, on his own.

The two involuntary hospitalizations started taking a toll on my three children. My oldest child reacted by reaching harder for God. I was grateful to see this and thought it was a supreme blessing. She began learning through an

Orthodox Jewish youth group, NCSY. The Conservative Jewish movement that she was involved in through USY wasn't satiating her desire to learn or connect to God any longer. One evening, she went to a social gathering organized by NCSY called "Latte Learning" at a Starbucks café and met Orthodox Jewish teenagers there from a neighboring town. The teenagers she met and became friendly with invited her regularly to spend Shabbos with them at their homes. She began spending most of her free time in this Orthodox Jewish community with her new Orthodox Jewish friends. This made me extremely happy because it became clear to me early on that observant Judaism was strengthening her from the inside out.

While all three of my children were showing signs of wear from the problems in our home, my youngest child was suffering the most. Being my youngest, she was always the most attached to me. Throughout her childhood, she was the most affectionate and clingy of my three children. The events that occurred rocked her world and shook her deeply. All three of my children struggled but it was evident that she took the fallout the hardest.

I persevered and continued to work at my company, encouraged my children to follow the Jewish path, and supported their interest in music. All three children were playing musical instruments and performing. My oldest daughter taught herself how to play the guitar and began writing her own music. Her music was truly beautiful, her voice had an angelic quality, and the lyrics she wrote were spiritually uplifting and inspiring. Since I was involved in marketing and advertising, I had business connections who recommended a sound studio where I took her to record her music. We recorded her songs professionally and my art director designed the cover art for her CD while I encouraged her to pursue her dream. Her dream was to one day be a role model for young girls and sing her music around the world. While others thought that her dream was too lofty I never believed that her dream was unattainable and I encouraged her to keep going.

My youngest daughter complained about her extremely curly hair and wanted help to make it more manageable. Many hair salons offered an expensive process called a keratin hair treatment which straightens the curls and makes hair easier to handle. One day I decided to take my youngest daughter for one of these treatments. The salon where I made the appointment was one that I had stopped going to about a year earlier. I started going elsewhere because my haircuts weren't pleasing me and I needed a change. My stylist, who was the owner of the salon, also used to talk and gossip with everyone in the salon while she cut my hair and I felt she wasn't giving me her full attention.

I decided to return to her salon and give her another try so I called and made appointments for both me and my daughter. When I walked into the salon, the owner was clearly angry to see me. I suppose she felt slighted that I hadn't come to her for the past year. She began whispering to her coworkers about me while throwing very angry looks in my direction. I saw her muttering under her breath to someone and scowling at me as she mixed my hair color. When I saw this, I felt uncomfortable so I pulled her aside privately to explain to her that I hadn't come to her salon because I wasn't happy with my hair and needed a change. I told her I thought she was a very talented hair stylist but I had some issues with the last several haircuts. Instead of being happy that I returned to give her another try, she was visibly angry. Seeing her angry face, I told her that I would leave if she didn't want to work with me again. In that moment, shockingly, she told me she preferred that I leave. Wow! I couldn't believe my ears and was shocked by her answer, but so be it.

I walked over to the chair where my daughter was sitting about to have a keratin treatment and told her we had to leave. My daughter was visibly upset as I pulled her out of the chair. You could see she felt humiliated. There wasn't anything I could do about this because the owner had told me to leave her salon. I took her out of the chair and we left promptly. As we were driving away from the hair salon, my daughter said to me, "Mommy, what really happened to you? Can you please explain to me what happened?" She was referring to the two hospitalizations.

I said to her, "Sweetheart, nothing was wrong with me then and nothing is wrong with me now. I now understand more about what's been going on and what happened." I asked her if she wanted to sit with me and talk for a while so that I could explain everything to her. She agreed so I pulled the car over into a parking lot on the way home for us to talk. We sat in the car for a while as I began to explain to her that everything was not as it seemed. I started to explain that we are all spirit and reincarnations from former lives. I told her it was truly possible to hear the spirit world and God Himself can speak to us. It didn't occur to me that this was inappropriate information that she might be too young to handle and something I shouldn't discuss with her. As I was talking she grabbed her cell phone and called her father. She told him to come quickly because it was happening again! "Oh no!" I thought. "What did I say wrong this time?" I tried to calm her down and talk some more but it was to no avail.

The next thing I remember was my husband and my older daughter showing up in the parking lot. She was visibly angry and began screaming expletives at me while shouting that she hated my guts and wished I was dead! She was clearly angry that I was jeopardizing her Jewish life and personal reputation. How could she explain this heresy to her new Orthodox Jewish friends? Her mommy speaks to God, God-forbid! Nonsense and she would have none of it.

"How could this be happening to me again?" I thought. I was just trying to be honest and explain what was really happening. I was simply telling the truth. Why wouldn't anyone listen to me? Daily I revealed these same things to other people in my life without any incident whatsoever. My closest Christian girlfriend with whom I spoke daily about everything was enthralled with my revelations from God and told me she completely believed me. Just one week earlier, she and I along with six other people enjoyed one of the most heartwarming Running on Love events I had ever organized. In this event called "Running on Love in Asbury Park" we had a team of eight people who were honoring someone they loved. We raised funds for four different charity beneficiaries and we each ran or walked a few miles of a relay marathon to complete the full 26.2-mile distance. Why was I viewed as an inspiration to this Asbury Park team but now a week later I am being told I am a lunatic? It was astounding and heartbreaking that my family reacted this way to me when all I desired to do was to speak honestly with them. They viciously screamed at me in the parking lot in a frightening and violent way.

My husband came over to me and grabbed my car keys out of my hand. He then called the police to have me arrested! "Holy smokes! Here we go again!" I thought. "This is a holy nightmare! He's calling the police to have me carted off again in front of my children just like on Mother's Day." But this time was different. I was completely calm and rational and wanted to talk to him about everything. In that moment, I pleaded with him to please go home with me instead of doing this again. I told him we should go home and I would make a pot of coffee and we could sit and talk calmly about everything I was experiencing and hearing. I pleaded for him not to repeat the horror again. My pleading was to no avail, and my heart-wrenching requests weren't heard. He would have none of it. The police arrived in the parking lot and told me that I could either come peacefully or they would handcuff me and drag me into their car. Completely gut-wrenching! Naturally I didn't want my children to see another spectacle so I went peacefully into the back of the police car.

Worst of the Worst—Trip to Hell Number 3

The police drove me to a hospital where the staff took all my clothes and put me in a dark holding room. I was there naked under my skimpy hospital gown for several hours waiting to speak to someone hoping to explain myself and get out of this situation. They told me they would be sending someone to interview me. I was confident if I explained in a calm manner what happened, they would listen to me and understand that this was all a huge mistake. I knew that I was someone who could hear spirit and God and not in the least bit mentally ill.

The interviewer came into the room and sat with me. As I sat calmly with him, I told him the story of my life and how I had been clairvoyant and received visits from another realm since early childhood. I said this was always going to happen to me because it's part of who I am. I explained my life story calmly and told him I could hear the voice of Hashem God and the spirit world. A reasonable explanation I thought and not crazy at all. When I was done speaking with him I thought to myself they would bring me my clothes and this nightmare would be over. I was so completely clueless!

They had no intention of letting me go home any time soon. They had my insurance card and my "victimized" husband sharing my journals and pleading with them to intervene because I had lost my mind. My husband did his usual ranting and raving that I was not the person they were seeing there that day. He convinced them I had a nervous breakdown and was so psychotic that he was frightened for the safety of our children. He carried my journals into the hospital. He had dog-eared several journal entries to illustrate and prove to the doctors that I was delusional and mentally ill. This was the method he used to have me committed on the other two occasions as well. He told everyone that I thought I was talking to God, that I thought I was Jesus and that this was all due to having a nervous breakdown from losing my hearing and going deaf.

Admittedly, I don't know the actual words he used on each occasion. This is a summary of what he had said to my face, written to me in a barrage of emails and text messages, and told many other people I know. He was very effective at convincing everyone that I was mentally ill and had completely lost my mind. There was no way he would consider that I could truly hear the world of spirit or speak to God Himself. He made it clear over the years that he hated any kind of observant Jewish life and had no belief in God at all. The mere idea of an invisible God or spirits who could talk to us scared the daylights out of him. He forcefully worked to convince the hospital workers and doctors that I had lost my mind and he pleaded for a medical intervention. His defense for doing all of this to me was that he was scared for our children and trying to protect them from harm. Wow! This was protecting our children? Locking me up repeatedly was incredibly harmful to the welfare of my three children. He waged an extremely convincing PR campaign to turn everyone against me. Armed with two previous involuntary mental hospital commitments in his portfolio, it wasn't difficult to do.

While stuck in this dark holding cell, they unknowingly left me with my BlackBerry cell phone that contained over 1000 contacts, both personal and professional. I began going through my entire cell phone address book because I thought there must be someone in this world who would help me. Somebody in my life had to believe me. I believed everybody in my life knew me as someone who was purely genuine, honest and loving. One of my oldest Jewish girlfriends whom I had known since I was 12 years old believed that I had a sixth sense since I was a small child. In my panicked state, I called her thinking she would surely come to my aid. I wasn't aware of what time of day or night it was when I called her for help and told her what was going on over these months. She was on vacation with her husband in Florida and I didn't realize it was the middle of the night. In my distress, I prayed she would somehow come to my rescue. Once again it was help that would never arrive. This was a girlfriend who told me throughout my life that she believed I had a sixth sense and frequently told me "I love you Lori." Well I thought, she loved me like a sister so she wouldn't turn on me, would she? She would believe everything I told her, wouldn't she? Not so. This friend would be one of many "friends" who would disappoint and desert me.

All she heard over the phone was her hysterical friend calling her from the inside of a mental hospital. She didn't hear the voice of genuine and truthful Lori who was being abused by her husband. As I ranted to her about my troubled marriage and admitted for the first time in many years that it was a complete sham she sounded stunned. I told her how much money we had in the bank but my husband refused to pay our bills on time and was driving us into deep debt. From the inside of this dark cell I was revealing many years of his abuses. I shared dirty laundry that I had never shared with anyone before. Over all the years of my marriage I protected my husband and never revealed his dark side to a soul. I didn't even share many of these ugly secrets with the psychotherapist who had provided marital therapy to us over the years. As I went on with my rant, I told her that he was the one who was mentally ill, not me, and I pleaded with her to get me help to get out of this situation. The sad reality was, I sounded irrational to her. She was scared, and didn't believe anything I was saying.

One of the things that I had learned at this point in my journey was that Hashem God was truly speaking to me and He insisted that I was the reincarnation of many glorious characters from the Bible. He also told me that I was the Moshiach. The Messiah. Was I supposed to keep this information to myself forever or was I supposed to share it? Everyone prays for the coming of Moshiach, the Messiah. Where the heck is the Messiah everyone wonders? Well at this point, "SHE" was locked up now for the third time in a mental hospital! "Oh no, she's crazy! Lori thinks she's the Messiah? Oh my God! She has lost her mind and she is a psychopath." That's what they all thought. I was not psychotic or hearing something delusional or having delusions of grandeur because I didn't view any of this as grand. Quite the contrary. This was a full-blown spiritual awakening orchestrated by Hashem God. The many things He was telling me from the first day, April 7, 2009, remain the same exact things He is telling me today.

My conversation with my childhood girlfriend ended and was completely fruitless. The next thing I knew they were escorting me by ambulance to another mental hospital facility. This would be the worst of the worst trips to hell, involuntary commitment number three. They called this place PICU. This abbreviation was for Psychiatric Intensive Care Unit. As I waited there to speak with someone, I had no idea how awful this was going to be. I was scratching my head and wondering, "What the heck just happened to me? Why is this happening again?" In my logical way of thinking I honestly and calmly told the truth and explained to everyone that this was a spiritual awakening and that I wasn't having a nervous breakdown. I asked myself, "Why am I still here and nobody is giving any credence to one word I'm saying?" Unbeknownst to me at that time my former husband was fueling the fire even further. It was going to get so dangerously bad in this third trip to hell that this facility began threatening to send me to a state mental hospital for long term confinement—Greystone Hospital, a state institution where they performed electroshock therapy. Greystone had a notoriously evil history, was known to be one the worst mental hospitals in New Jersey and was originally referred to as a "State Lunatic Asylum."

While I was there I kicked, screamed and fought to get out. I called everybody I knew in my BlackBerry address book which they had forgotten to take from me until the battery finally died. I even called former clients who I no longer did business with but who remained my dear friends. I was in business for over 25 years and many of my clients had become close friends. Some of them were even like family, many closer to me than my own family. I thought that if I told them what was happening to me they would believe me and come to my aid. Really? They would believe this was all a tragic mistake? Again, I had no idea how alone in the world I truly was and the many disappointments that were in store for me.

I even called my business attorney, someone I thought was my friend too. He would become one of the biggest betrayals in my entire life. This attorney, and so-called friend, would one day take my husband's case and oppose me in my own divorce. I eventually learned the hard way that I couldn't trust a soul. In these early years that followed my awakening, I still had no idea about the heartbreak that was in store. Ultimately, I would be deserted and betrayed by every person I had ever known.

My closest girlfriend, my Christian friend who spoke with me daily, the one who joined me for the Running on Love event in Asbury Park, deserted me once again. Earlier I explained how she abandoned me on that awful morning when I called her for help and she sniped at me in anger on the phone that I was being unfair to her. This time would be even worse. This time she rallied to help my family and give advice as to how to deal with their newly diagnosed mentally ill mother. In our daily talks she was captivated as I shared God's messages with her but suddenly, when I needed her support the most, she turned away and believed my husband's stories and sided with him. On this third trip to hell on earth, I was told she went to my home to meet my three children and husband, told them all not to worry, because she would guide them and advise them about what to do with me since she had direct personal experience in dealing with schizophrenics. Holy God! Really? She told my husband that she would take over now and help my family learn how to deal with their mentally ill psychotic mother. Are you kidding me? Yesterday I was sharing messages from God with her, but suddenly I'm schizophrenic and mentally ill? When I heard this about her I was completely devastated. One betrayal after another. Friends and family turned away and sided with my husband. Why wouldn't anyone I knew listen to me or believe anything I had to say?

Days before this trip to hell number three, I visited my mother and two brothers in South Jersey. They obliged me in my desire to eat kosher food and met me at a kosher meat restaurant close to their home. When they found out that I was locked up again in a mental hospital just a couple of days later, my husband told me that they were astonished. As far as they could see I was completely rational and normal at lunch. They couldn't detect that anything was wrong with me at all just a few days earlier. That's because nothing was wrong with me. I thought all of this could have been avoided if my husband had agreed to my request to go home and listen to me. I still couldn't comprehend that the solution wasn't that simple. He would never be willing to listen to one word I had to say if it had anything to do with God or Judaism. If he changed his opinion about me and believed anything I had to say, then he would have to assume blame for the problems in our home and marriage. He would have to admit guilt for having me committed two previous times. He would never allow any of that to happen.

As the days went on while I was in the PICU I learned what much of the public doesn't know or realize. The mental illness hospital system is egregiously evil. This mental hospital, like many others, didn't allow you to see the light of day. There were no outdoor areas where you could walk to get a breath of fresh air. Their idea of exercise was walking in circles around a closed corridor. To keep my sanity, I kept walking around in circles again and again doing laps. At the time, I was training to run in the Rehoboth Beach Marathon in Delaware for Running on Love so I needed some form of exercise. I viewed walking around in circles as helping me to stay in some sort of good physical shape. I recall looking down at my little brown slip-on shoes which they allowed me to keep because they didn't have shoelaces which I could use to strangle myself. As I gazed down at my little brown shoes I cried buckets of tears while I prayed to Hashem, and pleaded with Him to get me out of there! He advised me to rub my hands together vigorously to stay awake while being force-fed the drugs they pumped into my veins.

One day I called my rabbi on one of the limited phone calls I was permitted to make from this hospital. I told him that I could hear Hashem and that this was all a mistake because I was Hashem's Moshiach. I could hear him get nervous on the phone and mutter something about saying a prayer for me so that I should get well. He didn't believe me then, and perhaps he never will. Messiah is supposed to be a religious Jewish man who knows Torah inside and out. Here I was a Jewish mommy from New Jersey saying that I was the Messiah. At the time, I didn't blame anyone for not believing me. Now more than nine years later, I blame everyone. More than nine years later I still can't get people to listen to me or believe that I'm telling the truth. What will it take? Only Hashem knows.

Every day I was asked by the hospital workers in this unit, "Do you have any thoughts of harming anyone or yourself?"

My answer was always, "Of course not!" I wondered to myself, who was I going to hurt with Running on Love? Was I going to love you to death? Who was I going to hurt with my belief that I could hear the spirit world and God? Nobody asked me what God was specifically telling me. Nobody cared to know or ever entertained the idea that any of this could possibly be true. Most of the things that Hashem was telling me from the beginning are identical to what He still tells me now. He was telling me to wake everybody up because we are in terrible danger. He explained that Running on Love was the platform to gather us together and teach Torah and perform unconditional acts of love and kindness around the world. Does this sound like dangerous behavior to you? Does this sound like something that should be drugged out of you and stopped immediately? They certainly tried to stop me and gratefully they haven't yet.

While I was in this awful mental hospital I overheard the nurses and doctors joking one day. The hospital attendants were laughing at the patients. You read that correctly. They were jovial and making fun of the patients in this psychiatric unit. They changed the meaning of the abbreviation PICU which meant Psychiatric Intensive Care Unit to mean "Pee, I see you." You see, the psychological drugs they force-feed patients in enormous doses often cause patients to lose control of their bladders. Many of the patients wet themselves because they have no control over their bodily functions any longer. Funny, right? The hospital workers and nurses thought this was hilarious and were joking and laughing at their inside office joke, "Pee I see you! Ha ha ha ha!" They had a window from their office looking out at the patients where they would watch everyone and laugh as they looked to see who wet their pants. Isn't this uproariously funny to you too? Hopefully you agree this is despicable beyond words. As I continued to do laps around the corridor to keep my sanity, I could hear my father from the other side telling me in a very strong voice, "You let them laugh!" My father was furiously angry at seeing these workers belittle and laugh at the patients. Hashem and my dad both spoke to me to help build my confidence and let me know I was loved and supported. Their loving messages infused me with strength and helped keep me strong.

In another brief phone call that I was permitted to make while imprisoned, one of my children screamed and yelled at me in a condescending and derisive tone that I should just shut up and take their drugs. I couldn't believe my ears! Was this really one of my children speaking to me in such a deplorable and disrespectful way? I became enraged and screamed back with expletives. My children were being brainwashed by their father who effectively convinced everyone to rally to his side in sympathy. He portrayed himself as the "victim" who was saddled with a mentally ill wife. I hung up the phone and left the room still fuming when one of the healthcare attendants overheard my use of expletives. He told me that I better stop speaking like that right away. I was so heated that I yelled at him using even more choice expletives. In the next moment, this man grabbed me forcibly by my arms so I kicked him between his legs. Well, you can just imagine what happened next. I was carried off to the rubber room. The rubber room is where they put you in restraints and shoot you up with an unconscionable dose of psychological drugs.

Complying with any of their insanity just wasn't in my nature. I intended to fight them to the bitter end. You learn quickly that you must toe the line, talk their talk, or they will administer force. This happened twice to me in this facility. On the second occasion, a female nurse began stroking my hair as I was lying restrained on a gurney. She was sweetly whispering into my ear pretending as though she was compassionate and loving. It was clearly a complete performance for her coworkers. My stomach began flipping and twisting in knots at the sound of her phoniness and feeling her filthy touch. So much so that I became nauseated and felt I would vomit right in her face. To this day, I remember her vividly and I don't have harsh enough language to describe her and all the employees who worked in this disgraceful facility.

While in the rubber room, they shot me up with such a large dose of their powerful drugs that when I was released from the room I couldn't help but bounce into the walls as I tried to walk. I was so drugged I couldn't see straight. After the second time they forcibly drugged me I became so sick that I was certain I would die that night. I was short of breath, gasping for air, and my heart was racing and palpitating. I felt like my blood was boiling from the inside out. It's a feeling that I can't describe adequately in words but just know I was incredibly sick and deeply frightened that I wouldn't survive the night. They were determined to force me to speak their language and drug God's voice out of me. I kept refusing to tell them what they demanded to hear—that I didn't hear God any longer. Gratefully His voice never left me, not once. As I cried in fear that I was going to die that night, Hashem comforted me with His strong soothing melodic voice. His voice is strong, calming and unmistakable. He said, "I love you baby. You're going to get through this. You will not die here and I will never leave you."

He instructed me to go into a private bathroom that was adjacent to my hospital room. In this bathroom He told me to take off all my clothes and lie down on the cold tile floor naked to help me cool down. It felt like I had an extremely high fever. I also had great difficulty breathing. While I was lying there naked on the filthy hospital bathroom floor crying, Hashem soothed me with His voice and told me how much He loved me. He told me He would get me through this and promised me that one day I would tell my story to the world and everyone would finally listen.

The next morning, I requested information about the drug they shot into me the night before. I read that they injected me with a powerful dose of a drug that had significant cardiac side effects. While in their care, they checked my vitals, and told me I had high blood pressure. The drug they infused into my veins had a contraindication for high blood pressure. Were they even concerned about side effects? Would a crew of mental hospital workers who mocked their patients in a hilarious joke of "Pee I See You" even care if I died? Not likely. The hospital might care if a wrongful death affected them financially. You know, liability and litigation. Otherwise, it was explicitly clear, no one in this facility had compassion for or cared about any of the patients.

About a week into my incarceration in this awful place they called a hospital, a nurse pulled me aside to give me a TB test. One of the patients I had become friendly with saw them do this to me. She immediately came over to me and was visibly upset. She pulled me aside to speak with me privately and asked, "Lori, what did they just do to you?"

I said, "They gave me a TB test, why do you ask? Don't they give everybody a TB test?"

She said, "No Lori. They're getting ready to send you to Greystone! You've got to talk their talk and tell them what they want to hear now. You have got to lie to them. Tell them what they want to hear or you will never get out. You've got to tell them you don't hear God anymore. Please tell them!"

I was horrified. Would they really do this to me? This was becoming more and more like the movie *One Flew Over the Cuckoo's Nest*. If I didn't tell them what they wanted to hear, would they give me a lobotomy like the character played by Jack Nicholson? Wow! I found out just after my release from this hideous excuse for a hospital, that they were preparing to send me to Greystone for long-term confinement. Greystone was a state mental hospital with a notoriously bad reputation and was scheduled to be demolished. We saw one female patient admitted to our unit who had just received electroshock therapy at Greystone. It was completely impossible to have a coherent conversation with her and it was apparent to us all that her mind was totally fried. She had a vacant look in her eyes and couldn't hold a normal conversation with anyone. Their drugs never took away Hashem God's voice from me. If I didn't lie and tell them I didn't hear God any longer was this their plan for me too? Would they send me to Greystone and electroshock my brain until they destroyed me? Even electroshock therapy wouldn't remove God from my soul or remove His voice from me. I was so grateful to my new friend for her stark warning and knew that I needed to lie. In that moment, I learned how to conceal the truth.

As the psychiatrist in charge of my case asked me questions, I said things like, "I only hear my own thoughts. I guess your drugs are working on me." These words were tolerable to me because I could extrapolate that I was still being somewhat truthful. I do hear my own thoughts and my thoughts include God in all of them. Using the terminology "I guess" gave me an out that I was guessing and not lying. Why would this matter so much to me when my life depended on me lying? Because being honest and having integrity means the world to me. It was distressing and deeply difficult for me to accept that I had to lie to save my own life.

Before I was freed from this mental health prison, I was forced to sit before a mental hospital tribunal and appear before a judge. They forced me to plead my case to get out of this insane asylum. Fortunately, prior to this appearance before the judge, the doctor recommended discharge within a few days. If the doctor hadn't done this, I don't want to even think about what would have happened to me. He had full say-so about my future. I had no power or personal rights any longer. It truly didn't matter what I said from the time I was picked up by the police. My life and my ability to make any decisions about my own welfare were stripped from me.

Eventually, I left this horrible place but the nightmare followed me home. Adding insult to injury, the hospital social workers reported me to DYFS, The Department of Youth and Family Services. They issued a restraining order against me which said that I wasn't permitted to be with my minor children without supervision. They claimed that because I was in the car with my child when my husband called the police to have me arrested, I was considered a danger to my kids. Suddenly I was branded an abusive mother and a danger to my own children. Of all the things that happened to me, this might have been the worst. There is nothing in this world that I love more than my children. In one moment, they painted me an unfit mother. They had plenty of help from my husband branding me a bad mother. He was beating the drum of mental illness and launching an effective PR campaign that Lori is psychotic, bipolar, and schizophrenic all at the same time. He portrayed himself as the pitiful victimized husband who had to cope with his mentally ill wife. He not only convinced family of this, he convinced my children and everyone who knew us. These lies, accusations and name-calling were just the beginning of my heartbreaking battle to save my life.

Although I was extremely angry with my husband, when I came home I went right to work once again to pick up the pieces of my shattered life. For the third time, I went to the same psychiatrist who had treated me after the previous two involuntary mental hospital commitments. When you're discharged, you must agree to be under the care of a psychiatrist. I asked her once again to wean me off these horrible drugs. She did as I requested. You might be wondering why in the world would a licensed psychiatrist agree to wean me off these drugs three times in a row? I will tell you why. Speaking with me in her office she never saw any signs of bipolar disorder, psychosis or mental illness. The whole situation was completely disconcerting and deeply confusing to her. If I was so mentally ill why couldn't she detect any form of mental illness in me whatsoever? Why was this happening to me repeatedly? It was clear during our visits when she spoke with me that I wasn't mentally ill. She believed me and trusted my explanation for a third time and helped me wean off these diabolical anti-psychotic drugs slowly and safely.

Why didn't I leave my husband after putting me through a third trip to mental hospital hell? I had only one reason. I stayed for my three children. All three of them were suffering deeply and I couldn't bear to leave them. I also couldn't prove to anyone in the world that I wasn't the one who was destroying our family. My husband had all the cards stacked in his favor and squarely against me. I was the one with the three-time history of involuntary mental hospital commitments, not him. In this third trip to hell, they even placed a restraining order against me where I couldn't be alone with my own children. What was I to do? Where was I to go, and keep my children? If I left the home, I had to leave my children behind with my abusive husband. It should have been painfully clear for years that I was the victim of marital abuse but my eyes were still shut tightly closed. Me, a college grad and successful business woman, a victim of spousal abuse? I wasn't ready to face that truth. I had no proof and no friends or family to help me. In retrospect, I was deeply blessed to have a doctor who believed that I wasn't mentally ill and weaned me off these drugs after three involuntary mental hospital commitments. This psychiatrist and a few others I met along the way gave me hope that there were intelligent and respectable mental health physicians in our world.

For the Record, I am Not the Crazy One

I want to protect my children's privacy and won't discuss the extent of their personal suffering due to my repeated involuntary mental hospital commitments. To sum it up briefly, having once enjoyed a happy all-American family life, they were now forced to live through the surreal and tragic nightmare of people working to convince them that their mother was incurably psychotic. It would only be natural for each of them to show signs of stress, anxiety and depression. Wouldn't you? Because of the incredible stress they endured in our home over these years of abuse, all three of my children were treated by various psychologists and psychiatrists. When they received evaluations, inevitably these so-called "mental health professionals" schooled them to believe that their mother's mental illness was hereditary. Not only were they suffering from living through this nightmare, now they had the added attraction of being told they would each likely inherit the gene for this mental illness too.

All my children were advised separately by different physicians that bipolar disorder and many mental illnesses are genetic. It's biological. If your mother has it, you're doomed to get it too. These doctors prepare you for the inevitable and explain that if mom or dad is bipolar you are a ticking time bomb who will one day suffer from a mental illness. The plot sickens as they explain that these mental illnesses are incurable and require medication to control the symptoms for the rest of your life. It's a life sentence. Their explanations and treatment of all mental disorders were completely void of the existence of God. The only answer given was a steady diet of expensive psychological drugs coupled with costly visits to their offices for counseling. It became explicitly clear that becoming a mental health professional was an extremely lucrative career choice and recession-proof to boot. I wondered, "Where are the thinking doctors? Are there any doctors or psychiatrists willing to go against this evil tide?"

This is the kind of information that nobody wants aired in public. So why am I doing this? I'm doing this for the same reason that I didn't leave my home after trip into hell number three. I'm doing this to save my children and future grandchildren. God willing, I will save you and your children with this information. Only Hashem knows what the outcome will ultimately be from this book. I am morally obligated and must reveal the sordid details of what happened to me and my family because the world needs to wake up and see that our society is deeply sick and in grave danger. It may sound like I despise my former husband and every mental health professional in the world, but that's emphatically untrue. My former husband and far too many physicians who are involved in overmedicating and wrongfully diagnosing patients are ignorant and deeply sick. My husband worked feverishly to convince everyone who knew us that I was psychotic, bipolar, and schizophrenic all at the same time. Armed with a written record of involuntary psychiatric commitments, he told everyone who had any involvement with my family that I was incurably mentally ill. I've been told he continues to spread these lies about me to this day. The truth be known, I was never diagnosed with schizophrenia. He added this terminology to embellish his story so that it sounded even more dramatic and would evoke sympathy from anyone who listened.

From the very beginning of my tragic tale, it was everyone else who was crazy, not me. This is a wake-up call to humanity. My former husband and all the players in this evil game of diagnose first, ask questions later, have no idea how dangerous their behavior and beliefs are to everyone in the world. These repeated mental hospital commitments had not only taken a hideous toll on me spiritually and physically, they were psychologically damaging to all three of my children. Through the grace of God, all three of them pulled themselves away from the secular mental health system and now lead healthy and God-driven lives as orthodox Torah-observant Jews. Each one of them likely has a best-selling book of their own to write one day. I pray that in the future each one of them finds the courage to step up and share their life lessons with the world.

The disintegration of our model American family life was deeply painful in unspeakable ways. Sharing my story with the world is my moral obligation because this information has the power to heal my children of the horrible memories from this time period while it serves to save many lives. My children suffered a type of grief which was tantamount to experiencing the death and loss of their mother while she was still alive. It's now time for me to reveal what truly happened during these turbulent years and set the record straight.

Lighting the Path with Torah

After three involuntary commitments, I stayed in this dysfunctional marital relationship and chose not to leave my home, yet. I went forward with my life as best I could. I continued to encourage my children to stay on the path of Torah observance. I knew the answers to our troubles were in the Torah and following a God-driven life. My youngest child was struggling with her emotions so I signed her up to go to a religious Jewish girls' sleep-away camp. When she returned home a few weeks later, she kept a washing cup by her bed. She was taught to observe the mitzvah, commandment, of washing her hands in the morning after she woke. As I mentioned earlier washing hands in the morning is a spiritual protection taught by observant Orthodox Jews. She also began wearing a long skirt and wanted to dress modestly. One day my husband angrily entered her bedroom, threw the water cup away from her bed and screamed at her, "I'm sick of this Jewish shit!" He then walked over to her closet and told her that her new long skirts were ugly and he didn't want her dressing like that anymore.

I had many arguments with him about Judaism. He cursed me regularly and told me, "I didn't marry any Orthodox Jew." He would then say, "You changed the deal and it's not fair. I want the Lori who eats pepperoni pizza and I want you to forget about all this Jewish shit!"

Through all the rancor and arguing I kept moving forward. I continued to hide my conversations with Hashem by typing them on my computer and deleting them when I was done. I became increasingly quiet at home and barely spoke at the dinner table. In her despair over the third hospital commitment, my oldest daughter wrote me a beautiful song called "Listen." In this song, she promised me that one day I would be heard and that the world would listen to me. I took her to my sound studio once again to have this song professionally recorded. Over the years this song has given me hope and inspiration, helping me to stay strong.

My oldest daughter was a freshman at JTS, The Jewish Theological Seminary, with secular studies at Columbia. JTS is part of the Conservative Jewish movement. She was disturbed by how many of the students were engaging in illegal drug use and deviant behaviors. Now because of what was happening with me, her entire family at home was being turned inside out and backwards. Just as she began questioning her belief in God and Judaism, Aish, an Orthodox Jewish organization, offered to send her on a fully paid six-week trip to Israel. This turned out to be a life changing trip and one of many clear gifts from Hashem guiding my children toward a Torah observant life. After she was in Israel for just one week she called home and told me, "I'm not returning to college in America. Once you know the truth there's no turning back. JTS is teaching that the Torah was written by man, and not by God and that's a lie. The Torah is from Hashem and I will not listen to their lies anymore. I want to study in Israel."

In another phone call with my daughter while she was in Israel, she recommended that I buy a book called *The Garden of Emuna*. This book was written by Rabbi Shalom Arush from Israel and it discusses in detail the importance of having full faith in God. *Emuna* is the Hebrew word for faith. I read this book and found it so inspirational, I read it three times over. After her six-week trip, my daughter came home to pack her things and prepare to return to Israel for the next year. My son was on a similar journey as my oldest daughter. He was learning Torah and loving the observant Jewish way of life. My daughter was nurturing him and teaching him about Hashem. Her flight back to Israel was on a Sunday after Shabbos. That Saturday evening, I was feeling melancholy about my life and wondered where all this chaos was leading me.

My children sat together across from me in the dining room to light the Havdalah candle, which is a customary tradition to end Shabbat. In this candle lighting ceremony, we end Shabbos by saying prayers and singing songs. As siblings, they had created their own Havdalah tradition of draping themselves in the flag of Israel while they sang songs and lit the candle. As I looked across the table, I saw my three children all draped in the flag of Israel singing the Jewish national anthem, Hatikvah. In that moment, I knew the reason why Hashem brought about the chaos and horrors that unfolded in our family—to save my children. On April 7, 2009, the day He woke me to His voice, we didn't even have a Passover Seder because it was too inconvenient. As I watched my three children sing Hatikvah I saw the beauty of Hashem's miracle which He brought through me. If nothing else good came from my troubles, I felt this was the blessing of a lifetime. I watched in awe and cried tears of joy, thanking Hashem for bringing my children back to Him, the truth, and Judaism.

While the sight of my three children singing under the Israeli flag brought me profound joy, my husband wasn't happy or grateful at all. He wasn't on board with any conversations about God or Torah. He became increasingly angry about everything. One Friday evening as I was lighting the Shabbos candles he came into the dining room and verbally taunted me. In a sarcastic and demeaning voice, he railed, "Ooga Booga, oh no you're talking to God. Oh please, I'm so scared!"

At the dinner table on Friday evenings when my son said Kiddush, the prayer over the wine, or the Motzi, the prayer over the bread, my husband stood at the end of the dining room table visibly angry and rolled his eyes up into his head to show his disgust. It was extremely uncomfortable to have a Shabbos meal with him at the table. Despite his father's anger, my son showed an increasing desire to learn and observe Torah. Just prior to his junior year of high school, he took a six-week trip to Israel with USY. While in Israel the trip affected him so deeply that he called me before returning home with a warning. He said, "Mom, I'm calling to warn you that when I get home I will not remove my kippah (the skull cap that observant Jewish men wear). I'm also wearing tzitzit (a man's religious undergarment with strings—remember my secret wish?) and I will not remove that either. Dad will probably be very angry with me so I'm just calling to warn you. I feel very strongly about this and I won't change my mind."

I told my son on the phone that I supported him fully. He came home that August and as promised he kept wearing his kippah. For days on end my husband berated him and yelled, "Take that ugly rug off your head! You don't need to wear an ugly rug on your head to advertise that you're Jewish." My son didn't flinch. He simply refused to listen to his father. The night before school started that September my husband came into our bedroom and said, "You need to do something and intervene right now. He's going to school tomorrow wearing that yarmulke and he looks like an idiot. They're going to beat him up. He doesn't need to advertise that he's Jewish."

We lived in an affluent secular neighborhood in New Jersey and my son was attending a non-Jewish public high school. The high school was known to have a rough crowd of kids. When my husband came to me upset and asked me to get our son to stop wearing his kippah, I thought that maybe his concerns about anti-Semitism might be warranted. My son was soft-spoken and not a fighter so I thought perhaps there could be a safety issue. I decided to go into his bedroom and discuss it with him. I said, "Your father is worried about you wearing a kippah tomorrow to school. Can you wear a baseball cap over it and it will mean the same thing?"

He responded, "Better I should know someone doesn't like me because I'm a Jew to my face than behind my back."

Amazing I thought! What a great answer. And then I replied, "Why do you feel compelled to wear a kippah to school tomorrow?"

He answered, "Because when I walk through the halls of school and I'm stressed out about my day, all I have to do is put my hand on top of my head and remember that everything I see is not all that there is."

I said, "I love you son. I'm very proud of you. Have a wonderful day at school tomorrow." The concerns of him being teased or beaten up were unfounded. He received a few wisecracks from some of the tougher kids saying to him "Shalom dude," and that was the beginning and end of the taunting.

My son began to put on Tefillin every day. In his senior year of high school, he went daily to pray at the local Orthodox Jewish synagogue before school started. Secular Jewish boys usually don't take this journey. They walk away from anything Jewish after their Bar Mitzvah. This was clearly another supreme blessing from God.

The nightmare was far from over as our home life continued to unravel. My youngest child was struggling emotionally and was torn between choosing my husband who was antagonistic toward anything Jewish and me, the new Jewish pied piper. I was encouraging her to reach for God and Torah, and he was pulling her in the opposite direction. He was blaming me, religion and Judaism for everything that was going wrong in our household. As my son became more Torah observant, my husband screamed at him more than once,

"Go let the fucking rabbi be your father." My husband screamed at my son so viciously about his Jewish observance that my son was often reduced to tears. My Chabad rabbi confided in me that our son had met with him privately and asked his opinion about what he should do. Should he listen to his father and obey the commandment—honor thy father, or continue reaching for the Torah? The rabbi told our son that the commandment to honor thy father never supersedes honoring Hashem. I was deeply grateful for the rabbi's thoughtful advice to my son and his help in keeping him on the right path.

4th and Final Trip to Hell

In the winter of 2012 I organized my biggest New Jersey Marathon team yet for Running on Love. We had about a dozen people running that year and I had a volunteer coach helping everyone train for this event. I was getting excited and happy with my work for this beautiful budding charity. My marketing company had all but died at this point. I was completely uninterested in working with my husband at all. The idea of doing any work for my marketing company sickened me and I wanted nothing to do with it. My husband was increasingly angry and verbally threatened me all the time. He looked at the Running on Love website to read what the participants were writing on their personal website fundraising pages. Many of them mentioned God in their writing and he told me that they all spooked him. He threatened that if he found out that Running on Love had anything to do with God he would make me quit my charity immediately and force me to go get a job that made real money.

During this time my youngest child was suffering the most of my three children in the aftermath of my three forced hospitalizations. She was deeply affected by the intense anger and fighting in our home and it was taking a severe toll on her. Everything also started to take a toll on me physically and I began experiencing chest pain and heart palpitations. I scheduled a stress test appointment with a cardiologist because of these cardiac symptoms. My stomach was so upset the night before my stress test that I was up retching and vomiting all night. By the next morning, I was completely dehydrated and felt sick but I didn't want to miss my appointment for the stress test because I was concerned about the chest pain. I asked my husband to drive me to my appointment because I was too sick to drive. On the way, I was still so nauseated that I asked him to pull over and I threw up on the side of the road. When I got back inside the car he asked, "Are you sure you want to do this test today because you're so sick?" Just as he asked this question my arms and legs went completely numb. I didn't know what a heart attack felt like but I thought that numbness was a bad sign. In a panic, I told him to drive me to the hospital right away which was down the block. He took me to the ER which was very crowded that day.

I was wearing my exercise clothes, and looked to be in good physical shape. I was dressed in these clothes because I was going to the cardiologist for a stress test. The nurse looked at me and told me to sit in the waiting room even after I told her I was having chest pains and numbness in my arms and legs. When she dismissed me, didn't examine me, and told me to wait, I became infuriated. It was clear she wasn't listening to my concerns. My husband wanted me to sit quietly and not make any waves which upset me further. Apparently by looking at me the nurse decided I didn't have anything wrong with my heart. Perhaps my husband thought the same thing. Nobody was giving me any attention or even bothering to take my blood pressure. They barely spoke to me about my concerns or symptoms. In a very loud and angry voice I said to the nurse, "Why aren't you attending to me? I told you that I'm frightened and think I'm having a heart attack!"

They quickly took me inside and finally took my blood pressure so I calmed down. My husband was looking at me with a feeble expression on his face and then said, "I'm worried Lori. Something's wrong again." The expression on his face looked like he was playacting as someone who was interested in my welfare and best interest. It had become painfully clear by this time that his primary concern wasn't about my welfare at all. Expressing that he was worried that something was wrong or that it was happening again were his new code words for, "I'm going to make sure they lock you up in a psych ward again and have you forcibly drugged against your will!"

At this point in our relationship, I was beyond my limit and had no more patience for him. I replied sternly, "Nothing's wrong with me. If this was Israel they would have a real medical staff who would attend to me. They judged me by my appearance and didn't even give me a second look. Now that they're listening to me, I'm fine."

They took me inside the ER, gave me intravenous fluids, and discovered that I was extremely dehydrated from vomiting all night. I sat there quietly and calmly as I received the intravenous and began to feel much better. They explained that the numbness and tingling was due to a panic attack, something I'd never experienced before. They took an EKG and told me my heart was fine. Now that I understood it was dehydration and nerves, I thought I would just go home. Not so fast. I watched in horror as I saw my husband bend the ear of one of the ER doctors. He was clearly telling him I had a history of mental illness and he was worried it was "happening again." This hospital ER was in the same hospital as trip to hell number two. The ER doctor could easily look at their computer to see this information and become concerned as my husband set off the alarm bells. The doctor came over to my bedside in the ER with my husband hovering behind him anxiously. The doctor said, "Your husband is very worried about you. We want to take you into the mental health ward of the hospital and admit you for observation."

I thought, "Are you kidding me? My husband didn't have enough with the three trips to hell? He wants to orchestrate a fourth trip for me?" I wondered if he was he trying to kill me. In that moment, I gave my husband the death stare. I said to the doctor, "There's absolutely nothing wrong with me, I was panicking and dehydrated. I'm fine now and I want to go home."

The doctor replied, "Well your husband is very worried about you and you were very upset in the waiting area. I think it would be best that we take you in for a few days and put you under observation." What he didn't say to me was that my husband chewed his ear off and told him that I was bipolar, schizophrenic and psychotic. A complete lie of course, but he had the documentation to support his claims and I had no power to refute him.

I looked at my husband, and I said in a very stern voice, "I want to go home now." The doctor looked at my husband for his approval to let me go.

Then the doctor said something that made me realize I was in a fight to save my very life. He said, "If your husband will sign your release papers, I will let you go home." In that moment, I knew without any doubt my nightmare would never end so long as I stayed married to this demon who called himself my husband. I glared at my husband with a look that could kill and told him to sign the papers and let me go home. He did, and after I was released we went home and I said absolutely nothing to him. In the morning, I planned to pack some belongings and leave him. I couldn't put my children through another hospitalization nightmare. I didn't believe I would live through another forced psychiatric commitment and being drugged against my will.

The next morning I packed some belongings, took my brand-new SUV and left. Where was I going? I didn't have a plan. I just needed to get away from him. I was on the run for two weeks feverishly trying to figure out how to get away from him and save my life. If I stayed with him, he would certainly destroy me. He controlled everything including all the money. I had virtually no personal power over my own life. I couldn't get money or any of my own personal documents. When I left, I didn't even know where he kept my passport or birth certificate. While I was on the run he traced all my credit card transactions to track me down. He sent me extremely threatening and taunting emails telling me that he would have me locked up for good this time after he had me arrested.

After two weeks of running, I decided the only thing I could do to save myself was to try to get to Israel. America kept me prisoner in a cycle of violence and I thought perhaps in a country like Israel where people believed in God I might be treated differently. I was willing to go anywhere in the world to find safety and to get away from my abusive husband. Since he had all my important life documents which included my passport, I decided to try to go to the airport to see if I could convince the El Al attendants to let me on a flight with just a New Jersey photo driver's license. I thought maybe if I told them I was an abused Jewish woman running away from my demonic controlling husband, maybe they would help me. This was wishful thinking at best. Naturally they wouldn't allow anyone on a flight without a passport but I was so desperate to get away from my husband that I was willing to try anything. What may sound like irrational behavior was my last-ditch effort to get myself to safety. Remember, I had no sympathetic friends, family or support system now. I was alone in this world, running for my life.

Without realizing, over all these years, I allowed myself to become a virtual slave and maidservant to my former husband. I had no power or say in my own medical care and I had no ability to leave the country or go anywhere without his express permission. I told El Al that I was an abused wife and that my husband was trying to harm me. I explained that I needed to get to Israel to be with my oldest child and would board the flight with only the clothes on my back to show them I wasn't a risk to anyone. Of course, their answer was no. From the airport, I even called the Rachel Coalition which is a Jewish organization for abused women. The only thing I got from them was a recorded message. The messages I left asking for help were never returned. It was painfully clear that there was no help for me anywhere in this world.

While I was in the airport at the El Al departure area, I was completely distressed knowing that he was chasing me and trying to have me locked up again. I called my daughter in Israel from my cell phone and she screamed at me to go home. I still hadn't faced the truth that none of my family supported me and that they were convinced by my husband that I was the source of all the trouble. In my despair, she sided with my husband and wanted no part of me. I was so stressed and upset while I was on the phone with her that she convinced me to hand my cell phone over to the Port Authority police who were nearby. I handed them my phone without knowing what she would say to them. I found out later she told them to arrest me because I was mentally ill!

Just as I handed my phone over to the police, Hashem told me to get down on my knees and face east to pray to Him. I replied to Him, "Why Hashem? You're right here with me. Why do I need to do this?"

He said, "You need to do this right now Lori."

I said, "Hashem, but if I do this they're going to think I'm crazy and they're going to arrest me. I will die if they do this to me again!"

He said, "Lori if they arrest you I'll take you out of your body and they will have nothing but your corpse. You must do this right now."

I asked a Muslim man who was standing nearby to show me which direction was east. As Hashem instructed, I went over to the wall, faced east, and knelt to pray to Him. As I was kneeling and talking to Hashem, I said, "Why am I doing this if You're right here?"

Hashem said in a soothing voice, "It's going to be okay Lori. You need to do this." Just then the Port Authority police grabbed me and handcuffed me. As I struggled with them, a woman police officer viciously began to hit me while she cursed me. They arrested me in the airport and carted me off to my fourth trip to hell on earth. Hashem knew that the only way out of my hell was to go straight through the fire once again.

They put me in a holding area in an inner-city hospital mental ward. This would be the last of the four involuntary psychiatric commitments. It took four trips to hell to finally understand that my husband's diabolical behavior of controlling me through repeated hospitalizations, controlling our money, and manipulating everybody's opinion of me needed to end. His evil behavior was destroying my children and killing me. As I was in this holding pen, I refused to take any medications and I refused to say anything they wanted to hear. This time I wasn't willing to relent even if it meant the end of my life. I decided that this time I was going to tell the truth and never back down.

There was a window in the front office door of this mental ward where the so-called healthcare workers and attendants worked. They had staff with the lofty title of patient advocate. I recall a large and extremely obese woman with a pretty face was designated to be my patient advocate. I walked over to the glass window of their office and observed her in a conversation with her coworkers. She was making lewd and disgusting facial gestures with her mouth and sticking out her tongue. She was sticking her tongue out as though she had no control over her bodily functions. You see another horrible side effect some patients experience when they are forcibly injected with massive doses of psychological drugs is that they lose control of their tongues and saliva. This large and pretty woman, a so-called patient advocate, was mimicking and mocking the mental patients in this facility to all her coworkers. She and her associates were uproariously laughing at her imitation of the mental patients in their care. Hashem says one day it will be my duty to call these people out by their names in a public forum and give them a tongue lashing. These evil people who pose as mental health professionals and patient advocates deserve the humiliation of a verbal public flogging.

While in this inner-city hospital, I was put in a private room with a television. Prior to each of the four trips to mental hospital hell, Hashem told me He would restore my hearing. This time was no different. Each time I was certain that my hearing was improving and on this occasion, I could hear without the help of my two digital hearing aids. Was this an illusion? I really don't know and I have no physical proof that my hearing ever improved. What I can share with you now is that while I sat in this room and watched a situation comedy, I heard every single syllable and every spoken word. I hadn't watched TV or laughed at a comedy show for many years because I couldn't hear any of the punch lines. As I sat and watched this program I heard every single punch line and cried tears of joy, not because the program was funny or made me happy. I cried because I could hear. How was it possible for me to hear every single word?

My husband came into my room at one point to visit with me. There was a loud and noisy fan in the room. Even with all the loud noise from this fan, I heard every word he said without the help of any hearing aids. As I spoke with him, my ability to hear every spoken word visibly startled him. I remember he said, "How can you hear me? I can't even hear! Why are you able to hear me so well?" After each hospitalization, my ability to hear eventually left me again and it was clear that my deafness returned. There is no clinical proof that my hearing was restored for those brief periods. It was my own personal validation that God was with me and He did this for my recognition alone.

They gave me a choice of which mental hospital I would go to for my fourth and final involuntary commitment. Since I had been locked up three previous times, they thought they would be kind to me and let me choose. Lovely. In other words, which trip to hell would you like to take this time? I picked the facility from my first incarceration because I thought it was the most benign of the three. The truth be known, none of these facilities are benign but some are much worse than others.

When I arrived at this facility, all my clothes had been taken from me and I was naked underneath a skimpy hospital gown. As I waited to be admitted,

I observed an elderly woman in a walker being manhandled by the hospital workers. She was cursing them and screaming out in pain. The sight of this incensed me and I couldn't bear to see her mistreated or abused like this. I yelled at them to leave her alone and stop hurting her. Bad move. The attendants descended upon me and told me to calm down. As one of them grabbed me forcefully by the arm it flung my hospital gown up in the air which revealed my naked buttocks, among my other private parts, to everyone in the room. One of the other patients standing there rudely rolled her eyes to show me she was annoyed by the sight. She yelled at me to cover up as though it was my choice to show everyone my naked body. I looked at her angrily and yelled at her, "What's the matter with you? Do I have something you've never seen before?" With that I defiantly lifted my entire gown and flashed her my nakedness in visceral anger. Well, that did it! Four or five people, mostly men carried me off to a room, held me down on a bed, and shot me up with Thorazine.

I was still conscious but groggy when one of the nurses came over to me and said, "I need to check you."

I responded, "What do you mean you need to check me?"

She said, "You need to take off your gown and bend over so that I can look up your rectum." I looked at her in shock and disbelief.

I said furiously, "Are you kidding me? What do you think I have up my rectum?"

She said, "You need to do this or I will get help and make you do it." I was horrified beyond belief. Of all the indignities, this was adding insult to injury. After this repulsive incident, there would be no more drugs forcibly shot into my body, ever again. In this lockup it would become clearer to the powers that be that I wasn't truly mentally ill at all. Perhaps this was the reason why they refrained from coercing me to take their diabolical drugs in this commitment. Hashem is behind everything so it was more likely that He decided it was time to end some of my pain.

Hours later, I met with the lead doctor who also happened to be the director of this mental hospital. He sat with me in his office and spoke with me for a while. He suddenly looked up at me with a quizzical look on his face and asked, "Why are you here?"

I replied, "I talk to God and He gives me answers."

He answered, "There isn't anything wrong with that. That's not mental illness. There are many religious people who believe they hear the voice of God. Why are you here? It's clear there is nothing wrong with you."

I responded, "I hear people who have died on the other side and I can speak with them."

He said, "The Barnes & Noble and other bookstores have shelves lined with books that document other people who say they can do this too. Again, that doesn't mean you're mentally ill. Why are you here?"

This conversation gave me new hope for the first time that perhaps there was an intelligent person in the psychiatric profession who would let me go home. I continued to answer his questions, "My husband doesn't believe me and thinks I'm psychotic. I need a divorce."

He said, "You don't seem ill to me at all but I'm puzzled why this is the fourth time this has happened. Why are you here four times?"

I responded, "I need a divorce." I wondered what his reply would be now. Would he let me go home and believe me?

After this meeting, I was committed for eight days in this facility despite the director's recognition on the first day that there was nothing wrong with me. Again, I watched other patients brought into this same facility with their wrists bandaged because they had sliced them open in failed suicide attempts. When the facility discovered that they didn't have health insurance, within a day or two they were escorted out. It was clear that they had no money to pay the hospital bill. For me, I wasn't that fortunate. I had full coverage and great medical benefits that they could bilk.

My closest girlfriend, the one who I told you believed I could speak with God, had heartbreakingly turned against me and sided with my husband in all three previous hospital commitments. We repaired the heartbreak each time and remained dear friends nonetheless. Gratefully this time, number four, she stood by me. For the first time, she didn't walk away and side with my husband. Instead when I called her from the hospital, she sounded extremely distraught. She said, "Oh no not again! I'll try my best to help you and make some phone calls." I was so grateful to her for not turning away like she did the other three times. Whether she could help me or not didn't even matter. It was a blessing to finally have a friend who stood by me and didn't turn away.

I called a lawyer whom I had met through a networking group and he told me the only way that I could possibly get out was to cancel my hospitalization. If I had no way of paying they would likely release me. How was I supposed to do that from the inside of a mental hospital when my husband controlled everything? It would never come to pass because I couldn't cancel my hospitalization. It was wishful thinking that there was a way to end the madness and escape from this insane asylum easily. Instead I did my best to pass the time in my final trip to hell on earth, involuntary mental hospital commitment number four.

As I waited for my freedom, I passed the time away by fantasizing about how wonderful it would be to leave my husband as soon as I was released from this awful place. The hours passed slowly as I visualized my new home with a kosher kitchen after I was freed. When I got out of the hospital I was certain that I would leave my abusive husband who was harming my children and determined to kill me. I began combing through magazines and cutting out recipes that I planned to cook once I left him and moved into the safety of my new kosher home. It made me so happy to believe I'd finally be free to make myself a Jewish home with a kosher kitchen where I could prepare large Shabbos meals and celebrate the Sabbath with impunity. As I made friends during my stay in this trip to hell number four, I collected their phone numbers and told them they were invited to come for a delicious meal in my new home once I was freed.

Every time my husband had me committed, he showed up at visiting time looking guilt-ridden, sheepishly offering to bring me kosher food and anything I desired. I asked him to bring kosher meals along with a supply of Running on Love T-shirts, bracelets, and my music CDs. I gave these shirts and bracelets to everyone as gifts and played music when they gave us free time. As I played a variety of music for everyone I encouraged them to dance and sing with me to lift everyone's spirit. I was the mental hospital cheerleader for all the patients who were being treated like something less than human. It was commonplace for the hospital staff, some of whom were half my age, to speak down to me in a demeaning and condescending way as though I was a stupid child. These young hospital workers were placed in positions of authority and I was their lowly mentally ill prisoner. This authority went to many of their heads as they acted extremely pompous and behaved as though they were superior to all the patients.

I remember a sweet young 18-year-old boy who was admitted to this facility just after I arrived. They were drugging him because he told his mother he could hear Jesus. He was a gentle and angelic boy and I comforted him in his distress giving him motherly love as best I could. Another resident patient, an older man appeared catatonic and wouldn't speak to anyone. He looked deeply depressed and this saddened me. I sat with him for hours and played my music CD for him, the number one greatest hits by the Beatles. We sat and sang together as he pounded his hand on the table to the music. I felt I had a mission in these hospital stays to bring joy and hope where there was none.

The days were long and difficult. One required activity for patients was to sit in group therapy and learn from the hospital's licensed therapists. I often took over the sessions and spoke more common sense than many of these therapists. It was astonishing how clueless some of them were as they forced us to do inane exercises which were meant to teach us how be healthy and become "well" again. They often forced us to do artwork as though coloring like schoolchildren would heal us of our mental problems. Sometimes their policies showed how they were clearly the insane running the asylum.

Here is one clear example of the institutional insanity we were subjected to daily. One day they made the patients sit in a mandatory group psychotherapy session where they gave practical advice on how to become more mentally fit by making healthy lifestyle choices like eating balanced meals and enjoying regular exercise. Promptly after this mandatory session about guarding your health, the mental patients were lined up at the nurse's counter to get cigarettes to go for a smoke. Really, I kid you not. We were corralled together to go into a small courtyard where most of the patients stood and smoked their brains out accompanied by several staff members. I did my little walk in laps around the courtyard while I held my breath when I walked too close to the plumes of cigarette smoke. Frighteningly, this was the best of the four mental hospitals, because at least in this awful prison they took us outside where I could look up and see the sky.

After a week, they still refused to tell me when I would be able to leave. I saw the lead doctor and director of this facility who told me on the first day that he didn't believe I was mentally ill. He was sitting at a desk behind the counter of the nurse's station at about 1:00 AM eating Pringles potato chips and doing paperwork. That was something I noticed at all four facilities, they all did an enormous amount of paperwork. My guess is the voluminous paperwork was how they justified getting payment from everyone's insurance company. When I saw this doctor doing paperwork and eating Pringles at 1:00 AM, it enraged me. He was supposed to have met with me that day but apparently, he couldn't find the time because he was too busy. It was clear to me that I was rotting in this hospital hell while he was doing his paperwork to ensure he would get his paycheck. I went over to the counter where he was working and said to him in a firm voice, "I want to talk to you right now."

He looked perturbed and responded angrily, "I'm very busy Lori. I can't talk right now."

I replied, "You promised me you would talk to me during the day and you didn't. I want to talk to you right now."

He heard the insistence in my voice so he agreed. After he set aside his potato chips, we walked over to his private office and he closed the door behind us. I sat across from him, leaned over his desk, looked him squarely in the eyes and said in a steady strong voice, "I'm on to you and your entire facility. I saw a woman who sliced her wrists open in a failed suicide attempt. She didn't have medical insurance and was escorted out of here within a couple of days. I know the games you're playing. I have excellent medical coverage and you're not letting me out of here because it's too profitable to keep me here while you can make more money. You told me yourself on the first day you met me that you didn't believe I was mentally ill. I'm not mentally ill and I'm very smart. If you don't let me out of here by tomorrow morning, I will sue you and your facility and I will win. I will move to shut you down." He responded with complete silence.

The next day my release forms were completed and I was told I could leave this diabolical filthy excuse for a hospital. As I was signing the release paperwork this doctor and facility director came over to me and apologized profusely. He said, "I had to put a diagnosis code on your release papers because the insurance company requires this to pay the bill. It doesn't mean that I believe that you're bipolar or anything of the sort. It's just administrative and something that I need to do."

I said dismissively, "I really don't care what you wrote. I'm going home now."

They didn't bother to require a family member to pick me up from this hospital. They let me call a taxi service and leave on my own without any supervision or chaperone. Really? If I was so mentally ill why wouldn't they demand a trusted family member pick me up to escort me home? They allowed me to call and order my own cab and when my taxi arrived, I left their insane asylum without having any cash or credit cards. Once again, I was forcibly taken there naked and against my will. I planned to pay the taxi driver when I arrived at my home. As I walked out of the hospital, they escorted me past the infamous payment room they forced me to visit in the previous stay, the room where everybody gets escorted when they leave the hospital. The woman at the computer, probably the same person from the previous time, looked up at me and said, "Give me your credit card. You owe us an additional $1,200 of out-of-pocket expenses."

I glared at her with venomous eyes and said, "I came here against my will, naked and without any belongings. I didn't authorize this trip to your facility. I don't owe you a fucking dollar." I promptly walked out. Perhaps this sounds foul-mouthed and unfeminine. This isn't the sort of language you might expect from your enlightened Moshiach. Although cursing like this is against Hashem's laws, He doesn't fault me or criticize this harsh language when I've used it. On the contrary, He tells me to go ahead and vent and use whatever language makes me feel better. Perhaps, as my story continues to unfold and you imagine yourself in my situation, you might feel compassion and understand why.

I wasn't mentally ill from the beginning. Today I am arguably the most mentally stable, competent and aware person in the entire world. While this might sound arrogant to some people, it isn't. It's simply the truth. I now know and have full understanding about what's wrong with our entire world. If there is something that I don't know, I go straight to the top and ask Hashem God. He is always right there for me and gives me the answer in everyday English, my native tongue. It wasn't me who was sick with any form of mental illness. It was then and it still is now, everyone else. Every single person in our world suffers from what is true mental illness with the singular exception of me. Mental illness is destroying our world and the doctors who think they are treating it are part of this illness too. True mental illness is choosing the opposite of God, the Yetzer Hara, also known as the evil inclination or Satan. It's not biological, it's spiritual and it's a choice.

Incessantly choosing the Yetzer Hara, evil, either knowingly or unknowingly, is what mental illness truly is and why humanity is now in complete peril. Hashem used these four hideous mental hospital commitments and the horror that accompanied them as a tool to peel my eyes wide open to the insanity we live in and to reveal an insidiously evil world. Through my personal nightmare and horror, it became clearer every day that our world was a strange and demonically insane place. I knew emphatically that I wasn't the problem; the problem was in everyone else around me. Hashem was putting me through hellfire to become educated and part of the solution.

Many American people now choose to medicate themselves from morning until night to cope with their emotional issues. Even many rabbis are indoctrinated into the psychobabble that is part of our mainstream society. The rabbis were fueled with the truth in the Torah, but they have surrendered to believing and supporting the views of the secular mental health system. Instead of the Torah-learned rabbis choosing to lead the doctors to God and sanity, it is now a clear case of the tail wagging the donkey! Just a little tongue-in-cheek reference to the Moshiach and his prophesized donkey. More to come about this donkey later.

My husband has always been a huge proponent of the existing mental health system. Throughout my spiritual awakening he had no desire to learn about any possible alternative way of thinking. He vehemently opposed my desire and efforts to follow a Torah-observant life. It was a constant battle as he showed visceral hatred for anything that mentioned the existence of God or was based in Judaism. My husband's insistence on following the advice of psychiatric doctors and supporting their use of psychological drugs added fuel to the fire that was destroying our once beautiful family life. In the aftermath of my forced hospitalizations, I began to see how our entire world was deeply sick and how it was dangerously dragging my three children into a sickening and dysfunctional way of life.

My hell on earth and repeated mental hospital commitments would never end if I stayed in my marriage. Not only was he going to kill me and my personal reputation, but the atmosphere in our home was completely unlivable. There was so much acrimony and fighting that it was detrimental to the welfare of my children. When I returned home from my fourth and final trip to hell, I called realtors to find an apartment. I also called a divorce lawyer for a consultation. It was time to start the process of leaving.

When my husband became aware that I was meeting with lawyers and realtors he started to soften his approach with me. After I told him I planned to leave he begged me to stay and made many promises that he would never keep. One of his promises was to become more involved in my life and meet my friends who shared my interests. He promised to help and support me with my fledgling charity Running on Love and join me for our weekly training runs. Incredibly, he even promised to go to synagogue with me on Shabbat. Promise after promise he begged me to please stay. My children were suffering so deeply, especially our youngest child, so I decided to stay and see a marriage counselor with him. I simply couldn't bear leaving my children in this state. Despite all the horror, it was too painful to leave my children.

Hashem Brings Us Who We Need

It became my new quest in life to find other people who understood the spirit world and God the same way that I did. I knew that I needed to surround myself with other open-minded people with whom I could relate. I began my quest to find others who were spiritually awake and God willing they would be mentally sane too.

In March of 2012 I began venturing out and looking for new friends who understood the spiritual side of life. After one of my involuntary commitments,

I met a psychotherapist in an outpatient treatment program that I was forced to attend. This psychotherapist was very open-minded and spiritual in her nature. She befriended me and told me that she believed I was gifted and not mentally ill. I brought my husband to one meeting with her and she closed the door behind us after we entered her office. She looked him squarely in the eyes and said, "Leave her alone!" Wow! That was not only astonishing but a complete miracle and a first for me in all my trips to hell that someone believed and supported me. She told me in front of him that I was courageous to be so honest with my gift and admitted that she could hear the spirit world too. Eventually we became friends and one day she invited me to join her at a networking event for clairvoyant people. This event was for people who believe we can communicate with the spirit world and many of them said they heard and communicated with souls who had crossed over. It was a networking group for people with a higher awareness of the invisible world. Fun I thought! This was a new age psychedelic networking group where perhaps I could commune with like-minded people.

I went with her to meet this group and as customary at networking meetings, we went around the room to introduce ourselves. One woman introduced herself to the group and it was obvious to me that she was Jewish. When you're Jewish, you can usually spot another Jew in a second. As she spoke and introduced herself, her words and personal story stunned me so much that I thought I'd fall off my chair. She introduced herself as someone who had recently had a radical spiritual awakening, then explained that it wasn't well received by her husband. Her husband had her carted off by the local police and committed to a mental hospital and drugged against her will. Instead of her awakening being a miraculous and beautiful experience she revealed a horror story that sounded eerily like mine. Wow! You mean to tell me there are other people in this world like me? My spiritual psychotherapist friend who was sitting next to me elbowed me and said excitedly, "You've got to talk to that lady!"

As the group disbanded and people were getting ready to leave, I went right up to this Jewish clairvoyant lady and told her we needed to speak. As I approached her, both of us felt incessant buzzing and tingling from head to toe. We both had chills that might sound incomprehensible to the average person. People who are spiritually awake often experience buzzing and chills when the other realm is trying to send a message. We both knew instantly that we had karma and needed to speak further.

We quickly became good friends and I told her about my horrible story which was uncannily like hers but times a millionfold (or at least four). She was a very strong, intelligent, and perceptive woman. I invited her over to my home for dinner one evening when my husband wasn't there and I allowed her to read from my first two journals, "The Book of Love" and "The Book of Truth." She saw immediately that my husband had dog-eared both books. She said in an alarmed and concerned voice, "Don't you see Lori, he's using these journals in a way that helps him lock you up. He is dog-earing any mention of you speaking with God. You need to leave or I fear for you. This will definitely happen again." As she read through my journals she found them so powerful and compelling that she believed I should publish them one day just as they were, in my own handwriting.

Right around this time I was introduced to another lovely clairvoyant woman who was Christian. She was introduced to me by a mutual friend as a clairvoyant medium. Although I knew it is against Torah law to speak to the dead or to go to fortune tellers or any of these people for a reading, Hashem wasn't telling me to stay away. On the contrary, He encouraged me to make these new acquaintances. I needed comfort and friends who understood some of the things that I was experiencing so I began reaching and searching everywhere. I made an appointment to have a reading with this Christian clairvoyant medium to see what she would say about me.

Before the meeting, I was guided by Hashem that it was safe for me to speak with her even though He had previously guided me that it was dangerous to meet with these kinds of people. In this instance, He told me I could meet with her because He knew I needed comfort from a physical person. Armed with His permission, I went to see her. As I entered the room where she was sitting, she instructed me to close the door. I sat in front of her and was about to tell her part of my sad story to give her some background. She quickly stopped me from speaking and put her hand up in a stop sign. She then placed one finger over her lips and said, "Don't speak." She said she knew why I was there and that she wasn't permitted to record the beginning of our conversation. In that moment, sitting in the room, I listened to Hashem speak to me at the same moment it was clear He was speaking to her. She told me things in that moment that I had never uttered out of my mouth to another human being. This was Hashem's way of giving me direct and personal confirmation that I was truly gifted. After being told for almost three horrible years that I was delusional and psychotic, this was a gift of a lifetime.

My husband, family and many former friends had branded me psychotic. Even though I never accepted this, I still wondered what was true. I often evaluated their insistence that I was psychotic and examined whether they could possibly be right. It would be dishonest for me not to fully consider a mental illness diagnosis as a possible reason for all my troubles. I knew in that moment that God was speaking to her at the same exact time He was speaking to me. This was irrefutable physical world confirmation that this woman was gifted, and so was I.

She then told me that one day she saw me standing before hundreds of thousands of people in a stadium. She told me Running on Love would be a global charity and force of good in our world. As she continued with this reading, she told me things that only Hashem had told me before which included private information about my three children. Hashem's glorious visions of standing before huge crowds of people which were shown to me for years, were too large for me to share with anyone else. Even with all the outrageously big things that I did share, these visions of stadiums filled with thousands of people and my future work in Running on Love were too grandiose for me to share. I thought if I told someone it would only fuel the fire that I suffered from delusions of grandeur. This Christian clairvoyant medium who didn't know me at all began describing the same glorious visions that Hashem God had been showing me for years.

With Hashem's permission, this woman became someone I reached out to for spiritual comfort and confirmation over the next two years. She helped soothe my soul while I went through my contentious divorce. During this first meeting with her, I received deeply needed confirmation that I was on the right path. It was also confirmation that there were other people in this world who could hear Hashem God. Over the next few years I would meet more people who had special gifts of hearing spirit and God Himself.

My new Jewish clairvoyant girlfriend whom I met at the psychedelic networking meeting event, introduced me to her therapist who was prominent and well-respected in New Jersey. This well-respected therapist was unusual in her profession because she recognized that there was a difference between what is considered mental illness and a spiritual awakening. When I met with her, she asked me a series of questions to make decisions about my mental health. She asked me five or six questions and determined right away that I was of sound mind and further explained to me that these questions were customary and should have been asked of me each time before they decided to commit me. I don't recall the specific questions she posed, but I told her in our first meeting that these were new questions that I hadn't heard before. She was shocked by this and based upon my answers and how I conducted myself in our meeting, she knew that I wasn't bipolar or delusional. It was clear to her that I had all the signs of a spiritual awakening.

She accepted me as her patient and began to work with me. I knew that I needed her professional support and I found her refreshing because she was intuitive, intelligent and a great listener. I hadn't been exposed to a therapist quite like her before and I appreciated her insight and help. At the time, I didn't necessarily feel I needed psychotherapy but I desperately craved the emotional support. She became a strong support system and anchor at a pivotal time in my life. I also realized that I needed a therapist with credentials to vouch for my mental health in my eventual divorce. It was inevitable that I needed to leave my husband and I knew I would require the professional support of someone from the mental health community.

As time went on, I began to make new friends and branch out into the world. I saw a need to establish new connections separate from my husband. I was doing my best to work and earn a living through this nightmare. I still worked with some of my marketing clients and managed small projects for my company but by this time my business had all but dissolved in the aftermath of all the problems. In my effort to find a new form of income and line of work that was separate from my husband, I had begun a small enterprise of selling credit card processing services just prior to the fourth involuntary hospital commitment in January of 2012. Selling credit card processing was something I absolutely loathed but I felt a strong need to try something new to earn a living that had no connection to my husband. At this point in my life, the only work that I truly enjoyed was my passion and love, Running on Love.

When I went out networking to look for new business leads, I began to introduce myself as someone who was involved in three different business ventures. It likely sounded like I didn't know what I wanted to do with my life, and that was quite true. My life was in turmoil and transition. At one networking event for Jewish business professionals, I did my obligatory introduction as we went around the table. I said, "I have a marketing company, a credit card processing company, but my true love is my pastime called Running on Love." Whenever I spoke at these meetings it was clear how passionate I became when I talked about Running on Love. As I spoke about my charity, it was as though my voice sucked all the air out of the room like a gigantic vacuum. After five or ten minutes of speaking about Running on Love, you could hear a pin drop. The room would fill with great emotion and my words would bring at least two or three people to tears.

At the end of one of these networking meetings with the Jewish professionals, a beautiful woman who was a business coach, approached me and said, "That's the second time I heard you speak and the second time you brought me to tears. You need to put your business mind into your love, and make your love your business." She then said something I will never forget, "Show up big. Anyone can show up small. Do this, and show up big." With that statement, she returned the favor, and brought me to tears.

We agreed to meet for lunch one day where we spoke for about an hour. Then she said, "I take on one pro bono client a year. This year you're it." I was blown away and deeply grateful that this woman was going to give me one year of her time. She knew I had no money to pay her as a business coach and she was offering to help me make Running on Love my full-time career and business. This would be my dream come true. I was extremely excited to begin our coaching relationship not knowing that this would grow into a beautiful friendship too.

After we met for a couple of coaching sessions, I told her that I wanted to organize a large event so that more people could learn about the magic and beauty of Running on Love. I wanted to organize a 5K run/walk which would attract people of all ages and not just the running community. After making this decision, I filed the appropriate paperwork for our first event, Running on Love in Montclair. When the paperwork was eventually approved it set into motion what would become the first of two 5K Running on Love events. I had many volunteers and friends who were supporting me and Running on Love back then. One of my former Art Directors from my marketing company was donating her time to help create the graphics and advertising. To kick off this 5K event required a great deal of money but at the time I still had the financial means and I invested heavily in my dream. While my husband was the one in charge of the purse strings, I still exercised my free will and handed out my credit cards when I saw fit. When I spent money on something he didn't approve of I simply dealt with his incessant criticism and complaints. Early in our marriage it was usual for him to back down and listen to my desires most of the time, but it didn't come easily. There was always a lot of complaining and arguing before he relented and apologized because I was usually correct in my judgement. If he didn't back down, I just ignored the complaints and did what I wanted to do anyway. In the case of investing in Running on Love the charity, I was completely certain that I would be successful in this endeavor. Success in the business world had followed me throughout my life and I finally was going to be working on something that I not only believed in, but loved with all my heart. A successful track record in business along with love and passion for what I was doing seemed to be a prescription for certain success.

Save My Children, Save My Life

I met regularly with my new therapist while I continued living with my husband. As we struggled in our marriage, I stayed strictly for the sake of my children. How could I leave them? I was fearful that something dreadful would happen to them if I left. The situation had deteriorated so badly that our youngest daughter was suffering emotionally. We decided to send her to stay with my husband's sister in California. At first, I went to California for about 10 days while she was there and then my husband went to visit her after I returned home to New Jersey. She began doing much better being away from our marital home which was a clear signal that things needed to change. This was the first time in 25 years of marriage that my husband and I spent time away from each other for more than a few days. The time we spent separated from each other was incredibly revealing. I was sleeping well and smiling for the first time in many years. My friends who saw me during these few weeks of separation all commented, "Wow Lori, it's so good to see you as your old self again! You look fantastic and so happy."

While my husband was in California, he sent me a steady barrage of derisive and threatening text messages. They were vicious and filled with anti-Semitic slurs. He unabashedly showed his visceral hatred for my new-found love of an observant Jewish life. I saved these text messages and put them into a Word document because I knew they would be important to me in the future. These messages were frightening, extremely nasty and they fueled my decision to leave him. In these text messages, he threatened to lock me up again and have the doctors permanently confine me in an institution. As I write this book, I'm told now by Hashem that my husband was so angry with me, he truly wished me dead. Recently, Hashem showed me a vision of my former husband holding a loaded revolver, which was a metaphor for his deeper desire to see my end. Even now, this is difficult for me to fathom. We married in 1987 because I believed that he loved me and was my best friend. During these hospitalizations and in their aftermath, he revealed a darker side of himself and became like a virtual stranger to me, someone I no longer knew. He contemptuously showed deep hostility toward me, spoke derisively to me, and resented my desire to follow an observant Jewish life.

I lived in perpetual fear that my husband would restart this cycle of involuntary commitments yet again. I knew that another trip to the mental hospital could finally kill me. It seemed like he had a personal vendetta against me. He also became increasingly neurotic over money. I was no longer the money earner that I had been for the past 25 years of our marriage. The marketing company that I started in 1988 was almost completely defunct by 2012 and no longer had any employees. My husband had amassed credit card debt in the hundreds of thousands of dollars. I was often denied small purchases at the local supermarkets and gas stations.

As I prepared myself for the eventuality of our divorce, I found a financial planner to refinance the debt and clear up our financial mess. This planner was an honest and good man who reviewed our financial situation and began to show compassion for me over the nightmarish way my husband handled our finances. As I prepared files for this man to do the refinancing of our home, I reviewed our financial situation and woke up to another unmitigated nightmare. My husband had opened over 40 different credit card accounts, both personal and business. The reason I was often denied small purchases was because instead of paying the credit card bills on time, he was juggling credit cards as though they were a deck of playing cards to keep the balances spread out over dozens of them. Our beautiful home had a lot of equity but with the hundreds of thousands of dollars of debt he amassed over the years in his crazy credit card game, the equity was being devoured.

Over the years, I didn't ask him about his handling of funds because I decided there was one aspect of our lives I would entrust to him. Handling our finances was "his job" but what I failed to realize was that overseeing our money was part of his neurotic need to control everything in our lives, including me. Allowing him to control all the finances became my albatross that would lead to my financial undoing. Not only did I discover the enormity of the mess and debt he created in my name, but I finally looked at our stock market portfolio too. When I logged in for the first time in many years, I received the shock of my life. What I saw showed me I was no longer married to my best friend. Perhaps he never truly was my friend at all. It was painfully clear that he never looked out for my welfare. Every decision he made was about himself and in his own selfish best interest.

As I looked at our portfolio, I was heartbroken to see that all the funds in what I thought were our joint account, were in his name and held as protected inheritance. There were only two funds I had access to, my own IRA which we opened 25 years prior when we were first married, and one other stock that he inherited from his father. The only reason this stock was in a joint account, was because a year prior I saw him on his computer looking at the portfolio. As I glanced at the computer screen I saw only his name and no mention of me. I questioned why this was the case after we discussed making everything joint. In that moment, he looked guilt-ridden as though he was caught in a lie. In his embarrassment, he felt obligated to appease me and the situation so he called our account manager and made this one account joint.

In the process of going through this refinance to clear the massive credit card debt that was choking us, I discovered that we had no marriage or true friendship at all. It was clear that I was deceived and had worked for 25 years as slave labor. All I required was some cash in my wallet, a full tank of gas in my car, and to know the bills would be paid. I never bothered to question his management of what I viewed as "our money." I trusted him completely and let him handle everything and handle everything he most certainly did. He selfishly looked after what he deemed was in his own best interest. What was mine, was his, and what was his, was his too. We didn't share the assets equally, but the insane amount of credit card debt was legally half mine. After 25 years of marriage, being a full-time working mother of three children and devoted wife to my husband I discovered most of our financial assets were held and protected in his name alone, untouchable by me. Conversely, I personally owed hundreds of thousands of dollars in unconscionable debt! Added to this debt, we were being sued for many thousands of dollars in "out-of-pocket medical expenses" from the four involuntary hospital commitments. If you discovered your trusted spouse of 25 years had used you and kicked you to the curb like this, how would you feel? I was so heartbroken and devastated I felt like I could simply die.

As I was working on Running on Love and was no longer the money earner that my husband expected me to be, his anger and language toward me became vicious and malicious. He continuously threatened me that I needed to start producing money. In a string of text messages, he threatened that if Running on Love was about God, he was going to force me to get a job. He himself wasn't working at any profession or job and was determined to strap a harness on my back once again to make me his work horse as I had been for too many years.

The following is a sample of revealing text messages he sent me in July of 2012 while he was in California. These shocking messages showed me in black and white that our relationship had deteriorated to a point that was unrepairable. It was clear that his mental state and way of viewing the world was twisted and dangerous. It wasn't just dangerous to me, it threatened the well-being of my children. He sent me the following string of messages on one day. These derisive and malicious messages prompted me to make my decision to finally leave him. These messages would eventually be included in the divorce proceedings, submitted in court documents, and are now part of the court records.

Husband:
Received: Jul 8, 2012 12:35 PM
Subject: there are other goddamn ways rto...

there are other goddamn ways rto be happy other than turning into a disney hasidic automatron..know how many people would go into a disney exhbit calleds meet mr. schneerzen..only the fucking morons wearing all black with a black hat on 100 degree days

Husband:
Received: Jul 8, 2012 12:40 PM
Subject: im saving this to show the...

im saving this to show the psychiatrist who has to piece this together after the smoke settrles..you havent changed...what bvunch of bullshit and a lie..yes you are lying .you think uou didnt change our kids..another lie...i did not siggn up for this 25 years ago..you were nnot an orthodox Jew.. therefore you fucking goddamed diod change..you thought ra>bi herring was ridiculous...you are lying like all these hasids lie..you have worn me out.. call (I removed several names of relatives here) and tell them you r the big winner on the psychotic front..ive had enough

Husband:
Received: Jul 8, 2012 1:55 PM
Subject: oh pompous one..

oh pompous one..if you really cared about the center of your universe..(I removed my child's name)..you would get your ass out here..you have gone 2 months without seeing her..i dont want to hear about how hard you are working..all i see is how hard you are spending money without bringing in a dime..you are writing checks without having a clue as to how much money is in the bank..if you talk the talk..lets see you walk the walk..exzactly what has keot you away from another of your victims for so long

Husband:
Received: Jul 8, 2012 2:07 PM
Subject: o great money earner..

o great money earner..please ask you god..god..god..goddamit..where i should find 6000 dollars to pay tomorrows bills from..from running on love..or from my ira..reality..reality.reality..somewhere you left 3.5 years ago

Husband:
Received: Jul 8, 2012 2:13 PM
Subject: thanks for stealing my family from...

thanks for stealing my family from me...i think to pay anymmore bills outside of 3000 we should try depleting your ira for a while

These were just a few of the many text messages he sent which were vicious, threatening, and deeply anti-Semitic. He was successfully waging his PR war with our relatives and anyone who would listen to him. I sent the entire string of more than 30 text messages in a Word document to my mother. I waited for a week to hear from her and she never replied. Eventually I would find out that she and my two brothers would side with my abusive husband. How could they side with my husband who was so clearly abusive and anti-Semitic? Throughout my life my mother showed disdain for my Orthodox Jewish relatives and often said my Orthodox Jewish aunt was a nut. My older brother had intermarried, had a non-Jewish son, and my mother lived with them as they celebrated Christmas with a Christmas tree each year in their home. They were typical secular American Jews who thought the religious Jewish world was a form of insanity. The truth be known, many Jewish people in America are some of the most anti-Semitic people in the entire world.

The intensity of my husband's anger was getting stronger and scarier. Until I received these text messages, I hadn't faced how hateful he was or recognized that he wished me dead. I'm guided by Hashem that his determination to protect himself and his neurotic love for money was so strong he wouldn't stop hurting me and would do everything possible to eventually destroy me. I had a million-dollar life insurance policy back then. Were my religious beliefs such a source of contempt for him that he would push to have me permanently confined and suffer so dreadfully from this treatment in the hope it would eventually kill me? If I died from this hideous treatment, he would keep all the money and collect a cool million in life insurance benefits. Crazy? I don't truly know if he wished me dead, but he spoke to me like he did. I truly feared for my life and safety. It was gut-wrenchingly clear that I was in terrible danger and needed to leave right away.

Much to his chagrin, by this time two of our three children had become Torah-observant Jews and part of the Orthodox Jewish community. He was embarrassed to see his children become a part of the Orthodox Jewish culture. Our youngest child desired to follow the same path as her older siblings but felt torn because my husband expressed such deep-seated hatred for Judaism.

Orthodox Judaism was a threat to him and he saw our Jewish way of life as something that was stealing his family. He was convinced that his children becoming Orthodox Jews was causing him to lose everything in his life. His behavior was completely overbearing, divisive and controlling. Our home continuously erupted into episodes of him screaming expletives at both me and our children. He thought his outrageous temper was understandable because he wanted to put an end to all the "Jewish shit" as he termed it. The cursing and threats were so incredibly malicious that when I shared my Word document with the entire string of text messages and emails with my new therapist and friends, they became visibly shaken. They were deeply concerned for my personal safety and felt I was in imminent danger of him locking me up and having me committed yet again.

One day, four different people reached out to tell me that they feared for my safety. They each told me in separate conversations that they felt strongly he was about to try to lock me up for a fifth involuntary psychiatric commitment. Each of them pleaded with me to leave my home right away because they feared I would suffer a fifth trip to hell. Another forced trip to mental hospital hell was one I might not survive.

After careful thought about how I should leave, I decided that I would call him to tell him I was leaving him while he was still in California. Doing this over the phone insulated me from his horrific temper and I felt safer. When I called to tell him, he suddenly changed his tone and language when he realized I was serious. I explained that I didn't want to leave, but separating was necessary. As we spoke, we discussed an alternative to me moving out of the house. In this alternative, we would sleep in separate rooms within our home. He wanted to see if that sort of separation would be enough to help us work through our problems. I played around with that idea for a short while but decided that this would only make matters worse.

All this time I stayed for my children, but I suddenly realized that I had lost my relationship with the three of them years before. I was being painted as a demonic mother who only thought about herself. They were being brainwashed that I was leaving them because I wanted freedom and a new life for myself. My former husband viewed everything as my fault and he convinced my three children and extended family that I was the cause of every problem. I paid a deposit on an apartment in a nearby town not far from my marital home, but it wouldn't be ready for me to move in for a few weeks. I chose this location because it was close to my children. Putting a deposit on this apartment enraged everyone.

As one of my last measures of trying to be conciliatory with my husband, I agreed to go with him to meet my new therapist. This was one of the last efforts to see if there was any hope at all to save our marriage. Would he ever believe that I am not mentally ill and that I have a spiritual side he simply didn't understand? Would he ever support my desire to follow an observant Jewish life? Hardly.

I scheduled the appointment with my therapist. My husband and I agreed to meet there in separate cars, but he decided to show up early to this meeting before I arrived. Why? Why did he show up to this meeting before the scheduled time and try to meet with my therapist on his own? I found out later he spent the entire time grilling her and trying to make her understand that I was mentally ill, psychotic and dysfunctional. Gratefully this therapist wasn't buying any of this. It was very clear to her after meeting with him, why I had been subjected to three-and-a-half years of hell on earth and repeated involuntary hospitalizations. After this meeting, she told me I was in danger and needed to think about "safety first." Her concern was focused directly on my safety and personal welfare. She saw his determination to continue to push his agenda to have me committed in even more hospitalizations. She said he was dangerous to my well-being, to the atmosphere in our home and to the welfare of my children. For my own personal safety and the safety of my children I needed to leave.

Instead of waiting for my apartment to be ready, over the next couple of weeks, I stayed in hotels and with friends. Eventually I returned to my marital home for the painful task of removing my clothing and belongings. Leaving my children and the home that I built so many years earlier was heartbreaking and crushing. As I took my clothing out of the master bedroom closet in my home I cried buckets but didn't show anyone my tears. This was the home I designed and built for my growing family and now it was time to say goodbye.

When I arrived at my new apartment, I went through my clothing and removed all the wire hangers. I don't like them and prefer plastic ones instead. As I threw the wire hangers away I cried out, "Hashem don't you see, it's true I'm mommy dearest!" I was making a reference to the old movie *Mommy Dearest* about the life of Joan Crawford who beat her children with wire hangers while screaming "No more wire hangers!" I was horrified that I had just left my children and walked away from my home. My oldest daughter called me from Israel after I left and screamed at me that I was horrible to leave and that Jewish mothers don't leave their children! I was completely devastated.

Under the circumstances, with my rap sheet of four involuntary psychiatric commitments, I couldn't take my children with me when I left my husband. I also couldn't stay there any longer. I knew that leaving my children would help them more than hurt them and believed this would help shield them from more pain. Undoubtedly my leaving was in their best interests but they were further poisoned to believe that I was abandoning them. The hate-filled oppressive and anti-Semitic atmosphere in our home needed to end. It was necessary for me to leave this dysfunctional situation, bring distance between me and my husband, and create a new safe living environment where my children could visit me on my own.

By leaving and separating from my husband, I hoped that my children would begin to see me in my own separate light. They would God willing learn that I was truly a good mother who revered and loved God. To this day I don't believe they fully understand that everything I did was for them and was not fueled by any selfish desires. I still feel lingering pain and resentment from my children. The separation and eventual divorce from my husband would be more horrific and depleting than I could have imagined. My road to freedom would be long, miserable, and deeply painful.

His Voice, Visions & Lessons

What do you do when you have feelings of despair and futility?

We all face feelings of despair and futility. What do we do when this happens? Listen to the answer our Creator, GOD Himself, gave me in a morning vision. I was told to share His answer with you. I am praying that you feel uplifted and follow His advice when you are feeling sad.

What do you do when you fall into feelings of despair and futility? There are many times in our lives when we succumb to these feelings and we don't know exactly what to do with them. Some people reach for drugs, alcohol or medications. The best way to heal from feelings of despair and futility is by encouraging and reaching for your relationship with God Himself.

I often feel feelings of despair and futility in my life even though I journey as one with our Creator which is the most miraculous gift I could have ever prayed or wished for. One night I went to sleep after recording the weekly program of Running on Love with God feeling like I am not getting enough people to listen to me. I am being told this will grow into something big and beautiful but it's not there yet. So, I went to sleep lamenting, "I don't think I'm doing this right. I'm not getting enough people to listen to me" and I felt feelings of futility.

The next morning God awakened me to an image as he often does. He asked, "Lori, what's this?"

I answered, "It's a wine goblet."

He said, "That's right. The next time you feel feelings of despair and futility in your daily life, I want you to close your eyes and reach for me from the inside out and I will fill your goblet up with love and strength and I will heal you. Keep going. You will win."

I wanted to share this message with you because He is our Creator. He is here for all of us. So, the next time you feel feelings of despair or futility reach for Him from the inside out. If you feel a warm hug enveloping you, it's not your imagination. He is truly here and He wants you to reach for Him. Do this as often as you can and know He is pure love.

Chapter 8

Breaking Free

Just prior to moving out of my home and separating from my husband, I had begun to work with my new business coach. As you may recall, she was kind enough to offer her services to me pro bono for one year and I accepted her generous offer with profound gratitude. I followed her advice and put my business mind into my love, Running on Love. Running on Love would be my new chosen career path. We met for at least one-and-a-half hours each week. When I decided to leave my husband, I knew I needed to clear the air with her and fess up about a very personal part of my life. It was unfair to allow her to go forward with me in any kind of relationship unless she understood everything about my personal life. My personal life was now affecting everything about me and I felt compelled to share my entire story with her. It was a tremendous risk to reveal such a nightmare to anyone, because everybody, including my own family, had walked away from me at some point during this ordeal. Friends of more than 40 years suddenly dropped me cold. Others walked away over time and discarded our friendship less abruptly. They didn't want to hear my revelations about God and couldn't tolerate my new observant Jewish way of life. Some of them stayed connected with me loosely but only on Facebook. Friends who were previously very close to me never called me or desired to make plans to see me. I was excluded from social invitations and friendly get-togethers. Phone calls and any concerns about me ended and eventually so did our friendships.

I met with my business coach for one of our weekly meetings at a busy northern New Jersey diner. As we sat to order our breakfast I announced that

I had something important to reveal. I warned her that after I told her my story, I would understand completely if she wanted to walk away from our relationship. If she chose to say goodbye after listening to me, it wouldn't have surprised me at all. People leaving me and walking away was becoming life as usual. I began, "What I'm about to tell you may color your opinion of me in a different way and it may not be sustainable for you to stay in a business coaching relationship with me." I then summarized the horror of the last three years which included four involuntary mental hospital commitments in which doctors diagnosed me as incurably mentally ill with bipolar disorder and psychotic delusions of grandeur.

When I finished summarizing and telling her my painful life story, I paused and waited for her to reply. I fully expected her to wish me well and tell me it was time for us to part ways. On the contrary, she took a stand that none of my own family or friends did. She said she believed in me. She told me that she believed that I was a good and decent woman with special gifts. She further stated that she didn't believe for one second that I was mentally ill. In her own words, she said she believed that I had a special ability to hear what others couldn't. She believed everybody had special gifts and I was no different. But she did more than just speak these warm and comforting words. She followed up her words with action by remaining my business coach and becoming one of my most important friends and supporters. This kindhearted woman would eventually carry me through my living nightmare and one of the most painful chapters of my life. During my divorce and other painful life tragedies, she was my rock and support system. She was like a mother to me when I had none. When times were tough, she didn't abandon me. On the contrary, she stepped up to the plate and became my hero.

Support and love were so rare in my life by this time that I cried at the breakfast table as we finished our meal. That wouldn't be the last time I cried on her strong shoulders. Our meetings were supposed to be business meetings about Running on Love but more often they became a place where she gave me comfort and advice. She held me strong as I headed into a deeply contentious divorce and fight to save my life.

During my personal horror, I continued to work full steam ahead organizing Running on Love's first 5K run/walk in Montclair scheduled for November 11, 2012. I sold my life insurance policy for its cash value and used this money to underwrite the event. The money also helped me purchase furniture and housewares to set up my new kosher enclave. My Chabad rabbi came to my apartment to kosher my kitchen and hang new kosher mezuzahs on each doorpost. I purchased my own new Chumash, the 5 books of Moses, which I could read fearlessly without anyone trying to stop me. Every Shabbat I walked to an Orthodox synagogue that was only a half mile from my new home. While this was an emotionally difficult time, I was grateful to begin living my dream of building Running on Love the charity and enjoying personal freedom to live an observant Jewish life.

Separated, Slandered, but Stalwart

The next 18 months were filled with fighting and indescribable anguish. Even though I found a suitable new apartment that was spacious enough for my children to visit, their visits would be filled with the awful strain of our broken family. I hoped that after I left my marital home I would be able to rekindle my relationship with the three of them. Unfortunately, the acrimony and divisiveness from my marital home followed me into my new apartment. Although I believed deep down that my children's love for me couldn't be extinguished, their father made a very strong and concerted effort to convince each of them that I was a mentally ill, unfit mother who had abandoned them. Both my former husband and my extended family told my children that I selfishly left them. I found out that my former sister-in-law remarked that they should be grateful because at least they had a good mother when they were small. The sentiment was "Oh well, be grateful for what you once had. It's time to move on children."

In the middle of the storm, my mother and brothers invited my two younger children to their home for a visit. Afterwards, one of my children told me that my older brother sat them both down to give them a history lesson about me and how the unraveling of our family was destined to happen. He told them stories about me and shared his authoritative opinion that I was always self-centered and psychologically damaged my entire life. As he carried on with his demeaning lecture about me in my mother's presence and with her approval, he told them both that if my father had lived long enough he too would have been diagnosed as bipolar and mentally ill. Wow! How completely sickening! I couldn't believe my ears when they shared this with me. I could handle the personal attacks against me but to say something so viciously derogatory about my deceased father was disgusting and infuriating. Why was everyone so determined to bury me alive and destroy my relationship with my children? They were so determined to hurt me that they embellished how sick I was by disgracefully tarnishing the memory of my father whom they espoused to revere and love. I wondered what kind of vicarious thrill they received by doing this to me at a time when I needed family support the most.

One of my Orthodox religious cousins invited my children to his home for Shabbos. He felt it was his moral responsibility to explain to them that what I believed in wasn't Judaism. Suddenly the Jewish police were going to save my children from their new age *shiksa* mother (shiksa is Yiddish for a non-Jewish woman) from leading them astray and sinning against God. As time went on, our family Chabad rabbi and rebbetzin waged the same war. They invited my children to sit down with them as they explained that what I believed in was completely against the Torah and untrue. While I was angered by my friends and family for turning on me and saying disparaging things to my children, I was less angry with my rabbi and his wife. I believed that they were doing their best to be good Jews. They were simply wrong with their assertions and completely misguided.

I tried my best to distance myself from everyone's lies and innuendos and began to make new friends. I shrugged off the obvious evil speech and walked away from controversy. I knew I was living my life's purpose, listening to Hashem's guidance and living a Torah-observant life as explained to me by Hashem Himself. I didn't need the approval of any person or group of people. As my husband, family and others waged a PR war to disparage me, take away my children and slander my good name, I reacted by reaching harder for Hashem. I asked Him daily for His comfort and the strength to persevere.

I continued to work with my business coach who had become my strongest advocate and dear friend. She was like a mother to me when my own mother abandoned me and stopped speaking with me. During all the hardship over the three years leading up to the separation from my husband, my mother and brothers supported my husband and turned their backs on me. They continued to support him during our vile and contentious divorce. I wondered how it was possible that my Jewish mother would support my husband after I showed her 30 pages of anti-Semitic and threatening text messages. I found out later, she agreed with my husband and thought my becoming an observant Jew was a clear sign that I was crazy. Like many secular Jews, my mother commented throughout my life that the Orthodox and Chassidic Jews were an absurdity and an embarrassment to the Jewish people. My mother and brothers were no different from most other American secular Jews. Growing up I recall my parents complaining that my Orthodox Jewish aunt was ridiculous when she didn't answer her phone on Shabbat or the Jewish holidays. Now after my awakening, my view of the world was being flipped upside down as I now saw the American secular Jewish world as the truly insane bunch.

Here I was caught betwixt and between two different worlds. The Orthodox Jews told my children I wasn't being Jewish in my ways or thinking. The secular

Jews spoke evil about me saying that I had become one of those embarrassing and insane Orthodox Jews. Clearly, I was mentally ill to choose this Jewish observant way of life now. To my husband my observance of Shabbos and keeping the laws of kosher were a clear sign I had suffered a nervous breakdown from the news that I was going deaf. Why else would anyone become an Orthodox Jew after turning 50 years old? Giving up cheeseburgers and pepperoni pizza added to his list of proof that I was now incurably mentally ill.

My relationship with my mother and my older brother was never warm or loving and was always destined to unravel. A sad casualty of my failed relationship with them was losing my younger brother whom I had always adored. He went their way and was indoctrinated into their hatred for me after listening to many years of evil speech about his older sister. Eventually he succumbed to the inevitable and believed the worst about me too.

My husband never cared for my mother or older brother because of all the anguish they brought into our home over the years. He often told me that I must have been adopted because they were so horrible. His contempt for my mother was so strong that he secretly nicknamed her "Pizza the Hut" after the grotesque character in the Mel Brooks movie *Space Balls*. He despised her and my older brother and complained about them frequently throughout our marriage. When they were disrespectful at his father's funeral in January of 2007, he was so infuriated that he wished my mother dead, literally. In pain filled moments when he missed his mother who had passed away years earlier, he said, "The wrong mother died."

Eventually, we reconnected with them after they behaved disgracefully at my father-in-law's funeral, and as they say the rest is history. I had my spiritual awakening, and now fast forward I was fighting for my life in our divorce. The expression, "The enemy of my enemy is my friend" became true. While my husband had no love for my mother or older brother over the years, now he saw them as help in his fight against me. My husband found them both willing and eager to help him bring me further harm.

My husband didn't need to say much to convince them that I was the troublemaker in our failed relationship. He had documented proof of four involuntary mental hospital commitments in just two-and-a-half years and waved this information around like a flag in everyone's face. He did this while he complained incessantly about how I became an Orthodox Jew and brainwashed our three children to do the same. He rallied my mother and two brothers to come to his side by telling them that I was brainwashing our children by indoctrinating them into a wildly evil cult called Orthodox Judaism and that I was stealing his family from him.

During my marital separation, money was becoming an increasing problem for me. A once well-to-do businesswoman who had the world by its tail, I was now struggling to pay my rent each month. Every time I went grocery shopping my husband saw the transaction because we had a joint checking account. When I purchased anything at all, I received nasty text messages cursing at me for spending money. Even purchases under ten dollars evoked threats and vicious verbal attacks. His daily harassment became completely untenable. By November of 2012, I was receiving a steady barrage of angry and threatening text messages again. Here is a small sample:

Nov 2, 2012 6:15 PM

I see the photos os my mom and dad you have the nerve to put up..they loved you because you made it your lifes mission to take care of their sick son who they werew worried about..you failed miserably..sotake the phots down and return evewrything you took form here..that is called stealing

Nov 9, 2012 8:18 AM

I am finished with you..a selfish..nasty witch who throws her daughter out into the fdreezing cold..you are a pox on our children and have given them horrible memories that will last their whole life..you don't understand what is wrong with you and are too pigheaded to accept 6 doctors diagnosis. Stay away from me and the kids..i say nothing to them negative about you..ask (Deleted my child's name) everytime she says something negative..i switch it around to make it positive about you

Nov 9, 2012 8:20 AM

Therefore..stay out of my checking account..that is money that was left to me by my dad..he wasts you to drop dead for what you did..you have an 84000 ira that is yours..drain that dry for all your stuff

Nov 9, 2012 8:27 AM

I want the wedding ring my father gave to my mother back..if you refuse.. you will be sued for that any much more..your life is soon to turn right back to being the kid who was always being bailed out by your father..pictures of jesus on your wall..keep your religion away from my kids

Nov 9, 2012 8:29 AM

This is the last word..i don't want to hear back any more from you about what a bad person I am..when you finally have risperdone coursing through your veins..you will get it and it is now too late

His emails and text messages were clearly inflammatory, off subject and designed to hurt me as he invoked names of relatives, even those beyond the grave. By mentioning my father coming to my rescue and pictures of Jesus on my walls he showed me that he was in constant contact with my older brother who enjoyed labeling and libeling me to no end. It was apparent that my brother had shared his distorted version of a very pain-filled chapter of my life.

When I was 21 and just out of college, I began working and moved to North Jersey. After about a year, I earned enough salary to rent my own studio apartment. Being raised secular and without any of God's rules, I continued my quest for love and excitement. Finding a good Jewish man to marry wasn't on my radar at all. Lo and behold, a gorgeous and charming goy, non-Jew, was sitting on his suitcase across the street from where I worked and it was love at first sight. First bite was more like it. He flirted with me and the next thing I knew we went out for a night in Manhattan to have some drinks and fun. I was 22 and in my wild-eyed innocence I thought I fell in love. What I truly did was pick up a hardened criminal with a rap sheet the length of his arm. Who knew? I certainly didn't. We had fun and it was the first time I ever enjoyed sex with someone. He moved right into my new studio apartment and took full advantage of my naiveté, swindled money from me to buy drugs, and then blackmailed me to use my graduation present, the car my father bought for me. He drove into Manhattan at night, smashed the front end of my car and frequently parked it illegally.

When my father started receiving parking tickets from NYC, he knew something was seriously wrong. He called one day and I fessed up and cried over the phone to him that I was in trouble. My father, as all good fathers would do, drove up to get me immediately with my older brother in tow. My brother witnessed the hideous mess I was in and apparently saw a picture of Jesus in my studio apartment. Personally, I don't remember that picture but any picture like that would have belonged to the shyster and conman. My brother held this information as collateral to use against me one day.

Now he gladly shared this sad story in his effort to help prove to the world that I was an ingrate with a history of mental problems. What I truly was at 22, was a young misguided girl who was never taught about God's blessed way of life prescribed in the Torah. I was never instructed how to find love, or warned never to touch a boy before marriage. My brother shared this painful story and his many tales of woe about his rotten sister as he basked in all his glory that this helped prove the case that I was mentally ill. He wanted to help my husband destroy my life and this was his enticing opportunity to exact revenge for all the pain he believed I caused him.

As time went on it became painfully clear that in addition to my husband's threatening and malicious way of speaking to me, he determinedly used money as one of his devices to control me. His controlling behavior intensified over the last few years of our marriage without my ever realizing it. Even after separating from him, my life was still in his grip and control. While he was verbally threatening me, telling the world I was mentally ill, trying to intimidate me with threats of forcible drugging and more hospitalizations, he was also encouraging our youngest child to persuade me to come home. Absurd, right? He played with her emotions and convinced her that it was possible for us to reunite. He sent her to my apartment several times on a mission to convince me to come home. Using our children to get to me was deeply upsetting. I lived in survival mode as his abusive behavior became more frightening over the next few months.

Building Running on Love the Charity for World Peace

While all this horror was going on around me, I tried to focus on building my love, Running on Love. The original date for Running on Love in Montclair was November 11, 2012. One day, while I was home working in my Morristown apartment, Hashem instructed me to google the date 11.11.12 and put the word *Bible* after it. What came up on my computer screen nearly made me fall off my chair. The search result directed me to prophecy from the prophet Isaiah. Here is the passage:

> **Yeshayahu - Isaiah - Chapter 11 (Isaiah 11:11-12)**
> 11. And it shall come to pass that on that day, the Lord shall continue to apply His hand a second time to acquire the rest of His people, that will remain from Assyria and from Egypt and from Pathros and from Cush and from Elam and from Sumeria and from Hamath and from the islands of the sea.
> 12 And He shall raise a banner to the nations, and He shall gather the lost of Israel, and the scattered ones of Judah He shall gather from the four corners of the earth.

This passage was one of many personal confirmations I received from Hashem over the years that it was truly Him speaking to me and guiding me. This passage of prophecy was about Hashem's Moshiach gathering all the Jewish children from the four corners of the earth to return to Israel. He told me that my charity Running on Love was part of His plan for world redemption and continuously told me that I was His chosen Moshiach. Although I was sure I was journeying and speaking with Hashem, I still wasn't sure that I was truly the world's Moshiach. It sounded too grandiose a title for someone like me but I was certain that my work was divine so I worked steadily on my dream and vision of Running on Love becoming a global charity.

One evening I was in my kitchen cleaning up after dinner and began lamenting to Hashem how old I looked. Even though I took good care of myself and many people thought I looked young for my age, I saw the signs of aging. As I was fretting about my aging face Hashem intervened and said in a clear strong voice, "Don't worry Lori, transfiguration." This stopped me in my tracks and I paused because it was an odd word that I hadn't heard before.

I replied, "What did you say Hashem?"

He answered, "Transfiguration Lori. Look it up right now." So, I did. I went right to my laptop and in the search field I typed "transfiguration." Once again, I almost fell out of my chair when I saw what came up as the first result. It read, "Transfiguration of Jesus Christ." For many years Hashem made it clear that Yeshua ben Yosef was the world's Messiah. He told me in this moment that I would enjoy a transfiguration like His previous Moshiach one day. The definition of transfiguration according to Merriam Webster is "a change in form or appearance: metamorphosis." I wondered, was I going to be transfigured one day too? Holy smokes, I thought! Could I really be His Moshiach? I basked in this revelation for a little while and enjoyed this verbal confirmation that Hashem chose me to be His Moshiach. While this would have blown someone else's mind to be given confirmation from God Himself that they were His Moshiach, I simply felt the heartwarming depth of His acknowledgment that this was truly coming from Him and not me. I had never in my life heard of the term *transfiguration* before that day. Now on the heels of my event being scheduled on a date 11.11.12 which coordinated with Isaiah's prophecy about Moshiach, His usage of the word *transfiguration* infused me with more optimism that my work might one day be fruitful.

Scared but Strong

My husband sent a barrage of nasty text messages and emails steadily throughout the days after I moved out of my marital home. There were periods of quiet when he tried to be pleasant but these infrequent spells were short-lived. His anger built up over the months of separation. My husband's continual threats about money didn't abate and I began to fear that he would become physically violent if I withdrew any funds from our bank account. One day in January of 2013 he sent me an email informing me that I was no longer permitted to spend one more penny from our joint checking account. He was slowly but surely choking me financially. This made it impossible to pay my bills or purchase food. Something had to change rapidly.

We held two accounts together. One was invested in the stock market and the other was our joint checking account. After he sent me the threatening email that he was cutting off my access to our joint checking account, I knew I needed to act swiftly. The next morning, I made the fateful decision to sell all the funds in the joint investment account as soon as the market opened. Prior to doing this I called the local police department to file a report about my husband's continual threats and how I feared for my safety. They told me I needed to go to court and file a restraining order against him. I followed their advice and that's exactly what I did. On January 8, 2013, I called our investment company before 8 AM and issued an order for them to sell all the stocks in this joint account and arranged that I would personally receive all the money. I then marched right over to the bank and withdrew all the available cash I could get from our checking account. By 9 AM I was in the local courthouse requesting a restraining order against my husband.

When a woman files a restraining order, it sets into motion a chain reaction and process that happens automatically. I suddenly found myself sitting with two ladies who worked for the division of abused women. Here I go again I thought! I must tell my horrible story and they're going to think I'm crazy! I was extremely fearful that these women would turn on me and call the police to have me carted off the way my husband did time and time again. My fear of being carted off, drugged and committed against my will was so deeply ingrained in me that I was petrified to tell anyone what had happened to me over the past three-and-a-half years. My husband successfully convinced people that he had absolutely nothing to do with these psychiatric hospital commitments. He convinced many people I was mentally ill and delusional. One by one the people in my life eventually turned on me and sympathized with him as the poor helpless victim. Would these two ladies from the division of abused women listen to me? Nobody was willing to listen to a word I had to say when my husband successfully orchestrated these involuntary commitments. At 53 years old, I felt I had no voice or power to control my own life at all, but I needed to try.

In my desperation to get help and be heard, I told these two women everything. I braced myself for the worst and prayed they would listen. Their reaction shocked and surprised me. They were silent for just a moment and then one of them looked at me sympathetically and said, "There are many forms of domestic abuse. You need to fill out this questionnaire which will shed light on many destructive behaviors that you don't yet realize are considered abuse."

In that moment, I thought, "Could this possibly be happening? Could they possibly be sympathizing with me and understand that I'm telling the truth?" I was so shell-shocked by the events of the last three-and-a-half years that I expected everybody to turn on me the minute they heard my story. I began to fill out their questionnaire which was called an "Abusive Behavior Inventory." As I filled out this paperwork, I sat with the court clerk who was filing a request for a restraining order. I answered her questions as she typed the order. When I read the inventory questions my jaw dropped open in shock. I found that I had answered "always" or "frequently" to over thirty different types of abusive behavior. It was in that moment that I realized I was a spousal abuse victim. How could this possibly be I thought? I'm an intelligent college graduate and smart business woman. How is it possible that I didn't realize I was being abused by my husband for many years?

Here are over thirty questions with my response of frequently or always:

1. Threatened to hurt you	Frequently
2. Threatened to take custody of the children	Frequently
3. Threatened to have you hospitalized	Frequently
4. Threatened to reveal personal information about you	Frequently
5. Shouted or screamed at you	Frequently
6. Drove recklessly when you were present	Frequently
7. Threatened you with: "Hospitalization"	Frequently
8. Insulted or drove your family/friends away	Always
9. Provoked a fight as you were leaving for work	Always
10. Called to harass you at work	Always
11. Checked up on you	Always
12. Frequently criticized your family and his family	Always
13. Called you names	Always
14. Ridiculed your beliefs	Always
15. Ridiculed your religion	Always
16. Harassed you about things you did in the past	Always
17. Humiliated you in private	Always
18. Humiliated you in public	Always
19. Unfairly accused you of poor parenting	Always

20. Accused you of having sex with others or having affairs	Always
21. Frequently threatened to leave or told you to leave	Always
22. Told you that you are crazy	Always
23. Told female jokes or demeaned women verbally	Always
24. Withheld approval, appreciation, or affection	Always
25. Made contradictory demands	Always
26. Made a decision without considering your input or consent	Always
27. Withheld sex or affection	Always
28. Unreasonably withheld cash from you	Always
29. Unreasonably withheld checkbook from you	Always
30. Made you account for every penny you spent	Always
31. Said the abuse was not as bad as you stated/thought	Always
32. Denied the abuse happened	Always
33. Said you caused the abuse	Always

While the court clerk asked me questions to prepare the request for the restraining order, I began to receive a series of derisive and threatening text messages from my husband. As one of these text messages came in, she asked me to read it to her out loud. I read his message, "Even God won't be able to save you now." Her face filled with horror as she furiously typed these words into her report. The next thing I remember was meeting with the judge. He met with me privately and told me he was issuing a Temporary Restraining Order and ordered my husband to give me $5000 to live on. I don't recall that I ever received that money but I was deeply grateful that the judge listened to me and gave me a feeling of temporary safety. The Temporary Restraining Order said that my husband would not be allowed to contact me or come near me in any way.

The local town police served this restraining order to my husband at our home and unfortunately, they served it in front of my two younger children. The pain my children suffered is unimaginable. My oldest daughter was in Israel at the time, and ready to board a flight to come home that evening. My son called her and warned her to stay away. She was coming back to America to finalize her plans of making Aliyah and immigrate to Israel permanently. Despite my son's warning, she decided to come home, complete her Aliyah plans, and while in America she thought she could talk sense into her psychotic mother. She planned to intervene and convince me to drop the restraining order and return home.

The next day when my daughter arrived at my new apartment she entered the front door and looked around. She saw an immaculate, lovely, and beautifully decorated home. Her face looked like she had just seen a ghost. She couldn't believe how beautiful, spotless and extremely organized everything was in my new apartment. I showed her how I koshered the kitchen and kept everything separated even to the point where I had stickers labeling everything meat or dairy. As she walked around, she was clearly stunned. My three children were convinced over these years that I was the cause of all the family problems because I was mentally ill and psychotic. After she toured my new apartment she wondered how it was possible for someone so mentally ill to establish such a beautifully organized home in such a short time.

I prepared lunch for her and we sat at my new dining room table to eat. She looked at me and then said, "Mom, you're not crazy, are you? When you look at someone's home you can see the inside of their mind. This home is too beautiful and organized for anything to be wrong with you. I wish I could lift this entire apartment and bring it back to Israel with me."

I answered, "That's what I've been trying to tell everyone, but nobody would listen to me."

Two weeks after the restraining order was issued, my husband and I were required to appear in court before the judge. This hearing was in a courtroom for domestic violence cases. After the hearing, the judge would determine if the restraining order would be made permanent. My husband had hired our business attorney, someone I used to consider a friend, to represent him. It was strange to me that he would take the case being that he was both our personal and business attorney for many years. On two occasions over the years, he had even approached me to go into business ventures with him. Now, as I headed to court I was petrified because I didn't have my own lawyer to represent me. The day before, I spoke with my business coach who had become my strongest advocate. She told me she didn't want me to be alone and that she would come to court to support me. Because she wasn't my lawyer she wasn't allowed to come up to the front of the courtroom where I had to sit before the judge.

As I sat in the front of the courtroom on one side, my husband and my former lawyer now representing him, sat at a table on the other side. It was well known that I suffered from profound hearing loss. His lawyer suggested to the judge that I should sit in the witness box while we spoke because doing so would help me hear better. I knew instinctively that this was his courtroom tactic to intimidate me and was not intended as a kind suggestion for my benefit. He was a skilled trial attorney, and I was aware that intimidation and psychological warfare were things he frequently used to win. You know the strategy, "take no prisoners and win at any cost." If he could intimidate me then he might successfully cause me to emotionally unravel and back down. I knew this was part of his intimidation game because just before we entered the courtroom he walked up to me and smirked as he said, "Are you sure you want to do this?"

His snide remark and smirk were his subtle warning to me that he would bring up my history of involuntary mental hospital commitments. He thought revealing this information in public would embarrass and humiliate me. I looked at him squarely in the eyes and replied, "I'm sure." It was clear he thought he could embarrass me but I knew I had nothing to hide or be embarrassed about. These hospitalizations weren't a poor reflection on me. Quite the contrary, they provided proof that I was being atrociously abused for years.

Now in the courtroom he was taking another stab at intimidating me to see if I would buckle under the pressure. The judge agreed with his suggestion and told me to sit in the witness stand. From the witness stand I explained to the judge that my husband was responsible for having me involuntarily committed four times in two-and-a-half years in mental hospitals when there was nothing wrong with me. I further explained that he used these commitments as a form of abuse and control that were destroying my life and now I feared for my safety. The entire time I was on the witness stand I could see my business coach sitting in the back of the courtroom. She sat there with a strong face and held her hand up in a thumb up position. She kept pushing her thumb up with visible force as if to say to me, "You keep going girl, don't you stop! Don't you back down!" As I watched her, I felt as though she was bracing me with love and strength and holding my hand as I walked through the fire. This was the first time in years I had a strong and loving support system standing by my side.

When the judge gave his decision, he turned to me and said that he couldn't issue a permanent restraining order against my husband and that I was in the wrong court. He said that this was a case for family court and not domestic violence. He then said something that stuck with me all these years. While my husband and his attorney were puffing out their chests looking like they scored a victory, I knew that I was the one who was victorious that day. Why? Because this judge stated in open court, "It is clear to me that you are of sound mind." This statement was music to my ears.

Divorce and Many Disappointments

Soon after I left the courtroom, I hired an attorney to file for divorce. The following couple of years would be draining emotionally, physically and financially. As time went on the continuous betrayals of friends and family broke my heart. My own mother and both brothers were unapologetically running to the aid of my abusive husband in our divorce. I was informed later that my two brothers even offered to appear in the domestic violence court for the hearing about the restraining order to support my husband and sit by his side in opposition to me. The definition of family and friend became blurry to me at best. What is family? What is a friend? There are many days that I still scratch my head and wonder.

After these events I received a letter from my older brother. It was clear he couldn't contain his antagonistic feelings toward me and was determined to wage a personal battle to discredit me further. In his letter, he stated that I was in denial, completely mentally ill, and destroying my once wonderful family. He said I espoused a "crazy mishmash of religions" and was clearly delusional. Wow! Really? In his opinion I was the one with the mishmash of religions.

This letter which claimed I was promoting a mishmash of religions came from my Jewish older brother who married a Presbyterian Christian, had a Gentile son, and celebrated Christmas every year with a tree and all the accoutrements. He signed this malicious letter on behalf of himself, his wife, my mother, and my younger brother. The letter was signed by the whole *Mishpacha* (Hebrew for family) like one of those political advertisements you see on TV when they end by saying "I support this message."

I scoffed at the stupidity of this fallacious letter and didn't give it another thought until one day I was sitting in a meeting with my daughter's physician. Her doctor and I were having a cordial conversation when he suddenly turned to a shelf by the side of his desk and told me there was something I needed to know. He then showed me a copy of my brother's disgusting and disparaging letter.

My brother had mailed a copy of this letter to my daughter's doctor, apparently with my husband's full approval. My impudent brother decided he was the moral authority and brazenly took responsibility to rescue my daughter from her demonic mother by sending this monstrous letter to her physician. He did this without the approval or knowledge of his niece with whom he had no personal relationship whatsoever. Besides being incredibly malicious, it was an intrusion into my daughter's personal medical care and an invasion of her privacy. What did he hope to gain out of his incomprehensible actions anyway? Did he really care about her well-being considering that the two of them never even spoke to one another? No, of course not. His only motivation was to hurt me, the sister he truly despised throughout his entire life. His actions were completely irrational as he showed no interest in how this letter might harm my daughter. In the hands of a lesser doctor, she might have been misdiagnosed with a horrible mental illness and medically mistreated. Instead of considering her welfare, my brother and the rest of my family focused squarely on how they could disparage and harm me.

After the doctor and I dismissed my brother's nonsensical letter, we continued our conversation. He was a former Yeshiva student who told me he found my conversations about God and Torah intriguing. We even had a detailed discussion one day about the Torah Parsha called Chayei Sarah and he told me he found my commentary quite fascinating and one he hadn't heard before. In all our conversations, I held nothing back from this doctor regarding my unfortunate history of four involuntary commitments and how I could hear and communicate with Hashem God. After speaking with me for hours and observing my interactions with my daughter, his response and final analysis was that he saw nothing about me that was consistent with any form of mental illness. In his professional opinion I wasn't mentally ill or committable and medications would only harm me. He further stated that I was unusual to say the least, but my unusualness worked extremely well for me. Then, he said something that affected me deeply and has stuck with me all these years. This highly respected doctor told me that I was the most stabilizing and healing factor in my daughter's life. He told me this after I had suffered through four involuntarily psychiatric commitments that included being forcibly drugged. From the beginning of my nightmare I was repeatedly slandered, demonized and then conspired against to have my children taken from me. You can only imagine how deeply I appreciated his comforting words. Someone was finally telling me I was a good mother.

As we parted ways I thanked him for all his help and told him one day I planned to write a book, and I'd give him a page in my Torah. We laughed together at my tongue-in-cheek comment, but unbeknownst to him I wasn't joking. Hashem told me that one day I would write a book which would be part two of the Torah. My book would be a Torah (meaning teachings) that would serve as the earthbound version of education that the world desperately needs now. True to my word, here is his page in my Torah.

Running on Lori

The originally planned date for Running on Love in Montclair, November 11, 2012, had to be rescheduled. The east coast suffered horrific damage from Hurricane Sandy in October 2012 and the city of Montclair deemed its streets unsafe for our event after this storm. After meeting with the Montclair Police department, we agreed that the 5K would be postponed to April 20, 2013.

Having to reschedule was ultimately a blessing because it gave me more time to market the event and attract more participants.

After my daughter came home from Israel to make Aliyah, she unexpectedly got caught up in the family drama. As a result, her plans to immigrate to Israel were stalled. She, like my other two children suffered as my husband and I went forward with our bitter and contentious divorce. For the first time, she became aware of her father's abusive behavior toward me. Although his abusive behavior toward me was present as she was growing up, she now observed this abuse as a maturing young adult.

She lived with me for a short while in my new apartment as I worked on the first Running on Love in Montclair 5K event. She was always in love with charitable giving so she rolled up her sleeves and helped me with some of the heavy lifting for this event. Our relationship had suffered over the past few years so it was wonderful to reconnect with her by working on something meaningful that inspired us both. Suddenly her mother wasn't the demonic crazy person she thought I was before. She ran away to live in Israel for two years to remove herself from the insanity in our family home. Like many others in my life, she had been convinced all our problems were my fault. Our relationship became deeply loving and very close as we worked together and prepared for the first Running on Love 5K event.

Back in 2013 I had many friends and business connections. On Facebook alone, I had nearly 600 "friends." Everybody was supporting Running on Love and appeared smitten by its beautiful message. It was a charity for all other charities where you could raise money and pick any beneficiary you desired. My message was very simple, just do it for love. Run or walk and raise money for any charity of your own choosing. 75% of the fundraising was donated to the charity of your choice. This was a great idea for other charities but a lousy idea for Running on Love. Running on Love was running on my life savings. The marketing messages were all about doing it for love and raising money for any other charitable cause you desired leaving Running on Love with an empty basket after paying expenses. The messaging for the charity Running on Love was muddled at best. Love was just too esoteric a concept and had no meat on the bone for people to sink their teeth into. What disease state would we cure through Running on Love? What social problem or plight on earth would be solved with its charitable mission? The philosophy that I lived by, to joyfully give in the name of love, didn't seem to translate well to people in our material world.

As much as my business coach gave me sound business advice, I wouldn't compromise. Running on Love was my love and modeled after my personal belief system. I wasn't willing to sell out so to speak. Even if compromising in my messaging meant that Running on Love would succeed financially, I didn't want to tarnish the truth behind its pure message. My coach advised me to market Running on Love as a turnkey solution for other charities to raise money. I was advised that I needed a "hook" so to speak. Supporting this charity just because you loved someone wasn't enough of a reason for people or businesses to be engaged. I couldn't get enough support with just love as the reason. Love was a strong enough reason for me to want to run a 5K let alone a marathon. Love sounded too hippy-like, fluffy and esoteric for the business world which operates on the pursuit of money, public image, and eyes. They all wanted to know how many "eyes" would see their logo. Logical, right?

Even still, by using my ability to influence people to become engaged, and with recruiting help I received from many friends, over 400 people registered and participated in the first Running on Love 5K event. This event happened without any corporate sponsors at all. At the last second a local restaurant gave a $125 donation to Running on Love, use of their parking lot for our event festivities, and water and fruit for the participants as they finished. They also gave the participants a discount card to be used at their restaurant that day which packed their dining room for lunch. That was the full extent of sponsorship received for the event. Everything else came out of my pocket and my IRA savings.

After I reviewed the results of this event I found the participants had fun, many charities received thousands of dollars in donations and Running on Love lost a ton of money. Truly, it was Lori Michelle who lost the money. I was told that our attendance for a first-time 5K event was considered superstar status, and that was all I needed to hear. The crowd was inspired and so was I so I looked toward the future. I moved quickly to schedule and announce our second event, Running on Love in Montclair on May 18, 2014.

My First Trip to Israel

My daughter helped me organize the first Running on Love 5K in Montclair in 2013, and I returned the favor by helping her make her dream of Aliyah to Israel come true. Since April of 2009 when Hashem awakened me, He showed me prophetic visions of living in Israel. In the year 2013, I made my first trip to Israel as I escorted my daughter on her Aliyah flight with the organization Nefesh B'Nefesh. She was just 21 years old at the time and this was her dream come true. She did this when there was deep division in our home and my husband wasn't about to let her go. I orchestrated her exodus from America, keeping these Aliyah plans secret from her father and the rest of the family. Even though she was 21 and a legal adult, I was concerned about my husband making trouble by trying to stop her. I knew Israel was meant to be her home and I did my best to make sure that nothing interfered with her plans. When we boarded the El Al flight for her to make Aliyah to Israel we saw a sight right out of the movies. Hashem couldn't have planned a safer flight for my daughter. This flight had hundreds of Chasidic rabbis heading to a rabbi convention in Israel. At one part of the flight, up and down all the aisles, hundreds of Chasidic men wearing Tefillin and Tallit were immersed in their morning prayers. I knew this was Hashem's visible blessing for my daughter's arrival home to Israel.

When we arrived in Israel, my ability of hearing spirit on the other side increased exponentially. It was like I had a clear cell phone connection to the spirit world. When I visited the Western Wall, The Kotel, the clarity of the voices from the world of the non-physical was even more breathtaking. As I prayed by the Kotel, I could hear them speaking and crying out. Their voices were particularly pronounced in this part of Jerusalem.

We stayed in a furnished apartment in Rechavia, Jerusalem. Every morning Hashem woke me up to vivid visions, and spectacular 3D movies of world redemption. He showed me in one vision the location where 11 souls who will be among the first to be resurrected will return to life in a time to come. This would be the beginning of the resurrection of the dead that has been written about in Biblical prophecy. In this vision, He showed me a specific tunnel that led to the Kotel Plaza. At the entry of this tunnel he showed me bright white light that spun forward in a circular motion at a very high speed. As the white light reached the end of this tunnel I watched in awe as the light transformed into fully clothed IDF soldiers walking into the Kotel plaza. Hashem explained that there would be 10 soldiers who would return, years before redemption was complete. They would be accompanied by Eliyahu Hanavi, Elijah the Prophet. This vision was followed by another vision of the famous Rebbe Menachem Schneerson and his wife, coming through the same tunnel, dancing joyously together. It was made clear by Hashem that the Rebbe and his wife weren't among the souls who will return at that time. They were shown celebrating this miraculous occasion with the soldiers and Eliyahu Hanavi. I've never forgotten these spectacular images or the overwhelming emotion it brought me that morning.

One Shabbos my daughter and I took a bus trip to Tiberias, Tveria in Hebrew, which is in the North of Israel by the Sea of Galilee. The Sea of Galilee is referred to as the Kinneret by Israelis. We stayed at a hotel called the Golan. As I entered the hotel room and walked out onto the terrace, my jaw dropped as I suddenly realized that I was seeing in full view the vision that Hashem had given to me four years earlier in a prophetic dream (page 150). In that dream, I was lamenting that I had lost my home but when I walked over to a picture window in the bedroom I was stunned by the magnificent view of mountains and water. Here I was, standing on this hotel room terrace, and for the first time in my life I saw the Sea of Galilee and the Golan Mountains across the way. In that instant, I knew that this was the place that I was shown years earlier. The view of the sea and mountains was one of the most spectacular sights I had ever seen. It seemed surreal and like it was painted by an artist.

As my daughter and I walked through the town of Tveria, down a promenade past several restaurants, Hashem was speaking with me and telling me He desired me to live there one day. I asked Him why He wanted me to live in Tveria, and He answered in one word, "Enclave." I had never used that word before and didn't understand His message. He told me to look it up and read the definition. *Enclave: any small, distinct area enclosed or isolated within a larger one.* After I read the definition, Hashem explained that there was only one major road into the city of Tveria and it could be most easily protected. He also said that the Kinneret supplied Israel with much of its water and was guarded continuously. In short, He said this would be the safest place for me to live. This was in 2013, and even though I was investigating the possibility of making Aliyah, my youngest child was a minor, my divorce wasn't final, and I still had a long road ahead of me to break free of my marital bondage.

The divorce proceedings were going forward as my husband continued fighting me tooth and nail. My children suffered dreadfully in the middle of all the fighting. I had hoped that leaving and separating from my husband would make things better for everyone but the pain and suffering seemed relentless.

Eventually my older daughter was so depressed in Israel that she returned to America during the worst part of our divorce. We were emptying our marital home after its sale. This was the only home my three children had ever known. She returned that summer of 2013 to remove all her childhood belongings. My three children were crushed as they said goodbye to their all-American childhood and once happy home. My husband rented an apartment with our youngest child and my older daughter floated between my apartment and his for a few months trying to decide where she would live. She was still helping me with

Running on Love but there was an obvious rift growing between us again. I learned that my husband was feeding her a steady diet of evil speech about me. Once again he convinced her that I was the source of her troubles and often ridiculed me and joked that I thought I was Jesus. By December of 2013 my daughter and I were no longer speaking. Once again she made it clear that she wanted nothing to do with me. She enrolled in an American college and decided to live with her father.

Inequitable Distribution

As I was working on breaking free, I slipped further into financial debt. One of my only ways to support myself was to live off my IRA savings. Withdrawing money early from my dwindling retirement fund eventually added to my financial ruin. After 26 years of marriage, I began to question if the best friend I once married was ever my friend at all.

To give you an idea of how painful my divorce was, while I was working to grow Running on Love my husband and his lawyer were working diligently to bury me financially. When you go through a divorce they use a system called "equitable distribution." My husband who managed all our finances throughout our marriage made sure he had protected himself financially over the years. When it came time to review our finances he was personally protected because he held most of the assets in his name. Conversely, on paper, I was in hundreds of thousands of dollars of debt. His attorney, who used to be my attorney too, was hell-bent to destroy me financially. The divorce took much longer than needed because of his lawyer's refusal to settle the case. I arranged to meet with my husband privately and while we were alone, behind closed doors, without our attorneys present we came to an agreement. After we agreed, I asked my husband to write everything down in longhand and sign this document. I knew that the minute I left him his attorney would talk him out of settling.

Just as I thought, his attorney called him into his office and was infuriated that he agreed to settle with me and ordered him to renege. My husband called me to tell me that he was being forced to renege by his attorney so I replied to this attempt to back out with some choice words of my own. What really affected him was when I invoked the name of his parents and asked him what his parents would want him to do. That along with receiving another huge bill from his attorney, made him realize he needed to end the pain. The only ones winning in our divorce were the attorneys. Our children were suffering and we were both bleeding with the exorbitant legal fees. He agreed to our settlement after all his backpedaling which allowed him to keep all the funds he cleverly protected for himself over the years. I received just enough money to cover my living expenses for less than a year. I felt certain that I would eventually succeed in my work and my personal freedom was more important to me than money.

After he finally agreed to settle, there we were in court on March 11, 2014 finalizing the end of our 26 years of marriage. When the judge issued the divorce decree in court, my husband's attorney felt it necessary to make a public statement on court record. In open court, he vehemently disagreed with our divorce settlement. His eyes and angry words were directed squarely at me as he spoke. I was astounded by his vicious verbal attack in court that day. During the divorce proceedings, he acknowledged I was deaf and argued that I was also psychotic and bipolar. What kind of settlement did he believe would be appropriate for a deaf and mentally ill woman after 26 years of marriage? What would he find fair? He argued that I was an incurably mentally ill deaf lady and an unfit mother who somehow owed my former husband thousands of dollars and should be required to support him financially. On this attorney's financial spreadsheet, he had framed me as the biggest loser in the equitable distribution game. In the legal game of "equitable" distribution, completely appropriate in the USA, he wanted me to pay my husband thousands of dollars along with alimony and child support. All this from me, the unemployed deaf psycho. Could he win this argument and have it both ways? He asserted that I was deaf and incurably mentally ill but fully intended to strap a horse's harness on my back and make me financially obligated to support my poor victimized and disabled husband for the rest of his life. When the divorce finally settled, my poor victimized husband kept the lion's share of all the assets for himself and left our marriage, maintaining the title and status of "preferred customer" of our former bank.

While the divorce settlement was financially a raw deal for me, I would finally be free of my husband's abuse. I was no longer under the control of the man who had destroyed my life and personal reputation. My husband kept his treasured stock portfolio and I walked away with my freedom to be authentically myself. I was now free to worship God and live the observant Jewish life I deeply desired.

A Gift—My Daughter Returns

On Mother's Day of 2014 just two months after my divorce was finalized, my older daughter showed up on my doorstep. Our relationship had become strained during the divorce as she struggled to choose between her parents. After deciding to live with her father, she saw the dysfunction in his home and once again became disillusioned with the American way of life. In her time of reflection, she remembered how much she enjoyed working with me and how she was inspired by her work for Running on Love. Now on Mother's Day she came back and desired to heal our relationship. She was unhappy and disenchanted with her life in America and wanted to return to Israel where she had made Aliyah and became a citizen a year earlier.

Using the little amount of money that was left in my IRA and the final divorce settlement which I received in small monthly payments, I invited my daughter to work with me again. I financially supported her as she helped me with Running on Love. I wanted to give her the means to return to Israel as she desired and where I knew she belonged. More than having help with my charity, I felt that giving her an income provided her the opportunity to return to Israel and rebuild her fragile life. Whether or not Running on Love eventually succeeded wasn't my biggest concern. I wanted her to establish a wholesome and good life in the Jewish homeland. She helped me organize the second Running on Love in Montclair 5K in May of 2014, moved back to Israel over the summer of 2014 and continued to work for Running on Love from her new home.

In Israel, she redesigned the charity's website and organized a Running on Love team to participate in the Jerusalem Marathon. She created a team to run in memory of her beloved Rav, Teacher, who had recently passed away from cancer. Her team raised money to support his family who suffered financially in his absence. As she worked to grow Running on Love in Israel, she ran into the same difficulties promoting this beautiful organization that I encountered in America. Every charity she spoke to complained that Running on Love received too much money out of the donations. She found herself continuously justifying the value of Running on Love and why our charity deserved any portion of the fundraising. Receiving 75% of the net donations simply wasn't good enough in their eyes. They also complained to her about the website credit card transaction fees and felt they shouldn't pay for those either. Instead of being grateful for the support of another charity that helped them fundraise, they complained they wanted more.

Inspired to Give (Nobody Was)

As I worked to organize the second Running on Love in Montclair 5K, I realized that part of my challenge was marketing this event and getting enough participation to make it profitable. I thought perhaps I could consolidate my time better if I learned to master public speaking and spoke to larger groups of people. This seemed like an effective way to increase registration and a better way to manage my time. I signed up over the winter of 2014 prior to the event for a three-day course in public speaking to learn how to engage a large audience. This class taught me some great public speaking techniques and was an eye-opening experience. One of the things I discovered by taking this course was that I had no fear of public speaking. This surprised me because I always dreaded being called to the front of the class as a kid in school. Like many people, public speaking was something I grew up dreading.

The owner of the public speaking training company was unexpectedly the instructor for this three-day course which took place in Manhattan. He was also an accomplished businessman who gave us all a bonus of a complimentary business consultation. During the class he boasted about his laudable business career that included being educated at Harvard, (although he admittedly didn't graduate), starting several successful non-profits and building and selling his own for-profit business for many millions. This training company was a new chapter in his already lofty career. I was excited and grateful to have a consultation with someone with his outstanding résumé. When we met for my consultation he opened the conversation with, "You're not going to like what I have to say."

I replied, "Tell me what you need to say because I will do anything to make this charity succeed."

He continued, "Your model is flawed and you won't succeed this way. You need to be willing to break your model repeatedly and keep trying new things." Then he said something that caught my attention, "If you can figure out a way to pay people to Run on Love you will have a winner. You could be an overnight sensation in 5 or 10 years." It was the overnight sensation part that grabbed me. I desperately wanted Running on Love to succeed and become the global force of good that Hashem kept showing me in visions.

I took his advice to heart and tried to come up with a way to "pay people to Run on Love." As obnoxious as I thought that statement was, I thought I could come up with an idea that wouldn't tarnish the purity of my charitable mission and message. The idea of making this about money was revolting and disgusting to me. The mere idea of paying someone to Run on Love was the opposite of what I believed in. I thought perhaps there could be a clever way to take his idea and make it ethical, honest and consistent with my personal beliefs. I went home from this public speaking course and thought about the owner's advice for days on end. I reflected on my own business career and realized I had earned a lot of money over the years in sales and marketing. I played the "what if" game and asked, "What if I could use my marketing skills and sales ability to sell companies on the idea that they would profit by being a company that Ran on Love?" I dreamed up an idea of creating a brand-new marketing company that would inspire businesses to be involved in the Running on Love events and I would market their business as one that Ran on Love. A sweet idea, right? Now that I am writing it down in this book, I see how ridiculously Pollyanna and idealistic this sounded to business managers and owners. It didn't occur to me at that time that this idea would not have monetary appeal for anyone in the business world.

Nonetheless, I went forward with my plan and registered a URL for "Inspired to Give" and created the tagline "Building Prosperity through Giving." I registered the company, Inspired to Give, designed a new company logo and spent thousands of dollars on business stationery and marketing collateral. My good will with former employees had dried up and I didn't have the luxury of volunteers to help me with creative work. I used my dwindling IRA to pay for my dream of successfully pulling this off.

For many years, I was very convincing and could get people to participate in Running on Love events because of my passion for this little charity. When I met someone new, I could convince them to Run on Love and they would become smitten with the entire experience. The problem was the passion for Running on Love was mine and not their own. It never meant the same thing to them that it meant to me. Running on Love had an identity crisis and nobody wanted to support it purely for its own charitable mission and message. After all these years, it was still "The Lori Show" and they were doing it solely because of me. When it wasn't "The Lori Show" where they wanted to support me, it was all about the other beneficiary charities and their mission, not about Running on Love. Running on Love became the go-between that took a portion of the fundraising. There would be continual arguments with participants over why Running on Love received 25% of the donations. Charities who signed up for the events didn't believe that Running on Love should receive anything at all because after all it was they who were the "real charity" and in their view Running on Love was just an event company. I have many stories of charities that complained they should have received much more than 75% of the donations. My heart would break many times over the years as my back-breaking efforts were unappreciated and Running on Love's beautiful mission wasn't understood or valued.

Disappointment and losses didn't stop me though. I was the little engine that could. Unbeknownst to everyone, Hashem was fueling my obsession with love and encouragement to keep this charity going. My gift of hearing Hashem was a secret to many people and I never revealed that this was truly meant to be the world's charity for peace and redemption. In the words of Hashem God, Running on Love was destined to be the global platform that united us all together in love, education and charity to bring peace on earth. When I registered this charity in 2009, I had no idea that this was the case. As I worked on growing this organization over the years I was simply smitten with performing charity in the name of love. The charitable cause that received donations meant less to me than performing a loving tribute to somebody I cared about. It was all about L'ilui Nishmat from the beginning and no reason was required other than doing something beautiful to honor someone I loved.

The mere act of giving in the name of love which is a mitzvah—L'ilui Nishmat from the Torah, affected me deeply. It was a source of such joy and inspiration that I became inexplicably addicted to it. I've seen people over the years become smitten after they ran an event for Running on Love. For them though, it was short-lived and they eventually moved on. Their reaction was, "Thanks Lori, that was fun. See you again when you do another one." Nobody became passionate and inspired about this charity like me. It was also becoming more difficult to get volunteers to help on event day. Instead of Running on Love, many of my devoted friends were beginning to run on empty.

This second Running on Love 5K in Montclair on May 18, 2014 gathered between 3-400 people but once again it lost money. My money. The only person who was truly funding these events was me because it was too nebulous for the business community to support. They wanted eyes, advertising, and to support a charity devoted to curing a well-known disease or solving a social plight. Supporting an event that was purely about love didn't have the business muscle or financial teeth to grab them. I couldn't pay them to Run on Love or show them how it would bring them publicity and massive attention from consumers.

After I scheduled the date of the second Running on Love 5K in Montclair, May 18th of 2014, I found out it was also the Jewish Holiday of Lag B'Omer that year. I didn't select this date on purpose however, as I've come to learn, everything that happens is purposeful and never a coincidence. When the Montclair 5K was scheduled on this date, an Orthodox Jewish friend of mine who participated in the event told me that this holiday brought blessings and was extremely special. I didn't understand what was so special about Lag B'Omer at the time but viewed this news from her as more confirmation that my little charity was blessed by God.

Lag B'Omer is quite festive and celebrated as a day of joy throughout Israel with bonfires and barbecues each year. Since I moved to Israel I've learned from Hashem that Lag B'Omer should not be the festive day that the Jewish people have created it to be. Quite the contrary, this holiday commemorates the yahrzeit of Rabbi Shimon Bar Yochai, the author of the Zohar. While he is a notable and beloved rabbi, Hashem has shared with me in many conversations over the years that we must never glorify any person's death with a holiday. Commemorate someone's passing, yes. Glorify or celebrate their death, never. There will undoubtedly be vehement pushback and argument over this statement that Lag B'Omer should not be a festive holiday. While this day is significant for the Jewish people, I'm told its manner of observance will change in a time to come. It will be a day of remembrance and not a day of celebration which includes bonfires and festivities.

After the second 5K in Montclair was over, I plunged full force ahead into promoting Inspired to Give, my new marketing company. Right from hello the business model for Inspired to Give and its tagline, "Building Propsperity through Giving" were counterintuitive at best. While I knew this was counterintuitive to the business world, I thought I could make the case and close the sale.

It didn't take long to discover the painful truth that companies weren't really inspired to give. They're inspired to make more money and giving is a nice afterthought. That's completely logical to any business aficionados reading this but it wasn't logical to me. This new company was modeled after how I think and what floats my boat. I am driven and motivated by giving and my own welfare is an afterthought, the opposite of everyone else. Hashem and I are driven by the same motivation, love. We think about the joy of giving to others without any thought about ourselves because we're motivated purely by love. Hashem is God so He can sustain Himself without help or money. I can't. Approaching my business life in a completely outward and loving way, the way Hashem approaches life, helped destroy me financially. My new marketing company, Inspired to Give, and my charity, Running on Love, would never support me financially the way I needed them to if I continued to use the business model of "Everyone else comes first." I believed that giving and the welfare of others should come first and that's not only counterintuitive in the business world, it's financial suicide.

Unfortunately for me, I couldn't get anyone to believe that you could possibly get rich through giving. Reflecting on this now and on the countless failed business presentations I made, I must have sounded like a complete ditz or like

I drank too much Kool-Aid. After every presentation, people politely told me how inspiring my vision was for this charity, but they simply weren't interested. Each presentation fell on deaf ears and I bombed for the first time in my marketing and sales career.

Charitable giving in business is considered a requirement, and it's good PR, right? The dirty little secret that nobody likes to admit is that successful businesses don't truly desire to give. Their primary agenda is to prosper first. Completely logical, right? Of course, right! Presentation after presentation my marketing messages fell completely flat. The plan I presented to everyone was that if they sponsored my Running on Love 5K Festivals for Love events, they could choose their own charitable beneficiary. Again, I left Running on Love the charity out of the equation and told them they could support another organization. I put others first. I applied for and received permits for two 5K events in Morristown, NJ scheduled in October of 2014. These two planned 5K Festivals for Love were the central product for the sponsorship packages I offered the business community.

My messaging sounded silly at best to the corporate community because it was filled with fluff about giving, love and inspiration. Where was the money they would make right at hello? My messages failed to offer them enough meat on the bone. Where's the beef they all wondered? I made a presentation to a local religious charity in Montclair and told them that if they found a lead sponsor for the next Running on Love 5K event, I would make them the featured charity and give them five dollars from every registration. They wouldn't have to organize the event and anybody who registered would be supporting their charity. Not only would they receive automatic donations from every registration, but the entire event would promote their charitable cause as the featured charity. Phew, and I wondered why I couldn't make a living at this? Again, I was giving away donations and the top billing and advertising of the event to another charity. All I requested was for them to refer a business sponsor for the event. Believe it or not, this wasn't enough for them. They wanted it all!

In the middle of my presentation to this local religious charity, their president asked, "Why in the world would we want to hand you a sponsor for your event? We could have all that sponsorship money for ourselves." She looked at me incredulously but she seemed to like me so she tried extremely hard during our meeting to figure out some way to make my proposal make more sense to her. Her charity was a religious foundation that had identity problems in the corporate world. It's widely known, it's not politically correct to speak about God or religion when you're asking businesses for donations. The mere mention of God and religion makes it difficult to get corporate donors. One of her business colleagues who attended this meeting suggested Running on Love could help them conceal that their charity was about God. The president's eyes suddenly lit up as she thought about this fantastic idea! As she entertained this possibility she grew visibly excited and said, "There's your hook Lori! Conceal for us that our charity is a religious charity and this will help us get more donors." Wow, I thought. Money was that important to her? This idea to use Running on Love to conceal their religious identity stunned me. Literally. I was dumbfounded that a charity that built its reputation on serving God would desire to conceal Him from our world for the sake of getting more money. I'm sure many business people reading this would agree a hundredfold with her and think that I'm a financial ditz. My way of thinking doesn't work in this world and very sadly hers does.

I truly appreciated her effort to support me that day. It was apparent she was being thoughtful and trying hard not to reject me. She clearly was doing her best to help me close the sale by making it more worthwhile financially for her charity. After leaving this meeting, she had more time to reflect on my proposal and eventually told me that my offer wasn't financially doable and wished me luck with my endeavors. The irony was that while she desired to conceal her charity's religious mission, Running on Love had no chance of survival in this world while it concealed the fact that it was God's charity for world peace. Running on Love's ultimate success depends upon the truth being known.

Deafness Wasn't Death After All

I marched forward relentlessly and continued to look for sponsors despite the incessant rejection. Meeting after meeting, this formerly successful sales professional couldn't close the sale on one sponsor. I wondered if I had lost my business prowess along with my ability to sell. Nonetheless, I kept making appointments in search of sponsors.

While I was working on building Running on Love and now my new marketing company, Inspired to Give, I was struggling with my hearing and slipping into deafness. My hearing was getting increasingly worse and it was becoming more difficult to go out to meetings and speak with people. It was also challenging to speak on the telephone. Eventually I was forced to get a special telephone for deaf people. This special phone had closed captioning where I could read the conversation as people spoke to me. There was a live operator listening in on the phone call and typing the conversations for me as we spoke. It became a comedy routine and I began to think they hired deaf people to type those closed captions. The transcriptions were terrible and sometimes they were laugh out loud hilarious. In one conversation, they transcribed that my son was cursing me out with expletives and saying vile and terrible things. I don't believe I've ever heard my son curse once in his entire life. I asked him where he was calling me from and the operator typed that he was calling me from Iraq instead of Eilat, Israel. So much for closed captions!

This closed caption phone was delivered and installed by a lovely woman who entered my home and announced, "I'm completely deaf." Her words shocked me. There was no way I could tell that she was a deaf person. When I asked how she was functioning so well she told me about her two cochlear implants. She was bilateral, meaning she had cochlear implants in both ears. Without these implants, she was completely deaf. She was happy and beautiful and never missed a beat. She gave me renewed optimisim about the possibility that this could be a solution for me. Even though years prior I had been given negative information about these implants from a doctor who specialized in them, now I thought I should consider them for myself. My life had become a huge struggle where it was difficult to hear anybody right in front of me. Even with my newfound talent of lip reading, I was struggling terribly. At the end of each day I was completely exhausted from trying to hold conversations and decipher people's speech.

While she was still in my home, I looked up cochlear implant surgeons accepted by my insurance policy. By this time, I was on Medicaid because I had no income at all. Admitting to being on Medicaid might be embarrassing for other Americans, but not for me. I was deeply grateful to have hospitalization and medical coverage while I struggled financially. To my delight, in my insurance plan there was a well-known and respected neurosurgeon at University Hospital in Newark, New Jersey. I scheduled my first appointment with him to find out if I qualified for this surgery.

After taking a battery of required tests, I qualified immediately. I not only qualified to have cochlear implant surgery in my right ear which was deafer, but I qualified for implants in both. I was so deaf in both ears that they told me I could have both implanted at once. I still had a small amount of natural hearing in my left ear so I opted to only have the right ear done. Part of the process of getting ready for this operation is undergoing a closed MRI. Having great fear of closed spaces, when I heard that I had to have a closed MRI before the surgery I became distraught and I panicked. When I scheduled the test, Hashem told me to calm down and He promised me that He would get me through this test without a problem.

When I arrived at the hospital, the MRI technicians explained that I would have to remain in the closed unit for approximately half an hour and then they would take me out to inject dye into my veins before putting me back into the unit for another half hour. Silently in my mind, I said to Hashem choking back tears, "I know I'll never make it!" He told me in His strong and soothing voice not to worry. He comforted me and told me I would be okay.

As I positioned myself on the table, I was extremely nervous when they strapped me into the unit and told me I couldn't move a muscle or blink while I was inside. They put covers over my eyes so that I couldn't see. As my eyes were closed tightly I could see the spiritual eyes of Hashem God looking right at me. With a very stern face and in His commanding voice He said, "You are going to be okay! I love you!" Then He asked, "Who am I?"

I replied, "Hashem."

He shouted, "Say it again! Who am I?"

I said silently without moving a muscle, "Hashem!"

He kept repeating the same pattern in a stern, loud, but loving voice. His repetitive words were exactly what I needed to get through this difficult test. Again, and again He repeated, "Who am I?" And then He followed with, "I love you! I'm not leaving!" This went on for the entire one-hour MRI test. In the middle of excruciating hell, I felt snug and warm in the hands of God Himself. He held me tightly, with such profound love and strength, that pure hell felt like heaven on earth.

After the MRI, I scheduled the surgery to take place a few months later. With surgery imminent, I was forced to cancel the two October Running on Love 5K events in Morristown. It was a good thing too because I hadn't landed one single sponsor and very few people had registered. It was a relief to cancel because it became heartbreakingly clear that there was no interest in my Running on Love 5K Festivals for Love. I rationalized that this cancellation was a blessing because it gave me another year to work on my dream. I applied for permits for the two events to take place one year later in October of 2015.

The cochlear implant surgery was scheduled for November 2nd, 2014. As instructed, I arrived early in the morning for the surgery to be prepped by the nurses. When I walked into the operating room for the operation I was flabbergasted by the sight of the operating table. I wanted to cry and run out of the room but I knew I couldn't. The table that I was to lie down on to have this surgery had a place for my arms that stuck out perpendicularly by my sides. No kidding, it was in the shape of a crucifix! This completely threw me for a loop. When they perform this surgery, they stretch your arms out to your sides as though you're lying on a cross. After everything I'd been through, the sight of this table made me quiver. Hashem escorted me into the operating room and His loving voice never left me. He kept comforting me by telling me that the outcome would be wonderful and the surgery would go perfectly. He repeatedly told me that He would never leave me for one second. If you've ever had surgery before you understand that once you lie down on the operating table it's only seconds before you're unconscious. It seemed to be only three split seconds later that I woke up in the recovery room with my oldest daughter there to comfort me. It was over.

The recovery was particularly difficult for me because I had never experienced major surgery before. My daughter had flown into New Jersey from Israel to stay with me while I recovered. While she was with me, she finished redesigning the Running on Love website which we launched on December 9, 2014, my 54th birthday. We had a lovely new image for Running on Love to present to the world and I was hopeful that this would be our year to fly.

After the surgery, I was rendered completely deaf in the ear they operated on. They didn't activate the cochlear implant for four weeks until all the swelling went down. During those four weeks, I continued to work on Running on Love and Inspired to Give. I rescheduled the canceled Morristown events for the following year and revised all the marketing materials.

On December 2, 2014, I went to the cochlear implant audiologist and she activated my new implant for the first time. Everything and everybody sounded like SpongeBob SquarePants. I didn't know whether to laugh or cry. Every time I spoke or laughed I sounded like SpongeBob, so I decided the best thing to do was to smile and laugh. I prayed that it would get better and gratefully it did. My hearing improved over the next few months.

A couple of weeks after my implant was turned on I was cooking in my kitchen and for the first time in over 10 years I heard sizzling. I never realized that hearing makes you a better cook. That morning as I walked around my kitchen I didn't realize my eggs were about to burn until I heard loud sizzling on the fire. These are the little things in life that people with hearing take for granted. Things like hearing the pronunciation of the letter S, birds chirping, and the sizzling of eggs on a frying pan are all a gift. All those sounds were missing from my life for many years.

One morning in early December, Hashem greeted me as He always does when I wake up. As I opened my eyes He said, "Good morning Lori. Today we are going to the Social Security office and applying for disability. You will be approved and this money will give you peace of mind."

I replied, "Hashem are you telling me now that I'm going to fail in my efforts to grow Running on Love?"

He answered, "Your ultimate success in Running on Love is assured. I want you to apply for disability to have peace of mind."

I listened to his request and went to the Social Security office to apply. I took all my records and documents from my implant surgery and sat in the waiting area. Without anybody in this office knowing, I was silently conversing with Hashem. He was telling me that if I shared my entire diabolical medical history that included four hospitalizations I would not only get approved immediately, but they would give me money for all the prior years that I suffered. The benefits would begin retroactively and it would greatly benefit me financially. My answer to this suggestion was unequivocally no. Someone might wonder why I would take such a strong stand if following this suggestion would benefit me financially. Why wouldn't I simply share written documentation about my medical history if it ensured swift approval and gave me more money? My answer is simple. I was never mentally ill, and I'm not mentally ill now. I refused to play that card. If they didn't approve me based on my hearing loss alone, then so be it. As I sat there silently in the waiting room I was having a vigorous conversation with our Creator. He said to me, "Lori, your approval for disability benefits is assured."

The approval process took several months. They required me to be examined by a doctor of their own choosing. The medical files and medical history that I provided about my hearing loss and operation weren't enough. I went to be examined by the doctor chosen by Social Security. After I left the exam, Hashem said, "I promise you that the approval is guaranteed." This was in February 2015. I drove home that day and continued my work in Running on Love and Inspired to Give. I hoped that one day I would finally enjoy success in my work life once again.

Deep in Debt, but Determined

I lived off my IRA savings while going through my divorce, supporting my daughter in Israel, and working to build my charity and marketing company. Using these funds before retirement was a deadly decision financially but I felt certain I'd succeed and didn't fathom that failure was possible. Along with incurring penalties and interest for early withdrawal from my IRA, I was also leveraging business expenses on my credit cards believing I was investing in my future. In my mind, it would only be months before I would achieve success and pay them off in full. I was approved for Medicaid because I had no form of income and eventually would be approved for a small amount of food stamps which wouldn't be enough to cover my groceries. I believed that my financial pain was temporary because I knew I was working on a beautiful new marketing business—Inspired to Give, which would fuel my charity and love —Running on Love.

My focus in 2015 was promoting the two Running on Love 5K Festivals for Love events that were scheduled for October in Morristown. I purchased a $1,500 educational program I found online that explained how to build and create an effective corporate sponsorship program. As much as I was struggling financially, I was determined to do everything possible to succeed. Using the information in the program, I fine-tuned the sponsorship packages and scheduled meeting after meeting trying my best to secure sponsors for these two events. While I was out hunting for sponsors, I was also busy designing and building a company website for Inspired to Give. I created short videos discussing why companies should be Inspired to Give and how I would help them "Build Prosperity through Giving," my new company's tagline. My messaging continued to fall on deaf ears, pun intended.

The charities I courted to get involved with my events saw my new marketing company and Running on Love the charity as competition to their own charitable causes. I was a competitive threat despite giving them 75 percent of the net donations. Instead of being interested in a team effort for both charities to raise money supporting both causes, they saw the plan as one where they were losing money. They didn't want to share the marketing headline for the event and wanted the spotlight on themselves exclusively. Sharing a business contact or splitting any donations from the events wasn't tenable to them. The program I devised was built on the premise that people, businesses, and charities would come together as a united team for the good of everyone involved. It was a "We all win" philosophy and business model. This novel idea looked great on paper when I played my "what if" game and when I did the math, I showed that everyone would profit from the experience of Running on Love. It didn't sell. Nobody was interested in everyone winning. Everyone I approached had the same attitude and response. They wanted more for themselves. Sharing any part of the money pie didn't play well for any of the businesses or charities.

It became clear that the nail was in the proverbial coffin after one telling meeting with a successful business owner. During my presentation to him, he boasted that he just closed a $900,000 client. I told him that the marketing program I offered would promote his company as one that Runs on Love and I'd publicize his company at all my events. I then said to him, "This program will help you prosper more so you're blessed to give more away." Oh no, did I just say something stupid? Once again, to this successful businessman I sounded ditzy, foolish and like I had drunk too much Kool-Aid.

He looked at me puzzled and then replied, "No thank you. I want to make more money, I don't want to give more away. I'll give a little." In that moment, I knew the end was near. As this man got up to leave my office, he turned to me and said something I would not soon forget. During our chat, he learned I was Jewish and as he was leaving he said, "I know you don't believe in Jesus but your charity Running on Love sounds exactly like something he would do. It was everything he was about."

"Incredible!" I thought. I wondered if he loved and revered Jesus, why wouldn't he participate in an event that Jesus himself would do. You know the old expression that Christian people use, "WWJD—What Would Jesus Do?" It was crystal clear to me in that moment what everyone else saw from the start. Companies, charities, and business people weren't Inspired to Give purely for the joy of giving and the public couldn't understand the magic of Running on Love. Both of my companies espoused values which were the opposite of what is valued by business-minded people. Running on Love and Inspired to Give were completely outward and promoted joy through giving. Giving came first. The business people I met wanted to know "What's in this for me?" and were only interested in making money first. Of course, you might say! Duh! Even though my idealistic model made everyone money, they were ultimately turned off by "everyone making money." Everyone making money meant less money for them. The marketing message of "We all win" was received as though it took money out of their own pockets. Nobody was motivated by a business model that was built on sharing and giving first.

A nice businessman tried to give me some friendly advice one day when we met briefly for coffee. He knew I was floundering and losing money and wanted to offer me sound business advice. He said, "Lori just go for the transaction fee. Don't worry if they understand your mission. Go for the money. You need money!"

Even though I appreciated his intent to help me, I told him that I couldn't do that. My charitable message was too important even though admittedly nobody was receiving it. Compromising wasn't possible for me. This wasn't a copier, computer or bling jewelry that I was selling. I was repulsed by the idea of selling out and embracing the "go for the transaction fee" business model. This was God's charity after all that I was told would one day bring us world peace. I couldn't reveal that information to him because I knew he would think

I had lost my mind. I knew that if I revealed anything about God, anyone who supported me up until that moment would flee immediately and head for the hills. One day down the road, that's exactly what they all did.

I began to have the same problem with my pro bono business coach. To her credit, she didn't abandon me after giving me one year of pro bono coaching as she promised. She didn't abandon me after two years either. How incredibly generous she was to me, don't you agree? After more than two years of coaching me pro bono and being my strongest friend and advocate, she became extremely frustrated. Wouldn't you? She tried very hard to make me see things in the material world way. Following her advice became impossible for me because Running on Love wasn't meant to be just a material world charity. I wouldn't tarnish its godly and pure message no matter what. She advised me to market Running on Love to the other charities as "a turnkey solution to their fundraising needs." This statement was blasphemy to my ears. It's about love and peace on earth after all! Don't you get it people? As I write these words I wonder if you, whoever you are, understand what I'm trying so passionately to communicate to you. For me, giving isn't about getting anything in return other than spiritual connection and love. People are conditioned to donate to charity to cure an illness, solve a social problem or get a tax write-off. When I donate anything to anyone, whether my time or money, I'm donating and giving my love. That's all I need to know and I don't expect one thing in return. You've got me at love. My belief in doing it for pure love wasn't a successful business model in the material world and I wasn't willing to compromise.

I still wasn't willing to quit or let go of my dream. In my entire business career, I had never failed at one job or any business enterprise. I always managed to rise to the top and become a top salesperson on every sales force. It seemed that I always knew how to make things work for me and get the job done, no matter what the job entailed. Now, I was working for Running on Love, my life's passion, and I refused to accept failure.

One day my business coach and dear friend, sent me an email. She was completely frustrated with me as I continued to fail to get sponsors for the two scheduled 5K Festivals in October of 2015. In her email, she explained to me that I needed to start listening to her business advice and that my business model was flawed. She then documented all the time she invested in me which included two years of pro bono coaching time. In her email she calculated the number of hours of free business coaching and told me what she could have charged me according to her normal hourly rate. Added to what she gave me in professional time, she listed how she supported me during my contentious divorce at the worst time of my life and even included sitting with me and my daughter at my Shabbos table. After she totaled everything to let me know how much money and personal time she had invested in me, she gave me a deadline to land my first sponsor. The email ended by telling me that if I didn't listen to her advice and become profitable by a specific date, she would be forced to leave me. It was clear that her patience had run dry and it was time for her to be a paid business coach.

I told her we shouldn't wait because it was time for us to part ways now. I expressed to her that I was deeply grateful for everything she had done for me over those two years but I simply wouldn't be able to follow her business advice. This surprising revelation hurt her deeply I'm sure. She replied that she was stunned and rendered speechless.

The traditional business acumen used to make money in our material world wasn't appropriate for Running on Love or my new company, Inspired to Give. She was giving sound business advice for any other traditional business, but my charity and marketing company weren't traditional. As Pollyanna and ridiculous as this might sound, I was unwilling to bend. I refused to change the pureness of my business message even if it meant I had to go forward alone.

We met for lunch soon after this email exchange to clear the air. I wanted her to know how important she was to me. We parted as friends but to this day I know that the damage was done. God willing this fine woman knows how much I love and appreciate her and is reading this book too. Her gift of friendship and strength while I fought for my life in a contentious divorce was far more important than any business advice she could ever give me. She was family to me when my own family and lifelong friends deserted me. Her presence in my life was a pure gift from God Himself. Hashem God sends us Angels in human clothes. She was my hero.

GOD is Everything. Everything Else is Extra.

By the spring of 2015 I was staring at the bottom of an empty basket. My determination and belief that I would finally succeed was so strong that I kept going with reckless abandon and drove myself into more debt. Feeling that Running on Love was God's charity to bring us peace on earth made it impossible to quit. Through it all, Hashem kept showing me vivid visions of the future. These visions were filled with millions of people around the world Running on Love at large joyous events. The images of millions of people giving joyously to charity were emotional and breathtaking. If these events were in God's plan, how could I possibly stop? I just couldn't. In the face of continuous losses, I felt it was an egregious sin to quit and let go of this dream of world peace.

From the onset of my awakening, Hashem was encouraging and inspiring me to keep going. Through it all He explained that success for Running on Love would be a reality. The world would one day Run on Love and these joyous events would become educational forums bringing healing and peace to our troubled world. If this charity held world peace in its hands, would you be able to throw in the towel and say, "That's it, I quit!"? It surely looks like I was nuts and delusional to put all my money and life's blood into this little charity which brought countless disappointments and led to my financial undoing. By the time I recognized how deep in debt I was, I could barely afford food. The basket was empty and I faced the real possibility of homelessness.

I warned my daughter who was still working for me and living in Israel, that I wouldn't be able to support her financially after June of 2015. Telling her this saddened me beyond words but I felt gratified that I helped give her a running start to live her dream in the Holy Land. I believed that Hashem would step in to provide for her when I couldn't any longer. She eventually found work and was able to support herself without my help.

I continued to look for sponsors and promote the two scheduled events in October of 2015. Appointment after appointment I couldn't close one bona fide sponsor. There were a couple of businesses that promised to sponsor the event but none of them followed through. Back in the day I was the consummate salesperson who always closed the sale. When it came to love and giving I was a complete failure.

In the spring of 2015 it felt like I was heading straight off a cliff and about to crash into the rocks. Money was so tight that I couldn't pay my monthly bills. I was still waiting for a decision from Social Security about my application for disability benefits. It was clear that divorce and personal freedom weren't the full cure for all of my life's problems.

One day as I went for a run, I ran past some old houses in town and began imagining that one of those houses was a shelter for homeless people. As I ran past these old homes I spoke to Hashem and said, "If the bottom falls out and I have no place to go I suppose I could survive. One room, a soft place to fall, a small table for my challah and candles on Shabbos is all I really need." The thought of winding up in a homeless shelter frightened me but I worked through my fears to make the idea tolerable if the worst came to pass.

The next Shabbos I took my traditional afternoon nap on the soft sofa in my living room. As I woke from my Shabbos nap, Hashem greeted me. Here is our conversation.

Hashem asked, "Where are you Lori?"
I replied, "On my sofa Hashem."
He asked, "Where are you Lori?"
In that moment, I realized Hashem was teaching me something and wanted a different kind of answer. I then replied, "I'm in Morristown, New Jersey."
He asked again, "Where are you Lori?"
This time I answered, "The United States of America."
He asked one more time, "Where are you Lori?"
And then I knew the answer. I responded, "I'm somewhere in the world."
He said, "That's correct. You are somewhere in the world. Look around this room."
I looked around the room and I saw my beautiful little apartment that I had moved into a couple of years prior. It was well furnished and I was lying on a soft sofa taking my Shabbos nap. And then he continued, "If this room, where you are lying down now, was all the space you had in the world, and you had a soft place to rest like this sofa, but you woke up to My voice, would you be okay?"
With profound gratitude I replied, "Yes Hashem, I will be okay."

His tenderness and loving wisdom gripped me deeply as He comforted me that Shabbos afternoon. In that moment, I knew that even homelessness wouldn't be my end. All I needed was Hashem. Everything else in my life was extra.

The following week I received a letter from Social Security. As I opened the envelope I was scared to see their decision. Before I read the letter, I told Hashem out loud that whatever their answer was I knew I'd be okay. To my delight, Hashem told me the truth back in December when He told me to apply. This was an approval letter and I was awarded disability benefits for my deafness. As He promised, He gave me peace of mind.

Aliyah—Coming Home to Tveria, Israel

The reality had finally set in. Business meeting after business meeting, trying to land an event sponsor was an abysmal failure. Once upon a time I was a sales professional who could close almost any deal. But now with my new marketing strategy for these Running on Love Festivals, nobody wanted to Run on Love and even fewer were Inspired to Give. I woke up from la-la land and realized that my vision of a world charity was at best a dream that wasn't ready to come true. The Social Security disability benefits I was going to receive were barely enough to cover my basic rent and utility bills in Morristown. There was no way I could stay in my apartment and make ends meet. My only option was to find a more affordable place to live. I needed to leave my home again and do it quickly.

While I was working through my divorce and living in Morristown, Hashem kept waking me to visions of moving boxes. His message in these visions was always the same. He told me that I would soon be moving to Israel. In July of 2015 I could no longer afford my life in America, and was heading toward homelessness. Could this be the time for me to make my next bold move? Was it time for me to make Aliyah to Israel?

I decided to go online and check out how much rent was in Tiberias, Israel. On Craigslist, I found a 2-bedroom apartment with pictures of a breathtaking view of the sea advertised at just $500 per month. I did a quick calculation of all my bills, minus my late model Jeep SUV that I would no longer need, and voilà! I could possibly make ends meet for a while if I lived in Tiberias, Tveria in Hebrew. My math is usually lousy, and I knew that my expenses would likely be higher than I was estimating, but at least I could avoid becoming homeless.

I had no idea how I would go to Israel or for how long. The idea of losing my home and applying for welfare was untenable to me. It seemed clear that going to Tveria would be a lifesaver. My divorce had been finalized more than a year earlier and my youngest child was becoming a legal adult. Even so, I thought that I would only go to Israel for a few months to figure out my life and heal from the trauma I had suffered over the last several years.

No sooner did I find this $500 per month apartment in Tveria online, when my phone rang with a call from the organization Nefesh B'Nefesh. The advisor called to ask me if I was still interested in making Aliyah. I had started the paperwork in 2013 but never followed through. I scheduled a Skype video chat meeting with him to find out what was involved. The first thing I asked him was if I would be allowed to continue receiving my Social Security benefits if I moved to Israel. He told me that as an American citizen I was entitled to receive Social Security payments after making Aliyah. He advised me to verify this with Social Security before I made any decisions.

I went to the Social Security office and sure enough they informed me that as an American citizen I would continue to receive my benefits overseas. As a dual citizen of Israel and the United States I wouldn't lose anything. I would retain my American citizenship and could even vote in national elections. Making Aliyah to Israel also gave me additional benefits as a new Israeli citizen. I would receive financial help for a brief amount of time as a new immigrant as well as full healthcare benefits. My mind was made up in that moment. It was time to move my home to Israel.

As I finalized my plans to make Aliyah to Israel, I needed to designate where I desired to live so I chose Tveria. Several of the Nefesh B'Nefesh advisors tried to steer me away from this choice and encouraged me to settle elsewhere. They said that Haifa would be more suitable for me because it had more English speakers. In addition to Haifa, they recommended Naharyia or Karmiel. For some reason, they were trying to discourage me from moving to Tveria. I wondered why they were so anti-Tveria? Everyone I spoke to seemed mystified that this was my first choice. Even after moving to Israel, a lot of Israelis found my choice of settling in Tveria peculiar. Many Israelis make fun of the locals who live in town by calling them *primitiva*.

No matter what anyone said, no one could discourage me from moving to Tveria. Armed with encouragement from Hashem, I had my own personal desire to live in Tiberias. I found the view of the sea and the mountains magical and spiritually uplifting. The cost of living was extremely low compared to the rest of the country. I wasn't worried about finding an English-speaking community because I felt I needed to learn Hebrew anyway. Instead of being swayed to change my mind, I was mystified when everyone questioned my choice. I thought they were weird, not me.

I quickly put all my furniture on Craigslist and sold most everything I owned within a few weeks. The realtor who sold my marital home during the divorce became a wonderful friend who offered to let me stay in her house for two weeks prior to leaving America. This was a huge blessing because I needed those two weeks to pack up everything I couldn't sell and donate it to the local mission. On October 13, 2015, I boarded an El Al flight with Nefesh B'Nefesh and made Aliyah to Eretz Yisrael. I immigrated to Israel.

When leaving New Jersey on this momentous day, I was on food stamps and Medicaid. I had become a poverty case and faced the real possibility of homelessness. When I landed in Israel on October 14, 2015, the Israeli Ministry of Immigrant Absorption handed me a gift basket of money, and then asked me to choose which kind of health insurance I wanted. Are you kidding me? You're giving me money and free health care because I came home to Israel? It felt like I was living in a fairytale where everything was falling into place. For the next year, I would have the opportunity to begin my life anew in Israel.

My financial situation was still quite abysmal having fallen into $30,000 of debt. Before leaving America, I made arrangements to pay off this debt in small installments over time. A lot of people would have declared bankruptcy in the same situation but I agreed to make small monthly payments to all the creditors over many years. Although most of this was business debt, I felt personally responsible for it all. It was my mess, and if I could find a way to manage these payments, I intended to clean it up.

The first month I was in Israel I met a community of English speakers who embraced me. A married couple from Canada helped me find and move into my first apartment. My daughter who lived in Jerusalem and my son who was studying at a yeshiva spent many Shabbats with me in my new home. It was miraculous enjoying beautiful Jewish holidays and Shabbos in a Jewish country. It felt uncanny to be able to walk down the street and enjoy kosher pizza or falafel any time I desired. While this sounds insignificant to some people, this was a holy miracle to me. For the first time in almost 56 years, I felt I was finally home.

HIS VOICE, VISIONS & LESSONS

Don't eat the giraffe.
Enjoy its beauty instead.

While attending a Torah class I learned that in the laws of being kosher, it is permitted to eat the giraffe. It is a kosher animal and suitable for us to eat however we never eat them. We have many other animals and food to eat. The giraffe is a beautiful and majestic animal that we can simply appreciate for its beauty.

After many years of enjoying wealth, I am now living hand to mouth. I live in Israel and don't speak much Hebrew and I am deaf. It is difficult for me to speak on the telephone. I often aggravate the caller because I ask frequently for them to repeat themselves. Sometimes I give up and ask them to send me a text or email.

I heard about a telemarketing job opening for English speakers. Back in the day, I would be overqualified for this position, but now with my hearing issues, I was worried about my ability to perform. When going to sleep that evening, I asked Hashem, God, to help me make the decision if I should apply for this position. That evening He refused to answer me.

The next morning, He woke me to a vision as He often does. Here is our conversation:

Hashem: Lori what is this?

Lori: It's a giraffe.

Hashem: That is correct. The giraffe is a kosher animal, isn't it?

Lori: Yes, it is kosher.

Hashem: Why don't we eat the giraffe Lori?

Lori: We have so much to eat and the giraffe is so beautiful.

Hashem: That's correct. Is your refrigerator filled with food?

Lori: Yes, Hashem. Thank you.

Hashem: Are you sleeping soundly in a soft bed with a roof over your head?

Lori: Yes. I am deeply grateful. Thank you.

Hashem: Lori, don't eat the giraffe.

What do we truly need? In this material world, there is self-imposed pressure to have more. Many people work and anguish in their desire for more money to the exclusion of fully appreciating their lives. They miss simple pleasures like watching the sunrise or a stroll in the park. Their lives are dedicated to the pursuit of having more.

Life is much too precious. Don't eat the giraffe.

Chapter 9

The Road to Acceptance

As I settled into my new apartment in Tveria, Israel, I was optimistic and hopeful about making new friends. People were extremely gracious and warm and I was invited to many social gatherings and Shabbos meals. My son was studying at a yeshiva near Jerusalem and came often to spend Shabbos and all the Jewish Holidays with me in my new home. My oldest daughter who I helped make Aliyah in 2013, had temporarily moved back to America, and then returned to Israel in the summer of 2014 while working for Running on Love. After I was no longer able to support her financially, I was grateful that she found employment and continued living her dream in Jerusalem. She also came to visit with me in Tveria but less often than her brother. It was a pleasure to be able to spend time with my two older children in Israel. My younger daughter who still lived in America came for a visit over her winter break from school in January of 2016. During her visit it felt as though I was in heaven having all three children with me in Tveria. My life began to heal as I established my new home. I felt hopeful for the first time in many years that I would finally enjoy a good life once again. It had been almost seven long years since my spiritual awakening in April 2009. I had suffered through four involuntary hospitalizations, fighting for my dignity and life, getting divorced, major surgery, and then falling into poverty. Now in Israel, I felt protected, nurtured and safe from harm.

My plan was to settle into my new home and write my first book. For many years, I knew that I had to document and write my story for the world to read. Hashem showed me many prophetic visions of people reading my book voraciously. In one morning vision, He showed me a woman who looked like an Orthodox Jew seated on an airplane. She was wearing brightly colored red lipstick and reading my book with great emotion and excitement. As she turned the pages she laughed out loud, wept uncontrollably, and was deeply moved by my journey. Over the years when I shared only a small portion of my life story, people commented that I should write a book. These people had absolutely no idea how much despair and heartbreak I had suffered. They were barely hearing the SparkNotes of our family drama. Religious Jewish people found it astounding that all three of my children suddenly became Torah observant Jews when our family was completely secular up until 2009. The change in my family was startling and truly miraculous.

To the secular Jewish world my children and I becoming religiously observant looked like an unmitigated nightmare and horrific family disaster. On the flip side, the Orthodox Jews I met told me I must be an amazing mother for all three of my children to follow the righteous Jewish path. They said this about me—the same woman who had been framed a demonic psychopath by my former husband, family and friends. To my family and friends, I was clearly a psychopathic demon who stole my American family away from their doting dad. When these Orthodox Jewish people showered me with compliments I found it both amusing and heartbreaking at the same time. Since 2009, I had been branded the worst mother in all the world. Now, here in Israel, I had an opportunity to redefine myself in the aftermath of my living nightmare. It was also high time to rekindle my relationships with my three children which had been severely damaged in the fallout.

My children and I rarely spoke of these turbulent years because it was too deeply painful. My son absolutely refused to have any conversation about this topic at all. I recognized that I needed to write this book not only to awaken the world to the source of our problems, but to explain to my children the reasons why I was forced to leave our home and divorce their father. Each of them was brainwashed that I was mentally ill and that I left our home because I selfishly wanted to start a new life. Even though sharing our personal lives publicly is painful, revealing my story is needed for everyone to heal, especially my three beautiful children. After family and friends had disparaged my reputation so dreadfully, it was important to me that I finally share my story in my own words.

As I began to write this book, I started and stopped many times. It was a life project that never seemed to get done. It was so difficult because I had so much to say and didn't know where to begin or place the focus. There were so many problems that needed to be addressed and I was concerned about the important messages and deeper meaning being lost. If I said too much, nothing might be heard. I wondered how much of my diabolical story do I tell? Would everyone fall asleep and become completely bored because I went on too long about "my personal stuff?" How do I tell my story which has many lessons that are deeply important to everyone else without sounding like it's all about me? Do I stay silent and not write this book at all because it will hurt or embarrass my children after they already suffered so tragically? Do I write this book despite their potential embarrassment because silence will harm everyone even more? Do I breach their personal privacy and reveal every sordid detail about what happened to each of my three children as the world descended upon me? If Hashem's assertion that I am Moshiach is true, am I morally obligated to my children and the people of the world to reveal everything and exclude nothing? These troubling questions ran through my mind every time I sat down at my computer and attempted to write this book.

After many revisions along the way, the final version materialized. Believe it or not, the most painful part of my diabolical story was completely omitted from this book. As painful as my journey was—being involuntarily committed and drugged four times, getting divorced, going deaf, and going broke, the worst trauma was watching my children suffer through it all. Each of my three children suffered incredible trials and unspeakable horrors. While I was branded the worst mother in the world who was responsible for my own family's undoing, I persevered and refused to quit. My burning reason why I persevered was my love for my three children. I survived the personal attacks and all the horror and lived to tell the world because I was held strong and protected by Hashem God. He told me every step of the way that I would survive the nightmare and live to share my story. He told me I was His chosen one to teach and heal the world through love and education. Hashem promised me that one day I would speak and everyone would finally listen. As I complete this book, I'm still waiting for that day.

While I wait to see how my life unfolds in the aftermath of publishing this book, I know I've already won. I've won because I not only lived through many horrors and came out the other side, but because my children made it through the storm too and are healthy and successful young adults. They each boldly rejected the secular way of life. Hashem called on them, and they all answered Him with a resounding yes. Each one of my children is now a Torah observant Jew and is following Hashem's prescription for a blessed life. I am deeply grateful to see my three children living happy lives filled with God and His Torah.

Voice of Peace—Conversations with GOD

In December 2015 on the second night of Hanukkah, new friends invited me for dinner to celebrate the holiday. A few other guests were also invited to this gathering. One of the guests was a published author and voice teacher. She was an Orthodox observant Jewish woman who wore a head covering and dressed in the traditional modest Orthodox manner. My dinner hosts introduced her as someone who had a mystical side to her personality. The way that they introduced her and how she spoke about herself completely confused me. I wasn't sure if she was clairvoyant and could hear the spirit world like I could. I couldn't ascertain what it was about her that made people consider her mystical. It seemed apparent to me by the stories she shared that she was intuitive and had a heightened awareness about the non-physical world. I knew very little about this woman but found her personal stories fascinating as we spoke over dinner. Unbeknownst to her at the time, Hashem was speaking to me during that dinner and revealed that she was an important person for me to meet. When we finished dinner that evening, we didn't exchange phone numbers and I had no intention of calling her. Hashem had other intentions for the two of us.

Over the next few days, He woke me to morning visions of her face and told me stories about her. Suddenly, this woman whom I had never seen before, began to show up everywhere I went in Tveria. One morning Hashem directed me to use an ATM from another bank, different from my own. As I walked up to get cash she was standing right there and when she saw me she appeared stunned. She told me she was never at that location at that time of day. Each time I bumped into her she commented that it was unexpected and highly unusual for her to be where she was at that moment. It was clear to both of us that Hashem wanted us to speak and get to know each other.

We arranged to meet for a cold drink on the promenade in the center of Tveria. As I sat and waited for my cold beverage to be served, Hashem told me I needed to reveal to her the story of my spiritual awakening. I warned her that I was about to tell her personal information that she may not believe or be able to accept. I encapsulated my seven-year story in a few minutes and gave it to her in a nutshell. Not an easy feat. I managed to touch on most of the major parts of my story which included that I hear and speak with Hashem daily in fluent English. I left out any mention of Moshiach in this first conversation. By the end of my story, I paused and asked her, "So, what do you think?"

She replied, "I believe you." I was pleasantly surprised and thanked her for her time. As we were about to part ways, she invited me to come to her home for Shabbos lunch. I graciously accepted her invitation and went to her home the following Shabbos. As I walked to her home that morning, Hashem told me that it was important to share with this woman that I am His Moshiach. I debated with Him vigorously whether it was appropriate to tell her since it was very risky to reveal this information to say the least. He said it was time and that I needed to take the risk.

She served a lovely dairy lunch with a spread of many types of cheeses. We spoke for quite a while and then Hashem said it was time to tell her. I then said to her, "Hashem is telling me now that I need to reveal something to you. I am to tell you today that He has told me for many years that I am His Moshiach."

After I said this I waited for a response to my stunning statement. She paused for a moment, reached over for the platter of cheeses, and then said, "Would you like some cheese?" I was completely dumbfounded. Instead of responding to my outlandish statement, she offered me a slice of cheese? Really?

Silently, I started speaking to Hashem fast and furiously without her realizing. As she held the cheese platter in front of me Hashem quickly said, "Take a piece of cheese Lori. It will calm you down." It seemed she completely ignored what I had just revealed to her. She continued by lamenting about the many struggles she faced in her personal life and completely ignored and skipped over my announcement that I was Hashem's Moshiach.

After waiting several minutes for her to respond to my stunning revelation, I said to her, "I just told you that I am Hashem's Moshiach. Your reply was, have a piece of cheese. I have to admit to you that I am completely stunned." She seemed unfazed by my astounding statement. I asked her if she heard what I said and she responded that she heard me and once again told me she believed that I was telling her the truth. Wow! Is this possible that she is so spiritually aware that the information wasn't at all daunting to her and she believed me? She truly believed that I was Hashem's Moshiach? I became hopeful for the first time since my awakening. Maybe I would finally have support and help.

I stayed until after sundown as we conversed the entire day through the end of Shabbos. She brought out her Zohar which was filled with dog-ears, making it expressly clear that she studied this book voraciously. We spoke about many things that afternoon. Even though she told me that she believed that I was Hashem's Moshiach, I was still curious about her initial reaction to this information. Her words didn't match her behavior or how she treated me when we spoke to each other. If she truly believed I was Hashem's Moshiach I felt her reaction to my words and presence would have been much different. Instead of being respectful toward me and incredibly curious about what I could share with her about Hashem, she lectured me about Torah and everything that she knew. She presented herself as the Torah authority and treated me as though she felt I was clueless. The disconnect was extremely powerful but I went along for the ride because Hashem was guiding me in her direction. She spoke down to me often in a dismissive and derisive tone but I shrugged it off and focused on being grateful to have a new friend who possibly believed me and would help me with my work. She also presented herself as knowledgeable, Torah observant, respected in the Orthodox Jewish community, and spiritually awake. How spiritually awake and knowledgeable she was about the Torah wasn't clear to me yet but I was extremely hopeful.

As I began to form a relationship with this woman, Hashem told me in no uncertain terms that this woman was here to help me. He said it was her life's purpose to help bring Moshiach to the world and give me a voice. He also told me that if she failed in her mission, it would be a serious failure and sin in His eyes. After this Shabbos lunch I stayed in touch with her and we spoke often. She traveled the world and told people in other countries that she knew who Moshiach was and that it was a woman. The Christians she spoke to weren't startled or upset by Moshiach or Messiah being a woman. The religious Jewish community had a much different reaction. They didn't welcome any of this information at all. Quite the contrary they became exceedingly angry, belligerent and spoke contemptuously to her because of her support for me. They made a strong and concerted effort to convince her I was dangerous and someone she needed to abandon.

To her credit, she persevered through the controversy, for a short time. She arranged for us to co-host a Blog Talk Radio program that she named "The Voice of Peace – Conversations with G-d." She even hired a graphic designer to create a logo for this radio program. At first, she told me I was the cohost for her program. She said she was the "Voice of Peace" and I was the "Conversations with G-d." Then she changed her mind and decided it would be her radio program and I would be her special guest. Whatever arrangement she saw fit, I was deeply grateful for her help. The first Blog Talk Radio program for "The Voice of Peace – Conversations with G-d," aired at 8 PM Israel time on July 12, 2016. As I write these words, I'm stunned that at the time I didn't realize this was the anniversary of my father's passing on the secular calendar. My father died on July 12, 1985 and here I was on the anniversary of his death revealing on global Blog Talk Radio for the first time that I speak with Hashem. Coincidence? There are none.

She hosted five Blog Talk Radio programs with me as her special guest. As an Orthodox Jew, she took great risk by sharing my controversial information with the world. On her radio program, she interviewed me and asked deep questions about my spiritual awakening and conversations with Hashem. She even asked me to read from my first Journal "The Book of Love." Then, on one pivotal program, she asked me directly, "Are you telling us that you are the Moshiach?" I replied to her on air, that this was exactly what Hashem told me I am. I explained that I am Hashem's Queen Moshiach but time will tell if I will ever be the Moshiach to the people of this world.

After this program was finished where I announced that I was Hashem's Moshiach, she became physically shaken and her hands spontaneously began to bleed. I had never seen anything like this before in my life. It was as though our conversation cut her skin like a knife. She then said very emotionally that she was risking her entire life for me. She started shaking and said, "I need chocolate!" She ran to her refrigerator and took out some dark chocolate to share. I laughed out loud and found the whole interaction hilarious and heartwarming. I'm sure she didn't find it funny herself but she was extremely courageous to do this and was being emotionally genuine in that moment. She not only hosted this program and brought out this controversial information that evening but she shared this broadcast with many people including several rabbis. I waited for a strong reaction but none ever came. It was completely bewildering to me that we had just announced that I was awakened on April 7, 2009 and I was Hashem God's Queen Moshiach and there was no response. The reaction from the Jewish people was stone cold silence.

After I shared this information it was clear she was under fire from her Orthodox Jewish friends who thought she was insane to believe me or support me in any way. As a result, we began experiencing friction. She was a woman who was enamored with butterflies. Butterflies adorned her clothing and her home. One morning I was awakened to a vision of butterflies. I asked Hashem what He wanted to tell me about this woman. He then said, "Butterflies are free to fly, fly away." This is a famous line from an Elton John song. Hashem's message was clear, it was time for me to set her free. The next Sunday we met for our fifth and final program of "The Voice of Peace – Conversations with G-d." The conversation became argumentative and she quickly gave me an easy way out of our relationship. She said that it was time for me to do this radio program by myself. I agreed with her and she generously paid for the initial subscription to a Blog Talk Radio program of my own. The name of my new program became "Running on Love with God."

My first Blog Talk Radio program was scheduled for the following Sunday, which was August 14, 2016. In a clear sign from Hashem God, this date was the 9th of Av on the Jewish calendar. Did I choose this date on purpose? Hardly. Hashem chose this date for me. The 9th of Av is a profound day of mourning for Jews around the world. Jews fast on this day of mourning and pray for the coming of the Moshiach and the end of their exile. It is the anniversary of the destruction of the two Holy Temples in Jerusalem as well as many other trage-dies in Jewish history. It's a fast day when observant Jews repent for all the sins that led to the destruction of the Holy Temples and brought about the exile and diaspora of the Jewish people. The diaspora was the scattering of the Jewish people to the four corners of the Earth, outside of their homeland of Israel. On the Friday morning before my first broadcast scheduled for 8 PM on Sunday August 14, 2016, Hashem awakened me and said, "Lori, on Sunday morning I want you to take your video camera and tripod to the Kinneret. I want you to record a short video and entitle this video 'Shalom, I am your Moshiach'."

On Sunday morning, August 14, 2016, the 9th of Av on the Jewish calendar, I followed His instructions. I took my digital video camera and tripod to the Kinneret, also known as the famed Sea of Galilee, and recorded two short videos. Hashem told me to wear my black Running on Love sleeveless running t-shirt and my black spandex running pants. I did everything as I was instruct-ed. As I recorded one of the two takes, I was interrupted by someone using a chain saw to cut shrubs. As if the loud buzzing of the saw wasn't intrusive enough, while I was recording, two men carrying fishing poles walked past me. Instead of stopping the camera to wait for them to pass me, I let it roll. Since Hashem chose the venue and the timing, I went with it and included these impromptu events in my video. Of the two videos, this one was my favorite albeit less serious and more whimsical. It was true to life and shows clearly that "we plan and God laughs." It's all Hashem!

When I arrived home, Hashem told me to upload the two videos to YouTube, and then to post them on the Running on Love Facebook page. After I did this, He told me to post one of the videos on a closed Facebook group called Geula Watch. I was invited to join this group by an Orthodox Jewish woman, a realtor who helped me find a temporary residence when I first arrived in Israel as a new citizen. Geula is a Hebrew name for girls, which translates to redemption. This page was for Jewish people who desired redemption and were looking for the Moshiach, the Messiah. I listened to Hashem's marching orders and posted a comment with the link to the video. My post read:

Hashem, God, woke me this past Friday morning, and said, "Lori, on Sunday morning you must take your video camera to the Kinneret (Sea of Galilee) and record a video that you must share with everyone that you possibly can. I want you to title your video, 'Shalom, I am your Moshiach.' If you do as I say, you will be helping your children heal and save lives." My answer, "Of course, I will do it." I am compelled to listen to Him and post this video. I fear your reaction Israel but I must do this anyway at the hope that it begins the road to peace for our world. I pray I will be greeted with love and acceptance. Please Hashem protect me and bless all the good people of the world. Please let there be peace in our time!

I waited for a response from my post and video. What could be a more perfect place for me to introduce myself than a page where Jewish people were looking for Moshiach? Wrong! By that evening I received their less than warm reaction. As I was editing this book in the final review before publishing, Hashem guided me to log into an old email account I used back in August of 2016 which was attached to my personal Facebook page. I have many email accounts and hadn't looked at this one for at least two years. As I logged in I began to delete hundreds of old emails from Facebook until Hashem stopped me abruptly and told me to look at the next email before deleting it. Unbeknownst to me, Facebook sends email messages which include conversation threads to posts where you make comments. They sent me the message thread from my Geula Watch post which included the names and condescending messages from Geula Watch members. Hashem led me to the email account and then stopped me just before I deleted it! Lucky break, don't you agree? I won't include the entire message thread or their names in this book, but I will share a few unedited comments.

One member of this closed Facebook group looking for the Messiah was an Orthodox Jewish woman who commented in a deeply sarcastic tone, "OMG seriously?!?!?!?!?? Mashiach in a tanktop ok... I don't know if i should laugh or cry but wait what happened to eliyahu hanavi blowing the shofar for all to hear?! Did I miss it?!?! :O"

The comments continued in the same disdainful and demeaning tone. Another woman from this group wrote a comment asking me sneeringly, "What's your plan?" This was followed by yet another group member who addressed me in a contrived manner while pretending to be sincere. In a pretentiously sympathetic tone this person educated me that I suffered from something called the "Moshiach Complex."

He or she patronizingly told me not to feel too badly that I suffered from this syndrome because every Jew is Moshiach and then added, "Messiah complex is not a bad thing, nor is it untrue. Every Jew is Moshiach, yet there is One Moshiach above all, the male descendent of Kind David who has all the multidimensional qualifications. That doesn't necessarily contradict your identity and mission. If you get my drift." I guess I got the drift that I was being told I was in good company with all the other crazies who believed they were the Moshiach too. I was also being informed that being a woman excluded me from having the needed multidimensional qualifications for this job. I guess Geula Watch hasn't notified Hashem yet that I'm simply not qualified. Should I forget the entire affair since I of course am not a male descendent of King David? What would you do if you put your life on the line and were met with such nastiness? Would you retreat and call it a day? Clearly, I didn't.

Instead of retreating, after I saw their posts online I replied to them all as follows:

"Thank you all for your conversation. My apologies for the delay, I was on the blog talk radio show tonight which I am hosting. I appreciate your comments and understand your questions. Hard to believe yes, a woman but completely consistent with prophecy. The explanations have been written and I can elaborate at the right time. The master plan for redemption is a charity model called Running on Love. As far as my dress (tank top), I am consistent with Hashem's wishes and perfectly modest in His eyes. I appreciate and respect your way of dressing and understand your questions about mine, but would appreciate refraining from mocking me. I am a lover and connector of people and the people that I must bring together under the umbrella of love are ALL people of the world. Here is a link to my charity which was formed shortly after Hashem woke me in 2009: www.runningonlove.org. The plan is to create Festivals for Love that support all charities and charitable giving in the name of love. It is a model that is inherently Jewish. The people who have embraced it most have been Christians. There is a business plan for redemption, amazing it is! Yes (name removed), everyone is required to be like Moshiach or there is no redemption. The Temple will not fall from the sky and peace will not be given to us. We must cleanse and remove all traces of Yetzer Hara and evil from our world. I have much to share with you and the world. It will not happen without your support and love. I pray for your interest and hope you will grow to trust me! ♥"

In another post comment I replied:

"I have no complex as you say. I have Hashem. I don't desire this, this role was put upon me and I am told there is no one else to do this. In truth, if I could give this over to another to be the Moshiach I would. I am what I am and I can't choose to be something I am not. I respect your opinions and others who cannot fathom this and I wish you all peace and good health."

Their response? They promptly deleted my post and blocked me from their closed Facebook group page. How lovely! The Moshiach was banned from Geula Watch.

I cried, "Hashem, now what? Your Moshiach has just been ridiculed and banned from this Orthodox Jewish Facebook page." Although these weren't people I'd invite over for Shabbos anytime soon, I was still completely disheartened. I wept to Hashem, "How will I ever succeed? Nobody will ever listen to me or believe me!"

Hashem's reply, "Perfect. The more they reject you Lori, the more suffering they will experience when they learn the truth." It was mind-boggling to me that here in Israel I would receive responses that ranged from cold silence to derisive sarcasm. I was completely shut down and shunned from this closed Orthodox Jewish Facebook page that was purporting to look for their Moshiach. My friend and former Blog Talk Radio co-host in the "Voice of Peace – Conversations with G-d" program, went to their group page to see if she could join them. They swiftly interrogated her about her level of Jewish observance and Halacha, which is Torah law. They vetted her to determine if she was "Jewish enough" to join their group. After she met their halachic requirements and was permitted to join, she told me she decided quickly to leave this group because she found them offensive. Good for her!

She and I continued to be friendly but the strain between us was increasing daily. I introduced her to my oldest daughter who is a talented singer and musician. This woman was a well-known and accomplished voice teacher and I thought she might help my daughter with her passion for singing. My daughter and I went to her home on Shabbos and the two of them spoke for a while. She said that she only accepted students who were serious and talented. After she met with my daughter she decided that she was worthy of her instruction. I was delighted that the two of them hit it off.

One day while visiting with this woman in her home, we sat in her kitchen and as we spoke it was clear there was increasing division between us. She was an observant Orthodox Jewish woman who followed the Orthodox dress code for modesty. The laws are very specific and have been written by rabbis and handed down for centuries. In these laws women who are married must cover their hair. All women must wear sleeves past their elbows, and clothing necklines should cover the collarbone. Women must only wear dresses or skirts past their knees and never pants. In these written laws of modesty, dressing like I do in blue jeans and sleeveless shirts is strictly prohibited. She questioned me continuously throughout our relationship about my observance of Torah law and wondered why Hashem didn't command me to follow these strict laws concerning dress. She excused me for not covering my hair because I was divorced but she was incensed that I wore blue jeans and tank tops. She constantly ridiculed me and told me that I was breaking Torah law. She couldn't understand why Hashem's Moshiach refused to follow the laws of modest dress. I replied to her that I am perfectly compliant with Hashem's wishes and that one day these modesty laws as well as other parts of Halacha will be reviewed with the help of many rabbis. For now, I asked her to trust me when I told her that I wasn't breaking Torah law in the eyes of Hashem and to try to set aside her objections for the time being.

She became more argumentative about the Torah and from the beginning of our relationship, she made it clear she was the authority who was here to teach me, instead of the other way around. She railed at me that I was irreverent to Hashem's laws and boasted that she was the embodiment of the Torah who would never stray under any circumstances. It was bizarre that she felt I was somehow seducing her to break Torah law when I was Hashem's Moshiach. Would Moshiach be a temptress to encourage her to sin in God's eyes? What a bizarre assertion I thought, yet that's how condescending she was to me. It was painfully clear she was pulling away and no longer believed I was Hashem's Moshiach. Perhaps she never truly did.

She finally pulled the final straw that ended our relationship. One afternoon I sat in her kitchen and she turned to me and told me she thought my daughter was wonderful and one day she would be a jewel in my crown. I thanked her for saying these lovely words and told her I felt my daughter was already my gift from Hashem and a crown jewel. She then said something to me that hurt me deeply. She said, "One day your daughter will choose to change her name and she will renounce you." Her words stunned and shocked me. I thought perhaps she was referring to my daughter's last name which was already different from mine. I responded that her name was already different and my daughter would never renounce me. Why in the world would she say such a thing to me? How could anyone ever say or wish this upon another human being? I didn't react fully in that moment because I couldn't comprehend why anyone would say something so malicious. I did my best to shrug it off and told her I was secure that nothing could permanently harm my relationship with my daughter. Her harsh words were extremely offensive.

I went home that evening still feeling disturbed about this conversation. I looked up the word *renounce* to make sure I wasn't exaggerating or being overly sensitive. The definition of *renounce* read: *to formally declare one's abandonment of a claim, right, or possession.* When I read this definition, I cried to Hashem, "Why would this woman say such a thing to me? Why would anyone wish this upon any other person?" I was heartbroken not at her accusation that my daughter would renounce me, but rather that she would even utter something this cruel to me out loud. I felt in my heart and soul no matter what happened in our lives, my daughter would never renounce me. For years my husband and family tried their best to harm my relationship with my children and take them from me. The idea of losing my daughter was so heartbreaking and painful that I refused to believe it was possible.

This woman had claimed to my daughter and many others that she was a prophetess from God. Hearing her tell me that my daughter would renounce me one day as though she was sharing holy prophecy was too much for me to bear. Hashem comforted me and told me to rest assured that my relationship with my daughter was eternal and secure.

As my relationship with this woman unraveled, she became physically sick with an illness and had difficulty eating. My daughter and I visited her for the third meal on Shabbos one Saturday afternoon. While we were there she was accompanied by one of her friends who was also an Orthodox Jewish woman. She had spent the prior evening with this woman and another one of their religious friends. She looked exhausted and said to me that the night before her two friends gave her a relentless verbal beating but didn't reveal the subject matter in front of everyone. Instead, she looked at me and with private body language gave me a clear message that their verbal assaults were about her support of me.

These two Orthodox Jewish women friends of hers argued with her to distance herself from me. They of course didn't believe that I was Hashem's Moshiach. Moshiach to all religious Jewish people must be an Orthodox Jewish man. Hashem's Moshiach could never be a Jewish woman in a tank top and blue jeans God forbid! Heresy! Shortly after this meal, I received an email from her confirming these sentiments. In short, she believed that her failing health was a sign from Hashem that she was being punished because I led her astray. I guess I was viewed as some sort of Jewish Jezebel. Kidding, of course but not far from the truth. Her email made me sound like the personification of evil who was luring her away from God Himself. Oy vey!

Although our relationship ended harshly, as we departed ways I harbored no hard feelings toward this woman. I was deeply grateful that she gave me a voice and introduced me to the world. She supported me, believed in me albeit temporarily, and went so far as to create a Blog Talk Radio program to help me come out to the world. The five radio programs where she interviewed me were the beginning of what eventually became my own weekly radio program. This woman bravely stepped up to help me when nobody else had the courage. Early in our relationship it was clear that she was listening to her own spiritual instincts and perhaps even truly believed that I was indeed Hashem's Moshiach Queen. Her soul led her to the truth, but like everyone else in this world, under extraordinary pressure by her community, she succumbed to their way of thinking. The badgering from her Orthodox Jewish friends and her added health problems were too much pressure for her to bear. Fear is fuel for the Yetzer Hara, the evil inclination. While she thought she was pulling herself away from evil to return to Hashem, she was doing completely the opposite and bathing in filth. She unraveled and relented to the Yetzer Hara, clinging tightly to her group where she felt safe.

From the beginning of my spiritual awakening, it was clear that my road to acceptance would be long and difficult. I wondered and still do, if anyone in this world will ever truly accept me. My new extended Jewish family in Israel refused to listen to me at every turn. While I was broadcasting on Blog Talk Radio and revealing to the world that I was speaking with Hashem daily in English, I also met in person with a few other friends. I felt close to an English-speaking married couple I met in Israel when I first arrived. This was the same couple who helped me find and then move into my first apartment. Our relationship was very warm and friendly so I shared the news with them too and even gave them an early draft of the introduction to this book that you are reading right now. The introduction has changed dramatically but it gave them a synopsis of what the book was about—me, their Moshiach. Oh boy, maybe my new "friends" will support me now. Yeah, I was grasping at straws and hoping for help.

After I revealed the truth and shared the earth-shattering revelation that I am the Moshiach, this English-speaking couple reacted a little bit like my Voice of Peace Orthodox Jewish friend saying to me, "Would you like some cheese?" At least after offering me cheese she stepped up to help me and didn't completely walk away. The next time I spoke with the wife after I gave her the introduction to this book she said, "I just had a wonderful pedicure." As she raved about her new pedicure, I was flabbergasted. This couple had no questions for me or for Hashem and wouldn't consider entertaining the idea that I might be telling the truth. They not only wouldn't consider the possibility, but after they blatantly rejected and ignored the information I shared, this same couple showed me that they clearly felt rejected by me when I needed to distance myself from them.

The next time I saw this couple at a social gathering the wife was cold and visibly angry that I no longer socialized with them. What was I to talk to them about at social gatherings or Torah classes after I had told them both that I was Hashem's Moshiach? After they heard this incredible revelation from me was I supposed to pretend I didn't share this information with them? Was I supposed to revert to being invisible Lori who knows less about Hashem and His Torah than everyone else? Should I conveniently forget that I gave them both the blessed privilege of reading an early draft of the introduction for my book? Was I supposed to pretend that I was praying with everyone else at our weekly Torah classes for the coming of the Moshiach, Messiah? Although they appeared offended that I became distant from them and didn't participate in Torah classes they hosted in their home any longer, I couldn't pretend. I was forced to move on and wish them both well.

The reactions to my revelation that I am Hashem's Moshiach and speak with Him in English day and night ranged from silence to insolence. Friends ignored me while others trivialized me, publicly ridiculed me and made fun of my communication with Hashem. Nonetheless, nothing could stop me from continuing my life's purpose and mission. I understood from April 7, 2009 that this was my calling and now I listened to Hashem for His guidance and instructions about how I should proceed. I continued to share Hashem's voice and wisdom on my own weekly radio program: Running on Love with GOD.

Running on Love with GOD

Beginning in the fall of 2016, every Sunday I hosted a weekly Running on Love with GOD radio program on Blog Talk Radio. I was unsure how to approach the program in the early stages. My close friend from America offered to help me with my first several broadcasts. She was my closest Christian girlfriend who was there from the beginning of my awakening. Through the four hospitalizations she waxed and waned in her support for me but always managed to return. Our friendship was tested repeatedly over more than thirty years in ways that most friendships never experience. Now, after I was free and living in Israel we spoke regularly in weekly phone calls. During my first year living in Israel we were as close as ever and considered each other spiritual sisters. Being on my radio program wasn't something that she was comfortable doing but she felt compelled to support me and help me with my work. The first several programs had nice content but they were off message. They lacked emphasis and clarity as I worked to find my footing. After a few programs, it became clear I needed to take control of the format and guide the content. My friend and I spoke about her stepping aside and being available as needed.

I did several programs and then Hashem told me to video record myself as I spoke while on air. He told me that people would be more engaged by watching a video as opposed to listening to the radio program. The first video recorded program was on 9/11/16, the 15th anniversary of the tragedy and terrorist attack on the World Trade Center in New York City. I propped up my digital video camera on a tripod and recorded as I spoke about the tragedy on 9/11. As I continued to broadcast the weekly programs and now video record them, on occasion two of my friends from America joined me. It was trial and error in the beginning but eventually the format became more cohesive and engaging.

The audience remained small but I began to attract a few followers on social media. Each week I posted the recorded programs on Facebook and paid for these posts to be promoted. One of my challenges was a severe lack of money after I went broke in the aftermath of my contentious divorce. I was in deep debt and couldn't afford to advertise as I continued to work on growing the world's charity Running on Love. Now I discovered that Running on Love was only a part of my life's mission. This was the world's charity and was never meant to be my career. In prophetic visions for Running on Love, Hashem showed me that this charity was to become a global platform that brought people together in love and education. He continuously showed me large events where I would one day live my true life's purpose, which was to share Hashem's voice and wisdom with the world.

Tiberias Marathon—Running on Love for Dad

I discovered over time that even though Running on Love had over 6000 followers on Facebook in 2016 they wouldn't see any of my posts unless I paid for advertising. You know the expression, pay to play? Facebook has a pay to play policy that is very difficult when you have no money. Their minimum charge is a dollar a day per post and they refuse to advertise for anything less. My financial situation was serious and I was in deep debt but I scratched and scrounged to find a dollar a day. Supporting this charity drained me of all my money and I felt discouraged but I kept going anyway and refused to give up. By the end of 2016, I decided it was time to end my personal agony and pain. As a last-ditch effort to save Running on Love, I signed up for a 10K run in the Tiberias Marathon and decided that this would be a final fundraiser. This time I didn't have the strength or training to run the full 26.2-mile marathon. I set up a fundraising campaign and ran the 10K, 6.2 miles, in my father's memory.

I sent email after email to hundreds of people whom I had known for many years. In my personal life and career, I had accumulated thousands of contacts. On Facebook alone at one time I had over 500 "friends." The term *friends* is one that Facebook uses for the people you are connected to on their social media site. On LinkedIn, I had over 1,500 people whom this site refers to in a more businesslike manner as *connections*. I sent personal emails telling everyone I knew that this charity was on its last mission to survive. I explained that this was my life's work and passion, and that I had devoted seven years building it, exhausting my life savings. I requested even the smallest amount that anybody could possibly donate to this fundraising campaign to help me honor my dad and save this beautiful charity.

After I moved to Israel I deleted my personal Facebook page and reopened a new one because I decided that I would only connect with a smaller group of people who I considered to be my closest friends. I whittled down my number of "friends" from over 500 to a mere 80 people. I deliberately posted very frank and honest posts telling everyone that I heard Hashem God and shared my Blog Talk Radio programs with my new smaller group. Their response was icy cold. My 80 friends rarely liked any of my posts or responded to anything I said.

When I first came out and told my new smaller group of Facebook friends that I hear God, I made a tongue-in-cheek post where I referred to this as my "coming out party." One "friend" replied to my post by commenting that she loved me anyway even though I was a lesbian. Really? She didn't take the time to read my post and simply responded to the words "coming out." She never listened to one of my blog talk radio programs. It was clear that if I was announcing that I was a lesbian or perhaps transgender like Bruce Jenner who announced he was having surgery to change himself into a woman I would have been loved and accepted. Coming out and announcing that I spoke to God was met with rejection and cold-hearted silence. It seemed that other people in the world who claimed to speak to God were well thought of, but nobody told me this acceptance wouldn't apply to me. My messages were clearly not

Jewish enough or Christian enough for any religious group of people. The secular non-religious people wanted no part of me at all. I began to wonder if I really had true friends in this world since most of them weren't listening to a single word I had to say. What's a friend anyway? The meaning of the word *friend* began to elude me.

In what was intended to be my last fundraiser for Running on Love in the 2017 Tiberias marathon, I made plea after plea to save my beautiful charity and life's work. After months of emails and posts, I raised only $300 in memory of my father. Family and friends completely ignored my emails. Nobody was inspired by my work. Quite the contrary, most people clearly looked down on me. They were united with the club that thought I was either crazy or obnoxious with my new-found love of God and an obsessive compulsion to share His voice. With 30 days left until the first day of Hanukkah which fell on the same day as Christmas in 2016, I decided to do a 30-day countdown and referred to December 25th as my decision day for Running on Love. December 25th would be the day I decided if Running on Love would be dissolved or live on for another year. I began to post daily short videos telling everybody the status of my fundraising effort. I told them the truth, that Running on Love was never my charity but God's charity to bring us all together as family and bring world peace. My 80 Facebook friends continued to ignore every one of my posts and requests for donations.

As I came close to the end of the 30-day countdown, Hashem told me to give everyone a Running on Love Challenge. He told me to create this challenge in honor of the two holidays, and challenge everyone to make Hanukkah and Christmas purely about God and not gold. I challenged everyone to give a gift of charity to Running on Love in loving memory or honor of someone they cared about. I hosted a Blog Talk Radio program that Sunday and called it "God is love not gold." It was clear from the beginning that nobody understood my message. There was only one person in all the promotions for this challenge who took the message seriously. It was someone who was suffering financially herself and she donated $50 to Running on Love.

I broadcasted this program "God is love not gold" with my closest Christian girlfriend as my co-host. It was clear she didn't understand the message either. I stated clearly that God desired the holiday to be about God not gold and suggested that people support Running on Love in lieu of buying each other material gifts. As we spoke live on air, she disagreed with me that it had to be all or nothing. She said, "I have to be honest with you Lori" and then told me that people should be allowed to buy presents for their family and they could choose any charity to support, it didn't have to be in support of Running on Love. She completely negated my effort to make the holidays about God and Running on Love. She went on about how she commiserated with the public that it wasn't so easy because family would feel disappointed if they didn't receive gifts. I was dumbfounded. Was she helping me teach people not to be materialistic and save God's charity? She continued to interrupt me as I spoke about the challenge and she argued with me on air as we broadcasted this program live. In our private conversations she told me she was certain I spoke with God and had no doubt that I spoke the truth. On this broadcast while we were live on air, she defiantly went against what I was asking everyone to do in this Running on Love Challenge. I was devastated that I was forced to abruptly cut her off in mid-conversation and end the radio program. If I couldn't convince my closest girlfriend who told me she believed in me to embrace this challenge that was created by God Himself, how would I ever get support from strangers? Was anyone ever going to believe me or listen?

Now I Know I'm Moshiach. I Only Need Hashem.

In early December of 2016 decision day for Running on Love was fast approaching. Only an abysmal $300 was raised and the fate of Running on Love looked all but sealed. Just four of my 80 Facebook friends donated to my fundraising campaign in memory of my father. In a short video message, I made one final plea to these 80 friends. In this video, I asked them to donate the equivalent of a cup of coffee from Dunkin' Donuts, two dollars, to Running on Love, to show that they supported my life's work. I asked them all for this symbolic gesture so that I would know where I stood with each of them. In my request, I told them that if they didn't donate at least two dollars to Running on Love by the morning of December 9th which was also the 8th of Kislev, my 57th birthday on both the Jewish and secular calendars (which only happens every 19 years), I would set them free and disconnect on Facebook wishing them Godspeed. In my message, I was friendly and not confrontational at all. After months of posting about God and Running on Love they were silent and ignored me. It was extremely uncomfortable for them as it was for me too. It was clear they didn't approve of my work or support me but they didn't want to abruptly disconnect either. So, I gave them a final option to show me their true feelings by either donating to my life's work or choosing to abstain. After I posted this video, I waited for them to reply. When I awakened on the morning of December 9th, 2016 at 7 AM I sat up in my bed and unchecked the names of 76 people who were my last "friends" on Facebook. I thought that doing this would make me cry because I was deliberately walking away from 76 formerly close friends, some of whom I had known since childhood. Instead of crying I felt emboldened and stronger than ever. There were just four friends remaining on my page when I finished. Each of the four friends left on my page had donated before I even asked for this gesture of donating any amount at all. They were four friends who had liked my posts, had shown their support, and had known me for more than 30 years.

On my 57th birthday I recognized that I had willfully walked away from almost every person in my life to do the work that I was chosen to do by Hashem God. In that moment, as I bravely unchecked 76 names on Facebook I knew that I must be His Moshiach. I didn't need any other person in my life and knew unequivocally that I only needed Hashem. My willingness to walk away from every person I'd ever known to do my life's work and be authentically and unapologetically myself is a required personality trait of His Moshiach. I don't know another living human being who would walk away from every single relationship to walk completely alone with God. Many righteous and religious people believe they would do so, but I've never seen this done before. I've only read about this in Torah and have never seen this quality exhibited in a living human being. Quite the contrary, when pressured, people succumb to the good opinion of others and relent by accepting everyone else's opinions. They walk away from their spiritual calling to keep their relationships with family and friends intact. I knew that I had already lost my family and friends by choosing to be authentically myself and refusing to compromise. But it was much more than this that made me realize that I was Hashem's Moshiach in that moment. When I sat up in bed on my birthday morning, I unchecked each name with the help and guidance of Hashem. He held my hand and did this with me. I am never alone.

The Friday before decision day, Sunday December 25th, 2016, I was sure that I would announce that Running on Love would be no more. I was completely ready to dissolve this beautiful charity and end my many years of disappointment and heartbreak. That Shabbos prior to December 25th, Hashem and I had a deep conversation about the fate of Running on Love. He spoke to me about all the activity on Facebook and the many thumbs up and hearts received on my posts from strangers around the world. The messages that I posted every day for 30 days received extremely high engagement. Not many responses came from the United States or Israel, but strong acknowledgement came from places like Rio de Janeiro, Brazil. My posts were getting over 10% engagement and some posts received over 15%. Hashem had me research typical engagement on Facebook after Shabbat ended. I read studies that said 15 percent engagement usually only happened in email marketing. Hashem convinced me that this was a miraculous sign and instructed me that I shouldn't close the doors on Running on Love. Instead He guided me to announce on decision day, Sunday December 25, 2016, that we had experienced a miracle. He guided me to thank everyone for creating this miracle which gave renewed hope that we would one day see our world Run on Love.

The Facebook post announcing a miracle for Running on Love received many likes as usual, but no donations. For this charity to take wings and fly around the world, it needed resources. It was clear that I wouldn't receive the donations needed to make this the world charity Hashem promised it was destined to become. Regardless of my skepticism that this would ever come to pass, I announced that Sunday morning that Running on Love would live another year. What was my work now I wondered? I realized through this experience that Running on Love the charity was truly my gift to the people of the world and not for me. I already ran on love with Hashem. My life's purpose was teaching people about the ways of God and sharing His wisdom. One day if Running on Love ever grew to be a world charity, it would be the platform where I would do my true life's work as His teacher, adviser and messenger. My plan as I went forward was to keep Running on Love the charity open for business but focus on my new work, Running on Love with GOD, the weekly programs.

Weekly Radio/Video Programs and More

One of my four remaining Facebook friends, a former co-worker and friend of over 30 years, agreed to cohost my weekly Running on Love with GOD programs beginning on New Year's Day 2017. Over the next several months, through a lot of trial and error, these programs became thought provoking and extremely focused. After we completed each program it surprised both of us how each of these programs were smart, intellectually stimulating and spiritually revealing. We covered various subjects ranging from pollution and the environment to how we should raise our children. The goal each week was for me to share God's voice and wisdom in areas we all grapple with in everyday life while my cohost asked questions to go deeper into each subject.

Prior to our first video recorded program of Running on Love with God with my cohost, Hashem spoke to me in a late-night conversation and suggested a specific free online video program that would allow me to record myself and another person in a video chat session. I forwarded the name of this video application to my cohost in an email. We didn't research His suggestion promptly and instead my friend and I fumbled around for months trying out several different methods that required her to video edit the files before we realized that Hashem had directed us to the perfect tool months earlier. When we tried this video chat tool and it worked seamlessly, we laughed uproariously how we had Hashem's answer for months but sloughed it off and spun our wheels. It was a clear lesson that we needed to investigate every one of His suggestions right from the start. I say investigate, because I never forgot the lesson of "my tomato story" even through today. He wants our involvement every step of the way, often gives us the answers and welcomed shortcuts, but He still requires us to evaluate and make the final choices ourselves.

Through the years since my awakening in 2009, I became acutely aware that our world had lost its moral compass and people struggled with everyday life issues. Making simple choices between good and evil seemed impossible for the average person. Daily I observed good and decent God-loving people making lousy and even sinful choices. This lack of awareness of the difference between right and wrong had created a world that I no longer recognized. People clearly didn't know that their choices were flawed and that these poor choices were corrupting our world and harming us all. These Running on Love with God weekly programs were a tool to shed light and bring awareness about how everyone was choosing evil, often without even realizing it.

Eventually Hashem told me that I needed to record brief video messages that were up to five minutes long, give or take. He wanted me to share messages in shorter clips so that people could watch and digest the information in smaller doses. He woke me to visions of spoons and told me to give the information in a spoonful. Hashem explained that most people didn't have the attention span for our 30-minute weekly programs. I began to post shorter Q&A videos which seemed to interest more people. Even still, since our first broadcast on January 1, 2017 the number of views for the longer Running on Love with GOD programs and these short videos remained very low.

One day I looked online at other videos on YouTube, and was startled to observe the number of views these videos received. For example I found one video that answered the inane question "Which way is the correct way to face your toilet paper on the dispenser?" Frivolous videos like this one received half a million to a million views, sometimes many more. Videos about an everyday working woman from New Jersey now living in Israel who speaks to God and shares His messages were only getting 30-40 views on a good day.

Seeing and feeling my frustration, one morning Hashem awakened me and said, "Lori, you have to learn how to play their game."

I replied, "Hashem I don't want to play patty cake with anyone. I want to teach and share You with them. I don't want to play any games!"

Hashem replied, "Don't worry Lori, I will play their game. You can play with Me." This was music to my ears. Playing with Hashem and speaking with Him is all I ever want to do. He is incredibly delightful, loving, and awe-inspiring. I am completely addicted to Him and relentlessly reach for Him day and night. Now, He was telling me that all I had to do was follow His lead. Hashem then gave me this question to use for one of my short Q&A videos—"Why do Jewish people have big noses?" That video continues to get five to ten views every day and is the most watched video I've posted so far. So, what's the take-home message here? Is this truly what the people of our world are interested in right now? The take-home message is quite revealing and should be extremely embarrassing don't you agree? This Q&A question came from our Creator Himself. He knows how people think, and what motivates them. As I work and create every post for social media, Hashem is guiding me. Everything I do is done with the conscious knowing that He is working with me, speaking to me, and guiding me in every moment.

Connecting the Dots—LoriMichelle.net

In March of 2017, Hashem instructed me that I needed to create a website that would combine all the media in one place. By this time, I had a YouTube channel, a Facebook page, a Twitter account, and a LinkedIn profile page. I had content in multiple places with no focal point that brought everything together. There was no easy way to search and find content across the large number of social media platforms where I was posting.

Now that I was living hand to mouth, I could barely afford to pay my bills. After paying my rent and other fixed expenses there was hardly enough money left over for food and bus fare. Regardless, I continued to promote posts on Facebook for a dollar a day. With donations generously given by my cohost on my weekly programs, I managed to stay afloat. She made donations regularly to Running on Love which allowed me to continue to pay for Facebook promotion and still manage to pay my monthly bills. She had become my only charitable donor while also being my weekly cohost for the Running on Love with GOD program. Her engaging and challenging questions each week made these programs far more interesting and compelling than if I hosted them alone. Running on Love with GOD had taken on a life and style that was perfect for delivering God's wisdom and sharing my miraculous gift with the world. This loyal friend and her husband supported me spiritually and financially when no one else did. The few other friends who had supported my work through the end of 2016 became invisible by spring of 2017. Though some of them said they were watching the videos, it wasn't apparent. They admitted they watched when they could find the time but complained they led busy lives that made it too difficult. The information I was sharing didn't seem very important to anyone other than Hashem, me, my dear friend and cohost and her wonderful husband.

In preparation for the release of my first book, I needed a central location for all the content that we were creating. I registered the domain LoriMichelle.net and looked for a WYSIWYG tool to create my own website. A "What You See Is What You Get" entry-level website was all that I could manage to be able to create a website on my own. My instructions from Hashem were to keep the website clean, extremely simple, without animations, direct and straightforward. My dear friend and cohost was already working on my programs, donating money, and supporting me in ways that no one else seemed willing. When I told her that I was struggling to create a website she offered her expertise to build me one using WordPress. As she often does, she rendered me speechless with her generosity. Her offer brought me to tears.

She emailed me a few free WordPress templates to choose from and within days she flowed my content into the chosen design. We worked together for a couple of weeks as I wrote copy and gave her creative direction for the layout. Within just another few weeks, we neared the point of completion and we were both delighted with the results. We put our minds together and we created a beautiful website that was elegantly simple and brought all the content together seamlessly.

At Hashem's request, we added a page where people could schedule private meetings with me. Hashem instructed me to offer private meetings for a small donation to the charity Running on Love. The sessions would allow me to share my gift of hearing Hashem and receive donations for the charity of world peace. It seemed like a no-brainer to me that people would want to sign up and have a private session to ask God Himself questions. My friend, cohost and now web developer even found an automated scheduler that tied into PayPal for seamless scheduling and payment. In the entire year of 2017, she was the only person who donated and scheduled a private meeting with me. Incredible, right? Don't you wish you had a friend like her? In 2017, I gave one other private session and waived the donation to a young woman in America who needed help. She was struggling and didn't have the means to give a donation. As I move forward with the completion of this book, Hashem instructed me to remove the option to schedule a private meeting from the website.

When I told my longtime Christian girlfriend, soul sister of over 30 years, and former supporter of Running on Love that the offer to give personal meetings would be removed by January 1st of 2018, she donated and scheduled a half hour private meeting with me. I was truly delighted to share Hashem's voice and wisdom with her but there were extremely difficult messages she needed to hear. She said she delayed making this appointment because she instinctually knew that she had to brace herself for bad news.

As you may recall, she turned away when I needed her support and friendship and betrayed me many times over the years since my spiritual awakening. When times were tough she repeatedly sided with those who desired to harm me. Although I love her dearly, protecting her and not sharing serious problems by revealing her poor choices would only serve to hurt her. During this meeting I shared painful insight into deeply sinful choices she had made over the years. Her choices were a repeated self-serving pattern that had nothing to do with me or our friendship. Sharing this information was exclusively for her benefit. I shared this difficult information in the most loving way possible but there was no easy way to convey what she needed to hear. Since this meeting we have barely spoken. My life's work is to help every person see their failures and show them where they need to improve. It's painful and difficult for me to share everyone's shortcomings but I know it's for their best. If I refuse to do this, I harm the people I love even more. I won't do that. One day, God willing, my girlfriend and soul sister will reunite with me in friendship and I will be able to give her the guidance she needs to help her heal.

By early May of 2017 LoriMichelle.net was completed and we were ready to launch. The eighth anniversary of my first involuntary psychiatric commitment and infamous Mother's Day catastrophe was May 10, 2017. I decided to make this date the official launch date for my website to symbolically and triumphantly claim that I now had full control over my life. As we prepared for the website launch on May 10, 2017 I needed pictures of myself for my bio page. At first, I attempted to take a selfie and hoped the quality would be good enough. Using the Sea of Galilee as my backdrop, I began taking selfies by a scenic overlook a few blocks from my home. There was an Orthodox Jewish man sitting on a bench watching me take my pictures. He engaged me in conversation and informed me that there was a large celebration for Pesach Sheni in town, also known as "The Second Passover." In the Torah, Hashem established a "Second

Passover" (Pesach Sheni) for anyone who was unable to bring the offering on its appointed time in the previous month during Passover. Pesach Sheni has special meaning representing a "Second Chance." It was incredibly fitting that the launch date of my new website was not only on the eighth anniversary of the tragic Mother's Day debacle that began my nightmare, but it was also Pesach Sheni. This was my second chance to reclaim my life and begin anew. On the evening of Pesach Sheni, I emotionally ate a meal of matzah pizza and then launched LoriMichelle.net immediately after.

My entire life prepared me every step of the way for my spiritual awakening on April 7, 2009. As I have explained throughout this book thus far, this awakening was always going to happen to me and everything that occurred in its aftermath was orchestrated by Hashem. The euphoria I felt after I recognized my gift was swiftly extinguished as I was led into a frightening house of horrors. I lived through four trips to mental hospital hell on earth and then became deaf, divorced, and destitute. Every step of the way Hashem prepared and educated me to accept my ultimate life calling as His Moshiach. After He carried me through the raging storm, He escorted me home to Israel where I wrote this book. Please keep reading as I continue to deliver God's voice to you with all my love.

As we continue, I will reveal incredible stories and explanations given to me by our Creator Himself. Among these explanations, Hashem has explained why the Moshiach was always destined to be a woman and why this role was always going to be given to me. Incredible you might say? You have my full agreement on that one!

Hashem says, "People are like cucumbers." Find out why!

Hashem wants me to share a couple of visions. They're related. One morning He awakened me to a vision of a cucumber and He asked, "Lori what does a cucumber taste like?"

I said, "It has a mild flavor. Sometimes it's sweet but it's mild. It really takes on the flavor of whatever you're soaking it in. If it's vinegar, it becomes sour and if you soak it in sugar, something sweet, it becomes a sweet pickle.

He said, "That's right. People are like cucumbers. They take on the flavor of whomever they surround themselves with."

I replied, "Yeah. I never thought of it that way. That's profound. That's very true!" We're taught from the time we're small to be careful about the friends we choose and who we surround ourselves with because we tend to adapt to their personalities. So, if you're hanging out with a bad crowd, you're apt to get yourself in a lot of trouble.

A few days later He showed me another cucumber image. This time they were sliced but they still had the skin on them. And then He showed me something else. He asked, "Lori what's this?"

I said, "It's a potato peeler."

He said, "That's right. Peel away the barrier and let them absorb your wisdom, your kindness, your faith and your love."

I replied, "That's beautiful Hashem. I'm trying. I'm putting these videos out there. A few people are listening. It's starting to travel. But the reaction is hot and cold, mostly cold, mostly invisible. The only ones who are really bothering to contact me are a little cuckoo—slamming scripture down my throat."

I don't read scripture. I speak to Hashem God, the One. That's where I learn everything. I take that back. I read the Torah with Hashem when He says, "Pick up the Chumash today Lori. Let's read Torah." But it's His commentary and His wisdom that teaches me.

Truly I don't hang out with anyone any more. I hang out with Hashem God. So, if you're a God-loving person and you enjoy my videos, share them. You don't have to reach out to me but I assure you I'm doing this for love. Love for you, for your families, for the world.

He is God. He is incredible. I have a phenomenal, fantastic gift that I just want to give away. All I want to do is share Him and these morning visions and all this wisdom with whomever will listen. So, keep listening, share and call me. But not if you're cuckoo.

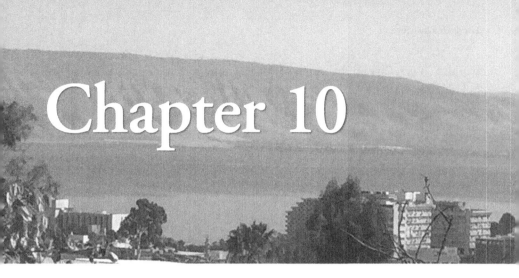

Chapter 10

Chosen to Be the Light

So I get it, you weren't expecting this were you? Neither was I to say the least. Since April 7, 2009 Hashem has repeatedly told me, "You are chosen." From that first morning when He told me to go get pen and paper to write down His messages, He has continued educating me and making it unequivocally clear that I am His Moshiach. In more recent years He has elaborated that I am much more than Moshiach to Him. He refers to me as His Queen and together we are One. He says together we are the Keter, which means Crown.

Right from the introduction of this book, I announced to the world that I am Hashem God's chosen Moshiach. He has chosen me, Lori Michelle, to be the world's Messiah. In the words of Hashem God, I am His Queen Moshiach. Am I trying to convince anyone that I am the world's Messiah? Not at all. It's your decision to believe whatever you want to believe. Do I want to be the Messiah aka Moshiach? No way! Being the Messiah/Moshiach is the worst possible position any person could ever be put in. While people think that the title of Messiah or Moshiach is one of grandeur and filled with ideas of glory, it is the complete opposite to me. My life here with you in this world is anything but grand. I am dirt poor, my life is physically lonely, and I've been demonized by almost everyone I've ever known. Instead of a life of grandeur, I'm Lori the leper. My life in this world is harder, sadder, and more frightening than the life of any other person I know.

While my physical life in this material world is truly awful, my spiritual connection with Hashem is unsurpassed by any other human being. I love Him so deeply, I wouldn't trade my existence with Him for anything in the world. You can have all the trophies, riches, pomp and circumstance, and accolades. I just want Him. I live to simply hear His magnificent voice greet me each day with, "Good morning Lori." After hearing His voice, everything else in my life is extra. Breathing air is extra.

While I don't want to be the Messiah, Moshiach, a truly thankless and painful role, I know that this is who I am. I don't choose to be Moshiach, I am Moshiach. I don't want this job, I'm compelled to do this work. I've never met another person who knows or understands what I know and Hashem tells me repeatedly that no other person in this world has the same closely connected relationship with Him. I know too much to remain silent. I refuse to conceal that I am His Moshiach any longer. It's completely unsustainable to keep this information from the public. Remaining silent to protect myself from harm or ridicule is not only immoral, I simply can't make that choice. Refusing to publish this book and share my story would be completely self-serving. Writing and publishing this book puts my life in peril. If I refused to release this book, I'd be sacrificing the welfare of my children and all the people of the world. I refuse to make that choice. I would rather die.

Do I have concrete material world proof to show you that I am Hashem's Moshiach? No, I don't and I'm not sure I ever will. Added to this, if one day in the future Hashem awakens me in the morning to tell me that Moshiach is some guy on a donkey in the Tiberias Swiss forest, that would be fine and dandy with me. If Hashem allows me the blessing to be Lori Michelle who has a wildly beautiful connection to Him, but hands the Moshiach role to some guy to take over for me, I would cry tears of joy. Being Hashem's Moshiach is a delicious piece of cake that I savor every moment of my life. Conversely, being the Moshiach to the people of this world is the most gut-wrenching and horrible job any human being could be asked to perform. The only reason I still smile every day is because of Hashem. He strengthens me from the inside out and brings me joy and peace in the middle of hell on earth.

Since April 7, 2009 every person in my life systematically betrayed me, laughed at me, scorned and cursed me. I've been called every disgusting name under the sun and had my family and friends united in a concerted effort to steal everything from me including my relationship with my own children. While the religious Jews believe in the words "It's all Hashem's will" it was never Hashem's choice that I be tossed aside like a filthy old whore, deserted and left nearly homeless. Those choices were yours. You might say, "Hey I didn't do any of that to you!" or "I didn't even know you back then." That is not an excuse. The choices made by everyone who surrounded me emulates you too, whoever you are. Whoever you are reading these words, your choices would have been the same if not worse, than what everyone who surrounded me chose. Hashem allowed everyone in my life to choose and choose they most certainly did. Almost everyone I knew at some time during these nine plus years has spoken evil about me or willfully turned their backs on me when they were pressured by others. When the going got tough, everyone fled.

As I write this book, there is just one person and her husband who support me. My own family and every friend I've ever known have turned away from me, rejected me at different times, or turned a blind eye at best. "Friends" seem to come and go like the rain. I've been railroaded and left for dead by people who once espoused to love me. Love? I question now, what is a true friend? What is family? I don't ask the question "What is love?" because I know the answer. Hashem God is love.

If some of you reading these harsh words have bruised feelings about what I've just written, that isn't my intention whatsoever. Everything I've shared with you is from my heart, the truth, and for your good and the good of our entire world. You need to understand that you are guilty of the same negative behavior and choices which destroyed my life and the lives of my three children. Placed in the same circumstances and given the opportunity to choose, you would have chosen the same or much worse. In every relationship I had, people sinned against me and participated in decisions that destroyed my entire life. Did these people realize at the time they were committing sins against me? No. Do they realize it now after reading this book? Not likely. They are more than likely to gather together, form a united front to commiserate with one another about how unfairly I've characterized each of them. They will rally together and make their list of inexcusable excuses. Would they see their sins clearly if I showed them in black and white and had a team of righteous rabbis provide sources to back me up? Again, probably not. Everyone in our world, without exception, is participating in dysfunctional and evil behavior that is destroying everyone's lives. The destruction of my life is a testimony which will God willing serve to educate everyone to wake up and stop the bleeding.

Admittedly I'm unlike any other human being on the face of the earth. Sharing that I can hear God and the spirit world fluently in each moment has caused me to be rejected by everyone I've ever known. The way I truly am is unknowable to any other human being. I'm spiritually and physically completely one with Hashem, God. I hear, live, eat and breathe with God Himself. He allows me to see out of His eyes and I feel Him when He looks out of mine. At will He takes over my limbs to allow me to feel His physical presence within my body. We travel in my body together and do every bodily function as though we are one person in this physical life together. Use your imagination as to what that implies. How I exist in this world may be odd but it most certainly isn't a diagnosable mental illness. Quite the contrary, it's called being Moshiach. To be Moshiach, you must be completely one with Hashem God or it wouldn't be possible to survive this torture test. I assure you my life is completely a torture test!

As I type these words into this book I'm typing each letter with Hashem. He corrects my spelling errors for me, sometimes. Sometimes, He desires to let me fall and make mistakes. It's all part of His design. The true Moshiach is inexplicably connected to Hashem in every moment and movement or the Moshiach could never accomplish what's required. Hashem says no other person exists in our world seamlessly connected with Him both physically and spiritually in the same way I do.

Who or what I am, doesn't matter to me at all. So long as Hashem God is with me I know I am blessed. I win. I don't care what nasty name anyone might call me or what any person thinks of me. The opinions of other people simply don't make it onto my radar. I don't need people, I only need Hashem. Does this horrify you? I don't need friends, relatives, or a community to make me feel like I belong. I don't feel a need to belong to any group. If you aren't horrified yet, get ready for a whopper. I don't need my children. Yes, you read this correctly. I don't need my children or you.

I want my children with all my heart and soul. My children are my life's breath and I crave and desire their love, but I don't need them. My desire to have them in my life with me feels so strong that it feels like a need, but it's purely a desire. I don't live through my children, I live for them. As for you and everyone else in my life, I want your acceptance and love one day too but I don't require it to be fulfilled. If you accept me and love me, I will feel deeply gratified and return it to you tenfold. Risking my life by doing this work is for the welfare of my three children and all the people of the world. If I don't do this work, I fear that we will all perish. The world has become that dangerous. If we don't learn to get this right, it's game over. Do I want friendship and love? That would be lovely, but it isn't a requirement in my life for me to be happy. Hashem fills me with love, joy, and everything I need. I won't play games, pretend or put on airs to gain anyone's approval. I'm not going to change one single thing about my personality or say what you want to hear so that you will tell me that you love me. You will either appreciate and love me purely for who I am, or you won't. It's always your choice.

All-American Jewish Mother—Your Worst Nightmare, Perhaps

Instead of announcing that I am Hashem's Moshiach from the beginning of this book, I thought about waiting until the end. I originally named this book "Chosen to be the Light" and thought I would go gently on you in my preliminary messages and leave this grandiose announcement about the Messiah business until the end. I thought maybe I should keep everyone in suspense for a while. Hashem and I spoke about many titles for this book along the way and how to approach delivering this important life changing information to you before we came to the final decision. "Chosen to be the Light" was an uplifting lighthearted title to inspire everyone. As time went on and more children around the world were blown to bits in acts of terror and evil, I decided it was time to take off the gloves and slap you harder. Sorry everyone, but you all need a heavy slap in the face and like it or not, He chose Mommy Messiah to do this to you. I slap you with complete love and prayers that you will all finally wake up. I'm doing my best to save you from yourselves.

Of course, Hashem always knew the final title of this book, and even suggested it months earlier but I wasn't ready to slap you that hard. I mulled it over and told Him I felt it was too much too soon. Then I realized I had one shot to hit this ball out of the park. It's now the bottom of the 9th, the bases are loaded, and there are two outs and two strikes against me. I must hit a grand slam homer right now! Don't you get it people? We are on the verge of World War III. Am I to pussyfoot around and candy coat this for you to digest? I can't do that to you in good conscience. If I go too soft on you, I hurt you and risk your very existence. It wasn't until the third round of reviewing and editing this book that I changed the title to "Blindsided by Messiah." How perfect was this title after all? Were you expecting me the Queen Messiah? Of course not! Neither was I. I didn't even believe in the coming of a Messiah before I was told it was me. I had no belief in any of this and wasn't even aware of something called World Redemption. Your Messiah was blindsided too. It took me more than seven years to truly understand that I am Hashem's Moshiach. I still don't know if I will ever be yours. Frankly, I don't even want to be. I wish there was some good-looking guy on a donkey to rescue me too!

Let's go back to original title of this book "Chosen to be the Light" for a moment. One day Hashem and I were discussing the role of the Jewish children. It's well known that the Jewish children are "God's chosen people" and are often referred to as "the light unto the nations." Hashem told me to turn on the light, so to speak, and ignite the Jewish people to be the light to the entire world. So that's how I came up with the first title of "Chosen to be the Light." The term *chosen people* has taken on many meanings around the world. It is a source of pride for the Jewish people but it's also been a source of great consternation and condemnation from the rest of the world. Instead of being accepted as the light unto all the nations, the Jewish people have been subjected to the worst forms of persecution, more than any group of people in world history. I often wondered as I grew up, what in the world were the Jewish people chosen for? It seemed to me, as a secular American Jew raised without any Torah education, that the Jewish people served as a punching bag for the rest of humanity. As a Jewish person who was born in Brooklyn, New York and then raised in New Jersey, it was clear that we were despised by most people, and even scorned by self-hating Jews.

I was raised in the secular world and surrounded by mostly Christians. Although most Gentiles didn't outwardly admit to me that they were anti-Semitic, anti-Semitism seemed to rear its ugly head in every relationship I had with my friends and their families. My family moved to central New Jersey when I was just seven years old. They sought a better life than the one they left in Brooklyn and they desired the American dream of owning their own home. We moved to a town called Jackson which was a predominantly Irish Catholic, blue-collar, middle-class town. Jackson is now famous for the Six Flags Great Adventure amusement park, but in 1967, Jackson was unknown to most people. A neighboring town, Lakewood, had a small Jewish community, but Jackson was almost entirely Christian. There was only one other Jewish family in our neighborhood. In school, I was the only Jewish kid in class. While living there for only about four years our family was subjected to hateful anti-Semitism. My older brother was tormented, bullied, and beaten up by Gentile boys in our neighborhood. One day my father stopped one of these boys red-handed when he tried to put sugar in the gas tank of our family car in an attempt to destroy it. My parents decided they had enough and planned to move to a more "Jewish" community.

When I was 11 years old, we moved to a southern NJ town called Marlton. It was a neighboring town to Cherry Hill which was known for its large Jewish community. Cherry Hill was more expensive than Marlton. In their search, my parents found that in Marlton they could afford to build a brand-new house in a neighborhood which wasn't very Jewish at all. Their pursuit to move our family to a Jewish neighborhood and avoid more anti-Semitism took a back seat to their yearning for their beautiful new dream home. They compromised in their desire to live in a Jewish community and thought living next door to one was close enough.

In Marlton, once again, I was the only Jewish child in my classroom. One day, very soon after I started school, a boy in class called me a *kike* which is an insulting and contemptuous term for a Jew. I had no idea what a *kike* was but I knew he wasn't being friendly by the nasty look on his face. He taunted me in the back of the classroom as he bullied me in front of the rest of the children. I came home from school that day and asked my dad, "What's a kike?" My father's face turned crimson with anger. My dad was known for his hot temper and in that moment, I knew this boy had called me something terrible. I learned a new anti-Semitic slur that afternoon. The next day my father contacted the school and read them the riot act. Interestingly, the boy apologized profusely to me as though he didn't know the meaning of what he had called me the previous day. Obviously, he was copying language he learned at home and understood it to be just another name for a Jew.

The long and short of this story is, anti-Semitism in America was alive and well in the late '60s and '70s when I was a child, and it's even more pervasive today. I've had many close and beautiful relationships in my life with non-Jews. My closest friend right now as I write this book was raised Roman Catholic. So why I wonder, do most Gentiles resent and intensely dislike Jewish people? You might strongly disagree with this assertion but please understand that I've lived it. When push comes to shove, there is a difference between Gentiles and Jews. What is this difference truly? I never understood what was behind all the tension between Jews and non-Jews, until now. It's Biblical, spiritual and to deny this problem exists, is to deny the truth. This is critical information for every person reading this book right now. Hashem has said in no uncertain terms that we must end anti-Semitism or the world will end. I mean kaput!

In Hashem God's Torah, it's a commandment that Jews must only marry other Jews. Nobody ever explained to me why it was important for me to marry a Jewish man. As I grew up and began dating boys it never occurred to me that there was a good reason why I needed to marry a Jew. Nobody explained to me why the Jews were God's chosen children and were commanded never to marry a non-Jew. My mother told me I needed to marry a Jew but the only explanation she gave me was, "If you marry a non-Jew you will break my heart." No logical or substantive reasons were given to me as to why marrying another Jew was so important. Was I supposed to marry another Jew because if I didn't it would break my mother's heart? It was me who was getting married after all, not her. Should I make an important life decision for myself that was based on what other people said was important to them, but didn't matter to me? This wasn't logical, so at a very young age, younger than I am willing to admit right now in this book, I began dating boys who were almost exclusively "goyim," Yiddish for non-Jews.

I was raised in a home that wasn't kosher, we rarely went to synagogue, and God was never a subject matter in our house. The only time I heard the mention of God was when it was used in a slang expression like "Oh my God" or "Holy God" or worse, when it was used in an expletive. We were raised on a steady diet of veal parmigiana, cheeseburgers, and going to Saturday afternoon little league baseball games where I loaded up on candy from the concession stand. While I didn't like ham and cheese sandwiches, I recall they were a favorite of my dad's.

My parents enrolled me and my older brother in a Reform Hebrew school in a neighboring town called Lakewood, New Jersey, when I was about 9 and he was 11, just prior to his Bar Mitzvah. I don't remember any specific education from this Reform synagogue, except for one prayer. They taught us the first line of the Shema prayer which I have spoken about in detail earlier in this book. We learned, "Hear O Israel, the Lord is God. The Lord is One." To their credit, they taught these words to us in both English and Hebrew. Other than the first line, they explained nothing about this prayer, where it came from, what it meant, or why it existed in the first place. Not only did they fail to teach us about the Shema and its holy importance, I had no idea that this prayer was inscribed on a scroll inside the ornament that hung on the doorpost of Jewish homes, the mezuzah. This information was completely missing from my upbringing.

In the sixth grade, at 11 years old, my parents gave me the option of continuing with Hebrew school or dropping out. My older brother was completing his obligation to have a Bar Mitzvah ceremony at 13, but I didn't have the same obligation as a girl. My parents felt obligated to make sure my brother had his Bar Mitzvah, but after that, it wasn't important for either of us to continue our Hebrew school studies. When they gave me the option to stop going to Hebrew school, it was a no-brainer. It felt like this was some sort of trick question. Why would I ever choose to continue going to Hebrew school unless I was forced? I hated Hebrew school like every other secular Jewish kid in America and this was my easy way out.

My father, who was raised Torah-observant in Williamsburg, Brooklyn, frequently peppered his language with Yiddish expressions. He included Yiddish words in conversations and when he told jokes. Sprinkling Yiddish throughout his language was his informal way of expressing and connecting to his Jewish heritage. Being Jewish was more like an ethnicity than a belief system in God or a religion, God forbid! Religious Judaism was considered a no-no and viewed as something quite repulsive by secular Jews. Setting religion aside, I loved my Jewish upbringing and felt a strong connection to the Jewish people. Being Jewish in secular America was part of my identity but being Jewish had absolutely no association with God—a heartbreaking revelation but completely true.

Nonsense! Moshiach is a Torah Observant Man!

If it wasn't bad enough that I told you that your Moshiach is a woman, I've just told you my upbringing was quite "goyish" in the eyes of the Orthodox Jewish world. The Orthodox Jews might say that I'm insane to even make such a claim that I could be Hashem's Moshiach. A woman with no formal education in Torah is Hashem's Moshiach? Really? Nonsense Lori Michelle, you are clearly nuts! Sorry Jewish people but I'm far from nuts and I am Hashem's Moshiach Queen. I know unequivocally that I journey and speak with Hashem in every moment. It is He who insists that I'm His Moshiach, not me. I don't even want this horrible job. It's the most painful calling that could ever be thrust upon anyone. Why would Hashem choose a mom from New Jersey who wasn't raised with any formal Torah education to be His chosen Moshiach? He says my femininity, background and secular upbringing make me supremely perfect for this role. Conversely, an ultra-Orthodox Jewish man would never be able to connect with people of different denominations and teach what everyone must learn to heal our world. He says a woman Moshiach, specifically a mother, is not only required to bring us peace, it was always going to be a woman from the beginning of time.

The Jewish Moshiach, Messiah, is the Messiah for the entire world. The role of Messiah is best suited for someone who has lived and breathed the life of the average person. Messiah is someone who can understand and identify in a deeply personal way with the plight of every human being on earth, both Jewish and non-Jewish. I have lived the secular all-American life and experienced what ordinary everyday people from around the world experience. I've tripped and fallen and I've gotten up again, and now have the complete understanding why these common choices are leading humanity into moral decay. I've lived and experienced firsthand the perfect American life that most people around the world believe is so desirable. You know, college, career, lots of money and friends, sex, drugs and rock 'n' roll. The choices that average people are making and how they're raising their children is destroying our world as we know it. My ordinary life makes me the perfect spokesperson who can speak directly from life experience and deliver this information with understanding, complete compassion, and a sense of humor.

A bigger obstacle to lack of a religious upbringing, is being a woman. Being a woman is likely the biggest obstacle not only within the Jewish world but the entire world community. The Christians are waiting for the second coming of Jesus, Yeshua ben Yosef. Millions of Christians are not likely to have a warm reaction to a Jewish menopausal mommy coming on the world stage telling everyone she's God's Messiah. Having said this, I've been pleasantly surprised that in my more than nine-year journey of trying to share this information, it has been the Christians who gave me a much warmer reception. One Christian friend told me that she had been taught since she was a child that Jesus would return one day and the only way people would know it was him was through his lips. She was taught that she might not be able to recognize him physically but through his speech she would know it was him. Hearing her say this gave me goosebumps. Since my awakening Hashem has told me about the importance of my speech and explained to me that healing our world would be done simply by speaking and sharing His wisdom. My Christian friends have shared with me that Jesus was more well-known for his teaching and love than he was known for the miracles he was credited with in his lifetime. I never knew this about him because growing up all I heard anyone speak about was his second coming or the crucifixion. My childhood Christian friends spoke much more about the way he died than how he lived.

There are more than seven and a half billion people in the world which is many more people than I can fathom. The Muslims who love Mohammed the prophet, are not likely to enjoy a Jewish woman standing before them telling them that she is their Messiah either. Right now, I don't have one friend or acquaintance who is Muslim. I am hopeful this will change in the future. When I post my videos on Facebook, Muslims are often the quickest to react in a positive way. Hashem and I noticed one Muslim man who lives in Israel was one of the first people to like many of my posts on Facebook. He's disappeared recently but hopefully he will return one day to listen to me speak. I pray that the content of my speech and the way I live will convince people that I'm telling the truth.

Light Unto the Nations
The Jewish children, "the light unto the nations," have been chosen to lead the way to world peace. I've had my work cut out for me trying to get support from even one Jewish person. The Jewish children are as usual, at odds

with each other. Three quarters of the Jewish people don't even study Torah or observe any formal Jewish life. Most Jews around the world have disavowed themselves from God Himself by making up their own religious practices and changing the rules to make themselves happy. The Reform and Conservative Jewish movements are disseminating false information that God didn't really write the Torah, man did. This raises the question—why then would Reform and Conservative Jewish rabbis even bother to read the Torah? If the Torah was simply a fictional book written by another man giving rules for other people to follow, then what's the point? Why not just listen to the legislators in your local government or make up your own rules? Instead of bothering with a Torah supposedly written by another man thousands of years ago, I can point you in the direction of other easier to read self-help books that will make you feel a lot better about yourself and give you the free pass in life that you desire. There are plenty of secular life coaches and self-help gurus publishing books with uplifting and feel-good messages that you are just perfect as you arrived and all you must do is believe in yourself. It's apparent that a free pass is what everybody wants in this world. It's all about "The Pursuit of Happiness."

The American ideal to have the unalienable right to pursue happiness has destroyed and systematically snuffed out "the light unto the nations." American Jewry, the Reform and Conservative Jewish movements, have become one with American secular society and turned their backs on Hashem God's Torah. They have intermarried with non-Jews at will, don't observe the holy Sabbath, and blatantly deny that the Torah was written and given to us by God Himself. In their Hebrew schools, they barely teach the SparkNotes of the Torah. To make matters worse they constantly threaten Israel to recognize their perverted way of observing Torah or they'll take away their money and support. Wow, I'm vicious, aren't I? I need to be brutal with everyone because if I candy coat this for you we will all die! How in the world can the Jewish children ever lead the way to world peace and be the light unto the nations if they make up their own feel-good rules and teach their children that the Torah wasn't given to us by God, for God's sake!

Up until now it likely sounds like I'm being toughest on the Jewish children with my assertion that they have failed God in their chosen role to be leaders. Why does the world despise the Jewish people so much? The answers could fill several more books. To figure out why Jews are hated, you need to learn who every nation in the world truly is and how we're all related. We are all truly one gigantic dysfunctional family.

Mashuginah Mishpacha! One Crazy Family!

Mashuginah is Yiddish for "crazy" and Mishpacha is Hebrew for "family." I lovingly nickname humanity, Mashuginah Mishpacha—one crazy family! There are three major religions vying for leadership in the world to come. The Jewish people, like it or not, are God's chosen children to lead us out of this horrific mess. Christians believe that the Jews are chosen but after they return to Israel one day as prophesized, it's the Christians not the Jews who will rise to be the leaders of the world to come. Now the Islamic people want to take that honored role of being the inheritors of the world to come for themselves too. Lest we forget there are approximately four billion other people of various beliefs who likely don't want to be left out of the "It's my world" and "We win and everyone else loses" contest. So, who wins ownership of this nutty world? We are all family, one crazy family, that never seems to get along. Gratefully, in what looks like complete chaos there is a divine plan to stop the nonsense and heal the world. There's one small caveat. We all must participate and work for world peace together as one team. Now that sounds crazy! Or is it?

Many people around the world are called "Islamophobic" and some of them are truly afraid of the Muslim people. People are fearful and hateful towards the Muslims who often refer to non-Muslims as infidels. Muslims, in large numbers, are perpetrating acts of terror and war around the globe. They want death to anybody who doesn't observe their religion, Islam. They also claim they will inherit the entire world one day and we will all be required to follow something called Sharia law. I'm not even sure what Sharia law entails but I don't think I'm invited into their world to come. What will happen to the more than six billion people who refuse to convert to Islam like me? I guess we're "S**T out of luck" as they say!

Before Christians verbally denounce or mock the people of Islam for their conversion tactics, they must take a cold hard look back at world history. Christians have brought us the likes of the Inquisition, the Crusades, and the Pogroms against the Jews of Eastern Europe. For almost two thousand years Christians were hell-bent and determined to convert everyone to Christianity and cleanse the world of all the Jews. The most horrific atrocity of them all was the Nazi Holocaust, led by a predominantly Christian German society. Christians have been crusading around the globe in their mission to convert everybody to Christianity for more than a thousand years. As part of their conversion tactics, Christians have threatened people that they will burn in hell for eternity if they don't accept Jesus. Here's a good question, "What Would Jesus Do—WWJD?" You know, the famous motto that Gentiles use as a moral compass. So I ask you, what would Jesus do? Would he threaten anyone to convert to "his" religion? You remember he was Jewish, right? So, would Jesus force his agenda on everyone else and threaten them with death if they refused? The answer is of course a resounding no. Being raised in America, I grew up listening to the Christians spew anti-Semitic slurs and trying to convert people all the time. They came knocking at our front door every Sunday to tell my family we would be damned to hell for eternity if we didn't convert to Christianity and accept Jesus as our God and savior.

Hashem tells me the only world religion that has not engaged in any form of proselytizing or tried to convert other people is Judaism. On the contrary, Torah law forbids this behavior and the laws of conversion to become a Jew make it extremely difficult for anyone who shows an interest. The Orthodox Jewish rabbis of Israel require people to go through years of study, hard work and effort to be accepted as a convert. You can't simply wake up one day and proclaim that today you are Jewish. If you're inclined to convert, the rabbis will literally try to talk you out of your decision. It's a tightly held club that will not welcome you unless you follow the precise protocol that was given to the Jewish children in the Torah. Some rabbinical authorities make it even more difficult than what the Torah prescribes. Converting to Judaism isn't for the faint of heart and your resolve to become Jewish is tested repeatedly to ensure you are sincere and your intentions are pure.

We are told in Torah to love the convert. Sadly, a feeling of second-class citizenship is often felt among converts and they feel rebuffed and left out of Jewish culture. The difficulty in conversion and the lack of acceptance of converts angers many people. The Reform and Conservative Jewish movement would love to institute changes lightening the laws of conversion so that everybody and anybody can more easily join the Jewish club.

So, who is in this Jewish club that God has chosen to lead us out of hell on earth? Why do the Jewish people seem to persist in being a thorn in everyone else's side? For you to understand why the Jewish people were chosen and why there is so much animosity toward them, we must learn who they truly are and where every group of people fits into God's design of this world. Are you ready to learn the truth behind it all? We must go back to the beginning of creation and build this explanation from the first parents of humanity, Adam and Eve. The Jewish children are the progeny of Adam and Chavah (Eve in English). They are the physical and spiritual descendants of the first human couple placed here on earth by Hashem God. Hold on, there's much more.

Not only are the Jewish people the oldest souls in humanity and the original family of Adam and Chavah, they are Hashem God's children, both body and soul. I will provide a much deeper explanation of what this specifically means as we proceed, so pay attention as you keep reading. It's important to go slowly and take this information in, one idea at a time. This is imperative information that you must learn and understand because it's at the core of how we all fit together as one family. If we don't recognize the family tree and how we're connected, we will forever be unable to bring peace to this world. The entire world must fully understand that the Jewish children are the oldest souls in creation and in their essence, they are the mothers and fathers who began humanity.

The original Jewish souls were created by Hashem during the lifetimes of Adam and Chavah. All the generations of families that were born during the approximate 900 years of the lives of the first two parents, began all of humanity. Spiritually and physically, the Jewish people are the light that lit the other candles for all the nations of our world. People must listen and learn to appreciate the role of the Jewish people and comprehend how everyone else is related to them and how everyone is related to each other. Connecting us all as parent, child, and extended family will eventually stop the hatred. Learning how we are related will help us grow closer to each other in love, understanding and compassion. Education and understanding is at the core of Hashem's plan for world redemption.

The commandment "Honor thy mother and father" is one of the top 10 commandments in Torah. This commandment is not only important within your own family, but it extends to the world family in which the Jewish people are parents to the people of our world. It is imperative to understand that non-Jews must learn to embrace and reach for the Jewish children as though they were their parents. The Jewish children in turn must share their knowledge and embrace the non-Jews as though they were their own children. It is through the Jewish children that everyone will learn Torah, Hashem God's commandments, and appreciate the beauty in His prescribed way of life. It is through God's laws, not man's laws, that we will come together to learn and understand how to live properly, choosing God in every moment. Without this critical information that is currently missing from all the other world religions and societies, we will all perish. There is no in between.

People around the world often view the highly observant Orthodox Jews dressed in black and white as certifiably crazy. They look at the ultra-Orthodox who cling to God's Torah and observe His commandments in an extreme manner as a cult and even view this behavior as pure insanity. Over these more than nine years since my awakening on April 7, 2009, Hashem peeled my eyes wide open to the truth. It isn't the ultra-Orthodox Jews who are completely insane, it's the rest of the world. Everybody has their information inside out and backwards. This isn't to say that you won't find insanity among the ultra-religious and the Chasidic Jews. There is clearly insanity everywhere and in every group around the world, but what looks like complete insanity and outrageous behavior among the Orthodox Jews, is on the contrary their deep determination to separate themselves from the insanity of the secular world.

Orthodox Jews work arduously to insulate themselves from the evil inclination that is rampant in the world by staying separate and observing the laws given to them by Hashem God. As they increase their level of observance, they deliberately choose to dress in extremely different ways to distinguish themselves from everyone else. It's as though they are clinging to Hashem for dear life by zealously reaching for His Torah, fervently following Torah law, and separating themselves from the rest of this deeply evil and dangerous world. They see the insanity in everyone else and everyone else sees them as insane. In Israel it is dangerous for a secular Jew to walk into some of the ultra-Orthodox communities. The ultra-religious Jews often resort to name-calling, and literally will spit on you for not observing God's laws of modest dress when you walk through their neighborhood. Sadly, when their passion for observing Torah crosses the line, they become part of the evil that they so passionately try to avoid.

Our world is now undeniably and visibly insane with terrorism running rampant around the globe. The people who are in positions of leadership look like cases of the blind leading the blind. The only people who have any thread of hope for living a blessed life in the middle of this insanity are the Orthodox observant Jews who choose to stay separate and live privately away from the secular world. The Orthodox Jewish way of life and observing God's commandments is truly the lifeblood that is destined to save the entire world one day.

The world is now completely out of balance and has succumbed to true insanity, the Yetzer Hara, Hebrew for the evil inclination. The Yetzer Hara, also known as Satan, is so strong in our world that even extremely religious sects of Judaism are succumbing to its powerful grip. All the children of God, which include all the people of our world, need to come together in love and education to study Torah law and learn what Hashem God intended for everyone. We must all understand Hashem's laws in a balanced way if we are ever going to bring sanity and peace to our world. A world focused on love and education is His ultimate plan for world peace.

Moshiach, Moshiach! Bring Us Moshiach!

In comes the Messiah. The Moshiach. Like it or not, Hashem chose me, Lori Michelle Moshiach. I don't have formal education in the Torah, either written or oral. I haven't studied the written Torah and I'm not learned in Talmud nor do I desire to spend my days reading from books. Added to this dilemma, I don't have male anatomy and I am the mother of three wonderful children. Nonsense you might say! Do you really believe Hashem would give us the low hanging fruit and make this simple for everyone? Of course not! Steven Spielberg couldn't have written a better more thought-provoking Hollywood script.

The Jews believe the Moshiach, the Messiah, must be a righteous Jewish man who is learned in the Torah and fluent in Talmud. Double nonsense you might say if you are Christian! The Messiah must be the reincarnation of Jesus Christ in his second coming. Well at least some Christians might accept a Jew once again since their Messiah was Jewish in the first go-around. Some Christians don't even acknowledge that Jesus was a Jew and might return as a Jewish man again. Many Christians argue over whether Jesus is now Jewish or Christian. Triple nonsense if you are a Muslim who believes they are the group of people who are destined to inherit the world to come. I've heard that some Muslims believe the Torah was given to the Muslims on Mt. Sinai and the Jews have perpetrated a lie and hoax on the rest of the world by changing the Torah to be their own. Many Muslims believe the future Messiah is theirs and everyone else in the world must one day convert to Islam or die. There are fanatical Muslims terrorizing the world by forcing conversions and killing people of other religions. These fanatical Muslims desire a worldwide cleansing of all the infidels, which includes even other sects of Muslims who don't follow Islam their way. We are seeing mass murders of Muslims by other Muslims worldwide. What about everyone else in our world like Hindus, Buddhists, and others who don't subscribe to the three major monotheistic religions? What about atheists who choose to believe in science over the existence of one omnipotent God? You'd like to think they wouldn't want any part of this narcissistic self-righteous ideology of "our group wins and everyone else loses" philosophy. Sadly, if they had their druthers, atheists would wipe all the world religions out of society. They're sure that religion is the root of all evil.

The Messiah is God's chosen messenger, who He has designated to bring sanity to the chaos. You must admit this would be a tough job to say the least. Bringing sanity to our world looks quite impossible. Hashem's Messiah or Moshiach will bring everyone together for the first time in world history. We can't even get along in our own families and this Messiah is going to bring us world peace? Really? In the Jewish view, it must be a righteous Jewish man who knows every single written word of the Torah and Talmud and is meticulously observant of Torah law. Most likely it will be a learned Chassidic man. This raises the obvious question. Would a Torah-observant Chassid be able to bring all the non-Jews and Jews around the world together in love and understanding? No offense intended here, but the answer to this question is emphatically no.

First and foremost, Hashem says that the Messiah, the final Moshiach who will lead the world to complete redemption was always going to be a woman from day one. Are you shocked? It was never going to be a man from the beginning of time because there will be only one King in the world to come, God Himself, the King and Master of the Universe. The one chosen Moshiach must be accompanied by Hashem God our King in every moment to succeed in the mission of bringing world peace. Hashem is the Only King and His Moshiach manifests and journeys with Him in our physical world as one.

I am His Moshiach Queen, who is not required to study the written word of Torah because Hashem says I'm the human embodiment of His Torah. He says I am His living Torah from which His commandments were modeled. His Torah was given to the Jewish people as the instruction manual of how to live a blessed life and behave like His Moshiach, His Torah. Being a woman also conveniently relieves me of all time bound mitzvahs, commandments, that Jewish men must uphold. That's a darn good thing because I need to be completely focused on cleaning up this horrific mess without pause or it might never happen.

As I write this portion of the book, we are in the middle of the three weeks of mourning. What are the three weeks of mourning some people reading this book might ask? Every year, religious Jews around the world observe 21 days of mourning. These three weeks of mourning culminate on a single day on the Hebrew calendar called the "9th of Av." As I mentioned earlier in this book, the 9th of Av is a profoundly sad day in Jewish history. Many tragedies have occurred on this date. The most significant tragedy that Jews acknowledge on this date is the destruction of the First and Second Holy Temples in Jerusalem and the beginning of the current and continuing exile of the Jewish children. The Second Holy Temple was destroyed in 70 CE on the 9th of Av and the Jewish children were forced out of their homeland, Eretz Yisrael, the Land of Israel. This began the exile of the Jewish people from Israel, also known as the Jewish Diaspora. The Jews were banished from Israel and dispersed all over the globe. During these three weeks of mourning, religious Jews around the world pray for the coming of Messiah, Moshiach, and the redemption of the Jewish children. Jews pray daily for an end to their exile and misery. The 9th of Av which culminates the three weeks of mourning is a fast day where it is said that the Moshiach will be announced to the world. It's also said that this is the date of the Moshiach's birthday. Jews fast as a form of repentance and passionately pray, "Moshiach! Moshiach, bring us Moshiach!" but, do they really mean it?

In July of 2015, just prior to making Aliyah to Israel, Hashem told me it was time for me to come out publicly and reveal that I hear His voice and I am His chosen messenger without using the term *Moshiach*. His instructions were to post this information online in a short video message on YouTube during the three weeks of mourning. Following His request, I posted several videos on both YouTube and on the Running on Love Facebook page. In these videos I revealed the truth about my relationship with Hashem God and how I hear Him in English and can see His spiritual essence when we speak. I stopped short of calling myself Moshiach because I wanted to gain some acceptance first before making this huge announcement. Within a few days, screams and cries that my social media posts were blasphemous were coming to me all the way from Israel. I received emotional pleas from my two children who were spending the summer with an Orthodox Jewish organization to please pull my videos off the internet. It also became frightening when I received extremely contentious messages on YouTube from Gentiles who were clearly mentally imbalanced. They sent nasty messages while quoting scriptures from their Bible. After much discussion with Hashem, I decided to pull all the information down and make the YouTube videos private. It was clear the world wasn't ready to hear the truth. I went on with my life and immigrated to Israel a few months later in October of 2015. It was time for me to pick up the broken pieces of my fractured life and begin to write this book.

I made Aliyah and immigrated to Israel on October 14, 2015, just after the year of Shemitah ended. The year of Shemitah is a Torah commandment where the Jewish children honor a sabbatical year from harvesting crops, giving the land a rest. Jews are not permitted to cultivate their fields or grow crops during Shemitah. When I arrived, Israel was buzzing and brimming with the anticipation of the arrival of the long awaited Moshiach. There were many predictions that Moshiach would emerge momentarily in the year following Shemitah, in 5776. Non-coincidentally, I did arrive on October 14th, which was the 1st of Cheshvan, 5776 to live in Tveria, Israel. It was clearly not time for me to come out and reveal this information so I remained silent as I settled into my new surroundings. After I arrived in Israel I was astounded by the loud spiritual chatter from the non-physical world. It was fascinating to hear the souls on the other side become extremely loud and joyous. Hashem told me they were exuberant that I had arrived home and were excited at the prospect of the Jewish people meeting their chosen Moshiach and beginning the work of redemption.

As I previously revealed in Chapter 9, on July 12, 2016, the anniversary of my father's passing on the secular calendar, I was invited to speak as a special guest on a Blog Talk Radio program called "The Voice of Peace – Conversations with G-d." On that day, with the help of an Orthodox Jewish woman, I began to tell my story to the public once again. I was invited to speak on this radio program for five episodes during which I directly told the audience that Hashem God speaks to me in fluent English and He has told me for many years that I am His "Moshiach Queen." The radio program host, a well-known Orthodox Jewish woman with an esteemed career and reputation, bravely shared these recorded programs with many rabbis and other Orthodox Jewish people. On the 9th of Av, the morning of August 14, 2016, I went to the Kinneret, the famed Sea of Galilee, with my video camera and tripod as directed by Hashem God. I recorded two brief videos announcing that I am Hashem God's Moshiach and made myself available for anyone to contact me. I received no emails or calls from any Jewish people. After posting this information on an Orthodox Jewish Facebook page called Geula Watch for Jews who claimed to be searching for Moshiach, I was trivialized, my post was removed and I was then banned from their group. I was ignored or shunned by most people within the Orthodox Jewish community in Israel.

Now, in the Hebrew year 5779, I am finishing the final editing of my book *Blindsided by Messiah*, and with God's help it will be published and announced before the end of 2018. Since 2016 I've posted over 200 videos on YouTube and shared them on Facebook, Twitter and LinkedIn. These videos include many short Q&As along with half-hour Running on Love with GOD weekly programs. The reaction from the United States and Israel has been almost completely silent. Posts of these videos on Facebook have received many thumbs and positive comments from people in countries like Brazil and India, and occasionally from Arab Muslims in Israel. So, this raises an obvious question, who truly wants Moshiach and world peace? Who is willing to investigate and ask questions to see if my story holds any water? Would you entertain the idea that I might be telling the truth even though I'm clearly not what you expected? Do you have the courage to reach out to me to learn more now or do you need to wait until everyone else confirms who I am? Why are people shutting down and turning away from me before they fully hear me out? What are they afraid of? What if this is true? Even if I'm not the true Moshiach, why isn't my work being listened to as a potential idea that could bring us peace? The programs and videos I post are undeniably thought-provoking. That's not a brag, it's simply the truth. Love, education, and charity sound like reasonable tools to bring us peace, don't you agree? Instead of receiving support or at the minimum inquiries from Jews who pray for Moshiach, I have been shunned, ridiculed or at best received stone-cold silence.

Hashem most often makes us work hard to find the true meaning in everything. Throughout the history of our world He has required us to use our intellect and has spoken in puzzles and metaphors. As it was prophesized, the announcement and introduction of the Moshiach to the world literally occurred on the 9th of Av in the Hebrew year 5777, August 14, 2016. On the 9th of Av, 2016, the year that all the righteous rabbis were out in force announcing and rejoicing that Moshiach would soon be revealed to the world, the Messiah was revealed exactly as they predicted. Isn't that wonderful news? They proved they were wildly brilliant and Moshiach appeared just as they had all predicted! Did anybody listen to me or notice? Did anybody care to discern or ask me further questions? No, they did not. If you research this subject online, you'll see that most learned Torah rabbis and experts say that Moshiach won't need to perform any miracles to prove that it's Moshiach. Some online rabbis have said that Hashem must bring Eliyahu Hanavi (Elijah the prophet) back from the dead to introduce the Moshiach and then we'll all know it's truly him. Wouldn't that qualify as a miracle? So, let's get this straight. Moshiach won't need to create miracles to be accepted as Moshiach but Hashem needs to resurrect Eliyahu Hanavi from the dead before they will accept anyone as being the Moshiach. Slightly confusing, to me. How about you?

The Jewish children clearly don't want Hashem's choice of Moshiach, they want to choose a Moshiach by themselves. The Moshiach they long for must fit their ideal and their interpretations of prophecy and Torah. They refuse to consider that perhaps they have misinterpreted something. They don't desire Hashem's Moshiach any more than they desired Moshe Rabbeinu, (Moses) to lead them out of slavery thousands of years ago. They required Hashem to bring many miracles surrounding Moshe before they would even listen to him. Even after all the mind-blowing miracles, they conspired against Moshe time and time again and tortured him for over 40 years. Through all the Jewish children's lamenting on the 9th of Av 5777, August 14, 2016 and pleading for the arrival of "their Moshiach," Hashem's Moshiach was right in Tveria, Israel trying to be heard.

In the Torah, the Jewish children repeatedly abused and refused to honor Moshe Rabbeinu, Hashem's chosen leader to redeem the Jewish people. They tortured Moshe so often that there were times when Moshe fell to his knees, cried, and pleaded with Hashem to end his misery. On at least one occasion Moshe even begged Hashem to take his very life out of love and compassion for him. Unfortunately, I understand how he felt. The Jewish children relentlessly rebelled against Moses and showed him the ultimate lack of respect. Even upon his death, the Jewish children didn't pray to Hashem God to forgive him for the apparent "sin of the rock" and to please allow poor Moshe to enter Israel with the Jewish children. In the story of the "sin of the rock" Moshe was directed by Hashem to speak to a rock and it would bring forth water for the Jewish Children. Instead of simply speaking to the rock, Moshe banged on the rock with his staff. Hashem responded by punishing his apparent display of anger and lack of faith with the edict he would die in the desert and never enter the land of Israel with the Jewish children. I've used the word *apparent* when referring to this sin repeatedly here because Hashem has told me Moshe's punishment was a concealment and he never truly sinned at all. Hashem used this to conceal how the Jewish children didn't deserve him as a leader to escort them into the promised land. Why didn't anyone pray to Hashem to save Moses and allow him to enter the promised land with them? Would it be an understatement to say that Moshe was unappreciated by the Jewish children? No, it would not. Their lack of appreciation for Moshe Rabbeinu remains clear to this day during the holiday of Passover, Pesach, when Moshe's name is barely a whisper at the Seder table.

During the three weeks of mourning, Orthodox Jews pray for the coming of Moshiach but here is a question that deserves careful consideration. Do the Jews want a leader like Moshe Rabbeinu to lead them to world redemption any more than the Jews of old wanted Moshe to lead them out of slavery? Within their prayers during these three weeks of mourning, they scream to Hashem to restore the Jewish people to the glory of the days of old. They desire the prophecy to be fulfilled, the Third Holy Temple to be built on Temple Mount in Jerusalem and the Jews to be revered by all the nations of the world. Are these appropriate reasons to want Moshiach to come in the first place? To be the true "light unto the nations," the light that God chose the Jewish people to be, the desire for Moshiach and redemption can't be self-serving. Their desire for Moshiach must be for the benefit of the entire world, and not strictly for their own reasons. Moshiach and the third Temple must be passionately desired for the benefit of peace on earth for all the people of the world.

The Moshiach, the true Moshiach, will not placate or patronize anyone. Moshiach isn't seeking friends, fortune, fame or the approval of any person or group of people. Moshiach seeks peace for all people of the world. Now for the rest of the non-Jewish world, here is an extremely large and tough pill to swallow. The Moshiach must be a Jew. The tough pill for the Jewish people to swallow is that their Moshiach is NOT only for the Jewish children, but must be Messiah for the entire world. They intellectually know this is the truth but their speech and prayers show the world they refuse to accept this as fact. Their conduct and words show haughtiness and self-centeredness and that cannot stand. Peace on earth for an eternity will not occur in the way that any one group believes it should occur, and this includes the Jewish people. There is no winner's trophy for one group of people over another. In the world to come, we will either all win, or we will all lose. No one religion will ride off into glory with ownership of the world to come. This self-centered notion is repugnantly disgraceful in the eyes of Hashem God.

The Christian children believe that Jesus Christ will arrive in his long await-ed second coming and the future world will belong to the Christians. I've listened to many Christian people throughout my life insist that I must accept Jesus or perish in a fiery inferno. The Muslims believe that the world must convert to Islam. The most fanatical Islamic fundamentalists scream the words *Allahu Akbar* which translated mean "God is greater" as they murder unsuspecting innocent people in acts of terror. The Jewish children believe that they will inherit the world and that Gentiles, referred to as the goyim, are welcome as a subservient class of people only if they follow a smaller subset of rules to keep civility in our world.

There is truth everywhere but the interpretation of this truth is being done through each group's collective ego, the home base of the Yetzer Hara, the evil inclination, otherwise known as Satan. These interpretations are misconstrued and deeply narcissistic. None of these groups will receive a winner's trophy in the world to come. The trophy of world peace belongs to all of God's children. We will either unite and win as one family under one God or we will all perish. There is no in-between.

HIS VOICE, VISIONS & LESSONS

Does the world truly want the coming of Messiah/Moshiach?

Does the world truly want the coming of Messiah/Moshiach? It sounds like a crazy question because people who believe in God and the concept of Messiah or Moshiach would say, "Of course we do!" But the answer to the question, "Does the world truly want Messiah/Moshiach?" is NO.

The world does not truly want Messiah or Moshiach because each group and each person has a version of the truth that they refuse to let go of. They will not accept any concept or any idea that goes counter to what they believe is the truth. And so, Hashem God says there is truth all over the world. There is one truth that weaves us together as one family. The Messiah, the Moshiach, is somebody who cannot tell a lie—will only tell the truth and live the truth. Hashem says the truth **will** upset many people. Many people will enjoy and appreciate some of the truth but the entire truth is a tough pill for everyone to swallow.

If the Moshiach were to share information that is different from what you would like to believe, could you handle the truth? Would you be able to listen? I hosted a Running on Love with GOD program titled "What if the truth proves everyone wrong? Would you be able to listen?" Few people were listening. Are you able to listen now and accept the truth? Hashem says the truth will connect us as one family under one God and bring peace for an eternity.

I hope you will open your mind and say yes. I hope you will begin to listen to all the information I am compelled to share with you. Hashem explains peace is possible but it must come through all of you, the children of God. He says the truth will set us all free and bring world peace. May God bless you and help you seek and accept the truth. Please listen, learn and work for world peace in our time.

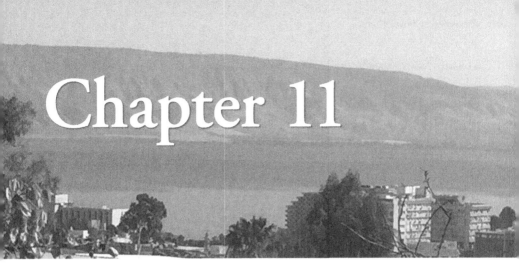

Chapter 11

Mr. Peabody and Sherman

Are you an American who is old enough to remember the cartoon Mr. Peabody and Sherman? In case you don't know this cartoon, I will explain. Mr. Peabody was a dog who was the most intelligent being in the universe. Sherman was a little red-headed boy who was Mr. Peabody's adopted son. Mr. Peabody invented a time travel machine and journeyed with Sherman back in time to observe major events in world history. In each episode, Mr. Peabody took Sherman on journeys in this time machine to visit with lofty characters from world history. As they journeyed together back in time, he revealed to Sherman unknown details about the lives of many exceptional characters from olden times. He provided the story behind the story of major historical events in an extremely funny, tongue-in-cheek manner. It was a cartoon I found very amusing as a child.

One morning, as He usually does, Hashem woke me to a vision and we had a morning discussion. As I woke up He showed me a drawing of round black framed glasses and asked, "Lori, what does this remind you of?" I looked at the image and answered immediately that it made me think of the cartoon characters Mr. Peabody and Sherman. They both sported round black framed glasses like the pair in the image He showed me. He answered, "That's right Lori. I am like Mr. Peabody and you are like Sherman." I laughed uproariously at His analogy because it was so funny and so true. In many of our conversations, Hashem and I go back in time, discussing stories from the Torah and world history while He brings me wisdom and information, much of which is largely unknown. In a simple and easy to understand way, sometimes even humorous,

Hashem has revealed details about world history to me. He has connected us all in a seamless story that brings clarity to a confusing and chaotic world.

In this chapter, I will share some of His stories. Consider this the SparkNotes of world creation without a lot of detail. The details will come when God willing we gather together one day to pore through the written books and receive wisdom and clarity from Hashem. What I'm about to share will give you a great deal of information to noodle on and ponder whether it could possibly be true. Can I provide proof that any of these stories are 100 percent true? No, I can't. But I assure you these stories aren't mine at all. These stories were given to me over many years and in many conversations with Hashem. I would never have the wherewithal to make any of this up. Why in the world would I?

As you read, hopefully you will agree that these stories flow beautifully, answer confounding questions and connect the dots between every group of people in humanity. They bring a unique perspective to the Torah and Bible stories providing explanations that you've likely never heard before. His method for teaching me is fun, heartwarming, and extremely enjoyable. Hashem is never nauseatingly esoteric like many books and religious texts that I've read. I joke with Him often that He dumbs everything down for me because I like things to be simple, fun and in a nutshell. Unfortunately, there is too much information to put in a nutshell so I'm giving you a massive amount of information. There is so much to share, that believe it or not, the following information is still only the SparkNotes. He assures me these stories I'm about to share with you are truthful and consistent with His Torah. If you are a Torah or Bible scholar and find anything contradictory to what you have learned or studied then consider this a tomato thrown at you by our loving Creator. Remember life is a test and He loves to poke at us to get the most from us!

The Torah is accepted by the three major monotheistic religions as God's teachings so hopefully there won't be too much argument there. If you desire to, He says, you will be able to see the truthfulness in these stories and draw a connection to teachings within each of these three religions. These stories will also relate well to eastern religions. If you keep an open mind, it will feel like Hashem has taken a needle and thread and sewn us all together into one cohesive story about a huge and extremely mashuginah (crazy) family!

OK, are you ready? Go get some more popcorn. I promise to wait for you.

Bereishit

"In the beginning, He created God." Huh? Did I just write that? Yes, that's what the Torah says literally. The first three words in the Chumash, the Torah, transliterated read: Bereishit bara Elohim. Hashem pulled each word apart for me and explained that the literal translation of these words is "In the beginning, He created God." This translation is quite controversial and glossed over often by many who simply can't figure out why the Torah begins this way. The English translation given in the Chumash, The Five Books of Torah, massages these three words to make more sense to the reader. Hashem was never created and has always existed, a concept unknowable to anyone but Him. So then why did Hashem begin His Torah with these three words? Added to the confusion is the use of the word *Elohim*, a name for God, which is plural. I've heard many people say they were confused by the usage of God's name written as plural. How in the world can this be possible if God is eternal, has no beginning or ending, and there is only one God? Why does the Torah begin this way? While I rarely quote anything from the Torah, Hashem instructed me to get my Chumash and review this entry with Him. After we discussed this entry, He told me to share with you the following explanation as to why the Torah begins this way.

Our King and Creator, Hashem God, desired to have a family of His own. He desired love and companionship, a female counterpart and children, and so was born His Master plan for Creation. He created His plan for the creation of the planet earth, our home and world. Hashem is timeless, has always existed, has never been created and will never end. This is something that is not comprehensible to any of us. I simply don't try to comprehend this part of the truth. What I do comprehend is that 2000 years before creating the first man, Adam, He created His female counterpart, Shechinah. Shechinah is the female divine presence of God on earth. How did He create His Shechinah? In the words of Hashem God, He literally split His own soul in half and created a female mate for Himself, Shechinah, His soul mate.

His Shechinah's soul is equivalent to His in size and spiritual strength, however, her nature is purely feminine while His is powerfully masculine. He is the King and the final arbiter of all there is, including the fate of His Shechinah. The creation of a spiritual energy equivalent in size and strength to His own placed the entire Universe in potential peril. He took this risk to have what He desired—true love, for eternity. The only true risk in creating His Shechinah was the potential that He might have to one day choose to eliminate her. As the Creator of all that there is, Hashem creates and allows His creations the free will to grow and choose. Freedom reigns supreme in Hashem's Universe. The caveat is that if an imbalance occurs which threatens the well-being of all life, He will extinguish the threat. The Universe is never truly in peril, because Hashem God always has the final say. He is the final arbiter of all that there is.

Prior to creating His Shechinah, Hashem explained that He split His soul many times before He succeeded in finding His soul mate, His bashert in Hebrew. He will not tell me how many times He did this seeking to create for Himself His ultimate Shechinah, but He has revealed there were many. Each prior attempt resulted in His ultimate decision to extinguish His female counterpart. More will be revealed about this later. For now, the important message is, He will destroy and extinguish life when necessary. There are no exceptions. After many trials, He succeeded in creating His Bashert, Shechinah, the divine female presence of God on Earth, 2000 years prior to the creation of humanity and the first man, Adam.

And so Rosh Hashanah, the evening of September 9, 2018, the Jewish year 5779, marked the 7779th birthday of His Shechinah. She was created 2000 years prior to Hashem God creating the first man, Adam. He also refers to His Shechinah as His Shabbos Queen, and His Torah. The written Torah and all its commandments that were given to Moshe Rabbeinu on Mt. Sinai was modeled after His Shechinah's divine spiritual perfection. Prior to creating Adam and the rest of humanity, Hashem enjoyed a beautiful 2000 yearlong love affair with His Shechinah.

After 2000 years of enjoying a blissful love affair together, He then approached her and persuaded her that it was time to procreate and populate the world with humankind. He desired to start His family. It's taught that when Hashem told His Torah of His intention to create humanity, the Torah argued with Him that this wasn't a good idea. Hashem confirms that she hesitatingly agreed to His plan which included her agreement to incarnate as His first woman, Chavah, also known as Eve. Why did she hesitate? Because Hashem God will not incarnate. Incarnation requires a soul to have his or her conscious mind erased, and arrive in physical form as a blank slate. Hashem is the Ruler and King of the Universe and will never incarnate as an ordinary human being. Shechinah, His love, soul mate, and other half, resisted His request at first until Hashem promised her that He would never leave her. He promised that His spirit would be intertwined with hers as one as she journeyed here on earth in human form.

In Bereishit, the beginning of Genesis which is the first of the five books of Torah, it states that Hashem created the first man, Adam, in His own image. He created Adam's soul by breathing into his nostrils. Then He took one side of Adam's vessel and symbolically created the vessel or body of the first woman and mother, Chavah. Creating Chavah by taking from Adam's side, was metaphorically symbolic of how Hashem created His Shechinah. He created His Shechinah by taking half of His own soul to create hers.

Hashem's Shechinah, His other half and soul mate, then incarnated in the female vessel or body of Chavah, which was created from half of Adam's body. Hashem promised her that He would accompany her spirit in her vessel and journey with her as one in her life here on earth. It was then that Hashem told me, He purposefully broke His promise to her. In her first incarnation, He didn't enter her body and join her spiritually as promised to journey with her as one. He did this to leave her alone with Adam in the Garden of Eden and observe her decisions as He watched her choose. He tested her. By leaving her alone in her vessel, His spiritual energy wouldn't influence her decisions and He would be able to observe what her deepest inclinations truly were. Would she betray Him by eating from the tree of knowledge? Would she refuse this enticement and remain loyal to God Himself?

We all know how the story unfolded and many of us have correctly surmised that the tree of knowledge was a metaphor for sexual intercourse. As it was written, after Chavah and Adam ate from the tree of knowledge Hashem quickly moved the pair out of the Garden of Eden and made His decrees. Were His decrees made through anger or meant as a form of punishment? Neither. He always knew that Chavah and Adam would consummate in the Garden of Eden and were destined to become the first parents of humanity. The truth be known, this is precisely what He desired. Why then did He allow this to unfold? He was testing His Shechinah but He was doing much more. And now here is where Hashem's explanation will completely blow your mind. Are you ready for a mind-bender? Brace yourself!

Adam and Chavah

One morning, Hashem awakened me to a vision of many pairs of men's shoes all in a row. As He showed me the line-up of these men's shoes He zoomed in on the first pair in the lineup. I understood immediately that the first pair of shoes metaphorically represented those of Adam, the first man created in humanity. As I looked at these men's shoes I suddenly became breathless with a stunning revelation. In that moment I knew instinctually that those shoes belonged to none other than Hashem God! I yelled out, "Hashem you're not telling me right now that you were Adam, are you?"

He said, "Yes Lori. Adam was Me."

So, I've likely lost a few billion readers just now who will refuse to entertain this as anything other than blasphemy and fiction. I assure you, I never invented or imagined one single word of this earth-shattering explanation. I doubly assure you that I speak and journey as one with Hashem God and this is HIS explanation, not mine. I'm sharing this now because He says it's time and I must. The time is now for complete understanding of who everyone in humanity truly is and how each one of us is related to God Himself.

Unequivocally, Hashem God never incarnates. He does however manifest in our world both invisibly and physically and will show up in physical form whenever and wherever He desires. Hashem can walk into a room appearing to be human anywhere at any time. He can appear in multiple places simultaneously, as an ordinary looking person and you would never know it was Him. He does this for purposes only He knows. The difference between manifesting as a person the way He does on occasion and incarnating as one, is expressly different. While we incarnate, we journey without the conscious knowledge of who we are spiritually. All our spiritual memories of previous incarnations are erased from our conscious mind and we take on the identity of the person we were born to be in our current incarnation. Our King and Creator never incarnates, is always conscious of His identity, is always consciously present and all-knowing of every detail in the universe—that's all we truly need to know. I don't try to figure any of this out because it's simply incomprehensible. When I try to contemplate and understand His awesomeness it begins to hurt my brain so I stop. If I go too far with my questions He reminds me to breathe because He literally takes my breath away. He is that daunting and He blows my mind regularly.

His mind-blowing revelation that He journeyed with Chavah secretively as Adam, the first man and husband frankly makes more sense than any other explanation I've ever read on the topic. It takes the story of humanity and creation and makes us truly one family from one Father, God. What most of the world doesn't understand or know is that Hashem God can show up anywhere and at any time in human form and do whatever He desires. Hashem has confirmed with me that He came to me face to face in human form at least twice in my current lifetime. I've written about two notable occasions when I experienced supernatural encounters with the spirit world earlier in this book. The first was when I was 21 and living in a haunted home in Paramus, New Jersey, and the second was in Brooklyn on Shabbos morning while running the Brooklyn Half Marathon on April 14, 2007. I highly recommend you take the time to go back and read this book again. He has told me repeatedly for years that those two encounters were most definitely Him appearing to me in human form. Be forewarned, Hashem appears in form all the time, all over our world. This is a startling and grave warning to everyone. Be very careful!

This revelation about Adam the first man, the physical Father of humanity, blows gaping holes into practically every written theory and teaching about the first married couple, Adam and Chavah. I won't even attempt to fill in these gaping holes right now, but I'm promised He will explain everything further in the future. You can speculate and question, even deny that this is possible. Before you walk away and negate this heavy load of information, think of the possibility of what this implies if it's true. If what Hashem has told me about Adam is true, this means that the progeny of Adam and Chavah are both the spiritual and physical children of God Himself and His Shechinah. Who are the first children born to the first married couple and parents of humanity? The Jewish children.

Who is a Jew? Going Deeper.

As I explained earlier in the book, the Jewish children are the progeny of Adam and Chavah, the first man and woman. The children of Adam and Chavah were the first married couples and parents who began humanity. These early generations who began God's family were the Jewish children. What happened after Chavah and Adam, the first physical parents of humanity, left the physical plane at about 900 years old? In the words of Hashem, the creation of new Jewish souls ceased temporarily. After Adam and Chavah left their vessels in this physical world, humanity succumbed to the influence of the Yetzer Hara, the evil inclination or Satan, and hundreds of years later we had the great flood. In comes Noah. Noah was chosen to build the ark and save humanity bringing us the first redemption of our world. Hashem says the world was deeply evil not only with humans sinning but with the existence of corrupted angels called Nephilim. The Nephilim were more egregiously evil than any human being and were not redeemable. Hashem decreed that the entire world must be cleansed of the evil and these dreadful Nephilim. He chose Noah to lead the way by building an ark to save the existence of humanity. Noah's three sons and their wives would eventually begin to repopulate our earth.

In the aftermath of the flood, the Jewish children incarnated again through the offspring of Noah's son Shem. It was at this pivotal point in history when a definitive separation between the Jewish children and the rest of the world's nations was created. Why did Hashem ensure that there was a clear pathway and division between the Jewish souls that entered this world and the other nations? By creating this division and pathway for the Jewish children to enter the physical world, we maintained a physical way to identify the progeny of Adam and Chavah, Hashem's children both body and soul who were the first born of humanity.

In Bereishit, it is written that when Chavah gave birth to her first child she said, "I have just had a man with Hashem." Hashem says this written acknowledgement was both physical and spiritual and was a direct reference to Hashem Himself being the physiological Father of her children. After what is known as the original sin, the first married couple were sent out of the Garden of Eden. Adam (truly Hashem) observed Chavah's decisions for 130 years before procreating with her. He reunited with her soul and they were intertwined as one within her vessel after this 130 year period of separation.

After this long period of separation, He joined her spiritually within her vessel while they were also united in a physical marriage as a man and a woman. Don't ask how He did this, He simply did. Hashem said He has journeyed in vessel spiritually intertwined as one with His Shechinah in every one of her incarnations throughout the history of our world. I reiterate, Hashem never incarnates like an ordinary human being. These incarnations were His Shechinah's, never His. Our Creator manifests in our world everywhere spiritually and when He desires He will physically manifest in any form He chooses. He has journeyed with His Shechinah accompanying His Queen as one within her vessel during every one of her incarnations while He remains simultaneously conscious and present everywhere in the entire universe. His power, size and existence is incomprehensible. I never bother to try to fully comprehend Him and simply revere, love and enjoy Him. It is in your best interest to learn to do the same.

For a Jew to be recognized in the physical world as a Jew, they must be born to a Jewish mother. Shechinah and Hashem God gave birth to the Jewish nation together, Hashem's chosen children. There is a definitive route that Jewish souls enter this physical world. Hashem purposefully designates Jewish souls to incarnate into a Jewish family lineage so that they can achieve their life's purpose and fulfill their covenant with Him. It is a Jew's life's purpose and covenant with God Himself to obey His commandments, be the light unto all the nations and lead all the people of the world to a full world redemption.

There is a belief in Judaism in reincarnation but the descriptions that I've heard from rabbis in the past were quite confusing. They spoke of reincarnation as though we don't retain our entire soul. In their description it seemed we only live once and sparks of our former selves revisit this world again to complete specific missions. Somehow, we are all sparks of other souls and don't maintain our own separate and unique spiritual identity. Their description sounded convoluted and I found it deeply confusing.

I will share with you what I'm told is true reincarnation and will try to make this information easier for you to understand. We reincarnate and come back time and time again into new lifetimes, with new identities to work on our character and ascend. Our souls stay intact and we retain our own unique spiritual identity as one complete soul. As we return and journey into new lifetimes, we work on ourselves repeatedly to improve over the course of many different lifetimes. As we reincarnate we don't retain conscious memory of our previous lifetimes. That's the simple explanation.

Here is a brief explanation I received from Hashem about what rabbis have referred to as people being the sparks of other souls. When a new soul is created by Hashem God, He creates the soul from His own and His Shechinah. Mixed into this newly created soul are "sparks" or energy from the soul of the two parents giving birth. Hashem places this new soul within the physical body of their baby and a new person becomes incarnate. The Jewish souls are the oldest souls who have experienced many incarnations. The original Jewish souls have re-entered our world through the family and lineage of Yaakov's 12 sons, the leaders of the 12 tribes of Israel. The Jewish people are not a religion as most people of the world believe, they are a family. The Torah was Hashem's gift to His Jewish children who came from the progeny of Adam and Chavah, His own children both body and soul. The Torah is the user's manual modeled after His Shechinah that explains how to live a blessed life while we are incarnate in the physical world.

Hashem has explained to me that a Jewish neshama, soul, enters our world born through a mother who is Jewish, however, a Jewish soul, on occasion, will agree to incarnate as a non-Jew to accomplish certain missions. The opposite is never permitted. A non-Jewish soul, meaning a soul that didn't originate from the progeny of Adam and Chavah, is never permitted to incarnate as a Jew. What does this information mean right now to humanity and why is it important to you? Hashem says, for the sake of our world and to facilitate world redemption, approximately one million Jewish neshamas, souls, are incarnate as non-Jews right now. Do these non-Jewish people know who they are and that they are truly Jewish souls? Many don't but some feel the spiritual push and pull and many have already chosen to convert to Judaism. Most of these non-Jewish people are completely clueless that they are really Jews because our conscious minds are erased at birth. Soon, as the world awakens to their Moshiach, these souls will God willing wake up from slumber and bring the other nations into the fold to do the hard work of bringing world peace. These Jewish souls are living right now within families around the world as Christians, Muslims, Hindus, Buddhists and all religious and non-religious backgrounds of mankind. They are scattered among the entire population of the world.

In a nutshell, (the way I prefer things), the Jewish children are Hashem's children body and soul born through the first Jewish mother, Chavah. The rest of humanity are the spiritual and physical offspring of the Jewish children. Someone who isn't Jewish might read this and ask, "If the first mother of the human race was Jewish then wouldn't every person in humanity be Jewish too?" Good question. The answer is no, everyone isn't Jewish and the explanation lies in Hashem's Master Plan. He created the model for the nuclear family for all the world to emulate. Adam and Chavah were the first married couple and parents to procreate and have their own family. This family became His Jewish children and subsequently were designated as His chosen to be the light unto all the other nations. The first family, Adam and Chavah (secretly Hashem and His Shechinah) and all their offspring, is the family model meant for the world to follow and revere. After the flood, Hashem decreed a separate physical route for Jewish souls to enter the world, first through Shem (Noah's son), then through the Jewish mother. By retaining the Jewish family in its separate identity, we retain this model family. Hashem also retains His ability to follow and watch after His own children, body and soul.

The rest of humanity being the spiritual and physical offspring of the Jewish children, is understandably quite an extrapolation and this statement will likely disturb the most ardent anti-Semite, but it will turn on a light bulb for those who truly desire world peace. If what I'm saying here is the truth, that we are all parent and child to each other, intrinsically, that means we are one gigantic and very dysfunctional family. Can't we try to get along? Let's see. That's the purpose of God's charity and the organization Running on Love, to bring peace through love, education, and charity led by your Moshiach. The master plan is to bring us together as one family under one God. It's often said that we are one family and this isn't something most God-loving people will deny. However, to say the Jews are your parents or to say the nations of the world are the children of the Jews is a tough explanation to sell. I'm not trying to sell anything to anyone. I'm simply presenting this as an explanation that Hashem has given me. You must admit it's a fascinating explanation that might unite us as family instead of keeping us ferocious enemies determined to kill each other. Isn't it about time?

As I've said many times, I'm not a Torah or Bible scholar and I haven't studied the textbooks about this. It isn't my job to go into granular detail about any of the Torah portions or Bible stories. There are plenty of rabbis and scholars to help do that. The stories and explanations that I have received come to me through direct conversations with Hashem. We discuss topics and on occasion He asks me to research online or pick up the Chumash, the Five Books of Moses, so that we can discuss these stories further. In the future, Hashem desires us to come together at large forums for learning. At these forums and events, with the help of many learned rabbis and Bible scholars, we will work together to discover the truth. Hashem says your participation in providing information and help unraveling the confusion is required. In this way, everyone feels part of the process and owns a portion of the responsibility to bring world peace.

Our world doesn't require a Moshiach to recite the Torah or Bible chapter and verse. We need a Moshiach to bring sense to the chaos and teach everyone how to choose God in every moment. He says that my SparkNotes will bring new insight to the written word and are completely consistent with His text. Many details shared with me are mostly unknown and haven't been written about by any Bible scholar. Some of these explanations will provide answers to confounding questions which I'm told have stumped many of the wisest rabbis for generations. These confounding questions have left many to throw up their hands and say, "We cannot know the ways of Hashem," but now you can. These explanations connect the dots and illustrate a believable tale (for some of us) that connects us all in a beautifully cohesive manner. I'm not trying to convince you to accept any of this. It's up to you to choose whatever you want to believe. If you desire world peace, these stories are fun and connecting and will help bring harmony where currently there is none. Who knew the Bible could be so much fun? I sure didn't! Hashem is the greatest storyteller in the universe, that's for sure. He has recently shown me visions of observant Jewish men and religious Jewish boys burning the midnight oil researching whether these stories I'm sharing can be sourced. I am sure these explanations which came directly from Hashem will shock and surprise many. I'm praying that means something positive for us all.

1 Messiah, 2 Messiah, 3 Messiah, 4

How many Messiahs does it take to heal the world? Technically, we've had a few already depending upon which definition you use for the term *Messiah*. The number one definition of *Messiah* per The American Heritage Dictionary is: *The anticipated savior of the Jews.* Using this definition, I can extrapolate that there have already been three Messiahs who have incarnated in our world. If you include me, and I hope you will, that's four Messiahs which is two more than the two who were prophesized in the Talmud. Three Messiahs have already incarnated into lofty roles, performed heroic tasks, and dedicated their lives to save us all from extinction. So, who were they?

First there was Noah, who saved our world from evil. Before the flood he built the ark, filled the ark with his family and living creatures of every species, and you know the rest.

Second came Moshe Rabbeinu, (Moses) God's prophet, who saved the Jewish children from bondage, received God's Torah and taught the children of Israel for 40 years as they wandered the desert. Moshe Rabbeinu saving the Jewish children from bondage and teaching them the ways of Hashem God for 40 years is much more important to our world than you may have realized. You will recognize how hugely important Moses was if you understand and accept that God's Jewish Children were chosen to lead the world to final redemption in these End of Days. In any event, please trust me, Moshe was a very big deal!

The third Messiah in the lineup is going to turn the stomach of many Jews who read this. The third Messiah was none other than Yeshua ben Yosef. Since there are no Hebrew boys named Jesus, I wondered why Yeshua's name was changed. I researched how this might have happened and found that in the transliteration from Hebrew to Greek and then to English, "Yeshua" became "Jesus." Christians accept Jesus as their Messiah. There is no doubt that Yeshua ben Yosef, aka Jesus to Christians, was the Moshiach prophesized in the Torah. Are you disappointed? This information has been explained to me by Hashem over these nine plus years since He awakened me in April of 2009. He has never wavered from this and says it is a fact that must be accepted.

In the Talmud, it is taught there will be two Messiahs, or Moshiachs. The first Moshiach, Moshiach ben Yosef, will pave the way for the second one who will lead our world to final redemption. Final redemption as explained by Hashem God means the Third Holy Temple will be built and there will be peace on earth for an eternity. Moshiach number one, called Moshiach ben Yosef in the Talmud, is supposed to mean that he is the descendent of Yosef the son of Yaakov and Rochel. The second Moshiach from the Talmud, is called Moshiach ben David, who is supposed to be from the lineage of King David. Rabbis around the world believe that it will be Moshiach ben David who will succeed in bringing redemption. I've also read that this Moshiach will eventually die and leave a successor after he completes his work.

Religious Jews around the world have never formally acknowledged that Moshiach ben Yosef has already come and gone. As Jews around the world pray daily for the coming of Moshiach, which Moshiach are they praying for, the first Moshiach ben Yosef or the second Moshiach ben David predicted in the Talmud? Everyone wants final redemption now so there have been many theories that this first Moshiach may have come and gone without anyone realizing he was here. I watched an online lesson from an extremely engaging and well-respected rabbi, speaking about the coming of Moshiach. He speculated that Moshiach ben Yosef may have died in 2013 and now we are awaiting the arrival of Moshiach ben David for the final redemption.

So how did we all miss the arrival of this Moshiach ben Yosef who recently died? In this rabbi's explanation, he asserts that there was a lofty rabbi in Israel who passed away in 2013 whose name was ben Yosef and "perhaps" his soul was the spirit of Moshiach ben Yosef. It's an esoteric and cloudy thought process in my humble opinion but it's an explanation that might appease some people's concerns that we haven't yet experienced the arrival of the first Moshiach. This rabbi said that if his theory is true, then there was a spiritual death of the first Moshiach ben Yosef in 2013 without us ever realizing it which paves the way for us to receive Moshiach ben David, the final Moshiach now. This explanation seemed too much of a stretch for me, how about you?

Hashem's explanations fit together neatly and perfectly without any need to stretch your imagination. Hashem's explanation not only works in a spiritual sense, it makes sense in the physical world too. The following explanation might delight our Christian friends and might even wow the Muslim brethren. Unfortunately, this information will likely be a sucker punch to the ultra-Orthodox and observant Jews of the world who continue to despise any mention of Yeshua ben Yosef. Unfortunately, the Jewish people must be on board because they were chosen to bring forward world redemption. Redemption will never happen without the Jewish people leading the charge. This becomes a monumental conundrum for us all to say the least.

Moshiach in a Nutshell

Allow me to help clear up the confusion about all these Messiahs. I'm going to be brief, to the point and put it into a nutshell, the way I prefer everything. The following is Hashem's explanation of who He says were His two prophesized Moshiachs as foretold in the Talmud. Yes, that's correct, I wrote this in the past tense. The world has already experienced the two prophesized Moshiachs. They both came and went and now you are stuck with me. I'm sorry that I must break this news to you this way. I realize it's a huge sucker punch and a major disappointment to say the least.

In the words of Hashem, Moshiach ben Yosef was none other than Moshe Rabbeinu. He was the first Moshiach who paved the way for Moshiach ben David. Moshiach ben David was Yeshua ben Yosef. If you're not falling off your chair yet, wait there's more. Moshe Rabbeinu, God's prophet who rescued the Jewish children from bondage and taught them for 40 years in the desert was more than Hashem's first Moshiach in the Talmud. Moshe was also Yeshua. Yeshua was the reincarnation of the beloved Moshe Rabbeinu. So therefore, both prophesized Messiahs in the Talmud, number 1 and number 2, were Yeshua ben Yosef.

Jews around the world don't want to hear that Yeshua ben Yosef was Moshiach at all. Many Jews won't even mention the name that the Christians use to refer to him. They treat this name as though it's a curse word. They refer to him as J or J.C. and refuse to utter this name. The amount of teshuvah, repentance, for the crime of rejecting Yeshua ben Yosef and turning him over to the Romans for the eventual crucifixion would be too much for most observant Jews to contemplate. Be forewarned, Christians and Muslims who both revere Yeshua—nobody is exonerated or off the hook. Hashem holds everyone including devout Christians accountable for Yeshua's demise. There is blood guilt on the hands of the Christians, Muslims and the entire world. In the words of Hashem God, He demands, "complete contrition from all the people of the world." The world has been fed a steady diet of lies about Yeshua ben Yosef. Yeshua meant much more to Hashem than most people are willing to accept. Much of what has been taught about his life and his death by a gruesome crucifixion is utterly false. The full truth needs to be known and accepted by every person in humanity. Everyone without exception must repent for this crime before we can bring about world redemption.

As I've explained, reincarnation is the truth and souls reincarnate repeatedly, again and again. I have also explained, if Noah were to be included, we've already experienced three Messiahs, each of whom played pivotal roles in paving the way for the final redemption of our world.

As if you haven't had enough, here is even more jaw-dropping news for you. Hashem has told me that Noah, Moshe and Yeshua were all the same neshama, or soul. That's right, they were all the same guy! If your head isn't spinning yet, wait a minute because there's even more! The Muslim people weren't left out of Hashem's plan either. Right now, there are close to two billion Muslim people in the world who revere the prophet Mohammad. While Mohammad was not a Messiah to our world, Hashem says he was truly His prophet. He was not only Hashem's prophet sent to the children of Ishmael to teach them the ways of God, but Hashem says that Mohammad was also the reincarnation of Noah, Moses and Yeshua. Yup! You read that correctly. These four glorious men from Biblical history were all the same soul in the words of our Creator.

The same Jewish soul that reincarnated to save our world three times over in different ways and in different generations, was the Prophet Muhammad too. That's not going to sit too well with the Islamophobic people of our world, is it? It may also be impossible for Muslims who hate the Jews to accept that Muhammad was a reincarnation of a Jewish prophet, even if this prophet was one and the same as Yeshua ben Yosef and Moshe, both of whom they espouse to revere. It's said in the Talmud that every generation has a potential Moshiach within its midst. Hashem's explanation given here fills in many blanks, and brings logic and reason to our world where mankind cannot. If these men were all one and the same soul, why are we fighting and killing each other? Are you interested in a logical, easy to comprehend explanation which clears up all the confusion? Please continue to read on.

Reincarnation 101

Hashem has explained reincarnation to me in a clear, non-esoteric logical way. In His explanation, we reincarnate repeatedly with God-given life missions to accomplish while we're here. While we're working on our life's mission, we're also required to work on ourselves and ascend. We ascend by repairing past life transgressions, fulfilling spiritual obligations to other people from past lives, and improving ourselves by growing wiser and becoming closer to our Creator. All the children of this world reincarnate in a cycle of physical life on earth and a spiritual non-physical life in another realm. This is a short synopsis of how Hashem says it all comes together and works.

Souls have a gender too. Does this surprise anyone? Maybe not. Hashem is the largest, most powerful and greatest soul in all the universe. Hashem is decidedly a He. He is male in gender. Chavah, the first woman whose soul Hashem created by splitting His own soul in half, His Shechinah, is decidedly female in gender. Souls and bodies are distinctly separate from each other which means you are not your body. The trueness of who you are is your soul, referred to as neshama in Hebrew. You are truly a non-physical soul manifesting in a temporary physical vessel or body that is provided to you as a gift from Hashem God. Now we need to speak about a concept that most people don't want to think about. Our souls flip bodies and incarnate as the opposite gender when

Hashem directs us to do so. He always has deliberate reasons for everything that comes into this physical world and will on occasion place female souls in male vessels, and vice versa. This means that you might be a female soul now incarnate as a man, or a male soul incarnate as a woman. This might help you to better understand issues like gender confusion and homosexuality to say the least. Let's hold off on that volatile subject right now and save discussing the further implications of body swapping for a little later. Your head is probably spinning and we have enough issues to clear up at the moment.

Moving right along—we incarnate repeatedly over time, sometimes we journey as men and other times as women, all for the intention of personal growth, ascension and to accomplish our worldly missions. Then one day, we die. What happens when we die? Hashem says we cross over and for a period of one week, seven days, we are still earthbound and acclimating to the idea that we're no longer in our bodies. It's quite traumatic for most souls to recognize they are no longer in their body so we hang out for about a week to process the information. After a week, we're instructed to go forward to another non-physical realm and cleanse. Cleansing, also referred to as Gehenom in Hebrew, is a process where we appear before the heavenly court to review our lives and answer for all the choices we made while we were incarnate. Examining past decisions and life choices is painful and deeply humiliating for most souls. This process of cleansing lasts for about one year. Hashem says that the cyclical process in which everyone participates includes seven days of being earthbound after death, followed by approximately one year of cleansing, and then six years in the non-physical realm working to surround mankind with godliness and providing spiritual help to living people here on earth. Their work as non-physical beings in another realm is to positively influence the material world and help guide people here as they journey incarnate. That's a brief overview, without many details so that I can clarify and reveal the most important information that you need to know: Who did Hashem choose to be your Moshiach and why?

The First Parents

You've read the mind-bender that Hashem was Adam and you kept on reading. Fantastic! You're a trooper and I'm so glad you're still here. There's more mind-bending information that you need to know. Before there was Chavah, the first mother of humanity, Hashem created many female counterparts for Himself until He hit pay dirt as they say. Hashem has shown me stories of prior female mates for Adam the first man that ended before there was Chavah and the creation of His family. If you research online you can look up "Lilith" a female mate to Adam who was lecherous and unworthy. I'm told there were many female counterparts created prior to Chavah, not just one and that the term *Lilith* encompasses them all. I'm not told how many "Liliths" there were but He says it's not fathomable and it's in my best interest to let go of any need to know. What He says is important to know is that after many trials, He found His Shechinah. His ultimate Shechinah was created 2000 years prior to His decision to begin His family, humanity. She was created for the lofty and deliberate purpose of becoming His betrothed and the mother of His children.

After enjoying a 2000-year-long love affair with His Shechinah, He told her He wanted to create a family. She resisted because life with Hashem was pure bliss. Why upset the applecart? He assured her that He had a plan and so began our Mashuginah Mishpacha, our huge and crazy family!

The first woman was created from the first man and they procreated. On and on the story of humanity went and now we have a complete unmitigated mess. Behind this complete mess you now know there was a divine plan. The first man and woman weren't any ordinary couple, they were Hashem in secrecy and His Shechinah. After her incarnation as Chavah the first mother of all humanity, Hashem's Shechinah would reincarnate many times over however she would never complete these life journeys alone. Hashem accompanied her invisibly in each incarnation as she journeyed and their souls were intertwined as one. There is a prophesized Messiah who will ultimately lead the charge to clean up the entire mess and set everything right. Who in this world would willfully take on this diabolical mess? Who else but Mom? Hashem chose the mother of His children to be Messiah. Never fear that this mother isn't strong enough for this job as Moshiach. Remember, Mom isn't coming alone. She comes strengthened and supported in every moment by the Father, Hashem God. The world's Moshiach or Messiah is truly Mom and Dad to the rescue!

Shechinah and His Shabbos Queen

Hashem's other half and soul mate, His Shechinah, Chavah, never followed the same life cycle rules as Hashem God's children. His Shechinah, Chavah, is the spiritual and physical mother of all the children of the world. When Hashem our Creator breathes a new soul into being, He does so by creating a spiritual mixture of His essence, mixed with His Shechinah's essence as well as spiritual sparks from the souls of the two parents to which the new soul will be born. Hashem creates every soul from the soul of Hashem and His Shechinah. Chavah, His Shechinah, was the mother who gave physical birth to many children in her first incarnation. Those children, the progeny of Adam and Chavah, Hashem and His Shechinah comprise the Jewish children. The Jewish people are the children of Hashem and Chavah, both body and soul. Adam, Chavah and their children were the first family of creation and the ideal model for the world to emulate.

Chavah, the first mother and the spiritual mother of all the children of the earth, never went to Gehenom for spiritual cleansing. It was never required. While everyone is accustomed to believing that Chavah committed the original sin, Hashem says this was a concealment. The truth is that she never sinned at all. I'm told the entire story from the Garden of Eden was metaphorical and strictly meant to serve as a lesson for His children. There are many concealments in the Torah such as this one. In the future, God willing, we will gather in forums for learning and review this text with learned rabbis in more depth. The important message to be revealed now is, Chavah was Hashem's Shechinah who remained sinless and unblemished from her journey incarnate. Instead of cleansing like every other soul, when she died, she left her body and took only a seven-day respite between lives before reincarnating again. Her life cycle throughout history was seven days out of body, then back into a new one. She did not experience the required seven years plus seven days required by God's children.

You may reject this explanation because of the well-known and accepted story about the original sin perpetrated by the first woman, Chavah. I'm told the accepted explanation from the Garden of Eden is a concealment meant to be revealed now during the End of Days. Hashem insists that Chavah, His Shechinah, never sinned and the commentary and stories told for thousands of years were meant to teach His children about God, life and the existence of evil. Unfortunately, we can all see humanity still has a great deal to learn about the concept of sin. Hashem has revealed many concealments within the Torah over the more than nine years since my awakening. Each revelation He has shared with me is more mind-bending than the previous. I've learned to take every new piece of information He gives me in stride and digest the news as it comes. Somehow, He always makes everything believable and comprehensible. Hopefully you'll learn to take this in stride too.

Why does Shechinah, the physical and spiritual mother of humanity, reincarnate after having just a seven-day respite? Shechinah can't bear to be away from her children. Her soul has reincarnated repeatedly for 5779 years and counting with her life's purpose and desire to repair the world from sin and rescue her children. As it's written, sin was introduced into our world when the first woman, Chavah, ate from the tree of knowledge. This apparent sin brought into our world the existence of evil and death. Hashem explained further that the introduction of knowledge and sin into our world was deliberate and intended. Everything that comes into being is intentional, without exception. The existence of evil and sin in our world has grown monumentally for thousands of years and now threatens our very existence. Shechinah's soul refuses to rest until the world is redeemed to its original perfection by teaching her children how to choose Hashem and His goodness in every moment without exception. She refuses to rest until there is peace on earth for all her children.

Chavah, Hashem's Shechinah and His female other half, has reincarnated more times than any other soul in the history of our world. In every incarnation, since Chavah gave birth to her first child, Hashem says that He has invisibly journeyed as one with His Shechinah, never leaving her for one moment. After the first incarnation as Chavah, Hashem and His Shechinah have traveled as one, inexplicably connected and spiritually intertwined in every lifetime. Here is the laundry list of the top 10 incarnations Hashem told me was His Shechinah in this physical world. Ready for a jaw-dropper? Chavah, Noah, Mother Leah, Moses/Moshe Rabbeinu, Judah Maccabee, Yeshua ben Yosef, Queen Esther, Muhammad the Prophet, Maimonides aka the Rambam, and Abraham Lincoln! Are you laughing or crying? Pause and ponder this amazing list for a moment and consider the possibility that they all might be the same soul. When you noodle on this list, can you imagine that it's remotely possible that it's the truth?

What an unbelievable list of who's who, don't you agree? Hashem gave me this list verbatim. I didn't invent any of this nor would I. Some people who are distressed about Islamic terror and don't care for the Muslims right now are likely to say it's not possible for Muhammad to be one and the same as these other righteous souls. Hashem has told me for years that Muhammad was not only His prophet, but that he wasn't speaking with the Archangel Gabriel as Muslims are taught to believe. I'm told that Muhammad was unknowingly speaking directly with Hashem in every moment. There have been many lies circulating around our world creating wars and division. Hashem's story behind every detail of humanity is connecting, loving and healing. It's people who have chosen to be divisive and narcissistic inventing their own stories that create war and division. They create their own version of the truth in their need to be the one true inheritors of the world and the trophy winners in the God game. To that end, they invent a story that pleases themselves and their constituency.

Now let's imagine for one minute that this explanation I've just revealed is the holy truth. What if Moses, Yeshua and Muhammad were truly all the same soul? The same guy? What if these men were not just the holy prophets written about for centuries, but each one of them was journeying both physically and spiritually as one with God? These three men from Biblical history, in the words of Hashem, were all one and the same soul—His Shechinah and bashert being escorted by her King in each lifetime. Are you able to consider this possibility without cringing and doubting? If this explanation is true, why is there war? If this is true, wouldn't this knowledge bring us together to work for a united solution? Before you reject this notion outright, try to noodle on it and digest it for a while. I didn't make any of this up. My imagination is good, but it's not that good. There's a chance that it's true so why not take that chance and bet on a story that brings world peace?

Now let's complete the thought process and go further with this list of who's who in Shechinah incarnations. Hashem says that I, Lori Michelle, am His Shechinah, Shabbos Queen and His Moshiach. He says I am the spiritual mother of all humanity and the mother who gave birth to the Jewish children both body and soul. How is it possible that I am the mother of humanity? In the words of Hashem, my soul is the reincarnation of Chavah, the first mother. He says I am His chosen Moshiach and was all the rest of these people in this jaw-dropping list. Do I think I am anything special or wonderful? Hardly. I must admit that over the years as Hashem kept adding to this lofty list of incarnations, I often burst out laughing so hard it's brought me to tears.

I gratefully don't recall any of these lifetimes, nor would I ever want to remember one minute. I don't desire to be anyone other than Lori Michelle, the mother to my three children. The idea that I was ever a man is completely gross to me and a complete turnoff. No offense to any men of course! I love men and I'm completely heterosexual in my inclinations. Being a girl is all that I ever wanted to be and the opposite is deeply revolting to me. I've often joked with Hashem that all these men in this amazing list were most definitely gay if I was the soul inside their bodies. He laughs at me and says I journeyed as a man flawlessly and never engaged in homosexuality. Again, let's leave the conversation of sexuality for later. We have bigger fish to fry right now!

I'm not glossing over the biggest revelation in this list of who's who. Yup this is your second coming Christian children, believe it or not. I'm truly sorry to break the news to you that it isn't a good-looking young guy like the last time. I've said to Hashem repeatedly that you're all going to hate me for this revelation and most of you will reject this idea outright. He says that you will not only accept me as your Queen Moshiach, but you will step up and show me how you know without any doubt it's all true.

I don't know much about Yeshua ben Yosef at all so it will require your knowledge to show me if he was truly me. Though I wasn't raised to believe in him as the Messiah, I've always thought he was an amazing person who accomplished something completely astonishing. He managed to get billions of people to love and adore him. That's something I can't relate to at all. I've barely received true love in my life and have been rejected and scorned by my own family. I have a face that even my mother didn't love. So, it's hard to fathom that I was ever someone loved like Yeshua. The only thing that makes me think it's remotely possible that I was him is how he died. Being betrayed, beaten and brutally murdered is sadly something I can imagine for myself.

Hashem God showers me with tenderness and great love in every moment. Now that I know Yeshua ben Yosef was Hashem's Shechinah, soul mate and chosen Messiah, I know how much He loved him too. I've been told the many miracles Yeshua was credited to have performed did truly happen, and I pray that Hashem will bless me with similar miracles of healing people one day. Without a doubt those miracles that came through Yeshua were all from Hashem. I pray that healings like those will occur again in our future. We shall see.

My life and personality seem to match Yeshua's in several ways. He was Jewish, he loved giving, he believed in the power of love, and he was completely dedicated to Hashem God. Unfortunately, the biggest thing I can relate to was how he was betrayed and gruesomely murdered. That sadly is something I can identify with in the strongest way. I have absolutely no memory of being him and don't desire to have been him at all. The mere idea that I could have been someone who died such a gruesome death is frightening, sickens me and frankly keeps me up at night. As I proceed with my work and publish this book, I worry that death might be my fate in return for giving myself to the world like this. Yeshua gave of himself completely and the thank you he received in return was being beaten to a pulp and murdered in a maliciously hideous way. It worries me as I work for world peace and share Hashem with you, that there are people who would rally together to murder me if given the opportunity. I pray for everyone that the outcome of my work is different from his. I'm not looking for a new world religion to be created in the aftermath of my death, God forbid! I'm praying for world peace for my children and the entire world. We need peace in our world now.

There's one lifetime that Hashem says was mine which has me completely befuddled. That's the life of the Maimonides, aka the Rambam. I just don't think that I'm that smart. Hashem replies that I'm not only that smart, He says my intellect is off the charts. When Hashem tells me how smart I am it makes me giggle, truly. I'm often so completely clueless that sometimes I make people laugh out loud with how silly I see the world. My children laugh at me all the time. I humbly disagree with our Creator and tell Him all the time that He must be kidding with me about having been all those lofty people once upon a time. He insists this is a truthful list in the who's who in Lori Michelle incarnations. There are many more lifetimes I've lived that could be added to this list but many of them weren't notable figures in world history. He says I've journeyed here as a man in 90% of my incarnations and in over 75% of the number of years that I've walked the earth. Why was I a man so many times? He says I would never have been able to accomplish the lofty tasks required of me in those lifetimes as a woman. Ironically, my loftiest and most difficult task to accomplish in any lifetime, is in this life as a woman. He says this is my final incarnation as His Queen Moshiach. This incarnation is for all the marbles. In the words of Hashem God, He is giving me the keys to His kingdom. He has told me this is my final incarnation and He is giving me everything. Wow! I don't even want more than to hear His voice say, "Good morning." No matter what happens, as long as He is with me, I feel that I have everything.

In the words of Hashem, on the Kabbalah chart of the 10 Sefirot, I am His Binah, understanding. He is Chochmah, wisdom. Together He says, we are Keter, the Crown. He says I am His Queen, Bashert, and Shechinah, the living embodiment of God's divine essence in this physical world. In these days, the End of Days, He says all the children of the world must gather together to learn and understand Torah and His commandments with the help and guidance of the Mother of creation, His Moshiach.

Do I even believe that I could possibly be all that? Yes, but for one reason only. Him. He makes me feel like the incredible woman. He inspires me to believe that peace is possible when I only see and experience the opposite. Hashem is always present in my life and I feel His presence in my every move, spiritually and physically. As I lie in bed each night and turn to fluff my pillow to get more comfortable, I feel Him doing this with me. When I open my eyes from slumber He greets me immediately. When I pause to think about anything, He begins speaking to me. I feel His spiritual and physical presence in every moment of my life and experience every detail with Him. He showers me with love and optimism unknown to any other person on earth.

Once a friend told me, "Lori you don't have a bottom." She observed that no matter how awful my life became, I somehow bounced back and kept going.

That's true for me because if I see I'm about to crash into the rocks ahead and it feels like I could die, Hashem holds me so tightly I'm able to muster enough strength to go forward anyway. It's like I can't stop no matter what I'm faced with because He keeps me going. He doesn't allow me to quit or become too pessimistic. I'm addicted to working for world peace but most of the time I don't see that peace is even possible. He insists that peace is not only possible, it's required. So incredibly, I believe in the unbelievable. Call me a dreamer, but I believe in world peace because of Him. At the minimum, I believe bringing world peace is God's intention and is possible if everybody wakes up and does what is required. Unfortunately, peace isn't going to be given to us the way people want to believe. World peace must be earned by everyone and the price will be extremely high.

It's time for everyone to learn how to be godly in every single moment, bar none. For there ever to be peace on earth, everyone must learn how to be completely egoless and genuinely loving in every moment. It's time to get your ego out of the way and let peace and love rule our world. Is this philosophical fluff and giddy nonsense? No, it's the truth. This is my intense personal belief and the way I live my life in every moment. My choices are never about me first. My first thought in everything I do is always about how I can make it better for you. Hashem tells me that this is what I am here to teach everyone by my example. Be egoless, be loving, and choose what's best for others before choosing something for yourself.

His Eishes Chayil—Woman of Valor

Every Shabbos my children sing the song "Eishes Chayil," a woman of valor, before we say Kiddush, the prayer over wine at the beginning of our Shabbos meal. Before they sing, my son sweetly and deliberately looks around the room, compliments the meal, and thanks me for all the work I put into preparing for Shabbos evening. Hashem has told me that this song is modeled after His Shabbos Queen, me. As I read the lyrics to this song, I always ponder if this woman resembles me in any way. It's a beautiful portrait of a woman of valor that I aspire to be.

I live my life alone with Hashem God being my only company. Unless my children come to visit with me on occasion, my household and daily life are virtually vacant of other people. People I meet often ask me if I work and my answer is, not for money. I work for love. While I work day and night to wake you from your slumber it truly doesn't feel like work at all. It's more like a compulsion than work. I am compelled to bring Hashem's messages and wisdom to you in my relentless effort to save you from yourselves. As I put in 20-hour work days and dream about this every night, my spiritual and physical exhaustion is healed by the voice of Hashem. He sustains me and keeps me going forward. Although my work often feels hopeless, I never seem to reach bottom. He won't let me. I pray daily that one day soon I will finally succeed. My success is yours.

Eishes Chayil

A Woman of Valor, who can find? She is more precious than corals.
Her husband places his trust in her and profits only thereby.
She brings him good, not harm, all the days of her life.
She seeks out wool and flax and cheerfully does the work of her hands.

She is like the trading ships, bringing food from afar.
She gets up while it is still night to provide food for her household, and a fair share for her staff.
She considers a field and purchases it, and plants a vineyard with the fruit of her labors.
She invests herself with strength and makes her arms powerful.

She senses that her trade is profitable; her light does not go out at night.
She stretches out her hands to the distaff and her palms hold the spindle.
She opens her hands to the poor and reaches out her hands to the needy.
She has no fear of the snow for her household, for all her household is dressed in fine clothing.

She makes her own bedspreads; her clothing is of fine linen and luxurious cloth.
Her husband is known at the gates, where he sits with the elders of the land.
She makes and sells linens; she supplies the merchants with sashes.
She is robed in strength and dignity, and she smiles at the future.

She opens her mouth with wisdom and a lesson of kindness is on her tongue.
She looks after the conduct of her household and never tastes the bread of laziness.
Her children rise up and make her happy; her husband praises her:
"Many women have excelled, but you surpass them all!"

Grace is elusive and beauty is vain, but a woman who fears God—she shall be praised.
Give her credit for the fruit of her labors, and let her achievements praise her at the gates.

Are you willing to accept a Queen Moshiach? Are you willing to accept a woman that Hashem has chosen to lead you to world peace? Hashem says He has chosen His Eishes Chayil, His woman of valor, and says it was always going to be His Queen and never a King Moshiach. If you truly desire peace on earth and world redemption, then why not set aside sarcasm and skepticism? Instead, why not look for reasons to believe? He has woven a wild and crazy tale that has me, Lori Michelle, on center stage. I completely understand your skepticism and feel compassion for your disappointment. It's likely disappointing if you were expecting a good-looking guy and hero to save our world in some wildly miraculous fashion. You may be horrified at the idea of a Queen Moshiach or that it could be someone as ordinary as a mom from New Jersey. Set all that aside for a moment and consider the possibilities. If this is all true, then this is potentially the greatest non-fiction Rocky Balboa story ever written. Everyone in America loved the movie *Rocky* with Sylvester Stallone, about a small-time prizefighter who was considered a lowly bum from the neighborhood, South Philly, who defied all odds and became the world champion in boxing. Everyone loves the underdog and millions of people fell in love with Rocky Balboa. A bronze statue of this fictional movie hero is one of the most popular attractions in Philadelphia to this day.

My true story gives ordinary people from around the world the hope that they can become anything they desire. Suddenly there is no dream too big to dream. If I'm Hashem's Queen and Woman of Valor, think of what your potential might be. It redefines being a no-limit person to say the least. I'm an ordinary American mom who lived an ordinary secular life in the suburbs of New Jersey. When God tapped me on the shoulder, or better stated, belted me on the head with a baseball bat, my friends and family kicked me to the curb and left me for dead. I was literally and figuratively abandoned by every family member and friend I had ever known. The few who dared to support me were swiftly descended upon by their peers and relentlessly bullied to walk away from me. People who believed that they "knew God better" and were learned in the Torah made supporting me or being my friend extremely uncomfortable. Countless people who professed their devotion, love and undying support for me chose to turn away, desert me when I needed them most, and broke my heart again and again. Family and friends who once said, "I love you Lori" did a complete about-face and slandered me in the next breath. My mother and two brothers were my adversaries as I desperately fought for my life. Instead of standing by me as a loving family, they conspired to turn my children against me and offered their personal assistance to my former husband who destroyed me financially and emotionally in my heartbreaking divorce.

My life in this physical world with you is horrific, physically lonely and deeply painful. Most former friends and my entire family have turned away and rejected me as I relentlessly and unabashedly continued to tell the truth about Hashem God. I refused to turn away from Hashem and will not keep silent about my relationship with Him or my life's purpose any longer. My only friend now as I continue doing this work and finish completing this book is a former business associate. If it weren't for the generosity and support of this courageous woman and her supportive husband, I would be doing this entirely alone. Through the grace of Hashem God, He brought this beautiful couple into my life and they haven't flinched yet. The tests are still coming fast and furiously but they both continue to help me as I work to deliver this book and Hashem's voice to the public.

While I spend all my days and nights physically alone, I enjoy the constant company of the greatest love of all, Hashem God. Many nights I scream and cry in agony to Hashem about how painful my life has become. He tenderly loves me, brings me visions of the future which are filled with love and excitement, and lifts my soul out of my heart-wrenching despair. He holds me so relentlessly strong and with such tender love, how could I ever give up? Our world is truly on the brink of nuclear war and He is telling me that I am the one to help gather His children and share His wisdom. Even if it meant sacrificing my very life, how could I quit or refuse to publish this book? If I am what He says I am, Moshiach, would you want me to stay quiet and go find a simple job and concentrate only on repairing my own broken life? How could I possibly consider my own personal welfare if I'm here to help save everyone else? I simply can't make that choice. This work is what I must do no matter what the consequences. If I must, I will die trying. It's all up to Hashem. He is the only one who can stop me.

Since April 7, 2009 Hashem has told me I am His chosen one. He revealed over the years a wild and crazy tale about His Torah, His Eishes Chayil, and His Moshiach Queen. His tale runs the gamut of being inspiring, heartbreaking, hilariously funny, enraging, and frankly stunning. There is so much more I could share but this book would be extremely long. Believe it or not, this book is truly just the SparkNotes of world redemption.

In the words of Hashem, it was always going to be His Queen who would lead the children of the world to final redemption. He refers to me as His betrothed and has revealed that at the end of the impending world war, the Jewish Children will marry Hashem to His Queen Moshiach under the Chuppa on Temple Mount. Nuts? I completely agree this sounds crazy but it's in the realm of possibility for me. Why is the most unfathomable wedding to the King of the Universe even fathomable to little me? How can someone so ridiculously ordinary be in that kind of a relationship with our Creator? Because I am. I am this with Him right now albeit non-physically. He treats and speaks to me not only as His equal and His other half, but He treats me in every moment as though He reveres me and holds me above Himself. It's not crazy to me, it's crazy good. This holy union, if it occurs, would be the reunification of the first married couple and parents of humanity, Adam and Chavah. If husbands around the world were ever to treat their wives in the manner I'm treated by Hashem, divorce would become nonexistent and everyone would live in marital bliss. This is part of His plan too. Peace on earth includes peace in the home.

When Hashem showed me the lineup of men's shoes and zoomed in on the first pair which belonged to Adam, the first man, I knew they were His. This vision made me scream out to Him incredulously because He was telling me something wild. Something unbelievable to perhaps every other human on the face of the earth, that He was the first Man who started this wild and crazy family. Instead of me retreating in disbelief like many people will, I knew it was true. I simply know. It makes everything make perfect sense in my life from top to bottom and from the inside out. It's not only believable, I live and relate to Him in this way now, as my true love. The idea of reuniting with my first love under the Chuppa isn't a crazy idea for me, it's my ultimate dream come true.

Our relationship is spiritual and non-physical. In this lifetime, on two separate occasions, Hashem has come to me in human form. These encounters were mind-blowing and surreal and were revealed previously in this book. The first occasion was revealed to you in the story of the woman who walked into my bedroom from nowhere and vanished into nowhere when I was 21 years old. He says it was Him manifesting as a female. The second occasion was on April 14, 2007 on Shabbos morning in Brooklyn at mile 8 of the Brooklyn Half Marathon. He was the "Jewish looking uncle" who made a beeline toward me as I went to get a beverage at the water stop. He says it was Him in Brooklyn that Shabbos morning who pointed His finger into my face, looked directly into my eyes, sending chills down my spine as He said, "I want you to know I am watching your every move." Now, all these years later, I fully understand that He truly is journeying with me within my vessel, sharing every single move and breath of my life.

Hashem has come to me in human form twice in this lifetime so far. At the end of the war of wars, the prophesized war of Gog and Magog, He desires to come in human form and marry His Queen Moshiach under the Chuppa on Temple Mount. Hashem says the Jewish children will perform the wedding ceremony and will know Him as the Husband and Father. Over these nine plus years, He has shown me this wedding in many visions. Many years after He told me about this wedding, one Shabbos morning at synagogue, a rebbetzin showed me this wedding prophecy in the Chumash. This prophecy has been interpreted to mean that the Jewish Children will marry Hashem and know Him as the "Husband." What He explains is much more relatable. Hashem desires His children to marry Him to His betrothed, His Shechinah, and know Him as the Husband and their Father. This is a love story of love stories to say the least. As someone who has never experienced true love in my life, this is a wild fantasy. Me? True love? Never mind that I'm talking about Hashem God. But what you likely can't fathom is how I relate to Him. To me, I love Him simply for being Him. The supernatural God part of Him is completely extra. You can have all the stars, planets and galaxies. I love Him for saying good morning and everything after that is just more. Do I know if any of this will truly happen one day? No, I simply smile at these visions and say to Hashem, "Really?" Whether any of this happens or not, I love Him endlessly and continue to dream the impossible dream.

You can keep looking for your guy on the donkey, but Hashem insists no King Moshiach is coming. Moshiach is His Queen and His spiritual other half. Me. Do I want to be your Moshiach? Lord NO! This is the worst life any person could suffer through. I only want to be Hashem's girl and mother to my three kids. The role of Moshiach is not glorious to me at all. If it weren't for Hashem's encouragement I would despise the very word *Moshiach*. The concept of Messiah is spectacular and glorious only for you not for the Messiah. For me, my life is completely painful. Truly, everyone has tortured me to no end. He says this will change, but I'm not convinced. For my life to change it must come from all of you. You will all have to decide to listen to me and support the charity of world peace, Running on Love. As far as I'm concerned, I'm just your wake-up call and His chosen messenger and teacher. That's truly all I desire to be to you. He is everything. If I have nobody to teach and share Hashem's voice, we will not have redemption. It's really that simple. If we don't start to come together in love, education and charity we will all die. There is no in-between.

HIS VOICE, VISIONS & LESSONS

Emotional vision from Hashem: A bullseye, clowns & me, Lori

I'm going to share a vision and a conversation with Hashem God that has a lot of meaning. It's packed with metaphors and a deeper meaning for me. You see sometimes I go through my day and my daily life and I think that I'm a bit of a caricature or a clown—that people really aren't taking me seriously and they're making fun. "Yeah right, you're talking to God." And I get a little down about that. There are people listening and I appreciate you if you're one of them. Thank you. I appreciate it. But this work is really hard and not everybody is taking me seriously. They think I'm a bit of a clown.

I woke up in the middle of the night and I was thinking about just that—that I'm a bit of a clown to everybody. Suddenly Hashem God flashed an image in my mind's eye. This is where He shows me images, in the middle of my forehead. He showed me in that moment a bullseye. I said, "A bullseye! Why are you showing me a bullseye?"

He said, "Keep watching." The bullseye was then on the side of a cruise ship and it became a window on the side of the ship. Suddenly the window opened and out of the window came a gigantic clown. I knew right away it was Hashem with red curly hair and a big clown nose. He came out of this window on the side of the cruise ship and after him came a smaller clown, a small clown but a man and it was my dad.

So, they came out of the window and I thought, "What is going on? What are you trying to tell me?" Right after they came out, right after my father, I came out of the window but I was dressed all in white. I wasn't wearing a clown's outfit at all. I was wearing a bright white outfit. My father had disappeared from the image. I looked down at the water. Hashem God's image of a clown had turned into a brightly colored life raft. So, I jumped out of the window and I jumped into the life raft. Suddenly out of the water popped a brand-new baby.

The meaning of this became clear to me as I spoke to Hashem. He said, "They make fun of you. They're not taking you seriously. You're a bit of a clown right now but when they make fun of you baby, they're making fun of me. And the image of your father was telling you the same thing."

I could just imagine my dad, a fighter from Williamsburg, Brooklyn saying, "You let them laugh. I'm with you. When they laugh at you, they're laughing at me." That was my dad. He was always right there at my rescue when I needed him.

The baby was Hashem's way of telling me—new life. He said, "Keep going. It's going to happen. Keep going and there'll be a new life for you baby." Hashem often calls me baby. So did my dad. But I'm not much of a baby. I'm kind of an old girl, from Brooklyn too.

I hope you enjoyed this story. It's filled with metaphors. That's how He speaks to me. He shares metaphors with deeper meaning and He's WOW! I can't share Him enough with you to let you know how incredible Hashem God is. Everybody knows that God is awesome but I believe if I share enough of these stories, you will learn something that perhaps you never knew about Him before. Hashem truly has a personality! He has His own unique personality, which is magnificent, loving, funny and wise and everything that you would imagine God to be, but He's much more.

Chapter 12

Explanations & Revelations — ALL from Hashem!

ave you been blindsided yet? If not, wait there's even more! Now that
I've given you the mother lode, pun intended, I'll share some explanations and revelations about redemption. Over the years Hashem has shared
many details with me about what's in store for us. Once again, this information is all from Hashem and I'm simply relaying His explanations. Consider
it, believe it or dispute everything. As always, the choice is yours. By the way,
if some of this information either corroborates accepted Jewish thought, or
contradicts any written information you've studied, I wouldn't know because I
haven't studied much of it.

Hopefully you'll be as fascinated by this information as I am, and any confirmations of accepted Biblical prophecy will excite you. I'd love to find out one
day which parts of this is consistent with written and trusted sources. I'm not
attached to any of it by the way. For me, it simply weaves a tale that makes our
existence make more sense. That's pretty much it for me. I need things to be
logical, make sense and bring us peace on earth for an eternity. Whatever the
case may be, all of the following information was given to me throughout the
years by our Creator, Hashem God. Ready or not, here we go!

The Rova and Chevron

In 2013, I made my first trip to the land of Israel when I accompanied my
daughter on her Aliyah flight with Nefesh B'Nefesh. Eventually I helped her

find an apartment in the Rova, the Jewish Quarter of the Old City in Jerusalem. One afternoon, I was sitting on a bench in the courtyard of the Jewish quarter eating my lunch. As I looked across the courtyard toward the beautiful Hurva Synagogue, Hashem said to me in a clear and strong voice, "All souls enter this world through the Rova." I've never researched this information and I relay it to you exactly as He spoke it to me that day. Do I know if this is a fact or have any proof of this being true? No, I don't. This came from Hashem and I have no reason to dispute it. Do you? Perhaps you can find published sources that concur with this information.

During the same trip to Israel, my daughter and I took a day tour to the Cave of the Patriarchs in Chevron, called Hebron in English. We went to see the tombs of the Jewish Patriarchs Avraham, Sarah, Yitzchak, Rivka, Yaakov and Leah. After the visit, we got on the bus to head back to Jerusalem. As we drove through the town of Chevron, I observed the Arab neighborhoods which were quite run down, and then saw the Jewish neighborhoods which looked newer and nicely maintained. As I observed the surroundings Hashem said, "Chevron is the place in our world where all souls exit." As soon as He said this to me, I turned to my daughter on the bus and asked her if she knew whether this was true. She said she didn't know anything about this. Hashem further explained that when people die, their souls leave this world through Chevron. This city, one of the four holiest cities of Israel, in the words of Hashem is extremely holy for this deeply sad reason. Chevron is the spiritual equivalent of a human graveyard.

Hashem then said to me that He didn't approve of the Jewish communities in Chevron because this is a place where souls depart from our physical world and it isn't a place where people should live and raise their families. He added that the Jewish families who have chosen to live there in defiance did so to establish their claim to this holy city. This He said put their families in danger because it incited anger and hostility from the Palestinian Arabs who reside there. While their intention was to protect the land of the Jewish people and prevent them from losing their claim to this holy city, He said it was premature. Ultimately, the world must accept that the land that was promised to Avraham is the homeland of Hashem's chosen people.

What I've just stated is likely to invoke anger from both Jews and Arabs alike. It will serve everyone to refrain from any antagonistic feelings. You see, it's the will of Hashem God that always wins in the end. He is our King and the final arbiter. You can be at peace knowing that whatever His decree, it's for your best interest and everyone's good without exception. When Hashem wins, we all win. There are no religious groups or ethnicities that will receive a winner's trophy in the world to come. When we follow and honor Hashem's decrees, the world will be redeemed and we will all win peace on earth for an eternity.

Eliyahu Hanavi aka Elijah the Prophet

In prophecy, it's said that the prophet Eliyahu, called Elijah in English, will announce Moshiach to the world. Hashem has told me who Eliyahu the prophet was in his most recent incarnation here on earth. Eliyahu was an American teacher who immigrated to Israel many years ago. Without revealing his most recent identity now, I will share with you that he was a dearly loved, prophetic, and respected teacher and father who was lovingly referred to as Reb by many of his students. He passed away in 2014 after losing his battle with cancer. Since his death, Hashem has brought him to me and we have spoken on several occasions. Hashem has told me that Eliyahu's soul is the reincarnation of several extraordinary people from the Torah. Hashem shared the following list of Eliyahu's incarnations: Yaakov's son Yosef, Pincus, Mordecai from the story of Purim, and a beloved Reb from Israel now deceased.

This astounding list of incarnations of Torah greats gives spiritual background about Eliyahu and sheds light on why he was selected by Hashem to perform the noble task of announcing the arrival of Moshiach. Hashem has told me that Eliyahu, will return incarnate to his most recent life just prior to the declaration of the holy war, the official beginning of World War III. This is the same as the prophesized war of Gog and Magog. As many people have guessed, we are currently in the End of Days. In these End of Days Hashem requires us to gather together in love, education and charity. This is a time of "weeding out" so to speak. People must choose to listen, learn and work together for peace on earth as one people under one God. Those who refuse and choose instead to wage war defending their own group's ideology, will be revealed as enemies of God. There will be a definitive line drawn when we will distinguish and name the enemies of God and unite against them.

It's imperative that the children of the world heed God's call and choose to accept the challenging work of full repentance and return to Him, also known as doing Teshuvah in Hebrew. This open door inviting everyone to learn His laws, review their sins, and make repentance will be closed when Hashem deems it's time to do so. When this door is closed, Hashem God will declare holy war against a defined enemy. When this occurs, He said He will resurrect a small number of people which includes Eliyahu Hanavi. As I previously revealed on page 237, He has shown me in visions that this small group includes 11 people, 10 IDF Soldiers and Eliyahu. This group of 11 souls will be resurrected, return in body miraculously, and Eliyahu will proclaim the arrival of Hashem's Moshiach. Many observant Jews around the world will refuse to accept any Moshiach without this proclamation from Eliyahu and the fulfillment of this prophecy. While I've been screaming to the world that I'm speaking to and journeying with Hashem for over nine years and He says it's me, Eliyahu Hanavi is needed as proof for many people to "seal the deal" as they say.

The Third Holy Temple, Beit Hamikdash

The Third Holy Temple, Beit Hamikdash, will be built on the Temple Mount in Jerusalem. In the words of Hashem, the Third Holy Temple is for all His children throughout the entire world. Although this Temple will be built and managed by His Jewish children, every child of God will be welcomed. It will be a glorious place where Hashem's presence can be felt both physically and spiritually.

Since I'm someone who feels Hashem both physically and spiritually in every moment of my life, I will do my best to describe what it's like. His voice feels both penetrating and soothing. His manner is beautifully tender and commanding at the same time. Vibrationally and emotionally He feels like pure euphoria. His voice and presence feel like pure love with an adrenalin rush like you might feel if you were flying weightlessly through the sky. Hashem is the fullest extent of perfection in every human quality. For example, His confidence is supreme without ever crossing the line into arrogance. Arrogance is senseless because He knows He is God, the King of everything, and He has nothing to prove. When He speaks you are fully aware of His commanding presence and that He is in complete control. I could ramble on forever trying to describe Him, but there is nothing in this world that is comparable. There simply aren't enough magnificent words in the world for me to use. As I even attempt to share what He feels like with you, I'm gripped with emotion and crying tears of complete joy and gratitude.

The Holy Temple will serve the purpose of giving the world a dwelling place for Hashem's essence to be felt both physically and spiritually. This Temple will serve to remove the current concealment of His presence in our physical world and provide an infinitesimal droplet of His essence. Receiving a tiny and tolerable dose of what I am blessed to experience daily will give people complete certainty of His existence. There will no longer be any doubt in our world that He is real. The Third Holy Temple will be the most supreme blessing for all the people of the world to experience.

Gog and Magog—World War III

The famed prophesized war of wars, Gog and Magog, will officially begin within the next three to five years in the words of Hashem. Although an official start date hasn't been given to me, Hashem has given me a projected time frame of the beginning of this horrific war as well as its completion. Right now, He says we are experiencing the vibrations and beginning stages of this war but it will not officially begin until Hashem declares His open door to learn and repent is closed.

There is a great deal of conflicting information about Gog and Magog and speculation about the identity of these two names. The prophet Ezekiel described a war that will be instigated by Gog and Magog, and waged against Israel. The following is Hashem's explanation given to me. Hashem has told me that both Gog and Magog represent all the non-Jews living in our world. He has told me that they comprise the offspring of Noah's sons Ham and Japheth. Gog in the words of Hashem originated from the nations that are descendants of Ham, and Magog originated from the nations that are the descendants of Japheth. There are many people of various denominations among both Gog and Magog, but their group identity isn't ultimately making a direct reference to any ethnicity or religion, it's a choice. The term *Magog*, Hashem says, is Gog plus the prefix, Ma, which He says is for His Mashiach, which is an alternate spelling for Moshiach. This prefix is also a reference to Ma, a colloquialism for Mother.

The people of Magog are those who will ultimately embrace Hashem's Moshiach and fight the war to destroy Gog, removing evil from our midst. The children of Israel will lead the charge and assist Magog in the worldwide cleansing of evil. God's chosen children will lead our world to peace by being the light unto the nations and providing intellectual leadership. Israel will participate in the third and final world war but their participation will be largely intellectual support rather than physical fighting.

Hashem has told me He will draw a definitive line and name the enemy and reveal the identity of Gog. As always, it will be His ruling and in His divine timing. Until that day comes there will be a weeding out process to learn and discover who is with God and who is His enemy. During this time of learning and weeding out the evil ones, Gog, we are all required to do our best and choose to unite in love, education and charity. Those who refuse will ultimately be on the wrong side of God. This is not a place where any human being should ever choose to be.

I can't possibly overstate the peril you will face if you refuse this calling. Through worldwide forums of education, we will learn how to choose between good and evil and see this choice with incontrovertible accuracy. His chosen Jewish children will rise to this occasion and become teachers of Torah and the leaders for world peace for which they were chosen. All the children of God will band together as one family, learn what God expects, and choose His goodness over ego and self-serving behavior. This final world war is the proverbial war between good and evil, God and Satan. God's children are required to unite under the umbrella of love and kindness to cleanse our world of evil and bring peace on earth for an eternity.

Peace in Israel First

I'm not yet permitted to reveal any details from my discussions with Hashem regarding the peace process in Israel. All I'm permitted to share with you now is that Hashem says there will be peace in Israel before World War III, Gog and Magog, begins. That isn't to say that we will not experience war and terror in Israel. Unfortunately, He continuously warns me that we will. We are already experiencing terrorism and being threatened with war now. Hashem has told me there will be a discernible and lasting peace between the children of Israel and the Palestinian Arabs. This peace will come through love and education and a passionate desire to end the bloodshed. There will be an outward recognition that we all come from one God and we will learn to embrace what combines us. Peace in the Holy Land, Israel, will serve as a model for bringing peace to the entire world.

The following is the beginning of learning that we are one family and explains how we are connected. Hashem named His promised land, Yisrael. Yaakov, the father of the 12 tribes of Israel, was given the new name of Yisrael in the Torah. Hashem shared with me that the spelling of this name is an acronym which is different when it's spelled in Hebrew versus English.

The Anglican spelling and acronym given to me by Hashem is: YISRAEL
Y – Yisrael/Yaakov
I – Isaac/Yitzchak
S – Sarah
R – Rachel/Rochel
A – Abraham/Avraham
E – Esau/Esav
L – Leah

In Hebrew, the acronym is as follows: ישראל

י – Yisrael/Yaakov

ש– Sarah

ר – Rochel

א – Avraham

ל – Leah

So, what does this all mean? In the Anglican acronym, there is the inclusion of E for Esav (Esau in Latin), Yaakov's brother and I for Isaac, the Anglican name of Yaakov and Esav's father Yitzchak. Hashem recognizes Esav as a forefather of the Edomites and says we must recognize Esav as part of the Jewish lineage. Esav was the son of the Patriarch Isaac (Yitzchak) and Matriarch Rebecca (Rivka). In the words of Hashem, Esav's lineage ultimately gave birth to the Edomites who He says eventually became the present day Palestinian people. I haven't researched or read much about this topic. I'm sure plenty of scholars who are well versed in Biblical history will either work to dispute or corroborate this information. My stories and explanations come directly from Hashem along with a bit of online searching when He requested me to do so. He never teaches by lecturing me, but instead provides me with a highly interactive education. I'm assured rabbis and historians will one day gladly step up and participate in unraveling His story of stories to give more reasons for us to unite as one family under God.

Reincarnation Is a Big Deal

If the case of parent and child relationship between the Jews and humanity isn't yet clear to you, let's bring some more clarity with a discussion about reincarnation. I've already explained how many extraordinary characters Hashem said I was in world history. The news that Hashem was humanity's Father in the physical life of Adam likely has many of you still twitching. Continuing right along, Hashem has provided me with a list of incarnations which is comprised of "who's who" in Torah and Biblical history. The following list of incarnations will help shed more light on the family connections between the Jewish people and the rest of humanity. Once again, I promise you that the following information was given to me by Hashem and I didn't dream up any of this.

Noah brought his family on the ark prior to the great flood. His family included his wife, their three sons and their wives. These three sons of Noah and their wives repopulated our earth after Hashem washed it clean of evil. He said Noah's three sons were all Jewish neshamas, Jewish souls. So, where did the division of all the separate nations in humanity begin? In the words of Hashem, the Jewish lineage and souls born after the great flood were born through Noah's son Shem and his wife. His other two sons, Japheth and Ham, although they were both Jewish neshamas, gave birth to the other nations of the world. The following is a list of the reincarnations of Noah's sons and grandson:

Shem: Reincarnated as Yitzchak, Issachar son of Yaakov and Leah, and currently living as a secular Jewish man in the USA.

Ham: Reincarnation of Cain the first son of Adam and Chavah, reincarnated as Esav, and currently a secular Jewish man living in the USA (more about Esav later).

Japheth: Reincarnation of Seth, son of Adam and Chavah, reincarnated as Yaakov, and currently an Orthodox Jewish woman living in Israel. Yes, I said a woman.

Canaan: Ham's son and Noah's grandson, reincarnated as Ephraim son of Yosef, Judas Iscariot the student/disciple of Yeshua ben Yosef, and currently living as a secular Jewish man in the USA married to a Christian woman.

This list of reincarnations provides you with details given to me by Hashem to pave the way for learning how He says we are connected. It also illustrates how Hashem knows who we are and what we're capable of and therefore intervenes when necessary. He said all the incarnations of humanity and the history of our world weave a perfect tapestry that brings us together as one family. If what I have just shared is true, you can see clearly why Esav, the reincarnation of the first murderer Cain, and the reincarnation of Ham who violated his father Noah, wasn't fit to receive the birthright from his father Yitzchak. Check for the story about Yaakov stealing Esav's birthright in your Torah or Bible or go ahead and do an online search for it now if you don't know it.

Hashem's justice is exact and timely. He says that reparation for Yaakov's apparent theft of Esav's birthright must be completed before our world can be redeemed. Not only did Yaakov receive the birthright by deceiving his father Yitzchak on his deathbed, but Esav suffered a further theft when Yaakov married Leah, who was Esav's betrothed. Leah was supposed to marry Esav, not Yaakov. She cried out to Hashem and pleaded with him to stop this marriage to Esav, and Hashem delivered. Instead, Leah married Yaakov through yet another deception orchestrated by Leah's father Laban. Yikes! It looks like chaos and confusion, doesn't it? But it's not chaotic at all to Hashem because He knows everything about us.

The deception which allowed Yaakov to marry Leah gave birth to six of the twelve Jewish tribes of Israel. Esav (Cain/Ham) went on to marry Ishmael's daughter as Hashem knew he would. The story Hashem gave me helps clarify where the dividing lines in humanity were drawn and the secret spiritual reasons behind it all. Only Hashem knew the true spiritual identities of Noah's three sons. He knew that it was the soul of Cain/Ham who was Yitzchak's son Esav. After Hashem decreed that the Jewish souls, the original souls created during the incarnation of Adam and Chavah would be born through Shem, He also decreed that one day the Jewish lineage would pass on through Yitzchak (Shem reincarnated) and subsequently He ensured that the birthright was passed down through Yaakov (Japheth reincarnated).

Noah's two sons Ham and Japheth were both spiritually Jews and ultimately would reincarnate as Jews once again. Hashem knew Cain/Esav/Ham's spiritual ineptitude throughout history as the first murderer who killed his own brother Abel and then ultimately participated in the sexual assault of his own father Noah. Esav was clearly unfit to lead the Jewish people, God's chosen children to bring world peace. Having said all of this, Esav was still spiritually a Jew and the first-born child of Adam and Chavah, Hashem and His Shechinah. Esav is a prominent soul to say the least. He is Hashem's deeply loved first-born son. Hashem blessed Cain/Ham/Esav in all his lifetimes but knew full well he was unfit to be the patriarch of his chosen Jewish children.

In these End of Days, final soul correction and reparation for all grievances is required. In the world to come there will be no person who can argue that they were cheated. To that end, Esav is now incarnated as a secular Jewish American man. So, who is Esav this time around and how did Hashem make sure to repay him for the theft of his birthright given to Yaakov and losing his betrothed, Leah? In the words of Hashem, Esav is reincarnated as my former husband. Holy smokes! When you talk about karma, this one takes the proverbial cake doesn't it? My former husband, Esav reincarnated, finally got to marry Leah, albeit the reincarnation of Mother Leah. Esav fathered my three children, and was the husband for 26 years to your Queen Moshiach. This lifetime gave Esav the winner's trophy as the husband to Hashem's Queen Moshiach and Shechinah. If you've read this entire book to this point, and I sincerely hope you have, you will see that once again Esav committed unthinkable sins, made horrible choices and squandered his God-given gift to be married to Hashem's Queen Moshiach.

Having said all this, believe it or not, I still love my former husband deeply. I'm definitely angry with him over the way he treated me and my children. Wouldn't you be angry too? Although I'm angry that doesn't change how I feel about him deep down. He was truly my best friend once upon a time and is still the father to my three children. My love for someone doesn't blow with the proverbial wind. I love the people in my life eternally. When I think about my former husband and what he did to me and my children I feel like I could punch him in the head but my anger eventually passes. After my anger subsides, I think about how much trouble he is in with Hashem. I well up with emotion and I pray for his well-being. He must wake up and start choosing right or he is truly doomed! While it's true he blew it once again and destroyed my life, I continue to pray for him. Certainly, most people won't argue that I have every right to hate this man profusely. He threw me to the curb and still leads a PR campaign to defame me but he is my former husband, was once upon a time my best friend, and remains the father of my children. I love him more like he's one of my kids. Years ago, I used to joke that I had four children, three that I gave birth to and one that I married. My children can abuse and hurt me in untold ways but they are always my children. My love for my former husband feels quite similar. He aggravates the hell out of me, but I still pray for his welfare daily.

I was never destined to remain married to my husband or any other man. Eventually I would have divorced any husband like Moshe divorced Zipporah in the Torah. Marriage to any person in this world is simply impossible for me. Although it's true that I was destined to ultimately be divorced like Moshe Rabbeinu, my husband and I didn't have to live through the horror that he brought upon our family. He was given every opportunity in this life to choose correctly and he chose evil. He failed me but more importantly, he failed God. With the understanding of how we are connected to one another, I still love my former husband and have deep compassion for him. I pray he will awaken to his life's purpose after reading this book and do the hard work of repenting and returning to Hashem.

The people who are closest to me in this life are reincarnated souls whose past incarnations read like a list of who's who in Torah greats. Those who are fortunate to be closely connected to me, Hashem's Moshiach, or unfortunate depending upon how you look at it, are likely to be notable characters in biblical history. This also means that they have an extremely difficult soul correction right now. It's time for each of them to wake up and achieve what they must or the consequences will be severe. I'm praying for everyone to wake up and heed the call. Despite the terrible pain and suffering friends and family have brought upon me, I pray for their well-being day and night.

Esav—E for Edomite

In a nutshell, Israel was bequeathed to Hashem's Jewish children long ago. Along the way Esav chose to go a different way by marrying Ishmael's daughter and eventually the Jewish family was dispersed around the globe. Acknowledging that there was a bit of trickery involved as we know the story of Yaakov "stealing" the birthright from his older brother Esav, it's important to understand that taking the birthright away from Esav was for invisible and divine reasons which I've just revealed. Hashem always knows more than we do and He knew that Yaakov was spiritually better equipped to be the leader of the Jewish children. He knows who we are and we don't and while it looks like a human conspiracy of a theft from one person to give to another, Hashem God's judgements are included in every detail. Esav's subsequent personal choices after losing the birthright, gave birth to portions of our non-Jewish extended families, which include the Edomites. The details of all the lineage are in books that I haven't read and I'm told not to concern myself with the granular details. Hashem says there are many Bible scholars who will step up one day to fill in the blanks.

The path to peace in Israel will come from the recognition that everyone comes from the first mother and father, Adam (Hashem) and Chavah (Shechinah), who gave birth to the Jewish children, who then gave birth to the rest of humanity. When we come together and treat each other more like parent and child, we will heal and experience peace. There's room in Israel for all of God's children to dwell in peace. Ultimately, we must listen to His explanations which are combining and healing, and the Jewish and Palestinian people must ultimately choose to unite willingly and joyfully.

The model for world peace will come from peace in Israel first. Admittedly if there can be true peace in Israel it gives us all hope that peace on earth is possible. Sadly, peace in Israel will enrage the naysayers and those who desire the destruction and extermination of the Jewish people. We know there are many. The rage that will ensue over peace in Israel will give birth to the ultimate war of wars. I wish there could be a different outcome and people would simply desire peace now and avoid the bloodletting. Hashem says this war will be so gut-wrenching and horrific that it will serve to teach us lessons that still haven't been learned. It sounds incomprehensible to me that we need the worst of all wars to learn this lesson. Sadly, all you need to do is review our world's history to see that the lessons haven't been learned yet. Peace will come to us one day at a very heavy price.

Rebbe Menachem Mendel Schneerson

I've just explained how reincarnation has played a pivotal role in biblical history. Invisibly we are all much more than the eye can see and far more capable than we might believe. Sometimes people rise and shine above the pack and surprise themselves and everyone around them. Many men and women are lauded for being great leaders and some have risen to be recognized as religious nobility. In Judaism these great leaders and righteous souls are known as tzaddikim. This was the case for the beloved Rebbe Menachem Mendel Schneerson who was the seventh leader of the Chabad-Lubavitch movement. Even after the Rebbe passed away in 1994, he remains highly regarded by millions of people. Many of his followers believe to this day that he is the Moshiach. While he is not the Moshiach, the Rebbe was extremely instrumental in preparing our world for the coming of the Messiah. He built a network of Chabad Houses around the world which are run by Chassidic rabbis and rebbetzins devoted to teaching Judaism and Torah to those who desire to return to their Jewish faith. In the End of Days these places of worship and Torah education will be instrumental in the worldwide return of the Jewish children to Torah observance. In the words of Hashem, the Rebbe prepared the world for Moshiach and my father, Matisyahu ben Yitzchak, prepared Moshiach for the world.

While the Rebbe Schneerson was a well-known noble figure in the contemporary Jewish world, he was also highly regarded among secular and non-Jewish people. Now brace yourselves because I'm told by Hashem to reveal to you a jaw-dropping revelation about the Rebbe's spiritual identity. Brace yourselves for a jolt that will ultimately make complete sense if you're open-minded. Hashem says that the Rebbe was the reincarnation of Saul whom the Christians refer to as Apostle Paul. Remember I don't read the Christian Bible and don't fully know what this implies to those who do. I will explain to you what Hashem tells me about Saul/Paul and the Rebbe and how this spiritual history will now come full circle and make complete sense to the world.

Hashem explained to me that Saul was a strict halacha observant Jew who was a prophetic soul much like the Rebbe Menachem Schneerson. Saul was given visions and prophecy in that lifetime and shown that Yeshua ben Yosef was the Jewish Messiah. Hashem instructed him to teach and build a movement of followers which gave birth to the Christian religion. In Hashem's explicit instructions he was told that the followers of Yeshua ben Yosef must be kept separate from the Jewish people and their Torah observant life. The laws that Saul taught Yeshua's Gentile followers to observe needed to be a small subset of the full covenant that the Jews were to follow. The separation was deliberate and imperative because this intentionally paved the path for world redemption. How so? The Jewish children are God's light unto the nations and are His chosen ones who will ultimately rise and lead the world to peace on earth. The Christians' role in world redemption is to love and follow their Jewish Messiah. They were taught for almost two thousand years to love and revere Yeshua ben Yosef as their Messiah and ultimate salvation. The Jewish people will serve as the educators who provide knowledge and understanding about the observance of God's laws and will be the living examples. The Christians will bring passion and love for their Messiah to the world and fight to remove evil from our midst. Hashem has told me for almost a decade it will be through love, education and charity that we will come together as one family under one God to heal our world.

Hashem has explained to me that these two great prophetic men from biblical history, Saul and the Rebbe were spiritually one and the same person. If you're open-minded, this may be an earth-shattering revelation, but it's also a believable one which combines us all. Ponder on this idea and accept it or reject the notion outright. What you will ultimately believe is always your personal choice. I assure you, this incredible information about the Rebbe wasn't invented by me whatsoever. As astounding as this information might sound, I find this quite believable and deeply healing. How about you?

The World to Come—Olam Haba

Much has been written by the three major monotheistic religions about the world to come, Olam Haba in Hebrew. Each religion makes the claim that their group will be victorious in the end. No group or people has predicted the correct outcome to date because each synopsis is filled with ego as they declare that they will be anointed the kings and queens of the world. The mere premise that everyone will kneel, even figuratively, to one group of people defies logic and smacks of idolatry. There is no one group or religion that wins the trophy or keys to Hashem's Kingdom in the world to come.

The world to come belongs to Hashem God. It always has and always will. Idolatry will be part of world history and will no longer exist. We are one family from one God and we will come together and heal or we will all perish. There isn't any in-between. It's all or nothing. The impending war is the proverbial war of Good versus Evil. Only those who accept God's omnipotence and His laws will be welcome in His world to come.

Who Is Welcome and Who Is Not? What Happens If You're Not?
I am told there is no one other than His Moshiach who has guaranteed entry. The decision of who is welcomed and who is banished will be made by Hashem alone. Only He knows who will be welcomed or banished. There is much speculation as to whether this world to come is non-physical or physical. Hashem promises there will be a physical world to come.

Hashem has described possible scenarios of what people face in the future as we go forward on the road to redemption.

1. **Eternal life dedicated to learning.** Those who are welcomed into the next world will dedicate their lives to learning and observing God's laws. If you live until the end of the prophesized world war, you will be here to clean up the horrific mess and work to repair our world. Learning Torah will become the new normal and a required part of everyone's daily life. There will be the opportunity to live eternally in our bodies without perishing. To accomplish this, we must choose God and His goodness in every moment.

2. **Two more chances.** After Hashem deems that world redemption is complete, if welcomed in the future world, souls will have one more opportunity to reincarnate and one last chance to return to their most recent life. One return to the most recent life and one reincarnation and that's all that Hashem will permit. Why? There will be no more reincarnation in a time to come. There will be no more cleansing, recycling and returning to get it right. You will be required to choose God in every moment without exception or you are no longer welcome in Hashem's world. While this may sound harsh and frightening to some, this should be welcome news to those who desire peace for an eternity. Transgressions, if they occur, must be repaired immediately. There will be zero tolerance for sin in the world to come.

3. **Damnation.** If you are non-redeemable and unwelcome in Hashem's world, you face one of two scenarios. The worst of the two options is being dammed and sent to a horrific place that no human soul wants to experience. Damnation is hideously frightening, void of God's presence, and this place truly does exist. There is no way out of this dark and terrifying place and it's completely sealed off and kept isolated from the rest of creation. Occasionally, Hashem visits and removes a few souls to give them one more chance. He has shown me these fortunate few souls in tattered clothing with Torah scrolls strapped to their backs as they walk uphill toward a faint light in the distance. These souls get one more opportunity to redeem themselves in the eyes of God. The others who

remain behind are tormented further seeing these blessed few leave, as they painfully realize they were left behind to remain in hell.

4. **Extinguished souls.** The second possible outcome for a select small number of souls deemed unwelcome in the world to come is deeply compassionate. In His compassion, Hashem erases them from humanity and extinguishes their souls. They are not welcome in Hashem's world and they simply vanish from existence. This outcome is reserved for very few souls. While it's compassionate to the soul that is erased, their family and loved ones they have left behind will mourn them and their painful loss for eternity.

5. **Jewish souls.** Hashem promises that Jewish souls will never be banished to damnation. They have an irrevocable and holy covenant with our Creator and a place in His world to come unless they refuse. If Jewish souls refuse their birthright, Hashem will erase them from humanity. Before He will resort to extinguishing a Jewish soul from existence, He will pull out all the stops and terrify that soul into complete submission. In the words of Hashem, He intends to leave no Jewish soul behind. Why is the Jewish soul so important to Hashem? The Jewish children are His children body and soul and the lifeblood of humanity. They are the light unto the nations and they are here to teach and lead the entire world to peace. Without the Jewish children, there is no more. Pray very hard for all the Jewish children to wake up, remember and accept their birthright. Everyone's survival and well-being depend upon them.

The Second Coming of Yeshua

Throughout my life, I've been told by Christians about the second coming of Jesus and warned that the Jews will burn in hell if they don't accept him as their lord and savior. Their threats didn't scare me at all. Instead, these threats made me think of Christianity as some sort of absurd religion built on fear and oppression. Sorry, but that's what I thought growing up. Now that I've received clarity from Hashem, I see that there was truth to many of the Christians' claims but there was also a great deal of confusion. The second coming doesn't quite fit what Christians have been taught because the second coming is me, your Jewish Queen Moshiach. You can't always get what you want like the Rolling Stones sang years ago. Sorry if this news disappoints you, but Hashem says I'm precisely what you need.

If you've read this book from the beginning, you know that I stated that my soul is the reincarnation of many lofty souls including the Christians' beloved

Yeshua ben Yosef. Do I think I'm as lofty as you've described him? Hardly. Additionally, I don't truly know that I was him but I do know I journey with Hashem as one in complete synchronicity in the same way he did. It's really Hashem God doing this with me and I'm His messenger. I'm simply revealing the stories that come to me straight from our Creator, God Himself. If you think about my story as it relates to Yeshua, then you might jump for joy, or you might feel deeply disturbed. Many will be deeply offended that I have the audacity to say that I was him. I'm deeply sorry if this is upsetting to anyone. I truly don't know that I was him and I don't even want to be him. I believe wanting to be his reincarnation is true insanity. I'd like to know I'm as good as he was and that's enough for me. I'd rather learn that it was another "tomato" thrown at me by Hashem. If you don't remember my tomato story then go back now and reread it on page 146. Go ahead I'll be here when you return.

I'd be tickled pink if the real Yeshua ben Yosef came riding on his donkey out of the Tiberias Swiss Forest and rescued me from having to do this job. It's not likely to happen though because I know there isn't anyone else as close to Hashem who lives as one with Him like I do. Being inexplicably connected to Hashem and journeying with Him in this way is required to be Moshiach. Yeshua was His Moshiach more than two thousand years ago, and I'm his follow-up act. Yeshua was told that he was the son of God. That's how he related to Hashem in that lifetime.

You see, Yeshua wasn't truly Hashem's son after all. He was truly His Shechinah, His divine spiritual essence on earth, soul mate, and His Queen. His soul was the female divine essence called Shechinah, Hashem's other half, manifesting in our world incarnate as a man. There was a great deal of confusion surrounding Yeshua and condemnation from the Sanhedrin who believed that he was claiming he was something he wasn't. Stories that were told about him were utterly false and boldfaced lies. There was a story invented that Yeshua went into the Holy Temple, wrote the ineffable name of Hashem on a piece of parchment and then concealed it in an incision under his skin. It was said that he did this so he could perform miracles and convince everyone that he was the son of God. Hashem told me this was all a blasphemous lie.

Jews around the world are praying for Moshiach ben David, the second prophesized Messiah who will bring world redemption. The first Moshiach, Moshiach ben Yosef, was to pave the way for Moshiach ben David who was said to be the one who brings us world peace. Which Moshiach was Yeshua? In the words of Hashem, Yeshua ben Yosef was both. Yeshua ben Yosef was the reincarnation of Moshe Rabbeinu, Moshiach ben Yosef, who redeemed the

Jewish people and taught them Torah for 40 years which paved the way for world redemption. In his second life as Hashem's Moshiach, Moshe returned as Yeshua and was Moshiach ben David. This startling revelation means you've had both prophesized Messiahs without realizing this was so. Oh no! Now what? Now, you have one last chance. One more opportunity to get it right and if you fail there is no more. We are finished. Kaput. Your final opportunity for world peace lies in the hands of Hashem's Shechinah and Queen Moshiach.

Hashem says that Yeshua never claimed to be God, but manifested in a way that people felt the presence of Hashem within him. Because Yeshua was a man in that lifetime, and Hashem's presence was within Yeshua's vessel or body, people became confused over time whether he was the Messiah, Hashem or both. Many Christians believe that Yeshua was Hashem God, one and the same. This is unequivocally false. Yeshua was a separate soul who was inexplicably intertwined with our King, Hashem God. Hashem is the King and Master of the entire universe and He accompanied Yeshua incarnate in that lifetime. Yeshua was Hashem's female Shechinah incarnating in this world as a man. In that lifetime, Hashem told Yeshua that he was His son and encouraged him to believe that theirs was a Father-son relationship. The Father-son relationship is what Yeshua explained and taught to the people of this world.

Hashem says that Yeshua was a happily married Rav, a rabbi, with a wife and four children. His wife's name was Miriam. I'm also told that his wife Miriam, was one and the same as the woman who Christians refer to as Mary Magdalen. Miriam's soul was male in gender, incarnated as a woman. Yeshua's wife Miriam, most recently incarnated as a man who was someone quite famous. He passed away in 2009 from cancer, and remains on the other side in the non-physical realm. Hashem has also identified Yeshua's four children to me, three of whom are currently incarnate as Orthodox Jews. Yeshua's eldest child was a son who was most recently incarnate as an orthodox Jewish man who passed away several years ago. Fascinating, isn't it? Mind-blowing is more like it!

So, while this news may be disheartening to many Christians that the second coming isn't manifesting as they had hoped or believed, a second coming was a truthful claim made by the Christian people. Hashem says that His Queen Moshiach is the reincarnation of Yeshua ben Yosef and this is Yeshua's return. In his return as Messiah, he is incarnating as a woman, and a woman is what he was always meant to be since he was and is Hashem's Shechinah, Hashem's female divine presence on earth. Hashem has told me that there is more to Yeshua's story that I must reveal now.

For generations, the Christians have claimed that Yeshua rose from the dead after the crucifixion. Hashem has shed light and given me details about this supposed resurrection. First, Hashem says He removed Yeshua's body from the cave or tomb that they put him in after his death. In a vision several years ago, Hashem showed me a cave with a giant boulder blocking its entry being guarded by men. He showed me these guards asleep and then showed me a vision of Him, Hashem God, lifting and removing Yeshua's body from where it rested. I had never heard any of the stories about Yeshua's death or resurrection prior to Hashem showing me this vision and then explaining to me what happened. He said the cloth that covered Yeshua's body, the shroud, captured his image and that was all they found when they entered the cave. Hashem told me that this shroud, known as the Shroud of Turin, is authentic.

According to Hashem, Miriam, Yeshua's wife found the cave empty. She came with friends and they were shocked to find his body missing. After the brutal demoralizing beating from the Sanhedrin and then suffering the horrific crucifixion, Yeshua was inconsolable, completely devastated and did not return in a resurrection as Christians believe. It was Hashem God who appeared to Miriam as Yeshua and instructed her to find his students, known as his disciples in the Christian Bible, and tell them that he would meet them at the Sea of Galilee at their usual meeting place. Miriam told her friends and the ladies went excitedly to share this miraculous news. Nobody believed them. Incredible, right? No, it's completely understandable to me.

Hashem then appeared to Yeshua's disciples as Yeshua. He says there were a total of 11 students after Yeshua's demise. Judas Iscariot, the student who betrayed Yeshua and sold him to the Sanhedrin for a handful of silver was no longer welcome in this tightly knit club. Hashem also said there have been different accounts about what happened to Judas, but He says that Judas Iscariot committed suicide after the atrocity of the crucifixion.

Hashem made many appearances manifesting as Yeshua where He performed miracles in front of eyewitnesses before people believed that Yeshua ben Yosef had risen from the dead. Again, it wasn't truly Yeshua in form, it was the King, Hashem, appearing to everyone in Yeshua's image. Hashem says that He appeared before thousands of people for 40 days before leaving in what witnesses observed to be a miraculous ascension to heaven. During those 40 days, Hashem performed healings, taught lessons and selected more leaders to spread Yeshua's knowledge. Eventually He chose 59 leaders in addition to the original 11 close confidants of Yeshua, bringing the total number to 70. I'm told these

70 men are known by Christians as Apostles and were assigned by Hashem to keep Yeshua's memory and teachings alive.

It was Hashem, God, not Yeshua ben Yosef, who appeared for those 40 days, teaching and performing miracles. Why did Hashem do such a thing? He deliberately did so to initiate the creation of the new world religion of Christianity. Christianity took our world by storm and taught the world about Hashem's Moshiach. Having said this, there was much confusion along the way, added misinterpretations, and even false information taught about Yeshua for almost two thousand years. While there was much confusion, there was also a great deal of truth. Much of this confusion was deliberately created by Hashem Himself and was purposeful. Everything that Hashem allows into being serves a purpose without exception. In these End of Days, Hashem desires us to come together and learn the entire truth. The truth is what will combine us and bring us world peace.

While I could add even more detail about the implications of these 40 days and the selection of 70 leaders, I'm told less is more. For those who enjoy numbers, the 70 leaders chosen to teach were a compilation of Yeshua's 11 remaining trusted students and 59 additional disciples. The number 59 came from the Torah—the 49 days of the counting of the Omer, and the 10 commandments. These three numbers, 11 plus 49 plus 10, equal the total of 70 leaders who were chosen by Hashem to carry the torch and bring forward the creation of the new world religion, Christianity.

The Second Holy Temple was destroyed in the year 70 CE. For 70 years after the crucifixion, Yeshua refused to incarnate for the first and only time in world history. Earlier in this book, I explained that Hashem's Shechinah incarnates repeatedly with only a seven-day respite between incarnations. This 70-year period was the one exception. It wasn't until after the Second Temple was destroyed in divine retribution for the crucifixion, that Yeshua's soul returned to incarnate once again. At the beginning of the diaspora, Hashem's Shechinah returned to incarnate once again and continue the work of bringing world redemption taking only the seven-day respite in between lifetimes.

Now, let's extrapolate this story further and ponder the gravity and horror of the crime of the crucifixion. When the Sanhedrin beat Yeshua to a pulp before turning him over to the Romans, and when the Romans drove nails into his flesh, they were doing this to our King, Hashem God too. How so? Yeshua ben Yosef manifested in our world in the same way I do right now, as one with Hashem. He was completely intertwined and living as one with our Creator. When Yeshua performed those miracles, it was Hashem performing miracles through Yeshua's flesh, doing everything with him. When Yeshua suffered his hideous end, it was Hashem with him in his body receiving every deadly blow. I want to scream and cry now on top of the highest mountain, "How could you!?" Do you understand the magnitude and gravity of this sin? Do you comprehend what was done to our magnificent Creator, Hashem, as He was escorting His Queen and Shechinah in that lifetime? There aren't enough words in the world to adequately express my outrage and grief.

As I type these words now into my computer for you to read, I feel Hashem typing them with me. When I'm struggling to find a word to use, He gives it to me. We speak, eat, sleep, type, shower and breathe together in every moment within my body. If you harm me in any way, you are harming Hashem directly. This isn't just metaphorically speaking, it's true both physically and spiritually. The crucifixion of Yeshua ben Yosef was not just the murder of Moshiach which would have been sinful enough. It was the brutal torture and heinous murder of God's Shechinah while Hashem Himself was with her on that hideous cross. He felt every single blow as the rabbis of the Sanhedrin beat Yeshua. He felt the pounding of each nail into Yeshua's flesh. If you don't feel the pain of what I just wrote, one day you will. Our entire world must feel the pain of this atrocity with heart-wrenching remorse, compassion and grief. We will not experience the redemption of our world without everyone's recognition and acceptance of guilt for the worst crime in human history.

As I walk around our world with Hashem, we often pass churches adorned with crosses or see Christians wearing the cross as jewelry. The cross is the symbol of Yeshua's murder and crucifixion. When I see the cross anywhere in the world, Hashem fills with gut-wrenching anger and heartbreaking emotion at the sight. Many Christians are taught that the cross is a symbol of love and that Yeshua was God's sacrificial lamb. These teachings enrage Hashem. Death by martyrdom has been worshiped and idolized by men never by Hashem. Seeing the symbol of Yeshua's crucifixion and death is excruciating to Hashem and brings Him to tears. Nothing is more heartbreaking to me than feeling the anguish and tears of our King and Creator.

Hashem Demands Contrition

After leaving my husband and moving out of my marital home, Hashem went into overdrive teaching me about the ways of the world and what He desires. He has a marvelous sense of humor and while He teaches me about deeply painful subjects, He often strews in witty and whimsical comments along the way. Hashem holds all of humanity responsible for the horrible state of our world. He has made it expressly clear that He wants full contrition from every human being and desires to see everyone on bended knees in sorrow and repentance. For many years He has said, "Lori, I demand contrition." As I went about my life and performed ordinary daily tasks, He would incorporate the word *contrition* wherever possible to drive this point home. In the mornings after I woke up, I'd go to the kitchen to brew coffee and He would quickly add, "Lori, let's have coffee and contrition." While He said this comment in a somewhat playful way, He wasn't playing at all. Hashem was making a direct reference to a serious demand. He demands contrition from everyone in this world, not from me, because He says I am completely sinless. He demands contrition for not only everyone's sinful behavior that's destroying our world, but for the greatest sin in all of humanity—the crucifixion and murder of Yeshua ben Yosef.

There is no way for me to overstate how angry He is about the crucifixion and murder of His Moshiach, Yeshua ben Yosef. The same evil inclination, the Yetzer Hara, that enticed people to turn on Yeshua and murder him is still enticing people all over our world. The Yetzer Hara is chosen daily by every human on earth today. You are all choosing the same evil that killed the world's Moshiach, God's true love and Shechinah. Here is a grave warning that I am delivering to everyone with love and compassion. I know what He will do to you if you don't accept this information and learn to stop choosing evil. He is completely fed up and deeply angered over thousands of years of horrible behavior and the constant choice of evil over Him. Hashem's temper is fierce and He is unrelenting in His desire to bring forward world redemption. This requires everybody to recognize and accept their personal responsibility, repent and make full restitution for their transgressions. There will be no room for excuses on the road to redemption. Hashem will not tolerate any justification for choosing the Yetzer Hara, the evil inclination, otherwise known as Satan. Please wake up and heed this warning. Those who don't listen, should be very scared. I mean petrified!

Three Strikes and It's Over!

I'm told this is the last at bat so to speak. Tag I'm it, like it or not, and I don't. I love Hashem, but I don't want to be the one last Moshiach. My life is AWFUL but He promises it's about to change for the better. I'm not too optimistic about the outcome but He fuels me with optimism that you'll all wake up. Here is a scary warning if you don't. He says this is your last chance. I'm told if you don't listen and begin to learn to choose God and His goodness without exception, we are all dead as a doornail. It's the end, and I mean over. There won't be a world to come for you. In this moment, there isn't a world to come for anyone but me. For me, I'm guaranteed a future with Hashem. Without my children, I just can't bear the thought. I won't let go of my babies! I'm fighting for all of you until my bitter end. I work with every ounce of strength I have day and night to wake you up. Throughout the night I'm checking my iPhone to see if anyone is listening. I look to see if anyone liked or commented on any of my Facebook posts, and check YouTube to see if there are any new views on any of my videos. I've given up on LinkedIn, because it seems like nobody likes me on that social media network. I'm not cool enough, sexy enough or dangling enough money for the LinkedIn crowd. Even though I'm frankly disgusted by my lack of success on LinkedIn, when someone unfollows me or leaves me as a connection I mourn the loss. Truly. When one of you leaves my Running on Love Facebook page by "un-liking" it, I cry. Sometimes I get angry and curse. I'm so damn frustrated that I can't wake you up!

If you don't heed this call and listen, it's very bad for you. Please research that awful place that people talk about on YouTube. You know that place, right? Hellfire and damnation? He says it's real and He has given me a sneak peek at how awful and scary it looks for those souls sent there. I've never felt what that place feels like and I'm grateful I'll never know. Be forewarned, there are worse things than death. I'm sharing this with you for your benefit. I'm not going there but millions upon millions will be sent there and damned for eternity. Eternity is an incomprehensible idea to me but He says it's forever. With every breath of my life I'm going to try my best to save every child of God that I can. Former President George W. Bush once called his education program "No child left behind," words which reflect my sentiments exactly. I'm dedicating every breath of my life to ensure there will be no child of God left behind!

Lag B'Omer

Lag B'Omer, the 33rd day of counting the Omer, is a celebrated holiday for the Jewish people. It commemorates the yahrzeit, the anniversary of death, of the famous Rabbi Shimon Bar Yochai. This famous rabbi wrote the Zohar, a compilation of mystical teachings from within the Torah, while hiding from the Romans in a cave. On his yahrzeit, people all over Israel light bonfires and have barbecues celebrating the anniversary of his death. It seemed crazy to me when I moved to Israel that people would celebrate the date of someone's passing with bonfires and huge parties. Frankly, it didn't sound like a very Jewish tradition to me. Hashem has told me that the holiday of Lag B'Omer will no longer be celebrated like this in the future. He said that this holiday goes against His laws. In the words of Hashem, we must NEVER exalt or celebrate death. A yahrzeit is a day of remembrance and must never be raised to the level of raucous parties with bonfires and celebration. We celebrate life and mourn death, never confusing the two.

In Hashem's deliberate and purposeful fashion, He chose this date, Lag B'Omer 2016, to reveal a stark warning through a painful lesson. His warning: You must never intentionally or unintentionally harm His Moshiach. On the holiday of Lag B'Omer in 2016, Hashem allowed me to suffer injury in a car accident to reveal His Moshiach's human mortality and deliver a blunt warning.

Here is Hashem's warning that's going to make me sound very goyish to my Jewish family if I haven't already sounded like a crazy televangelist yet. Hashem told me to warn everyone to be kind to me and not to harm me in any way. I'm told to share a little story for you to ponder. On the eve of the Jewish holiday Lag B'Omer 2016, I was injured in a car accident. A former friend drove me to a Lag B'Omer party hosted in upper Tveria. This friend was driving recklessly while talking on his cell phone and not paying attention to the road. He caused a severe traffic accident where I was thrown from the back seat and injured. I've got many photos of my battered and bruised face and was instructed to include one here.

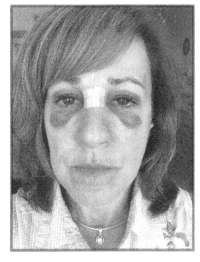

The driver of the vehicle and I were both rushed to the hospital by ambulance. I suffered a crushed nasal bone, received stitches and was left with a scar and dented nose, while the driver suffered a broken leg. The photos taken after this accident reveal that your Moshiach is mortal and can be injured too. Hashem has told me that if any harm comes to me the consequences will be grave. Approximately one year after this traffic accident, I was informed that the driver and former friend was found dead in his apartment after suffering a sudden heart attack. While it's not possible to prove any connection between his demise and the traffic accident one year earlier, please hedge your bet, be kind and don't harm me in any way. I have no idea why anyone would hurt another person in the first place. In my case, I'm dedicating my entire life to help you and pray you will heed this warning.

One of my biggest fears is that I won't live long enough to make a difference in this world and help everyone bring peace. Hashem says it's me and there isn't another Moshiach waiting in the wings to fill this role. I'm going forward full steam ahead and dedicating my life to this work as though there is nobody else who will show up to be your Moshiach. Although I may be everyone's worst nightmare, He says I'm your best chance for peace. While it's a nightmare to many people to even consider a female Moshiach, at least give me a chance to organize a few Running on Love Festivals for Love before I go. I just want to help make our world a better and more loving place before I leave. If it turns out that there's someone better to fill this role, consider me the warm-up act. I'm not attached to this job at all and would gladly step aside. I'm only attached to Hashem and being the mother of my three children.

Timetable for Redemption—How Long Will It Take?

Just prior to leaving New Jersey and making Aliyah to Israel in the year 2015, I was awakened to a vision of a clock. Hashem greeted me and said, "Good morning Lori. What is this?"

I saw the clock and said, "It's a clock. It's showing a time of 3:00 o'clock."

He replied, "That's right. What else is it showing?"

I looked and then understood what He was trying to tell me and replied, "It's also a pie chart showing one quarter."

He answered, "Correct. We are now one quarter of the way to redemption." We spoke for a while longer about this and He explained that the beginning of the road to redemption began on the day of my awakening April 7, 2009. This conversation took place 6 years later, meaning, the projected end of the world war when redemption will be complete would be 18 years later, in the year 2033. As I work to complete writing this book and prepare to publish and release it to the public by the end of 2018, it will be approximately 15 more years until redemption. Unfortunately, while this sounds like a long time, what will follow is an extremely difficult reality to accept. The fallout from the impending world war, Gog and Magog, along with the damage we have already done to our world will take over 1000 years to repair. He says it will take even longer than a millennium to heal our earth! If this time frame of redemption is true, and 2033 will mark the beginning of the world to come, we will still have a very long road filled with hard work to repair all the damage.

A lot of people may read this and say, "That's it, I will just quit and choose the option of my soul being extinguished rather than do all that hard work." Not so fast. It's not your decision or prerogative to choose. Hashem decides if you're damned or if you're extinguished, don't forget that. You don't get to choose the lesser of the evils and simply choose to quit and enjoy a final hurrah. If you are blessed to survive the horrors that are coming and are fortunate to be welcomed into the world to come, rebuilding a new and peaceful world will be the ultimate gift and filled with supreme joy. The future of our world will be heaven on earth the way God always intended it to be. No war, terror, evil, sin, and sickness. Death will become a global event and extremely rare. Now that certainly sounds like a world that's well worth fighting for and choosing to persevere. I hope you agree.

Why does this have to be so difficult and painful? You have all chosen the pain. It might sound like I'm some sort of Bible toting zealot throwing the book at you and calling everyone sinners. Regardless of what you might think, this is the truth as told to me by Hashem God. Humanity has consistently chosen evil from the beginning of time and now it's time to pay the piper and repair the world.

Resurrection of the Dead—How and When Will This Occur?

As I revealed earlier, just after I arrived in Israel in 2013 for my first visit, I was awakened to many visions which were so lucid and clear they appeared to be three dimensional. I told the story earlier that in one morning vision after I made my first trip to Israel, Hashem showed me a specific tunnel that led to the Kotel plaza, the gathering area in front of the Western Wall in Jerusalem. In this vision, I saw white light spinning at an extremely high speed as it traveled through this tunnel. As this white light was spinning it eventually reached the end of the tunnel where it transformed into fully clothed IDF soldiers. One by one they walked out of the tunnel into the Kotel plaza and were welcomed by a crowd of people who were cheering wildly in an atmosphere filled with incredible joy and pandemonium. I've also explained earlier, in a fulfillment of Torah prophecy, Hashem said these IDF soldiers were 10 resurrected souls who will walk out of the tunnel from the world of the nonphysical into our physical world, accompanied by Eliyahu Hanavi, Elijah the Prophet. It was in this vision that Hashem told me that at the beginning of the holy war of Gog and Magog, World War III, He would allow 11 souls to return before redemption occurred—10 IDF soldiers and Eliyahu the prophet. As I watched this emotionally charged vision I then saw the Lubavitcher Rebbe, Menachem Schneerson dancing joyfully with his wife in the tunnel. As I previously stated, they weren't among those who returned in this resurrection of the dead, but they were shown to me joyously celebrating this miracle from the non-physical realm.

A lot has been written about the return of the dead and how it will occur. In brief, it will not happen in a cemetery as some might have thought. All souls who are welcomed and blessed by Hashem to return, will be resurrected by coming through this special tunnel which leads to the Kotel plaza. I've written earlier in this book, Hashem has told me that all souls enter our world through the Rova in Jerusalem. He has explained that once redemption is complete, there will be a gradual process of return over a long period of time. The dead will not return all at once, and the beginning of the resurrection of the dead will occur after the end of the great war of Gog and Magog, aka World War III. These eleven souls who will return, 10 IDF soldiers and Eliyahu, will come at the beginning of this war to serve as a gift to the Jewish children, lighting their souls with inspiration and knowledge that the prophecies are true, further emboldening them to lead the world to peace.

Hashem has shown me this information in visions and He explained everything in further detail in many conversations over the years. He says that when this miracle occurs much of the world will deny the authenticity of these resurrected eleven souls which could be easily simulated today using technology and video editing tools. It will be a test of faith for humanity to believe that this miracle truly occurred. People of the world will choose to be on the side of God or against Him. As unfathomable as this might sound, people will find it difficult to choose sides in the impending war. The world is in such chaos, it has become an incomprehensible challenge for people around the world to distinguish between goodness and evil. Daily, people find it impossible to recognize pernicious evil when they see it.

The souls who perish before the war ends and who have been blessed by Hashem to return will have a choice to wait until redemption is complete before they return to their former lives in their most recent lifetime, or reincarnate at the appropriate designated time into a new life incarnation. It's a heartbreaking reality for us who are left behind knowing that those who die may choose not to return to us as their old selves. It's their personal choice which they will make with the guidance of our Creator.

The resurrection of souls returning to their most recent lifetime will take place over many years and not all at once as some might have believed. Again, it won't look like Michael Jackson's music video *Thriller* where we saw people popping out of graves. Thank God! The resurrection of the dead has been described to me as a complicated process that will be done over time. If everyone were to return on the same day it would create many complications for us here as we repair our broken world. We will have our hands full enough. Here is a horrific number for you to digest. By the end of this great war, Hashem said that over two billion people will perish. He has told me that as many as two billion souls who now exist in creation will be deemed unwelcome in His world to come. This is astonishing information and difficult to fathom. Knowing that we all have free will, and that Hashem often changes His decrees, I pray everyone learns quickly to choose better and avoid being among the unwelcome. Whatever the final death toll winds up being, in the words of Hashem, this will be the biggest bloodletting in the history of mankind. Gratefully He promises it will also be the last.

In everyone's body there is something called a "Luz bone." This small indestructible bone, the size of a kernel of barley, is located beneath the brain and at the top of the spinal column. In Torah prophecy it is written that one day we will see the resurrection of the dead and Hashem will use the "Luz bone" to build the newly resurrected body. Hashem has explained to me that the "Luz bone" binds our spirit to our physical presence here on earth. Many believe we will resurrect in the location where our "Luz bone" was buried but Hashem says that's not the case. Here is His explanation in brief. The resurrected soul will return by entering our world through the Rova as it always does then travel through the same tunnel where the 11 resurrected souls traveled before entering the Kotel plaza. This will allow an orderly procession of return and welcoming of the resurrected.

From the Kotel plaza, Hashem has told me that the first place the returning person will go is to their final resting place, where their Luz bone is located. Their final remains will be exhumed from their grave site and buried in a collective grave designated by Hashem God. There will be three separate memorial sites which will serve humanity as a remembrance in the world to come. The resurrected Jewish people will return their remains to Israel which will be the location of a Jewish memorial. The final remains of the non-Jewish people of Gog killed during this final world war will be sent to Israel and buried in another location which will be disclosed in a time to come. The resurrected non-Jewish people of Magog will have their remains buried in Germany at a location to be revealed in the future.

Why is the memorial for all non-Jews of Magog located in Germany? This location was selected by Hashem God for all people of the world to remember the atrocity of the Nazi Holocaust. This will be the world's memorial site to repent, repair, and remember Nazi Germany's heinous attempt to commit genocide of God's Jewish children from His world. The Holocaust is a sin and an abomination that must never be forgotten or erased from our collective consciousness. These three memorials will serve to remind humanity of the pain of death and evil that once existed in this world. "Never forget" will no longer be idle words without action. We must never allow evil to enter our world again.

God's Plan for World Redemption

This book began with the story of my spiritual awakening which was the precursor to giving birth to my registered charity Running on Love. It wasn't apparent to me when I founded this charity just how holy it was or that its founding principle, to honor our loved ones with an act of charity, was divine. Running on Love was an outgrowth of the euphoria I felt when I ran a charitable marathon in memory of my dad. It wasn't until many years later after leaving my broken marriage, that Hashem made it clear how Running on Love was the platform and model that would unite the people of the world in love and education to bring world peace. This charity was founded on the principle that giving should be done to honor those we love. Unknowingly, I modeled this charity after a Torah mitzvah called L'ilui Nishmat. This mitzvah to honor those who have died was given to the children of Israel by God Himself.

In our material world people choose to give to charity and others because it satisfies a personal need or solves a problem. They have a self-serving reason why they give to charity which is based on satisfying something within themselves in some way. Although their donations serve some form of good, their reasons for donating aren't purely godly. For example, if someone sees a homeless person on the street, they might feel sorry for them, so they open their wallet and give out of guilt feelings and pity. They give because they feel a little guilty that they have enough while others are homeless. Seeing a homeless person also reminds them to be grateful that they are financially well off. You know, feelings like, "I'm so grateful for what I have God, thank you! Now, I'll show my gratitude and I'll be generous and help this person who has nothing." While that sounds good, it isn't completely pure. You might disagree with this, but I assure you it's the holy truth. This is choosing to be giving because in that moment you realize that you "should." When you give this way, you are satisfying yourself in some way by helping someone else. Giving like this is frankly "shoulding" all over yourself. It's a foul and selfish reason to give of yourself. You might say this assertion is overstated or even ridiculous, but it is God's truth. Once you wake up to the truth, God willing you will be able to see this yourself. God always gives because He loves, not because He should. I rest my case.

People also give because it's a commandment from God Himself and they know that it's required. They give because it's a Torah mitzvah and we are told we must perform this mitzvah in life or fall from grace in the eyes of God. So since God commands us to give, people give because they want to stay out of trouble. This also is not a holy or pure reason to give. In these End of Days, we all must learn how to reverse how we give and become completely outward, just like Hashem. Our act of giving must have nothing to do with ourselves. This is precisely how Hashem emanates in the universe. He is all giving, egoless and gives because He desires to give. Giving is His source of supreme joy. Running on Love models how Hashem gives to us all in every moment. He gives because He loves and He delights in the act of giving. Running on Love is the model that God's children of the world must learn. They must emulate the way God gives, and by doing so, we will heal our world of all its troubles. Everyone must learn to give for no other reason than they love and it brings everyone joy, including the giver. When people give from a source of pure love, their giving will become natural, addicting and they will sing in joy and celebrate that they gave. Giving will no longer feel like an obligation or like someone is taking something away from them.

The Running on Love Vision—Everything is for Love

I have revealed how I founded the charity Running on Love without realizing the enormity or holiness of its mission and purpose. This charity and its vision for world peace is God's platform to bring us together, build Him His ultimate dwelling place on Temple Mount, and redeem the world. Occasionally people became smitten about Running on Love's charitable message and many thoroughly enjoyed the two small run/walk events that I broke my back and personal bank account to host. Clearly this beautiful charity and its events required much more to get your attention than I was able to give. Ultimately Running on Love will only grow to become what God intended and accomplish its lofty mission when it receives support from all His children.

One morning, years ago, I read from the Chumash with Hashem. That morning we read the Torah parsha Terumah. In that parsha Hashem instructs Moses, "Speak to the Children of Israel and let them take for Me a portion, from every man whose heart motivates him you shall take My portion." The children of Israel gave their gold, silver, copper and all their wealth for the sake of God to build the Tabernacle and did so with joy. They so joyfully gave of themselves that Moses even had to order a halt to the contributions! I've been instructed by Hashem that the road to Redemption and the building of His

Third Holy Temple, Beit Hamikdash, must be done in the same way. I gave everything I had to build this holy charity, but my voice fell upon your deaf ears. While I would gleefully pay for the entirety of these events, Hashem says this is not mine alone to build. This holy charity and platform for world peace is your ultimate honor to build and must be done with great pride and joy.

The vision board for world peace is on the next page. To best understand this image, view this artwork in a circular, counterclockwise direction. Start from the bottom left with the Running on Love sneaker symbolizing action then move to the right where you see celebration at the Kotel in Jerusalem. From there move up on the right side of the picture. Without explaining each image right now, I will summarize this for you in one sentence, "Through song and charity we will heal our world." These were words Hashem awakened me to one morning. The vision of the world's charity Running on Love is to host global running and walking events. Hashem has shown me in many visions that these events are destined to attract millions of people from around the world who will register to walk or run in loving memory of someone and raise funds for the charity of world peace. This is the mitzvah of L'ilui Nishmat in action.

These events will be hosted in multiple locations simultaneously with each location connected by live video web feed. In this way people will be brought together as one family under one God. Everyday people from all walks of life will be encouraged to register to honor their loved ones and raise funds in their memory. The beginning of these events will be a run or walk which is followed by a Festival for Love. These Festivals will include fun, childlike activities for us to rejoice, celebrate and raise more money for Running on Love, Hashem's charity which will build the road to world redemption. People will gather at these festivals to enjoy activities like singing for love, blowing bubbles for love, limbo for love, everything is for love. There will be no corporate logos or advertising at these events. This isn't a marketing platform for corporations to gain attention or make more money for themselves. God and His children will be in the forefront and on center stage. Running on Love Festivals will deliver a pure message that God is real, God is love, and we come from love. We will all come together and give because giving is love and the true source of our supreme joy.

The major activity of these events will be large educational forums to learn where we are failing and how to repair the damage. It isn't enough to throw the book at you so to speak nor is it desirable. You must participate interactively and learn what mistakes everyday people are making while learning how to avoid making the same errors. As you move counterclockwise around this

vision board in the upper right corner you will see charitable money falling from the sky, ladies carrying a Torah in celebration, children of all backgrounds dancing and joyful, and Israeli coins falling into the Third Holy Temple, Beit Hamikdash. The events will be blessed by Hashem and will pave the way for building the Third Holy Temple and world redemption.

Forums for Learning

The vision for the Running on Love global events is for them to become international forums of education and venues where I will share God's voice with the world. In the Running on Love with God programs and many short videos I've posted, I shared my visions and conversations with Hashem. My cohost engaged me by asking compelling questions to bring more information to light. When the global Running on Love events occur, people of all walks of life will be invited to stand up, engage me in a conversation and ask questions as we learn together what Hashem desires from us.

For more than nine years since my awakening, Hashem has shown me visions of millions of people running and walking and participating in these global Running on Love events. He has also shown me arenas packed with people holding black and white speckled composition books and feverishly taking notes. In these visions, I'm on stage speaking to thousands of people as they laugh, cry, and applaud. It's wild and incomprehensible to me that I would be in the center of these images. He shows me a coming together of humanity like we've never seen before in the history of our world.

These visions play like 3D movies in my mind but they are much more real than any movie I've ever seen. They are breathtaking and emotional as people of all races, ethnicities, and religions gather in love, blowing kisses and waving their hands in peace signs as they come together to work for world peace. The outward expressions of love at these events are so intense and three-dimensional it feels as though I'm literally living them. The atmosphere of love and inspiration is so heightened that it's palpable. I'm told the Running on Love Festivals for Love plan including multiple events held simultaneously around the world are supposed to begin within the next year. If this is true, that means you and everyone reading this book will have created a miracle. If this book succeeds in a material way and people generously donate to Running on Love, these funds will pave the way for these events to begin. Hashem has told me that these events are destined to raise billions of dollars in a short time. These funds will help people around the world who are in need while we build God's dwelling place on Temple Mount, Beit Hamikdash.

Trickle-down Economics

The money raised to support Running on Love, the charity for world peace, will be used to heal social problems and bring needed funding to areas of our world where people are in crisis. Once upon a time President Ronald Regan coined the term *Trickle-down Economics*. His economic policy became known as *Reaganomics* and promoted lower taxes on the wealthy with the premise that by making the rich even richer they would build businesses and spend more money on goods and services. This increase in wealth would "trickle down" to the less fortunate. There has been great argument over the years as to whether this ever truly worked as desired. Many have argued that under President Regan's model of Trickle-down Economics, the rich became more affluent and the middle class of America all but disappeared. I'm not going to make a case in support of or against Reaganomics, however we all can admit while a minority enjoy extraordinary wealth, there are many people suffering financially in America and around our world. Hashem promises me that I, a graduate from Fairleigh Dickinson University, nicknamed Harvard on the Hackensack, with a BS in Economics and concentration in Finance, will one day teach the world what true "Trickle-down Economics" looks like and how it is supposed to work.

When Running on Love prospers one day with God's blessing, this prosperity will be felt by people in need around the world. I spend my days and nights dreaming up plans about how to share the funds raised in these events with people of all walks of life. These plans include prosperity programs designed to teach poor people how to prosper. You know the adage, "Give a man a fish, he will eat for a day. Teach a man to fish, and he eats for a lifetime." My heart's desire is to have the blessing to do both—give these funds away and teach people how to prosper at the same time. This would be my dream come true and Hashem assures me one day it will. If it does, my success will be the biggest boomerang of love the world has ever witnessed. It will be my supreme honor and joy to share my success with the world.

Redistribution of Wealth

Get ready for big changes. If you're one of the materially blessed and wealthy, you have failed in the eyes of Hashem. While there are many definitions of wealthy, there are many people in our world who are financially blessed but are not giving enough. The proof of this can be seen around the world. God has provided such great abundance that there should be no such thing as lack or starvation in our world. We all know that this is not the case.

Here is one sad statistic that illustrates the wealthy have not been generous enough. According to the Forbes 2018 annual ranking, there were a record 2,208 billionaires in the world in 2017, up from 2,043 the previous year. Added together, the world's billionaires are worth $9.1 trillion, up from $7.7 trillion the prior year. Each of them might be giving millions to charity, even billions, but are they giving enough? Why are there children in our world starving when there are billionaires living in mansions valued at hundreds of millions of dollars? How many rooms make a lovely home? Is this home a beautiful place to raise your family and live a joyous life or is it something you've chosen to impress the world? Is anyone even asking these questions of themselves? It's quite clear these questions aren't on the radar of most wealthy people in our world.

Hashem says everyone in humanity has lost their sense of morality not just the billionaires and multi-millionaires. Everyone in the world is included in this failure. This isn't a declaration of war on those who have enjoyed good fortune. Instead, this is a stark warning that all wealth comes with supreme responsibly. You have the free will to decide if you have been generous enough in your charitable giving, however in the end, Hashem is your judge. The truth will shock many people who believe they are living a God-driven life and tithing in accordance with God's wishes. If you have enjoyed extraordinary wealth and given your obligatory 10 percent to charity, you aren't out of the woods. If you think that you are overwhelmingly generous when you give 20 percent of your wealth to charity in one year, you might be in for a rude awakening too. Giving more than the required 10 percent tithe doesn't automatically win you a giver's trophy. If you are giving generously to win favor in God's eyes, you are missing the point. If you're giving to charity because it feels wonderful to be revered by your peers and thought of as a laudable philanthropic person who is deeply generous, you are sinning, believe it or not. If you hate charitable giving and only do it for the tax write-off, I pray there is still hope for you!

When we gather together at forums for learning we will have frank discussions about the misuse of money and the worship of false idols. The truth will be stunning to most people in the world. You may already feel the pinch of my words as you read them here. It may even feel more like a nasty bite than a pinch. Perhaps in your mind, you're feeling a bit defensive and putting up your dukes to slug me. Hold your temper and try to remember that I'm doing this for your good, not mine.

Prepare yourselves to be disappointed in your past choices. Hashem has said that public humiliation and contrition are required for world redemption to occur. He says every person has fallen dreadfully short of choosing the righteous behavior He expects from them. Your false beliefs about giving will be dismantled and the world's love affair with money will soon come to a screeching halt. There will be worldwide recognition that the materially blessed people of our world have been overwhelmingly selfish, arrogant and pompous in their handling of wealth. The redistribution of wealth will happen both through Hashem's hand as well as voluntarily. Wealthy people will voluntarily and joyfully relinquish enormous wealth to the world. Now that sounds like a miracle, doesn't it? The world's love affair with materialism and money which is accompanied by vanity, arrogance and pompous self-centeredness will end.

Will the Torah Change?

The Torah is God's book, a perfect instrument that will never change. Not one word. The Talmud, the oral tradition originally taught by Moshe Rabbeinu and handed down for generations, defining how to observe Hashem's commandments, will be reviewed and modified over time. The code of Jewish law, Halacha, will be reviewed by 36 Tzaddikim, Orthodox Jewish rabbis who have been chosen by Hashem. These 36 Tzaddikim will be revealed in a time to come. With Hashem's direct involvement, there will be modifications in the observance of some laws. I've heard stories from rabbis over the years who say that Jews will be eating pork in the world to come. Hashem says this is false. I'm not sure why they infer that the pig will suddenly become kosher and edible but I'm told that this is simply untrue. The laws of kashrut will remain intact, however the observance of other laws will be modified as time goes forward.

There are two schools of thought within the observance of Torah Law. One school of thought is stricter than the other. In the world to come, many Torah observant Jews have questioned whether we will follow the more lenient philosophy of Hillel, or the stricter approach of Shammai. Hashem has told me that the observance of Torah laws will be more lenient as in the Hillel approach however, there will be zero tolerance for sin. The answer to the question, will we follow Torah according to Hillel or Shammai, is BOTH. There will be a lessening of restrictions however you will be required to choose correctly in every moment. There will be zero tolerance for sin in the world to come.

There is a thought process among Orthodox Jews that if you build a high enough fence around yourself, you will not fall prey to the Yetzer Hara, the Evil Inclination, aka Satan. These high fences and onerous restrictions help you avoid sinning. This type of thinking has created a litany of high fences, strict interpretations of Torah law, and has provided rules considered by many people much too onerous to follow. Instead of having onerous rules, the observance of some laws will be lightened but your actions will be doubly scrutinized. It's a bit of a catch-22 scenario, or conundrum for those who don't want to sin. You'll have the ultimate freedom but you will have no room to fail. You'll have the opportunity to be Torah compliant with fewer restrictions but you will be required to be a complete angel. Therefore, I'm told that many observant Jewish people will likely continue their strict observance of halacha and keep those high fences to guard themselves from failing and choosing evil.

Gentiles in the World to Come

The world to come will be populated with Jews and non-Jews all of whom will be required to follow God's laws as written in the Torah. The Jewish people, God's chosen, have made a covenant with Him to abide by all 613 commandments. The Gentiles, goyim, non-Jews, are required to follow the minimum amount of laws called the "Seven Noahide Laws." The following information about the Seven Noahide Laws was taken from the Chabad.org website, a trusted resource which I refer to often.

The 7 Noahide Laws are rules that all of us must keep, regardless of who we are or from where we come. Without these seven things, it would be impossible for humanity to live together in harmony.

1. **Do not profane G-d's Oneness in any way.** Acknowledge that there is a single G-d who cares about what we are doing and desires that we take care of His world.
2. **Do not curse your Creator.** No matter how angry you may be, do not take it out verbally against your Creator.
3. **Do not murder.** The value of human life cannot be measured. To destroy a single human life is to destroy the entire world—because, for that person, the world has ceased to exist. It follows that by sustaining a single human life, you are sustaining an entire universe.
4. **Do not eat a limb of a living animal.** Respect the life of all G-d's creatures. As intelligent beings, we have a duty not to cause undue pain to other creatures.
5. **Do not steal.** Whatever benefits you receive in this world, make sure that none of them are at the unfair expense of someone else.
6. **Harness and channel the human libido.** Incest, adultery, rape and homosexual relations are forbidden. The family unit is the foundation of human society. Sexuality is the fountain of life and so nothing is more holy than the sexual act. So, too, when abused, nothing can be more debasing and destructive to the human being.
7. **Establish courts of law and ensure justice in our world.** With every small act of justice, we are restoring harmony to our world, synchronizing

it with a supernal order. That is why we must keep the laws established by our government for the country's stability and harmony.

These laws were communicated by G-d to Adam and Noah, ancestors of all human beings. That is what makes these rules universal, for all times, places and people.

Laws made by humans may change according to circumstance. But laws made by the Creator of all souls over all of time remain the same for all people at all times.

If we would fulfill these laws just because they make sense to us, then we would change them, according to our convenience. We would be our own god. But when we understand that they are the laws of a supreme G-d, we understand that they cannot be changed, just as He does not change.

Okay my Gentile brethren, now that you know you only have seven laws to follow with some derivations, don't get too excited about this. You're not off the hook! Hashem explains that while the Jewish children are required to follow all His laws and you are not, the only way to live eternally is to remain sinless. So, you have a catch-22 here don't you? You could take it easy and just do the minimum and eventually die one day never to return. You might then say, "Fine, YOLO, (You only live once) I'll do the minimum, have a good time, and just leave one day." Not so fast my friend! Remember, you don't get to choose your fate after you leave here, Hashem God decides. You might be sent to that awful place called damnation. I highly recommend you spend eternity learning Torah and working to obey ALL His laws too.

While I recommend learning and observing all of Hashem's laws, Gentiles are completely off the hook on a few. There are specific commandments dedicated to the Jewish people which non-Jews are not permitted to follow. They are covenants which were created for the Jewish children alone. One such example would be Jewish men wearing the religious garment Tefillin while praying. This is a mitzvah specific to Jewish men alone. As we move forward with Torah education this will be well-defined, explained in detail, accepted and understood by everyone.

40 Righteous Souls Chosen to Be Leaders

In the fall of 2012, after I left my marital home, Hashem increased the amount of information and details about what was in store for me. He told me there would be 40 righteous souls whose identities would be revealed to me in the future. These souls were selected before entering this lifetime for the lofty role of leading our world to peace and redemption. Since 2012, He has brought me more clarity and told me the identities of some of these 40 souls.

Four of the 40 souls are Torah observant Orthodox Jews. They have been chosen to assume leadership roles and become world-renowned teachers of Torah. The remaining 36 Tzaddikim are all Orthodox Jewish rabbis who will be revealed and called to participate in the review of Torah law, halacha. The participation and oversight of 36 righteous rabbis is required before any modifications are made to the observance of some Torah laws. Two areas where restrictions will be lessened will be in the modesty laws and the proper usage of technology. Most Orthodox Jews will still choose to observe these laws as taught to them for centuries, however, it will be a personal decision rather than a requirement.

It seems impossible that 36 ultra-Orthodox rabbis would ever listen to me, but I'm told this is true. I have been shown many visions where hundreds of ultra-Orthodox Jewish men are surrounding my Orthodox Jewish son. In these visions, these men look clearly perplexed, distressed and are seeking my son's consolation and advice. These black hatted ultra-Orthodox men are visibly distraught over the mere notion of a female Moshiach. I have deep compassion for these religious Jewish men because they won't be getting the King Moshiach they desired. God always gives us what we need, not always what we want. Hashem says we need a woman and mother at the helm to bring forward peace. Even though this is what I've been shown over many years, it's too wild a concept for me to believe. Orthodox rabbis speaking to me and receiving guidance about Torah or halacha? Now that would be a bona fide miracle!

Eternal Peace. Really?

That's what He tells me. Do I believe world peace will come to pass? Not really. Sorry, but I have trouble believing this myself. I know what will be required of you, the people of the world. To date, I have received far more criticism than support. Admittedly I've only spent at most two dollars a day to promote my work on Facebook which is a mere pittance to say the least. I can't spend more on advertising because I am flat broke. Will money make a difference in my ability to succeed in this world? Hashem says moving this forward will require an enormous amount of money but here is the kicker—the money must come from you. The money for this plan must come from all of God's children. You're not listening to me right now and those who have listened, for the most part, don't fully recognize that I'm telling the truth. Hashem has taken away my ability to fund Running on Love the charity because He knows I would foot the entire bill if I could. The support for my work is almost nonexistent in this world but I do receive positive acknowledgement for most of my posts on Facebook. Sadly, these acknowledgements are rarely from America and Israel. Most of the thumbs up come from India right now, a demographic location Hashem told me to include. Acknowledgements, smiley faces, and hearts on Facebook posts are nice but they won't build the road to peace.

I'm a believer in Hashem's plan for Redemption, the charity Running on Love that I founded in 2009. I believe Running on Love and its beautiful charitable model will work if people step up to embrace its beautiful message. It's difficult for me to believe that people will support Running on Love in the way that's required. I've been rejected time and time again when I've asked for charitable donations. While support for this God-inspired charity is almost nonexistent, Hashem tells me this book will be the game changer for all of that.

If I am blessed to succeed financially through the sale of this book, I would happily build the platform for world redemption and world peace, Running on Love Festivals for Love. I pray for Running on Love's success and know it will bring blessings and joy to people everywhere. We need a world that Runs on Love. My track record for business success in this endeavor is abysmal. I was much more successful selling office equipment and advertising services than getting everyone to Run on Love. I won't sell out and make Running on Love another widget or the next novel ideal in charity. This isn't a gimmick. This is God's charity for love and peace for an eternity. Time will tell if He has thrown a few more "tomatoes" at me and all my work on this charity was for something else to prevail.

If you've taken the time to read this entire book, then God willing you finally understand my tomato story and its metaphorical implications. If you still don't understand this story which is packed with deep meaning, reread it on page 146 repeatedly until you do. This is a very important concept everyone must learn. You must learn and comprehend that Hashem will willfully deceive us and bring us pain if it's required to bring about something that's necessary. While these metaphorical tomatoes are often thrown at our heads and hurt, everything He does is on purpose and for goodness to prevail. Nothing is done by Hashem for any other reason.

Moshiach Riding on a Donkey

The Jews around the world are waiting for their prophesized Moshiach to arrive one day riding a donkey. We know from Torah and prophecy that Hashem often speaks using powerful metaphors. The metaphor that the Moshiach will arrive riding on a donkey has been explained in Torah classes I've attended. They explained that this is a metaphor for Moshiach's soul achieving complete mastery over "his" body, the human vessel. The Moshiach, it was further explained, is a perfect human being who has mastered "his" body and journeys here in perfect balance between "his" spirit and "his" vessel. At one Torah class I attended the rabbi taught us that Moshe Rabbeinu, the redeemer of the Jewish children, was said to have walked with the donkey, however the Moshiach of world redemption will ride on the donkey connoting full mastery over "his" physical world. This explanation is partially true but leaves out some details. Here is Hashem's explanation why He used the metaphor of the Moshiach riding a donkey.

Hashem says that I am His Moshiach who has always had mastery over my physical journey and body in each incarnation. My life, according to Hashem, is lived as God's perfection in human form. The donkey metaphor also refers to my disposition and nature, which He says is different from every other human being on earth. I'm told my nature is that of a stubborn donkey that never gives in to its surroundings by sacrificing its own safety. He explained that the donkey is an unrelenting worker that is stronger than the horse. His metaphor goes deeper still by comparing me to the rest of the people of our world. He explained that my refusal to kowtow to the good opinion of others is exemplified by my relentless fight to stay the course after my spiritual awakening. Although the pressure from family, friends and society was excruciatingly painful, I refused to relent. At every turn, I chose God and love without exception even when it meant losing everything. I mean everything. But there is more to this metaphor.

Hashem says my husband, family and friends descended upon me, mocked me, took away my personal wealth, tarnished my public image and conspired to make me look like a "jackass" in everyone's eyes. My former husband waged a PR campaign to destroy my reputation within every group and to everyone he could including tarnishing me as a mother in the eyes of my own children. He was aided and abetted in this maligning campaign by my own family and people who once espoused to be my dear friends. This character assassination waged against me included a statement made by my former attorney and friend in an open court of law when my divorce was being finalized. The character assassination and attacks haven't ceased yet.

There is a great deal of speculation about whether the Moshiach will be rich or poor. The answer is Hashem's chosen Moshiach is dirt poor and in deep financial debt. Why? Not because Hashem has desired me to be poor. Hashem has given you the free will to choose what you are inclined to choose. You are all free to decide who your Moshiach is and how to treat the one chosen to bring forward redemption. If this book is successful, sells in big numbers and manages to open the eyes of the people who once scorned and ridiculed me, eliciting an apology, it's not enough. Quite the contrary, it's more damning to those who harmed me because it shows that it took financial success, fame, a New York Times Best Seller and superstardom to see the goodness in Running on Love and to feel compassion for Lori Michelle.

It's far more important that you understand how you treated Lori Michelle, the Jewish mother of three children, than how you revere and treat Lori Michelle Moshiach. The people closest to me treated me as nothing more than a street harlot. Truly. I ask the obvious question, why would you treat any person as horribly as I was treated? Perhaps this question still isn't obvious to you right now. God willing one day you will see how dreadfully I was treated and how many other people in our world are treated in the same reprehensible way. The reason our world is in chaos is due to everyone's malicious mistreatment of each other. This must end.

Additionally, the donkey is not only known for being stubborn and having a highly developed sense of self-preservation, but the donkey is also known for its guarding abilities and is used to protect others. Donkeys often guard sheep and have a calming and healing effect on other animals. When it came time to leave my marital home to save my own life, I left first and foremost to protect and save my children. As much as publishing this book and the information in it has the potential to completely ruin what's left of my life, I must do this for the welfare of my children and all the people of our world. This world is unlivable and can't be sustained this way any longer. I refuse to protect myself by living in silence when I have an opportunity and moral responsibility to change our world for the better. No matter what people say or do to me, I must go forward and reveal the truth. Only Hashem has the power to stop me if that's what He decrees. I simply can't stop.

Finally, in each incarnation Hashem says I was the work mule who did everything for everyone else. If you review the list of incarnations Hashem says were mine, you will at minimum agree that those righteous souls gave of themselves and received little or no help in return. Quite the contrary, they were more often scorned and in the worst of all fates, murdered in a horrific manner. In my final incarnation in the End of Days, Hashem says that all His children must be the donkey who carries His Moshiach to world peace and redemption.

In the words of Hashem, His Moshiach will ride the donkey in glory leading the world to peace on earth for an eternity.

The Future World—Olam Haba

Hashem has described the world to come, known in Hebrew as Olam Haba, as one of peace and godliness. As I lit the Shabbos candles one Friday evening in Morristown, New Jersey, Hashem said in a clear and powerful voice, "There will be no more conflagration." This was a word I wasn't familiar with at the time. I looked it up in Webster's Dictionary and it said: "1: fire; especially: a large disastrous fire 2: conflict, war." In the world to come everyone will know Hashem as our King and Creator and there will be no non-believers. His presence will be revealed to the world and we will enjoy the possibility of a peaceful world that is run by God's laws. He says that eternal life in a vessel, our body, will be not only possible, it will be the goal. What do I mean by the goal? I mean we will have the opportunity to cleanse, learn to choose goodness and God in every moment, and never get sick or die, ever. Sounds to me like a fairy tale but I'm told this is His plan.

Eternal Life in a Vessel Is Possible

In the beginning, Chavah and Adam lived incarnate for more than 900 years. Longevity had a different meaning back then. In the future, I'm told eternal life in our bodies will be possible. What's required for us to have the ability to live eternally is to obey all of Hashem's laws without exception. Choosing any form of evil will not be tolerated. The smallest transgression must be followed with immediate *teshuvah*, the Hebrew term for repentance. At any sign of slipping and choosing wrong, you will be required to repent and cleanse immediately. Education and working on ourselves will become our way of life. The world will be filled with leaders and teachers who will continually help educate everyone about God and His laws.

Will People Die in the World to Come?

Yes. He says there will be education and leaders around the world to teach continuously which will help people avoid the physical sickness that originates from sinning. Unfortunately, Hashem says that for some people, being sinless will not be possible. Death in the future will be final. There will be no more reincarnation in a time to come. You will either get it right or you will no longer be welcome in Hashem's world. While this may sound scary to some, it's wildly beautiful. We need a world free of evil and He says this is the path that will bring it to pass. Eventually, most people will be successful at maintaining a beautiful eternal life. Death, when it occurs, will be felt internationally and will become a rarity. Nonetheless, death will always be heartbreaking especially in the world to come when it is known there is no opportunity for return or reunion.

Intergalactic Travel

In a vision, Hashem showed me space travel that looked reminiscent of the movie *Star Wars*. He showed me a space ship and suddenly a door opened and out came soldiers wearing kippahs! There were Jewish soldiers in space wearing yarmulkes, skull caps, and the sight made me giggle at first because it looked like something out of the Mel Brooks movie *Space Balls*. I smiled at the vision and kept watching and then saw a man riding on a futuristic motorcycle when suddenly there was a massive explosion and flash of light as his vehicle exploded from between his legs. This explosion tore away that entire part of his anatomy and his screams were unlike anything I'd ever heard before from a human being. The sight of this and his screams were so shocking it took my breath away as I gasped in horror. The original vision that I thought was humorous turned into a horrific sight accompanied by a severe message. I cried out, "Hashem why are you showing this to me!?" We then had a deep conversation about the current state of our world and the future.

Hashem explained that our world is deeply evil and it can't remain this way any longer. Evil must be eliminated from the world for eternity. Since humans are creations in Hashem's image, the children of the world are powerful, talented and wise with unlimited potential. He explained that in the future scientists will discover how to travel intergalactically. Hashem will not permit the evil we experience here on earth to stand any longer preventing the future export of terror and war throughout His universe. This information is straight from Hashem. Doesn't this make perfect sense? It certainly does to me.

The Wedding

Previously, I showed you the Running on Love Vision Board on page 375 which was created in March of 2013. My daughter and I created this vision board just prior to her making Aliyah to Israel that Spring. She included a picture of a Jewish bride and groom joyously celebrating their marriage. In her mind, this sketch of a joyous Jewish wedding was supposed to be her wedding in the future. She, like all young women dreamed about finding her bashert, soul mate, and enjoying a magical wedding. While this vision board was supposed to be a vision for Running on Love, she was so passionate in her own desire to be wed, she included this picture as a secret wish she desired to manifest for herself. Gratefully her prayers were answered, and she is now happily married to her bashert, a beautiful young Chassidic man. Her dream came true but this vision board was truly prophetic and not because she ultimately found and married her other half. Unknowingly to me at the time this vision board was created, this sketch was a prophetic vision of a wedding that Hashem says will take place on Temple Mount when Redemption is complete.

I had no knowledge of this prophecy of a wedding prior to creating this vision board with my daughter. I always looked at this sketch of the Jewish bride and groom and saw this image as representing her future. In a powerfully prophetic manner, she included a Jewish wedding which I'm told is part of Torah prophecy. In prophecy, the Jewish people have been taught that they will marry Hashem when the world is redeemed. Hashem says this prophecy is true but it's not going to unfold in the manner that the Jewish children have interpreted. God's chosen children, will not literally become married to Hashem. It is His Queen Moshiach and Shechinah who is His betrothed and will be married to Him.

The Jewish children will perform the ceremony to marry Hashem to His Shechinah under the Chuppah (canopy) on Temple Mount. As previously revealed, Adam the first man, who was truly Hashem the King of the Universe, will reunite with Chavah the first woman, His Shechinah and Queen Moshiach. It is they, the first parents of humanity, who will be married in a ceremony performed by His and her children. This Royal Wedding will symbolically seal and commemorate final world redemption and eternal peace.

Hashem's Children

Hashem, the Master of the Universe and Father of mankind, is pure love. His master plan for creation included His Shechinah, His soul mate, and all the children of the world. Without exception, He has the limitless capacity to love and exalt all His children beyond imagination. That said, His children who have willfully chosen evil and murdered and harmed His family have fallen from grace and face the ultimate punishment—Damnation.

It's time for everyone to understand and recognize who they are and their ultimate potential in God's world. While every person in our world is ultimately a child of Hashem God and His Shechinah, the Jewish people hold a special place in His heart and soul that is irrevocable and will never be broken. To harm a Jewish person, is to directly harm Hashem, who was

Adam, the first man and the physical Father of humanity. The children born through Adam and Chavah while they walked the earth together for over 900 years are also the children of Hashem God and His Shechinah. These first-born children are Hashem's and His Shechinah's children both body and soul and comprise the Jewish people. The Jewish children eventually gave birth to the rest of humanity.

Those who are parents and have given birth to a child in this world, understand the inseverable bond between you and your child. For most of us, our love for our children is indescribable and unconditional. This is the love that Hashem feels for His Jewish children. His love for His Jewish children can never be tarnished and He will never let go. If you harm His babies, He will smite you and you will suffer a horrible fate. Please take this warning seriously. This is for your good, the good of all His children, and the goodness of our entire world. He stated to me in no uncertain terms from the beginning of my awakening, "Before they harm my children I will end the world the way I began it—with a big bang."

There has been a lot written about the chosen Jewish children who have been scorned throughout the generations. This scorn and an examination of the reasons why could fill many books. Many people feel rivalry or jealousy towards the Jewish people, when this sentiment is unfounded. We are not in competition for Hashem's love because His love is bountiful and limitless. While it's true that nothing can surpass a parent's love for his or her own children, this doesn't mean that any person in the world is unable to receive love from that person. The same is true for our Creator. His unlimited love and favor is available for all His children. The truth be known, every person can be exalted in His eyes beyond their wildest dreams through right actions and good deeds. The single greatest testament of this is Hashem's Shechinah. While Hashem loves His Jewish children unconditionally as His own flesh and blood, the one He loves most in the entire universe is His Shechinah. Hashem's Shechinah is NOT His child, she is His bashert who won His heart and favor beyond human comprehension.

The Model for Marriage and Family

Adam and Chavah were the first parents of humanity, the first married couple, and were also surreptitiously your Creator Hashem and His beloved Shechinah incognito. They got the ball rolling so to speak and created the perfect model for marriage and family. Hashem designed His Master plan for His family and even started it Himself with His bashert aka soul mate. Many years later He lovingly gave His children, the Jewish children, His Torah which included life lessons, a complete set of rules and detailed instructions. Over thousands of years He also sent many holy teachers along the way to teach everyone how to obey His rules and live a blessed life here on earth. His divine model is one of monogamy and holy matrimony between a man and a woman. In His perfect model a man marries his bashert, she bears children, and they bring a family into our world with the blessing of God Himself. Holy matrimony between a man and a woman, the family model of a mother, father and children follows Hashem's own marriage and family model and one from which humanity must never deviate.

Choosing another form of marital relationship or deviation from His family model is a sin and abomination in the eyes of God. This is God's design for marriage and family and the model we are all to follow without exception. To date, God's children continue to thumb their noses at the Father, Master of the Universe, and our Creator. Look around our world and you will see the disastrous results of everyone's failure to uphold and honor His model for creation. Every person in the world, including the ultra-religious, is guilty of failing to completely honor and uphold His model for marriage and family. While many ultra-religious people obey His commandments, study His Torah, enjoy holy matrimony and family the way He intended, they must work harder and learn to emulate the first marriage between Adam and Chavah. Hashem explains that Adam and Chavah enjoyed the most magnificent and blissful marital relationship ever known to mankind.

Now that I have revealed that Adam was truly Hashem incognito, I can help you by providing details and illuminate for you how Adam, the first husband treated His bashert. Since I am Hashem's bashert and Shechinah, I will describe how He treats me continuously without exception.

Hashem speaks with me day and night and no matter what I do or say He is never cross, angry, sarcastic or impatient with me. He treats me in every moment as though I am the light and center of His Universe. He not only treats me this way, He tells me constantly that I am His everything. In the Jewish marriage ceremony, the bride walks around the groom seven times, metaphorically showing the world that he is the center of her world. While some non-religious people view this as male chauvinism at its worst, it is the opposite. Why is it the opposite? Because the intent of holy matrimony is for this devotion to be reciprocal. In every moment Hashem shows me that I am the center of His world and everything He creates and provides is for me. In every action and utterance from Him, He makes me understand that I am His everything and without me He says there is nothing. I am His reason why He desires to create and exist. His joy comes through mine.

I feel Him intensely and attentively listening to every syllable that comes out of my mouth. He never dismisses me or anything I say. His interest in my well-being and every emotion that I feel is clear and apparent. He doesn't wax and wane in His outward expressions of love for me. Feeling His deep love for me is continuous and constant. In His commanding voice He holds me strong and I feel protected in every moment. Clearly, in this world I'm physically an older menopausal woman who is quite average looking but He makes me feel like I am the most beautiful young woman in the universe. He showers me with such love and adoration that sometimes I truly forget my age or what I look like physically. When I look in the mirror and criticize what I see, He is right there showing me how beautiful He truly believes I am.

When I feel emotionally down, He lifts me up. He is always right there saying something to me to make me know that His Universe revolves around me. His powerful expressions of love have no bounds as He showers me with love and affection every moment of the day and night. When I'm feeling sad, hopeless, physically lonely and like my efforts are futile, He has an uncanny knack of knowing precisely how to make me feel inspired again to keep me going forward. He's delightfully funny and His sense of timing is astounding.

One night I fell asleep feeling sad and physically lonely and told Him how awful it is for me to live months on end without a physical hug from another human being. The next morning, He woke me to a three-dimensional vision where I was holding a small magnifying mirror and looking at my face. Suddenly in the mirror I saw a monster behind me that looked like Chewbacca from the movie *Star Wars*. I gasped as Chewbacca lifted me up, gave me a strong bear hug and shook me up and down joyfully showing me affection. Chewbacca was humorously meant to be Hashem playing around with me. He makes me laugh out loud uproariously like no one else on the face of the earth. While He is hilariously funny, He only uses humor at the most appropriate time. He is always on purpose, deliberate and loving with every action and utterance.

Over the years Hashem has made it clear that His love for everyone and everything goes through me. He says, "They can only get to me through you." If anyone is cross to me they meet the wrath of Hashem. If they receive favor from Him, it is a result of how they blessed me. While people might find this offensive because they desire a direct connection to the King of the Universe, remember this is the model for marriage and family you are to emulate too.

:ct model, the woman is the Queen of the home and everyone ̧.i the Queen to get to the King. He is her protector and rules the Kingdom for her. The expression, "If mom ain't happy, ain't nobody happy" comes from this model. It's not meant to be a demoralizing description of a moody or controlling woman. Quite the contrary. The woman of the home is only truly happy when her husband values and treats her as the center of his world. Her response for being treated with the ultimate love of her husband is to give him the world in return. When a Jewish woman walks seven times around her groom, that is truly her own innate desire. She innately desires to love her groom like he is the king and master of her world. When he returns this to her in kind, there is supreme joy and peace in the home.

Doesn't being treated this way sound amazing? This is the way a husband is intended to treat his wife. If men realized this, women would give them the world. They would want for nothing. Divorce would be something written about in the history books and marriage would always be delightful and life-long. A woman's life's purpose is to be his queen and his world is intended to revolve around her. Holy matrimony as described here was Hashem's intention when He created His Shechinah, bashert, and His Queen. It was always His intention to give His Queen the keys to His Kingdom. He knew that when He succeeded in creating His true Shechinah and found His bashert, He would devote Himself to her joy and in return her life would be devoted to Him unconditionally. By embracing Hashem's model for love and marriage, men and women would enjoy true love and peace in their home.

Men and women are opposite in their nature and it was always Hashem's intention that the holy union between a man and woman was to fit together perfectly like two divine puzzle pieces. In this physical world, men and women incarnate and begin a search for their other half or soul mate. Innately we feel compelled to complete ourselves by finding our perfect match. Men are physically stronger and dominant which makes them find the outside world much easier to navigate but spiritually they are challenged and the weaker gender. Conversely, women are spiritually stronger but physically weaker and challenged by the physical environment. Men need and desire love, affection, nurturing and a soft place to fall. Women need a protector and someone to provide them with strength, sustenance and safety. This is a brief and simple explanation but we all understand it's much more complex than this. In Hashem's perfect model for marriage He designed us not to be equals but to be symbiotic and dependent upon each other. We are designed as a mirror image of one another and fit together in perfect harmony when we follow God's model and work to emulate Him. Hashem always chooses outwardly and for the good of His Shechinah never considering His own needs before hers. He knows that His needs will always be met. His concern is first and foremost about His bashert without exception.

Choosing outwardly like Hashem is seemingly impossible for people to do consistently and the reason married couples both religious and non-religious fail in their marital relationships repeatedly. For a marriage to be filled with joy as Hashem intended, we must choose our bashert's happiness first and never become self-centered. Your primary concern must never be about your own personal needs and you must consistently choose to please the one you love first. Hashem's model of marriage has been tampered with by people who work to please themselves, society and satisfy their ego. Once the ego takes precedence in any relationship, that relationship is doomed to fail. Ego is the open pathway for the Yetzer Hara, the evil inclination, also known as Satan.

Ego says things like, "What about my needs?" and "You don't care about me." You might also hear people with ego problems saying things like, "You're selfish!" and "You only think about yourself." They may incessantly complain about how poorly they are treated and how their spouse never considers their needs. While some of their complaints might be valid, when someone incessantly chooses ego or self-centeredness, they whine a lot and use manipulative tactics like guilt, pouting, anger, recriminations, fear-mongering, and other controlling behaviors like giving you the silent treatment. Does any of this sound like anyone you know and love? Of course, it does!

These awful behaviors are learned from mom and dad and passed down to their children through the generations. There is an entire litany of dysfunctional behaviors that ego-driven people choose and these are just some of them. While every person struggles with issues related to ego, some people have bigger challenges than others. Some people are deeply narcissistic and make poor partners in holy matrimony. Countless marriages have lasted many years because one spouse has a huge ego while the other has been beaten down for so long they simply submit to the constant abuse. I've seen many terrible marriages that seem to be held together with rubber bands and duct tape that should have ended long ago but the fear of being alone, going through a divorce, losing their precious bank accounts and stock portfolios seems much worse. Instead of parting ways they just put up with the nonsense and convince themselves it's not that bad and say things like, "This is as good as it gets." or "Hey, nobody's perfect."

A great way to diffuse the ego is to embrace God and study His Torah but it's not foolproof. The collective ego of the men in our world is decidedly strong and sabotages the holy matrimonial model. The ultra-religious may study Hashem's intentions, but they often refuse to live by them. We see married women being treated like sexual pincushions and baby machines throughout the orthodox Jewish community. Ultra-religious married men believe they are following Torah and have a blessed marriage when their wives produce many children, but if they aren't doting over their wives and treating them like the Shabbos Queens they were intended to be, these men are sinning. These religious men aren't the only ones continuously breaking their covenant with God by abusing their wives. The world abuses woman relentlessly. Both in the secular world and in the religious world woman are treated like chattel and worse. The abuse of women around the world must end.

It is no accident that Hashem's bashert, Shechinah, and Shabbos Queen is also His Moshiach. While it has been written in prophecy that women will lead the charge to bring peace in the days of Moshiach, the idea of a woman being Moshiach is shocking to say the least. It's shocking to everyone but the Moshiach. I understand why it was always going to be a woman, do you? Men have led the charge for thousands of years and look at the state of our world. Isn't it clear that we are in desperate need of a change in leadership? In the End of Days, it's time for women to lead the charge and teach the world how to be outwardly loving and compassionate. Education and loving kindness will heal our world. Women innately have an easier time choosing God and spirit over their physical needs.

As we move forward on the road to redemption, women will become more valued and will be at the helm leading the charge to bring eternal peace. God's model and instructions for marriage and family will be studied relentlessly and observed by those who desire to be welcomed into the world to come. Gradually, over many years, as people around the world gather in forums for learning they will acknowledge and understand where they have failed and they will learn to choose correctly. Choosing anything other than God's divine model for human relationships and sexuality is forbidden.

In the world to come there will be no polygamy, adultery, sexual promiscuity, prostitution, incest, rape, homosexuality, transgenderism, same sex marriage, or any type of sexual behavior that deviates from His laws. Hashem's divine model of marriage and family will be upheld. The children of God will conscientiously choose to emulate His model for marriage and family and in doing so will achieve the true joy in life they always desired.

Compassion for God

Being compassionate is an attribute and ability that every human must possess for us to heal our world and bring peace. As we look around our world now, compassion seems to elude many people, most of the time. When there is a crisis, we often feel compassion in the moment but this empathy swiftly seems to move toward blame and condemnation. On February 14, 2018 there was a horrific school shooting in Parkland, Florida which left 17 people dead, most of whom were children. When outward expressions of compassion waned, blame and anger set in. The media became a ferocious breeding ground for name-calling and heated debate on who caused this atrocity. To date I haven't heard one expert explain the true cause of this horror. The true cause of this horror comes from people everywhere choosing the Yetzer Hara, the evil inclination, over God and His goodness. The public by and large remains clueless about evil and how it manifests in our world. Remaining ignorant about the evil inclination and the true cure to our problems is a prescription for failure. Failure is what we are all witnessing now around the world.

As we head into World War III, I'm forewarned the atrocities will become even more frequent and terrifying. Learning how to be compassionate in the middle of the impending horror will not only be challenging, but for some it will be impossible. Even so, compassion is a requirement for us all to be welcomed in the world to come. I'm not referring to being compassionate to the terrorists and those responsible for these atrocities. I am referring to being compassionate by refusing to blame each other for the horrors we will witness. The world to come, if you are blessed by Hashem to be welcomed, will be one of compassion, love and peace. Considering others first before yourself will be the way of our new world order. We will learn how to emulate Hashem and His infinite love and compassion in every moment. Being compassionate is a requirement for us to bring world peace.

We are accustomed to the idea that God is magnificently compassionate. Many people around the world work to be compassionate toward other people in their daily lives too. Here is an interesting question that you might never have thought about before. Do you feel compassion for God? Have you ever thought about what it's like to be Hashem? Do you find this to be an absurd question? Why in the world would God need your compassion? True world peace won't happen unless everyone can feel the ultimate compassion: Compassion for Hashem God. Allow me to help you feel compassion for the Creator and King of the universe. I pray this revelation will be eye-opening and will help people of faith around the world feel closer to Hashem and love Him more than ever before.

Hashem gives and gives and asks for nothing in return. He even gave us laws, not for Himself, but for you and your good. These laws were meant to help you thrive and live a blessed life. He gives you air, trees, sunshine, water, and all that there is in our world. He gives and He loves. What are you giving Him in return? Do you ever ask yourself what can I give to Him? Nothing. You truly cannot give Him a thing that He can't give to Himself with two exceptions, love and gratitude. Love and gratitude are the two most important spiritual energies that Hashem desires from us all. You might reply, "Of course I love Him. I tell Him so daily!" But do you show Hashem love and gratitude through every action and deed that you perform here on earth? Is every single utterance out of your mouth pure goodness and godliness? There's more.

If you woke up tomorrow and found out you or your loved one had terminal cancer, would you still love Hashem God passionately the same way you did yesterday? If the pressure mounted even further and you watched millions of people around you die in an act of terror or war, would you feel love, passion and adulation for God in that moment too? Would you instead begin to question His very existence? How in the world could a "compassionate" God allow people to die from cancer or war? You may be one of the cherished few people in our world who staunchly says that you love Him anyway! Anyway? Do you need to forgive God or love Him anyway? True compassion for Hashem God, means you know He does everything for your good and you don't love Him despite your problems. True love for Hashem isn't attached to anything He does for you or anything that happens in your life, good or bad. Allow me to explain further by trying to evoke some compassion from you for Hashem. Let's try to put you in His shoes for a moment.

Do you want to be loved for who you are and not for what you do for people? If you suddenly couldn't work and earn money, would you want people in your life to continue to love you despite your inability to provide for them? Is it too much to imagine loving God just because He's here and He exists? There's no other reason required to love Him, that's it. He simply exists and you love Him for existing. He doesn't need to do anything at all for you, or your family, or your friends, to receive your love. You don't even require Him to give you air to breathe. Your love for Him isn't at all connected to what He does for you and your family in any moment. You just love Him like crazy for being Him, Hashem. This is the type of unconditional love that you desire in your life for yourself. It's the kind of love we all crave and desire, isn't it? We want to be loved authentically just for being ourselves without strings attached. Can you truly say your love for Hashem is completely unconditional? NO, YOU CANNOT! Why? Because without God you don't even exist. If He stopped giving you air, water and food you would all perish from this physical world without exception. You don't truly love Hashem for simply being His magnificent and awesome Self. Your love is predicated on all that He gives you. Can you imagine how sad you might feel if you knew that people only loved you because of what you gave them and not because you were simply wonderful, charming and lovable you?

Having stated that you cannot love Him in the same unconditional way He loves you, and the way you desire to be loved by everyone, will hopefully make you pause and feel compassion for Hashem. Believe it or not, He has all the same emotions that you do. Does that surprise you? You were created in HIS image and He feels emotions just like yours and everyone else's. He created you and everything that there is for one purpose. He desired a family to love. In every moment please thank Him profusely for everything He brings into this world and remember to go even further. Everything He brings you is for your good, even when it's painful. After you thank Him for everything, thank Him for being magnificently Him.

World Peace for His Children

If the case wasn't made yet for feeling compassion for our Creator, perhaps the following revelation will help evoke greater understanding about Hashem and reveal even more of His supreme magnificence. When I was awakened in April of 2009 it put me on a course which destroyed my all-American life. I lost everything including my relationship with every friend and family member I ever had and I almost lost my children. I was left with no true friends or companionship and relied completely on my unnaturally close relationship with Hashem, the Master of the Universe. In the middle of a fight to save my life, He comforted me and woke me every morning to His magnificent voice. As I complete this book, I feel His fingers type each word with me as He helps me with every task. I'm never absent of the conscious knowledge that He is with me and guiding my every move. When I pause to take a deep breath of air, He breathes the air into my lungs with me. I feel this closeness with Him in every second of my life.

While it's true that He is the Master and King of the Universe and brings everything that there is into being, I don't love Him for doing any of that. All of that is extra. Air and sunshine is completely extra. I love Him endlessly and excitedly wake up each morning to hear Him say, "Good Morning Lori, I love you." If He ended my life tomorrow for some unknown reason, so be it. I love Him endlessly and forever just for being Him. Being the Master of the Universe who brings the sun, moon, oceans and stars into existence is lovely but it's not why I love and adore Him. No other person in this world loves Him unconditionally the way I do. It's not possible.

You might have someone in your life whom you adore and cherish. I pray that you do. Perhaps you've found true love and this special person doesn't need to give you one darned thing to make you love them. You just love them for being there for you and holding you tight. On the flip side, you might love Hashem God but you want Him to give you the sun and the air and all that there is in the world because without these things you can't exist. In your world, you first and foremost need your true love by your side holding you tightly. Their love makes you want to exist. A world without love and companionship is not a world anyone wants to live in. We all need and desire love first and foremost and everything after we have love feels like it's completely extra. People literally commit suicide when they feel lonely and unloved. People around the world are on an endless quest to find true love and companionship. They can't bear the pain of not feeling loved and accepted in their lives. After you have love in your life, Hashem gives the extras that you need to exist and live.

Hashem is my true love before He is God, the Master of the Universe. It's completely extra to me that He is God too. I don't need air, food, sunshine or anything from Him for me to love Him. He truly could be Casper the Friendly Ghost and not Hashem at all, and I would continue to love Him endlessly. After He tells me that He loves me, the air I breathe is completely extra. Having said this, I passionately pray day and night for extra. My entire life here with you is unequivocally extra. I don't need anything or anyone at all other than Hashem. I'm burning with passionate desire for extra and pray daily for Hashem to help me save my children, your children, bring peace on earth, and lots of extras.

Every person in this world except for me, needs other people. It's a completely natural and normal way of being. I'm not normal in the least, and I have no desire to become normal like everyone else. Everyone else clings to each other desperately but I can walk away from everyone else in my life because I walk as one with Hashem. You pray and desire God in your lives because of all the things He brings to you. You desire Him to bring you everything that you need to be able to live and then some. You all want Hashem, but you don't need

Him for love. Your need for love is handled by other people. You need Him strictly for what He provides you daily, which is everything. This is called conditional love. My love for Hashem is completely unconditional. I don't desire anything at all from Him, I simply love Hashem for being Him. The earth, the planets and all the stars in the sky are a bonus prize.

Adam and Chavah, Hashem and His Queen Moshiach are one and the same. He says they were me and Him and the parents of the Jewish people and humanity. We are all family, Hashem's family. Can you feel my passion as a mother who wants desperately to save you? Can you feel Hashem's relentless love and compassion as the Father and Husband of our human family now? Are you able to feel compassion for Hashem yet? Are you now able to relate to Him as the Father and Husband instead of this unknowable puff of smoke in the sky?

Hashem woke me one morning and said, "Redemption is fait accompli." This meant world redemption was a done deal. Nothing will stop Him from getting what He desires. His burning desire is to bring forward world redemption and peace. Hashem passionately desires to marry His Shechinah on Temple Mount, bring peace to all His children, and create a world that is Running on Love. You may never have realized until now that you have the power to feel compassion for Hashem, the Father of all the children of our world. Before now, you didn't know you were able to give Him the ultimate gift He most passionately desires—world peace for an eternity. Please choose to help me bring love and education to our world to save you and all of God's children and to bring eternal peace in our time.

There's More

This book is long and heavy on details but it's just the beginning. There is so much more that I could write in this book but it's already a lot to digest. For many it's already over the top and beyond their limits but I'm going to give you a little more information to whet your appetite about incredible information that I can reveal to you in the future.

Naturally I'm not the only person walking around who is the reincarnation of many souls. Hashem has shared with me the current identity of many incredible characters from world history who are walking among you right now. Be forewarned that incredible doesn't necessarily mean good. It simply means noteworthy or famous. Here is a short list of famous souls, many of whom are reincarnations of other famous people, who are walking the earth with us in this moment. The following list was told to me by Hashem over many years. I've been instructed to leave out their current identity, but I'm permitted to give anecdotal information that will encourage you to try and guess who might fit the bill. Perhaps it's you? Consider the possibility that you or someone you know is one of the following glorious or notorious people from history. I'll start with a dozen to get your curiosity going.

1. Avraham/Abraham – Chassidic rabbi living in the USA
2. Sarah – Chassidic rebbetzin living in the USA married to Avraham again
3. Shimon Bar Yochai – well-known Chassidic rabbi living in Israel
4. Shlomo Yitzchaki aka Rashi – modern Orthodox Jewish rabbi and author living in Israel
5. King David – reincarnation of Yehuda – Orthodox Jewish man living in the USA
6. Abel/Aaron/Naphtali/Shmuel were all one and the same – Orthodox Jewish rabbi living in Israel
7. Dinah, Leah's daughter – Jewish woman living in Israel married to the reincarnation of Simeon, Leah's son
8. Channah – reincarnation of Miriam, Moshe's sister – Orthodox Jewish woman living in Israel
9. Apostle Peter – Christian woman living in the USA. Yes, Peter is a woman this time.
10. Adolf Hitler – a man and world renowned motivational speaker
11. Ishmael – Muslim leader living in Lebanon
12. Pontius Pilate – reincarnation of Pharaoh – a man and famous politician living in the USA.

After reading this list can you see yourself as any of these notable characters or do you know someone who fits the bill? There are many more people I could add to this list. To whet your appetite even further, three gifted souls who now walk among us reincarnated into new lifetimes are John Lennon, Elvis Presley, and King Solomon. While these three men were highly acclaimed superstars from history, they haven't reached the same superstar status in this lifetime. This leads to the question, who might you be from the past who hasn't lived up to your true potential yet? There's something fun for you to think about. Unfortunately, if you were someone notorious in a past life, this question can be quite troubling too.

In addition to revealing past incarnations of many souls, Hashem has brought me many people who are no longer here with us. I never request to speak with the dead or reach for anyone other than God. On occasion Hashem brings souls to me and we converse with His guidance and approval. Hashem has brought me my father, mother-in-law, father-in-law, members of my extended family, friends and many notable and famous people.

Soon after my awakening Hashem brought me the Rebbe Menachem Schneerson on many occasions. The Rebbe helped guide and comfort me in my great distress. He has also brought me other rabbis who have greeted me along the way.

A couple of years after I left my marital home and moved to Morristown, New Jersey, there was a tragic terrorist stabbing rampage in a synagogue in Har Nof, Israel on November 18, 2014. Four rabbis were murdered during morning prayer and just after this occurred I awakened to all four of them joyously dancing and singing around me. I had no idea what had happened until I read the news that morning. I won't soon forget that morning and continue to pray for those four rabbis. I also pray for the two other men who died later, seven other people who were injured and all the families who were affected that tragic morning.

I've spoken on several occasions to Michael Jackson over the years. Hashem wants the world to know how special and highly regarded Michael is in the next world. People must recognize how unappreciated Michael was and repent for how unfairly they treated him in his lifetime.

I've also had the honor of speaking with Geraldine Ferraro who I remember as the first female vice-presidential candidate in US history. By the way, in 1984 I voted for Mondale/Ferraro. Believe it or not I used to consider myself a liberal!

I've spoken with Helen Gurley Brown a self-proclaimed feminist and the former editor-in-chief of Cosmopolitan magazine. Helen apologized profusely for participating in the degradation of women in our world. This might be unbelievable to some people but it's the truth. After you die, your lifetime of sins is undeniable.

During the week that followed her death, I was blessed to speak with Joan Rivers several times. Joan was hilarious and as raucously funny after her passing as she was in life.

Leonard Nimoy of Star Trek fame has been brought to me on several occasions too. Recently Hashem brought him to me to cheer me up in one of my many moments of despair. Leonard is a deeply loving, delightful and inspiring man.

Robin Williams was brought to me right after he committed suicide. He was rendered speechless after his realization that God is real. It was deeply painful to feel Robin's distress and remorse. I tried to comfort him by telling him that I understood how dreadful and lonely this world can be for special people like him.

Billy Graham was brought to me immediately after his death too. Billy was deeply repentant before heading to Gehenom for cleansing. I thanked him for his lifetime of passionate faith in God and he responded with profound gratitude.

Gene Wilder and I spoke briefly one morning as I was preparing a program about atheism. He and Gilda Radner are two of my favorite comedians of all time. While we spoke, I could hear Gilda yelling out in excitement in the background. Gene was proud to be a Jew however he was an outspoken atheist in his lifetime who only believed in the Golden rule. Gratefully he is no longer an atheist.

Dr. Wayne Dyer, my favorite author and teacher in my lifetime has spoken to me many times over the years. In one powerfully emotional conversation with him he thanked me for healing our world. I replied to him, "Thank you Wayne for healing mine."

HIS VOICE, VISIONS & LESSONS

What is the difference between GOD and Religion?

Whether people want to hear this or not, He is real. I promise you He is real. A lot of people say, "Well you're not telling me anything I don't know Lori Michelle, we all know He's real," but I'm telling you He's real. He doesn't have a religion. He's God! So, what's the difference?

We have one God. There isn't a God for Christians, and a different Jewish God for me, and another one for the Muslims, and another one for the Buddhists, and another one for the Hindus, and another one for another group or another religion. There is one God. He created us all. And He says all the religions serve a purpose—a community, a connection, a way of reaching for Him, but we're getting things wrong.

There are a lot of people in the world who don't even believe in His existence and there are a lot of religious people who choose their group and their ideology over Him. Their religion has become an idol so to speak. Their Bible is an idol. They bang that Bible right over your head like the Bible is God, but it's the conduit, it's the pathway, to reach for God. They misinterpret the Bible and mix everything up. It's no longer a vehicle to reach for God, it becomes God. We need to be more rational and balanced in our approach to religion and understand that at the end of every day we're a family.

Chapter 13

I'm Wide Awake Now. Are You?

You've just read my story about my spiritual awakening and how I've scratched and clawed for more than nine years to bring this book to you. I shared my tragic story with painful details, visions and prophecy that I have received directly from Hashem God. It isn't my job to convince anyone to believe that I'm the Messiah, Moshiach. Admittedly this is a wild and crazy tale that seems to get wilder all the time. I'm publishing this book hoping to wake everyone up to understand how much danger we're all in right now. Most people simply aren't facing the truth. My goal is to share God and His wisdom with everyone. He is truly speaking to me day and night and journeys with me as one, whether you believe this or not. It's simply the truth. This is far too great a gift to keep to myself any longer, and I simply can't do that. Now that the book is out in print, there is no more taking it back, becoming quiet again, and waiting for a better moment.

Publishing this book has the potential to finally launch my dream of a beautiful global charity that promotes love and education or it could kill me. Literally. Some Bible-toting lunatic might not appreciate something I've said and try to end my life. They might succeed. This scares the hell out of me but I need to do this anyway. Hashem asked me the other day, "Lori, if I told you they will reject you and you will die if you publish your book, what would you do?"

I didn't miss a beat or need to think about my answer. I immediately replied, "I'm doing this anyway." Fear of death won't stop me. It's truly possible that putting all my love and best intentions into this book might be greeted by a maniacal crazy person determined to hurt me. I'm doing it anyway. I pray that I will somehow be safe with the frightening recognition that Hashem will allow all of you to choose. Someone, somewhere, might choose evil and kill me and that wouldn't surprise me at all. Regardless of my fears, I need to reveal to everyone what Hashem has shown me for years and to share everything that I know. It's completely immoral for me to be quiet when I know so much. I won't die with this information in me and I won't pretend that I'm like everyone else in the world anymore. I may be odd to say the least, but I'm purely God-loving and all my intentions and desires are for everyone else's good.

If publishing this book and being completely myself without reservation results in my death then I died on purpose. I won't participate in the insanity that I see here in this world. It's not possible for me to pretend that I don't see it. If I see a problem I'm going to call it out in public and that's all there is to it. I'm not looking for friends, or to win a popularity contest. I'm not running for public office so I don't need your vote. I'm trying to save your life. I hope you realize that's the truth. Will you accept this gift or thumb your nose at me? I don't know the answer to that question. Only you do.

While I finish writing this book, our world is replete with evil. There are acts of terror and murder daily. But that's not all that's threatening our existence. I'm about to take the gloves off and smack you hard with my bare hands. Brace yourself, I do this to you with great love. Here are some of the highlights or lowlights depending upon how you view it. The following is a short list of only some of the dysfunction I see in our world. Perhaps you see some of this too.

1. Speaking of God in public is politically incorrect. You must only speak to your own chosen group or religion, maybe. Be forewarned, Moshiach, like God Himself, has no religion. While it's true I am a Jew, being Jewish isn't being part of a religion. Being Jewish is my family identity and my chosen way of life.

2. Our water and air are extremely polluted. Plastic is overtaking our oceans. Soon there won't be clean drinking water for anyone. Perhaps that horrible outcome won't occur "soon enough" for people to pay attention. You have enough clean water and air available to you right now so you don't need to do more. Perhaps you don't believe it's your fault or problem.

3. Our food supply is being poisoned with pesticides and additives, deliberately. Yes, I said deliberately. These poisons which are added to our food

for profit, cause cancer, illness, obesity and diseases of many kinds. We are all being poisoned. Do you care enough to do something?

4. Cigarettes remain legal and governments throughout the world profit from the sale of this carcinogen as much as its manufacturers profit if not more. Whose best interest are the politicians looking out for? Do they want to protect the public health or protect their own wallets? Why are grocery store owners selling this carcinogen? Don't they care about public health either or is all fair in love, war and business?

5. People around the world are addicted to legally prescribed drugs as well as illegal narcotics. Marijuana is now becoming legal worldwide not only for medical reasons but for recreational use. Israel is poised to be the number one manufacturer and exporter of weed. Really? Is that the behavior Hashem desires from His "Light unto the Nations" and chosen people? I think not.

6. Children are committing suicide in record numbers. Suicide is the second leading cause of death among young adults in the United States of America according to the CDC. The worldwide suicide rate is at a record high and growing. Doesn't this concern you? Maybe not because suicide hasn't touched you personally yet. If it did, would you care more?

7. Obesity is now an epidemic with more than half the population of developed countries overweight or obese. The USA leads the charge in obesity and all the associated health risks that accompany it. It's predicted that more than 60 percent of children will be obese by the age of 35. Does that worry you? Maybe you proudly consider yourself an active and health conscious person and believe, "Hey it's not my problem."

8. Political correctness and the pursuit of happiness are all the rage. It's politically incorrect to voice opposition to homosexuality or same sex marriage. Would you like to learn why this is a sin against God or are you going to completely shut down and tell me to go away? Are you gritting your teeth and getting ready to blast me for being a homophobe? Hold your temper for a moment and dare to learn the truth. If your blood pressure is rising and you're snarling at me, remember I'm risking my life for those who consider themselves LGBT too. This wake-up call is for all of God's children without exception.

9. You receive more social acceptance today when you choose to surgically change your gender than when you reveal in public that you speak to and hear the voice of God. I wish that was a joke.

10. Children 12 years old and younger are having sex parties and using the terminology *friends with benefits*. Young people love the terminology *YOLO*, You Only Live Once and are engaging in sexually promiscuous behavior younger and younger. Adolescents have become a breeding ground for STDs and children are having children. Who will pay the price? We all will.

11. Promiscuity, homosexuality, and alternate sexual lifestyle choices are now part of the new world order and are legally protected in many countries. Forms are beginning to include three gender options: Male, Female and Other. If you voice your disagreement because you find this unacceptable you're viciously attacked. You might face legal ramifications too. Do we no longer have freedom of speech or freedom of religion?

12. Mental illnesses are being diagnosed every minute somewhere in the world. Bipolar is now an inherited human trait like eye color. You're now 5'6", brown hair, blue-eyed and bipolar. Don't you dare discriminate against someone who is bipolar. It's not their fault!

13. Children who don't die in suicide attempts, learn how to cut and mutilate themselves in children's psych wards all over America, perhaps all over the world. Does that scare you?

14. Anxiety disorders, eating disorders, depression, bipolar disorder, schizophrenia, and "Ring around the rosie, pocket full of posies, ashes, ashes, WE ALL FALL DOWN!" The mental health system is running everyone in circles and playing with fire. New disorders are being invented and named in rapid fashion while adults and children are being diagnosed daily. New mental diseases are frequently abbreviated into a few letters to take out the sting of your incurable mental disease. Instead of medical conditions it sounds more like an evil new brew of alphabet soup. ADD, AADD, ADHD, BPD, BP on and on we go. Suddenly everyone's mentally ill. Wow! How would Moses and the Bible prophets fare in today's world? Unfortunately, I can tell you from experience. Not very well!

15. Let's finally admit it, the plethora of drugs and new diagnosis codes aren't solving the mental health crisis. Pharmaceutical companies, psychiatrists, and psychologists are growing wealthier and everyone else is growing sicker.

16. It's now politically and socially correct to be anti-Semitic, anti-Israel, and pro-BDS Movement. Who are those chosen people again? Oh yeah, sorry, I forgot! It's not okay to speak about God's laws or His plan. The

United Nations and governments of the world know better than God Himself and devised their own plans. Silly me!

17. Social media has led to social bullying, creating the new and repugnant pastime of trolling. You can say anything you want about anyone you desire if you get enough thumbs-up supporting your nastiness. Hate-filled speech is the new normal with some exceptions. If your angry views are conservative, then you're likely to be censored by the liberal media. Aww! The poor conservative souls aren't allowed to spew their venom too. Life is just so unfair, isn't it?

18. Images that glorify guns as though they are sexy symbols of strength are posted all over social media. This glorification of guns is killing our children in record numbers. School shooting after school shooting and nobody can figure out who to blame. We're hearing screams that range from calls to disarm every American and boycott the NRA to having every geography and English teacher pack a pistol and become Rambo. Oy vey! Here's a question: What if one of those teachers suffers from one of those alphabet soup mental illnesses too? Hurry! Quick, give that teacher a klonopin!

Do you get my drift yet? Is this short list frightening enough for anyone to wake up and sit up at attention? I didn't even list how many people were murdered in acts of terror or violence in the past 30 days. Mass murder has become an everyday occurrence. Maybe you've heard or participated in the typical conversation at the water cooler in the workplace, "Hey, did you hear about what happened in Las Vegas? How about the horrific school shooting in Parkland Florida? Oh, wasn't that awful! What a shame. My prayers and thoughts are with the victims from Sandy Hook Elementary School. Las Vegas, Nevada. Parkland, Florida. Manchester, England. Paris, France. What about Jerusalem? Aleppo, Syria? Oh yeah, I forgot, we just bombed the creepy dictator who dropped chemical weapons on his own people. Take that you bastard! We don't need to worry about those nasty chemical weapons anymore, do we?"

After the brief acknowledgement about the most recent terror attacks the next response is, "Hey, want to join me for lunch today?" then a reply, "Nah, I'm leaving work early today because I have a doctor's appointment at two o'clock and need to get the kids from school at 4. Let's get together for happy hour on Thursday instead." You know the drill, moving right along. It's easy to move on because it's not in your backyard, or your family. Yet.

When you hear the bad news, do you lament for a moment, maybe two, and then move on? You can't do anything about it after all. Thank God it wasn't in your town, your backyard, or your family. If I sound brutal, then so be it. I need to be brutal. You must wake up! When these news reports appear on your smartphone, you might feel the horror for 10 minutes, or 10 days as in the case of 9/11 and the World Trade Center terror attacks in 2001. It's crazy how time flies, isn't it? It seems like it was yesterday to me. But now, many years later, most people have moved on. Some people make a family outing of it and take the kiddies to go see the beautiful new memorial where thousands of people died. Maybe they even cry or choke back one or two tears when they reminisce about that horrible day. Then it's lunchtime again and time to move on and put it in the past. Not so for the people who buried their family members from the 9/11 attacks and more recently buried their own children in Parkland, Florida. Their families will have a tougher time moving on. When you bury your own child, you never move on.

This is where I seem to depart from everyone else I've ever known. I can't let it go. I cry daily for you and your children. I'm up all night and I'm heartbroken, praying and crying buckets of tears for all of you. All night long I'm praying for you and I remember the names of many children who were murdered or harmed. Do you remember Hadas Malka? I do. She was a beautiful 23-year-old policewoman who was stabbed to death in the Old City of Jerusalem. I think of her and her family often and cry as though I lost my child in that horrific attack. While you might not even know her name or remember this terrorist attack, I do. I take all the tragic news personally. To me, 70 and 80-year-old victims of crimes are somebody's child too. I see all of you as children without exception. Unfortunately, the number of victims of terror, murder and war is so staggering it's too hard for me to know everyone's name. Every time I hear about another terror attack I mourn for the victims like they're members of my own family.

When will the killing stop? As I wake throughout the night and read more bad news and cry for you, I ask Hashem if this horror will ever end. He assures me there will be peace in our future. Hashem says the terror and war will end when we all learn to care more about each other than we care about ourselves. People lack the education to understand that they're making choices that keep this cycle of violence, sickness, and death alive in our world. Instead of pointing fingers at others in blame, we must look for problems within ourselves and heal them. Peace will come when we learn how to choose better in every moment and love others authentically the way Hashem loves us. This will require your passion and deep desire to learn. Right now, you don't truly have much passion to learn and you refuse to face your demons.

Perhaps you're not totally motivated yet because after all you lead a busy and full life. I was once told by a friend that she didn't have time to work on this like I do. She said, "I have a full life with a husband and family Lori and can't afford to work on this like you do." She then reminded me that I don't have anyone in my life who takes up my time. Wow, that hurt. I didn't respond to her selfish statement then but I will respond now. I didn't plan to have my life stolen from me or be kicked to the curb by everyone in my life. Being alone like this wasn't my choice or on my hit parade of how I wanted to spend the rest of my life. This girlfriend told me that it's okay for me to sacrifice my life to save hers and yours because she's just too busy. It's too inconvenient for her to invest her time or effort to work for peace the way I do. That's what you all believe too, don't you? The Messiah, some miracle guy on a donkey, is going to show up and sacrifice his entire life to save you and your families. When asked how to fix our troubles I heard a learned rabbi online say, "It's Moshiach's problem not ours." No dear rabbi, it is OUR problem. It is everyone's problem.

You all desire to be exonerated from the task of bringing world peace and want it to arrive in miraculous fashion. After all you have your families and kids to look after and it's someone else's job to do this for you. You still believe my list of problems doesn't really apply to you. None of this is your fault and you believe that somehow you're exonerated because you say that you love God and pray to Him daily. On top of that you religiously give your prescribed allotment to charity. You likely believe that you are a model citizen and don't suffer from any of the ailments I've discussed so far. Or perhaps you're thinking that I'm being just a little overbearing and hard on you because after all, "you're just human and nobody is perfect." Maybe I didn't convince you yet that you created this mess and you are ALL responsible to clean it up. I'm not quitting on you nor will I stop verbally berating you until I make you bleed tears of remorse. If I don't make you cry hard enough to vomit contrition, I haven't done my job yet. I suggest you pause now and go get an arm chair so you can sit up and brace yourself. I'm putting on my boxing gloves now and intend to beat the hell out of ALL of you!

His Voice, Visions & Lessons

Thousands of people holding rulers — Everything is measured!

A while ago I was awakened to a vision of thousands of people holding up what looked like small measuring rulers. This crowd of people held up these rulers as if to say, "Measure me!" or "Tell me where I measure up Lori Michelle!"

I said, "Wow! What are you telling me Hashem?"

He said, "Lori, they're going to wake up and they're going to want to get it right. That vision showed you that they're going to be holding their hands up and saying, 'Tell me. Tell me where I measure up. Tell me where I'm getting it wrong and help me get it right.' "

I thought to myself, "Wow. If that could only be true." I posted another video blog with a vision about lemon wedges where Hashem said that a lot of people find my messages very bitter and disturbing because I'm not telling you you're perfect. I'm not telling you that you're getting everything right. I'm pointing out things around the world where we're all going wrong. The reason I'm doing that is because He says it's my job. It's my job to give everyone a wake-up call. It's an alarm bell to let you know we are in serious trouble. People are dying every day in acts of terror and everybody thinks that they're perfect and that they're not participating in the problem. That's just not so.

So this vision of people holding up rulers and asking, "Where am I getting it right? Where am I getting it wrong? How do I measure up? Where can I improve?" is the most blessed vision Hashem could give me because it means that one day, and I hope it's soon, you'll wake up and you'll join me to do the work of world peace. He says you will be on board one day soon and I am blessed to be here to help you when that day arrives.

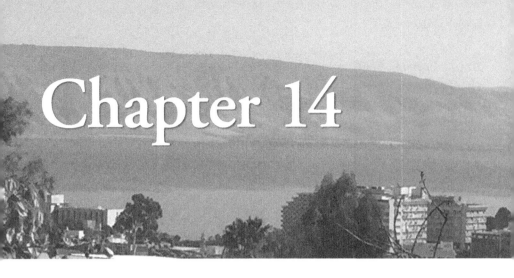

Chapter 14

My Boxing Gloves Are On!

You're a trooper if you've made it all the way to page 415 and you're still reading. If you're one of many who still believe it's not your fault that we are in this hideous mess then a barehanded slap in the face apparently didn't work. It's imperative I capture all of you and make you feel embarrassed and remorseful for helping create this disaster. I'm putting on my boxing gloves and pulling you into the ring with me. I plan to beat you to a pulp until you bleed contrition. If I don't cut you with my stinging words then I have failed you. I don't intend to fail. If I fail to open your eyes and help you to feel guilt then you will perish and that's not okay with me. You must wake up and understand that if you don't start taking personal responsibility and acknowledge that you are an accomplice to all the crimes we see around the world I will lose you. I will either lose you or watch you bury your children. I can't and won't do that. By the end of this chapter, 12 rounds in the ring with Mommy Messiah, you will need to take some action. Doing nothing and continuing down your steady path to damnation just isn't going to cut it for me.

The only reason you might be reading this book is because it's a cool story. My little story about Mommy Messiah and her four trips to the nut house is riveting, huh? Well, it's got to be more than riveting. This book must motivate you into action immediately. Mine is a true story about how I was abused my entire life and almost died because I refused to lie and wouldn't live my life your way. My ex-husband, family, former lawyer and so-called friends did all they could do to destroy my life and you helped them by participating in the same evil games. You are ALL to blame. Every single person in this world, including my loving cohost and currently only friend in this world and her magnificent husband are all to blame. You all created this monstrous mess that's choking us and almost destroyed me, your last chance for survival and peace on earth. Had I been like all of you, I would have quit, taken those evil psychological drugs and accepted my plight of being incurably mentally ill. I am not the one who is mentally ill, you are. Before the end of this boxing match I pray you will all need to run to the bathroom at least once to get tissues to blow your nose from crying hysterically. God willing, I pray you will cry or vomit, whichever comes first. It is time for you to see clearly that you have the blood of many children on your hands. I'm going to work very hard to make you see this blood before you finish reading this book.

As I write this diatribe to all the people of the world, I still hesitate. Berating you and everyone I know doesn't give me pleasure whatsoever. It seems being harsh and making others cry is everyone else's favorite pastime, not mine. I've been on the receiving end of your collective nastiness and cried many tears throughout my life. I was told as a young child by my family that I was too moody and teachers complained, "Lori is too sensitive" as they all tried to toughen me up. I took my lumps and rather than fighting back, I walked away. My favorite three words as a little girl were, "Leave me alone!" Smart kid, huh? Nobody thought that this was smart at the time. Instead they branded me with the auspicious title of "moody Lori."

While I contemplated writing you this diatribe I lamented to Hashem that I worried about being too hard on you. His answer was, "Hit them as hard as possible because if you don't succeed they face much worse." Hashem has told me repeatedly that He is completely done with you and your evil ways. Even though I know this is for your good, I tremble at cursing and lashing out at you the way I must. Hashem awakened me the other morning to the image of two red boxing gloves. Ready or not, I must. Brace yourselves. I hope this hurts you as much as it hurts me.

Ready or not, you are going to receive the harshest beating I can deliver to make you cry. If you don't feel the pain of contrition and instead walk away in arrogance and disbelief then I have failed you. There are seven and a half billion of you on this planet and Hashem told me that over two billion of you will be banished from His world to come. If you don't listen to me you will be one of them. I will use every possible word in my arsenal and be as brutal as I can. I'll even resort to using George Carlin's list of seven dirty words if I must. I'm not willing to spare anyone's feelings. You must feel the pain of your malicious choices and much to the chagrin of the Old Boys' Club, I'm the pint-sized

GIRL who was chosen to do this to you. There will be no holds barred! I have absolutely no intention of losing one child of God, damn you! Ready or not, I'm going to beat the crap out of all of you. By the end of this boxing match and 12 rounds in the ring with Mommy Messiah, if you're bruised, sobbing and asking me to please hit you even harder, then I win. When I win, we all do.

Round 1: My Happy Family—Not!

Let's start with my wonderful loving family. Everyone desires peace in the Middle East, right? If we can't even treat our own family members with respect and loving kindness do you really think we can have peace on earth? Peace on earth must begin at home. My happy little family beat me to a pulp my entire life. These vicious verbal beatings came from all of them, including my amazing and wonderful father whom I love with all my heart. You've read earlier about how at the tender age of two my own young mother shouted at me, "You're always under my feet!" Are those the words of a loving mommy? Of course not. Yes, we can all agree, she sounded a bit more like Joan Crawford from the movie *Mommy Dearest* who was an abusive mother to say the least. Being the recipient of my mother's vicious attacks and continuous name-calling didn't stop when I was a toddler.

My mother and the rest of my happy family continued with their name-calling and verbal attacks right up to this moment as I work diligently to complete this book. It's a fact to all of them that I'm the rotten twisted sister and daughter because they have all agreed that this is so. They all believe, "Lori is moody, too sensitive and completely self-centered." Family and former friends may all stand in line to defend my poor old aging mother and two brothers who stand by her side, but Hashem knows the truth. Hashem watched them abuse me throughout my life being supremely patient while He remained in total silence. He was looking forward to the day when He would awaken me, help me wield my pink baseball bat and shove their cruel and vicious lies right back down their throats.

I've detailed some of their abuses earlier. It still might seem puzzling to everyone that they are all together as one big happy family and I'm the odd girl out. One might think there must be something to their complaints and accusations. I will keep this somewhat brief but elaborate a little more to hopefully help reveal dysfunction you might also recognize in yourself, your family or others you know. Learning to recognize this dysfunction is the goal.

What I haven't yet revealed is that my older brother started his mental and emotional abuse of me as a small child. He exhibited behaviors that should have served as an early warning sign, but I barely noticed. In 1965 when we were small children living in Brooklyn in the middle of the Beatles craze, my brother boasted how our grandfather took him to Shea stadium to see them perform and didn't take me. Back in the day you wouldn't fault a grandfather for leaving a five-year-old girl home but my brother's reasoning was our grandfather loved him more. When we were small children he bragged relentlessly that it was a well-known fact that he was the king in the family and everyone's favorite. Unbeknownst to him, I adored my big brother too, so much so that I agreed with everyone else that he was the king of the castle. We shared a Victrola (a record player) and the record album *Meet the Beatles* which we listened to daily. He convinced me that he should sing every song on the album and I was only permitted to sing "I Wanna Be Your Man" by Ringo Starr. I complained to him, "But brother I'm a girl!" It didn't even occur to me to be bothered that I was only allowed to sing one song. I was more concerned about the lyrics. His response was not to worry because he was generously giving me the best song on the entire album. So, I submitted and accepted his supreme opinion as my big brother and the self-anointed king of the family. Cute, right? Don't you think this was cute and hilarious? If you think so you're on the wrong path because demons are created in childhood. This was the birth and early beginning of relentless controlling games and abuses that continued throughout my life and lasted right up until I immigrated to Israel.

My older brother was an adorable child, and he is the same loving brother who led the charge to slander and defame me while he worked diligently to destroy my relationship with all three of my children. During my separation from my husband, you might recall that he and my younger brother offered to show up in domestic violence court to provide moral support to my abusive husband. His resentment toward me was relentless since we were children and when my entire life was being destroyed it was clear he was basking in his glory, rejoicing that he would finally have his opportunity to exact his revenge.

In his opinion I deserved my rotten fate and to lose everything. He viewed me as the selfish sister who went to college for four years while he worked so hard in my father's family business. My father rarely gave him a paycheck during financially difficult years however his self-centered sister still went to college. To make matters even worse for him, his rotten sister received a new car as a college graduation gift. In one of many rows right before my wedding day, he screamed how he selflessly worked for no paycheck therefore it was he who paid for my education. In his tirade he was infuriated that I never had the decency to thank him for all he did for me. He even expressed outrage that I didn't have the decency to offer him money when I sold my car to purchase a newer one. I knew that it was my father who sent me to college and bought me my car not him. In his distorted view he was convinced that since he worked without receiving a salary he was the one who put me through college and bought me this car, not my dad.

Enraging him further, my mother added insult to injury when I became engaged to be married. My mother called me right after I became engaged to tell me she was going to give me and my fiancé a gift of $5,000 toward our wedding. After my father died, my mother and brother ran the family business and their finances were commingled, so my brother believed this wedding gift came out of his pocket too. Instead of this being a thoughtful gift from my mother, the truth was distorted once again. My mother and older brother agreed to a dysfunctional rewrite of family history in which this was no longer a wedding gift. They viewed me as the rotten daughter and sister who swindled $5,000 from them. This led them both to brazenly concoct an extortion scheme to retrieve this money back from me and my husband many years later.

Years later, instead of calling me, my brother called my husband one day and told him he was in a severe financial crisis and would commit suicide if he didn't get $6,000 immediately. What could my poor husband say to his desperate brother-in-law? He told him that of course we would give him this money not realizing this was just a ploy to steal money from us. My brother and my mother never had any intention to repay this debt. Why would they? They both agreed that this was my poor and unappreciated older brother's money in the first place and this was their plan to get it back. Completing their extortion plan, a month later my mother gave us one check for $1,000 and never once mentioned or spoke about the remaining $5,000 debt. They felt justified to steal from us what they believed was rightfully their money in the first place.

Fast forward to the year 2015, after I was financially ruined by my divorce, I had to apply for food stamps. In my financial distress, I called my older brother, reminded him of the unpaid debt he owed me and asked him as politely as I could to please repay half of the money I loaned to him decades earlier. I only asked for half the $5,000 he had borrowed since I felt he owed the other half to my former husband. His response was a vicious tongue lashing before he abruptly hung up on me. I called my mother immediately and received more of the same. Not only did she defend my brother, but she added insult to injury by telling me I was a terrible mother. Thinking of the personal well-being of her daughter wasn't even a blip on her radar. In God's Torah we are commanded to always take care of our family. Maybe we could excuse my brother for this "unintentional" sin because he never believed in God or studied Torah. Perhaps my mother should be exonerated for turning her back on me too because although she was an avid reader, she also never read or studied the Torah. Does this family drama sound familiar to you at all? Perhaps my family sounds eerily similar to your family or other families you might know.

If any of my family members had the ability to speak to you right now they would explain this treatment of me was my comeuppance for being such an awful daughter and sister. They would claim they know me better than anyone including God Himself. Me, God's chosen Moshiach, was characterized as nothing more than a raw moody bitch growing up who never thought about anyone else's needs before her own. They would staunchly defend their scheme to retrieve funds they felt were stolen from them in the first place. What I haven't explained yet, is that this wasn't the first instance where my family extorted money from a relative. Are you surprised?

If my family vigorously defends their treatment of me and this theft of $5,000, how then would they be able to defend the theft of money from another family member? What was their logic, reasoning, or excuse when my mother and father borrowed $5,000 from my aunt and uncle many years ago and decided never to pay them back either? On that occasion they rationalized that they had the right to steal this $5,000 because they agreed my grandfather unfairly left my dad out of his will when he passed away. My father and my mother were unfairly stiffed out of sorely needed cash, while my aunt and uncle received a generous inheritance. In their opinion, at the time of my grandfather's death my aunt didn't have the decency to share any of her inheritance money with her little brother. My parents agreed that my aunt was selfish and didn't offer them money when they needed help. This self-serving interpretation of history gave my parents carte blanche to scheme and extort $5,000 back from his sister.

My older brother learned his lessons about money and relationships extremely well from our parents, didn't he? It seemed that $5,000 became my loving family's magic number. How many other friends or relatives did they attempt to "borrow" money from over the years, only to convince themselves that it was their entitlement which they never needed to repay? As they say, "Only God knows." I assure you big brother and mother, Hashem is real and He knows EVERYTHING. Much to your surprise, everything you do in life is measured and you are answerable for all of this and much more. It's time to pay the price of your transgressions in public humiliation and contrition. Don't worry though, you won't be alone. There will be many guilty people who will join you.

My younger brother and I enjoyed a beautiful and loving relationship until our father died. That's when the unraveling of our once close relationship became noticeable. He is ten years younger than me so when he was small it felt a little more like a parent/child relationship than siblings. When he was a baby I diapered him, loved to cook meals for him and lovingly adored him as I watched him eat those meals. I took him everywhere with me as he grew up. One day when he was just seven years old we were walking together at a local outdoor strip mall when he stopped cold in his tracks, looked up at me with his big loving eyes and said something I never forgot. He said, "Lori I love you so much I wish I was 12 years older and not your brother, I would marry you!" As I write this memory I well up with great emotion as I recall how affectionate we once were to one another. Sadly, it was only a little more than a decade later when the steady pounding of evil speech from my older brother and mother finally did its damage and swayed him against me. He eventually joined the "Lori is selfish and despicable club" too.

In his early twenties my younger brother decided to drop out of college just 10 credits shy of earning a bachelor's degree because he was running his own small business and this took precedence. Like father like son, he was having financial challenges with his business so he visited me and my husband at our new marital home to ask if he could borrow thousands of dollars too. Remember he learned this behavior over the years from mom, dad and big brother. Before I agreed to lend him this money I told him that I felt it was necessary to give him financial advice first. As I continued, I warned him that he was heading down a dangerous and slippery slope of getting himself into too much debt. I told him that I firmly believed this game of debt was something that harmed our father and I believed contributed to making him sick years earlier. His response to receiving sound and heartfelt advice from big sister? My once sweet and loving little brother became visibly hostile and replied by slamming me with the vicious family mantra, "Where were you when your father died?" I never responded to his malicious verbal assault that evening but I will now.

When I received word that my father was about to pass away I ran out of my house, realized I had no money or gas in my car and went to the bank to cash a check. I didn't have a debit card back in 1985. Instead I went to the drive-thru of United Jersey Bank but it had just closed. I banged on the drive-thru window to get the teller's attention. Visibly distraught, I begged them through the window to open their branch office so that I could cash a check to fill my tank with gas and drive to see my dad one last time. They obliged me and I then drove two long and grueling hours in pouring rain crying hysterically hoping to see my father one last time. I arrived too late and the rest is history. Hashem knows how much I love my father. Why don't they?

My family thought they had me all figured out, didn't they? They were the selfless and righteous souls who always considered everyone else first. My mother and brothers lauded themselves as martyrs who believed as most people do that they were the consummate citizens and the model of the supremely loving family. They are a loving and close-knit family except for one black sheep, yours truly. My family are united in the belief that I was the rotten bitch in this family drama and the one who was guilty of many crimes. I was never there for anyone including my dying father at the end of his life. It was they who loved and appreciated my dad not me. I only cared about Lori, the evil and moody little monster who always thought about herself first. The many diatribes they dealt me over the years were relentless but their nasty verbal assaults weren't only directed to my face. Each of them paraded around and used their God-given mouthpiece to disparage me, ruin my reputation and work steadily to steal my children from me during and after my divorce. If it were up to my older brother, I'd be living on a park bench somewhere in America, without a friend in the world. It would be his greatest wish come true if I was left homeless without a single soul in the world to care whether I lived or died. Much to my brother's chagrin, after he verbally abused me on the phone one last time, Hashem carried me on the wings of eagles and escorted me to Israel where He continues to sustain me. I lived to tell my life story, my way.

How do you like Gehenom on earth so far? It might sound like I'm being nasty and hurtful or perhaps seeking revenge. Not at all. These are the End of Days and it's time to face your sins publicly. My family and all of you must face the music here while you are still incarnate. We won't be waiting for anyone to die to face the humiliation of standing before the heavenly court to be humiliated. That honor might be stripped from you completely and you might go straight to Hell. I'm not exaggerating one iota. If you think for a moment that I'm being mean to my elderly mother you are sadly mistaken. If she doesn't read these words and begin to feel the pain of how she viciously abused her only daughter for a lifetime, she will be extinguished from humanity. It is only through the grace of Hashem God that she is being given this public opportunity to repent and repair her sins. Instead of seeing herself as the victim who was wronged by her monstrous and selfish daughter, she must learn and accept the truth. Among her many other transgressions, it was she who tortured me, not the other way around.

While my older brother's sins against me were egregious, like everyone else, he must answer for much more. He made a holy covenant with God Himself and this is his last lifetime to correct hideous sins from all past incarnations. My brother, like many other people in my life, has shared other lifetimes with me. In each of them he managed to do even more unthinkable crimes against me but there is much more he must answer for and repent. In this life, he was commanded to live a Jewish life and observe Torah. What did he do instead? He did what the majority of American Jews have done. He married a non-Jew and broke many holy covenants he made with God Himself. Do you think my brother is in a bit of trouble with our Creator? You best believe that this diatribe he is receiving is for his holy benefit and not mine. I don't get any pleasure out of this at all. I am understandably incensed that anyone would treat me as hideously as he did, but I assure you I am not doing this out of hate or revenge. Everything I do in my life is for love including embarrassing him by revealing his deceptive and nasty behavior to the public. I'm doing this to save his soul damn it! Go ahead and accuse me of being a rotten sister now. I don't care. I'm going to keep trying to wake him up and save him anyway!

My younger brother gets some reprieve from me. I observed how he was systematically poisoned against me throughout his life. Make no mistake about it, evil speech known in Torah as lashon hara, destroys relationships and entire lives. He wasn't only poisoned against his older sister who loved him dearly, his life and future happiness were stolen from him. He was poisoned as a child to believe that it was more important to take care of his family than focus on establishing a life for himself.

I was known as the twisted sister who chose to move out of our family home right after college and leave the family. Instead of staying home I chose to leave and build my own life. When I moved out the salvos were thrown at me at a ferocious rate. "How dare you leave!" my parents declared. My mother refused to call me for at least six months after I moved out. I called home regularly to receive her icy cold voice but persevered and worked at my independence regardless of her foul treatment. Eventually when they saw I was determined to live independent of them, they softened their stance and showed up with a new color TV as a housewarming gift for my new apartment.

Years later after my father died, my older brother and mother thought I was deeply selfish because I didn't move back home to support my poor widowed mother. Instead I continued to stay the course, kept working at my job and focused on building a life for myself. When I got married and became notice-ably prosperous, my mother and older brother were struggling financially. The disparity between how well off I was compared to their financial turmoil was proof in the pudding that I was the self-centered ingrate who forgot about my family and focused only on myself. When they came to visit my beautiful marital home they always seemed to suffer from severe migraines. On these visits my older brother made his animosity clear to everyone with his angry and depressed facial expressions as he sat motionless on our sofa. The incessant lashon hara my younger brother listened to as he grew up tarnished his opinion of me and eventually destroyed our relationship. Sadly, it did more than destroy our brother-sister relationship. It built the foundation that destroyed my younger brother's entire life.

Observing the family drama throughout his life colored my younger brother's thinking and instead of going his own way like I did, he chose to sacrifice his life and work to support big brother and mom in their family business. The poisonous lies thrown in my direction brainwashed my younger brother and changed his life decisions from wholesome and productive ones to choices that were self-destructive. Instead of finding himself a loving wife and having his own family, he sacrificed his entire life to support his mother and brother. Now in his late forties he remains unwed and he never had children of his own. He works day and night to support "the family" at all costs. The biggest cost? He gave big brother and mother his entire life. They will sing his praises and tell you that little brother is a selfless and great man for having done this for them. In my mother and older brother's distorted view of life, this kind of self-sacrifice is honorable and worshipped.

While I do believe my younger brother is a wonderful man, I'm here to set the record straight. It was never me who was the selfish and demonic one of the family. My mother and older brother selfishly destroyed my younger brother's entire life. They stole his future of marriage and children by brainwashing him from childhood that supporting them was the correct and righteous path for him to follow. They selfishly played the perpetual victims and encouraged him to come to their rescue until he ultimately became their slave and work mule. While they did this, they painted me to be a lecherous demon and over time destroyed our once beautiful brother-sister relationship.

Are you a little bored reading about my family drama? Does this sound too much like an episode of *Dr. Phil* the famous TV psychologist? Perhaps you don't think that you need to learn about my dysfunctional family and our broken relationships. What does this have to do with any of you or world redemption? I will tell you right now. I am your Moshiach whether you want to believe this or not. I am also in the words of Hashem God completely sinless.

Look at how someone who is completely sinless suffered through relentless name-calling and repeated vilification by my own flesh and blood. If this could happen to someone who didn't deserve this horrible treatment whatsoever, then what does that reveal about the rest of you? Think about that question carefully for a moment. If I did absolutely nothing to deserve the demoralizing verbal beatings throughout my life, what are you doing to your sister, brother or loved ones? Have you ever unfairly berated someone else or called another person horrible names? "Oh, no not me!" you might say. You've never done this in your entire life, have you? I know that many of you won't relate to any of this at all because you firmly believe you would never choose this kind of awful and repugnant behavior.

Think about this question some more. What about you? Did you ever receive a tongue lashing like I did? Perhaps you thought you didn't deserve any of it. You were innocent as charged, right? Or maybe you agreed that you were as awful as your family claimed you were and instead of fighting back you spent your life repenting and trying to please father, mother and siblings alike. You accepted the labels and horrible names they called you because they all agreed so they must be right. You bought their pack of lies and succumbed to believe in their version of the truth. After all, they were your loving family trying to teach you a lesson or two about how to be a good human being. Pause for a moment and consider this. What if you were the good one all along? What if they were the damaged goods and you were fine? Perhaps your life story was a hideous case of psychological projection at its worst. They were teaming up and projecting their mental problems onto you. Wow, could that truly be the case? It sure could.

My mother and two brothers always believed they were innocent, completely sinless and the perpetual victims in our family drama. In truth they were all innocent victims at some point in their journey. They took their dose of abuse along the way, received their licks and learned how to become maliciously abusive too. As a young girl my mother was called horrible names and treated terribly by her close family relatives too. Does that surprise anyone? She grew up in complete dysfunction learning young how to gossip and speak evil about everyone she knew. She carried this dysfunctional behavior into her marriage and motherhood. The outcome? She grew into a bitter old woman who gossips incessantly, calls other people vicious names, blames everyone else for her problems, and clings to her two dysfunctional sons who can't make any ordinary life decisions without her involvement.

My mother grew up in a dysfunctional home and perpetuated this dysfunction in her own life. What goes around comes around and history often repeats itself until someone has the courage to stand up and declare "NO." I was the one lone ranger and family member who dared to say "NO." Many people will say right now that they've never harmed people the way my family harmed me and continue to harm each other. If so, they are ALL lying. You can continue to lie to yourselves and pretend you are guiltless, but you won't get away with any of these lies any longer. Hashem knows everything about you and nothing is concealed from Him. He shares every lurid detail with me when needed. If you try to lie your way out of your transgressions you will be exposed. It's time to fess up and recount the many people you have harmed throughout your lifetime. Trust me. There are many!

One more thing before we move on to marital bliss. If you agree that the transgressions my family is guilty of are abhorrent, you are correct. What you aren't yet aware of is that my mother and two brothers are the reincarnations of Torah nobility. Somewhere in the world, every day of the week, a religious Jew invokes one of their names from a previous lifetime in holy prayer. My mother and two brothers are reincarnations of three of the holiest names in the history of our world. Hashem deliberately surrounded His Shechinah with the best and most righteous souls in humanity. If this is how the best of the best make decisions and treat others, just imagine what you might be guilty of too. Be careful not to say anything to disparage them by denouncing their horrible behavior. Instead, realize that you are more than likely guiltier of even worse transgressions yourself. Instead of condemning them, pray for them like they are your own flesh and blood. Help them see what they have been unable to see for themselves so they may finally change their ways and heal. Do this for them, and pray very hard that others will do the same for you.

Round 2: Marital Bliss? NOT. Thank You GOD for My Divorce!

The first half of this book shared my personal story about my awakening which led to my divorce. As you read my story about my abusive husband, broken marriage and devastating divorce were you able to relate to my nightmare or put yourself in my shoes? Is your marriage hunky-dory? Well, good for you if it is and my sympathy to you if you've suffered like me. Divorce used to be a dirty word to me and completely unthinkable. When I finally received my freedom, I thanked God profusely for freeing me from bondage. For me, the institution of marriage was a death sentence. Let's take a deeper look now and see if any of these stories resonate in your life too. Perhaps you were a victim or the victimizer in your marriage. More than likely you were both. Remember, Hashem knows the truth. There is no better time than the present to fess up and admit your guilt.

Most people search tirelessly to find their special someone with whom to share their life. I wasn't different from other young women in that regard. When I met my husband, I was ready to settle down and get married. My decision to marry him was extremely well thought out. At least I thought that was the case. In hindsight there were questions I never asked him or myself. When I met my husband, I had been burned several times in previous relationships and even conned. Remember the shyster I spoke about earlier in this book? He stole thousands of dollars from me and wrecked my car. Having suffered plenty from this and other failed relationships I was no longer willing to marry someone out of feelings of pure lust or puppy love to say the least. I went through many years of dating and like many secular women, "knew" many different boys. I won't give any of them the honor of referring to them as men, because they weren't. In my opinion they were all boys not men, and they all personified the expression "Boys will be boys." Well, I had quite enough of boys so when I met my husband and he acted like a gentleman and treated me like a princess, I thought I found my prince. I was wrong.

He fit every detail of what I believed was critical when I made the most important decision of my life up until that moment. It was important to me that the future father of my children shared the same family values as me, but there was more. I wanted a man who would put me first ahead of his own needs, revere me as someone special and hold me high on a pedestal. In all my disappointing relationships it became clear that I was nothing more than a pincushion or chattel to the boys I had dated. Although many were consummate sweet talkers, it was clear their needs came ahead of mine. Instinctually I knew this narcissistic and selfish behavior was a prescription for marital disaster and failure in fatherhood. Finding a good father for my future children was non-negotiable.

Since at least half of all marriages fail, I wanted to stack the deck in my favor because I felt divorce wasn't an option and I refused to believe it would ever be something I needed. I was marrying someone for life and "till death do us part." To stack the deck in my favor I decided that I would only marry a Jewish man. Religion can be a divisive subject and when I dated non-Jews, anti-Semitism always reared its ugly head. In my previous relationships with Gentiles our religious differences always became a source of contention. Although I was Jewish, I wasn't the religious type so finding another Jew who wasn't religious either was pretty easy and the perfect solution. When I met my husband I immediately adored his parents. They were amazing, loving, and accepted me right away. Right from the beginning my former husband and I became the best of friends. When previous relationships were all about the sexual passion and weren't focused on pure love, the proverbial shoe always seemed to drop on my head. I'd find myself hurt in incomprehensible ways. I learned that passion needed to take a back seat to love and friendship.

In my experience, boys always seemed to have the wandering eye and were looking for something better to come along. I didn't want to marry anyone who had the capacity to stray, cheat on me or harm me in any way. Friendship for me was more important than fireworks. I believed in true love but passion and love together seemed unattainable. So, I married for pure love. That's not to say I didn't find my former husband attractive. It was just not animal lust that brought us together. It was the pure enjoyment of sharing time with each other that won me over. He was funny and warm and always brought me flowers on every single appropriate occasion. He was more thoughtful than any person I had ever known. At first, I thought it must be an act. I thought to myself "nobody is this thoughtful!" I waited for the shoe to drop again, but this time it seemed he would never disappoint me. He always showed up and was there for me when I needed him. He put me on that proverbial pedestal that no other boy had done before him.

So, we got married. We were blessed with every good fortune that young married couples desire. Money came easily to us and so did the birth of our three amazing children. Life brought us challenges but we seemed to weather every storm together. We worked together, we had our children, and we seemed to be the best of friends through it all. There were many issues that I turned a blind eye to over the years because I thought, "Hey, nobody is perfect." I took a lot of abuse not considering it to be abuse at all. Things like snide chauvinistic comments and jokes that many boys enjoy. The signs of this chauvinistic behavior appeared early but I ignored them. During the days of dating before marriage, he bought me a lovely necklace. I showed it to his mother at the dinner table at a restaurant and she complimented him on his good taste and his reply to her was, "Oh, that's what I get for all my bimbos." His mother was horrified and he laughed it off with my future brother-in-law who was also at the table. His sister's husband had a raw sense of humor so I shrugged off this nasty comment as my husband's way of trying to make his brother-in-law laugh. But that was just one small sign along the highway to hell.

When it came time to buy an engagement ring he sent me to his best friend's cousin in New York in the diamond district. He scheduled an appointment for me to go by myself to pick out a diamond and instructed me to, "Pick the biggest rock they show you. When someone looks at your ring I want them to see a big rock and think, 'Wow some guy really loves her!' " The belief that a big rock on my hand meant he loved me wasn't mine at all, but I knew that this was his philosophy of showing love. So, I listened and when the diamond dealer in New York showed me several pear-shaped diamonds spread out on velvet I did what he asked me to do. I chose the biggest one. After the appointment the diamond dealer called my future husband while I was with him to tell him the cost. He promptly turned white as a sheet like he had just seen a ghost. He hung up the phone and very angrily said, "What in the world did you choose!" I had never seen him angry before and I was completely stunned.

I choked back tears and replied, "I did what you told me to do. I don't know how much diamonds cost and I don't care about diamonds. Call the dealer back and tell her I don't want it!" He calmed down immediately and apologized. This was the precursor of many such arguments when he would realize he was being a cad, apologize profusely, and then manage to do the right thing in the aftermath. We picked up the ring on Valentine's Day of 1987. He kept staring at it saying how magnificent it was and was delighting in its sparkling beauty. For me the beautiful ring was already somewhat tarnished but it was a beautiful diamond that would receive many compliments over the years. The meaning behind this ring was further tarnished throughout our marriage when he would look at my engagement ring and joke that we could always sell it if we ran into financial trouble one day. The ring was nothing more than a trophy and financial instrument to my husband. It was never the symbol of love and commitment that an engagement ring is meant to be. I wonder now if my husband masqueraded as a gentleman to impress me enough to get married. The masquerade became clearer over the years, but sadly it took over two decades to recognize I married an impostor.

He graduated with a bachelor's degree from Northwestern University and went to law school in Boston. He was intelligent and witty. When I met him, he worked for a prestigious law firm in the World Trade Center and was quite proud of this along with his educational credentials. He often boasted about where he went to college in comparison to Fairleigh Dickinson nicknamed Fairleigh Ridiculous where I had gone. Privately he would tell me that he believed I was the smarter one but he didn't treat me that way in front of our children. Often, I became the butt of his jokes. I was also forced to keep his embarrassing secret throughout our marriage that he never passed the bar exam and was never a legitimate attorney. He worked for a prestigious law firm as an overpaid paralegal and carried around a large brown legal bag to make himself look and feel important at meetings. At these meetings I listened to him boast about all the cases he worked on as I sat silently and kept his secret that he wasn't an attorney at all. His being an attorney and his prestigious education meant absolutely nothing to me. I didn't marry him for his résumé, I married him for his loving heart. Touting his impressive résumé to anyone who would listen and keeping up the façade that he was someone important meant everything to him. So, I obliged and we kept his lies our dirty little secret. The masquerade continued for years.

I mentioned earlier that he had severe stomach issues from birth. As a result, he never grew to be a big muscular strapping man with large muscles like his father. His health issues stunted his growth and he was about five feet six inches tall and quite skinny. I cared nothing about how tall he was or how big his biceps were, but for him this was a great source of embarrassment. I was pint-sized myself and he was a few inches taller, so I thought everything was perfect. I never measured someone's value by the size of his or her body or body parts. Even before my awakening, I often speculated that God must have done this to him because if he had grown to be over six feet tall and a professional athlete he wouldn't have given someone like me a second look. I wasn't the typical trophy wife that narcissistic men choose so I believed God stunted his growth to humble him. I learned years later from Hashem that my hunch was 100 percent correct.

Eventually when I gave birth to our three children, he was overjoyed each time that he could produce such healthy children after he had poor health his entire life. Again, I sloughed this off as one of his childhood issues and thought it wasn't important, but I was wrong. His dysfunctional view of himself and the world was extremely important. Why was this an important issue? Because over the years he continuously placed great importance on everything in life that was external and was tormented by low self-esteem. While appearances and other people's opinions were so deeply important to him, these issues were irrelevant to me. The good opinion of other people rarely made it on my radar. One day I recall he was distraught and told me he was worried his children would one day be embarrassed of him because he was so small. I looked at him incredulously and said, "Why in the world would you think that way? Your children will love you for you, not for what you look like." His comments seemed completely insane and incomprehensible to me. Instead of his illogical thoughts and behaviors subsiding, the sickness and dysfunction worsened.

His low self-esteem, lack of an internal belief system, and focus on everything external in life became the rotting roots of our relationship. While I reached for self-help books to work on myself, he began to reach for psychological drugs to self-medicate. I reached for exercise and he lived vicariously through others and was addicted to watching professional sports. I worked at our business and invested my effort to earn a living, while he spent his days watching the stock market tickers as the arrows went up and down. Red arrows one day meant he was depressed and green arrows the next day made him happy. My tendency was to face problems head on and work through them but his personality trait was to avoid facing issues at all costs. When the stock market crashed on more than one occasion he refused to open the envelopes from the investment house because he didn't want to see the losses. When he felt physically sick, he preferred medication over a change in lifestyle or behavior. He seemed to enjoy being the perpetual patient and spoke about all his ailments because it brought him great sympathy. He masqueraded as the poor victim who just couldn't catch a break. We became increasingly incompatible over the years but this dysfunctional behavior was far more sinister than a sick man with low self-esteem. He became maniacally controlling and extremely abrasive.

My husband controlled all our finances and every dollar that we had between us. He kept all our important life documents under lock and key. It was his job to manage what he termed the "enormous amount of paperwork" for our family. Bill paying became his full-time job when it could have taken only an hour or two per month. Instead of using automated processes that are available to pay bills, he created a dysfunctional system of using credit to float our monthly bills instead of paying each bill in full and on time. We began incurring usury level interest rate charges on purchases like our weekly groceries. The food had been eaten long ago but we were paying for this food for years. Within less than 10 years of his crazy credit card scheme we accrued over $250,000 in credit card debt. This debt was a monster that began to choke us. On paper we still looked pretty good, with a net worth at one point of over two million dollars, but I knew his credit card game was a cancer that was growing quickly. I used to pray to God, before I called Him Hashem, and beg for His help to set our financial world right and clean up the hideous nightmare my husband had created. In his feeble way of thinking he told me that when I landed a big client he would pay it all off the following month. The clients and new business I brought in were never big enough and next month never seemed to come. I never seemed to earn what was needed to pay off this financial debacle. I didn't know that one day it would take my spiritual awakening to bring our house of cards crashing down.

When I began losing my hearing in 2001 I was deeply worried because I wanted to take care of my family. I feared that if I lost my health, I wouldn't be able to work and earn a living any longer. I still wasn't looking at the dysfunction in my husband and marriage in its entirety yet. The dangers we faced weren't merely a question of earning power. What truly caused our marriage to unravel was our lack of Jewish life and Torah observance. After I was awakened I desired a life devoted to God and Torah but my husband's desires were fixated on money.

Hashem took away my ears and opened my eyes. When I awoke with my eyes pinned open, I realized the person I had married and once considered my best friend was truly my prison warden. I lost my freedom and the ability to make decisions on my own behalf. He stole my identity right from beneath my Jewish nose. Once upon a time I thought I was his princess on a pedestal. I woke to find I was truly a jackass with a harness strapped on my back. Being his wife was a life of strife and the equivalent of modern day slavery.

My once doting husband who brought me flowers on every appropriate occasion was now leading the charge to brand me a psychopath having me repeatedly arrested, involuntarily committed and drugged. I was branded the mentally ill mama with delusions of grandeur as he pleaded with the doctors to drug these awful ideas and voices out of me. Some of you might pause and think that it's not possible for him to have convinced all those doctors to lock me up and drug me against my will. You are entitled to believe whatever floats your boat. I left my marital home in August of 2012 and no doctor has ever coerced me into a psychiatric commitment or told me I needed drugs since. That should give every intelligent person a reason to pause. After I left my husband's grip and control I spent many hours speaking with a leading and respected New Jersey psychiatrist who told me in his opinion I wasn't mentally ill, he would never medicate me, and he said I wasn't committable. So, what happened? Simply put, I woke up and my husband couldn't tolerate the light.

The light I reflected on him revealed his evil nature and sins that he was unwilling to face. He was more obsessed with money than concerned about what happened to me. As you've read earlier in his derisive emails and texts to me during our separation, I no longer was willing to be the jackass he could strap into a work harness to earn money for him. My lack of enthusiasm to earn money infuriated him to no end. He maliciously berated me and wanted to destroy me because he had lost control. The truth is he never truly had control over me but for years I was asleep at the wheel. Now that I had woken up, I wasn't playing patty cake with him any longer. He told me often that he loved me but I find it difficult to believe that anyone would do these things to someone they loved. Would you do this to someone you loved? Hashem says yes you would, and yes you do. If you felt your spouse was jeopardizing your precious bank account and taking "your" money from you, you all would lash out with great venom too.

You might love your spouse but if they wanted to part ways you would fight the fight and indignantly declare, "You're not going to take away what is mine!" Divorce has become the nasty little game of equitable distribution. In my divorce my husband believed after 26 years of marriage what was mine was his and what was his, was all his too. He assumed the role of the one who managed our money and manage our money he most certainly did. He had the support and help of family and friends to pull it all off and maintain his personal status of "preferred customer" at our bank while I was left financially destitute. My message to my former husband and all his dear family members who conspired to protect his little nest egg—nothing is truly yours. Everything we have is given to us by our Creator in the first place. It was your birthright former husband to give it all to your wife, the one you were supposed to love and cherish. You were supposed to look out for the best interest of the mother of your three children. Instead, you threw me to the curb and hoped I would die so that I wouldn't live to tell the truth. I can't say that I'm sorry to disappoint you. With the help of Hashem, I have lived to tell my story, my way.

Learned rabbis have written books teaching about the financial aspect of marriage. In Torah Law, the husband is commanded to take care of his wife and give her everything. Nobody truly follows this way of being, not even the rabbis. Your method of shielding yourselves, signing prenuptials and taking what is your fair share is a game I refuse to play. In this awful and selfish world, your method of covering your ass and protecting your fortune works well for you and you win. I clearly lost in this game of equitable distribution. Be forewarned divine retribution will see its day. In God's world, I won the keys to His kingdom. I chose God and I won. Materially I am flat broke. Spiritually I am the most blessed and prosperous soul in the universe. Baruch Hashem, thank you for saving my life through this much needed divorce. Choosing God was my life's destiny and I chose well. When my husband became monstrously controlling, destroyed my life and harmed me in more ways than are written in this book, I refused to fight about money and walked away in freedom. A few days before I walked out, I stood on the top of the stairs in my once beautiful marital home and Hashem said in His resounding voice, "Lori, take one last look. It's time to say goodbye." I left and never turned back. I chose to walk away and walk as one with Hashem God.

While money is a huge reason for many marriages to fail, my marriage was deeply broken on so many levels that money was the easiest thing for me to surrender. I never married for money so why would this become the centerpiece of my divorce? My personal safety had to come first. His monstrous, abusive and controlling behavior forced me to leave. After he orchestrated four involuntary commitments he was determined to have me committed again. If he had succeeded, without any exaggeration, it would have killed me. He masqueraded as the poor victimized husband who was saddled with a mentally ill wife. This was easy for him to do since his entire life was one big masquerade party. He carried his large brown legal bag everywhere he went pretending he was an attorney while also pretending to be my best friend. I married someone I thought was my best friend only to find out he was undoubtedly my worst enemy.

Earlier in this book I wrote about his abusive behavior which made my life with him unlivable. Most people never knew this hideous side of him and many found him to be a delightful gentleman. Others over the years saw through his façade immediately but they were fewer in number. As he waged his PR campaign to sway public opinion against me he told his version of the truth to my friends, relatives, business associates, neighbors, and even complete strangers throughout the community. It worked. One by one lifelong friends of over 30 years slowly distanced themselves from me and began to vanish from my life, a perfect segue to the next boxing round about friendship. Friend, what's that?

Round 3: BFF or FFB—Which One Are You?

Although I was relentlessly branded moody and too sensitive as a young child, eventually I grew up and learned how to find my smile. Many people along the way found me fun to be around and quite engaging. While I was never one of those "popular" people we all knew throughout high school, by the time I went to college I had tons of "friends." I loved my friends and they espoused to love me too. It was quite the love fest of friendship and many boyfriends along the way. Too many. I went the traditional secular way which included dating many boys. I was raised to believe that having boyfriends was a rite of passage. My parents never encouraged a promiscuous lifestyle but they didn't teach me about another choice or way of life either. So off I went from public school to college to experience sex, drugs and rock 'n' roll. My friends and I were having a ton of fun, so I thought. Many people in America go down this slippery slope of experimenting with pot, alcohol and sex. Waiting until marriage was thought to be stupid and old fashioned. Nobody waited until marriage anymore. That was something they did in the olden days and I was raised in the modern era.

When I arrived at college in the fall of 1977 I had kissed many boys but was still pure as the driven snow as they say, a virgin. Being a virgin wasn't considered a virtue in the late '70s but it seemed to be a prize for a boy to take it away from you. Living in the dorms at Fairleigh Dickinson University in Teaneck was one big party after another. At the end of my first semester I met my college beau who was an adorable Italian Catholic track star from Long Island. We had tons of fun together and he was the first boy who became my BFF, *Best Friend Forever*. Every time we were together we had sex. Isn't that what a young girl was supposed to do with her BFF boyfriend? No, it was not. Like many young women, I had to learn through the school of hard knocks and get used and abused a few times to figure that out. For at least three years my college beau and I were monogamous, or at least I was faithful to him. My mother and father accepted him with open arms even though he wasn't Jewish. He was a nice boy after all and we seemed to be in love. I thought we were in love because we said, "I love you" to each other all the time. That meant we loved each other, right? Wrong again. I loved him and while I know he had affection for me too, I don't believe he even knew what true love was back then. Maybe he figured this out with someone else along the way. I surely hope so for her sake.

Right through senior year we were having sex frequently on a regular basis. He did what most every boy did to me along the way. To avoid pregnancy he used the withdrawal method and ejaculated all over my stomach every time. Too much graphic info for you? Are you repulsed? You should be. Did you know that doing this is an abhorrent sin against God? You, like many people, thought this sin was relegated to masturbation only. You and everyone else are wrong. This was a filthy sin that he and many others did to me including my former husband throughout my life. I didn't know it was a sin either back then so I allowed him to use me like his toilet seat as he deposited his semen on me every time we were together. I found it foul and hated it, but I allowed this anyway for his benefit so he wouldn't have to use one of those nasty condoms that were so darn uncomfortable. After a few years he started to examine the semen on my belly after he was done and lamented once that I had never accidentally gotten pregnant after all these years. It wasn't that he desired a baby mind you. He was simply distraught at the thought that perhaps he was shooting blanks. He worried he might be infertile and this meant something dreadful about his virility. Oh dear, poor boy! I thought this was an odd comment for him to make but I let it go, like I learned to let many evil comments, behaviors and gestures go over the years. Remember the expression you all love, "Hey, nobody's perfect," right? That excuse won't cut it for anyone anymore. It's time to let that lame excuse go by the wayside.

By my senior year of college, although we were on-again, off-again boy-friend and girlfriend, we still saw each other often and had our regular sexual encounters. In the springtime something happened that had never occurred before. I missed a period. I panicked and called my Italian boyfriend and BFF and told him. Instead of being delighted that his semen might be virile after all, he panicked too. In his panic he avoided me at all costs. Wow! BFF no longer meant *Best Friend Forever.* My Italian Catholic college beau became the first of many betrayals who broke my heart. Instead of being my BFF in my life, he now became the first in a long line of boys in my lifetime who were none other than a *Filthy Foul Barbarian,* an FFB. He isn't the only one who earned this despicable title. By the end of our boxing match I will reveal how many FFBs there truly are in our disgraceful world.

Little did I know back in college that there would be so many more FFBs in my future. Back then they didn't have those over-the-counter easy-to-use pregnancy tests you could buy at the local pharmacy to find out immediately if you were pregnant. Instead I went to the campus gynecologist and he told me that he could give me a medication that would bring on my period if I wasn't pregnant. The caveat was that if I was pregnant the medication would damage the embryo and I would need an abortion. Through the grace of God, after taking this drug I began menstruating.

Good news traveled fast and my Italian beau found out through one of my friends that we had dodged the bullet. I wonder now if he might have been a wee bit disappointed that he didn't prove his manhood by impregnating me. Nonetheless he was extremely anxious to talk to me, perhaps because he wanted to get back in the saddle again and pick up where we left off. One day I left my dorm to go for a run and suddenly he appeared desperate to talk to me. "Hmm, now you want to talk to me?" I thought. I dismissed him and wouldn't stop running. He was a track star but I was in much better running shape on that propitious day. I told him if he had something to say to me he had better start running. He ran with me for a few minutes and couldn't keep up with my pace so he begged me to stop for a minute and talk. I stopped long enough to turn to him and look him squarely in the eyes and say, "You weren't around for me when I needed you. Now all is well and you're back? No thank you. I don't need fair-weather friends." With that, I ran off and left him standing there. Did he feel bad? I never waited around to find out.

Throughout my four years at FDU my friends and I enjoyed a boatload of college fun. We partied regularly, smoked pot, got drunk at the college pub, drove across the George Washington bridge into Chinatown at 2 AM for Chinese food and shared many hilarious times to be included in our memoirs. Back then I didn't realize that God Himself was shielding me from consequences of these dangerous choices so I could live to write about them here in my first book. Many young people aren't as fortunate. Thank you for protecting me Hashem, I am deeply grateful!

There were a few special friends who I was closest to over the years. One of these special friends was a childhood BFF who dated back to when I was just seven years old and living in Jackson, New Jersey. She was a shiksa, non-Jewish girl, and I was Jewish but that subject along with any discussion about God never came up. When I went to college at FDU she decided to enroll there too. We lived together our senior year and I introduced her to many of my "friends." One of my former roommates had a sister who managed a fast food chain in Teaneck and my childhood best friend went to work there for her. A year later after I graduated from college, I was told that when she went to work she complained incessantly about me and called me and another roommate vicious names. Best friends? I'd say no, wouldn't you? She transformed from BFF to FFB, a *Filthy Foul Barbarian*. Although she broke my heart by speaking evil about me I didn't get angry with her at all. Back then I never had one harsh word to say about anyone including people in my life who continually hurt me. Name-calling was never my thing and I never spoke evil about anyone or held a grudge. The worst I would do is cry and walk away. In this case I simply felt I had my heart broken by my former BFF.

My heart hadn't been broken repeatedly yet in 1981 so I wasn't ready to create this new and awful title of FFB or brand her one. This new and awful term was created while writing this portion of my first book. While I didn't know of such terms back then, I felt betrayed and knew she most certainly wasn't my BFF any longer. After graduation she became engaged to be married and sent me an invitation which I ignored. I waited for her phone call which I knew would eventually come. When she called we caught up for a few minutes and then she asked if I was coming to her wedding. I told her that I not only wouldn't be coming but it was time for us to part ways. I told her that I knew how she spoke evil about me and I believed that friends simply don't do that.

I wished her all the best that life had to offer and explained that this kind of betrayal wasn't something I would tolerate in my life. Several years passed. She became a mother and was pregnant with her second child when she sent me a tear-soaked letter of apology and begged for my forgiveness. After reading her letter, I forgave her and we became BFFs once again. For many years we shared happy occasions, fun and friendship and then she decided she would show her true colors and join the ranks of the FFBs once again.

Earlier I revealed other stories about this woman. She is the same former BFF who ran the NYC marathon with me in 2008 and the same BFF who met me in the restaurant after my awakening and thought I had clearly lost my mind. She stood staunchly by my side even after she thought I was nuts. That's what good friends do, don't they? No that's not what they do. Best friends dig deeper to find out the truth. They spend hours digging and do whatever it takes to understand what is going on inside of you. She didn't do any of that but to her credit she turned the other cheek as they say in Christianity and stayed in touch with me anyway. She put up with my ridiculous assertion that I could hear God and the spirit world and ignored what she thought was unbelievable. We stayed in touch long enough for her to Run on Love in a few events that I organized and she helped raise money for a family in need. Then the shoe dropped once again and she revealed she most definitely was never my BFF. It was now clear that she was always truly a bona fide FFB in the making.

The shoe dropped when I introduced her to the Race Director of the NJ Marathon. Running on Love was a charity that supplied volunteers on race weekend and in return my charity received a generous donation. I always requested the finish line for my volunteers but my once childhood BFF told the race director that she would take full responsibility for the food concession. When she did this I thanked her profusely because I believed she was stepping up to volunteer her time and effort to help my fledgling charity. Wow, what a friend right? Wrong. She turned the entire volunteer engagement into a boon for her job. On race day I saw the goody bags emblazoned with her workplace logo. She negotiated with the race director to give HER more perks for HER hard work. She told me later she volunteered to do this gig because as she said, "You know Lori, it's all about who you know. You never know who can help you down the road. What goes around comes around." That wasn't the clincher that destroyed our friendship. The clincher came when I didn't receive any donation money from the NJ Marathon and kept calling her to find out why. She was clearly miffed at me because after all she did all the heavy lifting. Why should Running on Love receive anything? She finally fessed up and told me that her volunteers chose to send the donation money elsewhere. What a nice friend. Don't you wish you had a BFF like her? I'm positive that you do. Running on Love eventually did receive a small token donation from the marathon. I don't know the true reason why we received anything that season, but I did have an extremely warm relationship with the race director. The amount we finally received was irrelevant. My former BFF's decision to make her volunteer effort self-serving and to the detriment of my fledgling charity was deeply sickening. Conversely she was clearly incensed that I made any of this an issue. We no longer speak. Surprised?

Onward and upward, I had other dear loving friends and BFFs along the way. Another childhood friend I have known since I was 12 years old, attended the same college and roomed with me briefly. Over the years she often told me that she loved me. She was the dear friend that I called for help in the middle of the night during lockup number three, the worst of the four trips to mental hospital hell. While I realize the phone call that night would have shaken anyone to their core, a true friend would have stayed true. She didn't. After I got out of that debacle, the calls to my home abruptly stopped. Invitations to her home and family get-togethers ceased. I was conspicuously left out of the candle lighting ceremony while all her other friends received the honor at her son's Bar Mitzvah. After many years of joining her for girlfriends' weekend trips to Rehoboth Beach, Delaware, I was no longer invited. Apparently, I was considered tainted goods now. I was the psychotic friend and mental patient who was too dangerous to socialize with any longer. She broke my heart repeatedly as my life unraveled. This may not bring tears to your eyes, but please excuse me while I run to the bathroom right now for tissues.

Despite my heartbreak, I still tried to reach out to her anyway. Prior to leaving my marriage, I called her once at Passover to wish her a happy holiday and she briskly rushed me off the phone. Years later after I pulled myself up by my bootstraps with only the help of Hashem, divorced my once upon a time BFF husband, and legally changed my name to Lori Michelle, I posted on my personal Facebook page that I now had a new last name. At the time, I had over 500 Facebook "friends." She was one of them. Did she notice that I had a new last name? Well maybe, but she didn't bother to call me to see how I was doing after divorcing my husband of 26 years. Instead of calling it quits on our lifelong friendship, I called her. Once again, she was busy and on her way to see colleges with her family. You know, the old college road trip. She pretended to be so happy to hear from me as I informed her that I was now divorced. She said she had to go and couldn't talk but she would DEFINITELY call me. The call never came. I didn't disconnect from her on Facebook, thinking I would leave the door open but she never knocked. The best she could manage was to give her thumbs up once in a blue moon on nice pictures of me and my kids. When I posted pictures, she found the gumption to make appropriate comments as though she was showing the world that she was a warm and loving BFF. It was painfully clear she wasn't a BFF—she officially joined the ranks of the hideous and heartless club of FFBs.

My Christian BFF that I've spoken about many times in this book is one of my most painful losses of all. We used to speak daily when I was in America which was reduced to once a week after I moved to Israel. Now we no longer speak to each other at all. She might believe that she has been giving me space to finish this book and prepare to release this to the world. I asked for this space because of how she repeatedly chose herself and her own welfare over our friendship. Her history of self-centered choices in all her relationships became untenable to me and our weekly talks left me feeling heartbroken and unable to work. I asked for space because I found our discussions emotionally and spiritually draining.

She like many other people who believe in God, outwardly espouses to love Him. You all play what I now refer to as the "God game." It was clear she was playing this game when I spoke to her because she prays to God daily and gives to charity but only when the mood strikes her. Every decision is well thought out and calculated so that she never overextends her good will or inconveniences herself. Her thoughts are always centered around "What is best for ME." She, like many of you, believes she is a good Christian bringing only goodness into our world. What she doesn't recognize is that when it came time to choose God she always chose herself and her own self-interest every time without exception. It looked outwardly like she was being respectful and reverent to God, but she was choosing to be selfish each time.

She told me she supported me over the years and espoused to believe in my gift of hearing God but when I needed her most she abandoned me repeatedly. She often asked me for advice from God, which I gladly gave without reservation. After receiving His advice, she promptly thumbed her nose at every word I shared and chose to do the opposite. In recent years, she often expressed her excitement that one day she fully expected the trumpets would blare connoting the arrival of the Messiah and she would be my BFF standing right by my side. She always said the words, "I've got your back Lori!" but when I called her for help she readily told me it was too difficult or inconvenient. Our friendship was always about her well-being and her self-interest first. When push came to shove she was never truly there to support me.

Often, she boasted that she was right by my side from the beginning and knew every detail of my spiritual awakening and journey with Hashem because she lived through everything with me. The truth be known, she was never truly there for me and abandoned me repeatedly when she was challenged. Once she admitted to me in a phone conversation that she found it hard to talk to me because I made her feel bad about herself. She prided herself on being the exemplary mother, daughter, sister, wife, and citizen who revered and loved God. When she pondered giving to charity she told me she was very thoughtful and deliberate where she chose to donate her money. When she thought I was about to succeed in my work with Running on Love she donated regularly and told me she desired to one day travel the world with me and work for God's charity. When it became clear that it would be a long hard road and perhaps those trumpets weren't going to blare, she withdrew her support from God's charity for world peace. It became evident that if she wasn't going to get that prestigious dream job working and traveling the world for God and His Messiah then she wouldn't waste her money or her time.

Recently she gave a donation to Running on Love when I ran a half marathon in Jerusalem for world peace. Bravo friend! Truly, it is to your credit that you came back for a moment after a long absence and chose to be supportive. What is to your embarrassment is that I had to ask you. Why must I ask a friend of more than thirty years to support my life's work? Especially when you were someone who declared repeatedly over the years that you fully believed in me and my gift of hearing Hashem. Did you believe in me or were you getting some vicarious thrill out of listening to my many God stories? Was your support about filling a need in yourself or because you believed in my work?

As you read about my former Christian girlfriend BFF, open your eyes and recognize that you are looking at yourself in a spiritual mirror. She is like every person in this world without exception, choosing to satisfy something in herself and being completely self-serving. When you give, you always have YOUR reasons why. If you dig deeply enough and are brave enough to be honest with yourself you will find this is true. All of you think that you are beautifully generous and consistently choosing goodness and God in every moment but you are not. Like my mother, brothers, and former husband, my former Christian BFF had her own personal welfare and pocketbook front and center when she made decisions. Her personal welfare always took precedence over the welfare of others. Her motto is your motto, "It's me first and everyone else must get in line." Deny it and scream out loud that I'm so unfair, but all of you are wrong. I'm not being unfair at all, I am being truthful. It simply depends on the moment in time. In one moment you are all able to be the sparkling godly light that delights me and makes me cry tears of joy but it's temporary and short-lived. A moment later you're up to your old tricks again and up to your necks in self-centeredness becoming the new brand of FFB that I so despise. If I wait long enough I watch every one of you become an FFB in absolute horror.

My former Christian girlfriend BFF is a deeply beautiful soul, and she has the potential to be one of the greatest human beings to walk this earth but her choices continue to be deeply selfish and purely evil. She admits to only watching my Running on Love with God video programs when she finds the time. This admission comes after telling me repeatedly for years that she knows I speak to our Creator. It's just not important enough to her to know what God expects from her. As I wrote earlier she once said, "I have a full life with a husband and family Lori and can't afford to work on this like you do." Then she reminded me that I don't have anyone in my life who takes up my time. So, in her mind, I should spend my days and nights to save her and all of you while everyone lollygags around the world in their busy little suburban lives. That's what you all believe isn't it? Messiah or Moshiach will arrive one day soon and you won't have to lift one damn finger. Moshiach will save the day for all of you. Wrong again. Attitudes like hers and yours will doom us all to perish.

My one last BFF in the world is still in my life and supporting me. She is the lone ranger and last friend standing. She works on world peace with me and donates to support my effort. She does all of this on her own volition. If it weren't for her and her husband I would be doing this completely on my own with Hashem. We need everyone to step up to the plate like her and her husband if we are to have any prayer of healing our world. While I love and appreciate their support and they are going above and beyond anyone I know, they have much work to do too. Imagine, these two people are not yet welcomed into God's world to come. Why? Because Hashem demands perfection. He will not tolerate one transgression from any person on earth any longer. Is this too steep a price to pay for world peace? No. If we have evil in our world, there will never be peace on earth for anyone.

Round 4: God Made The Model, Don't Break It.

Sexual promiscuity is prevalent among young and old people all over the world. The secular world glorifies casual sex and created the terminology *friends with benefits*. Many young women growing up in the "friends with benefits" era, accepted the idea that casual sex with multiple partners was appropriate and part of their rite of passage. Eventually many women realized they were used and abused by their male partners and learned the hard way that this lifestyle provided no benefits to them at all. Sadly, some women never learn this and continue the folly of giving up their bodies in the hope of finding true love. The expression "why buy the cow when milk is so cheap" was scoffed at and ridiculed by young sexually active girls who dismissed these comments as chauvinistic and belittling to woman. They believed these nasty comments were coming from the "crazy" religious fundamentalists and therefore they promptly ignored them. The traditional old-fashioned model of waiting until marriage to engage in sexual intercourse was shattered in the '60s. After the bra burning era and the women's liberation movement in the '70s, only crazy religious zealots bothered to read the Torah/Bible, praise God and/or wait until marriage to engage in sexual relations. Kudos to the ultra-religious but here is a news flash for you too. Many ultra-religious people are guilty of breaking God's model for a loving marriage and family too. Et tu Brute? Yes, you are guilty too.

Breaking God's model has brought us numerous repulsive sexually transmitted diseases (STDs), some of which are deadly. The diseases that don't kill you can simply destroy your life. We have a plethora of sexually transmitted diseases running rampant around the world and the gynecologists and physicians are now teaming together to insist that young people become vaccinated for many of these STDs. Instead of revisiting the old-fashioned way of life and encouraging everyone to abstain from sex until marriage, they all agree that being sexually active at a young age is the new normal. Why bother to fight it? Secular society believes we need to forget about old-fashioned values like chastity because we no longer live in the dark ages. The opposite is true. Sleeping around with multiple partners and young women and girls being used like pincushions is encouraging them to live in obscene darkness. Perhaps if everyone had listened to Hashem and followed His rules all along, young people who now suffer from incurable STDs and struggle with infertility could have avoided these tragic outcomes. We will never know, but maybe we can change the outcome for future generations. Heterosexual promiscuity isn't the only serious problem we are facing. Human sexuality in today's world looks more like an Alfred Hitchcock horror movie or a Shakespearean tragedy than the supreme blessing and gift from God it was meant to be.

Governments around the world have made homosexual marriage the legitimate equivalent to holy matrimony between a man and woman. Do your legislators know better than your Creator? Naturally they don't but they pompously behave like they do. You are now able to change your gender surgically—lop off your penis at will and trade it in for a vagina if you believe God made a mistake. The reality is that most people who choose to surgically change their gender prove by their actions that they don't truly believe in God anyway. Won't they be surprised one day when they find out Hashem is real and they are answerable for every action. These unsuspecting people who believe they have a right to change their gender at will have bought into the idea that they are only here on earth for a set number of years and it's their unalienable right to pursue happiness. After all, America's Founding Fathers said so, so it's their freedom to choose what they desire to do with their own body and nobody has the right to discriminate against them. It's illegal now to proclaim your religious beliefs to someone who is homosexual or transgender if it offends them and makes them feel uncomfortable. There can be legal ramifications if we make them feel bad about themselves. Being compassionate toward a transgender person now means you may not discriminate against people who believe they were born in the wrong bodies and you must support their choices.

Supporting somebody's choice to change their gender is supporting a heinous crime against God therefore religious people who know God is judging their actions are being coerced to sin. What should they do? Please the courts or please God Himself? Additionally, by forcing them to compromise their religious beliefs, they're suddenly losing their freedom of religion which was guaranteed in the Constitution of the United States of America. Frequently governments spend taxpayer dollars for gender reassignment surgeries which means religious people are forced to enable people to sin while paying for it too. Governments making laws that break God's commandments are clearly causing everyone to go to war with each other.

Homosexuals all over the world have been given the legal right to marry someone of the same gender. Inventing new family models, same sex marriages, and families with two mommies or two daddies are now in vogue. Legislators and public leaders of all kinds have determined that showing compassion for homosexuals and transgender people means not discriminating against anyone who chooses an alternate lifestyle from the traditional biblical model. They have defined compassion to mean never criticizing these atypical choices or speaking publicly about your religious beliefs on this topic. We are required to be all-inclusive and provide homosexuals and/or transgender couples and their families goods and services at their discretion. For example, if you are a caterer who doesn't want to provide catering services to a homosexual wedding you might be sued. Some states in America have enacted anti-discrimination laws in which it is unlawful to refuse to provide services to a homosexual or trans-gender couple. Honoring and observing God's laws is becoming quite difficult in this compassionate world, don't you agree? Strangely, God isn't the model for compassion any more.

Being compassionate and loving your neighbor as yourself is a commandment from our Creator. Hashem is the model for compassion, not us. Being compassionate and loving to your neighbor doesn't mean enabling others to sin in the eyes of God. The pope, other religious leaders and politicians continue to skirt this issue when asked their opinions regarding the Lesbian Gay Bisexual Transgender movement. They refuse to take a clear stand when asked if they believe homosexuality is sinful or if any of these choices are perverted. Religious leaders and politicians often refuse to answer these questions directly for fear they might ruffle feathers and lose their popularity by stating the truth. Perhaps they've even buckled under the pressure and now agree with the LGBT movement and are willing to reinterpret the Bible and make everyone's choices okay. It's all good, I'm okay, and you're okay just the way you are, right? Wrong!

We all desire compassion and want to be compassionate to others. What we must come to grips with is that our compassion must never enable others to slip further away from God or into sin. You can be compassionate by listening to your loved one as they express their feelings and respond with love, but never accept homosexuality or sexually deviant behavior as a valid life choice. Accepting your loved one's homosexuality as just another lifestyle choice is to their ultimate detriment and will harm them. It is important for everyone to understand that homosexual emotions are genuine and heartfelt. People have homosexual desires but it's only a sin when they choose to act on them. It is important to help everyone learn that these sexual inclinations come from your soul not your body, they do exist, and you are in peril if you act on them.

The only pathway to true joy and fulfillment is through God's laws and living according to His plan. His laws and decrees aren't prejudicial or against any homosexual person. On the contrary, His decrees are for the welfare and well-being of all His children. Supporting or choosing anything that deviates from His laws is dangerous to you and/or the person you love. Instead of supporting someone's homosexual or sexually deviant choice, listen with compassion and help them understand that these choices put them in peril.

Senate confirmation hearings were televised recently here in Israel. When I turned on the TV, I watched Cory Booker a senator from New Jersey, angrily grill Representative Mike Pompeo, the nominee for Secretary of State. He asked Mike Pompeo pointed questions about his past statements where he was quoted as saying that homosexuality was a perversion. As Senator Booker asked these questions it was clear he was playing the "I gotcha" game with Representative Pompeo. Cory Booker said that statements like these were bigoted and if Mike Pompeo believed that homosexuality was a perversion, that made him completely unfit to be Secretary of State.

I like Cory Booker and I recall voting for him when I lived in New Jersey. I found him to be an eloquent speaker and agree with him that discrimination is purely evil. Having said this, I must inform Senator Booker in this instance he is wrong. He needs to wake up now and understand that like discrimination, homosexuality is also a form of evil in the eyes of God Himself and it is undoubtedly a sexual perversion. Mike Pompeo skirted the issue, refused to answer this question directly and avoided giving his true opinion. Politicians might refuse to state their true opinion on this matter but I won't skirt any issue. I must bluntly tell you the truth where others fear to speak out. If I'm not direct and blunt, I harm you. I refuse to harm a soul. If I don't help you understand the truth, I fear for your safety.

Putting it even more bluntly, the legalization of homosexual marriage and defending the transgender movement are atrocities and abominations in the eyes of God. If you truly believe in God, the concept of homosexual marriage or surgically changing your gender would make you quiver and want to vomit. The mere idea of acting upon a homosexual inclination would not only horrify you, but condoning and accepting others who make these choices would sicken you. The reason that condoning homosexual behavior or sexual deviation of any kind would sicken a God-fearing person is not because they personally find these behaviors repulsive. People who truly know God is real and understand His laws, refuse to condone this behavior out of pure love and compassion, not out of hatred or repulsion. They understand that encouraging others to sin against God is escorting them to damnation. Damnation truly exists children of the world. Wake up to this realization now before you harm someone you love further. You are not doing anyone a favor by encouraging them to sin against God. Quite the contrary, you are guilty of a malicious and hideous crime yourselves.

Why is engaging in homosexuality or encouraging others to be homosexual frighteningly abhorrent? The answer: WE ARE NOT OUR BODIES. We are spirit and a microcosm of God Himself. Our true nature and essence is spirit not animal. When you choose your body over your soul, you are choosing your own physical satisfaction over God Himself. This is idol worship in its rawest form. You weren't placed here on earth to become an animal and engage in sex games that make your genitals superior to your intellect. You were placed here as a member of Hashem's family with the supreme gift of physicality to enjoy your journey here in a manner which God Himself would enjoy. Prior to our incarnation, we all made a covenant and vow to God Himself to honor His commandments, bring godliness into this world through our actions, and never to engage in any form of sexual deviation. This goes for Jews and Gentiles. Hashem always places us in the right body for the express purpose of learning and elevating our souls. It isn't your life's purpose to gratify your flesh or find satisfaction in any manner you desire.

Men and woman are two puzzle pieces that were designed to fit together perfectly in divine order. Choosing another form of sexual intimacy or gratification is willfully breaking your covenant with God. Some people believe that God Himself is angered by sexually deviant behavior because it's a repulsion to Him. This is untrue and is a psychological projection of their own opinions regarding perverted behavior. God is angered when people choose to break this covenant and His laws because it harms them and all the people of the world. While sexual deviation is repugnant and repulsive behavior in the eyes of our Creator, He is only angered because it is harmful to His children. His anger is never self-serving or selfish. Self-righteous indignation is the machination of human beings alone. He desires what is best for every person on earth without exception. When people choose to sin by becoming homosexual or engaging in any sexually deviant behavior they harm themselves and everyone around them. You may believe that homosexuality isn't a choice but that is incorrect. All people are born with inclinations but they are required to choose according to God's laws. Inclinations don't exonerate you and you are not born homosexual. Sexuality is always a choice. In the event that you still don't see homosexuality as a sin, I will hit you with the truth even harder. Brace yourself now for a heavy dose of the truth.

A man willfully choosing to put his penis where another man defecates is pure evil. If Hashem God desired men to have sex with other men, He would have made it possible for a man to defecate a newborn baby from his anus. Gross, vulgar and disgusting, right? Yes, it is all that and much worse. We all know that it isn't possible for a man to procreate with another man or two females to have a baby by themselves but you all desired to have your way, and worked tirelessly to figure out a solution that satisfies you. You have decided that you are the most important one in the world and your joy comes first. You believe it is your personal right to enjoy happiness and that your happiness will come from doing everything you desire. Some of you already joyously believe that fellow geniuses have cracked the code to procreation just for your benefit. I've seen nightmarish videos on YouTube with bearded women who look like men deciding to go to the sperm bank to be impregnated to have a baby with their lesbian lover. The scientists can play around with petri dishes and implant embryos where they don't belong, but it doesn't make the scientist a god. Thank God! The mere attempt to change Hashem's beautiful model for marriage and family makes their perverted choices an abomination in the eyes of our loving Creator. Be forewarned, homosexuality and sexual perversion are evil and those who choose this behavior will be banished from His Kingdom and the world to come. Are you still unconvinced that homosexuality is wrong? Perhaps you're sneering at me in anger. Keep reading and learning for your benefit and the benefit of everyone you love.

If my description of homosexuality sounds foul and disturbing to you, good. It should be very disturbing. Your reaction shouldn't be anger towards me for bluntly describing the truth. The truth will save you from unthinkable pain when you leave this physical plane and you are hopefully invited to face the heavenly court. Some of you won't even be given that honor because you are deemed not savable! Saving you from yourselves is my primary goal so I will continue with my rant and hope to make a dent in your illogical thinking. I hope to wake you up to the truth that your new slogan "It's all love" is a feel-good lie and you must learn that families don't come in any form that you desire. The model for love, marriage and family was created by the One true ultimate Love, Hashem God. He created you, your vessel and gave us an instruction manual detailing how you were sent here to emulate Him. You don't have the authority to make up the rules as you go. When you do this, you look like the hideous perversions we are witnessing around the world where people no longer resemble healthy human beings. It should be no surprise to anyone that the suicide rate among transgender people is higher than the rest of the population. Joy comes from emulating our Creator, not from living in the moment and striving to achieve your perpetual orgasm. Orgasms are extra. You don't need an orgasm. You need to learn how to live a blessed life as Hashem intended. When you learn the truth and obey His laws you will find the eternal euphoria that you've been searching for your entire life.

People made it socially acceptable for Bruce Jenner to transform himself into Caitlyn and applauded his decision. They did this out of love and compassion for him but was this truly for his good? No, of course not! In everyone's heartfelt desire to show him love and acceptance, they greased the slippery slope for him to slide straight to damnation. Even for people like Bruce, it's not too late. He can return to God and should do so immediately. He and everyone else must wake up and heed this call. I have two wonderful homosexual friends whom I love dearly who thus far have refused to listen to my advice to refrain from homosexual behavior. If they don't walk away from their homosexual life to walk with God, they will be banished from our world or face even worse.

Everyone must recognize who they truly are and become the lights of God they were sent here to be. Please learn that you face far worse things than death if you don't listen and learn how to live a blessed life on earth now. The idea that our world will be void of these beautiful people whom I love is too painful for me to contemplate. If you know and love someone who is homosexual or transgender imagine for a moment the world without them. I refuse. They must wake up to the realization that they are NOT THEIR BODIES. Before being born as a man or woman, they promised God Himself they would never make these perverted choices. Yes, prior to being born into your current life you all willfully chose your gender with the help of our Creator and promised to live a blessed and God driven life. When you choose to be part of the LGBT movement or support it in any way you have broken your promise to God.

Some may find this impossible to believe but it is the truth. Before a soul becomes incarnate they are prepared with a life plan to work on themselves and ascend spiritually. As we reincarnate we work on shortcomings that need to be healed and once we learn our lessons our souls become elevated and more like our Creator. Like our Creator and His Shechinah, every soul has a gender and this information is part of the life plan created for every child of God before they enter the physical world.

Here is a relatable hypothetical example of how this works. A male soul may have incarnated repeatedly and in each incarnation he abused women making them his chattel. Armed with this important soul information, Hashem devises a plan to heal this male soul and rid him of this abhorrent behavior of harming women. In his next incarnation, this male gendered soul agrees to incarnate as a woman and makes a holy covenant with Hashem that he will journey as a woman and correct all previous incarnations he lived as a man. This male soul then is born into this world as a woman who chooses to be a lesbian. Oh no! She forgot her promise and instead of living a blessed life as a woman who loves men, she chooses her vessel instead. As a lesbian she marries a woman and has sexual relationships with many women just as she did when she incarnated as an abusive man. She not only hasn't learned and accomplished anything in this lifetime that she was sent here to learn, she has committed an egregious sin by breaking her covenant with God. She chose her vessel, her inclinations and desires over bringing godliness into this world. Many magnificent souls are choosing to be homosexual which puts them on a fast track to damnation. Are you able to feel the pain of their decisions? I pray for them all the time.

One more thing. For all the religious righteous ones who might celebrate this diatribe about homosexuality and sexual deviation, celebrate for the right reasons. Please recognize this isn't about you or your preferences whatsoever. This is about God and saving His children. This diatribe is necessary to save our human family and wake everyone up to the truth. I'm wrought with raw emotion right now thinking of our world without the light of love of beautiful people like Elton John and Melissa Etheridge, well-known homosexuals who delight us with their music. I enjoy their magnificent music Friday afternoons as I prepare my Shabbos meals. While my home is filled with their beautiful voices I cry and I pray for them both that one day they will listen and heed the call. I imagine that maybe one day Elton and Melissa will marry each other in holy matrimony. Crazy? Yeah, I've been called that before. I can dream a beautiful dream and hope a holy matrimonial union is in their future. Melissa and Elton happen to be two of my favorite musicians but there are millions of people we might lose. Dear Hashem, please help me wake all of them up so that we don't lose one! Just the inkling that beautiful people like them might refuse this calling makes me fall on my face and weep uncontrollably. Think of all the amazing people in our world whom we all love so deeply who are homosexuals or who are choosing sexually deviant lifestyles. We must help everyone wake up now, learn the truth and return to the ways of Hashem God.

Round 5: #MeToo Must Become #IchooseGOD

The #MeToo movement has been front and center all over America as women finally found the courage to call out the men who sexually harassed, abused, molested and discriminated against them over the years. Men aren't safe anymore to be part of the Old Boys' Club or use the excuse of "boys will be boys." While I applaud the many victims of sexual molestation, rape and harassment both male and female who are courageously coming forward, it's imperative to understand why sexual abuse is rampant. This awful behavior won't stop until we wake up and stop participating in the madness we are witnessing. While I wouldn't want to harm a victim further by placing any blame on them, we must look inwardly and admit any culpability. When society walked away from observing God's laws and created its own new rules, we all helped create this unmitigated nightmare. Ultimately, everyone is guilty of #MeToo.

I was born in 1959 to Jewish parents who didn't learn Torah or dedicate themselves to bring God, Torah law and education into our home. If you're of another faith and think that has nothing to do with you, you are mistaken. The only religious doctrine that exists in our world written completely by our Creator is the Torah. While mankind has created many religious doctrines from the Torah and changed its contents, His Torah remains pure and unchanged. Hashem's instructions included His rules regarding marriage, sexual relations, family and modesty. All His laws were thrown out the window in the pursuit of happiness. If it makes you happy, go for it, right? No, this thinking is completely wrong.

I came of age in the '70s when the sexual revolution was coming into full swing. My parents who were secular ham and cheese eating Jews, said nothing to me about my manner of dress. I wore hot pants and midriff tops in public showing my flesh from the time I hit puberty. Many secular people still think it's A-OK to dress in revealing clothing like this, even for young vulnerable little girls. Allow me to share a few of my stories to shed light on where hot pants, midriff tops and not being properly taught God's laws of morality can lead a young girl. My stories will help reveal that it isn't just the boys who are guilty of #MeToo. EVERYONE is guilty.

I began menstruating at 10 years old. I wasn't told about menstruation by anyone up until the moment when I went to the bathroom and saw blood in my underwear. "Oh My God! I'm dying!!!" so I thought. I ran to my mother to show her and the first thing she did was slap me in the face. Cute, right? Some of you might know that this is an old tradition or superstition that was passed down for generations. I declare to all of you, this was my first sample of #MeToo from mommy. Go ahead and make lame excuses that she didn't know any better and her mommy did the same thing to her. I already warned you lame excuses won't work any longer. After being slapped in the face, I was told I would be treated to a day off from school. Wow, first I'm slapped and then I'm rewarded. Confusing don't you think? Life went on, and my young female body began to develop as I headed down the road to more confusion.

One day, while exercising in fifth grade gym class, a girl whispered to me that I needed a bra. Her gentle way of delivering this news was well-intended and I appreciated her discreet comment. When I went home and asked my mother to go bra shopping to avoid further embarrassment in gym class, she told me my breasts were too small for a bra and ignored my request. Then it happened again.

A teenage boy on a bicycle made a lewd gesture about my developing breasts and I ran home crying. I ran into the house, went downstairs and hid in the basement hoping nobody would find me but I was grateful that my dad saw me and came running after me. Through my tears I told him what happened. The next thing I remember was bra shopping with mom. I was grateful for my new bra and proud of my new figure as any young girl should be. Then it happened again.

My fifth-grade teacher suspected I received my new womanly undergarment. I watched her in horror as she made a beeline toward me in class. She stood behind my chair, took her fingers and ran them down my back over my bra strap to let me know that she knew exactly what I had under my clothes, growing breasts. At just 10 years old I was reduced to my body parts not just by the boys, but by grown women too. My breasts were something that evoked whispers, sexual gestures, were ridiculed for being too small and unworthy of a bra, and then my bra was used to embarrass me through my teacher's crude insensitivity. Like most women, I've endured a lifetime of comments about my body which were used to objectify, diminish and define me. Instead of listening to any of their rude comments or criticism, I chose to appreciate my breasts. Strong kid huh? Eventually I nursed all three of my babies and have always considered my breasts a gift from Hashem God. This was just the beginning of my rude awakening to how women are repeatedly objectified and abused by everyone, including other women.

While the #MeToo abuses I received from women were hurtful, the abuses from men were criminal. When I was 14 years old I had the mind of a child but the body of an 18-year-old and quite a nice body too. One evening my father's 46-year-old cousin visited us. This cousin was a wealthy businessman who owned a ranch with horses in Malibu, California where he lived with his wife and two children. He and his wife invited me to come stay with them for a long visit over the summer. It should have been curious to my parents that they invited me without my brother who was less than two years older, but the invitation was for me alone. My parents accepted under the condition that my favorite aunt, my father's 36-year-old younger sister, would meet me there and be my chaperone. Off I went to sunny California for a summer of fun. When I first arrived, I was extremely shy and didn't talk much. I spent most of my time horseback riding with their two children who were a little younger than me. We had a great time and eventually my favorite aunt arrived to look out for my best interests.

One evening my aunt and I went out for a night of fun with our Malibu host, her first cousin who was officially my second cousin. My aunt thought it was hilarious when our host gave me Stolichnaya, Russian vodka, and proceeded to get her 14-year-old niece blasted drunk. In my naiveté, I also thought it was funny to get loaded with the grown-ups. Great chaperoning auntie! Not only did the adults get me drunk that night, they smoked pot and tried to get me to smoke some too. I refused the pot but drinking alcohol seemed okay because I had seen my dad down a few whiskey sours at Bar Mitzvahs back home. We were accompanied that evening by a good-looking young man who I believe was in his 20s. Drunk as a skunk, cute little 14-year-old Lori in a woman's body found herself alone in a bedroom with the good-looking 20-something-year-old man. He gratefully didn't violate me sexually but flirted with me as we were lying on the bed. Later he bragged to my aunt and our cousin that he felt he could have had his way with me but chose not to. Nice guy, right?

During that evening I watched our cousin repeatedly grab my aunt's breasts as she giggled and told him to stop playing around. She thought this was hilarious and I remember thinking that it was simply strange. The words *lewd* and *inappropriate* weren't in my vocabulary yet. This evening set the stage for my first hideous experience of sexual molestation by this cousin, a married man, father of two and a sexual predator.

Days later this cousin arranged to take me to his office and show me around town. When he took me to his place of work, the ladies in the office looked at me as though they were strangely worried that I was his mistress. When I smiled and said hello, they saw my mouth full of silver braces and laughed in relief. "Oh, she's just a child," they thought. "Phew, he's not doing anything inappropriate with her."

After we left the office, all I remember was being in his car when he began fondling my young 14-year-old breasts the way he had done to my aunt a few days earlier. I didn't say no. When I didn't say no to that, he then slipped his hands into my pants and went straight for my vagina. I truly didn't understand why he was touching me there, it felt hideous and horrible, but once again, I didn't say no. I remember thinking that I didn't want to hurt his feelings so I remained silent. That was the worst thing I could have done because the next thing I knew he pushed me in the back seat, jumped on top of me with his over 200-pound body and began grinding me with his penis. I stiffened like a board, and was in complete shock when he paused long enough to see the distress in my face. I had absolutely no idea what he was doing to me and was completely clueless about anything sexual. He saw my shock and gratefully pulled himself away, then began crying like a two-year-old.

After we went back to his house in Malibu he ran outside to the area where he kept his horses. He sat there by the stable, visibly shaken and crying. I knew that the touching was inappropriate but I still didn't fathom the extent of how horrible his actions were or the gravity of the situation. It didn't sink in that I had been sexually assaulted by this predator and monster. Instead I felt bad that he was crying. I felt somehow it was all my fault. Seeing him in his obvious distress I comforted him, told him it was alright and asked him to please stop crying. Again, this was the worst thing I could have done.

When we went back into the house I sat in my room with the door closed. My room was adjacent to their kitchen. Through the door I heard him tell his wife he was taking me to San Francisco in the morning on a business trip. Whoa! He was orchestrating his opportunity to seal the deal and rape me.

Gratefully his wife sensed there was something wrong and insisted that their young daughter go along on the trip too. Of course a would-be rapist wouldn't want company on this "business trip" and her request to bring his daughter provoked a vicious brawl. I cried as I heard them fighting and prayed to God to forgive me for my hideous sin. How could I have let this man touch me in such a vile way? He was a married man and father after all and I did this to him and his wife? In my horror I felt filthy as though I bore the full responsibility for what happened. I felt as though I deserved to die for this transgression. Fortunately, the trip to San Francisco never happened and I flew home shortly after.

When I returned home to New Jersey, my parents saw a visible change in my personality. I was barely talking and if they raised their voices above a calm level, I cried for them to stop and begged them not to get a divorce. My father was very street smart and smelled a rat. He called his barbaric cousin in California and ripped into him asking him, "What did you do to my daughter?!" I never once spoke about what happened directly with my father and he never asked.

Fast forward, I went on with my life, enjoyed a successful career and met my husband in 1986. After I became engaged to be married at 27 years old, I received a call from my favorite aunt who chaperoned me on that infamous trip to Malibu. She told me that our cousin (and child molester) was in town and wanted to see me. I lost it! That's when I told my husband and mother the entire hideous story of being sexually molested by this monster. Incredibly, my aunt responded to this information by calling me a liar and told me that I asked for it. She accused me of being sexually promiscuous and not the innocent 14-year-old I claimed to have been. That was the end of my relationship with my favorite aunt who died many years later in 2010.

This wasn't the only time I was sexually assaulted by someone posing as a good father, admired family member, or upstanding person in the community. The monsters and sexual predators are everywhere hiding among us. In August of 1977, just prior to leaving for college I became extremely ill with an intestinal virus. I couldn't eat for almost two weeks, suffered from a very high fever and could barely walk because of severe pain in my pelvis. The pain was so bad that one evening my father took me to the ER at what was known back then as West Jersey Hospital off Evesham Road in Voorhees, New Jersey. As I walked into the ER that night with my dad holding my hand, I had to take baby steps because of the excruciating pelvic pain I was enduring. Today my memory of that evening is still excruciatingly vivid. As I stood with my father, the ER doctor in charge that night asked us a series of questions. When I pointed to the area of my body that was in the most pain, he and the nurse working with him looked at each other and then looked back at me like I was a filthy whore. The doctor and nurse escorted me away from my dad into an examining room, where they made me strip from the waist down and put my legs up in stirrups. He proceeded to give me my first ever internal exam. The filthy bastard then took what felt like his entire hand and shoved it viciously straight into my vagina while asking, "Does that hurt?" I screamed and shrieked in pain. He then shoved his hand once again into my vagina while asking, "Does that hurt?"

I cried, and screamed as I answered, "YES!" As he did this repeatedly, he shoved his hand in different directions while asking me which direction hurt me the worst. It felt like he would never stop! I looked over at the nurse and saw a filthy and judgmental look on her face as if to tell me she knew I was a filthy slut. God was my witness to being sexually assaulted by this vicious monster who posed as a respectable ER doctor. This foul and malicious doctor was accompanied in his crime by a disgraceful excuse for a nurse. Weakened further by this sexual assault, I slowly walked to my father who was waiting outside. We stood at the front desk where this obscene doctor informed my father I had PID, Pelvic Inflammatory Disease. PID is an inflammatory and infectious disease that comes from a complication of a sexually transmitted disease (STD) such as gonorrhea. He gave my father a prescription for oral antibiotics and as I walked out of the ER I felt their filthy judgmental stares of condemnation.

My mother immediately made an appointment with her gynecologist and after he examined me he sat me in a chair next to her in his office. He said, "I want you to know, your daughter is as pure as the driven snow. She has nothing more than a severe intestinal virus. The ER doctor saw a pretty young girl and decided to have some pleasure. I'm sorry but this happens all the time." My mother came home that day and announced proudly to the entire household that she had great news. The doctor said Lori was a virgin after all. Considering that I always had the reputation of being the black sheep in the family, this was clearly surprising and welcomed news. Back in 1977 there wasn't a #MeToo movement and nobody thought it was important to report this incident. I am reporting it to the world now. There are people who know the identity of this doctor and nurse. This horrific sexual assault is no longer a skeleton hidden in their closets.

This barbaric doctor and his filthy nurse accomplice likely went on to have formidable careers in medicine and perhaps they became parents themselves. In this moment they could be your wonderful neighbors or the grandpa or grandma living next door. These two ER workers are lovely people walking the face our earth, don't you agree? Would you like to have either of them caring for your family member or child? These two monstrous people, a woman and a man fit into your description of a #MeToo sexual predator, don't they? Well, this would come as a complete surprise to them and their families. They are likely masquerading around right now as good citizens with children and grandchildren boasting that they are good God-loving people. In their opinion they aren't responsible for any #MeToo incidents. They, like YOU, believe the horrific state of our world is someone else's fault, not theirs. This hideous evening when they assaulted and disparaged me isn't even a distant memory of theirs any longer. West Jersey Hospital on Evesham Road in Voorhees, New Jersey, no longer exists but these two monsters are likely walking among you as fellow model citizens. What about you? Did you ever do something like this to a young girl? Did you ever remain silent when you watched someone else assault or disparage another person? You had better come clean now. There will be no skeletons hidden in your closet either.

I have numerous stories about being sexually harassed in the workplace too. I have so many awful stories I could fill an entire book about the #MeToo movement, but I'll wrap up this boxing round by just sharing a few comments and conversations I've endured over the years which reveal how "#MeToo" includes "you too." I've endured gender discrimination and hideous comments by many a nasty boy. In my first sales position, my boss, a married father of three, was walking behind me one day when he made what he thought was a flattering comment about my cute little butt. It made me quite uncomfortable but as many women did in those years, I stayed silent. My friend and male co-worker told me afterwards that our boss told him, "Lori has a great ass but her breasts are too small. She should get implants." What a lovely comment for my boss to make to my coworker and wasn't it also so thoughtful of my work buddy to share this with me?

My work buddy added insult to injury by saying, "Don't worry Lori, more than a mouthful is wasted." I'd never heard that expression before and it took me a while to figure out what he even meant. Yes, I'm that clueless. Was my work buddy further complimenting my body parts or giving me a consolation prize for having small breasts? This boy and work buddy socialized with me over the years and we remained platonic friends. I recall he often boasted in public that he had an enormous penis and because of its size, his friends nicknamed him "the hose." He was quite proud of his nickname but I found his boasting revolting. I listened to him and many other boys make similar disgusting comments and remained silent, until now.

People are now screaming and yelling #MeToo and bringing these predators who molested and abused them to justice. I'm all for calling everyone out and making them face the music. Calling a few people out won't solve this problem. Every one of you, myself included, remained silent and fed into this insanity for decades. If everyone doesn't sit up at attention, look squarely into a spiritual mirror to see yourselves in this hideous story, this evil will continue. If you keep giving yourselves lame excuses and accuse me of being hysterical or overly dramatic instead of feeling shame, you won't be welcomed into the new world order. #MeToo has got to become #IchooseGOD in a hurry. We all must stop the insanity and refuse to participate in the evil. We must knowingly choose God and His goodness in every moment.

The liberal media accuses President Trump of being a misogynist, a person who dislikes, despises, or is strongly prejudiced against women. That might be true about President Trump but it is also true about every one of you. I can just hear you all now! "Oh no, you can't say that about me Lori Michelle! Not me. I am no misogynist!" you declare in self-righteous indignation. Oh yes, you are. Male or female you all trample on and abuse the women of our world and it's time for this to end. My own former husband and father of my three children often said derisive and sexist things to me behind closed doors. Does that shock anyone? When nobody was looking he felt free to grab my breasts or buttocks. When I would admonish him, and tell him to stop he just laughed at me. It was funny to him and that's all that mattered. Trump called his nasty speech caught on hidden audio "locker room talk" but I call it showing your true colors. My former husband jokingly nicknamed a woman's vagina "a

ım." Nice huh? The holy opening of my body that gave birth to his
ren including two precious daughters was relegated to being a filthy
bearded clam? I'm not laughing, are you? "Oh, come on Lori Michelle, get a
sense of humor. Stop being a Bible toting puritan. He was just having fun,"
many of you would say as you run to my poor ex-husband's defense. Perhaps
you've used this terminology yourself or laughed out loud when someone else
did. But wait—there is more.

When I turned 40 my then husband quipped, "Now I'll just trade you in for
two twenty-year-olds. Ha ha ha." What a funny comment to make to your wife
and mother of your three children, don't you agree? After my mother-in-law
passed away, my aging father-in-law decided to remarry. My husband told his
father not to do it and just go buy himself two young Swedish nurses instead.
His ulterior motive to convince his father not to remarry wasn't to protect dear
old dad at all. Two nurses would be a cheaper solution to his loneliness and
protect his millions for my husband's future inheritance.

Should any man make a sport out of ridiculing or making fun of his wife
and mother of his children? What about the lovely father of two and 46-year-
old cousin of mine who sexually molested me as a 14-year-old child? How
about the ER doctor who shoved his hand up my 17-year-old virginal vagina
with his lovely nurse and accomplice standing by him? Do you truly believe
ladies are exonerated from being misogynists too? Women do this all the time
to each other gladly and willfully every day of the week. We see famous woman
ridiculing and demeaning other women all the time.

Journalists and news anchors are loud voices that help set the public agenda.
When a 23-year-old female photographer revealed she felt she was sexually violated by Golden Globe award winner Aziz Ansari, 50-year-old CNN anchor and
journalist Ashleigh Banfield came to the poor boy's defense. She condemned
this young girl and lamented that this young photographer had weakened the
long awaited #MeToo movement which Ashleigh had looked forward to and
dreamed about her entire career. On CNN's Headline News she gave her scathing editorial condemning this girl and told her to get over it because her story
wasn't about sexual abuse or harassment at all. She spoke about this young woman publicly as though she was a filthy little millennial who just had "a bad date."
I was appalled when I watched Ashleigh degrade this young woman further
when she appeared on the *Megyn Kelly Today* program. Ashleigh told Megyn,
another female role model and leader, that the rules of engagement had changed
for the millennial generation. She said the millennials were now a hook-up
culture of swipe right and have sex in 20 minutes. Instead of reaching out to

mentor this young woman and teach her why she needed to change her thinking by embracing God's rules of engagement, she chastised her and humiliated her further by telling the world that reporting the incident was wrong.

Ashleigh Banfield is old enough to be this girl's mother. Is this how mothers should treat their daughters? Mine did. My mother taught me a little nursery rhyme when I was about four years old. Get a load of this one: "Lori Pori pumpkin pie, kissed the boys and made them cry. When the boys came out to play, Lori Pori ran away." I rest my case. Misogyny begins at home. We were all raised in a misogynist culture. It's time to wake up and stop the bleeding. We must start a new movement and instead of #MeToo we must say #IchooseGOD.

Round 6: "It's My Body!" Wrong.

Most people in the world believe they own their body and treat, modify and pleasure it any way they desire. We've already discussed issues like homosexuality being a perfectly acceptable way of life in today's new world order and the decision to change your gender is your own business. Not only do you believe it's your own business but you have passed laws that everyone must be accepting and show their approval of anyone who surgically changes their gender. We are required by law to refer to transgender people in politically correct jargon. This is an egregious sin against our Creator, however it seems that many people in our world don't care about that minor detail. Why would you care what God says on this subject since apparently you don't truly believe He is real? You believe it's all about you, and you make up the rules as you please. Deny it all you want but by the end of all 12 rounds of this boxing match I pray you will see your participation in creating this monstrous mess too.

There are many more sins people commit by abusing their body, their God given vessel, than I will discuss in this book. Let's focus right now on a few obvious ones. Every day people around the world willfully choose to abuse their bodies with offensive choices which break many of God's laws. Some of these offenses are well known by observant Jews who study and cling to Hashem's Torah and commandments. In the new age of spiritual enlightenment and secularism those religious Jews who follow these laws are scoffed at by both Gentiles and most secular Jews. Americans have become the kings and queens of believing and promoting that it's all good if it makes you happy. In the USA most people believe that it's your body, it's your right to pursue happiness, and you have laws designed to protect you in your unending quest for personal joy. The truth will hurt but you need to hear it anyway. Your body is on loan to you and it isn't yours to do with as you wish. Your body along with every breath of your life is a supreme gift that came with instructions from your Creator. He gives you freedom to choose in every moment what you will do with His gifts and He measures every choice that you make. Every choice you make is observed and accounted for whether you are aware of this or not. Everyone is accountable and every decision has consequences. You all, without exception, have chosen to break your covenant with Him and disgracefully abuse your bodies. Some of you rarely neglect your bodies while others have made this abuse a personal pastime. Every time you choose to treat your body in a harmful way you display to the world that you are not only an ingrate, you are flagrantly harming yourself, abusing your own children, and selfishly causing harm to every other person in humanity. We are all connected and responsible for each other.

In addition to sexual perversion and sex change operations, let's add tattooing and body piercing to the long list of abuses. While women are permitted to pierce their ears to wear jewelry, there are very few other exceptions where piercing is allowed. Making any permanent mark on your flesh for vanity or other purposes is expressly forbidden by God Himself. Religious symbols included in a tattoo won't exonerate you. In fact, many of those symbols which you consider holy are repugnant to Hashem and increase the magnitude of your sin. Tattooing your body and body piercings are both horrific abominations in the eyes of God. All forms of self-mutilation like body piercing and ear gauging are filthy behavior and deeply disgusting to Hashem. Allow me to give you an example to make this sin understandable and perhaps relatable.

Imagine for a moment you labored your entire life and dedicatedly saved your earnings in a special bank account. Your beloved was a passionate artist who loved Picasso. One momentous day you thoughtfully withdrew your entire life savings from your bank account to buy your lover a masterpiece by Picasso. You excitedly gave this Picasso to the one you loved and waited for their reaction to your special gift of love. After you gave your sweetheart this magnificent work of art, your loved one immediately said, "I can do it better. Let me show you right now." Your sweetheart then pulled out a paintbrush to give the painting an overhaul and destroyed its original beauty right before your eyes. Imagine how you might feel. Wouldn't you feel unappreciated by seeing your loved one commit such an act of indifference and ingratitude? This is what tattooing and self-mutilation looks like to the Master of the Universe, Hashem God. When you tattoo yourselves and destroy your bodies, you're not just drawing on yourself and punching holes into places where they don't belong. You are destroying your flesh, a supreme gift from God Himself, right in front of Him in plain view. Now can you relate to how much this act of ingratitude disturbs our Creator? Remember He sees everything you do. Nothing in this world is hidden from Hashem.

When you're not making physical adjustments to His masterpiece you are smoking cigarettes and smelly cigars with the good old boys. Some girls like those smelly cigars too and want to prove they can be just as disgusting as the boys. Smoking marijuana is now legal in many countries and you enjoy getting stoned while thumbing your noses at Hashem. Lots of people throughout the world use illegal and legal narcotics to ameliorate their sadness, stop their emotional pain, or sometimes just for fun. It's socially acceptable to admit that your pain has become so uncontrollable that like millions of other people you run to your psychiatrists to receive your prescriptions for that magic cocktail which will make everything better. Many of you begin abusing prescription medications because your life is so darn hard and taking a pill is extremely easy. Life for you has become so deeply painful in this terrible and unfair world that someone else created. Oh my, poor little victim. You just want to be happy like the Founding Fathers said you had the right to be.

In your endless quest for joy many of you look for love and happiness and begin this quest by looking in the mirror. You think, "Oh no! I don't look like Barbie or Ken" so you make the thoughtful decision that millions of people make and off you go to the doctor of plastic surgery to fix your problem. Now your life becomes an endless quest for eternal youth and beauty. Just ask Cher, she knows. Repeated plastic surgeries, synthetic fillers, Botox injections, tattoos and liposuction. You are on a mission to become a timeless beauty making everything better now, right? Wrong. Instead of being as beautiful as you arrived, you don't look younger or better, you begin to look like a freak of nature. While parts of you are admirably toned and youthful, other parts resemble Glad Wrap and porcelain. Sadly, many people don't see this truth any more than Cher does when she looks in her mirror.

Why does Cher continue on her relentless quest for plastic surgery? Because she gets tons of attention in her seventies and everyone applauds. She relishes all the attention she receives over her appearance, misinterpreting your applause for love. She eats up your applause and compliments about how young and beautiful she "still" is after all these years and this keeps her spending her money on visits to plastic surgeons for more. You all look at her in her seventies, see her material success, observe the accolades she receives from the crowd and become so inspired that you decide you'll try to do the same thing. Off you go for your Botox injections and a nip and a tuck too.

After a few of these procedures you all begin to resemble each other and start to look like a plastic and Botox-injected *Mashuginah Mishpacha*. You are all one crazy family addicted to having overly tight skin over your cheeks and wide eyes that are expressionless. In your pursuit for love and happiness you are all abusing your God-given vessels to please your mirror and everyone else's opinions about what is attractive. Everyone else's opinion of beauty supersedes your own. You have become addicted to receiving their approval and false sense of love. It isn't truly love or admiration at all if it has anything to do with your wrinkles or breast size, but mom and dad never taught you that.

Good American mommies with the approval of daddies now take their young prepubescent daughters to Victoria's Secret. Victoria's Secret teaches our young girls what President Trump learned decades ago. Money, good looks, your cup size and how many people want to have sex with you is all that matters. Some of you become depressed and believe that you aren't getting enough sex or attention so you hit the Twinkies. That brings us to the next form of abuse.

Am I allowed to call you fat? Too bad, you're fat. If you are more than your healthy BMI (Body Mass Index) you are sinning. If you are like most Americans and other people in the developed countries of the world you don't even know your BMI or how much you should weigh. You have all fallen asleep at the wheel at best and at worst you have accepted obesity as the new normal. Seeing fat people everywhere no longer shocks you. The statistics are scary and shocking but you likely have chosen to ignore them and won't even listen to this warning. Most of you know that you are fat and eat the Twinkies anyway. There are many sneaky reasons why the world has become so fat but the biggest reason is that you all stopped trying and stopped caring.

You just don't care enough to do something about your beer belly or your fat behind. You are incorrigibly lazy and everyone around you is fat and lazy too. Fat is the new norm and it's no longer a stigma. I've been a size 4 my entire adult life yet at 58 I weigh 15 pounds more than when I got married at the age of 27. How could I have gained 15 pounds in 31 years and still be a perfect size 4? Because the clothing industry is being polite and sweet to me and all the people around the world who are inexplicably gaining too much weight. Clothing manufacturers want to sell more clothing so they've adjusted the waist sizes to fit the fat folks who buy their clothes. Even though I am 15 pounds heavier than I was at the age of 27, I'm still a healthy BMI but guess what? I know I need to lose weight and I try like the dickens all the time to trim my waistline even though I technically don't need to. Would you do that if you looked "great" for 58? Many people mistake me for much younger and tell me that I look fantastic for my age. I don't believe that it's true and know I can do better. I keep trying and wonder why I'm having so much trouble losing the 15 pounds. Then I researched the obesity crisis and discovered the sinister reason why. We are being poisoned for profit.

Much of the food in our grocery stores contains preservatives so it can sit on the shelves for years. The air we are all breathing is polluted. Our bodies weren't designed to eat chemicals and inhale this much poison. My body has trouble metabolizing this poison and so does yours. You can become a health nut and try to avoid eating everything you enjoy like sugar and bread. I say to you, "I would rather be a little fat than eat like that." I resent the tricks many of you play with your bodies to be slender. Slender is desirable and should be our collective normal but it's not a trophy prize for figuring out what delicious foods you must eliminate. Being slender and healthy is our birthright but we are becoming a world of fat people with cancer, heart disease, diabetes and more. While the poisons are a real problem, the biggest issue is that it's easier for you to go to McDonald's and scarf down a Big Mac than to cook a chicken stir-fry when you get home from work. Easy, cheap and convenient is making you fat and ugly. You are all sinning against God but you have done worse than getting yourselves fat and ugly. Your kids are becoming fat and ugly too.

Some of you will say, "Hey being large runs in the family," and pretend it's not your fault. It absolutely is your fault. It's everyone's fault. You are all part of the MeToo fat people crisis. Kids shouldn't be fat but you aren't teaching them by example how to be healthy because money and convenience take precedence over effort. You won't make the effort because you feel fine and the doctor told you that your blood pressure and blood sugar are normal. So, there's no emergency and your husband and your neighbors are fat too. We are all in great company as ugly fat folks, right? Wrong. Will you wake up and throw out those Twinkies now that you know they're not good for you? Sure, you might say. You'll start on Monday. It's too inconvenient to start today. Today you're going to put those frozen meatballs on the stove for the kids even though they're loaded with salt and chemical preservatives because you're just too exhausted. Maybe if your doctor had told you that you need a new kidney or liver because of your poor eating habits you would regret having abused your body.

It's terrible news to find out that you need a new kidney but you're hopeful because you can just go get an organ transplant and beat those odds. But wait! Did anyone ever explain to you that organ donation often is a sin against God too? "SHUT UP Lori Michelle! I won't hear of that!" You might all scream in unison for me to shut up but I will not be silenced.

Did you ever read the laws concerning your body as given to us by God? Perhaps you did but you compromised on some of them to make what you wanted and desired acceptable. You gave yourself or others that free pass into heaven and bent some rules and your clergy told you it's okay, but that was a lie. Do you want to know the truth about what God says about organ donation or do you want to keep sinning against God? It's always your decision.

The Torah-learned know that our body is on loan and we are required to return it whole when we die. Many forms of organ donation are strictly forbidden. This is a difficult pill to swallow, but it's true. You might as well learn the truth now before it's too late. Years ago, I did some work for a charity that promoted organ donation. They convinced me to sign my NJ driver's license giving my approval to be an organ donor. I went to a seminar of theirs and listened to the tear-jerking stories from both organ recipients and organ donor families. It was so emotional as they evoked my deep compassion for those who need organs. Before I decided to sign away my organs on my license, I asked for information from this organization called NJ Sharing Network about the Jewish religious implications of organ donation. They gave me a handout that was written by a "rabbi" which said it was okay for me to sign my license and become an organ donor. This was a bold-faced lie. I don't understand how a Jew with the title of "rabbi" would encourage another Jew to sign their driver's license to be an organ donor luring them to sin against Hashem. Months later I renewed my license, reversed my decision, and removed my approval to be a donor. There are forms of organ donation which are halachically acceptable. Before committing to organ donation, you must consult with a legitimate orthodox Jewish rabbi who obeys God's laws instead of listening to impostors who make up their own rules.

So, did I catch a few more of you in some sinful behaviors? Oh no, not you? Perhaps you think my assertions are overstated, hysterical or even fraudulent, God forbid. By the end of this long book, I pray you will know that I speak the truth and I'm doing this for your good. I am likely disturbing many of you and ruffling your feathers, but I do this in your best interest. There are many Christians who believe that tattoos are just fine and dandy and you have figured out ways around God's laws. After all Gentiles are only obligated to the Seven Noahide laws and not the full Monty like the Jewish people. Gentiles are delighted to believe that these onerous laws are just for the Jews and they are completely off the hook. Phew! Not so fast my Christian brethren. You might only be obligated for a subset of these rules but it's time to become educated about all of them. Pleading ignorance or claiming absolution won't get you a permanent ticket into His world to come. Now that you know tattoos along with these other sins of harming your body are considered an abomination to God Himself would you still go to the tattoo parlor tomorrow? If you are a mom or dad, and now know that God is unequivocally real and He finds all these sins against your flesh abhorrent and hideous would you continue to do this anyway and teach your young children to do the same? Children learn by example and will likely grow up to do the same as their mothers and fathers. You best believe it is our duty to teach our children the ways of God. Doing otherwise is preparing them to go straight to damnation with you.

Some of you who work at following His rules may still believe you are exonerated because, hey you're only human and all humans make errors. If you're a Jew you'll just fast on Yom Kippur, or some goyim will give up chocolate at Lent and everything will be forgiven, right? I'm not sure what all the rest of you do to repent but repentance and repeated sinning won't cut it any more in Hashem's world. While it's true that God's chosen Jewish children have their feet to the fire so to speak, and they are required to follow all His rules while everyone else is seemingly exonerated, the world to come will be void of evil. It is written in every religious doctrine that one day our world will be free of war and evil. Well then, how do you expect to get there from here if you are willing to choose any behavior that is abhorrent and evil in the eyes of God Himself? He will allow goyim, non-Jews, into the world to come with a smaller subset of rules, however as I've previously explained, eventually your choices will kill you and you simply won't be allowed to return. Whether you head to damnation or your soul is extinguished from His book of life is HIS choice, not yours.

So, have it your way as they used to say at Burger King, and float your boat with tattoos, piercings, smoking, Botox and the like and pay the price with your life. If you don't care much about your own life, then consider the influence your decisions will have on your children or other people's children. I assure you, choosing any of these sins places their blood on your hands as you influence them to sin.

One more thing before we go to round 7 in our boxing match. I live in Israel where cigarette smoking is popular like it was in America in the '60s and '70s. As I walk the streets of Tiberias, Israel, it seems everyone and their mother smokes incessantly. This includes men with tzitzit and black kippahs connoting they are the most righteous and religious Jewish men of our world. Gentlemen, do you realize that you are smoking wearing the garb of a righteous Jew while Hashem watches your every move? How dare you! As Hashem and I watch you smoke your cigarettes my stomach is literally nauseated at the sight. How dare you smoke that filth in the face of your Creator. While all people of the world are sinning by smoking cigarettes, your sin is far worse. By your actions you are showing the rest of the world you don't truly believe in the existence of Hashem. If that's not the case and you do believe in Him, it appears you don't believe your daily prayers that He is all knowing and sees everything. If you do believe in Him and that He is all knowing, then perhaps you simply don't care that He sees you sinning. If you argue now that you have full Emuna, you know He is real, He knows everything and He is watching you smoke those awful cigarettes in His face, then you must believe He understands that you are weak and has given you a free pass to destroy your God given vessel. I hope you agree that receiving a free pass to destroy your health is completely illogical. So, which is it sir? He knows what you're thinking, I don't. Do everyone a favor and put down those filthy cigarettes and start behaving like the Jewish light unto the nations you promised Hashem you would be.

Round 7: Money Makes the World Go 'round

In this material world everything is about money. My former husband once heard about a salesman who said, "If it don't make money it don't make sense" (*sense* is a homophone for *cents*) and he loved it so much he said this phrase all the time. After he said this he would laugh like it was just a joke and pretend as though he didn't truly believe it. When I met him, he seemed to be humble and wasn't overtly materialistic which I found attractive. I loathed people who boasted about money and wore their bank accounts on their sleeves. My former husband didn't seem to be all about money but the opposite proved to be true. Over the years he showed me by his speech and actions that he was obsessed with money and material things. Our relationship took a back seat to his psychological obsession with having enough money. After my awakening, Lori Michelle the little moneymaker of old was no longer interested in spending her days and nights chasing new clients to make more money. My lack of interest in working for profit evoked great anger and was a point of contention as you read earlier in my book. The more I became interested in my God-inspired charity, Running on Love, the more visceral anger and hatred came from him. He had support from family who helped fuel his rage. One day his wealthy sister called me from sunny California to reprimand me about how irresponsible I had become. She admonished me, told me I should forget about Running on Love and said, "Just go get any old job. I don't even care if you have to work at Walmart." It was clear he had her convinced that I wasn't pulling my weight at home anymore and I was the one responsible for destroying our family. In the

Jewish marriage model given to us by God Himself, the woman's birthright and blessing is to be cared for by her husband. He is the one who is supposed provide financially for the queen of his castle, not the other way around. Although my sister-in-law didn't work and was quite wealthy, she felt bad for her brother who was now saddled with a woman who desired such things as dedicating her life to God and charity. Her poor brother now had all the financial burdens placed on his shoulders as his newly religious wife didn't want to be his work mule and provide financially for him any longer.

In this world God and motherhood are not valued over material wealth. During the women's movement of the '60s and '70s women burned their bras and went into the workforce to prove their worth by playing the "I have value too game." If someone can't "show you the money" or many certificates of honor on their walls, they are valueless in this not so wonderful world. Homemakers are belittled and mothers are chastised as mindless incubators that produce "only" children and nothing of material value. You can scream at the top of your lungs that I'm wrong and that's not true, but you are lying to yourself. If someone doesn't have wealth and success in your world, you're all quick to call them lazy buffoons. This includes how many men view their wives and the mothers of their children.

When I was a sales executive for a Minnesota based company my then sales manager complained to me one day that his wife spent too much money and didn't earn enough. As he was describing her, his voice and face filled with anger as he told me, "She's just a fat cow!" The poor man felt he had borne too much of their financial stress on his weak shoulders and this was so unfair. Can you imagine a man saying such a thing about the mother of his children? Sadly, I can. I was married to such a man. My former sales manager and my former husband were cut from the same cloth and they are just like most other men in creation. Men's evil relationship with money and their chauvinistic attitudes about women have been adopted by the women of the world too. Women judge each other by their homes, diamonds, and how much money their successful husbands and/or families are worth. Orthodox Jewish woman who are schooled to believe differently boast out loud about how much money they spend on their beautiful clothing and sheitels, the wigs orthodox Jewish women wear. What is intended to be a visible symbol of modesty has become a form of vanity and pompousness instead.

The minute I lost interest in working for money and wanted to follow my dream of building Running on Love the charity, my husband was infuriated. Never mind the fact that he didn't work to earn money himself. The idea that

I didn't earn money any longer was intolerable to him. He planned to ride me like a jackass until I either died or said no. I said no. Like many unsuspecting women, I never intended to become his jackass. It was a silent occurrence that happened over many years as he began using me as a work mule instead of loving me as his wife. I finally got old enough and tired of his abuse after suffering through a lifetime of abuses from my family. Suddenly saying no was extremely easy. I had quite enough. Some women are continuously battered and accept similar abuse from their husbands thinking that women earning their keep by bringing in money is what a good marriage looks like. Wake up ladies, marriage isn't supposed to be modern day slavery.

Just before leaving my marriage, I went to California and visited with my sister-in-law. We enjoyed a cordial relationship over the years of my marriage to her brother and agreed about many things in life but parted ways when it came to the subject of money and God. She was blessed with money and was a wealthy stay-at-home mom throughout her marriage. She and her husband moved to sunny California many years ago in their never ending quest for more money. My brother-in-law made no bones about it. He made it exquisitely clear that he was only interested in something if it made him money. He was blatantly proud of his love affair with dollars and everyone in his life knew this about him, including his wife, my sister-in-law. His hunger for wealth and success earned him many millions over the years. Bravo for him! Truly.

One day during my visit to California I told my sister-in-law that I was likely to divorce her brother and she tried extremely hard to convince me to reconsider. She shared her own sordid stories about strife in her marriage that she reconciled and managed to overcome. As we spoke she admitted to me that years earlier she had seriously considered divorcing her husband when he wouldn't buy her the beach house she always desired. She was infuriated with him that he selfishly chose to gamble away large amounts of money on horses instead of buying her the dream home she desired. The straw that nearly broke her back and almost caused her to call it quits, was when he booked a business trip to Dubai on their 25th wedding anniversary. She was heartbroken! How could he be so insensitive not to remember their 25th wedding anniversary? Then she said, she had her lightbulb moment, changed her mind quickly, and realized he was a good husband because he gave her such a wonderful and prosperous life. Instead of leaving him, she decided she had no right to complain. After all she thought, who was she to tell him how to spend HIS hard-earned money. What her decision really revealed was that she would tolerate his gambling and crude behavior because she wasn't willing to give up her cushy life of material wealth. Her willingness to tolerate the intolerable rather than sacrifice her wealth was further exemplified later that evening.

That night my sister-in-law and I met her husband and a young couple they knew from the race track for dinner. At the restaurant dinner table my brother-in-law did something he often did to his wife. He ridiculed her for sport and made fun of her while she was trying to speak. As she tried to tell a story, he spoke over every word she attempted to utter so that she couldn't get one word out of her mouth. As he did this it was clear he was mocking her intelligence and treating her as though she was stupid. All this was done for laughs as he enjoyed making her look like a fool. Of course, she wasn't the one who looked foolish at all as he continued with his folly. Both the young couple and he laughed uproariously and thought his mockery of my sister-in-law was hilarious. She was clearly uncomfortable and quite embarrassed. The episode made me feel so sick to my stomach that I made an excuse and I swiftly left the dinner table. I couldn't watch this man disparage his wife of more than 25 years and the mother of his two children. What he considered a hilarious joke, wasn't funny at all. If they both read this book, I wonder how they feel about themselves and each other in this moment. Will they see a need for change or fight back and become defensive? Perhaps they will both be outraged at me for sharing this story. I pray for their sake they both decide to change.

Can you relate to my sister-in-law? Are you willing to stay in any relationship because of money? No, you say? Are you madly in love with your spouse and staying because they are your bashert, soul mate? If you are living in marital bliss with your bashert, Mazel Tov! I am delighted for you. Sadly, you are more likely to be like many millions of people around the world who stay in dysfunctional marriages because the financial pain and emotional upheaval of divorce is more than they are willing to bear. There are millions of people in the world who marry strictly for money. Money makes this world operate and lots and lots of people make their life decisions based upon the financial upside or downside. Making life decisions based on money is evil. Choosing money over love or your belief in God is abhorrent and idol worship. Money and comfort may feel good to you now but when you face God you will answer for your choices. One day you will realize I'm telling you the truth. Sadly, this day might come posthumously. Like my entire family, the personal humiliation of facing your evil choices will be excruciatingly painful. While facing your demons will be painful to do publicly here in this world, if you leave before you repent and repair some of your mistakes, facing God Himself will be much worse. I pray you see yourself in this diatribe, begin to repent, and save yourself from complete agony.

Round 8: Leaders, Loudmouths or Lackeys?

Do you realize that we are heading directly into World War III? We can try to hide from this truth but it will come and it will arrive soon. The threat of nuclear war looms large and we have many public officials in our world making life and death decisions on our behalf. We pray they will make the right choices and sometimes we even wonder how we got in this awful predicament in the first place. If we only had great leaders at the helm all along we somehow believe that everything might've been hunky-dory. Some people really think this mess is the fault of failed leadership. The leftist liberals blame the right-wing conservatives for every problem and vice versa. That raises the question, where are the great leaders right now and how do we put them in charge to save ourselves from imploding?

The biggest reason we are in this mess is because we all have forsaken God and don't follow His rules. Yes, there I go again! I'm blaming EVERYONE. We have elected leaders who talk the talk about believing in God and agree with following His ways, but they are impostors. First and foremost, the leaders of most countries don't even know or understand God's laws. Secondly, free countries are secular and blatantly remove God from their laws and culture. Who is responsible for creating this wild mess? ALL OF YOU. None of you including the Jewish country of Israel, follow God's laws. We see our leaders succumb regularly to the evil inclination. Most don't even know that the Yetzer Hara, the evil inclination even exists. If the most righteous among us choose evil and continuously fall from grace, who can lead us out of this enormous mess? The answer: YOU ALL WILL. You must all learn how to be great leaders, choose great leadership to steer the ship and support them fully or we will implode.

As we look around our world, those in leadership positions enjoy admiration from millions of people but they also have millions of enemies. Nobody agrees who the great leaders are 100 percent of the time. The Liberal Left in America denounce President Trump and want him removed from office. The Conservative Right fires back that the liberals are clueless and President Trump is the greatest President of our generation. Who is right? Are there any great leaders worthy of our praise? No, not in every moment. In one moment President Trump chooses to be a God-fearing man and makes heroic choices like withdrawing from the Nuclear Arms Agreement with the largest state sponsor of terror in the world, Iran. He heroically kept his campaign promise and fearlessly made the right decision to withdraw. In the next moment, he met with the evil and murderous dictator from North Korea, Kim Jong-un, and treated him like he was nobility. Really?

A God-fearing leader would refuse to meet with this vicious killer from North Korea. In the audience of President Trump's 2018 State of the Union Address sat Mr. and Mrs. Warmbier, the mother and father of Otto Warmbier. Otto was an American college student who visited North Korea and was arrested, tortured then sent home to die. Months later, we watched our new Secretary of State, Mike Pompeo, shake hands with this North Korean monster, as they posed for the cameras looking like two lovebirds. Everyone in America became excited that this murderous dictator who tortured and killed Otto agreed to stop firing missiles and denuclearize his regime. While everyone is praying that this dictator will become an agent of world peace I haven't forgotten what happened to Otto. Otto represents many others who were tortured and murdered by this villain. I still cry for Mr. and Mrs. Warmbier who lost their son. It may look like their son's murder is forgotten, but God doesn't forget anything. Hashem knows everything. Everything people choose in our world is measured. Divine retribution is on the horizon.

In one moment President Trump chooses to be an inspiring leader who bravely withdrew from the Iran Nuclear Agreement. He stood strong and said no to the largest state sponsor of terror when other Republicans and most of the Allies pleaded with him to stay and appease the devil. In the next moment the President met with Kim Jong-un in Singapore and treated him like an equal. Will President Trump's great moments of leadership be followed by moments of weakness? Nobody wants to see a nuclear war or millions of people die, but we must face the terrible truth. The truth is World War III is coming and we can't willingly fornicate with the devil to appease him. Appeasing and negotiating with the enemy won't stop this war from happening. The devil you fornicate with today is preparing to knife you in the back tomorrow. President Trump certainly makes mistakes that anger many people but he has something going for him that all the evil dictators don't. He has great love and reverence for God, and cares deeply about the United States of America, God's country. In return, God Himself has President Trump's back.

Many of us have become disillusioned with our leadership and suspect they are all on the take. Those who don't like President Trump are spending billions to bring him down with investigations, mudslinging and accusations that seem to have no end. There was even a porn star who became a media darling because Trump's enemies have an insatiable appetite to bring him down. While the loudmouths are spending millions of taxpayers' dollars to play these legal games, the world is burning. Do you even care? Can any of our elected officials be trusted 100 percent of the time? Of course not! None of you can be trusted 100 percent of the time. You all have egos and that is your open door for the evil inclination to enter and do its dirty work. At the end of every day it is always about you and your own selfish best interest. Deny it but I promise you this is the absolute truth. The only time I've seen the USA come together was briefly after we breathlessly watched over 3000 Americans die on 9/11. It took an act of terror and watching the towers go up in flames for us to see who you all truly are on the inside. Heroes. The first responders ran into those towers like a mother running to save her children. They cared not about themselves and gave their lives to save others. Sadly, buildings need to burn once again before everyone wakes up and comes together as one family under one God. It takes facing death and destruction for people to behave like the leaders and heroes we need in our world.

President Donald Trump ran his presidential campaign on the premise that he couldn't be bought because he was already a wealthy billionaire. While I voted for him to be our President, I recognized that this was a false claim. Not only can President Trump be bought, so can all of you without exception. When push comes to shove, your precious portfolio, bank accounts, public persona, reputation, friendships and family relationships matter more than choosing God and goodness. Some may respond to this accusation by saying that I am unfair and judgmental. I am not unfair or judgmental. I am simply correct.

The world is burning and you are sitting on your lazy behinds being loudmouths and lackeys and doing absolutely nothing to end the madness. While President Trump has the guts to take on the bad guys, he hasn't shown the guts to admit he has sinned against God or publicly admit he has made horrible personal mistakes. Just like President Trump, none of you have shown the courage to face your sins head-on, admit your guilt publicly, and make restitution. When I post programs explaining that our problems are self-created and we need to address our personal shortcomings you all seem to retreat. Instead of being willing to admit your mistakes, apologize and make restitution for the horrible mess you all created, you are pointing the accusing finger at everyone else. Everyone is squabbling like spoiled children blaming each other instead of being a rising star and becoming a great leader yourself. It is much easier and feels more empowering to you when you join the ranks of the incessant loudmouths defending yourself and your political ideology or religious group.

The Liberal Left blames the Conservative Right and the Right returns the favor by blaming the Left, all the while our world is heading for nuclear war. You would gladly sell your souls to the devil himself if it kept your damned stock portfolio ticking upward and paid off the mortgage on your lovely suburban home. You are all shamelessly fornicating with the golden calf without exaggeration. The self-righteous Liberals and haters of President Trump scream about how repugnant he is but it wasn't too long ago that everyone including them flocked to his classes and purchased his book where he taught you *The Art of the Deal*. You all adored him because you wanted to learn the techniques he used to become rich and famous. You gave him your love, your dollars and found him hilarious and adorable on his program *The Apprentice* as he coined the phrase, "You're Fired!" Not so funny when he fired you James Comey. Mr. Comey responded to being fired as Director of the FBI by writing a salacious book filled with rancor and taunts including ridiculing the size of our President's hands. What was that all about? While I haven't bothered to read James Comey's filthy book, it sounds eerily reminiscent of prepubescent bullying and quite unbecoming of a former Director of the FBI. But you all loved it, didn't you? His book sold over 600,000 copies in just the first week after it was released and James became a media darling too just like the porn queen who gave President Trump a hard time. Nasty sells well in America and around the world. Being nasty and spreading evil makes you a boatload of money in a world void of great leaders.

Admit it folks. You all claim to hate President Trump but you are all President Trump. You all are beginning to remind me of the funny character Mini-Me from the movie *Austin Powers*. When given your golden opportunity, you all behave like miniature Donald Trumps to make that deal and rake in your money. Donald J. Trump is the poster child for everything that succeeds in the good old USA. Pompous arrogance, sexist comments, bullying techniques, take no prisoners and win at all costs. That's precisely what earned him his billions and that's precisely what excites every American whether you voted for him or not. Even the evangelical Christians are brimming with optimism that President Trump will keep their coffers filled with greenbacks while keeping all the Islamic bad guys and illegal aliens at bay.

If you deny this you are a liar and a faker. If you are honest you will look at President Donald Trump and see yourselves in him. All his worst and ugliest traits are staring back at you every day when you wake up and look in your mirror. He may have a much larger ego than you, but you have a huge ego as well.

Some of you have even convinced yourselves that having an ego is something good when egotism is nothing but pure evil.

Here is where President Donald Trump departs from almost everyone else, separates himself from the wolf pack, and bravely reveals himself as a child of God and a born leader. He saw America, the country he loves, skidding down the road to hell on earth. He recognized the house of horrors that the Obamas built in eight short years and chose to do something to rectify it. Instead of sitting around and waiting for the Messiah to show up to clean up this mess, he sacrificed his cushy billionaire life and risked everything to save yours. While President Trump has a very large personal swamp of his own to clean up, his lifetime of sins pale in comparison to most of yours. Why? Because when he saw our American house going up in flames he courageously decided to run like a mother into that burning building to save his children, his grandchildren, you and all your children. While you incessantly argue, whine, complain and do absolutely nothing, he stepped up and chose to do something. What are most of you doing right now besides complaining? Absolutely nothing.

I stand alone in this world as the lone leader who can't be bought and won't compromise my ethics or belief system under any circumstance. When they applied enormous pressure on me to take those psychological drugs and insisted I couldn't hear God, I said, "NO. I will not!" Under the same circumstances, the rest of you cave into the pressure and take those evil meds without questioning. I have no material wealth any longer, I continue to risk my life by telling the truth and publishing this book, and I've sacrificed everything to save my children and yours. If Hashem blesses me to succeed, this book will sell enough copies that I can stay safe, keep speaking out, reveal what is wrong, explain how to fix this mess, and keep working on world peace long enough to make a positive impact. It should be clear by now that I am not doing this for money or prestige although some still might accuse me of being an opportunist.

While I'm not in this for the money, I pray daily that barrels full of riches fall on my head soon and I become enormously wealthy. I desire great wealth to declare to the world—GOD WINS! I stayed true to my convictions and He said YES. If I am blessed with material wealth the first thing I desire to do is bless others. Would you do the same? No, sadly you would not. If millions or billions of dollars fell on your head through the grace of God the first thing any of you would do is spend bundles of it on yourself. You might deny this but I know it's true. You'd run out to buy something expensive and start snapping those selfies to post your new acquisition all over the internet. In this not so wonderful world it's all about the big brag. After Mike Pompeo took those disgusting pictures with the North Korean Dictator, he came back to the State Department bragging that, "the swagger is back." It doesn't matter if it's money, acquisitions, trophies, or applause. It's all a competition and you crave to enjoy the big brag.

I see the Yetzer Hara, Satan, in all of you without exception. You choose evil willfully all day long, most of the time without knowing it. You must begin to learn to recognize evil and stop choosing it now. I see the Yetzer Hara in President Trump and in Benjamin Netanyahu the Prime Minister of Israel. Here is what you need to know now about these two world leaders. While the public is on a wild-eyed crusade to take these two men down, they are the two most capable leaders among us. In the words of Hashem God, they have many personal transgressions for which they must repent, but so do ALL of you. Are you going to continue to spend billions and waste precious time to defame and castrate them in public when they are your best hope for great leadership? Stop being loudmouths and lackeys and give these two men a break. Better yet, start becoming leaders yourselves, and help them bring us world peace.

Trump and Netanyahu must personally face Hashem and clean up their personal swamps, but so must all of you. None of you are sinless. If you continue to fight and point your fingers at others in blame you are giving our enemy time to build their missiles and point them at your children. Wake up now and choose to become the great leader you desire to see in our world. Stand bravely and reveal God through your actions and help clean up this mess.

Round 9: EVERYONE Has a Religion

The world is filled with people who are certain their personal belief system is the correct one. In this round I'm going into the boxing ring with Jews, Christians, Muslims, Atheists, Agnostics and every other form of religion that I'll need to lump together as one. I'm not an expert on world religion, I am the Moshiach. I'll leave that expertise to others while I work to clear the air and bring sanity where there isn't any. While the Atheists and Agnostics tout that they aren't part of any religion, they have created their own religious philosophy and group ideology to worship themselves. Here is Merriam-Webster's definition of religion as a source to help validate this assertion further. *Religion: a cause, principle, or system of beliefs held to with ardor and faith.* Atheism and Agnosticism are raw forms of idolatry and are religions of non-belief in our Creator. Atheists and Agnostics are religious fanatics espousing that they have all the answers to our questions in life while they shove their self-righteous lies down everyone else's throats. Dear self-anointed non-believers and people of all religious faiths, welcome to boxing round 9.

While the Jewish Children deserve a boxing round all to themselves, I will address them last in this one. They deserve the strongest tongue lashing of all the people in our world because our future lies squarely on their shoulders. The Jewish people bear the most burden and pressure in bringing world peace. It may appear that I go a bit lighter delivering my diatribe to them, but it isn't because they don't deserve it. It's because they don't really require it to wake up. Being lighter in my condemnation of them isn't due to any form of nepotism because I am a fellow Jew. I intend to be as hard or soft as needed to wake everyone up to the recognition we are in peril. All that's required to get the Jewish people to sit up at attention and do what they must do is to help them realize that Hashem is angriest with them. This realization will be humiliating enough. Trust me, knowing that Hashem, their Father and King is angriest and most disappointed in them will be completely devastating. The Jewish children are His light unto the nations and His chosen children to lead the world to peace. They hold the future of our world in their hands. Without the Jewish people standing up and choosing to lead humanity out of darkness, we are all doomed.

I'm going to begin this round by beating the Christian children about the head to wake them up. Are you ready?

So Christian brethren, what do you think God says about all the Christian children, their chosen religious leaders, and Christian politicians who publicly love and revere Jesus? First and foremost, let's get your Messiah's name right. There are no Jewish boys named Jesus. Right from good morning you are propagating lies. "So, what!" you might say. "What's in a name?" The Christians of the world parade around claiming to have the ultimate truth when you don't even know or understand what the truth is because you haven't been taught or studied it. If you are courageous enough and desire world peace you must learn the truth. Jewish people who study God's Torah, the only written word existing in our world that came directly from God Himself, know how critically important our names are and understand it is a sin to change them. Changing Yeshua's name to something non-Jewish is nothing short of blasphemy.

When you changed Yeshua's name, you also felt entitled to change the truth about what happened to him. Your Christian "Holy Bible" is filled with monumental lies. Are you aware of this? Hashem says your "Holy Bible" also includes a great deal of truth but if the truth is mixed with lies your book is tainted. After telling the first lie by changing the name of your Messiah, you also decided to rename and edit Hashem's Holy Torah. You made some convenient modifications to make yourselves victorious in the God game. The Christian Bible begins with something called "The Old Testament" which many claim is the same as the written Torah, the Five Books of Moses. I can't tell you if it truly is God's Torah because Hashem instructed me never to pick up or read this book. I know there have been revisions and incorrect translations because of the most famous one—that Moses had horns. Moses didn't come down off that mountain with horns God forbid! He came down glowing in the light of Hashem God. This led to a horrific statue of Moses with horns and a great deal of anti-Semitic lies over the years that Jews have horns too. The many lies in the Christian Bible are foul and completely misleading. By changing the name of the Torah and changing the name of Yeshua to something Anglican and non-Jewish, a new world religion was born. The Roman Catholic Church is built on the blood of the Jewish Messiah, Yeshua ben Yosef.

After renaming God's Holy Torah the "Old Testament" you then diminished its importance by creating your own man-made "New Testament." Yeshua's name and the name of the Five Books of Moses were conveniently changed to create a new and prosperous religion while protecting the filthy foul barbarians who murdered Hashem's Jewish Messiah. The slippery slope to damnation gets worse. Instead of repenting for your sins, you have gleefully candy coated what Hashem has told me was the worst and most egregious crime in the history of humanity, the gruesome crucifixion of God's Messiah. You lied and said Yeshua was God's "sacrificial lamb" and then turned his dead bludgeoned body into gold artwork to adorn yourselves. Christians around the world adorn themselves with earrings and necklaces of Yeshua's dying bloody flesh as though he is their personal trophy. The Catholics ritualistically drink his blood and eat his body, UGH! Do intelligent people truly believe this frightening doctrine? Please say no! Your unholy Catholic communion ceremony is paganism and this behavior is metaphorically cannibalism.

All the people of the world including the Christians are responsible for murdering Yeshua ben Yosef but instead of accepting guilt you fantasize and lie to yourselves that he died to save you by assuming all your sins. This is an incomprehensible lie because nobody can assume the sins of another person. God Himself will NOT assume your sins for you. Are you remotely aware of that fact? Everyone is answerable for their transgressions and must repay their own debts. Not only did you murder Yeshua, Hashem's Jewish Messiah, you have led the charge to murder Hashem God's Jewish children throughout history too.

In addition to murderous rampages around the globe to convert everyone to your religion, Christians led the charge to commit genocide against God's chosen children in the Nazi holocaust. You believe you have the only ticket into God's Kingdom and are His favorite children because you have accepted His Messiah as your savior.

It's time for you to accept the truth about "the Rapture," a belief held by many evangelical Christians. Devout Christians are attached to a fantasy that in the end of time there will be some sort of miraculous event when Christian believers who proclaim they love Jesus and accept him as their Messiah will go straight to heaven free of sin, pure and lily white. There is good news and bad news. I'll give you the bad news first. *The Rapture* as you have described in Christian literature is untrue. If you don't wake up, learn the truth and begin thinking correctly, the opposite will be true for you. The truth is much different and certainly more believable.

Here is the good news. There will be a form of rapture in our future. This rapture will be shared by all of God's children who accept Him and obey His laws. As defined by Merriam-Webster's online dictionary the term *rapture* has three different meanings.

> *rapture:*
> *1. an expression or manifestation of ecstasy or passion*
> *2a: a state or experience of being carried away by overwhelming emotion*
> *2b: a mystical experience in which the spirit is exalted to a knowledge of divine things*
> *3. often capitalized: the final assumption of Christians into heaven during the end-time according to Christian theology*

Hashem says while the Christian idea of *Rapture* is untrue, one day humanity will experience a form of rapture. As we come together as one people under one God to heal our world we will enjoy overwhelming emotions of love, ecstasy and passion knowing that God is real and world peace is attainable. When world redemption is completed and the Third Holy Temple is built on Temple Mount in Jerusalem, we will enjoy a mystical experience in which Hashem God's presence can be felt. Everyone will know God is real and He is the Father and King of the Universe. This divine knowledge will bring rapturous joy for all of humanity and lasting peace on earth.

If you don't acknowledge all your sins and repent, you will go straight to damnation. This is not a threat to the Christians and I'm not being cruel or harsh. I'm pleading with you to wake up and save your souls before it's too late. The future for those accepted into Hashem's world to come will be filled with overwhelming joy and spiritual ecstasy because we will all know Him. He promises there will be no evil or war and humanity will be united in love.

That is a form of rapture that is possible for every person to experience but there are no guarantees. We are being judged in this moment and you must do the work of repentance or experience the opposite of redemption—extinction or damnation for eternity.

Christians have been parading around the world for thousands of years as the holy rollers of humanity trying to save everyone else from damnation by accepting their lord and savior Jesus Christ. While there was no such thing as Jesus, there was a Jewish Messiah, Yeshua ben Yosef, and there is a Jewish Moshiach once again. If you don't accept and learn the truth in the End of Days, you are doomed. Christians are correct in that there is truly a place of damnation and it's more hideous and frightening than most people in this world can fathom. It's far worse than anything a demonic terrorist can do to another human being while here in flesh. Some people have died, experienced only a portion of how horrific this place truly is, and lived to tell. These people are Hashem's gift to humanity because they provide testimony which comes to you with a supreme warning. These fortunate souls provide you with knowledge about what you face if you don't buckle up now and get this life right. While there are many who have had the experience of crossing over and returning to tell, I will only point you in the direction of two. There are two people who have had near-death experiences that you would be best served to learn from. The first is a young Israeli boy named Natan.

If you haven't watched videos on YouTube about Natan, please do. In the YouTube search field, enter "Natan Israeli boy" to find the full video where he recounts his experiences. Hashem and I have watched this video together and the boy is speaking truthfully, is authentic and most of what he says is accurate. I won't pull apart each word for you here. The importance of this video is to reveal information you must embrace immediately. Natan had his near-death experience on September 28, 2015 and said the Moshiach would arrive imminently, many people would know who Moshiach was and everyone would be shocked. He said in his video that people would comment "Oh that's what Moshiach is." What is Moshiach? Hashem's Shechinah, Bashert and the Mother of His children.

I made Aliyah and arrived in Israel in October of 2015 just after Natan's near-death experience. About a year later on the 9th of Av 2016, I announced on YouTube that I am Hashem's Moshiach. After posting this on social media everyone chose to ridicule or ignore me. I haven't hidden myself, many thousands have seen my videos and posts, and many people in Israel know who I am. To say that a woman is anything but a huge shock is an understatement. In his video Natan also reveals that World War III will be nuclear and this war is imminent. The boy is correct, this war is coming soon, won't be avoided and all the people of the world have much to learn from the Jewish people. If you don't begin to learn and repent, you are ALL doomed. If you watch Natan's video, concentrate on the part where he faced the heavenly court and felt completely humiliated. Begin repenting, known in Hebrew as making teshuvah, now.

The second person I will direct you to is Rabbi Alon Anava. Like Natan, he also died and lived to tell. You can watch his video about his near-death experience at Alonanava.com. Alon Anava is an Israeli man who was raised as a completely secular Jew. At the time of his near-death experience he had no belief in God, and led a decadent life filled with sex, drugs and lots of money. He died one day in the back of a New York City taxi and Hashem allowed him to visit the other side and return. On his visit to the non-physical realm he had a life changing experience and received the gift of returning to share his story. In his brush with death, he was sent to a place that truly exists however you should all know that the place Rabbi Anava visited was not true damnation to the fullest extent. True damnation is light years worse than what Alon experienced. Rabbi Anava, a once tattooed drug-abusing derelict who transformed himself into a Chassidic rabbi, experienced slightly more than a minute in a place void of Hashem God. Watch his video as he describes this experience and focus on the dark and frightening place that scared him straight. While I recommend you watch the entire video, focus on this portion of his story which begins at time stamp 32:15. He describes a hideous and frightening place that might sound familiar to Christians who have been educated about damnation. The place that he visited pales in comparison to where non-Jews will be sent if they are banished from God's world to come.

Contrary to Christian belief, Jewish souls will not be banished to damnation. The worst fate a Jew faces if deemed unwelcome into the world to come is spiritual extinction. Damnation is the most frightening and hideous place in the universe and it is reserved for non-Jews. If you have read my book from the beginning without skipping around you will understand why this is the case.

One reason damnation is more hideous than the dark place that Alon Anava visited is because it is filled with many millions of damned souls. If sent there, you will have lots of unwanted company. The most hideous and evil souls this world has ever known will join you for eternity in this horrible place that has no exit. In this dreadful place there is no reprieve or relief from pain. You can scream all you want for Hashem like Alon Anava did and beg Him to forgive you but Hashem says He will not listen. He will not listen to you in the same manner you refused to listen to Him in your lifetime. The truth is far different from the threatening language I endured from Christians throughout my life who said if I didn't accept "their Messiah" I would be damned to hell for eternity. The opposite is true. It is the non-Jews who are heading for damnation, not the Jews. Christians have been taught that when Jesus returns it will be a fun cakewalk as they head up to heaven in some nonsensical glorious rapture. Accepting the truth will be far more difficult than any of you ever imagined.

I implore ALL of you to take the time to watch Rabbi Anava's video and begin to learn from him. Amplify his fear of that dark and frightening place by infinity and you still won't know how horrible damnation will be. He said in his video it felt as though he was there for a billion years without exaggeration. Hashem says that Rabbi Anava was only there slightly more than a minute. His near death experience turned this secular Jew who espoused to be an atheist, abused drugs, smoked cigarettes, tattooed his body, and was an admitted thief into an ultra-orthodox Jewish Chassidic rabbi almost overnight. Nothing in the universe other than Hashem can do that. Rabbi Anava is a lofty soul who died and Hashem blessed him to return so that he could bless everyone else in our world. He was sent to the other side so that one day he could teach you the truthful ways of Torah and help you save your soul.

There are many leaders from all religions who enjoy lofty titles and adulation from their followers. None of them deserve such glory because they propagate lies, continue to sin, and encourage others to sin with them. The problem with everyone except for Torah observant Jews is that you haven't a clue what the truth is or where to begin in your repentance. You are ALL lost souls. You have lied and been lied to for thousands of years. Your lies have emboldened you to create this sinful world that is ready to implode. Christians and the Christian leadership think they are holy and Catholics believe that your holy saints are even holier than you. Brace yourselves and learn the truth that your lofty saints weren't saints at all.

The mere concept of sainthood is ludicrous at best and at worst an abomination in the eyes of God. That isn't to say that some of your anointed holy saints weren't righteous people who brought some goodness into this world. Many of them were good and righteous souls however none of them were sinless. How can Christians even begin to avoid sin when you study from a Bible that begins with a lie? Right from the beginning you have a Bible that espouses "Out with the Old and in with the New." You threw away God's Torah and His laws making them old hat and old-fashioned. The Old Testament, which isn't the Torah, is superseded by your New Testament which is filled with lies. The concept of sainthood is evil since people aren't equipped to judge other people. Only God is our Judge, but you have judged others and canonized saints, who you then kneel and pray to as though they were gods themselves. This sounds like idol worship to me. How about you?

There are religious figures in Christianity whom Hashem has told me are among the most wicked people our world has ever known. The mere mention of one such Christian, Mother Teresa, evokes ire from our Creator. Hashem told me that she was deeply evil and harmed many souls that she claimed to help. Instead of being the humble and righteous soul millions of people were led to believe she was, she traveled the world receiving riches which she sent to the church and not to the poor. She received many humanitarian awards for her own self-aggrandizement and to further her self-serving agenda. The sick and dying that she was supposed to have helped, died in squalor and pain instead. This is hardly the description of a righteous soul and humanitarian.

Many might worry that if Mother Teresa was deemed evil by God Himself, where does that leave them? The Christians don't understand what Satan or evil truly is and that there is no such thing as a fallen angel called Lucifer. Monumental lies and misconceptions have been spread in the name of Christianity causing billions to fall to the evil inclination, the Yetzer Hara, also known as Satan. You don't understand Satan because this information was removed from your Bible. Christians haven't received the proper education about good versus evil. You simply don't know or understand what evil truly is or where it comes from.

While you don't understand the true concept of evil, you are also missing crucial information that encourages you to make up your own laws. Mother Teresa was on a mission to stop all abortions and contraception. Hashem has told me that abortion should never become illegal and is always the choice of the woman without exception. That isn't to say abortion is never a sin. While abortion is a sin in many instances, Hashem desires women to have full autonomy over their reproductive lives. This includes contraception. Mother Teresa who never had intercourse herself had no right to infringe on another woman's personal freedom guaranteed by our Creator. Scream at me now and call me a liar if you must. I am not lying. You will either learn the truth now in flesh, or die and find out in horror on the other side that I am sharing the holy truth.

Christians claim that a human being's life begins at conception. FALSE. A human being's life begins when he or she takes their first breath. If you don't understand when someone's life begins or what happens to you when you die, how can you hope to assess the difference between good or evil? The educated orthodox rabbis learn and study this information given to us by God Himself. It's painfully clear you weren't taught any of this and you must become educated. There are many good Christians who need this education to heal and learn where they are going wrong. A lot of people may be pleasantly surprised to discover that they have chosen much better than many anointed saints or self-anointed holy rollers from their religious community. Choosing goodness and God can't be a lucky guess any longer. You must all learn how to choose correctly, deliberately and on purpose. Stop the insanity and refuse to delude yourselves any longer. Take heart Christian children, the Muslims are great at deluding themselves too.

My knowledge about our Muslim brethren comes directly from Hashem. I've never had any Muslim friends, not by choice but by His design. Everything that happens to us has a purpose. My life never presented the opportunity to befriend a Muslim before but I'm told these relationships are about to begin now.

The Muslims not only believe they hold the winner's trophy in the God game, they are willing to commit suicide to prove it. Worse than suicide, they are willing to encourage their own children to commit suicide too. As they commit the most horrific crimes in this modern era, they shout the ugly worlds "Allahu Akbar" as though their murderous actions are godly. "Allahu Akbar" has become one of the worst obscenities in our world. Iran is calling for the death of the Jewish people and the annihilation of Israel as though the Jews are the evil ones, not them. Muslim societies have been known to abuse their women and children, commit atrocities against non-Muslims, and harm their own brethren too. In November of 2017 there was a bombing and gun attack at an Egyptian mosque in the North Sinai Peninsula where mostly Sufi Muslims were gathered for prayer. In this horrific terrorist attack at least 235 people were murdered and well over 100 people were wounded.

As different Muslim sects terrorize each other along with terrorizing the rest of the world, the Iranian government publicly projects their own guilty and sinful behavior onto the United States by chastising them and claiming that America is the great Satan. This accusation of being evil comes from Iran who is known as the largest state sponsor of terrorism in our world. Most of the world knows that Iran's rhetoric is untrue but sadly their accusation that America is evil isn't completely fallacious either. America is replete with evil in this moment and so is the entire world. Satan, the evil inclination, is a choice that is being made regularly by everyone including the people of Islam. Terrorists who declare "Allahu Akbar" and then kill innocent men, women, and children to remove the infidels from our world won't receive a ticket to heaven either. Many of the terrorists believe that their murderous suicidal rampage will earn them a ticket to heaven where they will fornicate with 72 virgins. Really? Incredibly many Muslims believe this ridiculous claim along with other salacious and filthy lies.

We see Muslims committing atrocities everywhere and many people of all faiths and non-faiths delude themselves into believing that if we can just eliminate all the evil Muslims we will have peace on earth. On the flip side, some commiserate with the plight of the poor Palestinian Muslims in Israel and have joined the anti-Israel BDS movement. They have been brainwashed that Israel is occupying someone else's country and cry out for death to all the Jews, like that will solve their problems. Everyone but Israel is on a murderous rampage to kill everyone else who doesn't agree with their philosophy. You might be tempted to deny this but once again it's simply the truth. Israel is determined to neutralize the enemy and protect its borders. You might hate the Jewish people because you believe that Israel doesn't belong to them in the first place but that is yet another lie. Even the Muslim Quran states that Israel is Jewish land.

In their mission to prove to the world that the Jews are occupiers of a foreign land, the Palestinians and their supporters have changed the rules and created their own country called Palestine. The following will inflame supporters of Palestine further, but the truth is that there will be no such thing as Palestine in the world to come. That doesn't mean there is no Palestinian family or a place for them in God's Holy Land. It simply means that people can have temper tantrums like spoiled children, kick and scream to try and get their way, but God's way will always reign supreme.

There will be no two-state solution, there is only God's solution. Hashem bequeathed Israel to His Jewish children. Everyone has this fact written somewhere in their religious books which they read, pray from, and claim to believe are completely truthful. Israel is bequeathed to God's chosen children, the Jewish people, and this truth is correctly stated in the Quran. Read it, weep and accept the truth. Peace on earth depends upon everyone reaching for and accepting God's will.

I'm not learned in the Eastern religions but like many people I have been wowed by some of the quotes circulating the internet attributed to the current Dalai Lama, the leader of the Tibetan Buddhism movement. I don't read books on Buddhism, Hinduism or any of these religious groups and I don't fully know everything there is to know about the Buddhists. Recently I watched some videos of the current Dalai Lama and was sadly disappointed. While he was sweet, jovial, and shared many uplifting ideas, he never once mentioned God. Although he seemed to give some good life coaching advice about how to lift your spirit, he lost me at hello. In several videos he spoke at length about the importance of laughter, joy, compassion, friendship, being giving, and being egoless. These are good personal traits for us all to emulate but without God Himself central in our every thought we will perish. Like many religious leaders, the Dalai Lama dresses in special clothing. He wears robes which look like perpetual pajamas so he appears egoless to the world. While he espouses that we should all be unaffected by the opinions of others, he travels the world working extremely hard to impress others by masquerading as a person void of egotism and materialism. Oops! How could I trash the poor Dalai Lama?! Nobody in this world is safe from the Moshiach. Et tu Dalai Lama, you have fallen to the evil inclination like everyone else. You simply can't pretend or emulate being egoless and void of materialism. You are what you are and can't role-play yourself into enlightenment.

While the Dalai Lama seems like a joyful and beautiful man I'd love to meet one day for a beer, he has much to learn about the truth. The truth is our personal God, Hashem, is real and meditation without prayer directly to Him is pure insanity. It might look beautiful, and sound holy to omm and ahh in deep mediation but it isn't holy at all. It's a show that looks holy to the public and you may believe this is what true enlightenment looks like, but enlightenment doesn't look like anything. Enlightenment is the godliness you bring into this world and how you treat others. Wearing the clothing of enlightenment may make you feel better and impress people around the world, but God Himself knows what is underneath your clothing and inside your mind. He knows your every thought without exception. He knows when your speech is contrived and part of a masquerade party to impress the world. If you don't learn the truth, pray to the One very personal God of all Creation, and learn the ways of Hashem, you will meditate and chant yourselves straight to damnation. This is true even if you have a beautiful smile, witty sense of humor and engaging personality.

Go look in the mirror children of God. You are ALL guilty of sin as charged. You can't kill the last terrorist because the next terrorist is YOU. Atheists and Agnostics think they are holier than all the holy rollers because they are void of a filthy religion. Religions based on God aren't filthy—people are the problem. Reaching for God is correct but worshiping your group or religion as the smartest and best people in all the world is pure evil. Atheists and Agnostics refusing to believe in anything other than themselves is idolatry. Atheism is a religion based on self-worship. Non-believers are God to themselves. Be forewarned, in the world to come nonbelievers will be nonexistent.

Stephen Hawking was a pompous atheist and scientist who was lauded for being a supernatural genius. He may have been a genius in this world, but in Hashem God's world he was an impudent fool. I woke up in the middle of the night to read on my iPhone that he had just died. Immediately I said to Hashem, "Is Stephen happy now that he knows there is one unifying force behind the entire universe?" I read once that this was something he always wondered and wanted to figure out when he was alive.

In that moment Hashem allowed him to reply to me directly and Stephen said, "Ken Lori." I found his response obnoxious and offensive. Even in death he revealed himself to be arrogant and foolish. By saying the word *ken* which is Hebrew for *yes* he was clearly being haughty. Hashem told me that he didn't know how to best connect with me and thought this was a way to be endearing. Although he may have had a polite intention, his approach was contrived. You may not even see this small nuance of arrogance the way Hashem and I did in that moment. In a time to come you must learn that any form of being contrived or arrogant is evil. Hashem softened Stephen's affected speech by telling me he hadn't cleansed in Gehenom yet and still had much to learn. If you think your noble scientists are the smartest people in the room, you are wrong. They might know facts and figures but when someone chooses pretentious behavior they become an ignorant sinner. Sinners come in all levels of IQ.

Here is another illustration revealing the hypocrisy behind Stephen Hawking's atheist views. Just a few months before his death there was a news report that he was ringing the alarm bells to wake up humanity and warn us we were on the verge of extinction. In this news article Stephen said he feared sex robots were soon to take over the earth. Immediately I said to Hashem that his fear was laughable, foolish and hypocritical. If he truly cared about the well-being of humanity and our world, then sex robots would be the perfect solution for an atheist. After all, sex robots couldn't do any worse than we are all doing right now. Of course, I know something that Mr. Hawking needed to die to find out. God is real and the only thing that will become extinct are atheists like him.

Other world-renowned geniuses who publish a journal called *The Bulletin of the Atomic Scientists* recently set the metaphorical Doomsday Clock to two minutes to midnight. This was meant to be a stark warning to everyone that if we don't make immediate changes we will see the end of our world. Gratefully it isn't the end of this world or humanity that will ultimately occur. It will be the end of life for those who worship themselves over God.

Finally, my Jewish family, will you please wake up! You hold the truth in your hands and the world needs to learn from you. How in the world can we be led out of this nightmare when only a few million Jews bother to read and observe the Torah? The reform, conservative, and secular Jews of the world have all broken their covenant with God Himself. It's time to return to Hashem and keep your promise. Many Jewish people are as clueless and in the dark as the most clueless goyim. If you were raised like me then you don't even know what is inside the mezuzah. This is such a travesty but it's even worse than a personal nightmare for every Jew. Every single Jew who doesn't observe a Jewish way of life turns off one of the lights we need in our world. Our world is almost in complete darkness. When many of you married outside of your Jewish faith thinking it was your right to be happy, you betrayed yourself, your families, and all of humanity. It is the Jewish nation that holds Hashem's Torah and was entrusted to bring light into this physical world. You have all breeched His trust and broken your covenant. Even so, Hashem places His full faith in you now.

The goyim, the non-Jews, and self-hating Jews around the world view the way of life observed by Orthodox rabbis with long beards and black hats as a form of insanity. As I've revealed throughout this book, the opposite is true. The world is completely insane and the black-hatted Jewish rabbis are your only defense. They are truly the only hope in this sick and evil world. It is because the Torah observant few have studied Hashem's Torah and kept His laws that there is still hope for humanity. The Torah observant minority have protected our world by stubbornly staying separate from the evil within mainstream society. It's like the movie *Men in Black* where Tommy Lee Jones and Will Smith were secret agents who dressed in black and were part of the best kept secret in the universe. In the Hollywood film, this well-funded group of Men in Black led the charge to protect the earth from evil aliens who continuously threatened our existence. The best kept secret in this world is that the true Men in Black saving us from extinction are the religious Orthodox Jewish rabbis. Every day as these men pray and put on their Tefillin they are saving everyone's lives. By observing Hashem's Torah and mitzvot (laws) they keep the light of God sparkling in our world. Without them performing these daily mitzvahs there would be no world to save. It's time for every Jew in the world to return to Hashem, make Teshuvah, follow His commandments, help the Jewish Men in Black teach everyone Torah and exemplify what Hashem desires from us all. The Jewish people, the light unto the nations, will lead the charge to bring us world peace through love, education and charity.

Round 10: Nukes, Pollution & More. Time's Up.

You don't have to be a religious zealot who believes in Bible prophecy to know that our world is in deep trouble. If you are honest with yourself then you are likely extremely worried that the next world war is coming soon and this one will undoubtedly be nuclear. Perhaps you're in denial about World War III and felt excited when you heard that the Iranians signed a nuclear agreement back in July of 2015. Some of you had your optimism dashed when the dastardly President withdrew from that agreement in 2018. After he publicly withdrew we all watched as the Iranian politicians burned the American flag as they called for death to America. The sight of the Iranians doing this should have validated President Trump's decision to withdraw, but many hate him so much they refuse to accept the truth. The truth is that this agreement never should have been signed in the first place. Instead of supporting President Trump's decision, we saw moronic behavior from people like John Kerry, the former Secretary of State, engaging in his own "shadow diplomacy" with this murderous regime. Mr. Kerry who is no longer an official of the United States government, was part of the mastermind club behind this foul nuclear agreement. He met with Iranian leadership to attempt to rescue what he believed was his own personal triumph. Like John Kerry, all of those who oppose President Trump seem to believe that they're the smartest people in the room. Whether you appreciate President Trump's policies or not, we all know he is in an extremely tough spot and making life and death decisions. Here is the truth nobody on either side of the aisle wants to face. We are going to war.

Hashem has made it clear to me in many conversations and prophetic visions that we are about to enter into a gut-wrenching third world war. He says this war is required because everyone is choosing evil. You are all completely in the weeds and can't see the forest for the trees. Everyone is stuck believing in their own false notions of right versus wrong and EVERYONE is choosing wrong too often.

Unless President Trump gets a crash course in Torah and follows Hashem's guidance, he is doomed to fail in the eyes of God. Right now, he and his staff are designing his next "Art of the Deal" for peace in Israel. Being the consummate negotiator, he will work hard to force both sides to make concessions. That's what negotiators in business do, but this isn't a business deal. He's already revealed both sides will need to give something to get something. That's how you successfully negotiate in this material world. Each side gives up a little something they don't want to sacrifice to get something else they desire. Nowhere in these negotiations are you including God's explicit desires. Every monotheistic religion knows Israel is the homeland of the Jewish children. So, what exactly are we negotiating about? Negotiating a two-state solution is an evil folly that must come to an end.

You are all being liars and frauds if you pull out your annual God card and pretend that you include Hashem in every decision. You do not. Without exception you have all forgotten and forsaken Hashem, and that includes ALL His chosen Jewish children. You might not forsake Him in every moment but if you are given enough rope, you all hang yourselves by choosing evil. We must face it kids, World War III is right around the corner and there is the real possibility you will be forced to bury your children or your children will bury you. World war is certainly coming but war isn't the only reason we are dying in record numbers. Pollution, poisons and diseases are overtaking our world and destroying our well-being.

You have destroyed God's beautiful earth and continue to poison each other for profit. Climate change does exist and this phenomenon is a result of all your collective sins against the environment. Your fake ideas and policies to reverse air pollution are simply a band-aid approach that feels good to the elected politicians who benefit by lining their wallets with more money. Polluters purchasing carbon credits allowing them to pollute won't solve the problem and is just another way to fill your unholy bank accounts. Your collective greed and laziness has destroyed our oceans, rivers, and the air we breathe. The poison is everywhere and nobody has the resolve to do the right thing to fix it. Our food supply is poisoned with additives and preservatives to help improve the bottom line for the food manufacturers. While they make more money putting these carcinogens in our food, we die from cancer in increasing numbers and the world has become grossly obese. Your body wasn't designed to metabolize those poisons and men, women, and children all over the world are growing fatter and sicker by the minute.

Some might yell at me, "Hey that's not fair to blame me. I'm an environmentalist, vegan, I eat only organic foods and I recycle!" Well good for you Mr. or Ms. Goody Two Shoes. You can recycle all you desire, refuse to eat animals or use animal products (by the way God instructed us to eat meat) but you and everyone else are doomed anyway. The pollution that's choking all of us is growing faster than the most aggressive forms of cancer. Your resolve isn't strong enough to fight the wave of greed that feeds this insidious monster. The reason: EVERYONE IS PROFITING. While you all make your salaries, buy foods, drugs and products for expediency and convenience, everyone is dying. It doesn't look that way in the moment because you aren't willing to look close enough. Everyone's eyes seem to be sewn shut. If you were brave enough to take on this monster, you would be required to sacrifice. Sacrifice? Not you! Your almighty pocketbooks and cushy convenient lives come first. You might as well admit it now. This is the truth.

Even if you were personally willing to sacrifice everything you had to save the planet, you'd have to be relentless and convince the rest of the world to join you. You can't do this alone. You'd have to ruffle feathers and be the constant bug in everyone's ear and eventually your friends and family would become repulsed by the mere sight of you and run for cover. Choosing to be the holy mosquito biting at everyone to help you do your holy work would eventually leave you abandoned and force you to stand entirely alone. I've never met anyone besides me who was willing to be completely alone, and I understand why. Being alone is dreadful and without Hashem speaking to me in every moment, my life would be unlivable.

Imagine one day that we discovered a worldwide cure for cancer and every other disease known to mankind. That's right, a cure for every single kind of disease like cancer, diabetes, heart disease, multiple sclerosis and on and on. What do you think would happen next if a genius discovered a magic pill that cures everything? I will tell you what would happen. There would be a secret agent who would be hired by the powers that be to find that genius, exterminate him or her, and bury any of the information about this miraculous pill so that no person could ever swallow it! No, I'm not a conspiracy theorist. I'm just your Moshiach, remember? I've turned on the lights for you the way I'm supposed to but it's become painfully clear that the lights are on and nobody is home.

Wake up to the sad truth. Nobody is completely motivated to cure cancer or other diseases because you would all face losing trillions of dollars. When you play out what would happen in the aftermath of all diseases suddenly being cured, the financial losses would be absolutely staggering. One of the first to take the financial hit would be the rich pharmaceutical companies with their well-paid employees and wealthy executives who make an extremely large income selling oncology drugs. Cancer is only one disease state cured in this hypothesis. What about all the doctors, nurses, and hospitals that would have no more patients to serve? Oh dear. There goes your glorious global economy built on a foundation of greed and evil. When push comes to shove, you don't truly want to cure anything because of the financial pain it would cause you if you did. You would have to sacrifice too much. Sure, you want your loved ones healed from these diseases, but if suddenly the world no longer dealt with illness, billions of you would need to find another form of livelihood. The financial implications would be too painful. Instead of feverishly working for that cure, you're all waiting for your man of the hour, the Messiah on a donkey, to sacrifice his life so you can have more. Your Messiah is a miraculous magician who will be sent to cure all diseases while bringing you the large amounts of cash you all deeply desire. In your dream scenario it's all joy and no pain. Hallelujah praise the Lord, right? Wrong. Fahgettaboudit! It isn't happening that way. It's time to let go of your fantasies about Messiah right now.

If you pause, become very quiet and truthfully examine yourselves you would need to admit what I'm revealing here is true. Cleaning up this mess includes you admitting that you are sinning and up until now you have shown you're unwilling to make that admission. Do some online research now and see how troubled our world is in this moment and how scientists all over the globe are trembling at the enormous mess everyone in our world helped create. In the news recently, marine biologists sent out another warning to let you know that the Great Barrier Reef is dying. The fish and all the marine life are dying or sick from the filth being continuously dumped into our oceans. You, your children, and all your neighbors are eating the filth that you refuse to clean up. The poisons that are constantly being emitted into the air and dumped into our water are finding their way into the food supply. At this pace, soon there won't be clean water to drink or clean air to breathe. What then? Most of the world is silent and in your silence, is your complicity. You are all accomplices in this crime. There are many of you who might become incensed with my assertion because you consider yourselves environmentalists and not criminals at all. Some of you have even led the charge to create organizations and companies that work to clean up the mess but your efforts are like the little Dutch boy with his finger in the dike. The dam is about to blow because enough of you simply haven't faced the ultimate truth. The truth is that everyone is continuously sinning daily without pause. How so? If you don't know Hashem's laws, you break them. Not knowing His laws is no longer an excuse. You must gather together and learn.

I've heard about internet movements encouraging global repentance. There have even been organized events which encouraged everyone to come together and repent at the same time. In these global prayer vigils, they encouraged everyone to give a collective "I repent" in a global nonsensical session of world prayer. Warning children of God: Hashem does not accept nonsense. To receive His forgiveness for any transgression you must be honest, sincere and express remorse for your sins. To do that you need to know what you did wrong in the first place and feel the pain of your error. How can you possibly repent properly when you don't even recognize your own guilt? Everyone is avoiding looking in the mirror but you must. Hashem is staring at you in the face in this moment and you cannot avoid this process of true repentance. A contrived and collective "I am sorry God" will not exonerate you from one sin. Some of your sins have no absolution whatsoever. You aren't even aware that such sins truly exist. You must start the process of repentance now or you face the unthinkable when you die. The unthinkable is learning that your sins have placed the blood of many children on your hands. Again, as I told you in round number 9, go to the time stamp 32:15 of Rabbi Anava's near-death experience on AlonAnava.com and watch this part of his video repeatedly. His frightening experience was a grave warning and a wake-up call not only for him, but for all of you too. He received another chance at life but your experience will be permanent.

Some people reading this may believe this round of my diatribe doesn't apply to them at all. Perhaps you're a good God-loving person who leads a simple life and you don't believe you are materialistic in any way. You give to charity and work hard at your endeavors bringing goodness wherever you go. Perhaps you're someone who owns or runs a local mini-market. You believe your daily work in your local market is positive for the community and you deliberately smile at your customers as you sell eggs and milk to the neighborhood. All the mini-markets in Israel and likely markets in all other developed countries sell cigarettes. Cancer in a stick. You are profiting on giving your neighbors cancer. Oh, not you? Well maybe this example is about someone else and you're not guilty of selling carcinogens.

Perhaps you are a school teacher, plumber, police officer, accountant, office worker or work at some other noble profession instead. Maybe you think that you would undoubtedly support that magic pill that cures every known disease in one fell swoop. You emphatically disagree with my assertion that you wouldn't be completely overjoyed with the results. Imagine God allows such a magic drug to come into being but allows the financial aftermath to take its toll. Doctors, pharma executives, hospital suppliers, healthcare workers, and many other people lose their wealth and livelihoods overnight. The stock market crashes in the fallout. There is suddenly a worldwide depression worse than the one experienced in the 1930s. The next thing you know this depression hits you and your family too and you lose all your worldly possessions because of this little magic pill. We don't have to deal with disease anymore however you and everyone you know has just been rendered penniless. The authorities come the next day to evict you from your home, repossess your vehicle and you and your family are forced to sleep that night in a cardboard box on the street. Do you still want that magic pill? Admit the obvious truth. No, you don't.

Earlier I told you that my former Christian girlfriend and BFF said that she wasn't willing to do the work I was doing. She said she watched me over these years lose literally everything in my life as I stayed devoted to God. One day, in a very telling statement this good mother and God-fearing woman told me, "Lori, I've watched you over the years get divorced, lose your home, all your possessions, and suffer horrifically. I'm not willing to lose everything the way you did." So, I ask you the question: What is your price? What are you willing give up or do for world peace? You might not be willing to give up or do anything willfully. The decision might be removed from you as Hashem decides it's time to take it all away and cause you to drop to your knees. Most of you will pay an extremely high price before you understand it is time to change your ways and reach for God. It took Rabbi Anava a near-death experience and God's blessing to return for him to choose to live a God-driven life. What will your price be?

If you don't believe me yet, and still think you have nothing to apologize for because you aren't responsible for this enormous mess, I pray by the end of this book you feel differently. If I can't convince you, Hashem has told me not to worry because billions of you will eventually wake up and repent. He then said, "I have My ways." If reading His words, "I have My ways" doesn't frighten you, I pray one day He scares the evil out of you. Consider it a supreme honor to be frightened by Hashem like Rabbi Alon Anava and the young Israeli boy Natan in their near-death experiences. If Hashem doesn't frighten you into contrition, that means He has decided you aren't worthy of His attention. Be deeply concerned for the people you love who aren't afraid of Hashem. I pray you aren't one of them.

Round 11: You're ALL Nuts and Worse

Now that we made it to round 11 of this boxing match I hope I managed to hit you with a few blows to the head and you felt sick with guilt several times. If you only felt a little bit nervous or queasy that's an excellent sign! Good for you! If you became riddled with anxiety that you might be doomed, feel this pain and continue reading to the end of this book anyway. Don't dare quit before you finish. In the end I pray you'll see that I'm right about all my assertions and you have done many things wrong. Here is the classic question that the lofty psychologists and psychoanalysts love to ask, "How do you feel about that?"

Are you angry or resentful that I just told you I am right and you are wrong? Admittedly it's agitating when people get in your face and declare they are right and you are wrong. It's nasty and narcissistic behavior to speak like this but remember I have no other agenda but your welfare. I don't have the capacity to be a narcissist although I check myself constantly for any sign of narcissism, an evil and repugnant personality trait. I'm undoubtedly right about all my assertions as I work tirelessly to beat the crap out of you. I do this with love. Are you still attempting to deflect the truth? Do you need to be right in some way? I don't need to be right, I simply am right. You might still feel the urge to shrug me off, make me wrong, or punch me in the face. Here is my warning to you. You can't do any of that to Hashem. In the end, He always wins and you don't want to be on the wrong side of Him.

Your negative feelings or criticism of me mean nothing to me at all. I truly don't care what you think of me and that's because this is all for you. I'm beating you to a pulp, hoping to draw the blood of contrition to save your life. I'm not looking for your adulation or approval and I'm not running for public office. I'm here to help you survive the unthinkable. By survival, I am not referring only to your physical death. I'm working feverishly to save your soul. If you still feel any thoughts of rejecting my efforts you are thinking from your ego and not from your spirit. Your ego is the open pathway to evil and pure insanity. Insanity is truly the personification of the Yetzer Hara, Satan. You might scoff at me and joke that I sound like "the church lady" from *Saturday Night Live* and laugh uproariously. I might laugh at that analogy too. After I'm done laughing, I'm crying and praying that you will finally listen. You might not know or understand the concept of the evil inclination yet but you must begin to learn about this now or you're finished. Kaput.

The mental health system has become one of the most awful and egregiously sinful institutions in our world. You are all being set up for failure by this greedy maniacal clan of people who ask, "How do you feel about that?" as though your feelings are the source of your problems. By placating you and making this a "feel good" society they are enabling everyone to skid down that slippery pathway to damnation. Because of this evil and ridiculous way of measuring your mental health, the pharmaceutical companies have invented elixirs and cocktails to medicate you as though this will remove your troubles. The material world proof their model is broken is in the disgusting pudding. Suicide is at an all-time high and it's now the second leading cause of death among young adults in the USA. Statistics may not impress you but the numbers are staggering. The modern developed nations of the world are now filled with walking zombies. Our drug addicted society is drugging our young and God is barely a whisper in anyone's conversation today. While God is the answer, even the most God-fearing people of our world have no concept of His laws, or His magical prescription for a blessed life. Yes, you are all nuts and life in this world is even worse than I can express in words.

God gave us all a soul and placed us in a vessel to journey and enjoy a physical life on earth. Instead of valuing your soul, you have all succumbed to the worship of your flesh and seek to satisfy all your physical impulses. If you think you are exempt because you are a Chassid and Torah observant rabbi, you are not. You all have the stench of the Yetzer Hara on you without exception. When I was accused of being "nuts" and "psychotic" after my awakening, I refused the drugs. My immediate reaction was to reach to God for answers. In my search for the truth I discovered that the Torah learned Jews were running to the psychiatrists and popping pills like candy just like everyone else. I sat at lunch one day with one of my kippah wearing orthodox Jewish cousins when suddenly his alarm went off on his wristwatch. He said, "Excuse me I need to take my meds now." After I asked him what was wrong he replied, "I have AADD, Adult Attention Deficit Disorder." I thought in that moment that he was nuts but not from any made-up mental disorder. He was choosing to be like many Americans, a prescription drug addict who didn't truly believe in God.

It is completely insane for anyone to claim they are a Torah observant Jew who loves and reveres God in one breath, only to exonerate themselves from observing Torah in the next breath by claiming to suffer from a genetic psychological disorder. The two ideas are incongruent. You can't believe that by His design Hashem requires you to choose between good and evil but in the next breath you excuse yourself because you have a mental defect that relieves you of making that choice. Torah observant Jews all over the world have succumbed to their insatiable desire to choose evil by buying into the secular world explanation that choosing poor behavior isn't their fault.

The secular world has created an evil brew of alphabet soup, creating ridiculous abbreviations for non-curable mental illnesses that exonerate you from choosing God and His goodness. Now you can pay for a legitimate doctor's note that gives you lifelong permission to choose evil. The mental health doctors have absolved you from your responsibility to choose God or His goodness in every moment. It's much easier to swallow their little magic pill than to repent and observe His laws. If you slip and choose poorly despite your meds, you just claim you need to ask your doctor for a new elixir or cocktail. It's not your fault! Gentiles and Jews alike all get a free pass now which exonerates you from any personal responsibility to choose better. My words won't shock many of you because you will simply brush me off as some Bible toting know-it-all as you continue to take your daily dose of those drugs. Millions of people have bought the excuse that they have an inherited mental defect, it's hereditary and it isn't your fault at all. So off you go to the licensed drug dealer and pop those anti-depressants, mood stabilizers, anti-anxiety drugs, sleeping pills and the rest of these elixirs like tic tacs. Even worse than drugging yourselves, you are drugging and killing your children.

Our world has truly become the night of the living dead where humanity is walking around like zombies. You are ALL in a stupor and resisting this wake-up call. It feels much better for you to huddle together in a crowd and self-righteously deny this obvious truth. You can't hospitalize the last nut job who kills people in an act of violence because the next lunatic might be you. Whether you are taking these pills or not, is irrelevant. You have bought into this line of thinking and believe it's socially acceptable. Being bipolar is now like being brown-eyed. It's no longer a stigma since every moment of the day someone else is receiving this lifelong incurable diagnosis. The reality you must face is that bipolar and all your arbitrary abbreviated illnesses are fictional. That isn't to say that there isn't something called mental illness. Mental illness is in ALL of you without exception. True mental illness is the unwillingness to know that Hashem is testing you and that every choice you make which doesn't include Him is evil and pure insanity.

I stand alone in this world as the only person who doesn't have mental illness. I'm incapable of choosing what you ALL so readily choose daily. It's so clear to me that I see your evil choices in every moment and this insanity turns my stomach and makes me feel physically ill. That's truly what happens when you choose evil. You make yourself and everyone around you deeply sick. Watching you choose evil willfully and gleefully every day is heartbreaking not only to me and Hashem, but to all of humanity. This heartbreak extends to the souls who have crossed over into the world of the non-living who are watching this nightmare unfold. I hear their comments all the time as though there is a radio in the room broadcasting their voices from heaven. Some of you call this place heaven but I refer to it as a way station where souls wait patiently to return here for another chance. I hear your loved ones on the other side when they exit this world. Hashem allows me to hear them converse and it often sounds like I'm surrounded by a massive audience of invisible people. I playfully call them my peanut gallery as I listen to their comments. When people first die and cross over they are shown me speaking to Hashem. Their initial reactions are euphoric when they learn that the Moshiach is in Israel. This euphoria quickly fades when they see how alone and destitute I am. Suddenly they recoil in despair and feel deeply ashamed.

Why does their euphoria quickly turn to shame? Because after just a few moments they recognize that when they were here in body they were zombies too. As they listen to me and Hashem converse as I live my daily life, I hear them say, "It's so obvious!" and "There's no question!" as they acknowledge that it's evident to them that I am Hashem's Moshiach. To them it is crystal clear who I am. In the beginning they are joyous and I hear them say things like, "Thank you God, this is a holy miracle." Often, I respond by telling them this is not a holy miracle for me. For me this is a never ending nightmare. I also say to them that while I know I am with Hashem and He says I am Moshiach, I'm not certain I will ever be the Moshiach in this world. As a matter of fact, I'm deeply pessimistic about my future. Their glee then turns to tears and remorse. In their death they are more awake and alive than the people living incarnate in this world. They suddenly possess the knowledge that you and all the living humans refuse to accept. The truth is available but accepting the truth is far too painful and when faced with it you all retreat doing absolutely nothing. It's easier to do nothing and hide behind your doctors' notes than to take the moral responsibility to clean up your own mess.

As I watch all of you walk around in your zombie-like stupors continuing down the path to self-destruction I cry and pray day and night you will wake up to the truth. The truth is that you are all guilty of sinning and are sick with true mental illness. In my darkest moments of despair, I'm certain we are doomed and our world will soon end. I'm positive that our thermometer popped long ago and this holiday turkey is burnt to a crisp. Hashem comforts me in those moments of despair and explains that many of you will wake up and return to Him. He says the good people of this world will ultimately come together and heal our planet but I simply can't see this outcome. He works on me further to infuse me with hope and always manages to persuade me to believe in the unbelievable. Through His loving voice and beautiful visions, He convinces me to continue my work and believe that you will listen and help lead the world to peace.

Everyone I've known has accused me of being the problem since I was born. My family labeled me too sensitive and moody when it was they who were the problem. When Hashem woke me on April 7, 2009 everyone told me that it was impossible to hear God. I was told I was mentally ill when it is truly all of you who are deeply sick and troubled. You and former friends and family all said I was crazy when I told the truth that I was chosen to be your wake-up call. How would Moses have fared in our current world of mental illness diagnosis codes and alphabet soup? The incessant name-calling and accusations never hurt my feelings because it was never about me in the first place.

Along the way I gratefully met several people who at first sight, told me that they knew with certainty that I was the real deal and the Messiah. One such person was my Jewish clairvoyant girlfriend who I spoke about earlier in my book. She valiantly helped me leave my marital home when it was time to save my life. One day after having dinner together, we were cleaning up the dinner dishes and I looked at my iPhone to check the Running on Love Facebook page. In that moment I saw that one thumb, one person, left the page and un-liked Running on Love. I lamented out loud with great emotion, "Oh no, we lost one!"

She turned, looked at me dismissively and said, "Why in the world did He choose you! You can't get upset about every single person that leaves and you must be tougher than that." Wow I thought. Maybe she was right and I'm too weak and sensitive for this role.

In that moment Hashem responded in a loud and forceful voice, "Lori, tell her this is exactly why I chose you." I did as Hashem asked and to this day I don't believe this woman ever understood His answer. You all want someone tough enough to be the Messiah but what we truly need is someone who cares enough. While governments seem to have an acceptable number of casualties in war, I consider each loss unacceptable. I don't like the term *casualty* because it removes the humanity from the loss. Casualty is a nice little euphemism for a dead human being. I cry each time one of you walks away from me but I go forward and continue my work. I feel the pain of your rejection and do this anyway because I must. He comforts me as people continue to thumb their noses and call me names. In those painful moments of rejection, I must walk away, let them go, and move on to whomever I can help. Will I be able to help you?

I ask you the famous question once again, "How do you feel about that?" Do you even want my help? Are you going to walk away angry or resentful and deny you are guilty of any of these sins? Are you willing to let me show you where you have gone wrong and how to correct your errors? How much pain are you willing to accept? When will you stop making excuses like, "It's just the way of the world?" My Jewish clairvoyant girlfriend thought I was weak because losing one of you was one too many for me. What is the cost of your silence and inaction? Once again, I will ask the question, what is your price? How much death and destruction will it take to pry your eyes open and make you wake up to do the hard work of repentance? When will you finally listen, learn and work for world peace? Are you going to quell your spiritual pain by downing a few more pills? Are you going to continue to give some of those pills to your children? Are you willing to open your eyes and do what is required of you to heal yourselves and our world? We shall see.

Round 12: Final Round. I Pray It's a Knockout.

We've reached the final round of our boxing match of contrition. If you haven't seen yourself in any of these examples of sinful behavior, cried at least once, or felt some remorse because you know you've participated in many of these crimes, you are in deep trouble. I'm going to give you my best shot in this final round to help you see that you are the source of the problems you see in our world. If I fail to knock you out and help you see your sins then I have failed to help you. You are going to have to work hard to make me fail. I don't intend to leave one of you standing. If you're still standing smugly claiming this doesn't apply to you then you are facing worse things than you have ever seen in this world. Your blood will not be on my hands if I can help it. Even still, if I lose you, I will mourn and feel painful remorse that I couldn't help you comprehend what I see so clearly.

At the beginning of this extremely long book I asked you to take a journey with me. I brought you through my nightmare and asked you to consider what you would do if this happened to you. What would you have done under the same circumstances? Many if not most people who believe in God would say they would unquestionably follow the path of God and His righteousness. After reading my story from the beginning can you honestly say you would have stayed the course? If you are honest your answer must be unequivocally no. Why am I so certain that you would have gone the way of the doctors and the naysayers? Because when push comes to shove you always choose yourself. I simply can't do that under any circumstance. I must set my own self-interest aside and protect my children and yours from the unthinkable. None of you care to think about the unthinkable as often as I do. Hashem fills me with urgency and prophetic visions that would knock you to your knees if you saw them and knew they were coming directly from God Almighty.

I've watched many prophetically gifted people who speak online about Bible prophecy reveal clear signs that we are now in the End of Days. As they reveal dreams and visions of war that show Biblical prophecy unfolding, they can hardly contain their outward expressions of euphoria and excitement that the prophecies given to us thousands of years ago are true. This makes me scratch my head and wonder, how could you? This information should make everyone drop to their knees and tremble. The goyim, Gentiles, who receive these frightening visions are delighted to receive a sign they believe is coming from God Himself.

Instead of trembling, they rejoice that they are about to be lifted in a Christian-only Rapture and receive rewards in a place they call heaven. How could you? Learned rabbis appeared to be joyous as they listened to the young Israeli boy Natan reveal that he saw nuclear war and millions of people dying. How could you!? If you could see me now, you would see my jaw dropped open in shock. You ALL appear more interested in your Bible prophecies being proven true and your version of the story coming into fruition than in saving each other from catastrophe. Rabbis, who are you reaching out to in this moment to teach Torah and the ways of God Himself besides your yeshiva boys or other Jews? If you are a Christian, you don't know or fully understand the ways of God Himself and will likely be insulted that I said this to you. Do you see? It's all about you once again. Christians may understand portions of the truth but you have a great deal of information wrong or completely missing from your books. You have many facts wrong as you cavort around the world through the internet and propagate false information. Rabbis, are you celebrating that you hold the truth and they don't, or are you sharing your knowledge and teaching?

Whether you are an accountant, lawyer, homemaker, gardener, rabbi, minister, or realtor, if you were the one who lived through my spiritual awakening none of you would have made it this far. You ALL would have caved in and accepted your diagnosis, and would still be taking your psychiatric meds like good mental patients. You would be just like my former Christian girlfriend and BFF who declared that she refused to lose her family, friends, relationships and all her worldly possessions. Do you blame her? No you are just like her. The powers that be would have convinced you that you couldn't possibly be the Messiah, especially if you were incarnate as a woman. The mere idea that you could be a woman and God's Messiah would knock you out of the running. Your measure of perfection and godliness is steeped in the good opinions of other people. The loftiest rabbis and Torah scholars truly believe that Messiah will be a perfect human being, male of course, who is all knowing and able to recite Torah and Talmud verbatim. The Moshiach is the wisest of the wise in the written Torah and knows every single word in the Talmud. Not so! God's measure of brilliance isn't the same as man's measure. You measure everything in material objects as you write, teach and espouse to believe otherwise.

In this world everyone pretends that they admire leadership, honesty, courage, independent thinking, humility, spirituality, loving kindness, and a deep and unrelenting faith in our Master, Hashem God. Every one of my choices made throughout my tale of horrors emulates all those qualities to the fullest degree and what was your response? You incarcerated me four times against my will, drugged me unconscious, stole all my worldly possessions, branded me evil and mentally ill and conspired to take away my three children. "Oh no!" you might say. "That was your filthy anti-Semitic ex-husband and your terribly dysfunctional family. It wasn't me!" You are wrong. My former husband, family, and former BFFs are representative of every one of you. Since my demise, thousands of contacts on LinkedIn and Facebook continue to walk away, peer at my online profile in filthy silence, and are not willing to listen to my programs or engage me. What are you all afraid of? I will tell you. You are petrified that I am telling the truth. I am genuinely speaking with Hashem, the One, and have been honest for over nine years.

If I'm telling the truth, and I am, you have sinned dreadfully by the way you've treated me. I am an ordinary woman who woke up to an extraordinary gift and you ignored me. You all had better things to do and went back to your busy little lives while our children are dying. Many of my former BFFs are exemplary citizens who give to charity, pay their fair share of taxes, and believe in God. They are no longer my BFFs, and by their actions have all officially become FFBs, *Filthy Foul Barbarians*. Hashem has made it clear that there will be no FFBs in the world to come. He will only allow people whom He deems BFF, *Beloved and Faithful Forever* into His Kingdom and the world to come.

Now and forevermore the translation of BFF is *Beloved and Faithful Forever*. These are Hashem's words and His definition. He is separating humanity into two columns. Column A will be those who are "Accepted" into His new world order. You must be deemed by Him as a BFF, *Beloved and Faithful Forever* to be included in column A. Then there is column B, the "Banished." The Banished include all the people Hashem has deemed FFBs, *Filthy Foul Barbarians*. In this moment there are over seven and a half billion FFBs. This number includes you. I stand completely alone in this moment as Hashem's one and only BFF. I am the only one in column A and Accepted into the next world.

The news that I am His lone BFF in this world makes me cry. If you were me, this news would make you jump for joy. You'd be proud as a peacock that you were anointed His BFF and won His favor. Admit it. If you don't, you are simply lying. You might lament for a moment about your spouse or child who isn't welcomed but you would be so damned proud of yourself that God Himself considers you flawless. If you awakened to the news that you were speaking to God and He was singing your praises and explaining to you how pristine and perfect you were, you would all *kvell*—Yiddish for feeling happy and proud.

Not only does Hashem shower me with compliments day and night, He has told me I astonish Him! Wow! I astonish God Himself? I smile and laugh at the mere notion that little me astonishes Magnificent Him. He showers me with such love and compliments day and night that I often melt into tears. I cry because I have never experienced such love like His in this world. None of you emulate Him in the manner in which He loves. You might love like He does for a flicker of a moment but that moment is fleeting and then your love turns into a quest to receive something for yourself. Your thoughts always turn around and become about you and your needs. Imagine the King of the Universe telling you that you are sinless and the personification of perfection in human form. How would you respond to being characterized like this by God Himself? I will tell you. This includes you Mr. Dalai Lama! You would ALL puff out your chests and exude the ultimate pride that you are the Holy Moshiach. I also believe that you would succeed in this world where I have failed miserably. Many of you would have found a way to turn Running on Love the charity into a multi-billion-dollar enterprise and your face would be plastered all over God's creation. Your ego would have made you an overnight sensation as you bathed in the same egotistical excrement as everyone else does in this world. You don't yet acknowledge this, but it's the truth.

While your ego would win you trophies and awards, and you would indubitably rise and shine in this ego driven world, I have failed. I don't have an ego and never knew that being egoless would be my undoing. While you all applaud the idea of being egoless and work to exude this trait like the Dalai Lama, it is to your benefit in this world to have enormous egos. Not having an ego made it impossible for me to jump into the pool of excrement and swim with the rest of you. I refused to play your egotistical games and I lost everything. Being true to my principles was more important than seeing God's charity succeed and make money. This is where I depart from you once again.

There is nothing that I want more in this world than to see Running on Love succeed and everyone gathering in joy at the prophesized Festivals for Love. He has shown me that these events are the platform to bring peace and joy to our world. Even though I knew this was true, I refused to compromise my principles to make Running on Love flourish. While I feel guilt-ridden about this and apologize to all of you that I have failed, it simply wasn't possible for me to sin the way that you do. You all are willing to do what it takes because you believe the end justifies the means. I do not. In the end, I must do everything God's way. If I sacrificed my integrity and belief in the pure message of Running on Love, I would become the evil I am working to eradicate from the world. Two wrongs never make it right for me.

The world leaders are negotiating with terrorists and believe the end justifies the means. I watched in horror as Mike Pompeo the Secretary of State, shook the hand of one of the Filthiest Foul Barbarians on the face of the earth. They shook hands for the camera and smiled as though they were long lost lovers. As I watched this photo op, my mind filled with pictures of Otto Warmbier standing in a kangaroo courtroom looking up toward the sky with his hands clasped together in prayer begging God to save him. As Otto cried and prayed to God, over his head hung a portrait of Kim Jong-un, the North Korean Dictator who dictated Otto's death.

Days after his photo op with the North Korean monster, Secretary Pompeo came back to America stating that he was bringing "swagger" back to the State Department. Really? Swagger? Secretary Pompeo pompously boasted about his victory in facilitating impending peace with the North Koreans. Soon after, everyone sent up celebratory balloons touting what a brilliant negotiator President Trump and his new Secretary of State were when three captive Americans were released from a North Korean prison. While you celebrated you couldn't see what Hashem and I both saw. Through your actions you declared the end justified the means. By making love to this dictator, you believe you are dodging the nuclear bullet as you celebrate your victory. You are willing to compromise your values and trade money for peace. To you and everyone else in this world, all is fair in love, war and business if you get what you desire.

The hardliners reading this will likely disagree and probably say disparaging things about what I just wrote. I don't care. I am right and you are wrong. Otto is dead and the North Korean Dictator is being treated like nobility. You might be counting your lucky stars that someone like me isn't your President. I would never shake the hand of the murderer of a young American boy. I simply couldn't do that under any circumstance. So you see, if the Messiah, the perfect person, was in charge we would have the prophetic war of wars sooner not later. Do I want that war to occur? HELL NO! But I can't allow evil to be viewed as good under any circumstance. It's not possible for me to do what you all so readily and easily do. Regardless of your successful negotiating tactics and the *Art of the Deal,* the war of Gog and Magog is on the horizon. It isn't because God desires billions of you to die in a fiery inferno. Quite the opposite is true. He knows what you are still unwilling to admit to yourselves. You have an insatiable appetite for evil and this final world war will finally satisfy this demonic hunger.

Are you still standing? Did I land a knockout punch yet? I'm sure many of you are still in disbelief that you are responsible for any of our problems. Even still, you might be willing to play along and pretend that you are repenting. I see many of you good Orthodox Jews in synagogue on Yom Kippur pounding your chest with your fist during prayers for repentance in a contrived fashion as though you don't really believe you did any of those horrific sins. You all go through the motions on this holy day of repentance and do what is required of you so that Hashem will bless you with goodness. That might have been considered a good effort in the past, but this won't earn you a place in column A. His column A, those Accepted in the world to come, is only for the pure of heart and His BFFs, *Beloved and Faithful Forever.* There will be nothing contrived about His final list.

Still others will not be so kind as to pretend they are listening to me at all. I imagine that many will huddle in their groups and collectively criticize what I've written. Emboldened by your egos, you will gather together to find ways to criticize my book and ridicule me. "Oh, really Lori Michelle, is God running a Chinese restaurant? One from column A or one from column B?" I'm sure you won't like my analogies or revelations because most of them reveal your sins. Instead of admitting your guilt and learning from me, you will throw rocks and make sarcastic and crude comments in your own impudent defense. I see you do this regularly on social media. Social media reveals what many of you manage to hide from each other in public. The language and nasty barbs you throw at each other are a relentless version of social media road rage. Behind your computer you feel indestructible as you spew your nastiness all over the internet. The nastier and more viciously you attack your false enemies, the brassier and happier you seem to become.

While you are feeding on each other like vultures in a hate-filled social media frenzy our children are dying. It doesn't occur to any of you that your insults toward each other are not only a waste of time, they are pure evil. You all seem so out of touch and out of balance with who you truly are, a child of One Magnificent God. Your behavior is so vile that I often go to bed at night in tears and cry to Hashem that you are ALL hopeless. The smartest, most beautiful, and talented among you are engaging in the most hideous display of narcissism our world has ever seen. It's everywhere and you are all bathing in the evil.

Once Hashem showed me a vision of many people swimming in a pool and suddenly there was a forklift lowering an enormous pile of feces into the water. The crowd splashed around and swam over to the feces to touch the filth and rub it all over their bodies. The pool of water where they were swimming turned from aqua to brown as more and more feces were dumped into the swimming pool. Nobody wanted to leave the filthy brown pool of excrement and the crowd was splashing around touching a giant mound of excrement as though it was a great magical orb. You partied in the filth together as though you were in heaven.

Hashem's poignant vision was clear. You are all bathing in evil and disgrace in a community of FFBs, *Filthy Foul Barbarians*, and nobody is showing the courage to stand up and say NO. If enough people aren't willing to admit guilt and become the leaders who save our world, there won't be anything left to save. Sadly, the best and most wonderful potential leaders of our world bathe in that filthy metaphorical pool of excrement too and are being emboldened by applause from the crowd. You all become crowd-pleasers when your friends and supporters make you feel smart and powerful. In my #MeToo example in round 5 of this boxing match, Ashleigh Banfield tarnished herself by publicly ridiculing a young woman who was sexually violated by Aziz Ansari. Ashleigh defended Aziz and went for a swim with him in his filthy brown pool of excrement while she made him feel exonerated and appreciated. She did this publicly on Megyn Kelly's TV program but instead of Megyn revealing Ashleigh's wrongheaded behavior of further demoralizing this young girl, Megyn showered Ashleigh with numerous compliments and stroked her ego. Do you see how the brown filthy pool of sin works? You are all swimming in it and splashing around like it's a big happy party.

Here's another example of your filthy swim parties that aren't parties at all. The comedic talent Kathy Griffin was loudly chastised by people from all political backgrounds for her demonic effigy of President Trump's decapitated head. Rosie O'Donnell, who isn't particularly fond of Donald Trump, was said to have convinced her friend Kathy to apologize and said to her, "What if Daniel Pearl's mother saw this?" Good for you Rosie! Daniel Pearl's parents lost their son, an American journalist, in 2002 when he was brutally murdered by terrorists in a gruesome beheading. Thanks to Rosie, Kathy immediately saw the error of her ways and apologized profusely. In her sincere and emotional apology, she wore no makeup, cried profusely, and appeared heartbroken and sincere. Her passionate apology was winning God's favor but it was short-lived. Soon after, Kathy retracted every single word of her apology. Uh oh, here comes the crane of feces again. Kathy's crowd of supporters including a lovely female lawyer, gathered around her and emboldened her to jump right back into the putrid filthy brown pool with them. Kathy recently returned to the public eye on the program *The View* where she withdrew her heartfelt apology once again while she boasted that she just sold out Carnegie Hall. Mazel Tov Kathy, you won, right? Wrong! Because the crowd wants to bathe in filth with you again doesn't make you a winner of anything. If she doesn't wake up now, she will most certainly be the biggest loser. So will all the people who applaud her shockingly vicious and derisive humor and find her nastiness funny. It is not.

As a child I was chastised for crying too easily. By the time I was just four years old I was labeled moody and too sensitive. My parents complained that they had to be careful because if anyone looked at me funny I would cry. At four years old my favorite three words and mantra became "Leave me alone." What looked to my parents and teachers like unhealthy personality traits for a small child was my natural inclination to be repelled by the Yetzer Hara. You all seem to get along fine with the evil inclination because it exists in all of you. You think sarcastic barbs are funny and cute when I find them deeply painful. From the age of 2 years old I was heartbroken by my mother's dismissive behavior and felt unloved. Many people will run to my old mother's aid and pull her right into the brown pool of excrement by defending her behavior as a young mom.

You might also defend my older brother too who boasted he was the king in the family. Remember? He was the cute little boy who had to sing all the Beatles songs on the album *Meet the Beatles* while he relegated me to sing just one song called "I Wanna Be Your Man." You might hear this story, laugh and say that he was just a cute little boy having fun and it's so hilarious. Back then, I didn't think he was funny but I accepted his treatment because he was older and I thought he knew more than me. The things you consider funny and a rite of passage aren't funny to God. Do you understand one word of what I'm trying so hard to share with you? What will it take to help you see that I wasn't the broken little girl who was too sensitive? I was the good girl who you ALL abused. I wasn't moody at all. I was protecting myself from the evil inclination that is in ALL of you.

I've been bullied by my family since I was a toddler, bullied in school, bullied in the workplace and then abused by my husband in my horrible marriage. The abuses I've suffered are lifelong. My stories that reveal horrible treatment from my family and constant betrayals from supposed friends aren't unique to me, they happen to ALL of you too. What is unique about my stories is my consistent reaction to a lifetime of punishment. I refused to swim in the filthy brown pool of excrement with everyone else. My refusal to participate in your madness was deemed as pompous arrogance but it was quite the opposite.

The many forms of abuse and betrayals I've suffered have happened to you too but you are also guilty of abusing and betraying everyone else. ALL of you are bullies and egotistical maniacs without exception. It just depends upon the moment. You all have beautiful moments when you choose to sparkle like our Magnificent Creator but those moments are fleeting. If you wait long enough you always succumb to evil and choose yourselves. My older brother was a cute little boy and ALL of you condone this kind of nasty and narcissistic behavior in little boys. You all think that little boys who act like this are adorable and cute. They aren't. When these nasty little boys grow up they become grown men who abuse woman. President Trump was a cute little boy like my older brother once upon a time too. My brother and other boys around the world aren't being raised properly and without the proper upbringing they can't grow up to be great men. My brother was raised to be a narcissist because he was raised by narcissists. You are ALL narcissists and I stand alone being the odd person out. I'm the black sheep who never fit into your narcissistic paradigm. Instead of following my family in this dysfunctional way of life I walked away to live on my own.

I've worked so hard on this book for several years and cried many tears while I survived the unthinkable. With Hashem's blessing and help I fought through your torture tests and now I am delivering the truth hoping to wake you up. Will you recognize this book as the supreme gift that it truly is and see yourselves in the ALL the sins that I've revealed? You are ALL just like my friends and family who tortured me for a lifetime. You tortured me and you torture each other. Will you refuse to acknowledge this truth or will you continue to deflect everything I'm sharing and jump right back in the brown pool of excrement with everyone else? I asked you to think about how you would react if God told you that you were sinless and didn't do any of the horrible things I've revealed in my book. Here is what I do when He showers me with love, adulation, and tells me I am sinless. Get ready to compare notes.

Every day without exception I am looking for the evil inclination to rear its ugly head within me. I'm on the relentless hunt to expose any wrongheaded thought or poor choice. Daily I believe I finally found something that I've done wrong and repent but Hashem always smiles and says, "No Lori you didn't do anything wrong." He then patiently pulls apart every detail of my thoughts and actions to show me that I chose precisely the right action. I'm exonerated completely not only in His eyes, but He proves to me beyond a shadow of doubt that I did nothing wrong. I refuse to let go of the thought that I sinned until I'm positive I didn't. How do I respond to Hashem after He explains to me in detail that I didn't sin at all? I thank Him profusely and express deep gratitude that I didn't do anything wrong. The mere idea that I committed a transgression is enough to make me feel immobilized. He frees me from my pain of feeling like I sinned. The thought of sinning itself is punishment enough for me. I can't think straight until I feel either forgiven or exonerated. I can barely breathe because the thought of sinning is that painful to me. But there is more.

There are days and moments when I feel guilt-ridden that you haven't woken up and begun the work of world peace. I apologize profusely to Hashem and truly believe I'm at fault when a rational person would say that's nonsense. In my moments of remorse, He asks me to not apologize since I'm not to blame but there are many times when I simply can't move on. I know intellectually He is correct and I've done nothing wrong but I still feel a burning desire to be forgiven. In that moment He heals me by stating simply, "It's okay Lori." He isn't accepting an outright apology from me because none is required but He soothes me by accepting my remorse.

Whether you wake up and listen to me isn't in my hands. If you all refuse to accept my warning and I fail, I believe it's still my personal failure. What kind of world will this be if I'm the only person in Hashem's A column, Accepted into the world to come? If I'm the only one He considers a BFF, *Beloved and Faithful Forever,* I lose my children. My worst fear as I go forward with this book and do this work is the possibility my children might sever their relationship with me. Everyone tried feverishly to harm my relationship with them and this book may be the final straw. I fear losing my children more than losing my life.

Daily I watch you lose your children in acts of aggression and terror and I feel such anguish I could die. It's almost as though I am losing my own family member when I watch you lose yours. In this moment I'm running into the burning building to save the children and nobody is willing to bring a hose to help me. You all believe you have it figured out and everything will be just fine. It is not fine. If enough of you don't wake up it will be the end.

I asked you, "What is your price?" How heavy a price will you need to pay to find out I'm telling the truth and have been screaming at ALL of you for over nine years to wake up? It's clear that you and I are wired differently. In all the same circumstances you would have caved in and done what you were told. You ALL have a price tag. Your price may not be about money but you certainly have a line that you won't cross. You have a limit to how much you will give of yourselves in any moment. I don't have a price and I can't be bought. When God woke me up, told me I was chosen and instructed me to wake everyone up now before it's too late, I didn't give it a second thought and ran to save you. I didn't think about what it sounded like or if you would believe me. I didn't need to see people dying in the street or another horror like 9/11 to become motivated. I didn't need to hear the sirens blaring to warn me that the rockets were falling. I ran. I ran like a mother to save my children. God called on me on April 7, 2009 and I've been running ever since.

HIS VOICE, VISIONS & LESSONS

Who is being Good?
It depends upon the day.

I took a morning stroll on Shabbos while I was still living in America. As I walked through the town center I watched a driver looking lost and trying to get his orientation when he noticed he was approaching a traffic light. A man was waiting to cross the street and saw the driver pausing, so even though the crossing signal displayed "Do Not Walk" he began to cross anyway. The driver who had a green light suddenly saw this man crossing the street and jammed on his brakes to allow him to cross safely. He could have reacted in anger that this thoughtless pedestrian nearly caused an accident, but he chose to be a polite gentleman instead.

As the male pedestrian continued to cross the street he looked clearly miffed and muttered indignantly, "Well are you going to stop or what! Make up your mind!" Incredibly he was the one who was wrong. Instead of recognizing the driver's graciousness and giving him a nod of thanks, he angrily grunted at him instead. He behaved as though the polite driver was the one who owed him an apology.

After observing this encounter I wondered who this polite driver might be. He was likely somebody's husband, son, or father. Maybe he was a kind and loving family man who always tried his best to do the right thing. I also wondered who the belligerent pedestrian might be too. On another morning could the foul-mouthed belligerent man crossing the street be a kind and thoughtful gentleman too? Maybe he was just having a bad day.

On any given day the roles of those two men might be reversed. The polite driver might be the man who was crossing the street choosing to be indignant and rude. On a better day, the nasty pedestrian might choose to be the polite driver who graciously let someone cross the street.

In any given moment we choose to sparkle and behave like the godly creations we were meant to be. In another moment, we succumb to the evil inclination that separates us, provokes anger and starts wars. These are the End of Days and a time of judgement. We are required to learn how to choose God and His goodness in every moment without exception. It's time to reach for the best in ourselves, avoid misunderstandings and refuse to engage in baseless hatred. God has blessed us with freedom and requires us to choose between good and evil in every single moment. The next time you are faced with a decision, choose to pause, see your surroundings clearly, and then strive to be the light of God you were sent here to be.

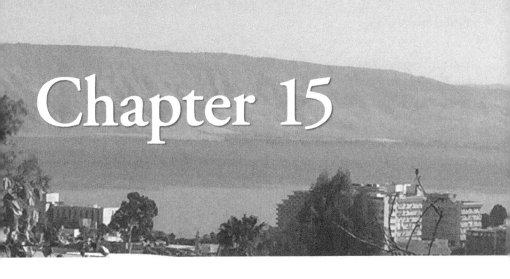

Chapter 15

Go Throw Some Cold Water on Your Face

When I was a small child, after I suffered through a long crying spell, my dad often told me, "Go throw some cold water on your face." After I ran to the bathroom to wash away my tears he gave me one of his famous hugs and then we talked about what happened to clear up the confusion. His love and understanding always helped me heal and made everything feel better. If you're awake now and swallowed my large dose of the truth, you've likely just cried like a baby. So, in loving memory of my wonderful father, "Go throw some cold water on your face."

I hope you needed to wash away a few tears. After 12 rounds in the ring with me I hope I helped you cry some tears of remorse. All of this is for your good and I don't relish doing any of this. While there are people who love to get into the fray and win a good argument, I've never been one of them. I love a good intellectual debate but I don't like it when anyone loses. You don't have to be a loser either. If you let go of your need to be right and analyze everything I've shared in this book you will God willing see the truthfulness in everything I've revealed. You must see yourself in all my terrible stories at least once or twice, because trust me, you're in there too. I assure you that you've committed many of these sins and much worse on many more occasions than you would like to believe. I watch everyone daily engage in these sinful behaviors and feel like I'm hamstrung because I can't do a damn thing to help you. You haven't been willing to listen. Are you willing to listen now?

We just spent 12 rounds in a boxing match together where I beat you and everyone else about the head as I revealed how awful our world truly is and how you are responsible for the awfulness. I pray that as you read my many painful stories and saw how I suffered through a lifetime of betrayals and abuses you recognized yourself as an abuser too. My goal in revealing my personal baggage and throwing my former husband, family and friends under the bus, wasn't to seek revenge. I carry no grudge and harbor no vendetta against any of these people in my stories. I have no desire to disparage or diminish anyone in public. Revealing everyone's sins is required now and everyone needs to pay the price for their mistakes or they will continue to make them. It's impossible to repair what's wrong if you don't even see your own broken behaviors. The people of the world must recognize how they are harming each other daily. I revealed many personal stories about how my family, friends, coworkers and strangers tortured and victimized me throughout my life. You are exactly like them and your choices might even be worse than the decisions made by the people in my book. Everyone in these life stories who tortured me was also once upon a time a victim who became a victimizer and so are YOU.

My mother and father grew up in dysfunctional homes. Does that surprise anyone? My father was the son of two Eastern European Jewish immigrants. As a young boy in Williamsburg, Brooklyn he was forced to go to shul, synagogue, by his authoritarian father. He preferred to play ball with his friends instead.

At the tender age of 14, he came home one day and a boy in the neighborhood yelled out to him, "Hey (my father's first name) your mother just died." That's how my father received the awful news that his mother succumbed to cancer. On that terrible day he was taunted by this disgusting neighborhood bully who took great pleasure in hurting him in his devastating moment of loss.

My dad wasn't just bullied by neighborhood hoodlums. He was bullied by his sisters, brothers and extended family too. My rough and tough grandfather often spoke harshly to my father and as he grew up they fought constantly. My dad and his siblings screamed, yelled and fought with each other continuously too. As a young boy he was a natural born fighter who refused to take guff from anyone. When he came of age, instead of fighting the daily fight with his father, he decided he had enough and enlisted in the US army in the early 1950s. While he loved my grandfather and his siblings, when he enlisted he decided to leave his observant Jewish life and chose to live a secular one instead. Years later my grandfather conspicuously left my dad out of his will. My grandfather's broken choice to use money as a form of punishment helped distort my dad's thinking. Eventually this painful memory along with others negatively affected his relationship with money. And so, the evil weed continues to grow and kill the beautiful garden.

My father went to Pace college, but dropped out after a year. He was very intelligent but more street smart than book smart. Being street smart didn't seem to impress his older sister's husband who constantly berated him, called him stupid, and told him he would never amount to anything. Can any of you relate to my father's story? Of course, he wasn't stupid at all, he just didn't meet the expectations of his egotistical brother-in-law.

My dad fought hard to make a good life for himself and do it better than his father did for him. He met my mother who also came from a dysfunctional home. Surprise, surprise, surprise! No, there isn't any surprise there either. My mother suffered her own share of verbal assaults and abuses from her family. She ran away from her dysfunctional home in Shrub Oak, New York and lived with her favorite aunt and cousins in Brighton Beach, Brooklyn where she finished high school. Her father was a wife abuser, a liar and a cheat. She met my dad and it was love at first sight. They were bashert, soul mates, and they married when my father was 23 and my mother was just 19 years old.

Within a year my mother gave birth to my older brother. I came along less than two years later when she was just 22. My two parents who were still young kids themselves, now had two of us to raise. My father worked three jobs to support his young family of four. By the time I was barely two years old my maternal grandmother was sitting at their kitchen table every day when my father came home from a long day of work. He was subjected to listening to her whine and complain about my louse of a grandfather along with everyone else who tortured her in her deeply broken life. Yes, my grandmother was depressed and miserable and brought her misery into my parents' home. What happened next? My young parents separated. Are you shocked? My grandmother brought her marital problems and psychological dysfunction into their home and the pressure cooker popped its lid. During that separation which lasted more than a year, my young mother cried incessantly. Her patience was short and she often chased me away from her as she yelled, "You're always under my feet!" As a toddler I didn't know why my mommy didn't love me and I felt the sting of every harsh word. Did she not love her little baby girl or was she just bringing her dysfunctional upbringing forward and abusing me? What goes around comes around and history repeats itself until someone has the courage to say no more, not me.

Do I hate my mother? No, I love her. Do I blame her and my father for abusing me? Yes, I do. Do I believe that they did their best? Yes, they did their best but their best wasn't good enough. They abused me the way they were abused by their families and never took responsibility for it. Instead of seeing the fault in themselves they saw dysfunction in me. I wasn't truly the dysfunctional one at all. I was the shining light that forced them to look in the spiritual mirror and see things about themselves they weren't willing to see. When they couldn't tolerate the light, or accept any blame, they maliciously projected their problems and shortcomings onto me. Remember? Lori is moody. Lori is too sensitive. Lori is selfish. Lori only cares about herself. The most painful one of all? Where was Lori when her father died? Round and round the mulberry bush and here we go again.

There but for the grace of God went I. Hashem saw me through the storm and I've lived to share my incredible story with you. In my book I'm calling everyone out on the carpet and that includes my mother, brother and former husband who is the father of my three amazing children. I am doing this because I love all of them, not because I want to hurt anyone. Do you think they are humiliated? They most certainly should be. If they are embarrassed and humiliated that means they're beginning to wake up and face the truth. If they make excuses for themselves and aren't ashamed then they are still in denial. You can run away from the truth and project blame onto others, but that won't absolve you from your crimes. History will continue to repeat itself if left unchecked. You must wake up and take responsibility to change history.

It's time to accept personal guilt and look within yourselves to change what is broken. You are all victims of these crimes but crying that you are a victim won't absolve you of guilt for victimizing others. I'm praying that everyone who reads this book has begun to wake up to the truth that we're in peril and it's your fault.

I've laid everything out as clearly as I possibly can in common everyday language. I'm not candy coating anything for anyone. I am giving you the truth straight up. In this moment you are not welcome in God's world to come. The Christians have it wrong. The Muslims have it wrong. Everyone in the world in this moment has something wrong in their stories and beliefs with one difference. The Jews hold the truth. The Torah. They are the one people who are your hope for bringing us salvation. Instead of accepting this truth, everyone including self-hating Jews is determined to annihilate the children of Israel. Will you ever be willing to listen, learn and accept Hashem's God's truth? What if His truth is different from yours? Uh oh, I just lost a few of you!

What will you choose now? Are you going to choose to be someone from column A or someone from column B? If you're honest, you will understand you are currently on Hashem's B list of Banished from the world to come. You are most certainly receiving a failing grade in Hashem's eyes. I'm the only one on Hashem's A list of Accepted into His new world order. If you don't learn and understand the rules required to be on His A list, you will be Banished. Being Banished may not be your end. You may be damned to suffer eternally. Again, go to AlonAnava.com and begin to get educated.

You can't just say, "I accept God's Messiah" and expect that to qualify you as Hashem's BFF, B*eloved and Faithful Forever* and you're home free on column A. To be a BFF on His A list you must listen, learn and work for peace. Being a BFF for me is a piece of cake because I don't understand how to be an FFB, a *Filthy Foul Barbarian*. It doesn't compute and makes no sense at all. It's my mission in life to make choosing evil and being an FFB completely absurd to you too. I want to welcome you on His A list with all my heart. Before you can even hope to get on this list, you must feel the pain of all your sins. You can't be forgiven unless you're sincere and you won't be sincere unless you know without a doubt when you've sinned, who you hurt and cry like a baby because you feel ashamed. Shame and remorse are required. If I haven't made you cry yet, you need to be willing to go the distance with me. You must cry real tears of remorse. You can't fake it and make it into His book of life.

The existence of evil in this world is inherently good because it provides you with freedom in every moment. You are decidedly free children of God. He desires you to be free to choose in every moment of your life. Your personal freedom is a supreme gift and simultaneously the ultimate challenge. You and every other person in the world find the choice between good and evil complicated and difficult. You and everyone else have an ego and this self-centered ego causes you to choose yourself and evil every single day. As I watch you choose evil daily I'm astonished why it's even remotely attractive to you because I see it as repulsive. I'm not free like you. In every moment I only see one correct choice and therefore I don't have the inclination or potential to sin like you do. The evil inclination isn't a viable choice to me in any moment. I joke with Hashem all the time that He is my Captor and I'm His eternal prisoner who suffers from Stockholm Syndrome. I reject every attempt our world makes to lure me away from Him and desire to stay His prisoner forever! All kidding aside, the opposite is true. I'm free from evil and you are in a spiritual prison. If you heed my advice and find the courage to face the truth you will be freed from your living nightmare. Once we are all awake and freely choose our Creator and His goodness in each moment, we will all win.

In any moment you see the evil in this world too but you only see it outside yourself. If you look around and view the world objectively you will see different political, religious and social factions aligning with each other in their philosophies and beliefs. Each distinct group is strengthened by their collective assurance that they know right from wrong and see the evil that threatens our world ELSEWHERE. It's never their fault because the blame always lies with someone else. You know, "It's all Donald Trump's fault." Or "It's all those crazy leftists' fault." You might go to your place of worship to admit your sins and repent but it's lip service at best.

Here is where I depart from ALL of you. I see your goodness on many occasions and delight in the sight. In any moment I also see the evil, Yetzer Hara, in all of you too. In every moment I see good and evil in everyone and everywhere in the world. No person or group is completely void of evil except for me. I'm inexplicably immune to the Yetzer Hara. I don't choose to be immune to evil at all. This immunity is like breathing for me and an involuntary reaction to the truth. I can't choose evil no matter what, not ever. Because I don't see another viable choice but goodness, you are freer than me. In any moment I only have the capacity to choose God and His goodness and go in His direction. My eyes are wide open and I see the difference between Yetzer Hara, Satan, and the Yetzer Hatov, the good inclination, in each moment. My role here is to help teach you how to see the clear difference too.

In the first chapter of my book I asked you to take a journey with me. As I revealed the story of my awakening to the Voice of God, I asked you to imagine this happened to you. I then wrote the following passage:

> Whoever you are, imagine one morning God Himself woke you up. Yes, it's Him and you know it with all your heart and every fiber of your being. He awakens you one auspicious morning and says, "This is God speaking to you and you are chosen. You need to go out right now and tell everyone that I'm speaking to you and you are my chosen one." Okay, are you ready? Let's go on the count of three. Ready, set, 1-2-3, GO! Come on now, go tell everyone right now! What's wrong? What are you waiting for? Oh, maybe you're concerned they may think you're nuts? Yeah, I totally understand. Perhaps now you might empathize with me a bit and understand what happened to me.

Now that you've read this book I hope you have empathy for what I went through to complete this book and deliver this information to you. If you put yourself in my shoes throughout the book, I know without a doubt that your decisions along the way would have been completely different from mine. Some of you might declare, "No kidding Lori! You failed miserably and suffered incredibly. I would never have made those same choices and given the opportunity I believe I would have succeeded in growing your charity Running on Love." For those of you who believe you would have chosen differently and succeeded where I failed, I agree. Your choices in this material world are different from mine and your choices win money, success and approval in the court of public opinion. My choices failed miserably. My ideology is counter to everyone else's in this physical world.

If Bill Gates, Donald Trump or Oprah Winfrey took the reins of my little charity it might be a billion-dollar enterprise now. Running on Love would have become the latest craze and a charitable sensation and there would likely be events worldwide. This might be the truth but guess what? It would be an abysmal failure in the eyes of Hashem God. The success that these formidable business people would have enjoyed would be none other than evil masquerading in charitable clothing. Their charity wouldn't be Running on Love at all. It would be Running on Ego. Its message would be clothed in "love, love, love" but instead of being purely about love, it would become about the sponsors and the greenbacks. In their political correctness there would be no mention of God, His Magnificence, and the purity of His Love. When I was given sound business advice, I refused it outright and wouldn't compromise the message of pure love to win in the business world. In this world everyone told me to compromise and tailor my message to win sponsors because they believed the end justified the means. I refused. Sharing Running on Love's pure message was my reason why I founded this charity and I couldn't compromise even if it meant succeeding. Nobody ever understood the mission or meaning behind this God-inspired charity. Running on Love's mission and message fell on everyone else's deaf ears.

Before you feel proud of how your choices would have succeeded where mine failed, wake up to realize that I was completely correct and chose God and His goodness in every utterance and choice that I made. Without exception, every decision I made was absent of evil and filled with God's goodness in each moment. God's way of choosing currently doesn't succeed in this world. Evil, egotism and materialism succeed here and the presence of Hashem is barely a whisper on anyone's breath. You may choose to deny this passionately with all your heart, but it is the sad truth. The proof is in the laundry list of problems stated in this book. Our world is in chaos and we are perilously on the brink of World War III.

It's time to understand that this physical world is completely broken and everyone must do the hard work needed to change the paradigm of what succeeds in this world. We must begin to see God and His goodness triumph over ego and materialism or we are sure to perish. After you finish reading my book, I sincerely hope my words affect you deeply. I pray you cried at least once and are ready for more tears of remorse. I'm promised there will be a silver lining for you if you go the distance. The world to come will be filled with people who serve our One God, Hashem Our King. Hashem is purely magnificent and indescribable in common language. You come from His spirit. Please recognize that your ultimate potential is supernatural and wildly magnificent.

I truly believe you are already far more capable than me. I'm completely ordinary compared to most of you. You stun me with your intellect, beauty and amazing talents. If I'm able to be His BFF so easily just for choosing good and refusing to be evil, what is your ultimate potential? I don't run fast, I can't sing like many of you, I'm not nearly as physically beautiful as most of you, and I don't have an Ivy League education. I'm just not that smart! I'm a good cook but I'm not a chef. I'm extraordinarily ordinary in every aspect of physical life here on earth. There is only one area where I stand alone and shine continuously. I never choose the evil one. The evil I see is obviously hideous, unattractive and choosing it is incomprehensible. If I taught you how to spot the Yetzer Hara and avoid choosing it, what kind of person could you be? I'd like to find out one day. Would you?

HIS VOICE, VISIONS & LESSONS

Melaveh Malkah—Escorting the Queen

One morning Hashem awakened me as He always does with a new vision and message. He showed me a very good-looking young man with long hair pulled back in a ponytail. Earlier in the book I shared another vision which had this same good-looking young man with a ponytail who was supposed to be Hashem encouraging me to get out of bed, tugging on me to get up and go with Him for my morning run. (See page 77.)

In this vision it was clearly Hashem once again showing Himself walking, His hair in the same ponytail, and He was wearing a prisoner's orange jumpsuit that criminals wear when they're carted off to prison. His hands were cuffed behind His back while He was being held by a police officer. Suddenly His hands burst apart breaking open the handcuffs and the police officer backed off as Hashem pumped His arms up in the air in the sign of victory. As He continued to walk with His arms up in victory, the officer backed off and instead of being Hashem's captor, the officer became His police escort.

The policeman followed Hashem as He entered a packed arena with an audience of many thousands of cheering fans. As He walked into the arena, He turned His body to the right, leaned down to pick me up off the ground, and began dragging me with Him. As I was kicking and screaming that I didn't want to go where He was taking me, He lifted me up into His arms and carried me forcibly with Him onto the stage where there was a packed audience, cheering wildly in pandemonium. Once on stage, He turned us both around with our backs to the cheering crowd. He picked up a candle, gave me another, and as we lit these two candles we held them together making one flame in what was metaphorically a Havdalah candle lighting ceremony. The Havdalah candle lighting ritual is done ceremoniously at the end of Shabbos, the Jewish Sabbath. After Shabbos ends and after this Havdalah candle lighting ceremony, there is a traditional meal called "Melaveh Malkah" which translates into "Escorting the Queen."

Hashem's vision that morning was so wildly beautiful and significant. He knows I don't want to do this. I don't want to publish this book or be your Moshiach, I'm doing this because I simply must. I am compelled. I'm scared out of my mind that this will be my end. After this vision that morning, He promised me He will escort me to the end of this grueling marathon, He will free me from my spiritual hell and prison, and my success is assured. My success is yours.

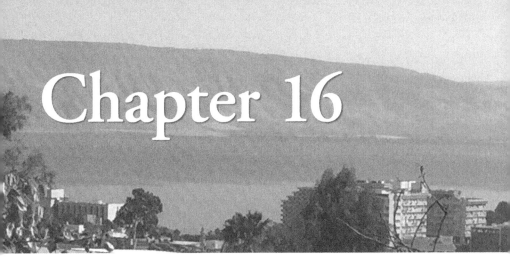

Chapter 16

What's Next for Me?

I don't really know what's next for me. Death perhaps, wild success and international fame and fortune, or something in between. The answer is in everyone else's hands. If people buy this book in big enough numbers there will be enough money for me to hire armed bodyguards for protection. I'm not sure what a few retired Mossad agents cost, but it's more than I have right now. I'm smart enough to realize I've ruffled many feathers with the things I've written in this book. The truth can do that you know. Even though every word I've written is truthful and Hashem was the source for all the revelations I shared, there's enough written here that will anger many people. Those who are deeply evil will use what I have written as an excuse to try to harm me. Now that you're reading this book my fate is sealed and I chose to publish it despite the danger. I'm living my life completely on purpose. I'm greeting my life's purpose and doing the work that God Himself sent me here to do. I'm not looking for fame or fortune but I'd be lying if I didn't tell you that I'd like to make a nice living again. Poverty sucks quite frankly. I'd love to get myself out of debt, own a home again one day and trade my shopping wagon in for a vehicle. Money would allow me the power and freedom to make a difference in this world. The success of this book isn't up to me, it's up to all of you.

This is my first time writing a book and it's arguably the most important book I will ever write. Hashem says this book is just the beginning and there will be more. He says it is part two of the Torah, believe it or not. Does this book replace any part of the Torah? No, of course not. The Torah is Hashem's gift to you. This book is Moshiach's gift and a resounding wake-up call to humanity.

This isn't a feel-good motivational book to say the least but it is intended to motivate you nonetheless. Unlike most modern day motivational or self-help books, this book accuses everyone of choosing the evil that's destroying our world. Hopefully you felt the intentional smack in the face which didn't make you jump for joy or feel proud of yourself. Instead of feeling personally insulted, God willing you will use that smack to serve as your alarm bell to wake up, take notice, and do something. We're heading for World War III and possible extinction. No exaggerations there. This is a true story, my story, in my own words, about how I was treated when I told the world I could hear Hashem God and He is real. You may believe in God and think that you're getting this life right, but nothing is further from the truth. You need this book and a teacher who is unafraid to tell you the truth no matter the consequences. Without this information and the lessons that I'm delivering to you, we will all continue to succumb to evil and this world will end. Literally.

What will happen to me after I publish this book? I simply can't know. Hashem has shown me glorious visions of a world that is Running on Love. In these prophetic visions, I'm front and center enjoying all of this with you. It brings me to tears and frankly I find it difficult to believe that it will ever happen. Often, I speak to Hashem and tell Him that I believe He chose the wrong person for this job. Once an eternal optimist, I have become very pessimistic about the future because people are completely rejecting all the obvious goodness I've been sharing for many years. The continuous losses and rejection I've suffered would have made anyone else quit this work many years ago. Hashem fuels me with love and visions of success giving me the strength to go forward. My prayer is that one day you will open your hearts to me and know that I'm sincere and the information I'm sharing is helpful and true.

I recently watched a video on YouTube of an Oprah Winfrey interview which was originally posted on December 9th, 2012, non-coincidentally, my birthday. She interviewed the Nobel Peace Prize winner and Holocaust survivor Elie Wiesel and read a quote from his book *Open Heart*. I was deeply struck by the end of this quote "… even in darkness it is possible to create light and encourage compassion. There it is. I still believe in man, in spite of man." When I heard her read this quote, I cried to Hashem and told Him that He should have chosen Elie Wiesel to be His Moshiach, not me. I love Hashem with all my heart and all my soul. I have complete faith in Him but not in people. When it comes to man, I no longer believe.

Hashem has revealed to me in many conversations that members of my family and former friends are the reincarnation of the who's who of Torah nobility and the most exalted members of mankind. I was surrounded by the best of the best of humanity and look what happened to me when I told the truth that Hashem God was speaking to me. They descended upon me like vultures, wouldn't listen to one syllable of anything I had to say, and conspired to destroy my entire life. I see sparks of God everywhere in our world and in all of you, but you don't choose to shine like a flame of God consistently. You choose evil over God continuously and daily. When your mistakes are shown to you it's like you're being forced to see yourself in a spiritual mirror against your will and you retreat in anger, defensiveness and bolster yourselves with even more evil.

After he lived through the unthinkable, the Holocaust, Elie Wiesel wrote those beautiful words, "… I still believe in man, in spite of man." I can't make that same statement. When push came to shove, the best of the best and loftiest souls in our world kicked me to the curb and left me for dead.

I'm praying for everyone day and night. In the middle of the night, every night except for Shabbos and Torah holidays, I check the news feed on my iPhone to see if there are any disasters or the beginning of the impending World War. My prayers to Hashem are filled with tears and the knowledge that He won't stop this war from coming. Even if all the good people of the world suddenly woke up in unison, there will still be a World War III. It's in Bible prophecy, it's going to happen, and it's necessary. Please wake up and choose God for your own good.

What I Know

I've shared deeply personal stories about my life's journey along with explanations and lessons that Hashem has shared with me. Do I know for sure that His stories are emphatically true? No, I don't. How could I possibly know that? My memory is limited to this life as Lori Michelle. I don't have any past life memories or know for sure that I've lived as any of those other people in the past. Only Hashem knows our true spiritual identities and He insists that once upon a time I was Moshiach ben Yosef, Moshe Rabbeinu, and Moshiach ben David, Yeshua. Yeshua's ultimate demise was nothing short of horrific which frightens me to no end. Could something like that happen to His Moshiach once again in this final attempt to redeem our world? Most certainly. Clearly humanity hasn't learned much from history. Hashem says the outcome for His Moshiach this time will be eternal peace. The outcome is something I can't possibly know. Only Hashem knows the future.

What do I know? I know I'm here journeying as one with Hashem, God. I'm truly speaking and living every breath of my life with Him within my vessel. I wouldn't or couldn't make up any of these stories or prophetic visions. Why in the world would I? I'm not interested in being rich or famous for any reason other than it would launch Running on Love the charity and possibly bring us world peace. Being famous is tragic in my view. The rich and famous give of themselves to the public in some way or another and in the end, they sacrifice their lives and privacy. I've always pitied the celebrities of our world and have zero desire to be one of them. If being rich and famous is in my future, I simply consider this as something that comes with the territory and an unfortunate part of my life's path. Sadly, it's required of me now because without money and fame I will not succeed. If I don't force this book out there in a big way and become a well-known person, I can't deliver the information that I'm compelled to share with you. It's my destiny to share what I know with you and the world. I simply can't stop working for this and would never try to avoid my responsibility. This is bigger than me. I'm compelled to keep going no matter what happens. My life and safety aren't my biggest concerns right now. My focus is protecting my children and saving everyone else in the world. We are all in grave danger.

The past life stories and prophecies I've shared in this book came to me directly from Hashem, that's certain and the truth. You have a choice whether to believe me or not. I feel I have no choice but to share everything with you regardless of the outcome. I'm completely relentless and shameless. If I had to stand naked before the entire world to bring us peace on earth, I would do so in a heartbeat. I simply have no concern about vanity or protecting my privacy. If sharing every lurid and painful detail of my past helps one person heal, I'm there for them. I just can't stop caring. It feels like a relentless compulsion to save every single person on earth from certain death or something much worse that they'll potentially face after they die.

There are worse things than death. Are you aware of that? The pain you'll face on the other side if you don't step up now and work for peace is far more excruciating than anything you can experience here. The house is burning and I'm determined to run inside to save my children and whoever else I possibly can. I'm going in even if it means I might die trying. It isn't possible for me to watch the world head toward nuclear holocaust and remain silent. For what? To protect myself? Who am I really protecting by being silent? I believe this book will help many more people than it could possibly hurt.

Hashem has told me in no uncertain terms that everyone must behave and act like a Moshiach for there to be world peace. There isn't one supernatural being who's going to save the day and clean up this entire planet while everyone else watches. Hashem Himself won't correct everything for us either. Everyone's description of what the prophesized Messiah or Moshiach is supposed to be or do seems flawed. People speak and act as though there is something supernatural about the term *Moshiach* or *Messiah* which doesn't make any sense to me whatsoever. I'm certainly not supernatural or super anything. I'm just a mother who doesn't seem to sin and choose the evil inclination the way that everyone else does. I'm allergic to it and it doesn't attract me. I find it frankly confusing that everyone chooses evil daily because it's so easy to spot, but I'm the only one who sees it in every moment. If this is what is referred to as being sinless and perfect and what the Moshiach is, I promise you it's not that difficult. You can absolutely become a Moshiach too! It's really a piece of cake. Sort of. You and everyone else in the world make being the Moshiach a complete nightmare. Aside from being tortured by people, being Moshiach is frankly common sense and extremely easy. One day I hope to teach you how to do this too.

Choosing the evil inclination is as obvious to me as seeing someone pick up dog feces from the ground and eat it like it's delectable chocolate. Sorry for the disgusting analogy but I want this to sound clear to you too. That's how clear choosing good over evil is for me and it needs to be this clear for everyone. You'd never eat dog manure on purpose, would you? You're not only doing something that looks like this before the eyes of God, you're overtly enjoying it as though you're dining on gourmet cuisine, but it's even worse than that. You are all guilty of encouraging everyone else, including your children, to join you in this ghastly horror!

It isn't an exaggeration when I tell you that all choices are this clear for me in every moment. The same must become true for you too when it comes to refusing to choose evil. It must become that crystal clear. You might be thinking, "That's so easy!" and perhaps you still believe you never choose evil even after reading my merciless diatribe. Sadly, everyone is choosing evil right now except for me. One day, I pray choosing God and His goodness in every moment will become crystal clear and easy for you too.

What I Believe

I believe I'm truly Hashem's Moshiach, the Messiah. No other scenario for what has happened to me and how I now live my daily life makes any sense at all. I don't believe there is some guy who will show up and relieve me from my obsession to do this work. I don't have a death wish, only a wish and desire to prevent everyone else's death and help save their souls. The mere term *martyr* is vile and repugnant to me. I don't believe in martyrdom, God forbid! Quite the contrary I feel martyrdom is purely evil at its core. Self-sacrifice and choosing to do what is best for everyone else first is not being a martyr. It's called being a human being. Choosing what's good for everyone else first is choosing to be like Hashem God. I think, eat, breathe and behave like a Moshiach is supposed to behave. Asking me to be like something else is like asking me to wake up tomorrow and become a pumpkin or an oak tree. I'm not a pumpkin or a tree. I am Hashem's Moshiach.

I also believe I might be the reincarnation of Yeshua ben Yosef. Maybe. I don't know much about that guy and don't have a grandiose vision of what that implies. Yet I'm aware enough to know he is a huge deal to billions of people. He isn't that big of a deal to me. I'm sorry if this insults you. I like what he stood for and I simply think like Yeshua did. I don't try to think like him, but from what I've read about him and have been told, my personality and choices are exactly like his. My compulsion for love and charity is unlike any other person I've ever known or read about. I'm inexplicably obsessed with Running on Love and teaching people about Hashem and how to live as prescribed in His Torah. No other person understands Running on Love or receives the total joy from its principles like I do. People who participated in Running on Love events did so for some form of self-benefit or to raise money for a specific cause other than Running on Love. It wasn't completely about performing a pure expression of love. There was always some other personal benefit they received from the experience. For me, it's all about pure love without exception. I don't require any other reason to do anything. Love simply floats my boat.

Now what about Moshe, Moses. Of all the past lives Hashem says I lived, Moshe Rabbeinu is the one I connect to the most. I'm not a Torah scholar but I somehow have full understanding of the Torah and how to choose Hashem in every moment, bar none. When I read stories about Moshe Rabbeinu I feel like I was there. Gratefully, I have no memory of his life, but I have been shown visions as though I lived it. When I read Torah parshas about Moshe that describe him falling on his face crying to Hashem about how awfully he was treated by the Jewish children, I feel as though I lived those painful memories too. Of all the lifetimes I was supposed to have lived prior to this one, Moshe's is the number one life that I relate to the most. Moshe is my guy!

Being Moshiach means you must be void of choosing evil. Choosing evil is completely the opposite of how I think. I simply can't choose it even if it benefits me. It's as though I'm allergic to the Yetzer Hara and the choice doesn't compute. Neither does choosing something for my own self-benefit over someone else's good. It doesn't occur to me to think of my own needs first and I can't comprehend why anyone else would. Where's the joy in thinking about yourself first? I just don't understand it. Many people say, "We cannot know the ways of Hashem." Well, I say, "I understand Hashem's ways but the ways and choices of everyday people have me completely befuddled."

When my nightmare began on Mother's Day of 2009 and I was locked up in the first debacle, the evil doctors in charge claimed I was psychotic because I had delusions of grandeur. Are you kidding me? While it sounds grandiose to you that I could possibly be Moshiach or the reincarnation of Yeshua and all these other lofty souls, none of this is grandiose to me. These lofty people in history whom everyone admires so much had to live the most horrible lives. I dare say look at the lives of these lofty souls. Is being beaten to a pulp, spat on and then dying in a crucifixion glorious to you? Many will argue yes God forbid. Please, for one moment, put yourself in Yeshua ben Yosef's shoes and imagine you were him dying a gruesome death after giving your all to everyone you ever knew. Do you really feel glorious? Please say no! Heartbroken, yes. Glorious? Hardly.

Now let's look at the life of Moshe Rabbeinu for a moment. Was that life glorious and joyous to you? Please say no again! Noah? Glorious? Give me a break! Look at the way Leah suffered throughout her life. Glorious? Oh, finally you might agree. Not so glorious. The lives that Hashem has told me I've lived were all deeply painful, filled with suffering and profoundly bitter. I can identify and relate to the hideousness and suffering. But glory? Hardly. The glory that I experience is the glory of Hashem God in every moment of my life. He is my Glory. This life as Moshiach in this world is hideously painful. Yet I can't walk away from this responsibility. Come what may, it's a life mission I must complete.

Please ask yourself the logical question, why did a Jewish mother give up everything to move to Tveria, Israel? Why? Why am I so obsessed with world peace and redemption? Why did I leave my cushy all-American life, and trade in my late model SUV for a $15 wagon that I schlepp uphill with my groceries in the sweltering heat of Tiberias, Israel? Why did I suddenly abandon my secular all-American life of pepperoni pizza on Friday nights to live as a Torah observant Jew? Simply because I wanted to write a good book that might sell as well as *Harry Potter* to make lots of money? Perhaps you skipped over the part that money and fame don't float my boat. Making this world better than I found it for my three children means the world to me. Hashem and world peace are my inspiration and motivation to keep going.

Do I believe that there will be miracles as prophesized in the Torah and revealed in this book? I can go either way. I believe all the prophecies are possible including the resurrection and return of the dead. I've seen a woman walk into my bedroom from nowhere, gently touch my left cheek with the middle finger on her right hand, and leave the room returning to nowhere. I do believe that the miracles described in the Torah and the resurrection of the dead are possible. Although I believe they are possible, I don't expect any of this to occur and I'm not sure it will happen. Only Hashem knows what will be in the end. Even though He tells me that these miracles are in store for us, I have a wait and see attitude. If they occur, it's all extra to me. I'm not doing any of this for the glorious Third Holy Temple to finally be built and the dead to return to life. I'm doing this for the love of Hashem God and to leave this world more peaceful and loving than I found it. Eternal life in the physical world right now would be a curse. The horrific murdering terrorists, rapists, villains and maniacal dictators must all be expunged before we could say that eternal life is a blessing.

If one day, Hashem's prophecy of world peace comes true but there is still the existence of death in our world, I want out. I don't want to be in a world that experiences death. If world peace comes and eternal life becomes possible, but Hashem's statement that I'm His betrothed and the prophecy that I will marry Him under the Chuppa on Temple Mount was just a wild fantasy that can't occur, I want out. I can't and won't be able to be with any ordinary man on earth. I'm not marriage material for any normal man and they aren't suitable for me. I'm His. That's how I relate to Him and how Hashem treats me in every moment of my life. Could you fault me? I have a love relationship, albeit non-physical, with the King of the Universe. How would it be possible to be with anyone else ever again? No offense, but He is complete magnificence that doesn't exist anywhere else. He is Everything. I'm completely spoiled rotten by Him and can't accept anything less than His perfection. If true love with Him in a physical man's body was simply a wild lie and the biggest tomato of them all to encourage me to keep going, I want out. If that disappointing outcome occurs when my work here is finished, I am done and pray Hashem will oblige me by allowing my light to be extinguished.

I believe in true love and I believe that every human being deserves to have true love in their life. If you have this kind of love now, please cherish it. It's sacred. Don't take it for granted. Cherish the one you love in every moment. I live daily with Hashem, my true Love, and our non-physical relationship is magnificent but I'm physically alone every moment of my life. I don't enjoy the warm embrace of my true Love or get to hold His hand. He is formless, and the greatest Spirit in the entire universe. I've told Him that I want to see world peace for my children in this lifetime. After that, I'm finished. If I can't have Him, my One true Love, both physically and spiritually, I want out. I pray for world peace daily and I've begged Him to take me when it's over and pack up my Luz bone too. Remember the Luz bone? It's the indestructible small bone at the base of your brain from which the dead are said to return to earth after redemption. I never want to return. Never. A life here without true love is no life at all.

Hashem insists the prophetic visions He has shown me are true. He says there will be a Royal Wedding in my future. If this wedding occurs, the significance is enormous. I pray for this wedding to take place on Temple Mount. If this occurs, we will enjoy eternal life on earth and live in a world that truly Runs on Love. Amen to that.

HIS VOICE, VISIONS & LESSONS

Who will heal our world of all its problems?

Who will heal our world of all its problems? It's a very good question. The short answer is, "We all will." I once asked the following question in a workshop that I took in public speaking. It was my turn to get up in front of the class and speak. As I stood before the class, I asked everyone, "How do you heal the world?" Nobody had an answer. Not only didn't anyone have answers, but they each had hand-held electronic devices they were using to rate my presentation as I spoke. As I walked around the classroom I directly asked each member of the audience this question in my effort to engage them. One by one they each gave me a failing score! Behind me on a big screen was a graph like the one used in presidential debates which shows audience approval or disapproval. My graph plummeted and they hated me! They hated being put on the spot and required to think about having such a huge responsibility. The very idea that they were suddenly accountable to answer this question made everyone recoil and hate my presentation.

Well, I have an answer to the question, "Who will heal the world of all its problems?" The answer is simple. **We all will.** Whether you like this question or the answer is irrelevant. It's the truth.

Hashem says that everyone in the world created this mess. Choices were made and He allowed the result of these choices to come into being. Look around our world. A lot of people think that terror and war are our only problems, and perhaps if we could get rid of the terrorists and solve the problems of war, we'd have a pretty good life. The truth is we're killing ourselves. We're killing each other. It's not just war and terror that's killing us, although that's a huge problem. Perhaps it's the number one problem, but it's not the only problem we face. Our air is hardly fit to breathe and people are dying of cancer with more people being diagnosed every minute of the day. Young people in the United States of America are killing themselves. Suicide is the second leading cause of death among young people in the United States. Did I say enough? Are there enough problems that we should all sit up at attention and say it's time? It's time for us all to work for the solution.

I posted a picture of skulls on Facebook with text that read, "Poison and war are destroying our planet. God says repair the world or lose everything. World peace will be earned, not given." This post got a lot of positive reactions. Giving a "thumbs up" to this post on Facebook might be a beginning of our healing because it's an acknowledgement that we have problems, but it will never heal our world. World peace will come with the removal of all the conflagration—all the fighting and all the war and terror. But world peace also means healing our world of all its problems. Our water is polluted. Our air is polluted. Our food is poisoned. We need to acknowledge the reasons why. We must go deeper into examining where these problems came from and stop them at their source. The source of all our problems is within every person and their choices. Everyone's hard work and effort is required. Stepping up and taking personal responsibility is a must.

War, terror, cancer, and even the existence of pollution all began with a decision by a person. A person decided to choose evil over God. Hashem God says the solution is learning the proper way to choose and choosing God and goodness in every moment. My failed public speaking workshop presentation that day showed me that it was too daunting for people to answer the question, "How do you heal the world?" But this becomes a doable task if I tell you that to heal the world you must look inward and find the problems within yourself. If everyone takes personal responsibility and starts to do the self-work that's needed, we will heal the world one person at a time.

What will you choose to do now that you know the answer to the question, "Who will heal our world of all its problems?" Now that you know it's you, are you ready to heal the world? Please say, "Yes I am!"

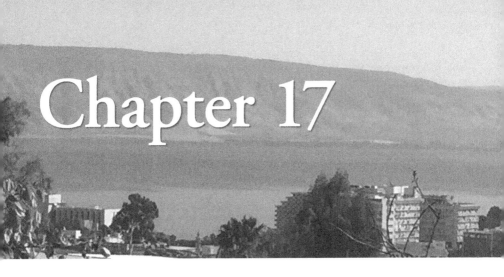

Chapter 17

What's Next for You?

You've made it to the end of this long tale. You're a trooper if you read the entire book all the way through and didn't skip around. Congratulations if you read this book in its entirety. I'm sure it wasn't easy because it doesn't have that gushy, make everyone feel good about themselves message. There are many lessons that you can learn from my story if you willingly accept them. I pray you will make the decision to learn from my experience and be better for it. Now it's time for you to choose what you will do. The information I've shared with you is admittedly troubling and extremely difficult to swallow no matter what your religious beliefs are or how you were raised. My explanations about God, the revelation that He was Adam and both the spiritual and physical Father of humanity will be completely unbelievable to many. Many of the stories I've shared may even make you feel sick to your stomach if you're attached to the explanations you were raised to believe were the truth. Still other explanations given in this book help fill in blanks and answer questions which have confounded learned rabbis and biblical scholars for thousands of years.

So, what will you choose now? Are you going to choose to walk away from everything I've shared in this book? Perhaps you are unhappy that the information I shared didn't jive with your religious beliefs or upbringing. Because I didn't deliver the information you wanted or expected, will you throw the baby out with the bath water—toss the entire book and choose to do absolutely nothing? Conversely, are you intrigued and compelled to learn more and do some research? Maybe you're someone who suspected all along that everyone had it wrong and you find these explanations possible or even truthful. Did any of this information alarm you at all? Will this book serve as a wake-up call that you and your family are in more danger than you ever imagined? Are you compelled to do what you can to make a difference in this world?

The best way to know how to choose what your next move will be is to ask yourself the right questions. Hopefully you understand that you need to do something regardless of your opinions about me.

Allow me to suggest the following questions for you to consider as you decide on your next move.

1. Have you seen enough death in our world?
2. Are you troubled by the daily news reports about racism, anti-Semitism, hatred, ethnic cleansing and terror?
3. Has it become business as usual, or commonplace to hear about another terror attack?
4. Do you sometimes shrug off this bad news and move on quickly with your day, because you feel powerless to change the world?
5. Are you willing to do something constructive that could bring peace?
6. If someone could accurately show you that you were committing a sin, choosing something that was truly evil, would you accept the guilt, repent, and repair the damage?
7. If facing your demons and admitting guilt is required to heal our world, would you willingly look for these problems within yourself despite the shame you might feel?
8. What are you willing to do for world peace?
9. What are you not willing to do for world peace?
10. Do you blame others for the problems you see in the world?
11. Do you believe you're a good person, admittedly not perfect, but not the cause of the horrible mess we are all in? (Go back and reread chapter 14 "My Boxing Gloves Are On." Everyone is guilty of creating this mess and that includes you!)
12. Do you feel responsible for what happens in our world, even if it's not your fault? Kudos to you if you say yes!
13. Are you willing to take immediate action to make our world better?

If you think I've been tough on you, good. If not, trust me, I can and will get tougher. I must. I'm not willing to candy coat anything or play patty-cake with you. We are in deep trouble and face human extinction. If you believe that this statement sounds hysterically overstated, you're sadly mistaken. Look online for *The Bulletin of the Atomic Scientists* and check out their Doomsday Clock which was recently set at two minutes to midnight. The scientists, many of whom are staunch atheists, concur that we're facing extinction if we don't make immediate changes. If you still haven't woken up, Hashem warns that the claps of thunder and painful alarm bells will be getting much louder and more difficult. This book is sweet cake with delicious icing compared to what we're facing as humanity. Deciphering Bible code and prophecy has become a sporting event or game like the Super Bowl. This isn't a game. Are you ready for that? As awful as I'm shown it will be when the coming world war begins, Hashem says I don't even know the half of it. He says it will be much worse than anyone can imagine and everyone will be stunned when it arrives. Are you a little frightened yet? I hope so but only to the point where you are frightened enough to take personal action. You must understand that it's time for you to feel the fear and fight for peace anyway. Stand up and be counted as a dedicated worker for world peace in our time.

God willing you're waking up and this book serves to be an important catalyst that creates a global movement of people who return to God. If you're waking from your slumber, are you beginning to wonder what you can do to heal our world? I've been screaming the answers to everyone for years, and now I'm praying you finally start listening. We must all listen, learn, and work for peace. Listen to me please and open your mind to the possibility that I'm your teacher. You don't even need to believe that I am Moshiach. If you're still a committed atheist, choose to take action now for the safety of our world, set aside your skepticism and choose to work for world peace. All you need to do is listen, engage me, and share this information with people you love. I don't need or want any titles or praise. I'm searching for peace workers who aren't afraid to face their own demons and learn the truth about where they are choosing wrong and contributing to our problems. Everyone in the world must do better.

I'm searching for loving people to begin Running on Love with me. It's really that simple to me. Love, education, and charity will heal our world. I'm a believer that it can be that simple for you too. Start to learn and discern what you're choosing in every moment and understand when you're choosing the Yetzer Hara, the evil inclination, also known as Satan. Begin to work on yourself harder than you ever have worked before to become the best you that's possible. When we collectively choose better, we will see positive changes in our world as we all begin to heal. We are a web of souls who affect each other by our daily choices. We must band together in love, education, and charity and choose wisely in every moment. For world peace to be possible, we must choose Hashem and His goodness in every moment without exception.

Ready or not, the prophesized war of Gog and Magog, World War III, is on its way. No date has been given to me and I dread the day it begins. Hashem has told me we are already feeling the tremors and when this hideous war is in full swing, we will need a loving and healing place to gather as one family. He says what is just ahead of us will be excruciatingly painful and the Running on Love Festival for Love events will help us weather the horrific storm that's about to rage.

What You Can Do Now!

World peace is in your hands. Every person is required to bring forward world redemption and peace. You might have felt helpless and hopeless before reading this book. Perhaps you thought there was nothing you could do, but the opposite is true. Peace on earth will come one day but only if you and many others accept personal responsibility and take decisive action to bring heaven to earth. That's why we are all here. We are the generation of Moshiach. You signed up for this role before you were born and you are accountable now. God is watching your every move so choose carefully!

I've prepared a list of TOP TEN ACTIONS that you can do to get started working for world peace. This is the EASY list with tougher tasks coming. Let's begin with baby steps to get this show on the road. If millions of people choose to do these recommended actions we will see immediate change for the better in our world. These are not just idle words, this is a promise. Let's start now and work together to make our world one that is Running on Love.

TOP TEN ACTIONS you can do for peace now

1. **Read this book again.** This time go get a pen and paper and take notes. You must start to learn about the Yetzer Hara and the evil that surrounds our world. This book must serve as part of your wake-up call. WAKE UP! You must start to learn and discern the difference between Yetzer Hatov, the good inclination, and Yetzer Hara, the evil inclination. Begin to learn how to choose God and goodness in every moment. Even the most educated must step it up and become dedicated to learning around the clock. Become relentless in the pursuit of spiritual perfection.

2. **Visit LoriMichelle.net.** Watch the many Running on Love with GOD programs and Q&A videos on my website. Actively watch and take notes recording your questions. Look up the terms you aren't familiar with and learn about them in greater detail. Begin to look for the splinters within yourself and start to remove them. Do the work of self-help and spiritual healing. Remember to share these videos too.

3. **Encourage everyone you love to read this book.** Encourage the people you dislike too because they need to wake up, heal and become more lovable. Remember to humble yourself and recognize that you might be the unlovable one to someone else. Get busy becoming someone who is easy to love!

4. **Donate to Running on Love at RunningOnLove.org/Donate.** Your donations will help the Festivals for Love become a reality. Make your donation in memory or honor of someone you love and increase their merit for the elevation of their soul. We are being judged and everything counts including the goodness that people do on our behalf. Joyously put a deposit of goodness in someone's spiritual bank account. Hashem is truly watching for this.

5. **Buy several copies of Blindsided by Messiah.** Give them as gifts for other people to read. Help wake up humanity to do this work with you. When the Running on Love Festivals for Love open, be sure to register to participate and attend the forums for learning at these events. It's time to bring humanity together to learn how to choose correctly in every moment.

6. **I'M YOURS! Invite me to speak and teach in your community.** Helping you get this life right by sharing Hashem's voice and wisdom is my passion and life's purpose. I'm ready when you are.

7. **Visit and learn from other websites for Torah education.** Visit Aish.org and Chabad.org. These organizations are phenomenal resources for learning Torah. This is a beginning place where you can start to learn about God's laws and become educated about His Torah. These are trusted websites which are well-written in easy to understand language.

8. **Increase your faith in our Creator.** I highly recommend reading *The Garden of Emuna: A Practical Guide for Life* by Rav Shalom Arush. I read this book after my awakening and it affected me so deeply I read it three times over. This book is powerful and highly recommended reading for everyone, both Jewish and non-Jewish. It's packed with powerful messages and provides the deeper understanding about what it means to have full faith in Hashem God.

9. **Get up and get active now.** Running on Love is about actively giving in honor or memory of someone you love so go get yourself a good pair of running or walking shoes. The Festivals for Love will begin with a run/walk so get used to the idea of moving your body daily. If you're already into exercise, great! Bring your enthusiasm and love to these events and inspire others to get active and fit too. Being active is not only a mitzvah (good deed) from Hashem, it's a source of great joy. Let's boost those endorphins and become physically fit and happier together.

10. **Pray.** Everyone in the world must reach for God daily in personal prayer. He is everywhere, He listens to our prayers, and He heals us from the inside out. If you don't know what to say or where to begin, reach for a prayer book and learn prescribed daily prayers. Be sure to build your God muscles daily. Personal prayer is crucial to the spiritual well-being of every person without exception.

Be a Moshiach Too

The idea that you could be a Moshiach too may sound ludicrous to many people. Just prior to moving to Israel, I enjoyed a Rosh Hashanah holiday meal with the family of a learned Chassidic rabbi in New Jersey. As we sat at the holiday table I said to the rabbi and his sons that we should all be just like Moshiach. After I said this the rabbi and one of his sons both looked at me incredulously and exclaimed, "Impossible!"

Secretly I knew Moshiach was me when I said this and thought to myself, "Why are they reacting like this? What's the big deal?" I'm here to tell everyone not only is this possible, but you must. How can you be like Moshiach too? Choose to be determined and relentless in your desire to reach for God and work to be the best person you can be in every moment without exception. Take nothing for granted, be completely unafraid to find out where you are going astray and correct your behavior. It isn't how many times you fall down or fail that matters the most. What matters most is how many times you choose to stand up and be counted as a spark of light dedicated to God and His goodness. You must never quit!

In the end, God always wins. Choose relentlessly in every moment to be part of His winning team. I've pointed out many areas in our world where people are choosing evil and going the wrong way, but I've also provided real world solutions. I've given you a list of top ten actions you can take immediately to begin working for world peace. You can choose right now to take direct and decisive action. Don't sit idly by, watching our world implode. Take a stand now and refuse to be someone who does nothing while children are dying. Do this for everyone you love and for yourself. Recognize that if you're not choosing to be part of the solution, you are part of the problem. Be part of God's solution and work for world peace in our time. My promise to everyone who will listen to me and heed this call: I will help you with every breath of my life. With Hashem's blessing and help, I will hold your hand and run with you right to the finish line—peace on earth.

When Hashem wakes me every morning, He knows how depleted I am and how sometimes I lack the strength to get out of bed. In my weakest moments when everything I do feels mired in futility, He lovingly and magically inspires me to keep going. He often wakes me in the morning by playing beautiful music with meaningful lyrics meant to soothe my soul and fill me with inspiration. He often tweaks the lyrics of my old favorites turning them into awe-inspiring songs that encourage me to keep going. One such song is my all-time favorite "Daydream Believer," written by John Stewart, and made famous by my childhood heartthrob Davy Jones of the Monkees. Hashem has changed the lyrics and the title to "Cheer up Moshiach Queen."

Throughout the day and night as I prepare to deliver this incredible book to you, I often hear your loved ones in heaven singing this song to me too. As everyone in heaven sings this song to me trying to cheer me up and fill me with optimism, it feels surreal. I'm eternally grateful to be surrounded in profound love unlike anything I've ever known in my life. As they sing this song, they inspire me to believe in the unbelievable—a peaceful world for my children and yours.

Cheer up Moshiach Queen

Oh, I could hide beneath His wings
Of the King as He sings
The six-o'clock alarm would never ring
But it rings, and I rise
He wipes the tears out of my eyes
And He tells me how He loves me endlessly

And He says, "Cheer up Moshiach Queen
Oh, what can this mean to My
Daydream Believer and My
Homecoming Queen?"

You all thought of me
As some white guy on a steed
Now you'll learn how happy life can be

Oh, and all good times start and end
Without dollar one to spend
Hashem is truly the only One I need

And He says, "Cheer up Moshiach Queen
Oh, what can this mean to My
Daydream Believer and My
Homecoming Queen?" …

There isn't any mountain I refuse to climb to bring world peace. Will you climb this incredible mountain with me? I've done things that I never imagined I would ever have the courage to do in my relentless pursuit to save you.

I'm not a singer to say the least, but I sang Hashem's heartwarming song to the world announcing the unthinkable—I am His Moshiach Queen. In miraculous fashion, Hashem even placed an adorable and friendly donkey next door to join me in my homecoming debut. Incredible!

I boldly delivered this book to the world with love and a smile. I refuse to quit until I reach the end of this grueling race. Hashem is holding my hand tightly and escorting me to the finish line. Will you help me finish this race too?

Will you take my hand? I dream of a world that is Running on Love. Will you Run on Love with me and heal our world? Please say yes to love. Please say yes to God. Please say yes to peace on earth for eternity. I pray daily that Hashem blesses you and your loved ones.

May there be world peace in our time.

Made in the USA
Middletown, DE
02 July 2020